Remedies for Torts and Breach of Contract

Third edition

Andrew Burrows MA (Oxon), BCL, LLM (Harvard), QC (Hons)

Norton Rose Professor of Commercial Law in the
University of Oxford; Fellow of St Hugh's College, Oxford;
Honorary Bencher of the Middle Temple

OXFORD
UNIVERSITY PRESS

OXFORD

UNIVERSITY PRESS

Great Clarendon Street, Oxford, OX2 6DP

Oxford University Press is a department of the University of Oxford.
It furthers the University's objective of excellence in research, scholarship,
and education by publishing worldwide in

Oxford New York

Auckland Bangkok Buenos Aires Cape Town Chennai
Dar es Salaam Delhi Hong Kong Istanbul Karachi Kolkata
Kuala Lumpur Madrid Melbourne Mexico City Mumbai Nairobi
São Paulo Shanghai Taipei Tokyo Toronto

Oxford is a registered trade mark of Oxford University Press
in the UK and in certain other countries

Published in the United States
by Oxford University Press Inc., New York

British Library Cataloguing in Publication Data
Data available

Library of Congress Cataloging in Publication Data
Data available

ISBN 0 406 97726 7

10 9 8 7 6 5 4 3 2 1

Typeset in Baskerville by Kerrypress Ltd, Luton, **www.kerrypress.co.uk**
Printed in Great Britain by Ashford Colour Press, Gosport, Hampshire

For Rachel

Preface to the third edition

The opportunity has been taken in this edition not only to bring the text up-to-date but also to restructure the material. My belief is that the new structure better brings out the underlying themes of the book. It may also make it easier to use. There are therefore now twenty-four chapters (rather than the previous ten) divided into five parts. The parts essentially correspond to the primary functions of the remedies for torts and breach of contract, namely compensation (which itself has fifteen chapters), restitution and punishment, compelling performance or preventing (or compelling the undoing of) a wrong, and declaring rights. Reflecting their increased importance in practice, and the considerable recent academic attention devoted to them, there is also a new final part and chapter on remedies for equitable wrongs, such as breach of fiduciary duty and breach of confidence. To that extent the book now extends beyond the scope of its title to provide coverage of judicial remedies for all civil wrongs. Most importantly, that last chapter reveals that there is a coherence of remedial function between remedies for common law and equitable wrongs.

The central objective of the book remains, as ever, to provide a clear and succinct analysis and critique of the principles governing judicial remedies. It is hoped that it will be a stimulating guide not only to students but also to practitioners.

This edition, over ten years on from the last, has required extensive rewriting. Huge swathes of new material have been incorporated, covering not only scores of new cases but also the Civil Procedure Rules, several new statutes (including the impact of the Human Rights Act 1998), a number of Law Commission Reports (especially on damages) and many recent academic articles and books.

In most areas, the new developments are to be welcomed. Excellent new decisions by the courts include, in the order in which they appear in the text: *Henderson v Merrett Syndicates Ltd*, HL (concurrent liability); *Brown v KMR Services Ltd*, CA (remoteness in contract); *Smith New Court Securities Ltd v Scrimgoeur Vickers (Asset Management) Ltd*, HL (damages for deceit, including remoteness); *Standard Chartered Bank v Pakistan National Shipping Corpn (No 2)*, HL (contributory negligence not a defence to deceit); *Lagden v O'Connor*, HL (removing the 'impecuniosity' restriction); *Gaca v Pirelli General plc*, CA (compensating advantages); *Ruxley Electronics and Construction Ltd v Forsyth*, HL (damages for breach of contract by builder); *Bence Graphics Int Ltd v Fasson UK Ltd*, CA (taking account of resales in assessing damages for the delivery of defective goods); *The Maersk Colombo*, CA (destruction of goods); *Voaden v Champion, The Baltic Surveyor*, CA (the betterment question); *Wells v Wells*, HL (calculating damages for future pecuniary loss for personal injury); *Malik v Bank of Credit and Commerce International SA*, HL (contractual damages for loss of reputation); *John v MGN Ltd*, CA (juries in defamation cases to be referred to personal injury awards); *Farley v Skinner*, HL (mental distress damages in contract); *Attorney-General v Blake*, HL (account of profits for breach of contract); and *Kuddus v Chief Constable of Leicestershire Constabulary*, HL (removing the 'cause of action' test for punitive damages).

In contrast, it is argued in the text that the reasoning in the following important cases has, with great respect, taken the law in the wrong direction: *South Australia Asset Management Corpn v York Montagu Ltd* ('*SAAMCO*'), HL (insofar as their Lordships advocated a novel 'scope of duty' restriction on damages, distinct from remoteness and intervening cause); *Burdis v Livsey*, CA (on damages for the cost of repairs consequent on damage to goods); and *Co-operative Insurance Society Ltd v Argyll Stores (Holdings) Ltd*, HL (which breathed new life into the unsatisfactory 'constant supervision' objection to specific performance). Also problematic is some of the reasoning of the House of Lords in *Alfred McAlpine Construction Ltd v Panatown Ltd*, which reflects a confusing approach by some commentators who have suggested that there has been a tendency in the law of contractual damages for the 'performance interest' to be subordinated to the 'compensation approach'.

There is never a perfect time to write a textbook on such an important and fast-moving area. The reader should be aware that, at the time of writing, we await: the decisions of the House of Lords in *Gregg v Scott* (damages for loss of a chance) and *Chester v Afshar* (on factual causation); the bringing into force of the provisions in the Courts Act 2003 allowing the courts to order (reviewable) periodical payments in personal injury and death cases; the publication of the seventh edition of the Judicial Studies Board's *Guidelines for the Assessment of General Damages in Personal Injury Cases*; the publication of the fifth edition of the 'Ogden Tables' for assessing damages for future pecuniary loss in personal injury and death cases; and the passage through Parliament of the Civil Partnership Bill (which has some impact on the Fatal Accidents Act 1976).

I would like to thank Paul Craig for his comments on the sections in chapter 1 on the Human Rights Act 1998 and European Community Law; Elizabeth Drummond and Henni Ouahes who were my research assistants; Katherine Frisby for all her hard work in typing the new text; and Jan Madden for her expertise and patience in seeing the book through from manuscript to publication.

The law is stated as at 23 July 2004.

While this book was nearing completion my mentor and friend Peter Birks, Regius Professor of Civil Law at Oxford, died of cancer at the age of 62. Words are inadequate to describe the enormity of my debt to him. He was one of my tutors at Brasenose College where I first studied law and he encouraged and assisted me at every stage of my academic career. The power of his mind and his deep knowledge of the law, combined with his passionate enthusiasm and generosity, made him a giant among English academic lawyers. It is with profound sadness, tinged with disbelief, that I close this preface knowing that the person who I would most have wanted to read this new edition will not be here to do so.

Andrew Burrows
23 August 2004
Oxford

Preface to the first edition

The aim of this book is to clarify and assess the principles applied by the courts in providing redress for a defendant's tort or breach of contract. While principally designed for students' use it is hoped that it will also be of assistance to practitioners.

Although there are several books dealing with one (or more) of the remedies for torts and breach of contract, as well as sections on remedies in books on contract, tort and equity respectively, this is the first book to treat the area as a coherent whole. This has the great advantage of enabling the many similarities, as well as the differences, between tortious and contractual remedies and their governing principles to be fully appreciated.

Moreover, it is a sad fact that many of the important and fascinating issues raised in this area have in the past escaped the attention of students, owing to the tendency in traditional contract and tort courses to concentrate on the cause of action rather than the remedies side of the law. It is therefore hoped that as well as being used in 'Remedies' courses this book will encourage greater concentration on remedies in the teaching of contract and tort, whether taught separately or as part of a joint 'Obligations' or 'Common Law' course.

In considering judicial remedies for torts and breach of contract only, an important objective has been to avoid the problems of superficiality and lack of context and structure that tend to beset attempts to examine all remedies. But having said that this book could happily be used alongside those on the law of restitution to provide an exposition of almost all civil law remedies. The temptation to expand this book to include all restitutionary remedies has, however, been resisted for three main reasons. First, knowledge of what constitutes a tort or breach of contract is basic to all law students, usually by the end of their first year and certainly by the end of their studies, whereas the same cannot be said of what constitutes an unjust enrichment. Secondly, in contrast to remedies for wrongs, it is unhelpful to consider separately the remedies for unjust (non-wrongful) enrichment and the unjust enrichment itself.

Finally, the recent expansion of the tort of negligence and the acceptance of concurrent liability between tortious negligence and breach of contract – as well as academic challenges to the division between tort and contract – have already rendered it commonplace for tort and contract to be taught as closely related subjects.

In writing this book I have been helped by many people. Peter Bromley first gave me encouragement with the project. Philip Davies, Peter Birks, John Davies, Alan Evans and Stephen Moriarty kindly read and made invaluable comments on various chapters. Five years of Manchester University third-year 'Remedies' students inspired and challenged my thoughts. Colleagues in the law faculty there were stimulating companions and friends over those years and furthermore generously allowed me study leave in Lent Term 1986. A research grant from the British Academy enabled me to make the best use of that time as well as helping with typing and other expenses. Jane Andrews and Gladys Allsop did most of the typing and made a splendid job of it. My parents provided support and encouragement throughout. Finally and most of all I would like to thank my wife, Rachel, without whom, quite simply, this book would never have been written.

Andrew Burrows
5 November 1986
Oxford

Contents

PART ONE COMPENSATION

Table of statutes

The numbers in the right-hand column are to page numbers. Those in bold type indicate where the statute is set out in full or in part.

Table of Cases

PARA

PARA

PARA

PARA

PARA

PARA

Decisions of the European Court of Justice are listed below
numerically. These decisions are also included in the preceding
alphabetical list.

PARA

Chapter 1

General introduction

1. JUDICIAL REMEDIES

The concept of a remedy has rarely been subjected to rigorous analysis.[1] Views may differ as to precisely what one is talking about. In this book, a remedy is used to denote the relief that a person can seek from a court.[2] The focus is therefore entirely on judicial remedies; and not on what are sometimes termed 'self-help' remedies, which are available without coming to court, such as out of court settlements, termination of a contract, and the ejection of trespassers.[3] Put another way, this book examines what a person can obtain from a court to counter an infringement (or threatened infringement) of his or her legal rights by a tort or breach of contract; but it is not concerned with any other legally permissible options open to a person to counter such an infringement.

A judicial remedy may be either coercive or non-coercive:[4] that is, it may be either a court order to do or not to do something, backed up by enforcement procedures[5] or a court pronouncement indicating or

---

1   Recent notable exceptions are Barker 'Rescuing Remedialism in Unjust Enrichment Law: Why Remedies are Right' [1998] CLJ 301; Birks 'Rights, Wrongs, and Remedies' (2000) 20 OJLS 1; Zakrzewski 'The Classification of Judicial Remedies' [2003] LMCLQ 477.
2   Or from an equivalent body (where appeals can be made to the courts), such as an arbitrator or employment tribunal.
3   For introductory examinations of some self-help remedies, see, eg Harris, Campbell and Halson *Remedies in Contract and Tort* (2nd edn, 2002) chs 2, 3 and 21; Lawson *Remedies of English Law* (2nd edn, 1980) chs 1–2. Note also that this book does not discuss judicial remedies available in a claim for judicial review (a quashing order, a prohibiting order and a mandatory order) even though, arguably, they can be awarded for a tort or breach of contract committed by a public authority: see, eg *Ex p Napier* (1852) 18 QB 692 at 695. Such remedies are better considered in books on administrative law. See Craig *Administrative Law* (5th edn, 2003) ch 22.
4   Lawson *Remedies of English Law* (2nd edn, 1980) pp 12–14.
5   Damages and the award of an agreed sum take the form of an award by the court which constitutes a judgment debt owed by one party to the other. That is, a court gives 'judgment for the claimant for £1,000' rather than saying that 'the defendant shall pay the claimant £1,000'. Such awards can still be regarded, loosely, as 'court orders' and they are certainly coercive because they are backed up by enforcement procedures. Indeed the same enforcement procedures apply to an award of damages as to an award of costs where the standard wording is in the form of a direct order to pay ('The claimant shall pay the defendant its costs of £1,000'). Note that an undertaking given by a defendant to the court and accepted in place of an injunction is enforceable and hence coercive even though, plainly, it does not comprise a court order.

altering what the parties' rights or duties are or were. Examples of the former are damages, specific performance, injunctions and the award of an agreed sum, while the declaration is the most obvious example of the latter.

This book follows the conventional practice of treating damages as a remedy. In the context of torts and breach of contract, the law of (judicial) remedies looks at the (judicial) relief available for a tort or breach of contract, and damages is one such remedy. There is another view, recently advocated by Zakrzewski,[6] which defines the law of remedies in terms of the judgment awards and orders made by the courts,[7] and their enforcement, and which treats the law of damages as being essentially concerned with secondary rights which, alongside primary rights, belong outside the law of remedies. While it may be analytically possible to treat the law of damages in that way, it seems unhelpful to do so. On the contrary, this book is based on the view that it is illuminating and practically useful to analyse the relief that a party may seek from a court for a tort or breach of contract. To see the law of remedies as including the law on injunctions and specific performance but not the law on damages cuts across that useful and illuminating approach.

2.   PROCEDURE

Our concern will be with the substantive law governing judicial remedies and not with the adjectival law dictating the procedure by which those remedies are obtained. For that, reference should be made to the Civil Procedure Rules and accompanying Practice Directions. It will also be assumed throughout that an English court has jurisdiction in respect of the claim[8] and that the claimant is proceeding within the appropriate English civil court.[9]

---

6   Zakrzewski 'The Classification of Judicial Remedies' [2003] LMCLQ 477.
7   For Zakrzewski there is a fundamental division of judgment awards and orders between what he terms 'replicative' and 'transformative' remedies. The former merely replicate the claimant's substantive rights, while the latter confer rights that are different from the claimant's substantive rights.
8   Dicey and Morris *The Conflict of Laws* (13th edn, 2000) chs 11–12.
9   Eg a personal injury action worth less than £50,000 must he brought in a county court: see High Court and County Courts Jurisdiction Order 1991, SI 1991/724. All the remedies covered in this book can be awarded by both the High Court and the county courts: County Courts Act 1984, s 38. But note that the County Court Remedies Regulations 1991, SI 1991/1222 (as amended), restrict the power of county courts to grant search orders and freezing injunctions.

3. ENFORCEMENT

There is a distinction between the coercive remedies granted by the courts for a tort or breach of contract, and the enforcement or execution of those remedies which may require further court orders. This book is not concerned with the latter secondary realm of judicial involvement. Suffice it to say that for some non-monetary remedies, such as injunctions and specific performance, enforcement is by proceedings for contempt of court, with the ultimate sanction being imprisonment; whereas for monetary remedies, such as damages and the award of an agreed sum, there are several methods of enforcing payment, examples being a writ of *fieri facias* (or, in the county court, a warrant of execution), an attachment of earnings order, a third party debt order or a charging order.

To give some general perspective to the role of the judicial remedies, two further points on enforcement are worth emphasising. First, enforcement of judicial remedies is at the claimant's discretion. This means that, even after it has been granted a judicial remedy, a claimant has the choice of settling for a different resolution of the dispute.[10] Secondly, even judicial methods may not succeed in enforcing the remedy. For example, a defendant who has insufficient assets cannot comply with a monetary remedy;[11] and imprisoning or fining a defendant for failing to carry out an order of specific performance does not guarantee performance.

4. ORDERS MADE TO ASSIST THE CLAIMANT IN COLLECTING EVIDENCE TO ESTABLISH ITS CASE

Although the case that the claimant is trying to establish involves a tort or breach of contract, orders made to assist the claimant in collecting evidence, like specific disclosure and inspection,[12] cannot realistically be described as remedies for a tort or breach of contract; rather, in so far as it is at all sensible to describe such orders as remedies, they are remedies to help the claimant in its attempt to show that a tort or breach of

---

10 The possibility of bargaining round non-monetary remedies has recently attracted much academic interest – see below, p 22.

11 The Green Paper *Towards Effective Enforcement: A Single Piece of Bailiff Law and a Regulatory Structure for Enforcement* (Cmnd 5096, Lord Chancellor's Department, 2001) para 1.31 states that only 35% of all warrants of execution issued (which account for about 85% of all enforcement effort) are paid and that the estimated value of unpaid post-judgment debt is more than £600 million per year. See, generally, Baldwin and Cunnington 'The Crisis of Enforcement of Civil Judgments in England and Wales' [2004] PL 305.

12 CPR 31.12.

contract has been committed. Or, to put it another way, on the assumption that a tort or breach of contract has been committed or is threatened, such orders are not the relief that the claimant seeks but rather are means towards obtaining that relief. They are therefore not considered in this book.

5.   TORTS AND BREACH OF CONTRACT

Tortious and contractual obligations are the two main types of obligations recognised in English law. A contractual obligation arises where one person makes a promise to another, provided generally that that promise is supported by consideration or is made by deed, and is not invalidated on grounds such as mistake, misrepresentation or frustration. The promisor is under an obligation to perform the promise and should she fail to do so the promisee has a cause of action against her for breach of contract. A tortious obligation, on the other hand, is an obligation not to wrong another by conduct that the different torts specify to be wrongful. Should a person break such an obligation, the person wronged has a cause of action against her for the tort.[13]

This book will, generally, not be concerned with the claimant's establishing such causes of action, ie it will not in general be concerned with how the claimant establishes the defendant's tort or breach of contract. Rather it will focus on the judicial remedies available to a claimant assuming that it can establish a tort or breach of contract or, more rarely, a threatened tort or breach of contract.

There are two major qualifications to this. The first is that in relation to torts actionable only on proof of damage, like negligence, nuisance and deceit (as opposed to breach of contract and torts actionable per se),[14] some of the principles that are concerned with establishing relevant damage, and hence generally[15] with establishing the tort, are principles of compensatory damages for an established liability in relation to torts

13   Birks 'Rights, Wrongs and Remedies' (2000) 20 OJLS 1, 22, has criticised this paragraph because it cuts across a taxonomy which distinguishes events from rights. But it is hard to see what is incorrect or unhelpful about lining-up alongside each other (primary) rights engendered by a contract and (primary) rights protected by torts. Crucially the breach of those (primary) rights (which is the wrong constituting the cause of action) then triggers judicial remedies. Birks' approach appears to produce the odd consequence that a (*quia timet*) injunction to restrain an anticipated tort is not concerned with a 'tortious right' because a tortious right cannot be anterior to the tort.

14   Most torts are actionable only on proof of damage. But libel, malicious prosecution (see *Watkins v Secretary of State for the Home Department* [2004] EWCA Civ 966) and trespass to the person, land or goods are torts actionable per se.

15   Sometimes the damage and hence the tort is clearly established and the dispute concerns further damage. One is then concerned only with compensatory damages.

actionable per se and breach of contract. Examples are factual causation, intervening cause, remoteness, and the restrictions on recovery for mental distress. So as to provide a rounded picture of such principles, this book includes cases dealing with them, even where they concern the establishment of a tort actionable only on proof of damage.

Secondly, for reasons there explained, liquidated damages and similar clauses are discussed in chapter 19 on the award of an agreed sum, even though the essential question is whether the clause is valid, and hence whether the defendant is contractually liable to pay the agreed sum.

6. CONCURRENT LIABILITY BETWEEN THE TORT OF NEGLIGENCE AND BREACH OF CONTRACT[16]

On the same facts and in relation to the same loss, the claimant may be able to show not only that the defendant has broken its contract but also that it has committed the tort of negligence. For example, where a carrier contracts to carry goods for the owner, it will usually be a term of the contract that the carrier takes reasonable care of the goods in transit. If the carrier then negligently damages the goods, it is not only in breach of contract but is also liable to the owner for the tort of negligence. The number of potential overlaps between breach of contract and the tort of negligence has increased in recent times. This is particularly so since the tort of negligence has been expanded to allow the recovery in some situations of pure economic loss (that is economic loss not consequent on physical damage).[17]

Clearly what the claimant cannot here do is to recover damages both for the breach of contract and for the tort of negligence, for this would be to recover double damages for the same loss. Moreover it would generally seem unacceptable, as being inconsistent with what the parties have themselves agreed, for the tort of negligence to impose a standard

16 See, eg French 'The Contract/Tort Dilemma' (1982) 5 Otago LR 236; Reynolds 'Tort Actions in Contractual Situations' (1985) 11 NZULR 215; Markesinis 'An Expanding Tort Law – The Price of a Rigid Contract Law' (1987) 103 LQR 354; Barker 'Are we up to Expectations? Solicitors, Beneficiaries and the Tort/Contract Divide' (1994) 14 OJLS 137; Cane *Tort Law and Economic Interests* (2nd edn, 1996) pp 129–149, 307–334; Burrows *Understanding the Law of Obligations* (1998) pp 16–44; *Chitty on Contracts* (29th edn, 2004) paras 1–105 to 1–147.

17 See, eg *Hedley Byrne & Co Ltd v Heller & Partners Ltd* [1964] AC 465; *Midland Bank Trust Co Ltd v Hett, Stubbs and Kemp* [1979] Ch 384; *White v Jones* [1995] 2 AC 207; *Merrett v Babb* [2001] EWCA Civ 214, [2001] QB 1174. But the recovery of pure economic loss for tortious negligence is still very restricted: see, eg *Spartan Steel & Alloys Ltd v Martin & Co (Contractors) Ltd* [1973] QB 27; *Candlewood Navigation Corpn Ltd v Mitsui OSK Lines Ltd* [1986] AC 1; *Muirhead v Industrial Tank Specialities Ltd* [1986] QB 507; *Leigh and Sillavan Ltd v Aliakmon Shipping Co Ltd* [1986] AC 785; *Murphy v Brentwood District Council* [1991] 1 AC 398; *Williams v Natural Life Health Foods Ltd* [1998] 1 WLR 830.

of liability that is more onerous than that laid down by the express or implied terms of the contract.[18] But provided consistent with the terms of the contract, there is in principle no objection to the claimant choosing to obtain judgment either for the breach of contract or for the tort of negligence, depending on which is more favourable to him. This was traditionally accepted where the defendant was exercising a 'common calling', for example if he were a carrier, innkeeper, bailee or farrier; and, after a period of some uncertainty,[19] the House of Lords in *Henderson v Merrett Syndicates Ltd*[20] fully accepted concurrent consistent liability for breach of contract and the tort of negligence. The case dealt with the liability of Lloyd's underwriting agents to Names at Lloyd's. Giving the leading speech Lord Goff said the following:

> 'My own belief is that, in the present context, the common law is not antipathetic to concurrent liability, and that there is no sound basis for a rule which automatically restricts the claimant to either a tortious or a contractual remedy. The result may be untidy; but, given that the tortious duty is imposed by the general law, and the contractual duty is attributable to the will of the parties, I do not find it objectionable that the claimant may be entitled to take advantage of the remedy which is most advantageous to him, subject only to ascertaining whether the tortious duty is so inconsistent with the applicable contract that, in accordance with ordinary principle, the parties must be taken to have agreed that the tortious remedy is to be limited or excluded.'[1]

Why might a claimant, who can establish a breach of contract and tortious negligence (or, conceivably, a different tort), wish to frame its cause of action in tort rather than contract, or vice versa? Leaving aside matters of procedure and conflict of laws, the most significant reasons are twofold.

First, the claimant may be entitled to a higher quantum of damages in contract than in tort or vice versa. This may be because the aim of the compensatory damages differs. In contract, the aim is to put the claimant into as good a position as if the contract had been performed. In

---

18 *Tai Hing Cotton Mill Ltd v Liu Chong Hing Bank Ltd* [1986] AC 80, at 107; *National Bank of Greece SA v Pinios Shipping Co No 1, The Maira* [1989] 3 WLR 185 (rvsd on a different point [1990] 1 AC 637, HL); *Greater Nottingham Co-op Soc Ltd v Cementation Piling & Foundations Ltd* [1989] QB 71; *Reid v Rush & Tomkins Group plc* [1990] 1 WLR 212; *Johnstone v Bloomsbury HA* [1992] QB 333; *Scally v Southern Health & Social Services Board* [1992] 1 AC 294; *Lancashire and Cheshire Association of Baptist Churches Inc v Howard & Seddon Partnership* [1993] 3 All ER 467.

19 This was particularly caused by influential obiter dicta of Lord Scarman giving the judgment of the Privy Council in *Tai Hing Cotton Mill Ltd v Liu Chong Hing Bank* [1986] AC 80, at 107. He said, 'Their Lordships do not believe that there is anything to the advantage of the law's development in searching for a liability in tort where the parties are in a contractual relationship.'

20 [1995] 2 AC 145.

1   [1995] 2 AC 145 at 193–194.

contrast, the aim of the damages for, for example, the tort of misrepresentation is to put the claimant into as good a position as if no contract had been made. The former will yield a higher measure than the latter if the claimant made a good bargain but a lower measure if the claimant made a bad bargain.[2] Again, some of the principles limiting compensatory damages are not applied in the same way to claims for breach of contract as they are to claims in tort.[3] For example, the rules on remoteness are traditionally more favourable to claimants in tort than in contract. And contributory negligence does not apply to reduce damages for many claims in contract, whereas it nearly always applies as a possible defence in tort. There may also be greater restrictions on the recoverability of certain types of loss, such as mental distress and loss of reputation, in contract than in tort.[4] It may also be that certain types of damages, for example, punitive damages,[5] are available for torts but not for breach of contract.

Secondly, the claimant may be entitled to a longer limitation period for commencing one cause of action rather than another. This may be because the statutory time period is longer. Or it may be because the different causes of action accrue at different dates so that the statutory time period starts running at different dates. Or it may be because of the application of the Latent Damage Act 1986, with its discoverability test, which applies to the tort of negligence but not to breach of contract.[6]

7. SHOULD ONE CONTINUE TO DISTINGUISH TORTS AND BREACH OF CONTRACT?

The acceptance of concurrent liability and the expansion of the tort of negligence to allow the recovery of pure economic loss in some situations raise the question whether the traditional division between torts and breach of contract (ie tort and contract) can be sensibly maintained. In particular, one interpretation of some of the cases allowing the recovery of pure economic loss in the tort of negligence[7] is that the courts are now recognising that a negligent breach of promise is a tort, enabling the recovery of damages, even by a third party, to fulfil expectations

---

2   See below, p 34.
3   See below, ch 6.
4   See below, chs 12 and 13.
5   See below, ch 18.
6   *Iron Trade Mutual Ins Co Ltd v JK Buckenham Ltd* [1990] 1 All ER 808; *Islander Trucking Ltd & Hogg Robinson v Gardner Mountain (Marine) Ltd* [1990] 1 All ER 826. See below ch 15.
7   Eg *Midland Bank Trust Co Ltd v Hett, Stubbs and Kemp* [1979] Ch 384; *White v Jones* [1995] 2 AC 207.

engendered by the promisor.[8] If this is so, the rationale of the division between torts and breach of contract is largely undermined. That rationale is that contract alone deals with liability for breach of a binding promise; and that such separate treatment is sensible because liability for breach of a binding promise rests on what, by convention, is treated as a voluntarily-undertaken obligation whereas liability for all other wrongs (essentially comprising the different torts) has no such voluntary basis and is simply imposed. Promissory liability therefore rests on, and respects and upholds, the parties' private intentions and arrangements; in this sense it may be thought to be more directly in line with 'laissez-faire' thinking than are tortious liabilities.

However, despite these developments in tort, this book continues to use the distinction between torts and breach of contract for a number of reasons:

(i) The judges continue to think and talk in terms of distinct actions for torts and breach of contract.

(ii) As regards remedies, while there are clearly many similarities between remedies for torts and breach of contract – for example, damages and injunctions are both available for torts and breach of contract, and most of the principles governing their grant are common to both causes of action – there remain significant differences. For example, remedies such as specific performance and the award of an agreed sum are available only for breach of contract. And, as has been referred to above, some principles of compensatory damages, such as remoteness and contributory negligence, and some types of loss, like mental distress and loss of reputation, are dealt with differently for torts than for breach of contract. Furthermore, punitive damages can sometimes be awarded for torts but not for breach of contract.

(iii) The view that some tort cases rest on recognising that a negligent breach of promise is a tort may not be their only possible explanation. Certainly where the defendant is liable to the claimant for breach of contract it may be thought odd to recognise a concurrent tortious liability resting on what is, on this view, essentially the same basis, ie breach of promise.

(iv) Even if the 'negligent breach of promise as a tort' interpretation is correct, an action for breach of contract still formally differs from the tort action for negligence in that it accrues before 'damage',

---

8   Burrows *Understanding the Law of Obligations* (1998) pp 26–40. See similarly Whittaker 'The Application of the "Broad Principle of Hedley Byrne" as between Parties to a Contract' (1997) 17 Legal Studies 169.

making it less favourable for the claimant as regards limitation periods. Furthermore a non-negligent breach of promise can still only be sued on by an action for breach of contract. In particular, this means that it will still only be for breach of contract that one can recover pure economic loss for non-negligent breach of an obligation, at least where that obligation is a positive one. Indeed strict liability, breach of a positive obligation, and pure economic loss are the standard features of most actions for breach of contract.

(v)   Even if the courts are treating a negligent breach of promise as a tort, one can of course argue that it is unsatisfactory for them to do so. Indeed, one can strongly argue that the reason why the courts may have done so is to evade some of the unsatisfactory differences between contract and tort (in particular, as a means of allowing the claimant the more favourable limitation regime operating in tort and as a means of avoiding the traditional privity doctrine in contract). In other words, to treat a negligent breach of promise as a tort is a pragmatic, rather than a logical or principled, development.[9] The strictly logical development would be to effect reforms (eg to the law on limitation periods) so as to eliminate any unwarranted distinctions between contract and tort thereby removing the incentive to use tort to overcome the deficiencies of contract.

8.   THE PRIMARY FUNCTIONS OF JUDICIAL REMEDIES FOR TORTS AND BREACH OF CONTRACT

The primary functions of the judicial remedies for torts and breach of contract can be expressed as follows: compensation, restitution, punishment, compelling performance of positive obligations, preventing a wrong, compelling the undoing of a wrong, declaring rights. A table (see below) is helpful to indicate which remedies correspond to which function.

These functions underpin the structure of this book and will be referred to throughout. This is not meant to suggest that there is no other way of expressing the primary functions; eg one can equally well regard most of the remedies for breach of contract as having the common function of fulfilling expectations engendered by the contractual promise. But taking into account all judicial remedies for torts and breach of

---

9   Burrows *Understanding the Law of Obligations* (1998) pp 26–34.

contract, the scheme below is considered the most helpful for understanding the role of and links between the remedies.

Remedies for Torts and Breach of Contract	
Primary function	*Remedies*
Compensation	Compensatory damages.
Restitution	Restitutionary damages. Account of profits. Award of money had and received.
Punishment	Punitive damages.
Compelling performance (of positive obligations)	Specific performance. Award of an agreed sum. Mandatory enforcing injunction. Appointment of a receiver.
Preventing a wrong	Prohibitory injunction. Delivery up for destruction or destruction on oath.
Compelling the undoing of a wrong	Mandatory restorative injunction. Delivery up of goods.
Declaring rights	Declaration. Nominal damages. Contemptuous damages.

Zakzrewski has recently argued that this classification, which he terms 'goal-based', is inadequate.[10] This is because one would need to unpack the goals of the rights triggering, for example, 'compelling performance' or 'preventing a wrong' and to do this would make the goals too diverse. With respect, this depends on the level of detail one uses to define the goals and there is nothing analytically impure in a classification of function that combines, for example, 'compensation' with 'preventing a wrong'. Even if there were an analytical impurity, it is submitted that this type of classification remains the most practically useful and illuminating one to adopt in understanding judicial remedies (for civil wrongs). In particular, as has been indicated above,[11] judges and practitioners are

---

10 'The Classification of Judicial Remedies' [2003] LMCLQ 477, esp at 493.
11 Above, p 2.

unlikely to find helpful Zakzrewski's view that the details of the law on specific performance and injunctions are within the law of remedies but the details of the law on damages are not.

9. LEGAL AND EQUITABLE REMEDIES

References will be made throughout to remedies being either legal or equitable. This is historical labelling indicating that the remedy was developed in the common law courts or in the Court of Chancery prior to the fusion of the courts by the 1873–75 Judicature Acts. It should be noted that, as a legacy of history, legal remedies, in contrast to equitable remedies, are almost all monetary.

Does it now matter whether the remedy for a tort or breach of contract is common law or equitable? For those who resist the fusion of common law and equity, the answer is 'yes'. They would seek to emphasise and retain the historical differences between common law and equitable remedies. In particular, they would point to equitable remedies being discretionary, and being subject to discretionary defences (such as 'clean hands', hardship and laches) in contrast to common law remedies being subject to clear rules and being available as of right. It is submitted that that approach is misleading. Both common law and equitable remedies are granted or refused in accordance with clearly established rules and principles. Some of the principles, including at common law, allow considerable discretion to the courts (eg the principles limiting compensatory damages and the availability of punitive damages) so that it is false to equate common law remedies with 'no discretion'.[12] True it is that there are some differences; for example, common law damages, in contrast to equitable damages awarded as a substitute for an injunction, cannot yet be awarded for an anticipated, rather than an accrued, wrong; and where a breach of contract or tort has been established, it appears that a court, if asked to do so, must at least award nominal damages whereas a claimant seeking an equitable remedy may simply be refused it. But it is submitted that the similarities far outweigh the differences; that the differences are relatively minor; that rationally there is no good reason for the differences; and that nothing would be lost, and some simplicity and rationality would be gained, if one took the small steps

---

12 The sort of discretion in play has been called 'weak' rather than 'strong', which goes back to a distinction drawn by Dworkin *Taking Rights Seriously* (1977) at pp 31–39. There is a school of thought that remedies should be decided by a strong discretion, which would allow the judge to choose the most appropriate remedy on the particular facts. For powerful criticism of this 'discretionary remedialism,' see Birks 'Rights, Wrongs and Remedies' (2000) OJLS 1, 22–24; 'Three Kinds of Objection to Discretionary Remedialism' (2000) 29 UWALR 1.

necessary to move to a fully-fused system of remedies where it would be unnecessary to use the labels common law or equitable.[13]

Certainly it is a grave error of some books and courses to perpetuate the historical division by treating equitable remedies separately from legal remedies as if they have no connection with each other. One of the purposes of this book is to emphasise that both legal and equitable remedies may be available to a claimant for a legal wrong, whether a tort or breach of contract. Indeed, in certain situations, the legal and equitable remedies perform the same or similar functions, eg an account of profits and the award of money had and received or restitutionary damages effect restitution, and specific performance and the award of an agreed sum compel performance of positive contractual obligations.

10.   EQUITABLE WRONGS

A useful classification within the civil law, articulated particularly by Peter Birks, is between causes of action that are wrongs and causes of action that are not wrongs.[14] Birks argued that a (civil) wrong means 'conduct ... whose effect in creating legal consequences is attributable to its being characterised as a breach of duty.'[15] Moreover, it appears that, with the conceivable exception of some statutory duties, a sure test for whether that definition is satisfied (ie whether the law is characterising particular conduct as constituting a breach of duty) is that compensation must be an available remedial measure for the conduct in question if loss is caused to the claimant by that conduct. Applying that test, torts and breach of contract are civil wrongs. In contrast, unjust enrichment triggering the restitution of money (or non-money benefits) rendered by mistake or for a failed consideration or under duress is a cause of action that is not a wrong. Restitution of the value of the enrichment subtracted from the claimant is the only available remedial measure; compensation for loss is not available for the unjust enrichment.

It also then becomes clear that, alongside torts and breach of contract, which are common law wrongs (because they were developed in the common law courts), there are equitable wrongs (developed in the Court of Chancery). Applying the above test, the equitable civil wrongs are breach of fiduciary duty, breach of confidence, dishonestly procuring or

---

13   Burrows 'We Do This At Common Law But That In Equity' (2002) 22 OJLS 1; *Fusing Common Law and Equity: Remedies, Restitution and Reform* Hochelaga Lecture 2001, pp 1–26.
14   Eg Birks 'Misnomer' in *Restitution: Past, Present and Future* (eds Cornish, Nolan, O'Sullivan and Virgo, 1998) pp 1, 8–9; Birks 'Rights, Wrongs and Remedies' (2000) 20 OJLS 1, 25–36.
15   Birks *An Introduction to the Law of Restitution* (1989) p 313.

assisting a breach of fiduciary duty and those forms of estoppel that constitute causes of action, in particular proprietary estoppel.[16]

It further follows from this analysis that the focus in this book on remedies for torts and breach of contract is on the common law wrongs only. On the face of it, one is putting to one side the analogous equitable wrongs merely because of their historical roots and not for rational reasons. Moreover, while it is still essentially true, as those wishing to perpetuate the historical divisions between common law and equity tend to stress, that only equitable remedies are available for equitable wrongs, it is also true that the same, or similar, functions are performed by the remedies for equitable wrongs as by the remedies for torts and breach of contract. In other words, there is a coherence in remedial function for civil wrongs that transcends the common law/equity divide.

In the two previous editions of this book, the importance of seeing that the functions of the remedies for equitable and common law wrongs are coherent was emphasised in the introductory chapter;[17] and the equitable wrong of breach of confidence (because so close to being treated as a tort) was dealt with throughout the book.

Developments in the last ten years – and, in particular, the increased number of cases of 'professional negligence' against, for example, solicitors, in which claimants have sought equitable compensation for breach of fiduciary duty as an alternative to damages for the tort of negligence or breach of contract – suggest that a more detailed treatment of remedies for equitable wrongs is now required. One way forward would be to examine remedies for equitable wrongs alongside torts and breach of contract under each of the four parts of this book devoted to different remedial functions. The possible disadvantage of that approach is in making the issues less accessible, and the text less easy to use, not least because our understanding of equitable wrongs, and the basic law on the central remedy of equitable compensation, is still developing. It has therefore been decided that the better approach is to devote the last part and chapter to remedies for equitable wrongs where the parallels – and contrasts – with remedies for torts and breach of contract can conveniently be explored. One should add that the inclusion of a chapter on remedies for equitable wrongs means that the coverage of this book, going beyond its title, is remedies for civil wrongs.[18]

---

16 Undue influence is not an equitable wrong because it does not trigger compensation: see Birks 'Unjust Factors and Wrongs: Pecuniary Rescission for Undue Influence' [1997] RLR 72 which discusses *Mahoney v Purnell* [1996] 3 All ER 61.

17 (2nd edn, 1994) pp 9–11.

18 But this book does not purport to cover any specialised remedies for particular statutory wrongs (eg the remedies that may be awarded by an employment tribunal for unfair dismissal).

11.   COMBINING REMEDIES

The question of the extent to which a claimant can combine judicial remedies for the same, or more than one, cause of action is a very difficult one. It has escaped the attention of commentators that it deserves.[19]

One should initially put to one side situations where a claimant invokes a self-help remedy and an inconsistent judicial remedy. For example, one cannot rescind ab initio a contract at the same time as claiming damages for breach of contract;[20] nor can one terminate a contract for breach of contract and seek specific performance of it.[1] The effect of the claimant's election to invoke the self-help remedy in these situations is akin to a claimant being barred from a remedy for an infringement of his or her rights because the claimant has affirmed, waived or acquiesced in the infringement. All rest on the justifiable policy that, where the defendant has relied on the claimant taking one course of action, it would unfairly upset the defendant's expectations for the claimant to change his or her mind.

But where judicial remedies are being sought the concerns about combining remedies are rather different. One is barely concerned, if at all, about the other party's expectations being disappointed. Rather it is the avoidance of the claimant having 'double recovery' or otherwise excessive recovery that is in mind. Labelling judicial remedies as inconsistent, and requiring the claimant to elect between them, is designed to avoid such double (or excessive) recovery.[2] Where there is no such problem, the claimant has a free choice to combine remedies.

So, for example, an injunction to prevent the continuation of a tort can be combined with compensatory damages for the tort that has already been committed. There is no double recovery problem.

In contrast, one cannot combine damages protecting the expectation interest for breach of contract with damages protecting the reliance interest for a tortious misrepresentation inducing that contract. Where the bargain was a good one, the former swallows up the latter and, where

---

19   An exception is the excellent article by Watterson 'Alternative and Cumulative Remedies: What is the Difference?' [2003] RLR 7.

20   Treitel *The Law of Contract* (11th edn, 2003) p 370.

1   *Johnson v Agnew* [1980] AC 367 at 392. Lord Wilberforce said, '[I]f the vendor treats the purchaser as having repudiated the contract and accepts the repudiation, he cannot thereafter seek specific performance. This follows from the fact that, the purchaser having repudiated the contract and his repudiation having been accepted, both parties are discharged from further performance.'

2   Watterson [2003] RLR 7, esp 18–21, argues that the most appropriate label to describe the objection is neither 'inconsistency' nor 'double recovery' but rather 'excessive remedial cumulation'.

the bargain was a bad one, the latter swallows up the former. To allow both would give double recovery. As alternatively expressed, it would be inconsistent: one cannot at the same time put the claimant into as good a position as if the contract had been performed and into as good a position as if no contract had been made. Again, it is clear law that a claimant cannot combine compensatory damages and an account of profits for, for example, an intellectual property tort. So, for example, if D, by committing a wrong to C, has made a net gain of £1,000 and by the same wrong has caused loss to C of £2,000, the effect of requiring D to pay C £3,000 would be that C is neither *just* compensated for its loss (but instead receives a windfall of £1,000) nor is D *just* stripped of its wrongly acquired gain (but rather has an extra £2,000 stripped away). An award of £3,000 would therefore be inconsistent with either of the remedial purposes being pursued and would constitute double recovery.

Where the law requires a claimant to make a choice, or election, of judicial remedy, the choice need not be made until judgment; and, even then, it can be changed if the defendant fails to comply with the judgment.[3]

One may question, however, whether the fear of double recovery necessitates the claimant making an election between judicial remedies. Provided one takes account of the other, double recovery can be avoided without requiring an election. In Watterson's words, 'English law's election orthodoxy is not a logical necessity.'[4] In the above examples, what is objectionable is *full* protection of the expectation interest and *full* protection of the reliance interest; or *full* compensation and *full* restitution. But there would be no objection to combining damages for the expectation interest and damages for the reliance interest if one modified the award protecting the expectation interest to take account of what one is awarding to protect the reliance interest. Similarly, the correct award of £2,000 in the second example above could be justified as restitution (£1,000) plus partial compensation (£1,000).

Viewed in this way, it can be seen that the great merit of requiring an election between judicial remedies is that, in a clear and straightforward way, it avoids double (or excessive) recovery. It avoids the courts having to decide, in assessing quantum, whether, and the extent to which, a particular combination of remedies gives double recovery. The

---

3   See, generally, *United Australia Ltd v Barclays Bank Ltd* [1941] AC 1, 19, 21, 30. See also below, pp 508–509 (specific performance).
4   [2003] RLR 7, 21.

disadvantage of requiring an election is that it is conceivable that a claimant may be deprived of its full entitlement by making an inappropriate election.

12.   THE IMPACT OF THE HUMAN RIGHTS ACT 1998

The enactment of the Human Rights Act 1998 (HRA 1998) has raised a number of novel issues for English law. But its impact on the law of remedies has been very limited. In particular, the 1998 Act does not mean that new and different remedies are suddenly made available. The impact of the Act on the subject matter of this book is best understood by clarifying that the Act can influence civil wrongs in one of two main ways.[5] First, and most obviously, HRA 1998, s 6(1) creates a new statutory cause of action constituted by a public authority's infringement of a person's Convention rights. This new cause of action is most conveniently viewed as a tort. It has been labelled a 'constitutional tort'[6] although, as it has been created by a particular statute, it is probably more straightforwardly seen as one of the many examples of a statutory tort. As a tort, it belongs within the coverage of this book.

But the 1998 Act is not confined to having that 'vertical' effect. As the definition of a public authority in HRA 1998, s 6(3) includes a court, the 1998 Act can have some 'horizontal' effect (that is, in actions between 'private parties').[7] While the Act does not require the courts to develop new civil wrongs, the courts may need to modify existing common law or equitable wrongs to take account of Convention rights. So, for example, it has affected torts by modifying the approach of the courts to 'immunities' from liability.[8] And while the Act does not create a new tort of privacy,[9] it has been a stimulus for the equitable wrong of breach of confidence to play a more vibrant role in protecting privacy.[10]

Under the first route of influence (and possibly under the second 'horizontal' way as well), when one turns to remedies, one must apply

---

5   That HRA 1998, s 3(1) requires statutes to be interpreted, where possible, in accordance with Convention rights, may also, albeit very rarely, be relevant to the subject matter of this book: see, eg below, p 297, n 5. On HRA 1998, s 12(3), see below, p 561.
6   See *Clerk and Lindsell on Torts* (18th edn, 2000) paras 1–04, 12–75–12–81.
7   For a clear recognition of this (contrary to the early doubts of some commentators) see, eg *Campbell v Mirror Group Newspapers Ltd* [2004] UKHL 22, [2004] 2 All ER 995, paras 132–133 (per Baroness Hale of Richmond).
8   But the very significant impact indicated by the European Court of Human Rights in *Osman v United Kingdom* (1998) 5 BHRC 293 has been backtracked from in, eg *Z v United Kingdom* (2001) 34 EHRR 97.
9   *Wainwright v Home Office* [2003] UKHL 53, [2003] 3 WLR 1137.
10   See, eg *Douglas v Hello! Ltd (No 3)* [2003] EWHC 786 (Ch), [2003] 3 All ER 996; *Campbell v Mirror Group Newspapers Ltd* [2004] UKHL 22, [2004] 2 All ER 995.

HRA 1998, s 8. By s 8(1) the court may grant any remedy, within its powers, as it considers 'just and appropriate'. By s 8(3) no damages are to be awarded unless, taking account of any other remedy granted, the court is satisfied that the award is 'necessary to afford just satisfaction' to the claimant. By s 8(4) the court must take into account in deciding whether to award damages, and the amount, the principles applied by the European Court of Human Rights in relation to the award of compensation.

HRA 1998, s 8(3) makes clear that, contrary to the position in English domestic law for torts and breach of contract, damages are not available as of right for a 1998 Act wrong and may be refused if other appropriate remedies render an award of damages unnecessary.[11] As regards s 8(4), while the principles applied by the European Court of Human Rights are notoriously unclear, there is no doubt that the basic aim of the compensation awarded, as in English domestic law, is to put the claimant into as good a position as if his or her convention rights had not been infringed; and both pecuniary loss and non-pecuniary loss can be compensated.

The indications are that, beyond the initial difference that damages are not available as of right, the English courts will apply essentially the same principles, and essentially the same approach to quantum, to compensatory damages awarded under the Act as to compensatory damages in 'domestic' tort cases.[12] So, for example, in *R (KB) v Mental Health Review Tribunal*[13] Stanley Burnton J pointed out that the requirement to take account of the principles applied by the European Court of Human Rights was difficult to apply given the inconsistencies of approach and 'lack of principle' in the jurisprudence of that court. More importantly, he thought that there was no good reason why compensatory damages for the new cause of action of a public authority's infringement of a person's Convention rights should be lower

---

11 So, eg in *Dennis v Ministry of Defence* [2003] EWHC 793 (QB), [2003] NLJR 634, para 31 damages for infringement of a Convention right were not awarded because compensatory damages were being awarded, irrespective of the Human Rights Act 1998, for the tort of nuisance.

12 One would therefore expect standard 'domestic law' principles of, for example, remoteness, contributory negligence and the duty to mitigate to apply.

13 [2003] EWHC 193 (Admin), [2003] 2 All ER 209. But two differences referred to by Stanley Burnton J are that, applying the jurisprudence of the European Court of Human Rights, no loss of a chance damages in respect of a favourable tribunal decision are awarded; and no punitive damages are to be awarded (see below, p 420). See generally *Damages under the Human Rights Act 1998*, Law Commission Report No 266 (2000) paras 4.59–4.91. With respect, the suggestion in the Law Commission's report that the European Court of Human Rights compensates loss of love, companionship and support, whereas English law does not, is incorrect: these non-pecuniary losses are clearly recoverable in English law where consequent on the claimant's personal injury and possibly in other contexts (eg for the tort of false imprisonment).

than for analogous torts in English domestic law. In relation to mental distress, he held that to be compensatable under HRA 1998 (at least for infringement of a right to liberty and security under the European Convention on Human Rights, Article 5) the distress had to be of sufficient intensity to justify an award.

In *Anufrijeva v London Borough of Southwark*[14] the Court of Appeal approved the approach of Stanley Burnton J but added that, in relation to maladministration by public authorities, courts may also derive guidance from the levels of compensation awarded by the Parliamentary and Local Government Ombudsmen.[15] This was not least because in English domestic law there is no direct tort of ultra vires maladministration by a public authority. The Court of Appeal stressed that there was no right to any damages under HRA 1998 and the judgment may be interpreted as suggesting, controversially, that the normal remedies in claims against public authorities under HRA 1998 would be those available by judicial review and not damages.[16] The Court of Appeal also suggested that the scale and manner of the violation may be relevant in deciding whether damages for non-pecuniary loss should be awarded, an approach which is reminiscent of the 'domestic' concept of 'aggravated damages'.[17] In so far as damages were to be awarded it was said that they should be moderate.

13.   BREACH OF EUROPEAN COMMUNITY LAW

There are two situations where an individual has a cause of action for damages for breach of EC law. The first is where there has been breach of a 'directly effective'[18] provision of EC law. 'Directly effective' provisions may operate both vertically and horizontally; that is, they may give a person rights against both the state and against other individuals. The second situation is 'state liability' as established in the leading case of

---

14 [2003] EWCA Civ 1406, [2004] 1 All ER 833.
15 The Court of Appeal therefore approved the approach of Sullivan J in *R (Bernard) v Enfield London Borough Council* [2002] EWHC 2282 (Admin), [2003] HRLR 4 who had derived assistance on levels of award not only from judicial awards for non-pecuniary loss but also from the Local Government Ombudsman.
16 See esp paras 52–56. Cf Sullivan J in *R (Bernard) v Enfield London Borough Council* [2002] EWHC 2282 (Admin), [2003] HRLR 4, at para 40, who suggested that, where a public authority explains what has gone wrong, apologises and assures the claimant that it will not happen again – and takes those steps reasonably promptly – 'Then it may well be the case that nothing more is required by way of monetary compensation in order to afford "just satisfaction" in very many cases.'
17 Below, p 339.
18 See, eg *NV Algemene Transporten Expeditie Onderneming van Gend en Loos v Nederlandse Administratie der Belastingen* Case 26/62, [1963] ECR 1; *Defrenne v Société Anonyme Belge de Navigation Aérienne* Case 43/75, [1976] ECR 455.

Francovich and Bonifaci v Italy.[19] 'State liability' is concerned to impose liability for harm caused to individuals by a 'sufficiently serious' breach of Community law for which the state can be held responsible. 'State liability' has now been extended from non-implementation of a directive to misimplementation, legislative acts and omissions, judicial decisions, and administrative decisions.[20]

English law has characterised the cause of action for damages for breach of EC law as a tort. It has usually been treated as an example of the tort of breach of statutory duty[1] although, not least because the link to an English statute (European Communities Act 1972, s 2(1)) is rather indirect, some have preferred to label it a 'Euro-tort'.[2] As a tort, it falls within the scope of this book.

In terms of remedies, most discussion has been in the context of directly-effective provisions and it has been established that the basic EC law principle is one of national autonomy.[3] The remedies available are a matter for the national legal system which is not required to create new remedies. But this is qualified to the extent that the remedies must be effective and adequate for the breach in question;[4] and must not be applied less favourably than those applying to similar domestic causes of action.

In practice, the remedies applied for Euro-torts, and the principles governing those remedies, have been no different from those applicable to domestic torts. One possible exception is that punitive damages may not be available (even if the case falls within the categories where they would be available for domestic torts).[5]

---

19 Case C-6&9/90, [1991] ECR I-5357. See also, eg *Brasserie du Pecheur SA v Germany, R v Secretary of State for Transport, ex p Factortame Ltd* Case C-46 & 48/93, [1996] QB 404; *R v HM Treasury, ex p British Telecommunications plc* Case C-392/93, [1996] QB 615; *Dillenkofer v Germany* Case C-178-9/94, 188–190/194, [1996] ECR I-4845; *Denkavit International v Bundesamt für Finanzen* Case C-283, 291 and 292/94, [1996] ECR I-5063.
20 Eg *Köbler v Austria* Case C-224/01, [2004] QB 848, ECJ (dealing with judicial decisions).
1   *Garden Cottage Foods Ltd v Milk Marketing Board* [1984] AC 130; *R v Secretary of State for Transport, ex p Factortame Ltd (No 7)* [2001] 1 WLR 942 (for the purposes of the Limitation Act 1980); *Crehan v Inntrepreneur Pub Co (CPC)* [2004] EWCA Civ 637. See also Brealey and Hoskins *Remedies in EC Law* (1998) ch 7. An earlier view that the tort in question was best viewed as misfeasance in public office (see, eg *Bourgoin SA v Ministry of Agriculture, Fisheries and Food* [1986] QB 716) was rejected in the *Brasserie du Pecheur* case [1996] QB 404.
2   *Clerk and Lindsell on Torts* (18th edn, 2000), paras 1–03, 12–80, 12–87; Lunney and Oliphant *Tort Law: Text and Materials* (2000) pp 523–527.
3   *Rewe-Zentralfinanz and Rewe-Zentral v Landwirtschaftskammer für das Saarland* Case 33/76, [1976] ECR 1989.
4   An example of EC law requiring a 'remedy', best rationalised as restitutionary, is provided by *Metallgesellschaft Ltd v IRC, Hoescht AG v IRC* Cases C-397–410/98, [2001] Ch 620.
5   See below, p 419.

14.   ECONOMIC ANALYSIS, BARGAINING AROUND NON-MONETARY REMEDIES AND THE CONSUMER SURPLUS

Over the past thirty years or so, there has been widespread interest by academic lawyers, especially in the US, in the economic analysis of law, which examines how far the law promotes economic efficiency. Indeed a good deal of economic analysis writing has focused on the civil law remedies considered in this book. Some commentators even seem to come close to using efficiency as the only important criterion for critically assessing the law, but this surely overplays its importance. The common law is best regarded as a coherent system of principle, reflecting a complex mix of 'moral rights' reasoning, modified and tempered by the desire to pursue certain long-term social policies. One important social policy is efficiency; but its place is alongside, not as a replacement for, moral rights reasoning, and this is how it is used in this book.

On a more detailed level, several other criticisms can be levelled at traditional economic analysis. To understand these, it is as well to set out very briefly how economists have tended to look at tort and contract.[6] There can be said to be three important steps in the reasoning. The first is that a system is efficient where those who place the highest value on resources have the use of those resources. Free-market voluntary exchanges, by which resources are moved to successively more valued uses, are therefore the necessary means for efficiency. The second step is the Coase Theorem,[7] stating that in the absence of transaction costs it does not matter what legal rights and remedies there are because the parties as rational maximisers of value will negotiate round them to produce the most efficient result. Say, for example, A's factory produces smoke ruining B's enjoyment of his land. If the value of the factory to A as it is (that is, the value attributable to the smoke) is £100,000 and the enjoyment of B's land is worth £70,000 to him, the efficient allocation of resources is to allow A to continue polluting. According to the Coase Theorem, even if A is legally ordered to stop the factory emitting such smoke, he will carry on as before, by paying B £70,000, or indeed up to £99,999. If we reverse the figures, then by the same reasoning the smoke will be stopped even if B is given no injunction because, according to Coase, B will pay A between £70,000 and £99,999 to stop the smoke. The final step is then economic analysis confronting the fact that in the

---

6   See also Harris *Remedies in Contract and Tort* (1st edn, 1988) pp 6–14 (that introductory section has been deleted in the 2nd edn, 2002); Howarth *Textbook on Tort* (1995) pp 15–19.
7   Coase 'The Problem of Social Cost' (1960) 3 J Law & Econ 1.

real world there are transaction costs. Hence the allocation of legal rights and remedies can be expected to affect efficiency. Free bargaining will not necessarily take place to correct 'errors' and, even if it does, transaction costs will be incurred. The courts should therefore strive to promote efficiency by deciding on legal rights and remedies that on a general level promote voluntary exchanges, and more specifically mimic the voluntary exchanges that the parties as rational maximisers of value would make.

This economic approach is troubling in several respects. First, the methodology being used is most unappealing to lawyers, who are used to dealing at a specific level with concrete facts and issues. In particular, lawyers are likely to be unhappy with individuals being portrayed as solely concerned to maximise value, when this does not correspond to the reality of human motivation. Secondly, it can be argued that efficiency is not a value-free notion, and that the approach outlined above rests on nothing more than right-wing, free-market ideology. Thirdly, even though applying the same general approach, economists differ as to whether particular legal rules are efficient or not. To give an example from the law in this book, it was for several years argued that it was efficient for specific performance to remain a secondary remedy to damages, but more recently the opposing view has been fervently put forward. It should not be thought, therefore, that the law can always turn to clearly agreed conclusions as to what is and what is not efficient. Finally, many of the arguments turn on the extent of transaction or other costs and yet there is little empirical data to support the views expressed.

For reasons such as these there seems little to be gained from detailed economic analysis. Moreover it should be reiterated that even where used at a general and relatively uncontroversial level, efficiency should in no sense be regarded as the sole criterion for assessing the law. Indeed it can be argued that, in the remedies field, the most significant contribution of the economic analysis movement lies not in showing that particular legal principles do or do not promote efficiency but rather in highlighting two legally important notions that might otherwise not have received the attention they deserve.

One is what economists term the 'consumer surplus', namely the subjective value that a consumer places on particular property or services, over and above the objective market value.[8] This is a useful way of explaining, for example, why a person having a wall built for privacy is, in the event of breach, unlikely to be put into as good a position as if

---

8   Harris, Ogus and Phillips 'Contract Remedies and the Consumer Surplus' (1979) 95 LQR 581.

the contract had been performed if she is simply awarded damages reflecting the difference in market value of her land with and without the wall; or why it is essential for the courts to award mental distress damages to compensate fully for a ruined holiday; or why specific performance is a preferable remedy to damages for someone buying a particular home.

The other notion is that the parties may well bargain around non-monetary remedies, like injunctions and specific performance, whether pre- or post-judgment.[9] Two views can be suggested as to the effect this should have on the remedies awarded. First, there is the view that the possibility of post-judgment bargaining should have no effect on a court's reasoning. The court should rather reach a decision according to what it thinks is just, and should regard it as entirely a matter for the parties if they then prefer a different solution. After all, the court cannot know in advance whether the parties will embark on post-judgment bargaining. Alternatively, it can be argued that the courts should be wary of granting non-monetary remedies, precisely because the claimant, who has been or will be awarded an injunction or specific performance, is placed in too strong a position in pre- or post-judgment bargaining; for to the extent that the defendant's gains from the wrong will exceed the claimant's loss, it will be in each party's interest to negotiate a deal whereby the claimant takes a share in the defendant's gains in return for the defendant being free to commit the 'wrong'. Moreover, there will be every incentive for the claimant to demand a huge share of those gains, going far beyond the compensation needed to cover the value to him of the right infringed. Both the consumer surplus and bargaining around the remedies are ideas that will be returned to at various stages in this book.

15. THE LAYOUT OF THE BOOK

This book is primarily structured according to, first, the functions of the remedies for torts and breach of contract and, secondly, the particular remedies concerned to effect those functions. So there are four parts corresponding to the remedial functions set out above[10] (compensation; restitution and punishment; compelling performance or preventing (or compelling the undoing of) a wrong; and declaring rights). Within each part, the particular remedy or remedies concerned to effect those

---

9   Sharpe *Injunctions and Specific Performance* (3rd edn, 2000) paras 1.150–1.170, Thompson 'Injunction Negotiations: An Economic, Moral and Legal Analysis' (1975) 27 Stan LR 1563.
10   Above, p 10.

functions are examined. A final part and chapter, for reasons set out above,[11] looks at remedies for equitable wrongs.

11   Above, p 13.

Part one

Compensation

Section one

General principles in assessing compensatory damages

Chapter 2

Introduction to compensatory damages: types of loss, compensatory aims, and theoretical underpinnings

1. COMPENSATION, COMPENSATORY DAMAGES AND TYPES OF LOSS

Compensation means the award of a sum of money which, so far as money can be so, is equivalent to the claimant's loss. The loss may be pecuniary (that is, a loss of wealth) where the equivalence to the claimant's loss can be precise; or non-pecuniary (for example, pain, suffering and loss of amenity, loss of reputation, and mental distress generally) where the sum to be awarded as compensation cannot be precisely equivalent to the loss and where the only way to ensure consistency of awards is through conventionally accepted tariffs of value.

The remedy concerned to achieve compensation for torts and breach of contract is compensatory damages (that is, damages concerned to compensate). This is almost always a common law remedy although, as we shall see in chapter 16 below, equitable compensatory damages awarded in addition to, or in substitution for, specific performance or an injunction, may also be awarded for a tort or breach of contract.

By an award of damages a sum of money assessed by the court is required to be paid by the defendant to the claimant.[1] The usual function of damages is compensation; that is, damages are usually compensatory. But it would be a mistake to imagine that damages and compensation are synonymous. This is because some awards of damages are non-compensatory: ie damages may also be punitive or restitutionary or nominal or contemptuous. In this part of this book, we are solely concerned with compensatory damages.

This and the following fourteen chapters examine in detail the law on compensatory damages. The first seven chapters (chapters 2 to 8) cover the general principles of assessment and equip one with all that is basically needed to assess compensatory damages, whatever the type of loss in question. The subsequent five chapters (chapters 9 to 13) then put

---

1   Strictly speaking, this refers to unliquidated damages. For 'liquidated damages' for breach of contract, see below, ch 19.

flesh on those bare bones by examining compensatory damages for the different types of loss. Chapters 14 and 15 deal with two factors of relevance to, while not concerning the assessment of, compensatory damages, namely, awards of interest and limitation periods. Finally, chapter 16 looks at equitable compensatory damages for torts and breach of contract.

It is convenient to consider in a little more depth here the fundamental division between pecuniary and non-pecuniary loss and to explain the further division of types of loss adopted in chapters 9 to 13.

So starting with the fundamental division between pecuniary and non-pecuniary loss, money can be complete compensation for the former but not for the latter. As Lord Diplock said in *Wright v British Railways Board*,[2] '[Non-pecuniary] loss is not susceptible of *measurement* in money. Any figure at which the assessor of damages arrives cannot be other than artificial ...'

This distinction does not mean that there are never any difficulties in assessing pecuniary loss; for while in some cases compensation for monetary loss is mathematically obvious and exact (for example, pre-trial expenditure), in most instances the uncertainties of what would have happened but for the wrong, and of what will happen in the future, make the assessment of even the loss of monetary income (eg loss of earnings) problematical. Similarly, while reliance on market values is often the most accurate method of assessing pecuniary loss for, for example, property damage, any attempt to put a value on anything, other than money itself, involves some approximation. So the distinction is not between losses where the compensation is precise and losses where it is imprecise. Rather it is between losses which are of wealth, and can therefore be readily translated into money, and other losses.

But as non-pecuniary losses are not losses of wealth, how exactly are they viewed and compared? The traditional judicial approach is to treat some heads of non-pecuniary loss, namely loss of amenity, physical inconvenience, and loss of reputation, as analogous to proprietary losses and as losses over and above the claimant's distress or loss of happiness; such heads of loss, in contrast to pain and suffering and mental distress, are therefore assessed objectively with the severe distress of the claimant or his unconsciousness being regarded as irrelevant. On this approach, while pain and suffering and mental distress are compared in terms of the degree of distress suffered by the claimant, the other non-pecuniary

---

2   [1983] 2 AC 773 at 777. For similar judicial statements, see *The Mediana* [1900] AC 113 at 116; *West & Son Ltd v Shephard* [1964] AC 326 at 346; *Fletcher v Autocar and Transporters Ltd* [1968] 2 QB 322 at 335, 339–340, 363; *Heil v Rankin* [2001] QB 272 at 293.

losses are compared by examining the extent of the interference with, and the importance of, the 'personal asset' affected.

An alternative and preferable view is that to treat any non-pecuniary loss as analogous to a property loss is unrealistic and that ultimately all non-pecuniary loss is concerned with the claimant's distress or loss of happiness. Taking this approach the different heads of non-pecuniary loss must simply be regarded as different types of distress with the head of 'mental distress' being a residual category. In practice this approach would rarely lead to different results than the traditional judicial one for the courts would need to treat a particular personal injury or physical inconvenience or loss of reputation as affecting individuals' happiness in essentially the same way, just as they already do, for example, in assessing pain and suffering damages. So adoption of the alternative approach would not mean that the claimant who has made the best of his misfortune would be likely to recover less than the claimant who has not, nor that a claimant would be encouraged to present a long face to the court. But the alternative view does provide a sound theoretical explanation for non-pecuniary loss and hence for why, for example, some non-pecuniary losses are regarded as more serious than others. Moreover, there would be at least two practical differences. First, severe distress suffered by the claimant would merit higher damages under any of the heads of non-pecuniary loss and, secondly, an unconscious claimant would recover nothing for non-pecuniary loss.

Whichever of the two approaches is taken – and as yet there is little judicial support for any departure from the first traditional view – there ought to be uniformity between awards. In other words, similar awards should be made for similar non-pecuniary losses and more serious losses should be compensated by higher awards. This is dictated by the essential justice of like cases being treated alike. It also gives some certainty to the law which in turn aids out-of-court settlements.

Since the virtual elimination of jury trials in personal injury cases, uniformity has indeed become the prime feature of damages for pain and suffering and loss of amenity, with judges relying on a tariff system. Similarly in Fatal Accidents Act 1976 cases there is a fixed statutory sum for bereavement. There would also seem to be an awareness of the need for uniformity in respect of other non-pecuniary losses, such as mental distress, although the survival of jury trials in defamation cases hampers putting this into effect for tortious loss of reputation.

Of course the emphasis on uniformity in no sense explains how the level of award is reached in the first place. Why, for example, should damages for loss of amenity and pain and suffering resulting from blindness be assessed at (say) £140,000 rather than £1,000? The courts are generally content to say merely that the level of awards must be fair and reasonable,[3] should keep pace with the times,[4] and should in no sense reflect the claimant's wealth.[5] This may be all that can be sensibly said. However, economists have suggested that a value can be put on injury or life by, for example, asking what people would be prepared to pay to avoid incurring that injury, or what they would be willing to accept to incur it.[6] But in general it is hard to see how either question can produce anything more than further guess-work and the latter would, in any event, produce astronomically high awards. Perhaps more hopeful is to think in terms of the cost of substitute pleasures; that is, a claimant should be enabled to buy whatever can in some sense be regarded as making up for the loss he has suffered or will suffer so that, for example, a blind man should at the very least be able to buy hi-fi equipment and compact discs, and the person disabled from skiing should be able to buy holidays in the sun.

It follows from this discussion that one way to divide the types of loss for the purposes of examining compensatory damages is simply to divide between pecuniary and non-pecuniary loss. But ultimately it has been considered preferable in this chapter to make a different and more detailed division of types of loss which, it is believed, accords more with the way lawyers are used to confronting and thinking about compensatory damages. The division adopted is therefore as follows: pecuniary loss (except consequent on personal injury, death or loss of reputation); personal injury losses; losses on death; loss of reputation; and mental distress or physical inconvenience (except consequent on personal injury or death).

It should be emphasised finally that this book's approach to compensation is novel in not dividing torts and breach of contract and then examining compensatory damages for different torts and contracts respectively. There are many common approaches to compensation, whether the cause of action be tort or breach of contract, and in order to bring these out it has been considered preferable to examine compensatory damages in respect of the different types of loss with the tort/breach of contract divide then being recognised, where helpful, under each of those types.

---

3   Eg *Rowley v London and North Western Rly Co* (1873) LR 8 Exch 221 at 231; *Scott v Musial* [1959] 2 QB 429 at 443; *Gardner v Dyson* [1967] 1 WLR 1497 at 1501; *Heil v Rankin* [2001] QB 272 at 294, 297.
4   Below, pp 186–187.
5   *Fletcher v Autocar and Transporters Ltd* [1968] 2 QB 322 at 340–341.
6   See Cane *Atiyah's Accidents, Compensation and The Law* (6th edn, 1999) pp 135–136.

2.　THE COMPENSATORY AIMS

The aim of compensatory damages for breach of contract is to put the claimant into as good a position as it would have been in if the contract had been performed. For tort the aim of compensatory damages is to put the claimant into as good a position as it would have been in if no tort had been committed.

These compensatory aims are of fundamental importance. They guide the whole process of assessment. They clarify in general terms – subject to the limiting principles considered in chapter 6 – the losses which compensatory damages are concerned to cover.

The classic contract case laying down the aim of compensatory damages is *Robinson v Harman*[7] in which Parke B said:

> 'The rule of common law is that where a party sustains a loss by reason of a breach of contract he is, so far as money can do it, to be placed in the same situation with respect to damages as if the contract had been performed.'

Lord Blackburn's statement in *Livingstone v Rawyards Coal Co*,[8] a case concerning trespass to goods, is probably the most cited tort authority on this. He said that the measure of damages was:

> '... that sum of money which will put the party who has been injured, or who has suffered, in the same position as he would have been in if he had not sustained the wrong for which he is now getting his compensation or reparation.'

Many subsequent cases contain equally clear expressions of these central aims.[9]

For shorthand purposes, the two aims can be linked by saying that the aim of compensation is to put the claimant into as good a position as if no wrong had been committed. However, if one does combine the two aims in that way, one must be aware that very different results may ensue depending on whether the duty broken was a positive or a negative one; and that typically contractual duties are positive (hence the separate

---

7　(1848) 1 Exch 850 at 855.
8　(1880) 5 App Cas 25 at 39.
9　Eg for breach of contract, *Wertheim v Chicoutimi Pulp Co* [1911] AC 301 at 307; *British Westinghouse Co v Underground Electric Rlys Co of London Ltd* [1912] AC 673 at 689; *Monarch SS Co Ltd v Karlshamns Oljefabriker* [1949] AC 196 at 220; *The Heron II* [1969] 1 AC 350 at 414; *Doyle v Olby (Ironmongers) Ltd* [1969] 2 QB 158 at 167; *Tito v Waddell (No 2)* [1977] Ch 106 at 328–334; *Radford v De Froberville* [1977] 1 WLR 1262 at 1268; *Rees v Darlington Memorial Hospital NHS Trust* [2003] UKHL 52, [2003] 4 All ER 987 at para 130. For torts, see, eg *Shearman v Folland* [1950] 2 KB 43 at 49; *British Transport Commission v Gourley* [1956] AC 185 at 187; *Lim Poh Choo v Camden and Islington Area Health Authority* [1980] AC 174 at 186ff; *Dodd Properties (Kent) Ltd v Canterbury City Council* [1980] 1 WLR 433 at 456; *Swingcastle Ltd v Alastair Gibson* [1991] 2 AC 223; *Rees v Darlington Memorial Hospital NHS Trust* [2003] UKHL 52, [2003] 4 All ER 987 at para 130.

formulation of the aim as being to put the claimant into as good a position as if the contract had been performed) while tort duties are typically negative (hence the separate formulation of the aim as being to put the claimant into as good a position as if no tort had been committed).

The difference in results – between compensation for breach of positive contractual duties and for breach of negative tort duties – is best illustrated by reference to tortious misrepresentations inducing contracts. Say, for example, the claimant buys a car. The seller falsely misrepresents to him, and gives a contractual warranty, that the car is only one year old. In fact it is four years old. The claimant pays £5,000. The market value of a one-year-old car (but with the other characteristics – apart from the age – of the car the claimant buys) is £5,500 but the value of the car he actually receives (given its real age) is £4,000.

If the claimant keeps the car and brings a claim for damages for the tortious misrepresentation (whether for the tort of deceit or the tort of negligent misrepresentation), the aim is to put him into as good a position as if he had never entered into the contract. His damages will be £5,000 – £4,000 = £1,000. But if he brings an action for breach of contract, that is, for breach of the contractual warranty as to the age of the car, the aim is to put him into as good a position as if the statement had been true. His damages will be £5,500 – £4,000 = £1,500.

If the claimant made a bad bargain, so that the market value of a one-year-old car of that type is £4,500, not £5,500, he would be better off suing for tortious misrepresentation. His damages in contract would be £4,500 – £4,000 = £500 whereas in tort they would be £5,000 – £4,000 = £1,000.

3. THEORETICAL UNDERPINNINGS OF COMPENSATION

(1) Breach of contract

Fuller and Perdue in their seminal article 'The Reliance Interest in Contract Damages'[10] labelled the principle of putting the claimant into as good a position as if the contract had been performed as that of protecting the claimant's expectation interest. They regarded this, on the face of things, as an odd kind of compensation since it often puts the claimant into a better position than if no contract had been made. Hence the central question raised by Fuller and Perdue was, why should

10 (1936–37) 46 Yale LJ 52 and 373.

contractual damages usually protect the claimant's expectation interest? Why, for example, should damages not be restricted to ensuring that the claimant is made no worse off than if the contract had not been made – in Fuller and Perdue's terminology why should not damages be restricted to protecting the claimant's reliance interest?

A famous illustration of the distinction between damages protecting the claimant's expectation and reliance interests is provided by the US case of *Hawkins v McGee*.[11] The claimant had burnt his hand and the defendant, who was a surgeon interested in skin grafting, contractually promised the claimant to restore his hand to a perfect condition by an operation. The operation went wrong and, instead of having a perfect hand, the claimant's hand was made worse than it was before the operation. Two possible ways in which the damages for the breach of contract could be assessed were examined. The first was to deduct from the value of the hand before the operation the value of the hand as it was after it – in Fuller and Perdue's terminology this would protect the claimant's reliance interest. The second was to deduct from the value of a perfect hand the value of the hand after the operation – this would protect the claimant's expectation interest. The court held that for breach of contract the claimant was entitled to be put into as good a position as if the contract had been performed; hence the second measure of damages was awarded. In other words the claimant's expectation interest was protected.

Fuller and Perdue ultimately thought that at least for bargain promises – promises supported by consideration – protection of the expectation interest could be justified on two main grounds. First, that the expectation interest is the best measure of the claimant's reliance interest given that the latter is difficult to prove, particularly with regard to the forgoing of opportunities to enter other bargains.[12] But this seems a weak argument[13] since it is often just as difficult to prove what position the claimant would have been in if the contract had been performed as it is to prove what position it would have been in if no contract had been made. Moreover, difficulty of proof does not justify picking what on this reasoning would be an arbitrary measure.

Fuller and Perdue's second justificatory argument is, in contrast, a forceful one. This is, in essence, that protecting the claimant's expectation interest for promises supported by consideration ensures that parties reap

11   84 NH 114, 146 A 641 (1929).
12   (1936–37) 46 Yale LJ 52, 60–61.
13   For a similar persuasive criticism, see Friedmann 'The Performance Interest in Contract Damages' (1995) 111 LQR 628, 635–636, 638. See also Stephen Smith *Contract Theory* (2004) pp 78–96, 413–417.

the benefit of their bargains and thereby encourages the practice of bargaining. This in turn upholds the working of the market economy under which, through bargains, goods and services find their way to where they are most wanted.[14]

A similar approach is taken by the economics and law theorists, like Posner,[15] who argue that contract law is a system of rules and principles furthering economic efficiency and hence overall social welfare. As expectation damages for bargain promises give the claimant no less and no more than the value it has placed on the defendant's performance, they provide the defendant with an incentive to exchange resources with those who place the highest value on them; the efficient result is thereby promoted. Say, for example, A contracts to sell to B for £100,000 a machine that is worth £110,000 to B (ie that would yield him a profit of £10,000). Before delivery C comes to A and offers him £109,000 for that machine. A would be encouraged to break the contract with B were he not liable to pay B £10,000 expectation damages. Given that damages do protect the expectation rather than the reliance interest, C will not be able to induce a breach of A's contract with B unless he offers A more than £110,000 thereby indicating that the machine really is worth more to him than to B. The expectation rule thus ensures that the machine ends up where it is most valuable.

In contrast to the above justification is Fried's theory of 'Contract as Promise'[16] according to which, contract rests on the moral bindingness of a promise.[17] This is essentially a revival of the will theory of contract whereby a contractual obligation as against, for example, a tortious obligation is regarded as resting on the defendant's voluntary acceptance of that obligation; and a promise, as a matter of convention,[18] is a voluntarily undertaken obligation. On this approach the expectation interest is the obvious and natural measure of damages for all promises, even if gratuitous, since it represents the monetary equivalent of the defendant's promised performance. Fried expresses this as follows:

> 'If I make a promise to you, I should do as I promise: and if I fail to keep my promise to you, it is fair that I should be made to hand over the equivalent of the promised

---

14 (1936–37) 46 Yale LJ 52, 60–62.
15 *Economic Analysis of Law* (6th edn, 2003) ch 4. See also Birmingham 'Breach of Contract, Damages, Measures and Economic Efficiency' (1970) 24 Rutgers LR 273; Beale *Remedies for Breach of Contract* (1980) pp 159–164.
16 *Contract as Promise* (1981); see Burrows 'The Will Theory of Contract Revived – Fried's "Contract as Promise" ' [1985] CLP 141.
17 Stephen Smith *Contract Theory* (2004) chs 3–4, esp pp 74–78, also supports a promissory rights-based justification of contract but for different reasons than Fried.
18 Fried *Contract as Promise* (1981) ch 2.

performance ... In contract doctrine this proposition appears as the expectation measure ... [it] gives the victim of a breach no more or less than he would have had had there been no breach.'[19]

On this view, based as it is on moral 'rights' or 'principle', 'policy' and 'consequentialist' arguments put forward in Fuller and Perdue's market economy and Posner's economic efficiency explanations provide merely additional reasons for protecting the claimant's expectation interest, where the promise is a bargain promise.

More recently, in a superb article,[20] Friedmann has argued that, while synonymous, 'performance interest' is more appropriate terminology than 'expectation interest'; that the explanation for the law's protection of the performance interest is that it is the natural and obvious concomitant of there being a valid contract which confers a legal right to the promised performance; and that Fuller and Perdue's promotion of the 'reliance interest' (at the expense of the 'expectation interest') was misconceived and has had relatively little impact on the substantive law.

However, it should be stressed that all the above approaches, purporting to justify the protection of the expectation interest, run counter to many of the writings of one of the most influential English legal academics of the late twentieth century, Professor Patrick Atiyah.[1] A major thrust of Atiyah's work was that while protecting the expectation interest may have been justified in the nineteenth century, when people strongly believed in the moral bindingness of promises, and in upholding the free-market economy, it was far more difficult to justify in the late twentieth century. He therefore argued that protection of the reliance interest should be the normal rule and, while he did backtrack to some extent,[2] his predominant view was that traditional contract law protecting the expectation interest and built up on, what he regarded, as nineteenth-century laissez-faire values was dead or at least in its final death throes.

But his attack grossly overstated the position; for while the law does and should enable a promisor to escape from a contract more easily than in the past – reflecting a greater concern in today's age for the weak – there is still a large area where the expectation interest is and should be protected for breach of a binding promise. Indeed the development of promissory estoppel and the reform of privity potentially open the way

---

19   Fried *Contract as Promise* (1981) p 17.
20   Friedmann 'The Performance Interest in Contract Damages' (1995) 111 LQR 628.
1   *The Rise and Fall of the Freedom of Contract* (1979); *Promises, Morals and Law* (1981); essays 2 and 7 in *Essays on Contract* (1987). Similar views are put forward by Gilmore *The Death of Contract* (1974). See also Collins *The Law of Contract* (4th edn, 2003) pp 405–422.
2   *An Introduction to the Law of Contract* (5th edn, 1995) pp 27–34, 444–464.

for more promises to be legally enforced. Moreover, while in the US Second Restatement of Contracts, restriction to the reliance interest is suggested as a possibility under promissory estoppel or where there is a disproportion between the consideration and the defendant's liability,[3] there is no indication in England of the courts preferring to measure contractual damages by the reliance rather than the expectation interest.[4] Contract law, and its central protection of the promisee's expectation interest, remains fully alive and is in no sense dying. As Friedmann has written:

> '[T]he main thrust of modern law has been in the very opposite direction ... [T]here are no signs of weakening of the performance interest. On the contrary, one of the major trends in modern contract law is the strengthening of the protection accorded to the performance interest. Traditional limitations upon the availability of specific performance and upon the recovery of performance damages have either been removed or severely curtailed.'[5]

One final point, which concerns Fuller and Perdue's interest analysis, is that it does not seem particularly helpful and indeed may be confusing to subdivide the expectation interest into damages protecting the (subsidiary) reliance and expectation interests, although this is an approach often adopted by commentators. All possible confusion is best avoided by using the expectation and reliance interests to refer only to the overall interest that the damages are seeking to protect. If so confined, *there is no question of combining the different interests since they are mutually inconsistent.*[6]

(2) Torts

In the tort realm (with the exception of misrepresentation)[7] the theoretical underpinnings of compensation have not been discussed in relation to any controversy over what the compensatory aim should be. On the contrary it is accepted without dispute that the compensatory aim is and should be to put the claimant into as good a position as if no

---

3   Ss 87, 90 and 351(3). See also ss 158(2), 272(2) dealing with recovery of reliance loss where a contract is unenforceable. Generally, see Young 'Half Measures' (1981) Col LR 19. On s 90, see Slawson 'The Role of Reliance in Contract Damages' (1990) 76 Cornell LR 197.
4   This is so even for non-bargain promises; Burrows 'Contract, Tort and Restitution – a Satisfactory Division or Not?' (1983) 99 LQR 217, 241.
5   'The Performance Interest in Contract Damages' (1995) 111 LQR 628, 648. For the trend in favour of specific performance, see below, ch 20. As regards a strengthening of 'performance' damages, Friedmann points to changes in relation to the date for assessment, the removal of the bar on damages consequent on impecuniosity, and the availability of damages for non-pecuniary loss.
6   Burrows (1983) 99 LQR 217, 223–224. See above, pp 14–15.
7   Below, pp 254–258.

tort had been committed. Nevertheless the justification for tort compensation is hotly debated,[8] with attention being particularly concentrated on the most fundamental question of all – should tort compensation (at least in the realm of accidents) be abolished altogether?

Most of the theoretical discussion has had in mind the usual type of tortious obligation, which is the imposed *negative* obligation; that is, the obligation not to make the claimant worse off. However, not all tortious obligations are negative, and arguably there is a growing trend to impose positive tortious obligations, that is, obligations to benefit the claimant. This will be discussed later. For the present, sole concentration will be on the justification for imposing on a defendant negative obligations and corresponding compensatory damages.

One explanation is again offered by economics and law theorists, like Posner,[9] who argue that tort compensation promotes economic efficiency. By making a defendant responsible for costs he has caused, it encourages him to take precautions to prevent those costs unless the costs of the precautions outweigh the costs caused to the claimant. The general tort standard of negligence precisely fixes liability on those who act inefficiently by not taking cost-justified precautions. The approach to negligence taken in *United States v Carroll Towing Co*[10] is particularly focused on as showing such economic reasoning. Judge Learned Hand there said, 'If the probability be called P: the injury L: and the burden B: liability depends upon whether B is less than L multiplied by P: ie whether $B < PL$.'[11] For Posner then, the liability to pay compensation for negligence promotes economic efficiency by deterring uneconomical accidents.

A different and more elaborate economic efficiency justification is advocated by Calabresi in his 'market deterrence' theory.[12] According to

8   In addition to the literature cited below in the text, see Ison *The Forensic Lottery* (1967); Williams & Hepple *Foundations of the Law of Tort* (2nd edn, 1984) ch 7; Cane 'Justice and Justifications for Tort Liability' (1982) 2 OJLS 30; Klar 'New Zealand's Accident Compensation Scheme: a Tort Lawyer's Perspective' (1983) 33 UTLJ 80; Hutchinson and Morgan 'The Canengusian Connection: The Kaleidoscope of Tort Theory' (1984) 22 Osgoode Hall LJ 69; Ogus 'Do We Have a General Theory of Compensation?' (1984) 37 CLP 29; England *The Philosophy of Tort Law* (1993) chs 1–6; Stapleton 'Tort, Insurance and Ideology' (1995) 58 MLR 820; O'Connell and Kelly *The Blame Game* (1987); Atiyah *The Damages Lottery* (1997); Bell and O'Connell *Accidental Justice* (1997); Cane *The Anatomy of Tort Law* (1997); Hepple 'Negligence: The Search for Coherence' (1997) 50 CLP 69; Schwartz 'Mixed Theories of Tort Law' (1997) 75 Texas LR 1801; Burrows *Understanding the Law of Obligations* (1998) ch 6; Harris, Campbell and Halson *Remedies in Contract and Tort* (2nd edn, 2002) chs 18 and 24; Morgan 'Tort, Insurance and Incoherence' (2004) 67 MLR 384.
9   *Economic Analysis of Law* (6th edn, 2003) ch 6.
10 159 F 2d 169 (1947).
11 159 F 2d 169 (1947) at p 173.
12 Eg *The Costs of Accidents* (1970); see Cane *Atiyah's Accidents Compensation and the Law* (6th edn, 1999) pp 374–392.

this, the costs of accidents will be reduced, and indeed, will reach the optimum level in terms of efficiency, where the cheapest cost avoider, who is a cause of an accident, is made strictly liable to compensate the injured party. It is essential to this theory that, while the defendant's ability to spread the loss is an important factor in deciding liability, the aim is not loss-spreading per se, but rather the reaching of the most efficient level of accidents by making the defendant bear the costs of the accident. So while for Calabresi 'non-fault enterprise liability' should replace the present legal emphasis on fault, the tort system of individual responsibility for accident compensation is preferable to a state compensation scheme. As Blum and Kalven put it, Calabresi's view is that: 'Social security "externalises" from the activities that produce accidents the costs of those accidents – bringing in its wake a loss of "general deterrence".'[13]

In contrast to such economic justifications for tort compensation is an explanation in terms of individualistic morality. It can be argued that it is a basic principle of corrective justice that, while one should generally be free to carry out one's own activities, one should generally not be free to interfere with or harm others by those activities; hence if one does cause harm, there is a good reason why one should compensate the injured party. This does not demand that the person causing the harm must actually pay the compensation but rather that that person must ensure that compensation is paid. Most obviously, there is no objection to a liability being met by liability insurance.[14] On this view, the traditional insistence on fault is arguably unnecessary and may merely add further moral weight to an already sufficient case for compensation: it is perhaps best explained (like consideration in contract) as being concerned to confine legal intervention in individuals' lives to the strongest cases.[15]

The leading modern theorist advocating a strict liability corrective justice approach to tort compensation has been Epstein.[16] He has stated his aim as being, '... to show how ... tort law can be viewed usefully as a

---

13 'The Empty Cabinet of Dr Calabresi: Auto Accidents and General Deterrence' (1967) 34 U of Chi LR 239, 243.

14 Burrows *Understanding the Law of Obligations* (1998) pp 122–123.

15 For a corrective justice theory requiring fault, see Weinrib 'The Special Morality of Tort Law' (1989) 34 McGill LJ 403; *The Idea of Private Law* (1995) chs 6–7. See also Coleman *Risks and Wrongs* (1992) ch 18 (albeit that he argues that true strict liability can sometimes be a matter of corrective justice).

16 *A Theory of Strict Liability* (1980). Cf Epstein 'Causation in Context: An Afterword' (1987) 63 Chicago Kent Law Review 653. See also Fletcher 'Fairness and Utility in Tort Theory' (1972) 85 Harv LR 537. For a different moral explanation of strict liability, which rests on the fairness of bearing responsibility for the results of bad luck, see Honoré 'Responsibility and Luck' (1988) 104 LQR 530. For criticisms of Epstein's theory, and strict liability in general, see Stoljar 'Concerning Strict Liability' in *Essays on Torts* (ed Finn) (1989) ch 11; and Weinrib (1989) 34 McGill LJ 403, 411–412; *The Idea of Private Law* (1995) pp 171–177.

system of corrective justice appropriate for the redress of private harms.'[17] His central proposition has been that he who causes harm by affirmative action should be strictly liable to compensate the victim, subject to certain limited defences. On this view causation is crucial and, while not developing any general theory of causation, Epstein has offered four examples of sufficient causal connections; A hit B; A frightened B; A made B hit C; A created a dangerous condition that resulted in B's harm. Epstein's approach is both simple and clear, but its prime importance, as far as we are here concerned, is that it emphasises that tort compensation can be justified on the basic moral principle of corrective justice albeit that, contrary to the present law, strict liability rather than negligence is regarded as the central standard of liability.

Strict liability for accidents has also been widely advocated by those who view loss distribution as a justification in itself for tort compensation.[18] Stemming directly from dissatisfaction with the fault system, this approach calls upon the courts to take into account insurance and other methods of spreading losses such as a manufacturer charging higher prices for its goods. Strict liability should then fall on whichever of the parties was most capable of spreading the loss or, as it can alternatively be expressed, on the party who was better able to guard against the risk of damage. The underlying rationale is that, while it is fair that individuals who have suffered loss from the activities of others should be compensated, it is also fair that the burden of compensation should not fall on one pair of shoulders but should be distributed. Fleming explained this as follows:

> '[I]f a certain type of loss is looked upon as the more or less inevitable by-product of a desirable but dangerous activity, it may well be just to distribute its costs among all who benefit from that activity, although it would be unfair to impose it upon each or any one of those individuals ...'[19]

Although the courts have traditionally purported to ignore insurance considerations, advocates of this theory regard some areas of traditional tort law, most notably vicarious liability, as best justified by loss distribution.

The major problem with this approach, as a justification for tort compensation, is that to apply it fully would undermine tort compensation altogether; for if loss distribution is the sole objective, a state compensation scheme where the loss can be widely distributed

---

17 *A Theory of Strict Liability* (1980) p 71.
18 Eg Jolowicz 'Liability for Accidents' [1968] CLJ 50.
19 *The Law of Torts* (9th edn, 2000) p 11.

among, for example, all taxpayers would be the best way forward. In other words, the 'fairness' underlying loss distribution is that of distributive justice but, followed to its true conclusion, distributive justice requires compensation by the state, and to leave it to tort compensation is to adopt an unsatisfactory half-way house.

This leads finally to those, who consider that a state compensation scheme on the lines, for example, of the industrial injuries scheme, should replace tort compensation for accidents at least where causing personal injury or death.[20] In contrast to all the above theories, this approach considers that distributive justice dictates state compensation, and that there is here no justification for the tort system based as it is on individual responsibility. Support for this is particularly sought in the vagaries and expense of the present fault system. But arguably the tort system would be harder to attack if strict liability were to replace negligence as the general standard of liability for accidents. Moreover, it should be realised that a state compensation scheme would have no deterrent effect at all on harmful actions or activities (though if this were considered a defect it could perhaps be overcome by, for example, extending the criminal law); nor would a state scheme fulfil the 'ombudsman' role of tort in helping to establish the true facts of a particular accident, which may be of benefit both to the public at large and to the immediate victims and their families.

All in all, within the realm of accidents (and few would ever seek to deny the need for tort compensation outside that realm, for example, in the area covered by intentional torts) it is submitted that the basic moral corrective justice principle of compensating those whom one has wrongfully harmed, has traditionally justified, and provides a convincing reason for continuing to impose on a defendant, negative tort obligations and corresponding compensation. This is to justify tort as a system of individual responsibility.[1] However, there is room for debate as to whether fixing the general standard of liability at negligence is an unsatisfactory cut-off point short of strict liability.

So far our discussion has been confined solely to negative tort obligations. But some tortious obligations, particularly those imposed by the torts of negligence or breach of statutory duty, are positive; that is,

---

20 This was most famously the view of Atiyah expressed in his *Accidents, Compensation and the Law* (3rd edn, 1980) ch 25. He has since dramatically changed his views so that, while still favouring the abolition of tort, he would now not favour its replacement by a social welfare system but would rather favour leaving individuals to choose whether to take out personal accident insurance protection: *The Damages Lottery* (1997) ch 8. Atiyah's original (rather than his later) views find more favour with Cane: see Cane *Atiyah's Accidents Compensation and the Law* (6th edn, 1999) ch 19.

1   Burrows *Understanding the Law of Obligations* (1998) ch 6.

the obligation is to put the claimant into a better position than he would have been in if the defendant had done nothing. For example, there is often a tortious obligation to use reasonable care to ensure that a person within your control,[2] or property belonging to you,[3] does not cause personal injury or property damage to others. Again, there is often a tortious obligation to use reasonable care to ensure that a person within your control does not himself suffer personal injury or property damage;[4] and there is sometimes an obligation to use reasonable care to perform properly services that are beneficial to a claimant with whom one is in a relationship of close proximity.[5]

What then is the justification for positive tortious obligations, and hence for the compensatory damages for breach of them? There has been relatively little consideration of this. What there has been has tended to concentrate on the classic hypothetical example of whether there should be a duty of care to rescue a drowning child. Posner[6] considers that there should be such a duty, wherever the costs of the intervention are less than the costs of the injury, ie wherever it is economically efficient to confer the benefit. Epstein, confining himself to corrective justice, considers that there should be no such duty.[7] But perhaps the courts' approach is best regarded as applying, albeit to a very limited extent, the moral notion that one should 'look after one's neighbour.' In most of the situations where a positive duty of care has been imposed, the defendant has been in a particularly good position to prevent personal injury or property damage being suffered by the claimant, and it is not merely efficient, but also accords with the idea of looking after one's neighbour, that the defendant should use reasonable care to prevent such harm. Applying this, a defendant in a particularly good position to rescue a drowning child should be under a legal duty of care to do so.

Where pure economic loss is in issue the justification for imposing positive obligations seems less obvious. One possible explanation of the cases is that the courts are recognising that a negligent breach of promise is a tort, and that the promisee's expectations are being fulfilled as in an

---

2   Eg *Carmarthenshire County Council v Lewis* [1955] AC 549; *Home Office v Dorset Yacht Co Ltd* [1970] AC 1004. Cf *Smith v Littlewoods Organisation Ltd* [1987] AC 241.
3   Eg *Goldman v Hargrave* [1967] 1 AC 645; *Leakey v National Trust* [1980] QB 485; Occupiers' Liability Act 1957.
4   Eg *Kasapis v Laimos Bros* [1959] 2 Lloyd's Rep 378; *McCallion v Dodd* [1966] NZLR 710.
5   Eg *Midland Bank Trust Co Ltd v Hett Stubbs and Kemp* [1979] Ch 384; *Junior Books Ltd v Veitchi Co Ltd* [1983] 1 AC 520; *White v Jones* [1995] 2 AC 207.
6   *Economic Analysis of Law* (6th edn, 2003) pp 190–191.
7   *A Theory of Strict Liability* (1980) ch 4.

action for breach of contract. If so, it may be thought preferable to recognise the action as one for breach of contract and not for tort.[8]

8   Above, p 9; Burrows *Understanding the Law of Obligations* (1998) pp 24–40.

Chapter 3

Factual causation

1. INTRODUCTION

A requirement that can be regarded as inherent in the compensatory aims is that the defendant's tort or breach of contract has been *a* cause of the claimant's loss. So the words, '... as if the tort or breach of contract had not been committed' correlate to the usual 'but for' or *sine qua non* test of factual causation; that is, the claimant must establish that but for the tort or breach of contract he would not have suffered the loss.

It should be emphasised that for torts actionable only on proof of damage, factual causation is a factor more often concerned with whether a tort has been committed than with damages.[1] But to provide a rounded analysis of the courts' approach, examples of factual causation are included even where they do go to liability rather than damages.

The approach to factual causation does not differ whether the claimant is suing for a tort or breach of contract. Nevertheless nearly all the important cases concern torts. This is because factual causation is usually a disputed issue only in respect of damages for personal injury or property damage, and such damages are generally sought in tort.

2. THE 'BUT FOR' TEST

The best-known case showing a straightforward application of the 'but for' test is *Barnett v Chelsea and Kensington Hospital Management Committee*.[2] A night-watchman, the claimant's husband, called early in the morning at the defendant's hospital complaining of vomiting after drinking tea. The nurse on duty consulted a doctor by telephone and he said that the

---

1   For the tort of deceit, it is arguable that the burden of disproving but for causation is on the defendant: see Burrows *The Law of Restitution* (2nd edn, 2002) p 47.

2   [1969] 1 QB 428. For other good examples, see *JEB Fasteners Ltd v Marks Bloom & Co* [1983] 1 All ER 583; *Tate & Lyle Industries Ltd v Greater London Council* [1983] 2 AC 509; *Rigby v Chief Constable of Northamptonshire* [1985] 1 WLR 1242. In *Messenger Newspapers Group Ltd v National Graphical Association* [1984] IRLR 397, expenditure incurred in anticipation of a tort was held recoverable: the 'but for' test shows that this cannot be correct.

night-watchman should go home and consult his own doctor in the morning. Five hours later he was dead as a result of arsenic poisoning. In failing to examine the deceased the doctor was in breach of his duty of care but the claimant's action failed because she could not establish on a balance of probabilities that the doctor's negligence had been a cause of the death since, even if the deceased had been properly examined and treated, he would almost certainly still have died.

3.   ADDITIONAL SUFFICIENT EVENTS

Where a tort or breach of contract was sufficient in its own right to bring about the loss and yet there was an additional sufficient event, application of the 'but for' test to each event would produce the result that neither was a cause of the loss. That result offends common sense. In this situation, therefore, the courts have departed from simply applying the 'but for' test and have relied on other reasoning to decide that each event, or one or other, was a cause of the loss. This therefore represents a minor qualification to the compensatory aim being to put the claimant into as good a position as if the tort or breach of contract had not been committed.

Additional sufficient events may be either concurrent or successive. The classic hypothetical illustration of the former is where two independent fires, negligently started by D1 and D2 respectively, converge on a house and demolish it, each being sufficient on its own to demolish it. Applying the 'but for' test neither defendant's breach of duty would be regarded as a cause because each could say that the claimant's home would have been burnt down even if he had not committed his breach of duty.

However, it has been established that the 'but for' test is not applied in situations of concurrent sufficient events and that D1 and D2 and can both be held liable for the loss. For example in *Crossley & Sons v Lightowler*[3] it was held to be no defence to an action for nuisance against the defendant for wrongfully polluting a river that the river was also being wrongfully polluted by others so that the claimants would not have had water in a fit state for use even if the defendant had not polluted it. One can say that the justification for this is that there is no more reason to pin the loss on one tortfeasor than on the other, and hence both should be liable.

---

3   (1867) 2 Ch App 478.

Although there is no direct authority, analogous reasoning from successive sufficient events[4] suggests that where the concurrent event is not a breach of duty but rather a natural event – for example, if one of the fires in the above example started naturally – the 'but for' test will be applied to the breach of duty so that the defendant will not be liable for the loss.

The facts of *Baker v Willoughby*[5] beautifully illustrate the problem of successive sufficient events. As a result of D1's negligence the claimant suffered an injury to his left leg. Later he was the victim of an armed robbery during which he was shot in the left leg by D2. The leg had to be amputated. D1 argued that he was liable only for loss suffered from having an injured leg until the date of the robbery: after that time D1's breach could not be regarded as a factual cause of that loss. But the House of Lords rejected that argument and held that as regards an action against D1 in a situation of successive sufficient causes the 'but for' test should not be applied; D1 should therefore be liable for the loss suffered from having an injured leg without any reduction on the ground of D2's breach. In other words, D1 was held liable to pay full compensation for the difference between a good and an injured leg. On the other hand, the House of Lords did consider that D2 would only have been liable for depriving the claimant of an already damaged leg, which represents an acceptance of the 'but for' test in relation to D2. This aspect is further supported by the earlier case of *Performance Cars Ltd v Abraham.*[6] The claimant's car was involved successively in two collisions brought about by the negligence of D1 and D2 respectively, and each necessitated a respray of the lower part of the bodywork. The car had not had this work done to it in between the two collisions. D2 was held not liable because he had not caused any additional loss in relation to what was an already damaged car.

The *Baker* approach in respect of D1 again shows the rejection of the 'but for' test. Of the three possible solutions left of pinning the relevant loss (that is, the loss for which D1's and D2's acts were sufficient – here the loss suffered from an injured leg after the date of the robbery) either on D1 alone, or on D2 alone, or on both D1 and D2, the Lords in *Baker* were taking the first alternative. This seems correct. It cannot be right for the claimant to be worse off, as regards damages, by being the victim of

---

4 Below, pp 48–49.
5 [1970] AC 467. See McGregor and Strachan 'Variations on an Enigma' (1970) 33 MLR 378. *Baker v Willoughby* was distinguished (but, with respect, not altogether convincingly) in *Heil v Rankin (No 2)* [2001] PIQR Q16, CA, in holding that the deduction for the vicissitudes of life, in assessing future loss of earnings in a personal injury case, did include vicissitudes of life that might be caused by a future tort.
6 [1962] 1 QB 33. See also *Murrell v Healy* [2001] EWCA Civ 486, [2001] 4 All ER 345.

two torts than if he had suffered just the first of them. And to hold D2 liable for more than the *additional* injury would infringe the normal principle, applied in *Performance Cars Ltd v Abraham*, that whether for better or worse one takes one's victim as one finds him, a principle that attaches greater importance to events that happen first in time.

On the facts a further possible reason for favouring the first alternative was that D2 was a man of straw. But as a matter of principle that should be irrelevant: *Baker* should still have been decided in the same way even if D1 had been the man of straw.

But what if one of the successive sufficient events is a natural event rather than a breach of duty? In *Jobling v Associated Dairies Ltd*[7] the defendants' breach of statutory duty had caused the claimant to suffer a back injury which meant that he could thereafter do only light work. Three years later and before trial he was found to be suffering from a spinal disease (myelopathy) unrelated to and arising after the accident but which in itself rendered him wholly unfit to work. The defendants argued that the onset of the myelopathy ended their liability for his loss of earnings resulting from the back injury; applying the 'but for' test to the breach of duty it could not be said that the claimant would not have suffered the loss of earnings but for the defendants' breach of duty. Moreover, they argued that this approach is implicitly accepted in the courts' practice of reducing damages for future pecuniary loss to take account of the 'vicissitudes of life'. The claimant, on the other hand, contended that *Baker v Willoughby* should be analogously applied, so that the defendants remained liable for the loss of future earnings as if no spinal disease had occurred.

The House of Lords found for the defendants. Much of the reasoning in *Baker v Willoughby* was heavily criticised, but it was left open whether that decision may remain valid for successive sufficient breaches of duty.[8] All their Lordships accepted the 'vicissitudes of life' argument and in effect therefore accepted the 'but for' test as applied to the breach of duty, but not to the natural event. But most of them also emphasised that at root the question was one of policy, and that it was only fair that the defendants' liability should here be cut down. Unfortunately there was

---

7   [1982] AC 794.

8   See also *Rahman v Arearose Ltd* [2001] QB 351, CA where it was said, at 367, per Laws LJ, that there was no inconsistency between *Baker v Willoughby* and *Jobling v Associated Dairies Ltd* because the essential principle is that 'every tortfeasor should compensate the injured claimant in respect of that loss and damage for which he should justly be held responsible.' The complex facts raised an issue that was analogous to the *Baker* case. A psychiatric illness had been caused by D1 but that psychiatric illness had been made very much worse by D2 (who had been solely responsible for the loss of the claimant's eye). It was held that (as regards non-pecuniary loss) D1 was responsible as to one-quarter for C's psychiatric illness and D2 as to three-quarters.

little clear articulation of why this solution was considered fair. Lord Wilberforce thought it relevant whether or not the claimant would be compensated from other sources. But irrespective of that, it would seem that the fairness of the decision rests on the notion, firmly embedded in the common law, that an individual has no right to compensation for natural injury and disease. In McGregor's words:

'It is one thing to protect the victims of multiple torts from falling between two stools: it is quite another to afford protection from non-tortious loss while our legal system continues to adhere to the principle that adequate compensation for injury and disease should be available only to those whose injury or disease has been tortiously inflicted.'[9]

Where the successive sufficient events comprise a natural event followed by the defendant's breach of duty, the 'but for' test will be applied to the breach of duty so that the defendant will not be liable. This follows from the notion of taking one's victim as one finds him and is consistent with *Baker* and *Jobling*. It is directly supported by *Kerry v England*[10] where a druggist supplied tartar emetic (a fatal poison), instead of bismuth, for an attack of 'flu to a fatally sick patient. Damages were reduced to nil on the basis that the tartar emetic had not accelerated to any appreciable extent an already imminent death.

In a recent important examination of the role and limits of the 'but for' test in the context of the tort of conversion, the House of Lords in *Kuwait Airways Corpn v Iraqi Airways Co*[11] clarified that one should not apply the 'but for' test in respect of multiple conversions (actual or hypothetical) of the claimant's property. The claimant was therefore entitled to damages for the defendant's conversion of six aeroplanes even though those aeroplanes would have been seized and converted by the Iraqi government had they not been converted by the defendant. Lord Nicholls, giving the leading speech, explained that, in respect of multiple wrongdoers, 'the but for test is over-exclusionary.'[12] He went on to deal specifically with conversion and to hold that each tortfeasor is liable for damages for the claimant's loss of possession of the goods. He said:[13]

'By definition, each person in a series of conversions wrongfully excludes the owner from possession of his goods. This is the basis on which each is liable to the owner. That is the nature of the tort of conversion. The wrongful acts of a previous possessor do not therefore diminish the plaintiff's claim in respect of the wrongful acts of a later

---

9   (1970) 33 MLR 378 at 382–383.
10   [1898] AC 742. See also *The Ferdinand Retzlaff* [1972] 2 Lloyd's Rep 120 at 128.
11   [2002] UKHL 19, [2002] 2 AC 883.
12   At para 73.
13   At para 82.

possessor. Nor, for a different reason, is it anything to the point that, absent the defendant's conversion, someone else would wrongfully have converted the goods. The likelihood that, had the defendant not wronged the plaintiff, somebody would have done so is no reason for diminishing the defendant's liability and responsibility for the loss he brought upon the plaintiff.'

4.   MATERIAL INCREASE OF RISK

The 'but for' test (provable by the claimant on the balance of probabilities) has also been departed from in a few other exceptional cases. These appear to be situations where: (i) the defendant has broken its duty to the claimant; (ii) by so doing the defendant has materially increased the risk of the type of injury or disease that the claimant has in fact suffered; (iii) not least because of the present state of scientific knowledge, the claimant cannot prove – but nor can the defendant disprove – that it was that breach of duty that caused the injury or disease; (iv) there is a very restricted number of causes of the claimant's injury or disease other than the defendant's breach of duty. Where all these factors are present, the courts in seeking to do justice to claimants are prepared to accept that factual causation is proved even though the claimant cannot satisfy the 'but for' test.

This was brilliantly explained by Lord Nicholls in *Fairchild v Glenhaven Funeral Services Ltd.*[14] He said:

'The law habitually *limits* the extent of the damage for which a defendant is held responsible, even when the damage passes the threshold "but for" test. The converse is also true. On occasions the threshold "but for" test of causal connection may be over-exclusionary. Where justice so requires, the threshold itself may be lowered. In this way the scope of a defendant's liability may be *extended*. The circumstances where this is appropriate will be exceptional, because of the adverse consequences which the lowering of the threshold will have for a defendant. He will be held responsible for a loss the plaintiff might have suffered even if the defendant had not been involved at all.'

Three main examples of where this approach has been applied may be given.[15] The first is the well-known Canadian case of *Cook v Lewis*.[16] The two defendants had negligently shot in the direction of the claimant,

---

14   [2002] UKHL 22, [2003] 1 AC 32 at para 40.
15   This approach may also be the best explanation of *Chester v Afshar* [2002] EWCA Civ 724, [2002] QB 356 where the Court of Appeal held that a doctor, who had negligently failed to warn a patient of the risks of an operation, was liable for the injury caused by the operation even though the patient could not establish on the balance of probabilities that, had she been warned, she would not have had that operation. This case has been appealed to the House of Lords.
16   [1951] SCR 830.

who was hit. Although the claimant could not prove which of the two defendants had fired the shot that hit the claimant, both defendants were held liable.

The second example is *McGhee v National Coal Board*[17] where the defendants had failed to comply with their duty of care by failing to provide showers for their employees who had been working inside a very dusty and sweaty brick kiln. The claimant employee had contracted dermatitis. He succeeded in his negligence claim against the defendants even though he could not prove on the balance of probabilities that he would not have suffered dermatitis had showers been provided. It was just as likely, for example, that the dermatitis might already have been inevitable before showering rather than being contracted in the period between when a shower would have been taken and showering at home. Nevertheless it was held sufficient that the defendants had materially increased the risk of dermatitis by negligently failing to provide showers. Although there are passages in some of the speeches in the House of Lords that treat the approach taken as an application of the 'but for' balance of probabilities test (which was plainly incorrect) or as reversing the burden of proof of the 'but for' test (which is an unhelpful description given that it was known that the defendants could not discharge that burden), the better view, as now established in the *Fairchild* case is that the 'material increase of risk' approach is a departure from the normal 'but for' test of factual causation.

The third, and leading example, is *Fairchild v Glenhaven Funeral Services Ltd*[18] itself. Here the claimant was suffering (or, in the claims by estates, had died) from mesothelioma. This was caused by exposure to asbestos dust at work. The complication was that the claimant or the deceased had worked for more than one employer each of whom, in breach of its duty of care, had failed to take measures to prevent the employees from inhaling asbestos dust. The claimants could not establish, applying the but for balance of probabilities test, which employer had caused the mesothelioma. Nevertheless it was held that, as each of the employers had negligently materially increased the risk of the employees contracting mesothelioma, they should each be regarded as causally responsible for it. Their Lordships openly recognised that they were departing from the normal 'but for' test as a matter of policy in order to ensure justice for claimants. As Lord Bingham said,

17 [1973] 1 WLR 1.
18 [2002] UKHL 22, [2003] 1 AC 32. For an interesting case-note see Morgan 'Lost Causes in the House of Lords: *Fairchild v Glenhaven Funeral Services*' (2003) 66 MLR 277.

'[T]here is a strong policy argument in favour of compensating those who have suffered grave harm, at the expense of their employers who owed them a duty to protect them against that very harm and failed to do so, when the harm can only have been caused by breach of that duty and when science does not permit the victim accurately to attribute, as between several employers, the precise responsibility for the harm he has suffered. I am of the opinion that such injustice as may be involved in imposing liability on a duty-breaking employer in these circumstances is heavily outweighed by the injustice of denying redress to a victim.'[19]

---

19 [2002] UKHL 22, [2003] 1 AC 32 at para 33. In *Barker v Saint Gobain Pipelines plc* [2004] EWCA Civ 545, *Fairchild* was applied to a case where the deceased (who had died from mesothelioma) had not only been exposed to asbestos by more than one negligent employer but had also been so exposed when self-employed. However, as the claimant had been contributorily negligent in exposing himself to asbestos (primarily, it would seem, when self-employed) it was thought appropriate to reduce the damages by one-fifth.

Chapter 4

Proof of loss and loss of a chance

1. STANDARD OF PROOF OF LOSS

(1) Balance of probabilities or assessment proportionate to the chances?[1]

(a) Past fact as against future events or hypothetical actions of third parties

Where in proving loss one is concerned with past facts the usual civil standard of 'proof on the balance of probabilities' is deemed appropriate. That usual standard is thought apt for facts which must be either true or false. But where in proving loss one is concerned with future events or with hypothetical actions of third parties, the balance of probabilities standard is thought inapt. Instead full damages are only awarded if the claimant can prove its loss with reasonable certainty. Below that, damages – sometimes loosely referred to as damages for 'loss of a chance' – can be awarded in proportion to the chance of that loss. No damages at all are recoverable where the chance of the loss is entirely speculative.

In *Mallett v McMonagle*[2] Lord Diplock summarised the law as follows:

'In determining what did happen in the past a court decides on the balance of probabilities. Anything that is more probable than not it treats as certain. But in assessing damages which depend upon its view as to what will happen in the future or would have happened in the future if something had not happened in the past, the court must make an estimate as to what are the chances that a particular thing will or would have happened and reflect those chances, whether they are more or less than even, in the amount of damages which it awards.'

This is indisputably an accurate summary of the law as regards past fact and future events. But, as we shall see below, the approach to hypothetical events is more complex than Lord Diplock's summary suggests.

---

1   See generally Cooper 'Assessing Possibilities in Damage Awards – The Loss of a Chance or the Chance of a Loss?' (1972–3) 37 Sask LR 193.
2   [1970] AC 166 at 176. See also *Davies v Taylor* [1974] AC 207, esp at 212–213, 219–220; *Malec v J C Hutton Pty Ltd* (1990) 169 CLR 638.

Before we turn to that complexity, however, it is helpful to consider two leading cases, one in contract and one in tort, which illustrate the application of Lord Diplock's general distinction between uncertainty about hypothetical events, where damages are assessed according to the chances, and uncertainty as to past facts, where a balance of probabilities test applies.

In *Chaplin v Hicks*,[3] the defendant, a theatrical manager, ran a newspaper beauty competition in which he offered theatrical engagements to those 12 contestants whom he should choose after interview from the 50 who secured the greatest number of votes of the newspaper's readers. Six thousand women entered the contest and the claimant succeeded in being voted as one of the 50 to be interviewed. However, because of the defendant's breach of contract, the claimant was not informed of the interview in time and the 12 winners were chosen in her absence from the remaining 49. This was a case where the uncertainty was as to the hypothetical actions of the interviewing panel: that is, would it have chosen the claimant at interview?[4] The Court of Appeal held that, while the claimant could not recover for the loss of a theatrical engagement, since she could not establish to the required degree of proof that she would have been one of the 12, nevertheless she should be given contractual damages for the loss of the chance of being one of the 12 (ie about a 25% chance, although the court did not need to be precise on this because the damages had been fixed by a jury and the court was simply concerned to confirm that substantial, rather than nominal, damages were appropriate).

In *Hotson v East Berkshire Area HA*,[5] the claimant injured his hip in a fall. The medical staff at the defendant's hospital incorrectly diagnosed his injury and he was sent home. After five days of severe pain he returned to the hospital where the medical staff realised its earlier mistake. The claimant developed a permanent hip disability and brought an action for negligence against the defendant claiming that, if his injury had been properly diagnosed at the start, his permanent disability would have been avoided. Simon Brown J found that, even if the defendant had treated the claimant properly, there was still a 75% chance that his disability would have developed. Nevertheless he awarded the claimant damages

---

3   [1911] 2 KB 786.
4   Although the Court of Appeal treated the interviewing panel as if it were independent of the defendant, careful examination of the facts shows that the competition rules had been changed and that the sole decision-maker was the defendant himself. This should have meant that 'loss of a chance' was irrelevant: see below, pp 147–153.
5   [1987] AC 750.

(25% of the full damages) for being deprived by the defendant's negligence of the 25% chance of avoiding the disability.

In overturning that award, the House of Lords stressed that what was in question was a matter of past fact to which the all or nothing balance of probabilities standard of proof applied. Lord Bridge said, 'This was a conflict, like any other about some relevant past event, which the judge could not avoid resolving on a balance of probabilities.'[6] In Lord Ackner's words, '… the judge had determined as a matter of fact, on the balance of probabilities, that the compression and blocking of the blood vessels had had no effect on the plaintiff's ultimate condition. In determining what happened in the past the court decides on the balance of probabilities. Anything that is more probable than not is treated as certainty …'[7] And according to Lord Mackay, '… the fundamental question of fact to be answered in this case related to a point in time before the negligent failure to treat began. It must, therefore, be a matter of past fact. It did not raise any question of what might have been the situation in a hypothetical state of facts.'[8]

So applying the balance of probabilities test to the judge's findings, the Lords concluded that the claim failed in that the claimant had not established that the negligence of the defendant had caused his hip disability.

The *Hotson* case was the subject of further careful judicial analysis in the difficult case of *Gregg v Scott*.[9] A doctor negligently diagnosed a lump under the claimant's left arm as benign when it was in fact cancerous. This led to a nine-month delay in the claimant receiving proper treatment. It was found that, on the balance of probabilities, the claimant would have been in the same position even if there had been no delay. It was also found that the delay had reduced the claimant's chances of cure from 42% to 25% (ie by 17%).

The majority of the Court of Appeal dismissed the claim. Simon Brown LJ thought that the case was indistinguishable from *Hotson*. What was in issue was a matter of past fact to which the all or nothing balance of probabilities test applied. Mance LJ thought that the case was not necessarily governed by *Hotson* because being cured from cancer raised uncertainties that were not so obviously matters of past fact. Nevertheless, as a matter of policy – in particular to avoid opening the

6   [1987] AC 750 at 782.
7   [1987] AC 750 at 792.
8   [1987] AC 750 at 785.
9   [2002] EWCA Civ 1471. This case has been appealed to the House of Lords. Judgment is expected in October 2004. The *Hotson* case was straightforwardly applied to an issue of past fact in the medical negligence case of *Geoffrey Hardaker v Newcastle Health Authority* [2001] Lloyd's Rep Med 512.

floodgates of litigation in medical negligence claims – Mance LJ thought that it would be wrong to extend the law to include such claims. Latham LJ dissented. He considered that *Hotson* could be distinguished because here the delay had clearly led to the spread of cancer and the enlargement of the tumour. Damages for the 17% reduction in the chances of cure were therefore recoverable on the normal principle applicable to quantifying the loss consequent on an actionable injury.

We must now turn to examine in more detail the approach to hypothetical events, where the law is more complex than Lord Diplock indicated in *Mallett v McMonagle*.[10]

The leading case on the approach to different types of hypothetical events is *Allied Maples Group Ltd v Simmons & Simmons*,[11] which concerned a solicitor's alleged negligence in the negotiation of a contract. The claim was brought in contract and tort. The question of uncertainty was as to what contract would have been concluded had the defendant solicitor given correct advice to the claimant. This in turn involved two more specific issues of uncertainty. First, would the claimant have acted on the advice?; and, secondly, and the principal issue on uncertainty, what terms would the other party to the contract have agreed to? The Court of Appeal held that, where the uncertainty was (solely) as to the claimant's hypothetical actions (eg what would the claimant have done had proper advice been given), an all or nothing balance of probabilities approach should be applied. But where the uncertainty turned on the hypothetical actions of a third party, a proportionate chances approach should be applied.[12] Although the explanation for this distinction was not clarified,

---

10 [1970] AC 166 at 176.

11 [1995] 1 WLR 1602. *Allied Maples* was applied in the contract cases of *North Sea Energy Holdings v Petroleum Authority of Thailand* [1999] 1 All ER (Comm) 173, CA, and *Bank of Credit & Commerce Int SA v Ali (No 2)* [2002] 3 All ER 750, CA (albeit that the reasoning in the last case is not easy to interpret): but in both those cases no 'loss of chance' damages were awarded because the chance was entirely speculative. See also, just prior to *Allied Maples*, the excellent judgment of Blackburne J in *Obagi v Stanborough (Developments) Ltd* (1993) 69 P & CR 573 (upheld 7 April 1999, CA) denying substantial damages for breach of a contractual obligation to use best endeavours to obtain planning permission because the chance of obtaining such permission was merely speculative. For (an uncharacteristically unconvincing) criticism of the *Allied Maples* case, see Stapleton 'Cause-in-Fact and the Scope of Liability for Consequences' (2003) 119 LQR 388, 402–411.

12 For damages for 'loss of a chance' being awarded in professional negligence cases, consistently with the reasoning in *Allied Maples*, see the damages awarded against solicitors for negligence in litigation or other work in, eg *Hall v Meyrick* [1957] 2 QB 455 (reversed on other grounds); *Kitchen v Royal Air Force Association* [1958] 1 WLR 563; *Hartle v Laceys* [1999] Lloyd's Rep PN 315, CA; *Sharif v Garrett & Co* [2001] EWCA Civ 1269, [2002] 1 WLR 3118; *Normans Bay Ltd v Coudert Brothers* [2003] EWCA Civ 215: *First Interstate Bank of California v Cohen Arnold* [1996] PNLR 17 (negligent misstatement by accountant): and *John D Wood & Co Ltd v Knatchbull* [2002] EWHC 2822 (QB), [2003] 8 EG 131 (in a contract and tort claim for professional negligence against a surveyor, damages of £120,000 were awarded for the loss of a 60% chance of selling property for an extra £200,000). For numerous other similar cases, see *McGregor on Damages* (17th edn, 2003) paras 8–038–8–045. A very recent and particularly

it presumably rests on the idea that the claimant can be expected to produce the best evidence possible of how it would have behaved. The court is therefore in as good a position to assess a claimant's hypothetical actions as it is to determine past fact. It should be able to decide one way or the other how the claimant would have acted. The same cannot be said of a third party's hypothetical actions not least because the third party is unlikely to be before the court. As is said in *McGregor on Damages*:

'At first glance it may seem somewhat strange to have different tests applicable to hypothetical acts of the claimant and hypothetical acts of third parties. But it can be seen to make sense. For a claimant can hardly claim for the loss of the chance that he himself may have acted in a particular way: he must show that he would have done.'[13]

Although the Court of Appeal did not itself have to determine the chances of the third party agreeing to particular terms – because quantification was not before the court – it decided (Millett LJ dissenting) that there was a substantial (ie more than speculative) chance of the third party agreeing to terms which would have avoided a particular loss to the claimant.

In the *Allied Maples* case no express mention was made of the hypothetical actions *of the defendant*. This is presumably because one is not concerned with assessing what the defendant would have done had no wrong been committed. Rather, as the wrongdoer, one assumes that the defendant would not have acted in such a way as to commit the wrong in question. Moreover, in so far as the defendant could have performed a contract in different ways, there is a principle, discussed in detail in chapter 6 below,[14] that no damages should be awarded beyond the defendant's minimum contractual obligation.

It is also important to appreciate that, what is in effect, a loss of the chance approach has been standardly applied to what one might term

---

interesting decision is *Dixon v Clement Jones* [2004] EWCA Civ 1005 in which the CA upheld an award of 30% damages against a solicitor for loss of a claim against accountants albeit that the trial judge found that, on the balance of probabilities, the claimant would not have relied on the accountants' negligent advice so that her claim against them would have failed: it appears that the important point justifying this decision is that the trial judge's view as to the claimant's reliance was not a finding at the trial of the action against the accountants (where that question would have been decided on all the evidence) and was therefore not caught by the all or nothing approach taken in *Allied Maples* to a claimant's hypothetical actions; a proportionate chances approach was therefore appropriate. Note finally that a loss of the chance approach, as regards the hypothetical decision of a tribunal, has been rejected by the European Court of Human Rights: see above, p 17, n 13.

13 (17th edn, 2003) para 8–035. See also Mance LJ in *Gregg v Scott* [2002] EWCA Civ 1471 at para 71: '[T]he rationale of the distinction ... must, I would think, be the pragmatic consideration that a claimant may be expected to adduce persuasive evidence about his own conduct (even though hypothetical), whereas proof of a third party's hypothetical conduct may often be more difficult to adduce.'

14 Below, pp 147–153.

hypothetical natural events in the assessment of damages for loss of earnings or loss of dependency in personal injury or death claims.[15] For example, in calculating damages for lost future earnings consequent on a personal injury some small deduction for the 'contingencies of life', which refers to the chance that the claimant would have suffered a loss of earnings irrespective of the injury, is factored into the assessment.[16] Traditionally there has been no categorisation of the hypothetical events in such cases and certainly no suggestion that a loss of the chance approach was permissible only if the uncertainty turned on the hypothetical actions of third parties. In *Doyle v Wallace*,[17] however, the Court of Appeal did think it necessary to apply the *Allied Maples* categorisation in deciding that damages for past and future loss of earnings consequent on a personal injury should be assessed on the basis that the claimant had lost a 50% chance of becoming a drama teacher because of her injury. It was reasoned that, in line with *Allied Maples*, a loss of the chance approach was to be applied because the case turned on the uncertainties of what third parties would have done. On the other hand, the *Allied Maples* categorisation was not mentioned in the leading case on the assessment of damages for women wrongfully dismissed from the army because pregnant, *Ministry of Defence v Wheeler*,[18] where it was held important in calculating the loss of earnings to consider the chances that the women might have left the army irrespective of the wrongful dismissal.

In the *Hotson* case, prior to *Allied Maples*, Simon Brown J at first instance had regarded the crucial question as being not whether the uncertainty was as to past facts or hypothetical events, nor as being whether the hypothetical events were actions of the claimant or third parties, but rather as being whether causation or quantification was in issue (with the all or nothing balance of probabilities approach applying to the former but not to the latter). And he had come to the conclusion that on the facts quantification, not causation, was in point. The House of Lords in *Hotson* disagreed. But the very distinction between causation and quantification is misleading because it does not perfectly match the central distinction – applied by the Lords – between past fact and hypothetical or future events. For example, if a claimant who has indisputably been injured by the defendant's negligence claims damages

---

15　See, eg *Mallett v McMonagle* [1970] AC 166; *Davies v Taylor* [1974] AC 207.
16　Below, p 281.
17　[1998] PIQR Q146. See also, prior to *Doyle v Wallace*, *Mulvaine v Joseph* (1968) 112 Sol Jo 927 (lost prize money consequent on personal injury); and, subsequent to *Doyle v Wallace*, *Langford v Hebran* [2001] PIQR Q160. Cf *Herring v Ministry of Defence* [2003] EWCA Civ 528, [2004] 1 All ER 44.
18　[1998] 1 WLR 637.

for pain suffered and expenses incurred, the questions of whether that pain has been suffered or whether the expenses have been incurred must be decided on the balance of probabilities albeit that they are most naturally regarded as going to quantification rather than causation. And while in almost all cases the question of whether a personal injury has been *caused by* the defendant's breach of duty (whether a tort or breach of contract) is one of past fact, one can envisage circumstances where this is not so. Say, for example, a claim is brought against an employer for failing to call in promptly a doctor to assist an employee who has been injured at work. Let it be assumed that, if a doctor had been promptly called and had immediately administered one particular type of treatment, the employee would have made a quick and full recovery. As it is, the employee is permanently disabled. Let us further assume that the employee cannot prove on the balance of probabilities that, had a doctor been promptly called, the doctor would have immediately administered the one particular type of treatment that would have avoided the permanent disability; but he can establish that there was a 25% chance that that would have happened. Here the uncertainty on 'causation' would revolve around what a doctor – an independent third party – would have done and, applying *Allied Maples*, it is arguable that damages could be awarded against the employer for the loss of the 25% chance of avoiding the permanent disability.

But while the causation/quantification distinction is misleading, there is a closely linked point, not adverted to in the *Allied Maples* case, which does complicate matters and which must be taken into account in considering the hypothetical example just given. It may perhaps best be expressed as turning on whether the hypothetical event goes to liability or quantification (that is, on the one hand, to whether a tort or breach of contract has been committed or, on the other hand, to the assessment of damages for an established tort or breach of contract). Here an important difference between contract and tort rears its head. Breach of contract is actionable per se. In the hypothetical example given in the last paragraph, *Chaplin v Hicks* would support the view that contractual damages could be straightforwardly awarded, there being no 'liability' question, for the lost chance of avoiding the permanent disability. In contrast, the tort of negligence requires damage to be established for liability. In the above example, if a tort claim were brought against the negligent employer, could one regard the necessary actionable damage as being the loss of the chance of avoiding the permanent disability? In other words, does the tort of negligence extend to where the lost chance of avoiding injury turns not on past fact (where, as in *Hotson*, a balance of probabilities test will be applied so that the injury, rather than the loss of the chance of avoiding that injury, is regarded as the damage) but on hypothetical actions of third parties (so that the loss of the chance of avoiding the injury is the actionable damage)? *Hotson*, because dealing with past facts, did not answer that question. The solicitor's negligence cases on loss of a chance such as the *Allied Maples* case[19] – where, as we have seen, the claim was brought in the tort of negligence for pure economic loss as well as contract – suggest that the answer is 'yes'.[20] Certainly in terms of policy one could not defend an approach, which counted loss of a chance as actionable damage in the tort of negligence for pure economic loss (eg for negligent financial advice) but not for personal injury. Nor is it clear why the concurrence of liability in contract and tort should make any difference to the justification of the tort claim unless, perhaps, the contractual relationship is seen as removing the fear that the floodgates of litigation would be opened.

It should finally be noted that, although English law clearly applies an all-or-nothing balance of probabilities approach to past fact, this is not an approach that is immune from criticism. For example, it can be argued that, where the uncertainty about past facts turns on the state of medical and scientific knowledge (as in *Hotson*), one should treat uncertainty about those past facts in the same way as future events. That is, as in practice, as opposed to theoretically, it is just as impossible to be certain of some past facts as it is to be certain of the future, one should apply the same approach (of assessment according to the chances) to both. In his dissenting judgment in *Commonwealth of Australia v Amann Aviation Pty Ltd*,[1] which concerned reliance damages for breach of contract, Deane J said the following:

> 'It is true that Lord Reid's reasons for rejecting the balance of probability test in the
> circumstances of *Davies v Taylor* could be applied equally to some categories of case in
> which a court is concerned with the determination of past facts. That does not mean,
> however, that the traditional approach for determining past facts should be applied to
> a case requiring the assessment of damages on the basis of what would have happened

---

19 See also the cases cited above in n 12. After *Henderson v Merrett Syndicates Ltd* [1995] 2 AC 145, which accepted concurrent liability, actions for professional negligence brought by a client should be regarded as equally relevant to tort as to contract.

20 This is also supported by obiter dicta of Lord Lowry in *Spring v Guardian Assurance Plc* [1995] 2 AC 296 at 327, approving a loss of the chance approach to a claim in the tort of negligence for a negligently supplied reference; and by Andrew Smith J's decision in *Smith v National Health Service Litigation Authority* [2001] Lloyd's Rep Med 90 (damages for 25% chance of avoiding injury in a medical negligence case). See further Mance LJ's obiter dicta in *Gregg v Scott* [2002] ECWA Civ 1471 at para 65: '[I]t cannot be necessary for a cause of action to exist prior to or independently of ... injury, or there would be a distinction between contract and tort ... It cannot make all the difference whether such a claim is put in contract or tort, or is against a part of the National Health Service or against a private, contracting hospital.'

1   (1991) 66 ALJR 123 at 147. See also, eg Fleming 'Probabilistic Causation in Tort Law: A Postscript' (1991) 70 CBR 136, 140–141.

or will happen. To the contrary, it lends support for the view that there is a need for modification or reassessment in some categories of case of the conventional approach that, in assessing damages for what has occurred in the past, a court decides on the balance of probabilities and assumes certainty where none in truth exists.'

But there has, as yet, been no sign of the English courts considering it necessary to carve out exceptions to the all or nothing approach to past facts. Indeed it may be doubted whether it is possible to recognise exceptions without shattering the conventional approach altogether.

(b) The scale of assessment proportionate to the chances

If, in line with what has been said in the last subsection, the case is one where damages are to be assessed according to the chances, the scale runs from reasonable certainty down to more than a mere speculative possibility. So at the top end of the scale full damages can be awarded for a loss that is proved to a standard of reasonable certainty. In *Ratcliffe v Evans*[2] Bowen LJ said:

'As much certainty and particularity must be insisted on, both in pleading and proof of damage, as is reasonable, having regard to the circumstances and to the nature of the acts themselves by which the damage is done. To insist upon less would be to relax old and intelligible principles. To insist upon more would be the vainest pedantry.'

This means that full damages may be awarded for a loss even though there is some doubt whether that loss will be incurred or would have been incurred irrespective of the breach of duty. Reasonable certainty is therefore a notch down from absolute certainty.

Interestingly, in the US in the nineteenth century some types of loss, especially contractual loss of profits, had to be proved with certainty. As such, and in contrast to England, certainty played a vigorous role in restricting damages alongside limiting principles, such as remoteness and the duty to mitigate. During the twentieth century this high standard has been relaxed so that, in the US too, the standard required is now one of reasonable certainty.[3]

Coming down the scale, if the loss cannot be proved with reasonable certainty, damages are awarded in proportion to the chance of loss. Leading cases accepting or applying this include, as we have seen, *Chaplin v Hicks*[4] and *Allied Maples Group Ltd v Simmons & Simmons*.[5] Common illustrations of the awarding of tort damages, in proportion to the lost

---

2 [1892] 2 QB 524 at 532–533.
3 Farnsworth *Contracts* (3rd edn, 2004) para 12.15; *McCormick on Damages* (1935) ch 4.
4 [1911] 2 KB 786.
5 [1995] 1 WLR 1602.

chances of gain, are provided by future earnings and dependency awards in personal injury and death cases, which take into account the contingencies of life (that is, that the claimant might in any event – irrespective of the defendant's wrong – have suffered that loss).[6] Similarly, common examples of damages being assessed according to the chance of a worsening in the future of the claimant's existing position are provided by personal injury cases, where there is a more than speculative future chance of the claimant developing epilepsy or osteo-arthritis.[7]

However, the claimant cannot recover any damages if it cannot establish that the chance of the loss is more than very small, ie if the chance is entirely speculative. The classic hypothetical example was given by Erle CJ in *Priestley v Maclean*:[8] '... supposing a lady to have been injured and disfigured in a railway accident, she could not say that she ought to recover damages because she was prevented from going to a ball, at which she might have met a rich husband.' In *Davies v Taylor*[9] the principle was applied in relation to a claim under the Fatal Accidents Act by a wife, who had deserted the deceased husband, and the latter had begun divorce proceedings against her. It was held that she had no claim because she could show nothing more than a 'speculative possibility'[10] of a reconciliation, and hence a pecuniary gain, had the husband lived.

(2) Sometimes loss is presumed

In several types of case English law eases the burden on the claimant by presuming that loss has been suffered: in other words, damages are sometimes 'at large'. The tort of defamation is probably the most important in this respect,[11] but the same applies, for example, to trespass to goods,[12] and inducing breach of contract.[13] Very similar is the tort of injurious falsehood where, although loss will not be presumed, proof of general loss of business is sufficient and the claimant does not need to prove the loss of any particular customer or contract.[14] The one clear

---

6   Below, pp 281, 304.
7   *Jones v Griffiths* [1969] 1 WLR 795 at 801.
8   (1860) 2 F & F 288 at 289.
9   [1974] AC 207. See also *Fielding v Variety Inc* [1967] 2 QB 841 – the Court of Appeal reduced damages for injurious falsehood from £10,000 to £100 because the loss was almost entirely speculative. See also the cases cited above at p 56, n 11.
10   [1974] AC 207 at 219 (per Viscount Dilhorne).
11   *Tripp v Thomas* (1824) 3 B & C 427; *Ley v Hamilton* (1935) 153 LT 384; *Jameel v Wall Street Journal Europe SPRL* [2003] EWHC 2945 (QB), [2004] 2 All ER 92.
12   *GWK Ltd v Dunlop Rubber Co Ltd* (1926) 42 TLR 376.
13   *Exchange Telegraph Co Ltd v Gregory & Co* [1896] 1 QB 147; *Goldsoll v Goldman* [1914] 2 Ch 603.
14   *Ratcliffe v Evans* [1892] 2 QB 524.

case of loss being presumed for breach of contract is in respect of pecuniary loss of reputation, caused by the defendant's failure to honour the claimant's cheques.[15]

2. DIFFICULTY OF ASSESSMENT IS NOT A BAR

Where loss or a more than speculative chance of loss has been proved or is presumed, a court will do its best to assess damages even if the assessment is difficult and is necessarily imprecise. So in *Chaplin v Hicks*[16] Vaughan Williams LJ said:

> 'it may be that the amount [of damages] … will really be a matter of guesswork. But the fact that damages cannot be assessed with certainty does not relieve the wrongdoer of the necessity of paying damages for his breach of contract.'

The most obvious example of difficulty of assessment is in respect of damages for non-pecuniary loss, such as loss of amenity or pain and suffering. Lord Halsbury LC emphasised the point in *The Mediana*:[17]

> 'How is anybody to measure pain and suffering in moneys counted? Nobody can suggest that you can by arithmetical calculation establish what is the exact sum of money which would represent such a thing as the pain and suffering which a person has undergone by reason of an accident … But nevertheless the law recognises that as a topic upon which damages may be given.'

But the same sort of approach applies also to pecuniary loss. For example, in *Simpson v London and North Western Rly Co*,[18] the claimant was a manufacturer who displayed samples of his goods at shows in order to attract custom. The defendants in breach of contract failed to deliver the samples in time for a particular show. The claimant recovered damages from the defendants for loss of custom and the defendants' argument that damages for the loss of custom could not be awarded because the amount of damages could not be precisely assessed was rejected.

---

15 *Rolin v Steward* (1854) 14 CB 595; *Wilson v United Countries Bank Ltd* [1920] AC 102.
16 [1911] 2 KB 786 at 792.
17 [1900] AC 113 at 116.
18 (1876) 1 QBD 274.

Chapter 5

Contractual reliance damages

1. INTRODUCTION

The term 'reliance interest' was coined by Fuller and Perdue, whose classic article 'The Reliance Interest in Contract Damages'[1] first clarified and explored the different possible objectives of damages for breach of contract. The aim of damages protecting the reliance interest is, according to Fuller and Perdue, '... to put the plaintiff in as good a position as he was in before the promise was made'.[2] This can alternatively and preferably be expressed as aiming to put the claimant into as good a position as he would have been in if no promise had been made.

For many years the debate concerning the reliance interest, in line with Fuller and Perdue's article, has been whether the protection of the reliance interest for breach of contract is a more obvious measure of compensation than is the usual protection of the claimant's expectation interest. But it now seems clear that that debate has tended to mislead. The protection of the expectation interest is the obvious and justified measure of compensation for breach of contract.[3] In this respect, breach of contract is to be contrasted with tortious misrepresentation where the wrong in question justifies reliance, not expectation, damages.[4] Where the courts have awarded reliance damages for breach of contract, this is best justified not as showing that reliance protection is as well-merited an aim of compensation as expectation protection, but rather that it affords a means of protecting the expectation interest where there are problems of proof. The best justification, which fits with the details of the law, especially the refusal to allow claimants to escape from a known bad bargain, is that the claimant is given the benefit of a rebuttable presumption that, had the contract been performed, it would at least have recouped its reliance losses.

1 (1936–7) 46 Yale LJ 52 and 573.
2 (1936–7) 46 Yale LJ 52 at p 54.
3 Above, pp 34–38.
4 Above, p 34. Below, pp 68–69, 254–260.

In the first two editions of this book, damages for breach of contract protecting the reliance interest were treated after examining the details of the law's standard protection of the expectation interest. However, in recognition of the preferable view that reliance interest protection in contract is not full-blown protection of the reliance interest (in contrast to a claim for tortious misrepresentation) but is rather a means of protecting the expectation interest where there are problems of proof, it has been considered better in this edition to deal with it here immediately following the general chapter on proof of loss.

2.   PROTECTION OF THE RELIANCE INTEREST WHERE DIRECT PROTECTION OF THE EXPECTATION INTEREST IS BARRED

While the English courts have generally not adopted Fuller and Perdue's interest terminology, there are decisions which may be viewed as protecting the claimant's reliance interest for breach of contract.

First, there are those cases to which the (now abolished) rule in *Bain v Fothergill*[5] applied. By this if, because of a defect in his title, a vendor without fault broke a contract for the sale of land by failing to complete or delaying in completion, the purchaser could not recover damages for the difference between the market value of the land and the contract price. Rather he was restricted to damages in respect of at least some expenses incurred in relation to the contract; and those damages could be viewed as at least partially protecting the claimant's reliance interest.

Secondly, there are cases where the claimant cannot directly recover damages protecting his expectation interest because he cannot prove what position he would have been in if the contract had been performed.[6] The Australian case of *McRae v Commonwealth Disposals Commission*[7] affords an excellent illustration. The claimants bought from the defendants an oil tanker together with its contents which the defendants had advertised as lying off a named reef. The claimants went to considerable expense to reach and salvage the tanker but it turned out that neither tanker nor reef existed. The claimants successfully sued the defendants for breach of contract, it being held that the contract contained a term that the tanker and reef existed. The claimants were not given damages based on the value of the ship and its contents, for

---

5   (1874) LR 7 HL 158. Abolished by the Law of Property (Miscellaneous Provisions) Act 1989, s 3.

6   See above, ch 4.

7   (1950) 84 CLR 377.

this was considered too speculative. Rather they were given damages in respect of the price paid for the tanker and for what it had cost to send out a salvage expedition to look for the tanker. Such damages may be viewed as protecting the claimants' reliance interest.

A similar English authority is *Anglia Television Ltd v Reed*.[8] Here the claimants, with the intention of mounting the film production of a play, sought to engage the defendant for the main part. For the purposes of the production they incurred expenditures to the extent of some £2,750, including fees for a director, designer, stage manager and supporting artists. The contract between the claimants and the defendant was made but a few days later he repudiated. In an action for breach of contract, the claimants did not claim profits that the play would have made since they conceded that these could not be ascertained. They sought instead to recover the £2,750 expenditure in organising the production. The Court of Appeal affirmed the lower court's judgment awarding the full £2,750. This may again be viewed as the award of the reliance loss to claimants who could not directly prove their expectation loss.

3.   MAY THE RELIANCE INTEREST BE PROTECTED EVEN WHEN DIRECT PROTECTION OF THE EXPECTATION INTEREST IS NOT BARRED?

Dicta of the majority of the Court of Appeal in *Cullinane v British Rema Manufacturing Co Ltd*[9] and of the unanimous Court of Appeal in *Anglia Television Ltd v Reed* supported the view that the claimant is always free to claim protection of his reliance interest. As Lord Denning said in the latter case, '... the plaintiff ... has an election; he can either claim for loss of profits or for his wasted expenditure'.[10] The decision in *Lloyd v Stanbury*[11] could also be regarded as supporting this although it concerned a contract for the sale of land and such contracts could, arguably, be regarded as special particularly given the *Bain v Fothergill* rule. But the answer to this question has now been put beyond doubt by Hutchison J's comments in *CCC Films (London) Ltd v Impact Quadrant Films Ltd*.[12] The defendants had there granted a licence to the claimants to exploit three films and the claimants had paid the agreed consideration of $12,000 for that licence. By the contract the defendants

8   [1972] 1 QB 60. See also *Nurse v Barns* (1664) T Raym 77.
9   [1954] 1 QB 292.
10 [1972] 1 QB 60 at 63–64. Clearly the profits referred to were gross and not net.
11 [1971] 1 WLR 535. The damages awarded here extended beyond 'wasted expenses', strictly construed, to include a sum for the claimant's loss of earnings.
12 [1985] QB 16.

were to send to the claimants video tapes of the films and were to insure them. In breach of contract the defendants sent the video tapes by ordinary post and uninsured and they were lost. The defendants were also in breach of contract in failing to deliver replacement tapes. The claimants could not prove any loss of profits and instead claimed damages in respect of the expenses of $12,000. Hutchison J held that they could recover those damages. Moreover he squarely addressed the question of whether a claimant's choice to claim reliance expenses is unfettered and said:

> '... the plaintiff has an unfettered choice; it is not only where he establishes by evidence that he cannot prove loss of profit or that such loss of profit as he can prove is small that he is permitted to frame his claim as one for wasted expenditure ... I consider that those cases [*Cullinane v British Rema Manufacturing Co Ltd* and *Anglia Television Ltd v Reed*] are authority for the proposition that a plaintiff may always frame his claim in the alternative way if he chooses.'[13]

But the crucial question that then arises is whether this means that the courts will allow a claimant to escape from what is clearly a bad bargain by recovering damages protecting his reliance interest. The answer, as laid down in *C & P Haulage v Middleton*[14] and *CCC Films (London) v Impact Quadrant Films Ltd*, is that they will not. In the former case, the respondents had granted a contractual licence to the appellant to use their yard for his car-repair business. With ten weeks remaining of a second six-month licence the respondents, in breach of contract, terminated the licence. Proceedings were begun by the respondents but the real controversy centred on the appellant's counterclaim for reimbursement of £1,767.51 to cover labour and material used in building a wall enclosing the yard, laying on electricity and transferring a telephone. The Court of Appeal refused to award the appellant anything beyond nominal damages. If we adopt the reliance interest interpretation, the reasoning was that a court will not award damages protecting a claimant's reliance interest if this will knowingly put him in a better position than he would have been in if the contract had been performed. To have awarded the appellant the damages he claimed would have contravened this because the respondents could have lawfully terminated the licence at the end of the next ten weeks and presumably the appellant could not during that period of time, nor indeed during a full six months, have recouped in profits his expenditure on the yard: but, in any case, as the local authority had permitted him to work from home

13 [1985] QB 16 at 32.
14 [1983] 1 WLR 1461.

the appellant had been able fully to mitigate his loss of profits during those ten weeks. Indeed his profits would be higher working at home since he was spared paying for the use of the yard.

In deciding that a claimant cannot escape from a known bad bargain by claiming protection of his reliance interest, the Court of Appeal took the same view as that prevailing in the US and Canada. Indeed Ackner LJ, giving the principal judgment, relied heavily on the decision of the British Columbia Supreme Court in *Bowlay Logging Ltd v Dolmar Ltd*[15] which in turn had cited with approval *L Albert & Son v Armstrong Rubber Co*[16] the classic US authority on this point. In the former, Berger J admirably summarised the underlying rationale of these cases in the following passage:

> 'Where it can be seen that the plaintiff would have incurred a loss on the contract as a whole, the expenses he incurred are losses flowing from entering into the contract, not losses flowing from the defendant's breach ... The principle contended for ... would entail the award of damages not to compensate the plaintiff but to punish the defendant.'[17]

C & P Haulage v Middleton was applied in *CCC Films*, where Hutchison J went on to stress, relying on the same Canadian and US authorities, that where the claimant claims reliance damages, the burden of proving that he has made a bad bargain, that is that he would not have recouped his expenses if the contract had been performed, is on the defendant.

The upshot of all this is that where the defendant (D) cannot prove that the claimant (C) has made a bad bargain and C's reliance loss exceeds the expectation loss that C can prove, it will be to C's advantage to claim reliance damages. But where D can prove that C has made a bad bargain C's 'free choice' to claim protection of the reliance interest is of no advantage to C because he will be confined to his lower expectation damages.

Ultimately, then, the reliance interest bows to the expectation interest. This is only right since it is the breaking of the promise, disappointing the claimant's expectations, that renders the defendant's conduct wrongful.[18] As such, damages for tortious misrepresentation provide an interesting contrast.[19] The very objection to misrepresentation is that the defendant ought not to have induced the claimant to rely on an untrue statement. If in reliance on the misrepresentation the claimant has, for

---

15   (1978) 4 WWR 105.
16   178 F 2d 182 (1949).
17   (1978) 4 WWR 105 at 117.
18   See above, pp 34–38.
19   See above, p 34. Below, pp 254–260.

example, entered into what is a bad bargain, he can and ought to be able to escape from it by recouping all his losses because if the defendant had not wrongfully made the representation the claimant would not have entered into the contract. In other words, unlike a contract-breaker who acts wrongfully when he breaks his contractual promise and not when he induces the claimant to enter into the contract, the misrepresentor commits a wrong when he induces the claimant by his statement to act to his detriment by, for example, entering into a losing contract.

In the difficult Australian case of *Commonwealth of Australia v Amann Aviation Pty Ltd*[20] the primary question in issue was the standard of proof faced by a defendant who seeks to discharge the burden of showing that the claimant has made a bad bargain (ie that the claimant would not have recouped his reliance loss).

The claimant had won a contract to conduct aerial coastal surveillance for the defendant. It committed large sums of money in acquiring the necessary specially-equipped aircraft. Several months after the contract commenced, and at a time when the claimant was itself in breach by having insufficient aircraft available, the defendant committed a repudiatory breach by serving an invalid termination notice. That breach entitled the claimant to terminate the contract and sue for damages, which it did. The majority of the High Court of Australia (Mason CJ, Dawson J, Brennan J, Gaudron J) held that it was entitled to full reliance damages of some $5.5 million (plus interest). Although the defendant had shown that there was a 20% chance that the defendant would otherwise have validly terminated the contract for the claimant's own breach, in which event the claimant's reliance losses would not have been recouped, the majority felt that no discount should be made for that chance because it was unlikely. A balance of probabilities, all or nothing, standard of proof therefore seems to have been applied. In contrast, the three minority judges thought that a discount should be made. Intriguingly each of them adopted different reasoning and conclusions. Deane J thought the appropriate discount from full reliance damages should be the 20% chance that the defendant would have validly terminated. Toohey J considered that, taking account of all the contingencies in the case, the discount should be 50%. On the other hand, McHugh J thought that reliance damages were inappropriate and that instead normal expectation damages, reduced by the 20% chance, should be awarded.

---

20 (1991) 66 ALJR 123; Treitel 'Damages for Breach of Contract in the High Court of Australia' (1992) LQR 226.

4. THE JUSTIFICATION FOR RELIANCE DAMAGES FOR BREACH OF CONTRACT

As the courts will not knowingly award reliance damages which put the claimant into a better position than if the contract had been performed, the best interpretation of the cases awarding reliance damages is that they are concerned to protect the claimant's expectation interest, albeit in a different way than the expectation interest is normally protected. That is, one can say that the law accepts an alternative way of putting the claimant into as good a position as if the contract had been performed, because it allows the claimant the benefit of a presumption, rebuttable by the defendant, that the claimant has not made a bad bargain. Hence where the claimant can prove its reliance expenses, this rebuttable presumption enables it to recover that amount on the ground that if the contract had been performed it would at the very least have made gains to cover those expenses. This was the interpretation strongly favoured by at least five judges of the High Court of Australia in *Commonwealth of Australia v Amann Aviation Pty Ltd.*

The great merit of this analysis is that it provides the only convincing explanation for why the courts do not allow claimants to escape from a known bad bargain by claiming reliance damages. If one were concerned to protect the reliance interest because that provides an alternative and valid aim of compensation for breach of contract (as suggested by Fuller and Perdue), it is hard to see why it should be limited by a known lower expectation interest.

On the other hand, it may at first sight appear puzzling why, on this interpretation, the courts are willing to give the claimant the benefit of a rebuttable presumption that it would have recouped its expenses. But it is submitted that this is simply a consequence of the fact that the defendant is a contract-breaker. It is as a result of breach by the defendant that one does not know what the position would have been had the contract been performed. It is therefore only fair and proper that the problems of proving that the claimant would not have recouped its reliance loss should fall on the contract-breaker and not on the innocent claimant.

One should also note that, as Berger J stressed in the passage cited above,[1] there is simply no causal link between a breach of contract and damages protecting the reliance interest. The expenses would have been incurred even if there had been no breach. This is another way of expressing the point that expectation, and not reliance, protection is the natural measure of compensation for breach of contract.

---

1   Above, p 68.

5. PRE-CONTRACTUAL EXPENSES

A further reason to prefer the 'rebuttable presumption of recouping reliance loss' explanation is that pre-contractual reliance expenses have been held recoverable. In *Lloyd v Stanbury* pre-contractual expenditure was recovered, and Brightman J said that this should be so, so long as the costs were of '... performing an act required to be done by the contract.'[2] Given doubts about whether contracts for the sale of land are exceptional, however, the clearest authority is *Anglia Television Ltd v Reed*. Here many of the expenses recovered were pre-contractual. Lord Denning, with whom the other two judges agreed, said:

> 'If the plaintiff claims the wasted expenditure, he is not limited to the expenditure incurred after the contract was concluded. He can claim also the expenditure incurred before the contract, provided it was such as would reasonably be in the contemplation of the parties as likely to be wasted if the contract was broken. Applying that principle here, it is plain that, when Mr Reed entered into this contract, he must have known perfectly well that much expenditure had already been incurred on directors' fees and the like. He must have contemplated – or at any rate, it is reasonably to be imputed to him – that if he broke his contract, all that expenditure would be wasted, whether or not it was incurred before or after the contract. He must pay damages for all the expenditure so wasted and thrown away.'[3]

The recovery of pre-contractual expenses is perfectly explicable if one adopts the view that the claimant has the benefit of a rebuttable presumption that the claimant would at least have recouped its expenses had the contract been performed. A claimant's loss on a contract would naturally take into account pre-contractual as well as post-contractual expenses. Put another way, a claimant could not be said to have 'broken even', if it recouped only post-contractual expenses.[4]

In contrast, if one applies the view that the reliance interest is awarded as a valid alternative aim of compensation, it is hard to see why pre-contractual expenses are recoverable. They would in any event have been wasted if no contract had been made with the defendant. The defendant has not induced the claimant to incur them.[5] And if one were

---

2   [1971] 1 WLR 535 at 546.
3. [1972] 1 QB 60 at 64. Note also that Lord Denning was here applying a normal 'reasonable contemplation' remoteness limitation to the 'wasted expenses'.
4   *Commonwealth of Australia v Amann Aviation Pty Ltd* (1991) 66 ALJR 123 at 161 (per Gaudron J); Waddams *The Law of Damages* (3rd edn, 1997) paras 5.200–5.250; Owen 'Some Aspects of the Recovery of Reliance Damages in the Law of Contract' (1984) OJLS 393, 396–399; McLauchlan 'Damages for Pre-Contract Expenditure' (1984–5) 11 NZULR 346.
5   In *Chicago Coliseum Club v Dempsey* 256 Illinois App 542 (1932) it was held that reliance damages for breach of contract did not extend to pre-contractual expenses.

to allow the claimant to recover some pre-contractual expenses, it is hard to see how far back one would go or where one would rationally stop.[6]

---

6   Cf Ogus *The Law of Damages* (1973) p 350 who writes, 'Perhaps the best solution would be for the reliance interest award to comprise those expenses incurred as from the time when there was substantial agreement between the parties.'

Chapter 6

Principles limiting compensatory damages

1. INTRODUCTION

There can be said to be five[1] principles limiting compensatory damages (ie which reduce the damages that full adherence to the compensatory aims would dictate)[2] for both torts and breach of contract, and the role played by each can be briefly described as follows:

Remoteness – A claimant cannot succeed if the loss was too remote from the breach of duty.[3] The tests for remoteness centre on reasonable foreseeability or contemplation of the loss.

Intervening cause – A claimant cannot succeed if an intervening cause is so much more responsible for the loss than the defendant's breach of duty that it breaks the chain of causation between the breach of duty and the loss.

The SAAMCO principle – The House of Lords in *South Australia Asset Management Corpn v York Montague Ltd*,[4] in the context of a claim for negligent valuation, held that the lenders' loss consequent on a fall in the

---

1   Consent, *volenti non fit injuria* and illegality are not considered because these defences are practically always concerned with liability rather than with damages (but for illustrations of illegality barring damages rather than the cause of action see, eg *Burns v Edman* [1970] 2 QB 541; *Hunter v Butler* [1996] RTR 396; *Hewison v Meridian Shipping Pte* [2002] EWCA Civ 1821, [2003] PIQR P252). Exclusion and limitation clauses are also omitted because, taken together, they are not purely concerned with restricting remedies and, in any event, space prevents an adequate examination of them. See generally Treitel *The Law of Contract* (11th edn, 2003) ch 7. Also not examined are special statutory provisions limiting damages: eg Carriage by Air Act 1961, Sch 1, art 22; Carriage of Passengers by Road Act 1974, Sch 1, art 13(1); Merchant Shipping Act 1995, s 185. Note also that, as between the parties, the costs of litigating (eg in relation to a tort or breach of contract) are only recoverable as 'costs' and not damages (subject to some exceptions as in, eg *Berry v British Transport Commission* [1962] 1 QB 306 and *Union Discount Co Ltd v Zoller* [2002] 1 WLR 1517; for an interesting note on the latter case, see Tan and Yeo 'Breaking Promises to Litigate in a Particular Forum: Are Damages an Appropriate Remedy?' [2003] LMCLQ 435).
2   Subject to the limiting principles considered in this chapter, compensation for both torts and breach of contract aims to be full compensation. This is sometimes referred to, in the context of personal injury compensation, as 'the 100% principle'. See Cane *Atiyah's Accidents, Compensation and the Law* (6th edn, 1999) pp 119–134, esp 130–131. See also *Wells v Wells* [1999] 1 AC 345 at 363, 382–383, 398.
3   Breach of duty is throughout used as shorthand for breach of contract, tort actionable per se, or in the case of a tort actionable only on proof of damage, breach of duty.
4   [1995] QB 375.

property market was not recoverable from the valuer. This exclusion was justified on the principle (the *SAAMCO* principle) that the loss was outside the scope of the duty. This principle was treated by their Lordships as distinct from remoteness and intervening cause. The validity and scope of this principle are controversial.

Duty to mitigate – A claimant cannot succeed if subsequent to the tort or breach of contract he or she could reasonably have avoided the loss.

Contributory negligence – Damages may be reduced where the claimant's negligence has contributed to, ie been a partial cause of, his loss. But this principle is not applicable to some torts and is inapplicable to breach of contract (other than of a contractual duty of care where there is concurrent liability in tort).

A sixth limiting principle – that, as established in *The Liesbosch*,[5] loss flowing from the claimant's impecuniosity is irrecoverable – has recently been authoritatively removed from the law, after 70 years of doubtful existence, by the House of Lords in *Lagden v O'Connor*.[6] We shall briefly examine its demise later in this chapter.

Five introductory points need to be made regarding these principles. First, for torts actionable only on proof of damage, such as negligence, and in contrast to torts actionable per se and breach of contract, remoteness, intervening cause and the *SAAMCO* principle are often concerned with establishing whether a tort has been committed (ie liability) rather than with damages. But in order to provide a full picture of the courts' approach to those principles they will here be examined even when they are concerned with establishing tort liability.

Secondly, since all these principles are concerned to limit compensatory damages it is not at all surprising that the same result may often be reached by applying more than one of them. So, for example, in *Compania Financiera Soleada SA v Hamoor Tanker Corpn Inc, The Borag*,[7] where the issue was the recoverability of interest charges paid on a loan taken out by the claimant as a consequence of the defendant's breach of contract, Templeman LJ said, '... in the present case if the interest charges were unreasonable, they were too remote: they were not caused by the breach; they were not part of a reasonable form of mitigation; all these matters hang together.'[8] But normally just one of these principles will be used to limit damages.

Thirdly, the distinction between remoteness and intervening cause is often not drawn and both principles are dealt with under the one head,

---

5   *Owners of the Dredger Liesbosch v Owners of SS Edison* [1933] AC 449.
6   [2003] UKHL 64, [2004] 1 AC 1067.
7   [1981] 1 WLR 274.
8   [1981] 1 WLR 274 at 864.

whether labelled 'remoteness' or 'legal causation' or 'proximate cause'. This is perfectly acceptable since both principles are essentially concerned with the same policy, namely that, as explained by Lord Wright in *The Liesbosch*, '... the law cannot take account of everything that follows a wrongful act: it regards some subsequent matters as outside the scope of its selection ... In the varied web of affairs, the law must abstract some consequences as relevant not perhaps on grounds of pure logic, but simply for practical reasons.'[9] In Ogus' words, 'A line has to be drawn somewhere so that the burden of liability will not crush those who have to pay the bill.'[10] However, in this book it has been considered helpful to separate remoteness and intervening cause for not only does each have a different focus of attention but also the principles applied to each are not the same.

Fourthly, where the claimant's unreasonable conduct subsequent to the tort or breach of contract has been a cause of his suffering loss, both the duty to mitigate and intervening cause *can* be regarded as denying damages for exactly the same reason. Hence in this situation the courts sometimes use the principles interchangeably.[11] But generally they are distinguished by using the duty to mitigate for the claimant's unreasonable inaction, ie his failure to minimise loss, while using intervening cause breaking the chain of causation for the claimant's unreasonable action, ie his augmenting of loss.[12] However, where the unreasonable action comprises incurring expense, this is generally viewed as an aspect of the duty to mitigate rather than intervening cause. These general usages are adopted in this book.

The role of contributory negligence (if applicable to the tort or breach of contract in question) also needs to be clarified in this situation. In particular it should be realised that contributory negligence has been applied to the claimant's negligence occurring subsequently to, as well as prior to or contemporaneously with, a tort.[13] Therefore the essential distinction between contributory negligence on the one hand, and

---

9 [1933] AC 449 at 460.

10 *The Law of Damages* (1973) (hereinafter cited as *Damages*) p 67.

11 Eg *Compania Naviera Maropan SA v Bowaters Lloyd Pulp and Paper Mills Ltd* [1955] 2 QB 68; *The Borag* [1981] 1 WLR 274 (per Templeman LJ); *Emeh v Kensington and Chelsea and Westminster Area Health Authority* [1985] QB 1012; *Schering Agrochemicals Ltd v Resibel NV SA* (26 November 1992, unreported) (per Purchas LJ); *Standard Chartered Bank v Pakistan National Shipping Corpn* [2001] EWCA Civ 55, [2001] 1 All ER (Comm) 822, para 41.

12 For express recognition of this, see *Schering Agrochemicals Ltd v Resibel NV SA* unreported (per Nolan LJ). A different distinction was drawn by Scott LJ in that case and by Phillips J in *Youell v Bland Welch & Co (No 2)* [1990] 2 Lloyd's Rep 431 at 461–462 to the effect that a duty to mitigate only arises once the claimant has actual knowledge of the breach: for criticism of that, see Burrows 'Contributory Negligence in Contract: Ammunition for the Law Commission' (1993) 109 LQR 175.

13 *The Calliope* [1970] P 172.

intervening cause and the duty to mitigate on the other, is that the former is a partial defence while the latter two are total defences; ie if a claimant has broken the chain of causation to the loss, or has failed in its duty to mitigate that loss, it cannot recover any damages for that loss, whereas if it has been contributorily negligent in relation to that loss, its damages are merely reduced to the extent that this is thought just and equitable.[14]

Finally, the burden of proof in relation to these limiting principles (provided liability has been established) is on the defendant.[15] That is, once the claimant has proved a breach of duty, factual causation and his loss – that is, once he has shown that prima facie he merits compensation – it is, and should be, for the defendant to prove that one of these limiting principles applies to reduce the damages.

2.   REMOTENESS

A principal restriction on compensatory damages is that the loss must not be too remote from the breach of duty. The tests formulated for deciding on this have centred on whether the loss was (in contract) reasonably contemplated or (in tort) reasonably foreseeable by the defendant. While broadly similar these tests have, in their detail, been traditionally regarded as having significant differences. The full recognition of concurrent liability, and the expansion of the recovery of pure economic loss in the tort of negligence, have rendered these differences particularly interesting, important, and controversial. The issue of whether the tests are different will be examined in depth in the contract section.[16]

In policy terms the remoteness restriction is based on the view that it is unfair to a defendant, and imposes too great a burden, to hold it responsible for losses that it could not have reasonably contemplated or foreseen. It has also been regarded as having an economic efficiency rationale in encouraging the disclosure of information regarding unusual

---

14 It is for this reason that *Tennant Radiant Heat Ltd v Warrington Development Corpn* [1988] 1 EGLR 41 is controversial as a decision on causation (as opposed to contributory negligence).

15 *SS Heranger (Owners) v SS Diamond (Owners)* [1939] AC 94 at 104 (contributory negligence): *Philco Radio and Television Corpn of Great Britain Ltd v Spurling Ltd* [1949] 2 KB 33 (intervening cause); contra *SS Singleton Abbey (Owners) v SS Paludina (Owners)* [1927] AC 16 (burden of proving not an intervening cause on claimant): *Roper v Johnson* (1873) LR 8 CP 167; *Garnac Grain Co Inc v Faure & Fairclough Ltd* [1968] AC 1130n; *Standard Chartered Bank v Pakistan National Shipping Corpn* [2001] EWCA Civ 55, [2001] 1 All ER (Comm) 822 at paras 33–41; *Geest plc v Lansiquot* [2002] UKPC 48, [2002] 1 WLR 3111; *LE Jones (Insurance Brokers) Ltd v Portsmouth City Council* [2002] EWCA Civ 1723, [2003] 1 WLR 427 at para 26 (all duty to mitigate).

16 See, generally, Cartwright 'Remoteness of Damage in Contract and Tort: A Reconsideration' [1996] CLJ 488.

potential losses, so that the defendant with full knowledge of the risks involved can plan and act rationally.[17]

(1) Torts

(a) The *Wagon Mound* test

Remoteness for torts has been primarily discussed judicially in relation to the tort of negligence; but as is explained below, it seems that with the exception of deceit and other torts that have been committed dishonestly or intentionally, the test applied to negligence applies to all other torts.

The old test for remoteness was that laid down in *Re Polemis and Furniss Withy & Co*:[18] according to this, a defendant was liable for all the direct consequences of its negligence suffered by the claimant whether a reasonable man would have foreseen them or not. But *Re Polemis* was effectively overruled by *Overseas Tankship (UK) Ltd v Morts Dock & Engineering Co Ltd, The Wagon Mound*[19] which established that consequences are too remote if a reasonable man would not have foreseen them. Here the defendants carelessly discharged oil from their ship into a harbour. Over two days later, molten metal from the claimant's welding operations on the wharf set fire to the oil on the water. The claimant's wharf was severely damaged. The Privy Council held that the defendants were not liable in negligence because, while they could have reasonably foreseen damage to the wharf by fouling, they could not have reasonably foreseen that the wharf would be damaged by fire when they carelessly discharged the oil. Viscount Simonds said: 'It is the foresight of the reasonable man which alone can determine responsibility. The *Polemis* rule by substituting "direct" for "reasonably foreseeable" consequence leads to a conclusion equally illogical and unjust.'[20] The illogicality he was referring to was that under *Re Polemis* the test for the extent of the defendant's liability (directness) differed from that for the existence of liability (reasonable foreseeability).

However, in applying the *Wagon Mound* the courts have chosen not to restrict the defendant's liability to the degree indicated by the reasoning of Viscount Simonds. Rather 'reasonable foreseeability' has been loosely

---

17 Posner *Economic Analysis of Law* (6th edn, 2003) pp 127–128; Beale, *Remedies for Breach of Contract* (1980) p 180; Harris, Campbell and Halson *Remedies in Contract and Tort* (2nd edn, 2002) pp 310–313.
18 [1921] 3 KB 560; Davies 'The Road from Morocco: *Polemis* Through *Donoghue* to No-Fault' (1982) 45 MLR 534.
19 [1961] AC 388. See Stauch 'Risk and Remoteness of Damage in Negligence' (2001) 64 MLR 191.
20 [1961] AC 388 at 424.

adhered to, so that the results produced differ little from those that would have been reached under *Re Polemis*. This represents a policy view that fairness to the defendant does not dictate quite such a rigid cutting off point as that favoured by Viscount Simonds. Five features of this loose case-law application of the *Wagon Mound* merit particular consideration.

First, so long as the type of physical damage which has resulted was reasonably foreseeable at the time of the negligence, neither the actual manner in which it came about nor its actual extent needs to have been reasonably foreseeable.[1] *Hughes v Lord Advocate*[2] is the classic illustration. Post Office workmen left an open manhole, in which they had been working, covered by a shelter tent and surrounded by warning paraffin lamps. The claimant, aged eight, was playing with one of the lamps when he stumbled over it and knocked it into the hole. An explosion followed and the claimant was thrown into the manhole and was severely burned. The defendants were held liable because, while it was not reasonably foreseeable that a child would be burned as a result of the actual sequence of events that had occurred, it was reasonably foreseeable that a child could be burned by playing with one of the gas-lamps. Nor did it matter that the burns were more serious than those that were reasonably foreseeable. Similarly in *Vacwell Engineering Co Ltd v BDH Chemicals Ltd*,[3] the defendants supplied a chemical and carelessly failed to attach a warning that it was liable to explode in water. A scientist working for the claimants placed a consignment in a sink and a violent explosion ensued causing extensive damage. The defendants were held liable because a minor explosion causing some property damage was reasonably foreseeable, and it did not matter that the magnitude of the explosion and the actual extent of the damage could not reasonably have been foreseen. Again in *Jolley v Sutton London BC*[4] a 13-year-old boy was severely injured when a boat, which had been left on the defendant council's land, collapsed on him while he was under it. The type of accident and injury (personal injury from meddling with the boat)[5] were reasonably foreseeable. It did not matter, applying *Hughes v Lord Advocate*, that the precise manner in which the injury came about (the boy with a

---

1   *Doughty v Turner Manufacturing Co Ltd* [1964] 1 QB 518 is difficult to reconcile with this principle, as is acknowledged in *A-G of the British Virgin Islands v Hartwell* [2004] UKPC 12, [2004] 1 WLR 1273, at para 29.
2   [1963] AC 837.
3   [1971] 1 QB 88.
4   [2000] 1 WLR 1082.
5   'Meddling with the boat' was emphasised by Lord Hoffmann as being the relevant type of accident. In contrast, Lord Steyn went so far as to accept the trial judge's finding that the precise accident – the collapse of the propped-up boat – was reasonably foreseeable.

friend had jacked the boat up to 'work' on it and it fell off the jack) or its extent (the boy was rendered paraplegic) may not have been reasonably foreseeable.

Goff LJ's judgment in the negligence case of *Muirhead v Industrial Tank Specialities Ltd*[6] contains an excellent passage stressing the need for only the type of physical damage to be reasonably foreseeable:

'... the true question to which the judge should have addressed his mind was simply whether damage of the relevant *type* was reasonably foreseeable by the manufacturers, ie physical harm to fish stored in a tank at a fish farm ... If he had found that damage of that type was reasonably foreseeable, then the fact that, by reason of the full stocking of the relevant tank, the fish died more quickly or in greater quantity was of no relevance, unless it could be said that overstocking of the tank constituted the sole or contributory cause of the disaster which took place.'[7]

Applying this, the manufacturers of defective circulation pumps were held liable for the loss of the claimant's entire stock of lobsters.

Secondly, the notion that it is the type of physical damage that needs to be reasonably foreseeable allows the courts considerable discretion in how wide to extend the defendant's liability, for opinions can differ as to how to divide up types of damage. Two cases can be usefully contrasted. In *Bradford v Robinson Rentals Ltd*[8] the defendant employers exposed the claimant van driver to extreme cold in the course of his duties and in consequence he suffered frostbite. It was held that a common cold, pneumonia or chilblains were reasonably foreseeable and since frostbite was of the same type of harm as these the defendants were liable. On the other hand, in *Tremain v Pike*,[9] the rat population on the defendants' farm was allowed to become unduly large and the claimant, a herdsman on the farm, contracted a rare disease, Weil's disease, through coming into contact with rat's urine. Payne J held that the defendants were not liable, for while the effects of a rat bite or food poisoning from contaminated food were reasonably foreseeable, Weil's disease was not and was 'entirely different in kind'[10] from such consequences.

Thirdly, the 'thin skull' principle, that the defendant takes his victim in the physical condition he finds him in, survives. A good example of it is *Smith v Leech Brain & Co Ltd*[11] in which a negligently-inflicted burn on the claimant's husband's lip resulted in his dying of cancer because he was

---

6 · [1986] QB 507. See also *Ogwo v Taylor* [1988] AC 431 at 444–445.
7 [1986] QB 507 at 532.
8 [1967] 1 WLR 337.
9 [1969] 1 WLR 1556.
10 [1969] 1 WLR 1556 at 1561.
11 [1962] 2 QB 405. See also *Brice v Brown* [1984] 1 All ER 997.

suffering from pre-malignant cancer and this was caused to develop by the burn. The defendants were held liable for his death. Lord Parker CJ's reasoning suggests that the thin-skull principle is merely an aspect of the principle looked at above: that so long as the type of damage which has resulted was reasonably foreseeable, its actual extent need not have been; but it is probably preferable, so as to avoid deciding whether the type of damage is the same as that which could have been reasonably foreseen, to regard the thin-skull principle as separate.

Fourthly, the *Wagon Mound* has not affected the principle that it is no bar to recovery that the pecuniary value of property damage or the loss of earnings/dependency resulting from personal injury or death is far greater than could reasonably have been foreseen.[12] So if the defendant negligently injures a multi-millionaire or negligently damages an antique vase, it is no defence that she could not reasonably have foreseen that the loss of earnings or pecuniary value would be so great and she will be liable so long as the personal injury or property damage was reasonably foreseeable. One *can* say that this follows logically because the damage itself is foreseeable, and it is merely the quantum that is unexpectedly high. But the line between damage and quantum is not an easy one to draw. Ultimately then the principle is best seen as a policy decision that such loss should not be regarded as too remote, even though unforeseeable. However, it is doubtful whether this principle extends to profits consequent on physical damage or to other pecuniary loss.[13]

Finally, what degree of likelihood of the loss occurring is required under the *Wagon Mound* test? This has rarely been discussed in the tort cases themselves. The main exception was *The Wagon Mound (No 2)*,[14] which arose out of the same fire that produced *The Wagon Mound*. In this case, however, the claimants were the owners of the damaged ship rather than the wharf owners, and they sued in nuisance and negligence. Somewhat different evidence was presented than in the first case and the Privy Council decided that the damage to the ship by the fire was not too remote, since it was reasonably foreseeable. One *can* distinguish the two *Wagon Mound* decisions because of the different facts found, but it does appear from the use of phrases like 'real risk' that in the second case, in contrast to the first, the Privy Council considered that only a low degree of likelihood of the loss occurring need be reasonably foreseeable in order for the loss to be recoverable. Thus Smith has written that *The Wagon Mound (No 2)*, 'makes a substantial change in *The Wagon Mound* rule

---

12 The usually cited authority is the dictum in Scrutton LJ's dissent in *The Arpad* [1934] P 189 at 202.

13 But see *The Liesbosch* [1933] AC 449 at 463–464; *The Argentino* (1889) 14 App Cas 519 at 523.

14 *Overseas Tankship, (UK) v Miller SS Co Pty Ltd (The Wagon Mound No 2)* [1967] 1 AC 617.

in that it limits ... the test of foreseeability of damage to possibility rather than to probability.'[15] Furthermore the House of Lords in *The Heron II*[16] (a contract case), in contrasting the contract and tort remoteness tests, emphasised that the tort test requires only a low degree of likelihood of the loss to be reasonably foreseeable. Similarly, in *H Parsons Ltd v Uttley & Co Ltd*[17] (a contract case) Lord Denning MR said that the *Wagon Mound* test was reasonable foreseeability at the time of the breach of the type of loss occurring *as a slight possibility.*

(b) Is the *Wagon Mound* the test for remoteness for all torts?

The *Wagon Mound* test was applied to the tort of nuisance in *The Wagon Mound (No 2)*. It was also applied by the House of Lords to liability under *Rylands v Fletcher*[18] in *Cambridge Water Co v Eastern Counties Leather plc.*[19] These cases strongly suggest that the *Wagon Mound* test is the appropriate remoteness test for all unintentional torts even though the liability is strict (as under *Rylands v Fletcher* and, arguably, nuisance) in the sense that the defendant may be held liable despite the fact that it has taken all reasonable care to avoid harm to others.[20]

However, as far as the tort of deceit is concerned, the Court of Appeal in *Doyle v Olby (Ironmongers) Ltd*[1] considered that reasonable foreseeability was too restrictive a test. Lord Denning said: 'the defendant is bound to make reparation for all the actual damages directly flowing from the fraudulent inducement ... All such damages can be recovered: and it does not lie in the mouth of the fraudulent person to say that they could not reasonably have been foreseen.'[2] This was confirmed as the correct approach by the House of Lords in *Smith New Court Securities Ltd v Scrimgeour Vickers (Asset Management) Ltd.*[3] It can be regarded as the survival of the *Polemis* test for the tort of deceit. Indeed one can strongly argue that the same should apply to other dishonestly committed, or intentional, torts on the ground that there is less justification for showing leniency and limiting compensatory damages where the defendant committed the tort dishonestly or intentionally (in the sense that the

---

15 'The Limits of Tort Liability in Canada: Remoteness, Foreseeability and Proximate Cause' in *Studies in Canadian Tort Law* (ed Linden) (1968) p 102.
16 *Koufos v Czarnikow Ltd, The Heron II* [1969] 1 AC 350.
17 [1978] QB 791.
18 (1868) LR 3 HL 330.
19 [1994] 2 AC 264.
20 This is also supported by *Winfield & Jolowicz on Tort* (16th edn, 2002) paras 15.19, 16.12; and *Clerk & Lindsell on Torts* (18th edn, 2000) para 2–68. For a contrary view in respect of liability under the Animals Act 1971, see North *The Modern Law of Animals* (1971) pp 47, 58, 107–108.
1 [1969] 2 QB 158.
2 [1969] 2 QB 158 at 167.
3 [1997] AC 254.

consequences were intended).[4] This is supported by obiter dicta of Lord Nicholls, giving the leading speech, in *Kuwait Airways Corpn v Iraqi Airways Co (Nos 4 & 5)*:[5] his Lordship thought that, although the tort of conversion is a strict liability tort, the *Doyle v Olby* 'direct' test of remoteness should be applied if the conversion was committed dishonestly. Otherwise the *Wagon Mound* test of reasonable foreseeability should be applied to the tort of conversion.[6] Lord Nicholls said, 'I can see no good reason why the remoteness test of "directly and naturally" applied in cases of deceit should not apply in cases of conversion where the defendant acted dishonestly.'[7]

Unfortunately the remoteness test laid down in *Doyle v Olby* was applied by the Court of Appeal in *Royscot Trust Ltd v Rogerson*[8] to a claim for negligent misrepresentation brought under the Misrepresentation Act 1967, s 2(1). This was on the ground that the 'fiction of fraud' wording used in the subsection left the court with no alternative but to apply the same test of remoteness as for deceit. This is a most unsatisfactory approach for it cannot be sensible to apply a different remoteness test under the Act than to the closely analogous common law tort of negligent misrepresentation. And the rejection of the *Wagon Mound* only seems justifiable where, as in deceit, there is a high degree of blameworthiness attached to the tortfeasor. Moreover the words in s 2(1) do not need to be read as dictating that the rules applicable to assessing damages for deceit apply in exactly the same way in every respect to claims under s 2(1).[9]

In a controversial decision in *Essa v Laing Ltd*[10] the majority of the Court of Appeal (Pill and Clarke LJJ, Rix LJ dissenting) held that it was sufficient in an action for the statutory tort of racial discrimination that the psychiatric illness suffered by the claimant was a direct consequence of the defendant's offensive racist remark even if a psychiatric illness was not a reasonably foreseeable consequence of that remark. Yet the majority did not think it necessary to consider the intentions of the defendant in making that remark. This, it is submitted, is to extend the

---

4   For an excellent clarification that intentional (as distinct from deliberate) conduct in tort refers to consequences, see Cane *The Anatomy of Tort Law* (1997) pp 32–33.

5   [2002] UKHL 19, [2002] 2 AC 883.

6   See *Saleslease Ltd v Davis* [1999] 1 WLR 1664: discussed below, pp 250–251. See also *Sandeman Coprimar SA v Transitos y Transportes Integrales SL* [2003] EWCA Civ 113, [2003] QB 1270, where the claimant's loss (from having to pay guarantees to the Spanish tax authorities when paper tax seals for bottles were lost) was held too remote in the torts of negligence and conversion.

7   [2002] UKHL 19, [2002] 2 AC 883 at para 104.

8   [1991] 2 QB 297. It was left open by the House of Lords in *Smith New Court* whether *Royscot* was correctly decided on this point: [1997] AC 254 at 267, 283.

9   For an historical argument to the contrary, written before the *Royscot* case, see Cartwright 'Damages for Misrepresentation' (1987) Conv 423.

10   [2004] EWCA Civ 2, [2004] ICR 746.

realm of the exceptional 'directness' test too far. The analogy with dishonestly committed torts required that the defendant must have intended (or possibly been reckless as to) the consequences of his remark. But it should have been insufficient to trigger the wider remoteness test that the defendant deliberately made the remark. The majority went on to indicate – and, with respect, this is again controversial – that injury to feelings and psychiatric illness were the same type of harm for the purposes of the remoteness test so that, even applying a reasonable foreseeability test, the psychiatric illness in question was not too remote given that injury to feelings was clearly reasonably foreseeable.

(c) A stricter test?

It is strongly arguable that, even for torts for which it is indisputably the general test, such as negligence, the *Wagon Mound* should not always be the tort test. For example, a stricter test should probably be applied where there is a contractual (or similar) relationship between the parties. This is discussed further in the next section.

(2) Breach of contract[11]

(a) What is the test for remoteness and how does it relate to the *Wagon Mound* test?

The contract remoteness test has been dealt with in five main cases. The first was *Hadley v Baxendale*.[12] The claimant's mill was brought to a standstill by a broken crank-shaft. The claimant engaged the defendant carrier to take it to Greenwich as a pattern for a new one, but in breach of contract the defendant delayed delivery. The claimant sought damages for loss of profit arising from the fact that the mill was stopped for longer than it would have been if there had been no delay. All the carrier knew was 'that the article to be carried was the broken shaft of a mill and that the plaintiffs were millers of that mill.'[13] The court held that the loss of profit was too remote and that therefore the carriers were not liable for it.

The test for remoteness was laid down in two rules by Alderson B. He said:

---

11 For an excellent discussion, see Beale *Remedies* pp 179–187. For a comparative account, see Treitel *Remedies for Breach of Contract* pp 150–162.
12 (1854) 9 Exch 341. Danzig '*Hadley v Baxendale*: A Study in the Industrialisation of the Law' (1975) 4 J Legal Studies 249.
13 (1854) 9 Exch 341 at 355.

'Where two parties have made a contract which one of them has broken, the damages which the other party ought to receive in respect of such breach of contract, should be such as may fairly and reasonably be considered, either arising naturally, ie according to the usual course of things from such breach of contract itself, or such as may reasonably be supposed to have been in the contemplation of both parties, at the time they made the contract as the probable result of the breach of it.'[14]

On the facts neither of these two rules was satisfied; the loss was not the natural consequence because it was felt that in the great multitude of cases the absence of a shaft would not cause a stoppage at a mill as usually a mill-owner would have another shaft in reserve or be able to get one; nor was the loss in the contemplation of both parties because the special circumstance that the mill could not restart until the shaft came back was not known to the defendant.

In the second case of the quintet, *Victoria Laundry (Windsor) Ltd v Newman Industries Ltd*,[15] the claimants, launderers and dyers, decided to extend their business and contracted to buy a boiler from the defendants. The defendants knew that the claimants wanted the boiler for immediate use in their business, but in breach of contract delivered the boiler five months late. The claimants sought damages for the loss of profits that would have resulted from using the boiler, including damages for the exceptional loss of profits that they would have been able to gain from contracts made with the Ministry of Supply. The Court of Appeal held, applying *Hadley v Baxendale*, that damages should be awarded for ordinary loss of profits but not for the exceptional loss of profits. The exceptional profits were too remote because they did not arise naturally and were not in the contemplation of the parties at the time of contracting since the defendants knew nothing about the Ministry of Supply contracts.

Asquith LJ, giving the Court of Appeal's judgment, correctly reasoned that the two rules of *Hadley v Baxendale* could be regarded as comprising a single rule, centring on reasonable contemplation or, as he preferred, reasonable foreseeability. If in applying the second rule one includes as important what the defendant should have reasonably contemplated or foreseen if he had thought about the breach at the time of contracting, then it can swallow up the first rule; for something arising naturally is something that should have been reasonably contemplated by the defendant if he had thought about the breach.

Since *Victoria Laundry*, while the courts have sometimes continued to talk of two rules of remoteness, they have tended, like Asquith LJ, to

14 (1854) 9 Exch 341 at 354.
15 [1949] 2 KB 528.

think in terms of one rather than two rules.[16] Indeed Lord Reid in *Heron II* (which we shall examine below) specifically said, 'I do not think that it was intended that there were to be two rules or that two different standards or tests were to be applied.'[17] And in *The Pegase*[18] Robert Goff J said:

> '*Hadley v Baxendale* is now no longer stated in terms of two rules, but rather in terms of a single principle – though it is recognised that the application of the principle may depend on the degree of relevant knowledge held by the defendant at the time of the contract in a particular case. This approach accords to what actually happens in practice; the courts have not been over-ready to pigeon-hole the cases under one or other of the so-called rules in *Hadley v Baxendale*, but rather to decide each case on the basis of the relevant knowledge of the defendant.'

It is hard to see that anything of substance should turn on whether one formulates the test in two rules or one; and some of the leading contract texts do provide illustrations of the two rules taken separately.[19] In particular, where one is talking about special circumstances that must have been communicated to the defendant in order for particular loss to be non-remote, it can be convenient to say that one is talking about the second rule in *Hadley v Baxendale*.

But what is incorrect is to treat the two rules as providing mutually exclusive, rather than overlapping, tests. This is not least because what occurs naturally will almost always be within the contemplation of the parties. Yet some courts have approached the rules as if they were mutually exclusive so that the first gives the remoteness test for 'general damages' and the second gives the remoteness test for 'special damages'.[20] This requires one to embark initially on an unnecessary, unhelpful and largely circular categorisation of loss as being either general or special. In truth, one shades into the other.

This was expressly emphasised by the Court of Appeal in *Kpohraror v Woolwich Building Society*.[1] The case was concerned with what damages were recoverable for the wrongful dishonour of a cheque where the defendant bank's error had been corrected, and the claimant informed that the cheque would be honoured, later the same day. The claimant

---

16 See, for example, Lord Denning in *Robophone Facilties Ltd v Blank* [1966] 1 WLR 1428; *Parsons v Uttley Ingham* [1978] QB 791.
17 [1969] 1 AC 350 at 385.
18 [1981] 1 Lloyd's Rep 175, 182.
19 Eg Beatson *Anson's Law of Contract* (28th edn, 2002) pp 605–609; McKendrick *Contract Law* (5th edn, 2003) pp 428–429.
20 See, for example, *Monarch SS Company v A/B Karlshamns Oljefabriker* [1949] AC 196 at 221 (per Lord Wright); *President of India v La Pintada Compania Navigacion SA* [1985] AC 104.
1   [1996] 4 All ER 119. See also *International Mineral and Chemical Corpn v Carl O'Helm AG* [1986] 1 Lloyd's Rep 81 (per Hobhouse J).

sought compensation for the damage to his credit and reputation and for the trading loss caused by being unable, as a consequence of the breach, to pay for and hence resell a particular shipment of goods. The Court of Appeal upheld the master's judgment awarding £5,500 for the injury to the claimant's credit and reputation but refusing damages for the particular trading loss. The reasoning was that there was no 'traders only' rule denying the claimant damages for the injury to his credit and reputation and that loss was not too remote. In contrast, the specific trading loss was too remote because the defendant bank had not been informed, and did not know, that a short delay in payment would cause the loss of a transaction. In particular, the bank had not been given notice of the need for immediate clearance.

The important point for us here is that in respect of remoteness the case had been argued by making a rigid distinction between the general damage to the claimant's credit and reputation which was presented as being entirely a matter for the first rule in *Hadley v Baxendale*; and the specific trading loss which had been presented as being entirely a matter for the second rule in *Hadley v Baxendale*. As the Court of Appeal clarified, the correct approach should have been to apply both rules to both types of loss. Evans LJ, with whom Waite LJ and Sir John May agreed, said:

> 'The contentions for both parties were presented as if in a straightjacket imposed by the strict application of the rule in *Hadley v Baxendale* so as to require the separate consideration of each of the two limbs ... I would prefer that the starting point for any application of *Hadley v Baxendale* is the extent of the shared knowledge of both parties when the contract was made (... including the possibility that knowledge of the defendant alone is enough). When that is established, it may often be the case that the first and the second parts of the rule overlap, or at least that it is unnecessary to draw a clear line of demarcation between them.'[2]

It is perhaps worth interjecting here that a rigid distinction has been drawn between the two rules in *Hadley v Baxendale* for the rather different purpose of defining 'indirect or consequential loss' in exclusion clauses. That is, in a number of decisions concerned with the construction of clauses excluding liability for 'indirect or consequential loss' the courts have laid down that the line between direct and indirect or consequential loss is drawn along the boundary between the first and second rules in

2   [1996] 4 All ER 119 at 127–128.

Hadley v Baxendale.[3] Direct loss is treated as loss that follows naturally from the breach within the first rule; while indirect or consequential loss falls within the second rule and is loss that is legally recoverable only if special circumstances were brought to the defendant's attention. Construing exclusion clauses is, of course, a different matter from deciding when losses are, and are not, too remote and one should not reason back from these cases to say that, for the purposes of remoteness, there is a sharp line between the two rules in *Hadley v Baxendale*. As Sedley LJ said in *Hotel Services Ltd v Hilton International Hotels (UK) Ltd,*[4] having referred to the rules in *Hadley v Baxendale*:

> 'This is not a dichotomous but a continuous classification, bringing into the region of recoverability all loss which the parties must in the nature of things or for known reasons have anticipated. It is the framing of exclusion clauses which has made it necessary to divide up its elements ...'

Returning to our quintet of leading cases, in *Heron II*[5] the House of Lords was concerned with the degree of likelihood of the loss occurring that needs to be in the reasonable contemplation of the defendant in order for the loss to be non-remote. The claim was being brought by charterers of a ship against the defendant shipowner for delivering sugar at Basrah, nine days late. During those nine days, 8,000 tonnes of sugar had arrived at Basrah with the result that the market price for sugar at Basrah had fallen. The shipowner had not known that the charterer intended to sell the sugar as soon as it reached Basrah but had known that there was a market for sugar at Basrah. The House of Lords held that, applying *Hadley v Baxendale*, as refined by *Victoria Laundry*, the loss of profit from the fall in the market was not too remote and was recoverable. The argument that the remoteness test for carriage of goods by sea was more restricted than that of *Hadley v Baxendale* was rejected. The Law Lords agreed that a higher degree of likelihood of the loss occurring was required in contract than under the tort remoteness test of reasonable forseeability laid down in the *Wagon Mound*[6] so that losses may be too remote in contract that would not be too remote in tort. Unfortunately, there was no clear consensus as to how the degree of

---

3   Eg *Croudace Construction Ltd v Cawoods Concrete Products Ltd* [1978] 2 Lloyd's Rep 55, CA; *British Sugar plc v Projects Ltd* (1997) 87 BLR 42, CA; *Deepak Fertilisers & Petrochemicals Ltd v Davy McKee (London) Ltd* [1999] 1 All ER (Comm) 69, CA; *BHP Petroleum Ltd v British Steel plc* [1999] 2 All ER (Comm) 544, Rix J; *Hotel Services Ltd v Hilton International Hotels (UK) Ltd* [2000] 1 All ER (Comm) 750, CA; *Watford Electronics Ltd v Sanderson CFL Ltd* [2001] 1 All ER (Comm) 696. Cf *Caledonia North Sea Ltd v British Telecommunications Plc* [2002] UKHL 4, [2002] 1 Lloyd's Rep 553 at paras 99–100 (per Lord Hoffmann).
4   [2000] 1 All ER (Comm) 750, at 755, CA.
5   [1969] 1 AC 350.
6   [1961] AC 388.

likelihood required in contract should be expressed. However, perhaps the clearest way of expressing the essence of their Lordships' reasoning[7] is that, while a slight possibility of the loss occurring is required in tort, a serious possibility of the loss occurring is required in contract. So, on the facts, the loss of profit from the market fall was not too remote because the defendant should have reasonably contemplated that loss as a serious possibility had it thought about the breach at the time the contract was made.

In some subsequent cases, additional complexity has been caused by the necessity for the courts to analyse in greater detail the 'fit' between the remoteness tests in tort and contract. The best known (and the fourth in our quintet of leading cases) is *Parsons v Uttley Ingham & Co Ltd*.[8] The defendants supplied to the claimants a hopper for storing pig food; in breach of contract they failed to provide for proper ventilation so that food became mouldy and 254 of the claimant's pigs died from a rare intestinal disease. The claimants sought damages for the loss of the pigs in contract. All three Court of Appeal judges agreed that such loss was not too remote. But the reasoning of Lord Denning differed from that of the majority, Scarman and Orr LJJ.

To take Lord Denning's reasoning first, in his opinion there are two contract remoteness tests depending on the nature of the loss.[9] To loss of profit, the stricter so-called contract test should be applied; '... the defaulting party is only liable for the consequences if they are such as, at the time of the contract, he ought reasonably to have contemplated them as a serious possibility or real danger'.[10] As *Hadley v Baxendale, Victoria Laundry,* and *Heron II* all dealt with loss of profits, this was why, according to Lord Denning, the stricter test was there applied. On the other hand, as regards physical damage, ie personal injury or damage to property, or expenses incurred, Lord Denning considered that the less strict *Wagon Mound,* so-called tort test, should be applied. By this '... the defaulting party is liable for any loss or expense which he ought reasonably to have foreseen at the time of the breach as a possible consequence even if it was only a slight possibility'.[11] As this case was concerned with physical damage (loss of pigs) Lord Denning applied the *Wagon Mound* (and *Hughes v Lord Advocate*[12] to stress that it was the type, rather than the extent or manner of the damage that was important) and thereby arrived at the

7   This fits in with Lord Denning's interpretation in *Parsons v Uttley Ingham* [1978] QB 791.
8   [1978] QB 791.
9   Lord Denning drew his analysis from Hart and Honoré *Causation In The Law* (1st edn, 1959) pp 281–287.
10   [1978] QB 791 at 802.
11   [1978] QB 791 at 802.
12   [1963] AC 837.

decision that the defendants were liable for the loss of the pigs, which in his view they would not have been if the stricter so-called contract test had been applied.

So for Lord Denning the important distinction is not so much the cause of action – contract or tort – but rather the nature of the loss – loss of profit as against physical damage or expense. In particular, he went on to emphasise that where a defendant is liable for physical damage to one man in contract and to another in tort – and he cited as examples, product liability, occupier's liability and medical negligence – there should be no difference in the remoteness test applied: 'Instances could be multiplied of injuries to persons or damage to property where the defendant is liable for his negligence to one man in contract and to another in tort. Each suffers like damage. The test of remoteness is, and should be, the same in both.'[13] One can go further to point out that a defendant can be liable for physical damage to one and the same claimant in both contract and tort. Indeed in *Parsons* itself, the defendants would surely also have been liable in the tort of negligence had the claimants so framed their claim.

There are at least two issues left unclear by Lord Denning's problematic judgment. The first is what test he would apply to loss of profit in tort. He adopts two tests for remoteness in contract, but he does not say whether a dual test for remoteness would also apply in tort. Would he, in other words, adopt a stricter test than the *Wagon Mound* for tortious loss of profit? The acceptance of pure economic loss recovery in the tort of negligence makes this an important issue. The simplest, neatest view is that Lord Denning would apply the *Heron II* stricter test to tortious loss of profit (albeit with references to the time of the contract replaced by appropriate substitutes, such as the time of the work commencing). The nature of the loss would then be the sole and simple determinant of the remoteness test to be applied, whether in tort or contract. If loss of profit, the stricter *Heron II* would be applicable; if physical damage or expense, the *Wagon Mound*.

The second uncertainty is where the exact division lies between Lord Denning's two categories. However, it seems safe to assume – particularly given his express reliance on the distinction drawn in the tort of negligence between pure economic loss and other economic loss – that Lord Denning's reference to loss of profit is to 'pure' loss of profit (as was in issue in *Hadley v Baxendale*, *Victoria Laundry* and *Heron II*) and not to loss of profit consequent on personal injury or damage to one's property.

13 [1978] QB 791 at 804.

What about the majority's judgment, given by Scarman LJ with whom Orr LJ agreed? They disagreed with Lord Denning's reasoning because they did not think that his distinction between the remoteness test for loss of profit and for physical damage was supported by the authorities. Rather, they considered that *Heron II* provides the single test for remoteness in contract but stressed that, in applying it, it is the type and not extent of loss that must be reasonably contemplated as a serious possibility at the time of contracting. Scarman LJ said:

> 'It does not matter ... if they thought that the chance of physical injury, loss of profit, loss of market, or other loss as the case may be, was slight or that the odds were against it, provided they contemplated as a serious possibility the type of consequence, not necessarily the specific consequence, that ensued on breach.'[14]

Applying that test to the facts, as it was reasonably contemplated by the parties at the time of the contract that, by reason of the failure to provide a hopper fit for storing pig food, there was a serious possibility that the pigs would become ill, and since illness could be said to be the same type of loss as death, it did not matter that the extent of that illness (that is the death of many pigs) was not reasonably contemplated as a serious possibility. Ultimately, therefore, the majority arrived at the result that the loss of the pigs was not too remote.

Three main points should be made regarding the majority's approach. First, it did not say how types of loss are to be divided up. One could argue, for example, that since illness and death of pigs were regarded as the same type of loss, and merely differed in extent, the majority's approach is irreconcilable with *Victoria Laundry;* for one could argue that the type of loss in issue there was loss of profits, and that the exceptional profits were merely a greater extent of that same type of loss. Presumably, the majority's answer to this would be that its test allows the courts a discretion as to how to divide up types of loss, and that *Victoria Laundry* is reconcilable by regarding the ordinary loss of profits as a different type of loss from the exceptional loss of profits. But such discretion and flexibility in the test is only achieved at the expense of certainty. However, some support for the majority's approach does derive from Megarry J's earlier holding in *Wroth v Tyler*[15] that the extraordinary and uncontemplated rise in the market price of houses was not too remote because the type of loss – a difference between the market and contract prices – had been contemplated. But it can be argued that the case is better regarded as turning on the fact that the claimants were

14   [1978] QB 791 at 813.
15   [1974] Ch 30.

'consumers', who wanted the house to live in, rather than businessmen. As such their loss was most accurately described as the loss of a home of a certain standard rather than a loss of profit. Viewed in this way, the loss was clearly contemplated, and remoteness and the type/extent distinction were not in issue.

Secondly, Scarman LJ's approach differed from Lord Denning's in that in applying his test to the facts, he regarded the breach not as that of supplying a hopper with inadequate ventilation but rather that of supplying a hopper unfit for the purpose of storing pig food. So that instead of asking, 'was it reasonably contemplated at the time of contracting as a serious possibility that supplying a hopper with inadequate ventilation would make the pigs ill?' to which the answer was clearly 'no', Scarman LJ asked, 'was it reasonably contemplated at the time of contracting as a serious possibility that supplying a hopper unfit for the purpose of storing pig food would make the pigs ill?' to which he was able to answer 'yes'. In other words, Scarman LJ's approach shows that, by defining the breach more generally, the loss is less likely to be judged too remote.

A third point is that there are passages where Scarman LJ seems at least to suggest that, where there is a contractual relationship between the parties, there should be no difference between the remoteness tests in contract and tort. For example he says:

'... the law must be such that in a factual situation where all have the same actual or imputed knowledge ... the amount of damages recoverable does not depend on whether, as a matter of legal classification, the plaintiff's cause of action is breach of contract or tort. It may be that the necessary reconciliation is to be found, notwith-standing the strictures of Lord Reid in *Heron II*, in holding that the difference between "reasonable foreseeability" (the test in tort) and "reasonably contemplated" (the test in contract) is semantic not substantial. Certainly Asquith LJ in *Victoria Laundry v Newman Industries* and Lord Pearce in *Heron II* thought so; and I confess I think so too.'[16]

But the difference between *Heron II* and the *Wagon Mound* tests is not to do with the terms foreseeable or contemplation; ie we can agree that the difference in these terms is semantic and not substantial; rather, even if one modifies the *Heron II* in the way that Scarman LJ does, it differs from the *Wagon Mound* as to the degree of likelihood of loss required – the *Heron II* test requiring a higher degree – and as to the time at which the contemplation or foreseeability is judged, being at the time the contract is made under the *Heron II* and at the time of the breach of duty under the *Wagon Mound*. It is submitted therefore that this 'reconciliation' between

16 [1978] QB 791 at 807.

the tort and contract tests is nothing of the kind. As such a reconciliation fails, this passage and others like it[17] must be interpreted in one of two ways. First, as suggesting that assimilation of tests *would* be desirable where there is a contractual relationship between the parties, while at the same time leaving the law without any such assimilation; or, secondly, as bringing about assimilation by laying down that where there is a contractual relationship between the parties, the *Parsons* majority test applies, even as the test in tort – that is, as there replacing *The Wagon Mound*.

It is submitted that this latter approach, assimilating the (stricter) contractual and tort test where the parties are in a contractual relationship, must be correct. If we think about the policy behind having different tests, this rests on there being an opportunity for a contracting party to inform the other party of unusual risks. That other party can then exclude or limit its liability or can negotiate a higher price. This is not an opportunity that a party suing in tort normally has because the defendant prior to the commission of the tort is a stranger. The classic judicial exposition of this policy was in Lord Reid's speech in *Heron II*. He said:

> 'In contract, if one party wishes to protect himself against a risk which to the other party would appear unusual, he can direct the other party's attention to it before the contract is made, and I need not stop to consider in what circumstances the other party will then be held to have accepted responsibility in that event. In tort however, there is no opportunity for the injured party to protect himself in that way and the tortfeasor cannot reasonably complain if he has to pay for some very unusual but nevertheless foreseeable damage which results from his wrongdoing.'[18]

But where the claim is being brought in tort in the context of a contractual relationship the parties are not strangers and plainly the claimant has had the same opportunity to inform the defendant of risks – and this can be reflected in the terms of the contract – vis-à-vis the tort claim as he has had vis-à-vis the contract claim. In that context, therefore, there is good reason to apply the stricter contract test to the claim in tort.

This assimilation of remoteness tests where the parties are in a contractual relationship derives support from the most important case on

---

17 [1978] QB 791 at 806.
18 [1969] 1 AC 350 at 385–386. See similarly at 411 (per Lord Hodson) and at 422–423 (per Lord Upjohn).

remoteness since *Parsons*, *Brown v KMR Services Ltd*[19] (which is the last in our quintet of leading cases). One question, in claims by Names at Lloyd's against their members' agents for breach of contract and the tort of negligence, was whether the loss was too remote. The defendants' argument was that the magnitude of the financial disasters that had struck, and the consequent scale of the loss, was unforeseeable and could not have been contemplated. No one would have predicted such a run of major catastrophes as had occurred in the relevant years (1988–1990).

The Court of Appeal held that the loss was not too remote because it was the type and not the extent of the loss that needed to be foreseen or contemplated: the majority's approach in *Parsons v Uttley Ingham* was approved and the decision in *Victoria Laundry* was distinguished. Hobhouse LJ, with whom Peter Gibson LJ agreed, said that the only type of loss in question was that suffered by being a member of a high-risk syndicate. Stuart-Smith LJ similarly regarded there as being only one type of loss in issue although he described that as underwriting loss. He distinguished *Victoria Laundry* saying:

> 'I accept that difficulty in practice may arise in categorisation of loss into types or kinds, especially where financial loss is involved. But I do not see any difficulty in holding that loss of ordinary business profits is different in kind from that flowing from a particular contract which gives rise to very high profits, the existence of which is unknown to the other contracting party who therefore does not accept the risk of such loss occurring.'[20]

There are three main points to emerge from this often overlooked, yet important, case. First, it clearly establishes that the majority view in *Parsons* was correct; applying the contract test, even for economic loss, it is the type of loss and not the precise loss that needs to have been reasonably contemplated or foreseen. Secondly, it is arguable that the contract test was applied even in relation to the concurrent claim in the

---

19 [1995] 4 All ER 598. See also *Berryman v London Borough of Hounslow* [1997] PIQR P83, CA, where the contractual remoteness test was applied to deny damages for a personal injury where the claim was framed in both contract and tort. For contract cases on remoteness since *Parsons*, which have failed to clarify the issues raised by that decision, see, eg *Rumsey v Owen, White and Catlin* (1978) 245 Estates Gazette 225; *The Pegase* [1981] 1 Lloyd's Rep 175; *Kemp v Intasun Holidays Ltd* [1987] 2 FTLR 234; *Seven Seas Properties Ltd v Al-Essa (No 2)* [1993] 3 All ER 577. Cf *The Borag* [1981] 1 All ER 856 (in which Lord Denning relied on his own judgment in *Parsons*); *The Rio Claro* [1987] 2 Lloyd's Rep 173 (in reliance on *Parsons*, the type of loss was stressed, albeit that the loss was held too remote); *The Forum Craftsman* [1991] 1 Lloyd's Rep 81 (in which an argument that the loss was not too remote, based on the 'type' emphasis in *Parsons*, was rejected). See also the very interesting Scottish case of *Balfour Beatty Construction (Scotland) Ltd v Scottish Power Plc* 1994 SLT 807, HL, in which it was explicitly left open whether *Parsons* was correctly decided. For discussion of that case, see MacQueen 'Remoteness and Breach of Contract' [1996] Jur Rev 295; Burrows *Understanding the Law of Obligations* (1998) pp 160–163.
20 [1995] 4 All ER 598 at 621.

tort of negligence. If this interpretation is correct, the Court of Appeal was adopting the assimilation approach that has been examined above – and argued to be correct in terms of policy – in relation to the majority's decision in *Parsons*. Admittedly both Gatehouse J and the Court of Appeal used only the language of breach of contract in expressing their conclusions; and, at the time of Gatehouse J's judgment, the House of Lords' decision in *Henderson v Merrett Syndicates Ltd*,[1] authoritatively accepting concurrent liability, had not yet been laid down. But the claims in *Brown* were for both breach of contract and the tort of negligence and the appeal in *Brown* was heard, and the judgment of the Court of Appeal was given, almost a year after *Henderson v Merrett*. Thirdly, the way in which *Victoria Laundry* was distinguished illustrates again that there is a wide degree of discretion open to the courts in deciding how to divide up types of loss.

It is arguable therefore that, despite little attention being devoted to it, the *Brown* decision provides the final major piece in the remoteness jigsaw. After it, we can describe the law, in a way that is relatively clear and based on sound policy, in the following three points.[2] First, there is a single contract test of remoteness which lays down that losses are too remote if, at the time the contract was made, the defendant did not contemplate and could not reasonably have contemplated that type of loss as a serious possibility. Secondly, the normal tort test, applicable in standard tort claims where the parties are not in a contractual relationship, is that losses are too remote if at the time of the breach of duty the defendant did not foresee and could not reasonably have foreseen that type of loss as a slight possibility. Thirdly, where the parties are in a contractual relationship, the above contract test applies even where the claim is being brought in tort because of the equal opportunity that the claimant has had to inform the other party of unusual risks.[3]

1   [1995] 2 AC 145.
2   For a different approach, see Cooke 'Remoteness of Damages and Judicial Discretion' [1978] CLJ 288 (advocating a wide judicial discretion, albeit with articulated considerations to be taken into account).
3   One can strongly argue that, wherever there is a pre-existing relationship, even if non-contractual, between the parties, the 'contract' test should apply even where the claim is being brought in tort because the claimant has had the opportunity, and should be encouraged, to inform the other party of unusual risks. Admittedly the scope for the defendant to deal with that information is more restricted than where there is a contractual relationship: in particular there is no price to modify. But the defendant can exclude or limit its tortious liability (eg for negligent advice) by a non-contractual disclaimer.

(b) Is the contract test too harsh on a defendant?

An argument can be made that the contract test is too harsh on defendants in that it does not directly take into account the amount of the contractual consideration to be received by the defendant. In other words, the fact that the claimant's losses are out of all proportion to what the defendant was to receive under the contract is an irrelevant factor in judging remoteness. For example, in *Hadley v Baxendale* itself, the fact that the claimant's loss of profits from delay were out of all proportion to the price to be paid to the defendant for carrying the mill-shaft was irrelevant. In the US this point has led commentators and courts frequently to suggest that the *Hadley v Baxendale* test does not restrict liability enough.[4] In accordance with this, the Second Restatement of Contracts, s 351(3) states: 'A court may limit damages for foreseeable loss ... if it concludes that in the circumstances justice so requires in order to avoid disproportionate compensation'; and by comment (f) 'disproportionate' means 'an extreme disproportion between the loss ... and the price charged by the party whose liability for that loss is in question.'[5]

Similarly, in a few English cases, particularly those concerning carriers, the courts have applied a different, more restrictive, test than that of *Hadley v Baxendale*. For example, in *British Columbia and Vancouvers Island Spar, Lumber and Saw-Mill Co Ltd v Nettleship*[6] it was held that a carrier would not be liable even if told of special circumstances unless he agreed to accept liability for the unusual risk as a term of the contract. Willes J said:

> 'Take the case of a barrister on his way to practise at the Calcutta bar, where he may have a large number of briefs awaiting him; through the default of the Peninsular and Oriental Company he is detained in Egypt or in the Suez boat, and consequently sustains great loss: is the company to be responsible for that, because they happened to know the purpose for which the traveller was going?'[7]

The answer was considered to be 'no' applying the approach that one needs both knowledge and actual acceptance of the risk of loss as a contractual term. However, this approach has clearly been rejected, not

---

4 Eg *Lamkins v International Harvester Co* 182 SW 2d 203 (1944); Farnsworth 'Legal Remedies for Breach of Contract' (1970) Col LR 1145, 1209.
5 See Kniffin 'A Newly Identified Contract Unconscionability: Unconscionability of Remedy' (1988) 63 Notre Dame LR 247; see also above, p 38, n 3.
6 (1868) LR 3 CP 499. See *also Horne v Midland Rly Co* (1873) LR 8 CP 131.
7 (1868) LR 3 CP 499 at 510.

only impliedly by the approval of *Hadley v Baxendale* in *Heron II*, but also specifically by the Court of Appeal in *GKN Centrax Gears Ltd v Matbro Ltd.*[8]

Moreover, it is submitted that the English approach is to be preferred. Once the defendant has been given notice of unusual potential losses, he can act accordingly, whether by refusing to contract, or by raising the price, or by reducing the probability of breach, or by excluding liability. Given such a choice, it seems perfectly fair and not unduly harsh to hold him responsible for reasonably contemplated losses flowing from what, after all, was his breach of contract. In any event, an approach like that advocated in the Second Restatement creates unacceptable uncertainty.

(c) The principle in *Cory v Thames Ironworks Co*[9]

Where the claimant's actual loss of profit is too remote, and hence irrecoverable, it is still entitled to recover a lesser sum measured by the loss of profit that would have been non-remote. The leading authority on this often overlooked principle is *Cory v Thames Ironworks Co* in which the defendants were in breach of contract in failing to deliver the hull of a boat on time. The claimants, who were coal merchants, intended to use the hull in a novel way unknown to the defendants. The defendants assumed that the claimants intended to use the hull for the usual purpose of storing coal. It was held that, while the loss of profit flowing from the special use was too remote, the lesser profit that would have been lost from applying the hull for usual purposes was recoverable. That was so even though the claimants had suffered no such loss in the sense that they would not have used the hull for storage.[10] Cockburn J said:

> 'The buyer has lost the larger amount, and there can be no hardship or injustice in making the seller liable to compensate him in damages so far as the seller understood and believed that the article would be applied to the ordinary purposes to which it was capable of being applied.'[11]

This must be correct. To overcome the objection that the claimant recovers for a loss that it has not suffered, the principle is best rationalised by saying that the claimant recovers that part of its actual loss of special profit that is *equivalent* to the ordinary profit that would have been lost.

---

8   [1976] 2 Lloyd's Rep 555. See also Lord Upjohn in *Heron II* [1969] 1 AC 350 at 422. Cf *The Pegase* [1981] 1 Lloyd's Rep 175 at 183–184; Treitel *The Law of Contract* (11th edn, 2003) pp 969–970.
9   (1868) LR 3 QB 181.
10   *Victoria Laundry (Windsor) Ltd v Newman Industries Ltd* [1949] 2 KB 528, above, p 84, was significantly different in that the claimants had suffered a loss of both ordinary and exceptional profits.
11   (1868) LR 3 QB 181 at 190.

3. INTERVENING CAUSE[12]

Even though the defendant's breach of duty is a cause of the claimant's loss, the claimant may not recover damages for it because an intervening cause,[13] combining with it to produce the loss,[14] is regarded as breaking the chain of causation between the defendant's breach of duty and the loss. The underlying policy behind this restriction is that, where an intervening cause is much more responsible for the loss than is the defendant's breach of duty, it is considered unfair on the defendant and is imposing too great a burden on her to hold her liable for the loss.

The principles upon which the decisions in this area are based have rarely been clearly articulated, and some judges have even resorted to saying that it is simply a matter of instinct or common sense.[15] However, unarticulated common sense or instinct is hardly a satisfactory basis for legal decision-making and therefore an attempt will be made to indicate the main principles that underlie the decisions in relation to each of the three main types of intervening cause: namely natural events (that is, where the event is not caused by any identifiable person); conduct of a third party; and conduct of the claimant.[16]

(1) Intervening natural events

In general, a natural event only breaks the chain of causation if the sole contribution that the defendant's breach of duty makes to the claimant's loss is that the claimant or his property is in the place where, at the time when, the natural event intervenes. Even then the natural event will not break the causal chain if it was likely to intervene.

This is illustrated by the well-known hypothetical examples of the claimant who, having been injured by the defendant's negligence and while on the way to hospital, is further injured by a falling tree or roof-tile

---

12 The leading discussion on causation is Hart and Honoré *Causation In The Law* (2nd edn, 1985). The analysis in this book is in agreement with theirs that causal limits should be kept distinct from other limits on responsibility such as remoteness; but it differs from theirs in regarding intervening cause as depending on a policy decision rather than on the largely factual question of whether there is causation in the ordinary commonsense meaning of that term.

13 Ie a factual cause subsequent to the breach of duty. A factual cause prior to or contemporaneous with the defendant's breach of duty cannot be correctly described as intervening so as to come within this section. But such a factual cause does not merit separate treatment elsewhere since it is very rarely regarded as the sole legal cause of the damage.

14 Contrast sufficient causes, above, pp 46–50.

15 Watkins LJ in *Lamb v Camden London Borough Council* [1981] QB 625 at 647; Glidewell LJ in *Galoo Ltd v Bright Grahame Murray* [1994] 1 WLR 1360 at 1374–1375.

16 In *Normans Bay Ltd v Coudert Brothers* [2003] EWCA Civ 215 the rare question arose of whether the *defendant's* own wrongful conduct (which was not actionable because of limitation) broke the chain of causation between the wrongful conduct of the defendant being sued for and the claimant's loss. Not surprisingly, it was held that, as a matter of principle and policy, it did not.

or, while in hospital, suffers further injury because of a fire there.[17] In each of these situations the sole contribution of the breach of duty to the further loss is that the claimant is at the place where, at the time when, the natural event intervenes; since, in addition, none of these natural events was likely to intervene the causal chain is broken. Similarly in *Carlslogie SS Co Ltd v Royal Norwegian Government*[18] the claimant's ship was damaged in a collision for which the defendant was wholly responsible. After temporary repairs rendering the ship seaworthy, she set out on a voyage to the US. On that voyage she suffered extensive damage due to heavy weather. The House of Lords considered that there was certainly no question of the defendant being liable for the heavy weather damage. Viscount Jowitt said that it '... was not in any sense a consequence of the collision, and must be treated as a supervening event occurring in the course of a normal voyage'.[19] More specifically it can be said that the chain of causation was broken because the sole contribution of the breach of duty to the heavy weather damage was that the claimant's ship was in the Atlantic at the time of that heavy weather, and moreover that heavy weather was unlikely to intervene.

In contrast, let us suppose that the defendant negligently sets fire to the claimant's field and later, fanned by gale-force winds, the fire spreads to and destroys the claimant's house; the winds do not break the chain of causation because the contribution of the defendant's negligence to the burning down of the house clearly has nothing to do merely with the claimant's property being in the place where, at the time when, the natural event intervenes. On the contrary without the defendant's breach of duty there would have been no fire at all.

A further example of a natural event not breaking the causal chain is provided by *Monarch SS Co Ltd v A/B Karlshamms Oljefabriker*.[20] The defendant's breach of contract in failing to provide a seaworthy ship for the carriage of the claimant's cargo of soya beans meant that the voyage was delayed, and that the ship could not reach her destination in Sweden before the Second World War broke out. The ship was ordered by the Admiralty to discharge the soya beans at Glasgow. The claimants thereupon had to pay for the beans to be forwarded to Sweden in neutral ships. They claimed damages for the cost of that transhipment. One issue was whether that transhipment was too remote in the sense discussed in the last section, but another was whether the intervening

---

17   See *Hogan v Bentinck West Hartley Collieries (Owners) Ltd* [1949] 1 All ER 588 at 601 (per Lord Macdermott).
18   [1952] AC 292.
19   [1952] AC 292 at 299.
20   [1949] AC 196.

events, in particular the outbreak of war, broke the causal connection between the defendant's breach and the transhipment. It was held that the chain of causation was not broken. Although the sole contribution of the defendant's breach to the transhipment was that the ship was within waters patrolled by the British Navy when the war broke out, that intervention, as Lord Porter stressed, was likely.[1]

This principle for natural events sets a fairly high standard for establishing that the chain of causation is broken; that is, it is relatively rare for a natural event to break the chain of causation. This should be contrasted with the approach to wrongful intervention by a third party or the claimant's own unreasonable conduct. The difference reflects sound policy; a defendant cannot attach blame to anyone else in the case of natural events.

(2) Intervening conduct of a third party

(a) The duty was to guard against such a third party intervention

Clearly in this situation the third party should not be regarded as having broken the chain of causation, and this is shown in a number of contract cases. In *London Joint Stock Bank v Macmillan*,[2] for example, the defendant customer of the claimant bank, in breach of his contractual duty to the claimant not to draw cheques so as to facilitate fraud, signed for a trusted clerk a cheque for £2 drawn in such a way as to enable the clerk readily to alter the amount to £120; the clerk then obtained this sum from the bank and absconded. The House of Lords held that the defendant was liable to the claimant for the forged sum. Lord Finlay LC said, 'The fact that a crime was necessary to bring about the loss does not prevent it being the natural consequence of the carelessness.'[3] More specifically, one can say that the reason why the intervening acts of the third party, albeit criminal, did not break the chain of causation was that the duty broken was to guard against a third party fraudulently obtaining money from the bank.

Stansbie v Troman,[4] in which the cause of action is probably best rationalised as breach of contract,[5] is a further and very clear example. A decorator was at work in a house and left it for two hours to get

---

1   [1949] AC 196 at 215.
2   [1918] AC 777. See also *De La Bere v Pearson* [1908] 1 KB 280.
3   [1918] AC 777 at 794.
4·   [1948] 2 KB 48.
5   See *P Perl (Exporters) Ltd v Camden London Borough Council* [1983] 3 All ER 161 at 170.

wallpaper. He was alone and had been told by the claimant householder to lock the front door if he ever left. Instead he left the door unlocked and during his absence a thief entered and stole some jewellery and clothes. The Court of Appeal held that the defendant was liable for the loss: the third party intervention did not break the chain of causation because the duty broken was clearly to prevent what had occurred. As Tucker LJ said, '... the act of negligence itself consisted in the failure to take reasonable care to guard against the very thing that in fact happened.'[6]

Similarly in *Home Office v Dorset Yacht Co Ltd*[7] the majority of their Lordships, with the notable exception of Lord Reid, framed the issue in terms of whether a duty of care in the tort of negligence was owed by borstal officers to the owners of nearby yachts damaged by escaping borstal boys. Having decided that there was such a duty, and that it had been breached, it obviously followed that the chain of causation was not broken by the intervention of the borstal boys. As Oliver LJ said in *P Perl (Exporters) Ltd v Camden London Borough Council*[8] in which the defendant was held to owe no duty of care to a neighbour whose premises had been burgled by thieves gaining access through the defendant's premises:

> '... the question of the existence of a duty and that of whether the damage brought about by the act of a third parry is too remote are simply two facets of the same problem: for if there be a duty to take reasonable care to prevent damage being caused by a third party then I find it difficult to see how damage caused by the third party consequent on the failure to take such care can be too remote a consequence of the breach of duty.'[9]

The same sentiment was expressed by Lord Goff in *Smith v Littlewoods Organisation Ltd*[10] in which it was decided that no duty of care was owed to neighbours whose property had been damaged as a result of vandals setting fire to the defendant's derelict cinema. 'Of course, if a duty of care is imposed to guard against deliberate wrongdoing by others, it can hardly be said that the harmful effects of such wrongdoing are not caused by such breach of duty.'[11]

The controversial decision in *Weld-Blundell v Stephens*[12] seems to be out of line with the principle being discussed and it is submitted that, for this reason alone, the minority view is to be preferred. The claimant, when

6   [1948] 2 KB 48 at 52.
7   [1970] AC 1004.
8   [1984] QB 342.
9   [1984] QB 342 at 353.
10   [1987] AC 241.
11   [1987] AC 241 at 272.
12   [1920] AC 956. The case was distinguished in *Slipper v BBC* [1991] 1 QB 283.

employing the defendant accountant to investigate the affairs of the company, libelled certain officials of the company in his letter of instructions to the defendant. The defendant negligently left the letter at the company's office, where it was read by a third party who related its contents to the officials, who successfully sued the claimant for libel. The claimant brought an action against the defendant for breach of contract, claiming compensation for those damages and the costs. The House of Lords held by a bare majority that the third party's act broke the chain of causation and that the claimant could therefore recover no more than nominal damages. The main ground of reasoning was expressed as follows by Lord Sumner:

> 'In general ... even though A is in fault he is not responsible for injury to C which B, a stranger to him, deliberately chooses to do. Though A may have given the occasion for B's mischievous activities, B then becomes a new and independent cause ... It is hard to steer clear of metaphors. Perhaps one may be forgiven for saying that B snaps the chain of causation; that he is no mere conduit pipe through which consequences flow from A to C, no mere part of a transmission gear set in motion by A; that in a word, he insulates A from C.'[13]

Such a generalisation is misleading and did mislead the majority in the case, for it fails to indicate that where, as on the facts of this case, the duty broken is to guard against such a third party intervention as occurred, even a criminal act of the third party, let alone a non-wrongful act as here, does not break the chain of causation. In the dissenting words of Viscount Finlay, '... the very thing happened which it was [the defendant's] duty to guard against'.[14]

(b) Third party intervention other than where there was a duty to guard against it

Rationalisation of the case law is here particularly difficult. However, it would seem that where the third party's intervention comprises wrongdoing it breaks the chain of causation unless it was a likely, or in the case of intentional wrongdoing, a very likely consequence of the defendant's breach of duty. Non-wrongful conduct of a third party will probably only break the chain on the same principle as for natural events. The policy is therefore one of showing more leniency towards the defendant if a third party's intervening conduct has been wrongful, so

---

13   [1920] AC 956 at 986.
14   [1920] AC 956 at 974.

that the claimant can claim against him, than if non-wrongful. Moreover, the greater the culpability of the third party's wrong, the greater the leniency.

Two cases involving multiple collisions can be used to illustrate a third party's non-intentional wrongdoing. In *Rouse v Squires*[15] D1 negligently jack-knifed his lorry across a motorway. D2 driving his lorry negligently, collided into D1's lorry and killed the claimant's husband who was assisting at the scene. D2 was held liable to the claimant. D2 now brought third party proceedings against D1. The question that arose was whether that intervening negligence of D2 broke the chain of causation between D1's negligence and the death of the claimant's husband. The Court of Appeal held that that chain of causation was not broken. Cairns LJ said that where a driver:

> '... so negligently manages his vehicle as to cause it to obstruct the highway and constitute a danger to other road users, including those who are driving too fast or not keeping a proper look-out, but not those who deliberately or recklessly drive into the obstruction,[16] then the first driver's negligence may be held to have contributed to the causation of an accident of which the immediate cause was the negligent driving of the vehicle which because of the presence of the obstruction collides with it.'[17]

Moreover, on these facts, once D1 had negligently jack-knifed, it was likely that another negligently-driven vehicle would collide causing injury or death to those on the scene.

On the other hand, in *Knightley v Johns*[18] D1 negligently overturned his car thereby blocking a tunnel. D2, a police inspector, was held to be negligent in not immediately closing the tunnel and in ordering the claimant, a constable, to ride back along the tunnel against the traffic in order to close it. While doing so, the claimant collided with D3's oncoming car and was injured. The primary question was whether the intervening negligent acts of D2 broke the chain of causation between D1's negligence and the claimant's injuries. Stephenson LJ said that the test to be applied was '... reasonable foreseeability, which I understand to mean foreseeability of something of the same sort being likely to happen.'[19] Applying that the Court of Appeal, not surprisingly, reached the conclusion that D2's negligent acts broke the chain of causation and that therefore D1 was not liable for the claimant's injuries. Some types of

---

15   [1973] QB 889.
16   These words were expressly relied on by the Court of Appeal in *Wright v Lodge* [1993] 4 All ER 299 in holding that the *reckless* driving in question broke the chain of causation.
17   [1973] QB 889 at 898.
18   [1982] 1 WLR 349.
19   [1982] 1 WLR 349 at 366.

risk-taking and even negligence by the police were likely to intervene; but the same could not be said of the acts of negligence that D2 had actually committed.

The well-known case of *The Oropesa*[20] concerned non-wrongful intervention. A ship of that name negligently caused a collision with another ship. The master of the latter ship decided to cross to The Oropesa in a small boat. The boat overturned and the claimant's son was killed. The question was whether the death was caused by the negligence of The Oropesa or whether the master's action in taking to the boat broke the chain of causation. It was held that the chain of causation was not broken. Lord Wright said:

'To break the chain of causation it must be shown that there is something which I will call ultroneous, something unwarrantable, a new cause which disturbs the sequence of events, something which can be described as either unreasonable or extraneous or extrinsic.'[1]

This is typical of reasoning in the area of intervening cause in not articulating the exact principle; but it does indicate that non-wrongful conduct will rarely break the chain. It is submitted that in accordance with this and with the approach to natural events, the underlying general principle is that third party non-wrongful acts will only break the chain if the sole contribution that the defendant's breach of duty makes to the claimant's loss is that the claimant is in the place where, at the time when, the third party intervenes. Even then the causal chain will not be broken if the intervention was likely. Applying this to the facts of *The Oropesa* the causal chain was not broken because the defendant's breach of duty contributed to the master taking out the boat, and its contribution was therefore not solely that the claimant was in the boat when it overturned. Similarly it is submitted that, had the events considered above under natural events[2] been caused by a third party's non-wrongful act, the same decisions on causation would be reached.

Where the third party's conduct comprises intentional wrongdoing, the intervention will break the chain of causation, unless it was a very likely consequence of the defendant's breach of duty. In *Home Office v Dorset*

---

20   [1943] P 32. For a colourful example of non-wrongful intervention of a third party being held not to break the chain of causation in the context of the tort of defamation, see *McManus v Beckham* [2002] EWCA Civ 939, [2002] 1 WLR 2982 (publication of defendant's slander did not break chain of causation).

1   [1943] P 32 at 39.

2   Above, pp 97–99.

Yacht Co Ltd[3] Lord Reid who, unlike the majority, regarded the primary issue as one of intervening cause rather than as one of duty, said:

> '... where human action forms one of the links between the original wrong-doing of the defendant and the loss suffered by the plaintiff, that action must at least have been something very likely to happen if it is not to be regarded as *novus actus interveniens* breaking the chain of causation. I do not think that a mere foreseeable possibility is or should be sufficient, for then the intervening human action can more properly be regarded as a new cause than as a consequence of the original wrongdoing.'[4]

Since on these facts it was very likely that as a result of the defendant's negligence the boys would escape and damage nearby yachts, the chain of causation was not broken.

Lord Reid's dictum was subsequently applied by Oliver LJ in *Lamb v Camden London Borough Council*,[5] albeit that he recast Lord Reid's test in terms of 'reasonable forseeability' and regarded intervening cause as an aspect of remoteness. The defendants had negligently caused the subsidence of the claimant's house with the result that the claimant had to leave it unoccupied. The question was whether in addition to their admitted liability in nuisance for the subsidence the defendants should be held responsible for the loss caused by the action of squatters occupying and looting the home. The Court of Appeal unanimously held that the defendants should not be liable for that further loss. Oliver LJ, applying Lord Reid's test, in effect held that as the third party's intervention was unlikely the chain of causation was broken. On the other hand the reasoning of the other judges is unhelpful with regard to intervention by a third party. Least satisfactory was Watkins LJ who regarded the loss as too remote because his instinct told him so. Rather more satisfactory was Lord Denning's primary reasoning by which he in effect decided the issue in terms of the claimant's failure to act (that is, the duty to mitigate) rather than intervening third party conduct; the claimant had unreasonably failed to secure adequately the empty house even after an initial intrusion by squatters.

Unfortunately even Oliver LJ thought that Lord Reid's test might not be stringent enough, and he said, 'There may ... be circumstances in which the court would require a degree of likelihood amounting almost to inevitability before it fixes a defendant with a responsibility for the act

3   [1970] AC 1004. For an excellent illustration, see the Supreme Court of Alberta case of *Duce v Rourke* [1951] 1 WWR 305 (theft of tools from car by third party after accident broke the chain of causation). For the intentional wrongful act of a third party breaking the chain of causation in a claim for breach of statutory duty, see *Horton v Caplin Contracts Limited* [2002] EWCA Civ 1604, [2003] PIQR P180.
4   [1970] AC 1004 at 1030.
5   [1981] QB 625.

of the third party over whom he has and can have no control.'[6] The hypothetical example worrying the Court of Appeal was that of an escaping borstal boy stealing a car and committing a burglary hundreds of miles from the borstal. While this was thought very likely, it was considered that the Home Office ought not to be held liable for it. But there is surely no need to qualify or reject Lord Reid's test to reach that result for it can be argued that the Home Office would owe no duty of care to the claimant in that situation. In other words Lord Reid regarded *Dorset Yacht* as raising particular difficulties over intervening cause rather than the duty of care, but he could still have regarded the duty of care as the problem issue on other facts.

In *Ward v Cannock Chase District Council*[7] there was no such qualification of Lord Reid's dictum which was applied, along with Oliver LJ's reasoning in *Lamb*, to reach the decision that the defendant council (which admitted negligence) was liable for damage to the claimant's house resulting initially from vandalisation of the defendant's empty house next door and later from direct vandalisation of the claimant's then unoccupied house. The chain of causation was held to be unbroken as it was very likely that unoccupied houses in that area would be vandalised.

(3) Intervening conduct of the claimant

The position here seems to be that, where there has been a tort[8] or breach of contract, unreasonable conduct of the claimant breaks the chain of causation (unless the duty was to guard against that intervention)[9] whereas reasonable conduct does not. In accordance with

---

6   [1981] QB 625 at 644.
7   [1986] Ch 546.
8   Separate consideration is not given to the claimant's conduct subsequent to a breach of duty but prior to a tort (that is, where there is as yet no damage and the tort is not actionable per se) because here even unreasonable conduct rarely breaks the chain of causation and usually amounts to contributory negligence. Exceptions are *Rushton v Turner Bros Asbestos* [1960] 1 WLR 96, and *Jayes v IMI Ltd* [1985] ICR 155 (in the latter the incorrect term '100% contributory negligence' was used); *Galoo Ltd v Bright Grahame Murray* [1994] 1 WLR 1360 (as regards the tort claim).
9   Eg *Reeves v Metropolitan Police Comr* [2000] 1 AC 360, HL where it was held that suicide did not break the chain of causation because the duty of the police was precisely to take reasonable care to prevent suicide. (Note that, as a case on the tort of negligence, this is also consistent with the general rule referred to in the previous note.) That the duty in question was to guard against the claimant's conduct is also probably the best explanation of *British Racing Drivers' Club Ltd v Hextall Erskine & Co* [1996] 3 All ER 667 (distinguishing the *Galoo* case discussed below, at p 107) where there was held to be no break in the chain of causation between solicitors' negligent advice to a company that its directors could go ahead with a transaction without reference to its members and loss caused to the company by that transaction.

the distinction explained above,[10] cases where the claimant has unreasonably failed to take action, or has unreasonably incurred expenses, are not discussed here but under the duty to mitigate.

(a) **Unreasonable acts**

The classic case is *McKew v Holland and Hannen and Cubitts*.[11] The claimant had suffered an injury for which the defendants were tortiously liable, and as a result he occasionally lost control of his left leg. Some days after the accident he was descending a steep staircase without a handrail and without the available assistance of his wife and brother-in-law when he lost control of his left leg and, in jumping to save himself falling, broke his ankle. The House of Lords held that the further injury was brought about by the claimant's own actions because, in placing himself unnecessarily in a position where he might be injured, the claimant was acting unreasonably; and even though unreasonable conduct was not unlikely or unforeseeable, it nevertheless broke the chain of causation. Lord Reid said, '... it is not at all unlikely or unforeseeable that an active man who has suffered such a disability will take some quite unreasonable risk but if he does, he cannot hold the defender liable for the consequences'.[12]

Two contract cases similarly illustrate the principle. In *Quinn v Burch Bros (Builders) Ltd*[13] the defendants in breach of contract failed to supply a step-ladder to the claimant, a sub-contractor. The claimant injured himself when he fell from an unfooted trestle which he had made use of in the absence of a step-ladder. The Court of Appeal held that the defendants were not liable for the claimant's injuries because their breach of contract did not cause them: the claimant's own unreasonable acts broke the chain of causation between the breach of contract and his injuries.

Again in *Lambert v Lewis*[14] a dealer supplied a defective trailer coupling to a farmer, who negligently went on using it after it was obviously broken. There was an accident resulting in injuries to other parties, when the coupling gave way. The farmer was found liable for those injuries and in an action for breach of contract against the dealer sought to recover an indemnity for the damages he had had to pay. The House of Lords held, however, that he should not be so indemnified because his

---

10   Above, p 75.
11   [1969] 3 All ER 1621.
12   [1969] 3 All ER 1621 at 1623.
13   [1966] 2 QB 370. See also *Beoco Ltd v Alfa Laval Co* [1995] QB 137, CA; *Young v Purdy* [1996] 2 FLR 795, CA.
14   [1982] AC 225.

negligence in continuing to use the coupling knowing of its condition had broken the chain of causation between the dealer's breach of contract and the accident.

The principle that unreasonable intervening conduct of the claimant breaks the chain of causation may be the best explanation of the well-known decision in *Galoo Ltd v Bright Grahame Murray*.[15] A claim was brought by a company for trading losses against its auditors. The claimant company argued that, had the auditors drawn up the company's accounts using reasonable care, they would have revealed that the company was insolvent. The company would thereupon have stopped trading. The auditors were therefore liable in contract and tort to the company for its continued trading losses after that time. But the Court of Appeal dismissed this claim on the basis that there was a break in the chain of causation between the auditors' negligence and the company's trading losses. Rather unhelpfully Glidewell LJ said the following: '[H]ow does the court decide whether the breach of duty was the cause of the loss or merely the occasion for the loss? ... The answer in the end is, "By the application of the court's common sense." '[16] It is arguable that behind this opaque reasoning lay the idea that the company's trading losses were essentially a result of its own poor decisions.[17] That 'unreasonable conduct' broke the chain of causation between the auditors' breach of duty to the company and those losses. But a possible difficulty with that argument is that the tenor of Glidewell LJ's judgment is that there would still have been a break in the chain of causation even if the trading losses were essentially attributable to market forces rather than poor decisions. Given that applying usual principle, natural events or the non-wrongful conduct of third parties relatively rarely break the chain of causation,[18] one may be led to the conclusion that the approach to legal causation in *Galoo* is inconsistent with normal principle; and that legal causation is being used to reflect a specific policy decision that an auditor's liability (in contract or tort) should be severely limited.

---

15   [1994] 1 WLR 1360. See also *Moore v Zerfahs* [1999] Lloyd's Rep PN 144, CA (unwise investment of a loan in a company, which fails, breaks the chain of causation between the defendant's breach of duty of care owed in tort in organising the loan and the claimant's loss).

16   [1994] 1 WLR 1360 at 1374–1375.

17   This derives some support from Laddie J's analysis of the Australian negligent audit case of *Alexander v Cambridge Credit Corpn* (1987) 9 NSWLR 310 in *Bank of Credit and Commerce International v Price Waterhouse (No 3)* (1998) Times, 2 April: 'Alexander's breach of duty was not regarded as the cause, in the legal sense, of the losses which arose simply from continuing trading. What caused those losses were the dangers inherent in the marketplace and the directors' management decisions which, with the benefit of hindsight, can be seen to have been the wrong decisions to take.'

18   Above, pp 97–99, 101–103.

(b) Reasonable acts

The contract case of *Compania Naviera Maropan v Bowaters*[19] illustrates that the chain of causation will not be broken by reasonable intervening acts of the claimant.[20] The defendant charterers were in breach of contract with the claimants by nominating an unsafe loading place for their ship. The master of the claimants' ship thought that the place nominated was unsafe, but placed reliance on the assurance of safety given by the defendants' experienced pilot. The ship was damaged and the question that arose was whether the master's actions had broken the chain of causation between the breach of contract and the damage to the ship. It was held that they had not because he had acted reasonably in the circumstances. Hodson LJ said:

> 'The question is one of causation. If the master by acting as he did, either caused the damage by acting unreasonably in the circumstances in which he was placed or failed to mitigate the damage, the charterers would be relieved accordingly, from the liability which would otherwise have fallen upon them.'[1]

Similarly in *Wieland v Cyril Lord Carpets Ltd*[2] the defendants negligently inflicted neck injuries on the claimant so that she had to wear a collar. She later fell down some stairs because she could not use her bifocal spectacles with her usual skill. Eveleigh J held that she was entitled to recover for her further injuries from the defendants because her own acts did not break the chain of causation. Again we can say this was because the claimant was not acting unreasonably when she fell down the stairs.

(c) Contributory negligence?

The all or nothing division between reasonable and unreasonable acts leaves out of account the possibility that contributory negligence subsequent to the tort or breach of contract might not break the chain of causation while allowing a reduction of damages. For breach of contract this mid-position is often unavailable because the Law Reform (Contributory Negligence) Act 1945 often does not apply to breach of contract.[3] But there is no such reason for forcing tort cases into the all or

---

19   [1955] 2 QB 68.
20   A relatively minor degree of carelessness by the claimant may be insufficient to break the chain of causation. See, eg *County Ltd v Girozentrale* [1996] 3 All ER 834, CA: chain of causation between broker's breach of contract (to claimant bank, which was underwriting an issue of shares, in telling potential investors of bank's intention to proceed on an 'all or nothing' basis) and claimant's loss not broken by claimant carelessly accepting indicative commitments from an investor which then pulled out.
1   [1955] 2 QB 68 at 99.
2   [1969] 3 All ER 1006.
3   Below, pp 136–144.

nothing straitjacket and contributory negligence has been applied to acts subsequent to a tort. In *The Calliope*,[4] a ship of that name sustained damage in a collision in the river Seine with another ship, attributable to the negligence of both. In view of the damage she had sustained it was decided to turn the 'Calliope' round and proceed up river to an anchorage to await the ebb-tide. The next day she was to be turned round again to proceed down river. Unfortunately, when the ship was being turned round for the second time she sustained further damage. Brandon J found that this would not have occurred but for the negligence of the 'Calliope' but he held that this negligence did not break the chain of causation between the other ship's negligence and the further damage; rather, some damages for that further damage should be given, albeit of a reduced amount for the contributory negligence of the 'Calliope'.[5] He said:

> 'Looking at the question from the point of principle, I cannot see any logical reason for denying to the court the right to apportion … liability in the circumstances contemplated. Where all relevant negligence on both sides precedes the original casualty the fact that A's negligence occurs later than B's negligence, and possibly also in a different place, does not prevent an apportionment of liability for such casualty. The view that it did so was enshrined in the so-called last-opportunity rule, which is, to this extent, dead and buried. I find it difficult to see why, as a matter of principle, it should make any difference that, in relation to a particular part of the damage arising or alleged to arise, from the casualty, the later negligence of B should follow rather than precede the casualty itself. Why should later negligence of B before the casualty be held not necessarily to break the chain of causation but later negligence of his after the casualty be held necessarily to do so?'[6]

This is an eminently sensible approach, and it is therefore surprising that contributory negligence was not even discussed, let alone applied, in the *McKew* case.[7]

4. THE *SAAMCO* PRINCIPLE

The House of Lords in *South Australia Asset Management Corpn v York Montague Ltd*[8] ('*SAAMCO*'), in the context of a claim for negligent valuation, laid down what was arguably a new principle restricting

---

4   [1970] p 172.
5   As the 'Calliope' had been contributorily negligent in relation to the original accident, there was a sub-apportionment.
6   [1970] P 172 at 181–182.
7   Millner 'Novus Actus Interveniens: The Present Effect of Wagon Mound' (1971) 22 NILQ 168, 178–179.
8   [1997] AC 191. See generally Stapleton 'Negligent Valuers and Falls in the Property Market' (1997) 113 LQR 1; Peel 'SAAMCO Revisited' and Butler 'SAAMCO in Practice' in *Commercial Remedies* (eds Burrows and Peel, 2003) pp 55–87.

damages, namely that loss is irrecoverable if outside the scope of the duty broken. This principle ('the *SAAMCO* principle') has subsequently been applied to various examples, in tort and contract, of negligent misrepresentation or negligent failure to provide information. To that extent it may be regarded as a general restriction on damages, which is therefore appropriately considered here (as a restriction separate from remoteness and intervening cause).[9]

The question at issue in the various cases being decided in *SAAMCO* was the extent to which, if at all, valuers who had negligently overvalued property provided as security for loans were liable in contract or tort for the losses suffered by lenders consequent on the collapse of the property market in the early 1990s. For example, let us assume that claimants had advanced £11 million on the security of a property valued by defendants at £15 million. The property's actual value at the time of valuation was £5 million and the claimants ultimately realised £2.5 million on resale. At first instance, Phillips J held that the claimants were entitled to be put into as good a position as if they had not entered into the loan transaction but that, on grounds of causation, they were not entitled to damages for the fall in the property market.[10] They were therefore entitled to the money lent (£11 million in the above example) minus the actual value of the property at the date of valuation (£5 million in the above example) plus interest from the date the money was lent. This was reversed by the Court of Appeal which held that, applying a 'no transaction' approach, the claimants were entitled to damages for the fall in the market.[11] They were therefore entitled to the money lent (£11 million in the above example) minus the value ultimately realised (£2.5 million in the above example) plus interest from the date the money was lent.

The House of Lords took a mid-position. Unfortunately Lord Hoffmann's speech, with which the other Law Lords agreed, is difficult to interpret. At one level, the reasoning can be expressed quite simply. A lender will be entitled to be put into as good a position as if it had not entered into the loan transaction but can never recover a greater measure than the difference between the represented value of the property and its actual value at the date of the valuation (plus interest). So in the above example the claimants would be entitled to the £8.5

---

9   For clarification that the *SAAMCO* scope of duty principle should follow the application of the basic compensatory aim – and be seen as a limitation on it – rather than preceding it, as Lord Hoffmann confusingly suggested ([1997] AC 191 at 210–211), see *McGregor on Damages* (17th edn, 2003) paras 1–022, 4–010.

10   [1995] 2 All ER 769.

11   [1995] QB 375, CA. Five other decisions, some contrary to Phillips J's, were also on appeal.

million (£11 million minus £2.5 million) plus interest because that falls within the outer limit of £10 million (£15 million minus £5 million) plus interest. But had the property been valued at £13 million rather than £15 million, the outer limit would have been £8 million (£13 million minus £5 million) so that only £8 million (plus interest) would have been recoverable.

The puzzle lies in determining whether and, if so, why that is the correct measure. Lord Hoffmann reasoned that this followed from carefully analysing at the outset the scope of the valuer's duty of care. The scope of that duty did not extend to protecting the lender against a loss that would have been a consequence of the transaction even if the representation had been true. Or, put another way, the scope of the duty extended only to the consequences of the information being wrong so that there was no liability for losses which would still have been incurred even if the information had been correct. In Lord Hoffmann's words in the *SAAMCO* case:

> '[A] person under a duty to take reasonable care to provide information on which someone else will decide upon a course of action is, if negligent, not generally regarded as responsible for all the consequences of that course of action. He is responsible only for the consequences of the information being wrong. A duty of care which imposes upon the informant responsibility for losses which would have occurred even if the information which he gave had been correct is not in my view fair and reasonable as between the parties. It is therefore inappropriate either as an implied term of contract or as a tortious duty arising from the relationship between them.'[12]

It is also of central importance that in *Nykredit plc v Edward Erdman Group Ltd (No 2)*[13] Lord Hoffmann clarified that the 'scope of the duty' concept was distinct from – and that the *SAAMCO* decision was not based on – remoteness or causation (or a cap on liability). In Lord Hoffmann's words, in the *Nykredit* case:

> 'It was not suggested that the possibility of a fall in the market was unforeseeable or that there was any other factor which negatived the causal connection between lending and losing the money. There was, for example, no evidence that if the lender had not made the advance in question, he would have lost his money in some other way. Nor, if one started from the proposition that the valuer was responsible for the consequences of the loan being made, could there be any logical basis for limiting the recoverable

---

12 [1997] AC 191 at 214.
13 [1997] 1 WLR 1627. This is also supported by the Court of Appeal's reasoning in the *SAAMCO* case that the fall in the property market was neither too remote nor a new intervening cause: [1995] 2 All ER 769 at 841, 842–855.

damages to the amount of the overvaluation. The essence of the decision was that this is not where one starts and that the valuer is responsible only for the consequences of the lender having too little security.'[14]

At first sight it might appear that, contrary to Lord Hoffmann's view, the same decision excluding liability for the fall in the market could have been reached applying remoteness and legal causation. As regards remoteness, we have seen that the courts have a wide degree of discretion in dividing up types of loss, perhaps especially so as regards economic loss.[15] The same conclusion as in the *SAAMCO* case could perhaps have been reached by deciding that the loss consequent on the fall in the property market was too remote because it was a different type of loss (and could not have been reasonably contemplated as a serious possibility at the time of contracting) from the 'ordinary lending loss' suffered because the property did not provide the security that the claimant had been led to expect. Alternatively, one might have reached the same decision as in *SAAMCO* by resurrecting the rejected 'acceptance of the risk as a term' remoteness test;[16] the valuers were not liable for the loss consequent on the fall in the property market because that was outside the risk that they had accepted under the contract to carry out the valuation.

Similarly, as regards legal causation, we have seen that the principles are flexible.[17] One could say that the fall in the property market was a natural event that broke the chain of causation between the valuers' negligence and the actual loss suffered by the claimant. The claimant was therefore merely entitled to recover for the direct loss consequent on the security being inadequate and not the indirect loss consequent on the fall in the property market.[18]

The difficulty with both these approaches – and ultimately supporting Lord Hoffmann's view that a different concept was in play – is that the approaches involve straining or rejecting the principles that have been developed for remoteness and legal causation. The 'acceptance of the

14   [1997] 1 WLR 1627 at 1638.
15   Above, pp 79, 90, 93.
16   See above, pp 95–96. For this analogy see also Wightman 'Negligent Valuations and a Drop in the Property Market: the Limits of the Expectation Loss Principle' (1998) 61 MLR 68, 75–76.
17   Above, pp 97–99.
18   At first instance, [1995] 2 All ER 769, 809, Phillips J reached a similar (but not identical) conclusion as the House of Lords using the language of causation: 'I do not see how the negligent adviser can fairly be said to have caused that loss unless his advice has been relied upon as providing protection against the risk of that loss.' In his extra-judicial lecture, given to the Chancery Bar Association on 15 June 1999 entitled 'Common Sense and Causing Loss' Lord Hoffmann conceded that one might say causation was relevant to the *SAAMCO* principle: but this was only in the trivial sense that, once outside the scope of the duty, the loss was not 'legally caused' by the breach.

risk in the contract' remoteness test was rejected in later cases; and to divide, for the purpose of the conventional remoteness test, the loss consequent on the fall in the property market from the other economic loss consequent on the negligent valuation would, at the very least, be highly controversial. Similarly, as regards legal causation, we have seen that normally natural events do not break the chain of causation. Indeed, it is ironic that, in the context of legal causation, the language of 'scope of duty' has been used to explain why what would otherwise have broken the chain of causation did not do so; that is, it has been used to extend normal liability. In contrast, the *SAAMCO* 'scope of duty' principle operates to limit liability.

The best conclusion is that Lord Hoffmann was correct to regard the *SAAMCO* principle as different from remoteness and legal causation. It appears to add another separate limitation on compensatory damages. But this conclusion only serves to highlight how controversial the *SAAMCO* principle is. Rather than being a standard application of remoteness or legal causation, it represents a novel development. So the question remains, how justified is the *SAAMCO* principle?

It is important to clarify that factual causation was not the basis of the decision. As was made clear in the *Nykredit* case,[19] there was no evidence that, had it not loaned money secured on the particular property in question, the lender would have loaned money secured on another property and would therefore have suffered the same 'property market loss' in any event. Similarly, as was made clear in the Court of Appeal in the *SAAMCO* case,[20] the finding of fact in relation to all the cases considered was that, had the valuers not overvalued the land, no loan would have been made (ie to use the old language frowned upon by the House of Lords, these were treated as 'no transaction' rather than 'successful-transaction' cases).

Much discussion has turned on Lord Hoffmann's celebrated mountaineer example. According to this, a mountaineer goes to the doctor about his knee and is negligently told that he is fit to go on an expedition. Had the doctor used reasonable care he would have informed the mountaineer that the knee was unfit and the mountaineer would not have gone on the expedition. He goes on the expedition and suffers an injury which is an entirely foreseeable consequence of mountaineering but has nothing to do with his knee. According to Lord Hoffmann, the doctor ought not to be liable and the justification for this is that the mountaineering injury is outside the scope of the doctor's

---

19 [1997] 1 WLR 1627 at 1638.
20 [1995] 2 All ER 769 at 841a.

duty. More specifically, if the representation had been true (so that his knee was fit to go on the expedition), the mountaineer would still have suffered the mountaineering injury.

However, it is important to note – and this weakens the force of the example – that the same conclusion would follow from a standard application of the principles of legal causation. Assuming that the accident was the consequence of a natural event (eg a rock-fall or avalanche) the chain of causation would be broken by that intervening cause. This is because the sole contribution that the doctor's breach of duty made to the claimant's loss was that the claimant was in the place where, at the time when, the natural event intervened: ie the injury was coincidental to the breach of duty.[1]

Moreover, one would still need to apply legal causation to reach desired results even if the injury were within the scope of the doctor's duty of care. Say, for example, having received the doctor's 'all-clear' on his knee, the mountaineer goes on the expedition. While there, his knee swells up requiring him to be carried down on a stretcher. While being carried down, he is hit by a rock-fall. Applying Lord Hoffmann's approach, it would seem that the rock-fall injury is within the scope of the doctor's duty of care because, had the representation as to the mountaineer's knee been true, his knee would not have swollen up and he would not have been hit by the rock-fall. Yet, applying standard principles, the rock-fall is essentially coincidental to the doctor's breach of duty and would break the chain of causation.

The point to emerge, therefore, is that Lord Hoffmann's mountaineering example does not justify or explain the need for his 'scope of duty' restriction. Standard principles of legal causation are sufficient and, in relation to variations of the example, are necessary in order to achieve the correct result.

A more fundamental criticism is that Lord Hoffmann's approach undermines the traditional link between the duty broken and the measure of damages, thereby upsetting the standard view that damages for negligent misrepresentation allow escape from a bad bargain. In comparing damages for breach of contract with damages for the tort of misrepresentation, it has been trite law that the former enables the claimant to reap the benefits of a good bargain (putting the claimant into as good a position as if the contract had been performed) while the latter enables the claimant to escape from a bad bargain (by putting the claimant into as good a position as if no representation had been made). In chapter 2, we gave the following simple example to illustrate that the

1   See above, pp 97–99. See also *Winfield & Jolowicz on Tort* (16th edn, 2002) para 6.24.

so-called tort measure of damages for misrepresentation may exceed the so-called contract measure of damages for breach of warranty.[2] A, in selling his car to B, makes a misrepresentation about the age of the car. The car is four years old but A tells B that it is one year old. B pays £5,000 for the car. The market value of a one-year-old car which otherwise has the same characteristics as the car A is selling is £4,500. The market value of the car, however, given that it is in fact four years old, is £4,000.

In this situation, B's damages for the tortious misrepresentation (including negligent misrepresentation) would be £1,000 (£5,000 – £4,000) whereas the damages for breach of warranty would be only £500 (£4,500 – £4,000). Yet it appears that this basic proposition, known to all law students, is inconsistent with Lord Hoffmann's approach. According to Lord Hoffmann one should put the claimant into as good a position as if no representation had been made only to the extent that this does not put the claimant into a better position than if the representation had been true. This is because the (normal) scope of the representor's duty is confined to protecting the claimant against the consequences of the information being wrong. It appears therefore that damages for the tort of negligent misrepresentation in the above example would be cut back from £1,000 to £500. The claimant could not escape from a bad bargain; or to use well-known academic terminology, the reliance interest would be limited by a lower expectation interest. That Lord Hoffmann was assimilating damages for negligent misrepresentation with damages for breach of contract in bad bargains meets his argument that 'it would seem paradoxical that the liability of a person who warranted the accuracy of the information should be less than that of a person who gave no such warranty but failed to take reasonable care.'[3]

Yet, in principle, this seems incorrect. Where one is suing for breach of contract, it is correct to measure damages according to the expectation interest. This is because the very duty broken was one to fulfil a promise that would have put the claimant in the promised position whether for good (under a good bargain) or bad (under a bad bargain). But misrepresentation (or breach of a contractual duty of care in giving information) rests on a duty not to induce the claimant to act in a particular way. Reflecting that duty, the aim of the damages should be to put the claimant into the position it would have been in if it had not been induced to act in that way (including not entering into a bad bargain).

2   See above, p 34.
3   [1997] AC 191 at 213–214.

The protection of the reliance interest is therefore the natural measure of recovery for misrepresentation and there is no principled reason why it should be limited by the expectation interest.

Jane Stapleton made a similar criticism in her excellent case-note on *SAAMCO*.[4] She wrote:

> '[Lord Hoffmann's] is not the correct approach to determining the scope of the duty of care. What makes the valuation wrongful is that it is careless, not that it is not true. The wrong is that the defendant did not use care: he valued the property at V when he should have valued it at V*. When dealing with liability for breach of an obligation of care the correct test is one based on the approach of the Court of Appeal: determining ... what were the consequences of the information being given carelessly and therefore asking where the plaintiff would have been had he received a careful valuation. ... In contrast, Lord Hoffmann sees the wrong as V not being accurate. He therefore focuses on the consequences of the information being wrong, and asks where the plaintiff would have been had the valuation which was given been accurate. ... Lord Hoffmann's approach in effect allows a defendant to take advantage of the fact that the plaintiff made a bad bargain, but in circumstances where it is inappropriate to allow the defendant to take such advantage.'

The flawed basis of the *SAAMCO* decision perhaps explains the difficulties the courts have subsequently encountered in applying it. Four such difficulties are adverted to below. Before examining these, it is worth clarifying the scope of the *SAAMCO* principle as applied in subsequent cases. The case itself, and the two House of Lords' decisions following on it,[5] concerned negligent valuations and losses consequent on falls in the property market. But subsequent cases have made clear that the scope of the *SAAMCO* principle is not so confined. Even putting to one side cases where the 'scope of duty' language has been used in traditional ways (eg to determine the type of loss for which a claim for breach of statutory duty could be brought),[6] the *SAAMCO* principle has been applied to a variety of negligent misrepresentations or negligent failures to give correct information. For example, the *SAAMCO* principle has been

---

4   'Negligent Valuers and Falls in the Property Market' (1997) 113 LQR 1, 3. For another excellent critical case-note, see Sullivan 'Negligent Professional Advice and Market Movements' [1997] CLJ 19. The SAAMCO case was distinguished, but without casting doubt on the decision, by the High Court of Australia in *Kenny v Good Pty Ltd v MGICA (1992) Ltd* (1999) 163 ALR 611. For a case-note pointing out the difficulties of interpreting the judgments in that case, see McLauchlan and Rickett '*SAAMCO* in the High Court of Australia' (2000) 116 LQR 1.

5   *Nykredit Mortgage Bank plc v Edward Erdman Group Ltd (No 2)* [1997] 1 WLR 1627; *Platform Home Loans Ltd v Oyston Shipways Ltd* [2000] 2 AC 190.

6   *Blue Circle Industries plc v MOD* [1999] Ch 289; for traditional use of this idea in this context, see, eg *Gorris v Scott* (1874) LR 9 Exch 125.

applied to information given by solicitors to lenders[7] or to purchasers;[8] to statements made by a vendor to a purchaser as regards the time within which the transaction could be finalised and the title registered;[9] to an architect's failure to warn of the consequences of his design;[10] and to statements made by a public or quasi-public body (the Intervention Board for Agricultural Produce) to a farmer as regards milk quotas.[11] One must also recall that Lord Hoffmann relied on his hypothetical example of a doctor making a negligent misrepresentation to his patient. It seems, therefore, that the *SAAMCO* principle has been treated as a principle of general application in contract or tort to negligent misrepresentation and negligent failure to provide information. In contrast, the tort of deceit was put to one side by Lord Hoffmann as raising different considerations where the *SAAMCO* limitation was inappropriate.[12]

A first difficulty encountered in applying the *SAAMCO* principle has been in ascertaining when the cause of action accrues (for the purposes of a tortious claim for negligent valuation) and from when interest should be paid. This was the issue for the House of Lords in *Nykredit Mortgage Bank plc v Edward Erdman Group Ltd (No 2)*.[13] Under the Supreme Court Act 1981, s 35A, a court can award simple interest on damages from the time when the cause of action arises. The standard approach to negligent valuation pre-*SAAMCO* was that the date of accrual of the cause of action in tort – and the date from when interest should be paid – was normally when the lender entered into the losing transaction.[14] While there may be variations on this,[15] the *SAAMCO* principle has made this basic position more complex because the relevant loss is now regarded not as that suffered by entering into the transaction as such but rather as that suffered because of the overvaluation. In *Nykredit* it was therefore decided that, while the cause of action in tort did accrue at the time of

---

7   *Bristol and West Building Society v Mothew* [1996] 4 All ER 698, CA; *Bristol and West Building Society v Fancy & Jackson* [1997] 4 All ER 582; *Portman Building Society v Bevan Ashford* [2000] 1 EGLR 81, CA; *Lloyds Bank Plc v Crosse & Crosse* [2001] PNLR 34, CA.

8   *Cottingham v Attey Bower & Jones* [2000] PNLR 557; *Peterson v Personal Representatives of Cyril Rivlin* [2002] EWCA Civ 194, [2002] Lloyd's Rep PN 386.

9   *Green v Turner* [1999] PNLR 28.

10 *HOK Sport Ltd v Aintree Racecourse Co Ltd* [2002] EWHC 3094 (TCC), [2003] Lloyd's Rep PN 148.

11 *Leidig v Intervention Board for Agricultural Produce* [2000] Lloyd's Rep PN 144, CA.

12 This has subsequently been confirmed, and the Court of Appeal's contrary approach in *Downs v Chappell* [1996] 3 All ER 344 at 361–362 disapproved, by the House of Lords in *Smith New Court Securities Ltd v Scrimgeour Vickers (Asset Management)* [1997] AC 254. The 'fiction of fraud' language used in the Misrepresentation Act 1967, s 2(1) may mean that the SAAMCO principle does not apply to s 2(1) damages as well as damages for deceit itself: *Avon Insurance plc v Swire Fraser Ltd* [2000] 1 All ER (Comm) 573.

13 [1997] 1 WLR 1627.

14 Eg *Forster v Outred & Co* [1982] 1 WLR 86; *Bell v Peter Browne & Co* [1990] 2 QB 495.

15 Eg *First National Commercial Bank v Humberts* [1995] 2 All ER 673.

the transaction,[16] interest was not payable until the claimant had suffered its full allowable loss (within what we may for shorthand purposes call the *SAAMCO* 'cap') which was not sustained until nine months later. Not only does *Nykredit* therefore require an unusual separation between the date of accrual of the cause of action in tort and the date from when interest is payable, it requires a difficult and time-consuming exercise plotting when it is that the *SAAMCO* 'cap' is reached.

A second difficulty is in the application of contributory negligence. In principle, one would have expected contributory negligence to be applied to the legally recoverable loss (ie the loss recoverable under *SAAMCO*) and not to a higher irrecoverable loss. If one considers the analogy of remoteness, contributory negligence is applied to reduce damages for non-remote loss. It is not applied to reduce damages for remote loss. So, for example, if contributory negligence were applicable in contract to a case like *Victoria Laundry (Windsor) Ltd v Newman Industries Ltd*[17] it would surely apply to reduce damages for the recoverable ordinary profits and would not first be applied to the irrecoverable exceptional profits. Yet in *Platform Home Loans Ltd v Oyston Shipways Ltd*[18] the majority of the House of Lords (Lord Cooke dissenting) held that a 20% reduction for contributory negligence applied to the claimant's overall loss attributable to negligent overvaluation and not to the claimant's legally recoverable loss under the *SAAMCO* principle. So where the claimant's overall loss (ie reliance loss) was £611,750 and the recoverable loss under *SAAMCO* (ie reliance loss limited by expectation) was £500,000, a 20% reduction for contributory negligence was applied to the first figure (giving damages of £489,400) and not to the second figure (which would have given damages of £400,000). This decision seems correct. But, applying the *SAAMCO* principle, this is only because, as Lord Millett explained, the contributory negligence (in not checking adequately the creditworthiness of the borrower and in having a general policy of lending 70% of the secured value) did not directly relate to the overvaluation as opposed to the overall loss. As Lord Millett said, 'Where the lender's negligence has caused or contributed directly to the overvaluation, then it may be appropriate to apply the reduction to the amount of the overvaluation as well as to the overall loss.'[19] It is not obvious that this qualification will be easy to apply in practice. Above all,

---

16   Surprisingly there was very little mention in *Nykredit* of the cause of action in contract which clearly accrued at the date of the valuer's breach irrespective of any damage caused. The decision that interest would be payable only from when the claimant sustained its full allowable loss would presumably apply equally to a claim for breach of contract.
17   [1949] 2 KB 528: see above, p 84.
18   [2000] 2 AC 190.
19   [2000] 2 AC 190 at 215.

the point to stress is that the *SAAMCO* principle has required the development of a novel approach to contributory negligence which requires a departure from the usual starting point of applying contributory negligence to legally recoverable loss only. Prior to *SAAMCO*, the same decision in *Platform Homes* would have been simply and straightforwardly reached without any departure from normal legal principle.

A third difficulty is that one can think of examples where, on the face of it, Lord Hoffmann's approach appears to produce clearly unacceptable results. Say, for example, a representation is made which the claimant relies on to forgo profits that would otherwise have been obtained. More specifically, let us assume that a claimant was given negligent legal information to the effect that developing a particular product (that would have been very profitable) would infringe a third party's intellectual property rights.[20] Relying on that information, the claimant did not develop the product and thereby lost profits. In this type of situation, to limit the claimant to the position he would have been in if the representation had been true would mean that the claimant could not recover for the lost profits (because had the representation been true the claimant would not have had the right to develop the product). That result is plainly unacceptable. The lost profits should be straightforwardly recoverable to protect the claimant's reliance interest. No doubt Lord Hoffmann would seek to arrive at the same result by distinguishing the *SAAMCO* case and by arguing that the loss of profit in this example was within the scope of the duty. But it is not obvious wherein the distinction lies.

A fourth difficulty is the distinction drawn by Lord Hoffmann between providing information and advice. His Lordship said:

> 'The principle thus stated distinguishes between a duty to *provide information* for the purpose of enabling someone else to decide upon a course of action and a duty to *advise* someone as to what course of action he should take. If the duty is to advise whether or not a course of action should be taken, the adviser must take reasonable care to consider all the potential consequences of that course of action. If he is negligent, he will therefore be responsible for all the foreseeable loss which is a consequence of that course of action having been taken. If his duty is only to supply information, he must take reasonable care to ensure that the information is correct and if he is negligent, he will be responsible for all the foreseeable consequences of the information being wrong.'[1]

---

20 This example was discussed in *Green v Turner* [1999] PNLR 28.
1 [1997] AC 191 at 214.

But it is hard to see the principled difference between these two situations and, as a matter of practice, one surely shades into the other. This is supported by *Aneco Reinsurance Underwriting Ltd v Johnson & Higgins Ltd*[2] in which all of their Lordships sought to explain the distinction being drawn by Lord Hoffmann in a way that was not dependent on the labels 'advice' or 'information.' For as Lord Millett said, '[the distinction] between a duty to provide information and a duty to give advice ... is a distinction without a difference, for the terms are interchangeable.'[3]

In the light of these difficulties in application –as well as the argument set out above that the basis of the *SAAMCO* principle is flawed – it is not surprising that the *SAAMCO* principle remains very controversial. This is borne out by the different views taken in the House of Lords, in their Lordships' latest application of the *SAAMCO* principle, in *Aneco Reinsurance Underwriting Ltd v Johnson & Higgins Ltd*.[4] Here the claimant insurance company sought reinsurance. This was arranged for them by the defendant brokers. Unfortunately the brokers failed properly to present the risk to the reinsurers who were able to avoid the reinsurance contract, and did so, for material non-disclosure. Under the insurance contract (the 'Bullen Treaty'), for which the insurers were seeking reinsurance, the claimant suffered a loss of $35 million. Had the reinsurance been valid, the claimant would have recovered about $11 million. That is, even if the reinsurance had been valid the claimant would still have lost $24 million. The claimant brought an action in contract and tort against the brokers on the basis that the brokers had negligently informed them that reinsurance for the Bullen Treaty was available in the market whereas, in fact, it was never available. Had the claimant known the truth it would never have entered into the Bullen Treaty insurance. It therefore sought damages for its full loss of $35 million. This claim succeeded (Lord Millett dissenting).

The majority of the House of Lords considered that *SAAMCO* was distinguishable. Here the scope of the duty of care was not confined to obtaining reinsurance and informing the claimant that reinsurance had been obtained. Rather it was a wider duty and extended to advising the claimant generally on what course of action to take (including whether to enter into the Bullen Treaty). In the words of Lord Steyn, the facts here fell on the other 'side of the line drawn in *SAAMCO*.'[5] In the light of that

---

2   [2001] UKHL 51, [2001] 2 All ER (Comm) 929.
3   [2001] UKHL 51 at para 62.
4   For an excellent discussion of this case see Peel '*SAAMCO* Revisited' and Butler '*SAAMCO* in Practice' in *Commercial Remedies* (ed Burrows and Peel, 2003) pp 55, 60–63, 71, 81–86.
5   At para 43.

wider duty, the wider measure of damages – putting the claimant into as good a position as if it had not entered into the transaction – was appropriate.

It is noteworthy that Lord Steyn presented the issue as one of disputed fact not law. He thereby avoided re-examining the correctness of the *SAAMCO* principle. While essentially adopting the same approach, Lord Lloyd suggested that *SAAMCO* was laying down a narrow principle for a special class of case (typically, but not exclusively, concerning valuers). That special class of case is where the scope of the duty is confined to the giving of specific information. Lords Slynn and Browne-Wilkinson agreed with Lords Lloyd and Steyn.

Lord Millett gave a powerful dissenting speech. In his view, this case was indistinguishable from *SAAMCO*. The defendants were not under a duty to advise in relation to the claimant's decision to enter into the Bullen Treaty. The defendants were brokers, not underwriters, and their only duty was to take reasonable care to ensure that the information which they did supply was correct. This was directly covered by *SAAMCO* so that the defendants were responsible only for the consequences of that information being wrong. Had the information been correct, the claimant would have had reinsurance of $11 million but would still have lost $25M. The correct measure of damages, in Lord Millett's opinion, was therefore $11 million not $35 million.

It is submitted that, applying *SAAMCO*, Lord Millett's speech is correct. The brokers could not be classed as general advisers. They were concerned with a specific task and had made a specific representation. On the other hand, the decision of the majority is to be welcomed in confining – albeit artificially – the application of *SAAMCO*. In most cases, there is no clear difference between a duty to give general advice and a duty to give specific information. This is shown by the fact that all general advice may be regarded as comprising a number of specific pieces of information. Albeit contrary to the *SAAMCO* principle, the important issue *should* be whether the claimant relied on the representation in entering into the whole transaction; if he did, damages for having entered the whole transaction should be recoverable. It is in contradicting that, that the *SAAMCO* principle is flawed. In this respect, it is again noteworthy that, prior to *SAAMCO*, the decision in *Aneco* would have been straightforward.[6]

It seems inevitable that the *SAAMCO* principle will continue to generate litigation as the courts struggle to break free from it. The

---

6   As was exemplified by the concession of counsel for the brokers in the similar case of *Youell v Bland Welch & Co Ltd (No 2)* [1990] 2 Lloyd's Rep 431.

cleanest solution would be for the decision in *SAAMCO* to be overruled or, at least, for Lord Hoffmann's reasoning to be rejected. If the courts wish to treat falls in the property market as irrecoverable against negligent valuers (contrary to standard principles of remoteness and legal causation) they should do so openly as a matter of specific policy. Needless confusion has been caused, and will continue to be caused, by Lord Hoffmann's attempt to deduce that specific policy from general principle.

5.   THE DUTY TO MITIGATE

The duty to mitigate is a further restriction on compensatory damages.[7] On the one hand a claimant should not sit back and do nothing to minimise loss flowing from a wrong but should rather use its resources to do what is reasonable to put itself into as good a position as if the contract had been performed or the tort not committed. On the other hand, it should not unreasonably incur expense subsequent to the wrong. The policy is one of encouraging the claimant, once a wrong has occurred, to be to a reasonable extent self-reliant or, in economists' terminology, to be efficient, rather than pinning all loss on the defendant.[8]

The term 'duty to mitigate' should not be thought to indicate that the claimant can itself be sued for failure to comply with its duty: rather the consequence of such a failure is simply that no damages are given for the avoidable loss.[9] The duty is best regarded as comprising two principles, the first focusing on unreasonable inaction, the second on unreasonable action.

(1) The first principle – unreasonable inaction

A claimant must take all reasonable steps to minimise its loss so that it cannot recover for any loss which it could reasonably have avoided but has failed to avoid. The classic judicial formulation of this is Viscount Haldane LC's in *British Westinghouse Electric v Underground Electric Rlys Co of*

---

7   The duty to mitigate is also sometimes used as a positive reason for awarding damages, ie one can recover reasonable expenses incurred in seeking to minimise loss. But it is simpler to view this proposition as a natural consequence of there being no relevant restriction limiting the compensatory principle.

8   Bridge 'Mitigation of Damages in Contract and the Meaning of Avoidable Loss' (1989) 105 LQR 398 argues that several policies are at play in explaining the duty to mitigate.

9   Theoretically, contributory negligence should apply as a mid-position to *reduce* damages but no case has been found allowing contributory negligence as a mid-position alternative to the duty to mitigate: cf above, pp 108–109.

London Ltd[10] (a contract case), who said that the principle '... imposes on a plaintiff the duty of taking all reasonable steps to mitigate the loss consequent on the breach and debars him from claiming any part of the damage which is due to his neglect to take such steps.'

Clearly whether steps should reasonably have been taken to minimise loss depends on the particular facts in question. However, some indication can be given of the sort of factors that have been considered important in past cases in deciding this.

(i)   Where the claimant has been wrongfully dismissed he need not accept an offer of re-employment from his former employer *if* factors like the following are present: the new work would involve a reduction in status; employment elsewhere would be more likely to be permanent; the claimant has no confidence in his employers because of their past treatment of him. Such factors were present in *Yetton v Eastwoods Froy Ltd*,[11] and it was therefore held that the claimant had not failed in his duty to mitigate by refusing his former employer's offer of re-employment. The opposite decision was reached in *Brace v Calder*,[12] where such factors were not present.

(ii)   In relation to a contract of sale, if the defendant makes an offer of alternative performance, it will generally be unreasonable for the claimant to turn it down if acceptance would reduce its loss. So in *Payzu Ltd v Saunders*[13] the defendants, who had contracted to deliver goods to the claimants in instalments, refused to deliver the second and subsequent instalments unless the claimants would pay cash on delivery. The claimants refused this offer and sued the defendants for breach, claiming damages based on the difference between the market and contract prices, the market having risen. It was held that although the defendants were in breach, the claimants had failed in their duty to mitigate, and they recovered merely £50 damages for the period of credit they would have lost by paying the cash on delivery rather than when stipulated in the contract. Contrasting with this is *Strutt v Whitnell*,[14] where the defendants offered to repurchase from the claimant a house, which they could not transfer to him with vacant possession. The claimant's refusal of the offer was held not to amount to a failure to mitigate; the offer

---

10 [1912] AC 673 at 689.
11 [1967] 1 WLR 104.
12 [1895] 2 QB 253.
13 [1919] 2 KB 581. See also *Sotiros Shipping Inc v Sameiet Solholt, The Solholt* [1983] 1 Lloyd's Rep 605. These decisions are criticised by Bridge 'Mitigation of Damages in Contract and the Meaning of Avoidable Loss' (1989) 105 LQR 398.
14 [1975] 1 WLR 870.

was not of an alternative performance but of no performance at all and was in effect merely equivalent to an offer by the defendants to pay the claimant damages.

(iii)   The claimant's conduct is unreasonable if he refuses an operation contrary to firm medical advice. In *McAuley v London Transport Executive*[15] the claimant, having been injured by the defendants, refused to have an operation strongly recommended by a doctor which, if successful, would have restored him to his previous earning capacity. It was held that his refusal was unreasonable, and the claimant was therefore able to recover his loss of earnings only until the time when he would have recovered had he undergone the operation. On the other hand in *Selvanayagam v University of West Indies*[16] the Privy Council upheld the trial judge's decision that the claimant had not been unreasonable in refusing to undergo a neck operation. A doctor had recommended the operation but, given the claimant's diabetic condition, the recommendation had not been a strong one. Similarly in *Geest plc v Lansiquot*[17] it was held that the claimant had not been unreasonable in not going ahead with an operation on her back where the doctor had made plain that surgery could not guarantee a cure and where he was clearly ready to respect her decision if she decided against the operation.

(iv)   It will generally be unreasonable for the claimant to refuse offers of help which would have prevented further property damage. In *Anderson v Hoen, The Flying Fish*[18] the claimant's ship was damaged by the negligence of those in charge of the defendant's vessel. After the collision, the claimant's captain refused aid and in consequence the ship was destroyed. The claimant was able to recover for the damage caused by the collision but not for the additional loss when the ship was destroyed.

(v)   The claimant need not take action which will put its commercial reputation or good public relations at risk. In *James Finlay & Co Ltd v Kwik Hoo Tong*[19] the seller under a cif contract tendered to the buyer a bill of lading which incorrectly stated the date of shipment. The buyer was unaware of this and entered into sub-contracts but the sub-purchasers, realising the error on the bill of lading, refused in breach of contract to take delivery. The buyer sued the seller for

15   [1957] 2 Lloyd's Rep 500.
16   [1983] 1 All ER 824. Note that in putting the burden of proof in relation to the duty to mitigate on the claimant this decision was disapproved by the Privy Council in *Geest plc v Lansiquot* [2002] UKPC 48, [2002] 1 WLR 3111: see above, p 76.
17   [2002] UKPC 48, [2002] 1 WLR 3111.
18   (1865) 3 Moo PCCNS 77.
19   [1929] 1 KB 400.

breach of contract and recovered substantial damages, the Court of Appeal holding that the buyer was not bound to reduce its loss by suing the sub-purchasers because to do so, when knowing of the error on the bill of lading, might seriously injure its commercial reputation. Similarly in *London and South of England Building Society v Stone*[20] borrowers from the claimant building society had covenanted to keep the house being purchased in good repair. In fact the house suffered from serious subsidence and was valueless and the claimant undertook repairs at a cost to itself of £29,000. The claimant had made the loan on the strength of the defendant valuer's report which had negligently failed to disclose the subsidence. In an action brought in contract and tort against the defendant valuer the claimant recovered as damages the sum lent (£11,880). The Court of Appeal rejected the defendant's argument that there should be a deduction of £3,000, as the amount the claimant could have recovered from the borrowers by enforcing the repair covenant because, to maintain its good public relations, it was reasonable for the claimant not to call upon the borrowers to pay for any part of the repairs.

(vi) The claimant need not take steps which would involve him in complicated litigation. In *Pilkington v Wood*[1] the claimant bought a house but when he came to sell it he discovered that his vendor had given him a defective title. The claimant sued the defendant, his solicitor, for contractual negligence and recovered damages based on the difference in value between the property with and without good title. The defendant's argument that the claimant should have mitigated by suing his vendor was rejected by Harman J because, '... the so-called duty to mitigate does not go so far as to oblige the injured party ... to embark on a complicated and difficult piece of litigation against a third party.'[2] But as a rare exception to this, the Court of Appeal in *Walker v Medlicott*[3] held that the claimant, who was suing a solicitor for negligent will-drafting, had failed in his duty to mitigate his loss by not first seeking rectification of the will. This rare exception appears to stem from the courts' belief that a negligence action against a solicitor is a less satisfactory solution to the problem of an incorrectly drawn-up will than is rectification of

20 [1983] 1 WLR 1242.
1   [1953] Ch 770.
2   [1953] Ch 770 at 777. *Pilkington v Wood* was distinguished in *Western Trust & Savings Ltd v Clive Travers & Co* [1997] PNLR 295, CA (lenders had failed in their duty to mitigate by failing to enforce their security by a straightforward possession action).
3   [1999] 1 All ER 685. This was distinguished in *Horsfall v Haywards* [1999] 1 FLR 1182, CA, which was another negligent will-drafting case.

the will. The duty to mitigate is therefore being used as a means of ensuring that a claim for negligent will-drafting is used as a last resort.

(vii) The claimant need not take steps which it cannot financially afford, ie impecuniosity is an excuse for failure to mitigate. This is examined in a later section.[4]

(2) The second principle – unreasonable action

Unreasonable action subsequent to a wrong is normally regarded as an aspect of intervening cause. But the unreasonable incurring of expense subsequent to the wrong is generally viewed as an aspect of the duty to mitigate.[5]

The principle is that a claimant should not unreasonably incur expense subsequent to the wrong.[6] As with the first principle, what is unreasonable depends on the facts, but a number of illustrations can be given in most of which the expense was held to be reasonably incurred.

So, for example, in *Holden Ltd v Bostock & Co Ltd*,[7] the defendants had sold sugar to the claimants for brewing beer. Unfortunately the sugar had contained arsenic. To prevent any loss of business the claimants advertised that they had changed their brewing methods. In an action against the defendants for breach of contract, the claimants were awarded, inter alia, the advertising costs. Again in *Bacon v Cooper (Metals) Ltd*[8] the high hire-purchase interest charges paid for a rotor to replace that damaged beyond repair because of the defendants' breach of contract were held to be reasonably incurred and recoverable. No doubt the most common example of recoverable reasonable expenses are the medical, hospital and nursing expenses undertaken following personal injury.[9]

---

4   Below, pp 144–145.
5   Above, p 75.
6   Although there appears to be no case in point, the principle of *Cory v Thames Ironworks Co* (1868) LR 3 QB 181, above, p 96, may apply by analogy: ie even though the actual expenses were unreasonably incurred a lesser amount, equivalent to what would have been reasonable expenses, may be recoverable.
7   (1902) 18 TLR 317.
8   [1982] 1 All ER 397. See also *Mattocks v Mann* [1993] RTR 13, CA, and *Burdis v Livsey* [2002] EWCA Civ 510, [2003] QB 36, where the cost of hiring a replacement car, while the claimant's car was being repaired, was considered reasonable and recoverable even though those repairs, through no fault of the claimant, had taken longer than they should have done (and the hire charges were therefore higher than they should have been).
9   Below, p 276.

A particularly colourful illustration is provided by *Banco de Portugal v Waterlow & Sons Ltd.*[10] Here the defendants contracted to print banknotes for the claimant bank. In breach of contract they delivered a large number of these to a criminal, who put them into circulation in Portugal. On discovering this, the bank withdrew the issue. It then undertook to exchange all the notes illegally circulated for others. In an action brought against them for breach of contract the defendants argued that they were only liable for the cost of printing new notes, which amounted to £8,922, and that the further heavy loss was due to the bank's own act in giving value for the notes. But the House of Lords, by a majority, rejected this argument and held the defendants liable for the further loss because the conduct of the bank was reasonable, having regard to its commercial obligations towards the public. Lord MacMillan emphasised that no great weight should be attached to the defendant's argument that cheaper measures could have been taken:

'[T]he measures which [the claimant] may be driven to adopt in order to extricate himself ought not to be weighed in nice scales at the instance of the party whose breach of contract has occasioned the difficulty. It is often easy after an emergency has passed to criticise the steps which have been taken to meet it, but such criticism does not come well from those who have themselves created the emergency … [The plaintiff] will not be held disentitled to recover the cost of such measures merely because the party in breach can suggest that other measures less burdensome to him might have been taken.'[11]

On the other hand, in *Compania Financiera Soleada SA v Harmoor Tanker Corpn Inc, The Borag*,[12] the claimants in seeking to gain the release of a ship detained in breach of contract took out a loan requiring very high interest charges. It was held by the Court of Appeal that such high interest charges should not be compensated since the claimants had not acted reasonably in incurring them.

It should also be stressed that the fact that the incurring of expense has overall augmented the loss, rather than minimised it, ie it has not been a success, does not mean that it was unreasonably incurred and is irrecoverable. A statement to this effect in the twelfth edition of *Mayne and McGregor on Damages* was cited with approval in *Lloyds and Scottish*

---

10 [1932] AC 452. For an argument that the bank, by issuing and transferring new notes, suffered no loss other than the printing costs, see Oditah 'Takeovers, Share Exchanges and the Meaning of Loss' (1996) 112 LQR 424, 437–441. See also below, p 602, n 20.
11 [1932] AC 452 at 506. This passage was approved in *Bacon v Cooper* [1982] 1 All ER 397 at 399; *London and South of England Building Society v Stone* [1983] 3 All ER 105 at 121; *LE Jones (Insurance Brokers) Ltd v Portsmouth City Council* [2002] EWCA Civ 1723, [2003] 1 WLR 427, para 26.
12 [1981] 1 WLR 274.

Finance Ltd v Modern Cars and Caravans (Kingston) Ltd.[13] *Esso Petroleum Co Ltd v Mardon*[14] may be said to illustrate it. Here the claimant had been induced to enter into a tenancy agreement for a petrol station by the defendant's false estimates of the potential throughput of petrol. In an action for negligent misrepresentation, or breach of a warranty that the estimate was made using reasonable care, the claimant was held able to recover all the loss he had suffered, until he gave up possession. This included the loss after he had entered into a fresh tenancy agreement. In the Court of Appeal's opinion, in view of the loss already suffered, the claimant was acting reasonably in attempting to mitigate some of that loss by entering into that new agreement: the fact that he actually suffered further loss as a result did not prevent recovery.

(3) When does the duty to mitigate arise in relation to the anticipatory repudiation of a contract?

Indisputably there is a duty to mitigate once there has been an actual breach of contract. This is reflected, for example, in the general rule that one assesses the market value of property at the date of the breach of contract. But the traditional approach is that, following an anticipatory repudiation, there is no duty to mitigate,[15] unless the claimant chooses to accept the anticipatory repudiation.[16] It is submitted that the better view is that economic efficiency should override the wishes of the innocent party to hold the contract alive and that, as in the US,[17] the duty to mitigate should arise once there has been an anticipatory repudiation. Such a reform is supported by departures from *White & Carter (Councils) Ltd v McGregor*[18] regarding the analogous question of the extent to which a claimant is entitled to outflank the duty to mitigate by an action for the agreed price.

---

13   [1966] 1 QB 764.
14   [1976] QB 801. See also *Hoffberger v Ascot International Bloodstock Bureau Ltd* (1976) 120 Sol Jo 130. *Banco de Portugal v Waterlow & Sons Ltd* [1932] AC 452 may be a further example, depending on what was regarded as the value of the bank's commercial obligations to the public. Somewhat similar is *Gebrüder Metalmann GmbH & Co KG v NBR (London) Ltd* [1984] 1 Lloyd's Rep 614.
15   *Tredegar Iron & Coal Co v Hawthorn Bros & Co* (1902) 18 TLR 716; *Shindler v Northern Raincoat Co Ltd* [1960] 1 WLR 1038.
16   As in *Melachrino v Nickoll & Knight* [1920] 1 KB 693. See also *Gebrüder Metalmann GmbH & Co KG v NBR (London) Ltd* [1984] 1 Lloyd's Rep 614; *Kaines (UK) Ltd v Osterreichische Warrenhandelsgesellschaft Austrowaren Gesellschaft mbH* [1993] 2 Lloyd's Rep 1, CA.
17   Uniform Commercial Code, ss 2–610a, 2–723(1). But see Goetz & Scott 'The Mitigation Principle: Towards a General Theory of Contractual Obligation' (1983) 69 Vir LR 967, 993–995.
18   [1962] AC 413. See below, pp 435–440.

6.   CONTRIBUTORY NEGLIGENCE

At common law, although it was unclear whether it applied as such to breach of contract, contributory negligence was a complete defence to many torts. In other words, where applicable, it nullified the causal potency of the defendant's breach of duty.[19] However, the Law Reform (Contributory Negligence) Act 1945 made contributory negligence a partial defence, by which damages are reduced but not completely denied. Section 1(1) of that Act provides:

> 'Where any person suffers damage as a result partly of his own fault and partly of the fault of any other person or persons, a claim in respect of that damage shall not be defeated by reason of the fault of the person suffering the damage, but the damages recoverable in respect thereof shall be reduced to such extent as the court thinks just and equitable having regard to the claimant's share in the responsibility for the damage.'

As far as breach of contract is concerned, the crucial question is whether the Act, and hence the defence of contributory negligence, applies at all. This will be examined after looking at the operation of the defence for torts, where generally it is clear that the Act applies.

(1) Torts

(a) **What must the defendant establish?**

In order for the defence to apply the defendant must establish three points. First, the claimant must have been at fault or negligent towards himself. To illustrate this by reference to cases of personal injury or death, the claimant is most obviously negligent towards himself if he negligently causes an accident (involving himself) or puts himself in an inherently dangerous position or renders an inherently non-dangerous position dangerous by failing to take safety precautions. The first situation is illustrated by the commonest of contributory negligence examples, where two motorists negligently collide. Examples of the second situation are riding on the towbar at the back of a 'traxcavator', as in *Jones v Livox Quarries Ltd*,[20] accepting a lift with someone who you know to have been drinking heavily, as in *Owens v Brimmell*,[1] or accepting

---

19 Where subsequent to the breach of duty contributory negligence was therefore indistinguishable from saying that the intervening conduct of the claimant broke the chain of causation or, where a negligent failure to act followed a tort, from saying that the claimant failed in his duty to mitigate.
20 [1952] 2 QB 608.
1   [1977] QB 859.

a lift in a car knowing that the brakes are defective, as in *Gregory v Kelly*.[2] The classic examples of the third situation are failing to wear a seat-belt while travelling in the front seat of a car, as in *Froom v Butcher*,[3] or failing to wear a crash helmet while riding a motor-bike, as in *O'Connell v Jackson*.[4] It should be added that the courts are reluctant to find that a child has been negligent towards himself – and the younger the child the greater the reluctance.[5]

Secondly, the claimant's negligence must have been a factual cause of his loss. The usual 'but for' test is used to decide this. So, for example, where two motorists negligently collide, as each person's negligent driving is a factual cause of the collision, so necessarily it is a factual cause of the loss suffered by each. A case like *Froom v Butcher* stressed that while not wearing a seat-belt could of course not be said to be a factual cause of the collision, it was a factual cause of the loss, and this was what was important. On the other hand in *Owens v Brimmell*[6] the claimant's negligence in not wearing his seat-belt was not established to be a factual cause of his injuries – they were no worse than if he had been wearing one.

Thirdly, the claimant's negligence must have exposed him to the particular risk of the type of damage suffered. In the standard negligent driving case there is no difficulty in establishing this since in driving negligently or in not wearing his seat-belt the claimant is clearly exposing himself to a particular risk of suffering personal injury in a crash. This principle, which can be regarded as analogous to remoteness, was discussed in some detail in *Jones v Livox Quarries Ltd*. There the claimant was riding on the towbar at the back of a quarry vehicle. Another vehicle belonging to the defendants was negligently driven into him and the claimant was injured. By so riding, the claimant exposed himself not only to the particular risk of falling off the vehicle but also to the particular risk of being crushed – as had happened. The claimant was therefore found to be contributorily negligent, although Denning LJ said that this would not have been the case if, whilst riding on the towbar, the claimant had, for example, been hit in the eye by a shot from a negligent sportsman – he was not exposing himself to a particular risk of suffering that type of damage by riding on the towbar.

---

2   [1978] RTR 426.
3   [1976] QB 286.
4   [1972] 1 QB 270.
5   Eg *Yachuk v Oliver Blais Co Ltd* [1949] AC 386; *Gough v Thorne* [1966] 1 WLR 1387.
6   See also *UCB Corporate Services Ltd v Clyde* [2000] 2 All ER (Comm) 257 (claimant bank's own negligence not causative of its loss).

(b) How do the courts decide the extent to which the damages should be reduced?

The Law Reform (Contributory Negligence) Act 1945 (LR(CN)A 1945), s 1(1) says that where contributory negligence applies, the damages '... shall be reduced to such extent as the court thinks just and equitable having regard to the claimant's share in the responsibility for the damage.' How exactly the courts apply these words is difficult to clarify; but what can be said, as stressed by Denning LJ in *Davies v Swan Motor Co (Swansea) Ltd,*[7] is that the courts consider both the causal potency and the comparative blameworthiness of the parties' conduct.[8]

Where the defendant is held strictly liable, it might be thought difficult to apply comparative blameworthiness, since the defendant is not blameworthy at all. But Ogus[9] thinks that one can still talk in terms of comparative blameworthiness by asking how far short of the standard imposed by law did the conduct of each party fall.

In *Froom v Butcher*[10] Lord Denning, recognising the difficulty of deciding to what extent to reduce damages and in a desire to avoid prolonging cases, suggested standard figures for reducing damages where the claimant has been contributorily negligent by not wearing a seat-belt. If the damage would have been prevented altogether a reduction of 25% should be made and if it would have been considerably less severe a reduction of 15% should be made. To have standard figures for very common instances of contributory negligence sensibly produces certainty and uniformity but it can only be adopted where, as with seat-belts, the blameworthiness of the contributory negligence varies hardly at all from case to case.

In *Capps v Miller*[11] the claimant moped-driver was severely brain-damaged when a car negligently ran into him. The claimant was wearing a crash helmet but, contrary to the Motor Cycles (Protective Helmet) Regulations 1980, the chin strap was unfastened and the helmet came off before the claimant's head struck the ground. Damages were reduced by 10% for contributory negligence in not fastening the strap. In arriving at that figure Lord Denning's guidelines were relied on but it was felt (Croom-Johnson LJ dubitante) that the true analogy to not fastening a seat-belt was not wearing a helmet at all. Wearing a helmet but not

---

7   [1949] 2 KB 291 at 326. See also, eg *Eagle v Chambers* [2003] EWCA Civ 1107, [2004] RTR 115.
8   For a suggested principled approach in applying these criteria, see Gravells 'Three Heads of Contributory Negligence' (1977) 93 LQR 581.
9   *Damages* p 105.
10   [1976] QB 286.
11   [1989] 1 WLR 839.

fastening the chin-strap was less blameworthy than not fastening a seat-belt (or not wearing a helmet at all) so that 10% rather than 15% was the appropriate reduction.

In deciding on the appropriate reduction contributory negligence must be kept distinct from the issue of contribution between tortfeasors. In *Fitzgerald v Lane*[12] the claimant was hit by two cars one after the other on a pelican crossing. The claimant and each of the drivers was found to have been equally to blame for the claimant's injuries. It was held by the House of Lords that the appropriate reduction for contributory negligence should have been 50% and not 33½%. In Lord Ackner's words:

> '... the determination of the extent of each of the defendants' responsibility for the damage is not made in the main action but in the contribution proceedings between the defendants, inter se, and this does not concern the plaintiff.'[13]

What has to be contrasted is the claimant's conduct on the one hand with the totality of the tortious conduct of the defendants on the other.[14]

Finally, although there has been little discussion of this, it is clear that, in general, contributory negligence is applied once it has been determined what loss is (otherwise) legally recoverable. For example, one would not apply contributory negligence to loss that is legally irrecoverable because too remote. This has been discussed above in the context of the *SAAMCO* principle and the decision of the House of Lords in *Platform Home Loans Ltd v Oyston Shipways Ltd*.[15]

(c) Contributory negligence subsequent to the tort

As has been discussed above,[16] in *The Calliope*[17] Brandon J applied contributory negligence in respect of the claimant's conduct subsequent to the tort. In terms of policy this is a sensible approach and there seems to be nothing in LR(CN)A 1945 to restrict the defence to contributory negligence prior to or contemporaneously with the tort.

---

12 [1989] AC 328.
13 [1989] AC 328 at 345.
14 See also the Australian case of *Barisic v Devenport* [1978] 2 NSWLR 111. For criticism of *Fitzgerald v Lane* as being too pro-defendant see, eg Chandler and Holland 'Apportionment of Loss: Collisions and Contributions' [1989] LMCLQ 30. See generally, Burrows 'Should One Reform Joint and Several Liability?' in *Torts Tomorrow* (eds Mullany and Linden, 1998) pp 102, 115–117.
15 [2000] 2 AC 190. See above, pp 118–119.
16 Above, p 109.
17 [1970] P 172.

(d) Is contributory negligence applicable to all torts?[18]

The crucial words are those in LR(CN)A 1945, s 4 which define fault in LR(CN)A 1945, s 1(1) as meaning '... negligence, breach of statutory duty or other act or omission which gives rise to a liability in tort, or would, apart from this Act, give rise to the defence of contributory negligence'.

For reasons discussed under 'breach of contract',[19] it is best to read this as comprising two limbs, the first – '... negligence, breach of statutory duty or other act or omission which gives rise to a liability in tort' – referring to the defendant's fault and the second – any act or omission which '... would apart from this Act, give rise to the defence of contributory negligence' – referring to the claimant's fault. In the context of torts, this two-limbed interpretation of LR(CN)A 1945, s 4 has now been authoritatively accepted by the House of Lords in *Standard Chartered Bank v Pakistan National Shipping Corpn (No 2)*.[20]

In this context, the first limb creates no difficulties; the defendant is at fault, whenever he is liable for a tort and it makes no difference which tort. So whether contributory negligence is inapplicable to some torts turns solely on the second limb of LR(CN)A 1945, s 4. One interpretation of the second limb is that it all depends whether, in relation to the tort for which the claimant is now suing, his (the claimant's conduct) would have given rise to the total defence of contributory negligence at common law. Since contributory negligence was probably not a defence at common law to intentional torts, like deceit and intentional trespass to the person, this view means that contributory negligence continues not to apply to such torts. That was the approach adopted by the House of Lords in *Standard Chartered Bank v Pakistan National Shipping Corp (No 2)* in deciding that contributory negligence is not a defence to the tort of deceit.[1] Lord Hoffmann, giving the leading speech, pointed to past cases where the fault of the claimant had been no answer to a claim to rescind a contract or damages for fraudulent misrepresentation.[2] Moreover, he thought that such a rule was based

---

18 See Glanville Williams *Joint Torts and Contributory Negligence* (1951) pp 318–319, 326–328; Hudson 'Contributory Negligence as a Defence to Battery' (1984) 4 LS 332.
19 Below, p 137.
20 [2002] UKHL 43, [2003] 1 AC 959 at para 11. See also *Reeves v Metropolitan Police Comr* [2000] 1 AC 360.
1 The House of Lords approved the decision to the same effect of Mummery J in *Alliance & Leicester Building Society v Edgestop Ltd* [1993] 1 WLR 1462. See also *Corporacion Nacional del Cobre de Chile v Sogemin Metals Ltd* [1997] 1 WLR 1396 in which contributory negligence was held inapplicable where the defendants had bribed the claimant's employee and the claims extended beyond deceit to include conspiracy, inducing breach of contract and the equitable wrong of assisting a breach of fiduciary duty.
2 Eg *Redgrave v Hurd* (1881) 20 Ch D 1; *Edgington v Fitzmaurice* (1885) 29 Ch D 459.

upon sound policy. 'It would not seem just that a fraudulent defendant's liability should be reduced on the grounds that, for whatever reason, the victim should not have made the payment which the defendant successfully induced him to make.'[3]

In terms of policy, this denial of contributory negligence is a response to the dishonesty of the defendant. A dishonest defendant ought not to have its liability cut back by reason of the claimant's own fault. In this respect, the approach is consistent with the application of a wider-than-usual remoteness test for the tort of deceit.[4]

On this policy basis, it would appear that the same denial of contributory negligence ought to apply to other intentional torts (eg intentional trespass to the person). Although Lord Denning MR in *Murphy v Culhane*[5] indicated that a widow's claim for damages for the death of her husband might fall to be reduced under LR(CN)A 1945, because it had resulted from a criminal affray in which he had participated, it would seem that that suggestion must be regarded as incorrect after the *Standard Chartered Bank* case.[6]

What it is important to avoid, however, is the wider view that contributory negligence is inapplicable to negligent misrepresentation. *Standard Chartered Bank* concerned only fraudulent misrepresentation. The non-availability of contributory negligence must be distinguished from the separate rule, originating in *Redgrave v Hurd*[7] and applicable to all misrepresentations, whether fraudulent or not, that one should not attach blame to a claimant who has relied on a misrepresentation without taking an opportunity to check the truth of the representation. This is a rule that that conduct of the claimant, in the context of misrepresentation, should be treated as non-blameworthy. As Lord Hoffmann made clear, this is not to deny that other negligent conduct of the claimant may reduce damages for negligent misrepresentation on the ground of contributory negligence. This is supported by *Gran Gelato Ltd v Richcliff (Group) Ltd*[8] in which Sir Donald Nicholls V-C held that contributory negligence can apply to the statutory tort of negligent misrepresentation in the Misrepresentation Act 1967,

---

3   [2003] 1 AC 959 at para 16.
4   See above, pp 81–82.
5   [1977] QB 94.
6   In the *Standard Chartered Bank* case, at para 45, Lord Rodger expressly left open whether Lord Denning MR's suggestion should be regarded as sound.
7   (1881) 20 Ch D 1.
8   [1992] Ch 560. One possible, albeit unattractive, argument against the applicability of contributory negligence to liability under the Misrepresentation Act 1967, s 2(1) is the 'fiction of fraud' wording of that subsection. This might be read as laying down that contributory negligence cannot apply to s 2(1) if it does not apply to the tort of deceit. Cf *Royscot Trust Ltd v Rogerson* [1991] 2 QB 297, CA, discussed above, p 82.

s $2(1)^9$ albeit that there was no contributory negligence on the facts because the claimant had merely failed to take an opportunity to check the truth, thereby falling within the rule in *Redgrave v Hurd*.

One should note that the interpretation given in the *Standard Chartered Bank* case by the House of Lords to the second limb of LR(CN)A 1945, s 4 is not an inevitable one. This is because one could interpret that second limb as meaning that the conduct of the claimant must be of the sort that at common law would have given rise to the total defence of contributory negligence, if the claimant had been suing for a tort to which the defence indisputably applied, for example the tort of negligence. But if that alternative interpretation of the second limb had been taken, the House of Lords would have had no scope to deny the applicability of contributory negligence to the tort of deceit because plainly, under the first limb, a liability in deceit is a liability in tort.

On the other hand, the interpretation taken of the second limb by the House of Lords might be thought to produce the oddity that the applicability of contributory negligence to torts would be entirely controlled by the state of the common law prior to 1945. The better view, which avoids this 'freezing of the common law' problem, is that when their Lordships referred to the common law they were hypothetically assuming the continuation of a common law of contributory negligence after 1945; and were deciding – as a matter of the normal interpretation and development of the common law based on sound policy – that contributory negligence was and should be inapplicable to the tort of deceit.

Whatever the correct interpretation of LR(CN)A 1945, it is important to add that the Torts (Interference with Goods) Act 1977, s 11, specifically lays down that contributory negligence is not a defence to conversion[10] or intentional trespass to goods. While the exclusion of intentional trespass is in line with the sound policy underpinning *Standard Chartered Bank* it is hard to see the justification for contributory negligence not applying to non-intentional conversion.

---

9   Sir Donald Nicholls V-C thought it important that the defendant was also concurrently liable for the tort of negligence at common law and drew an analogy with the approach to contributory negligence as a defence to breach of contract laid down in *Forsikringsaktieselskapet Vesta v Butcher* [1989] AC 852. On the face of it, this was to focus on the *defendant* being at fault within the first limb of LR(CN)A 1945, s 4. But there would be no need to find concurrent liability if one took the view that the Misrepresentation Act 1967, s 2(1) itself creates a liability in tort (ie that s 2(1) is a 'statutory tort').

10 This is qualified by the Banking Act 1979, s 47 so that contributory negligence does apply in favour of a banker being sued for non-intentional and non-negligent conversion.

(2) Breach of contract – does contributory negligence apply?[11]

The correct approach to construing LR(CN)A 1945, s 4 in relation to breach of contract was first put forward judicially as late as 1989 in obiter dicta of the Court of Appeal, confirming Hobhouse J's reasoning, in *Forsikringsaktieselskapet Vesta v Butcher*.[12]

The case concerned the reinsurance of underlying insurance that the claimants had given in respect of fish lost on a fish farm in Norway. The claimants asked their brokers, who were the defendants, to sort out the reinsurance for them. They specifically told them in a telephone call that they did not want one of the terms in the underlying insurance (requiring a 24-hour watch over the fish) to be relevant to the reinsurance contract. But in breach of their contractual (and tortious) duty of care to the claimants, the defendants failed to delete that term in the offer of reinsurance.

Ultimately it was held by the Court of Appeal, and upheld by the House of Lords, that the reinsurers were liable to pay the claimants for what they had had to pay out in respect of a loss of fish irrespective of the '24-hour watch' term. The defendants' breach of contract did not therefore cause the claimants any loss. But if that term had been crucial the claimants would have had an action for substantial damages against the defendants for breach of contract. And it was in relation to that action that contributory negligence was discussed, as obiter dicta, by the Court of Appeal (there was no examination of the point by the Lords): for the defendants argued that the claimants were contributorily negligent in relying on just the one telephone call to bring about the deletion of an important contract term, especially as the claimants had asked for confirmation that the deletion was acceptable to the reinsurers and the defendants had never given that confirmation.

The Court of Appeal thought that, had the breach of contract caused loss, contributory negligence would have here applied – and Hobhouse J's reduction of damages by 75% at first instance was supported – because the defendants would have been liable not only for breach of a

---

11 Swanton 'Contributory Negligence as a Defence to Actions for Breach of Contract' (1981) 55 ALJ 278; Palmer and Davies 'Contributory Negligence and Breach of Contract – English and Australian Attitudes Compared' (1980) 29 ICLQ 415; Chandler 'Contributory Negligence and Contract: Some Underlying Disparities' (1989) 40 NILQ 152; Glanville Williams *Joint Torts and Contributory Negligence* pp 318, 328–332.

12 [1989] AC 852, CA; affd on a different point [1989] AC 880, HL. Authoritative confirmation of the obiter dicta in *Vesta v Butcher* has been given by the Court of Appeal in, eg *Barclays Bank plc v Fairclough Building Ltd* [1995] QB 214; *UCB Bank plc v Hepherd Winstanley and Pugh* [1999] Lloyd's Rep PN 963.

contractual duty of care but also in the tort of negligence. Hobhouse J's threefold classification of cases for dealing with contributory negligence was approved.

A 'category one' case is where the defendant is in breach of a strict contractual duty. A 'category two' case is where the defendant is in breach of a contractual duty of care. A 'category three' case is where the defendant is in breach of a contractual duty of care and is also liable for the tort of negligence (or would be so liable, if pleaded). In terms of that classification, this was a category three case and hence contributory negligence would have applied.[13] And according to the Court of Appeal it is in a category three case only that LR(CN)A 1945, s 4 allows contributory negligence to be a defence to breach of contract.

How does one arrive at that conclusion in interpreting LR(CN)A 1945, s 4?[14]

The initial problem is whose fault does LR(CN)A 1945, s 4, or the different parts of s 4, refer to? The view taken by Pritchard J in his influential judgment in the New Zealand case of *Rowe v Turner, Hopkins and Partners*,[15] which was in effect approved by the Court of Appeal in *Vesta v Butcher*[16] – and is an approach that, in the context of the tort of deceit, has subsequently been applied by the House of Lords in *Standard Chartered Bank v Pakistan National Shipping Corpn (No 2)*[17] – was as follows.

The first limb of LR(CN)A 1945, s 4 – '... negligence, breach of statutory duty or other act or omission, which gives rise to a liability in tort' – refers to the defendant's fault: while the second limb – any act or omission which '... would apart from this Act, give rise to the defence of contributory negligence' – refers to the claimant's fault. To divide s 4 in this way is sensible: for on the one hand, it is hard to see how any act or omission which 'would apart from this Act, give rise to the defence of contributory negligence' can refer to the defendant's fault, since such an act or omission might not even be actionable; and on the other hand, it seems irrelevant to establishing the claimant's fault whether his acts or omissions give rise to a liability in tort.

---

13 The Court of Appeal considered itself bound so to hold in a category three case by *Sayers v Harlow Urban District Council* [1958] 1 WLR 623, CA: but there was no detailed reasoning on this point in that case and it is possible to interpret the reasoning as supporting the application of contributory negligence in category two as well as category three. For other relevant decisions, prior to *Vesta v Butcher*, see the second edition of this book at pp 82–83.

14 LR(CN)A 1945, s 4 has been set out above, p 133.

15 [1980] 2 NZLR 550; revsd on liability [1982] 1 NZLR 178.

16 But, while stressing that the practical effect would be the same, O'Connor LJ preferred to regard both parts of LR(CN)A 1945, s 4 as applying to the *claimant's* fault: [1989] AC 852 at 862.

17 [2003] 1 AC 959: see above, p 133.

But so to divide LR(CN)A 1945, s 4 does not end the problem of statutory interpretation, for each of the two limbs can be interpreted in various ways.

Taking first the second limb defining the claimant's fault, on one interpretation the essential issue is whether the claimant's conduct would have given rise to the total defence of contributory negligence at common law had the claimant been suing, as he is now is, for breach of contract. Assuming, as seems correct, that contributory negligence was not a defence at common law, this interpretation concludes that the Act does not apply to breach of contract.

However, there are at least two alternative interpretations according to which the second limb sometimes does apply to breach of contract, even accepting that contributory negligence was not a defence to breach of contract at common law. One of these, or an equivalent, must have been adopted in *Rowe v Turner* and *Vesta v Butcher.*

The first is that where the defendant is concurrently liable in tort, then if the claimant's conduct would have been a total defence at common law to that tort, had the claimant framed its action in tort, the Act applies even though the claimant has now framed its action in contract.[18] The second interpretation is that it is irrelevant to consider the defendant's actual conduct, or what the claimant is suing for in the instant case. Rather the second limb refers to the claimant's conduct being of the sort that at common law would have given rise to the total defence of contributory negligence, if the claimant had been suing for a cause of action to which the defence indisputably applied, eg the tort of negligence. On this second interpretation, the claimant's fault in the second limb is kept rigidly distinct from the defendant's fault in the first limb.

The common feature of these alternative interpretations is that the second limb of LR(CN)A 1945, s 4 does sometimes apply to breach of contract, so that the applicability of contributory negligence rests on the first limb of s 4 defining the defendant's fault. So turning now to the first limb (which was primarily focused on in *Rowe v Turner* and *Vesta v Butcher*) does 'negligence, breach of statutory duty, or other act or omission which gives rise to a liability in tort', include the defendant's breach of contract?

One possibility is to regard the first limb as comprising three separate clauses, ie 'which gives rise to a liability in tort' does not qualify 'negligence'.

But such an approach seems to ignore the word 'other', and in *Rowe v Turner* and *Vesta v Butcher* it was considered that 'negligence' (and 'breach

---

18   Palmer and Davies (1980) 29 ICLQ 415, 445; cf Swanton (1981) 55 ALJ 278, 280–281.

of statutory duty') is qualified by 'which gives rise to a liability in tort'. One might then think that, as breach of contract is not liability in tort, the Act does not apply to breach of contract. But in *Rowe v Turner* and *Vesta v Butcher* it was considered that the words do cover where the defendant is being sued only for the breach of a contractual duty of care provided he would also be liable for the tort of negligence on the ground that that is then 'negligence ... which gives rise to a liability in tort'.

Whatever the technicalities in construing LR(CN)A 1945, it has now been confirmed in a number of subsequent cases – and is therefore now clear law in England[19] – that, in line with *Vesta v Butcher*, contributory negligence applies as a defence to breach of contract in category three but not in categories one and two.

The leading case on category three is *UCB Bank plc v Hepherd Winstanley and Pugh*[20] in which, confirming the obiter dicta in *Vesta v Butcher*, the Court of Appeal applied contributory negligence to reduce damages. The claimant bank sought damages from its solicitors in relation to loans made by the bank. It was held that the solicitors had been negligent and in breach of their contractual duty of care in failing, contrary to the wishes of the bank, to ensure that full collateral security for the loans was obtained. As a consequence, when the borrower defaulted and the security was enforced, the bank received £107,151 less than it would have done had it had full collateral security. The Court of Appeal nevertheless reduced the damages by 25% because of the bank's own fault constituted by the failure of its relevant employee to read properly the letter sent by the solicitors. Chadwick LJ said,

'Properly understood this is a category (3) case within [the] classification in *Vesta v Butcher*. Accordingly the damages which UCB may recover in respect of HWP's breach of duty must be reduced to such extent as the court thinks just and equitable having regard to UCB's own share in the responsibility for its loss. In my view, the appropriate reduction in the present case is 25%.'[1]

In contrast, contributory negligence was held to be inapplicable by the Court of Appeal in *Barclays Bank Plc v Fairclough Building Ltd*[2] because this was a category one case. The defendant had been in breach of contract in cleaning the roofs of the claimant bank's storage warehouse. The roofs were made of asbestos cement sheeting and the result of the defendant's cleaning, without proper precautions being taken, was that the

---

19 In *Astley v Austrust Ltd* (1999) 197 CLR 1, the High Court of Australia (Callinan J dissenting) held that the identical Australian legislation should be construed as meaning that contributory negligence can never apply to breach of contract even in a category three case.
20 [1999] Lloyd's Rep PN 963, CA.
1   [1999] Lloyd's Rep PN 963 at 971.
2   [1995] QB 214.

warehouse was contaminated with asbestos fibres and dust requiring remedial work of £4 million. The defendants alleged that the claimant bank was partly responsible, through its property division, for proper precautions not having been taken and that therefore there should be a reduction for contributory negligence. It was held that contributory negligence could not here apply so that full damages were awarded. This was because the facts fell within category one. The claimant's loss followed from the breach of the defendant's strict obligations to carry out the work in accordance with the specifications and to achieve the standard specified. The breach was not merely one of a duty of care. While the Court of Appeal accepted that contributory negligence could apply in a category three case, it was emphatically laid down that it should not apply in a category one case. Indeed Nourse LJ went so far as to say the following:

> 'It ought to be a cause of general concern that the law should have got into such a state that a contractor who was in breach of two of the main obligations expressly undertaken by him in a standard form building contract was able to persuade the judge in the court below that the building owner's damages should be reduced by 40% because of its own negligence in not preventing the contractor from committing the breaches. In circumstances such as these release, waiver, forbearance or the like are the only defences available to a party to a contract who wishes to assert that the other party's right to recover damages for its breach has been lost or diminished. It ought to have been perfectly obvious that the Law Reform (Contributory Negligence) Act 1945 was never intended to obtrude the defence of contributory negligence into an area of the law where it has no business to be.'[3]

Since the House of Lords' acceptance of concurrent liability in *Henderson v Merrett Syndicates Ltd*[4] it will be very rare to find a case that falls within category two but outside category three. *Raflatac Ltd v Eade*[5] is such a rare case. Here the defendant head-contractor had broken its contractual duty of care as regards acts of a sub-contractor in negligently damaging the claimant's property. Although the defendant head-contractor was in breach of its contractual duty of care it was held that it had no personal or vicarious liability in tort for those acts of the sub-contractor. This was therefore a category two case and contributory negligence was held to be inapplicable.

---

3   [1995] QB 214 at 234. In third and fourth party proceedings in *Barclays Bank Plc v Fairclough Building Ltd (No 2)* (1995) 44 Con LR 35, CA, the sub-sub-contractors, who had actually carried out the cleaning work, were held liable for breach of a contractual duty of care to the sub-contractors. Ironically there was a 50% reduction because of the sub-contractor's contributory negligence, this being a category three case. *Vesta v Butcher* was applied.
4   [1995] 2 AC 145. Above, p 6.
5   [1999] 1 Lloyd's Rep 506.

But while the law is now clear, how satisfactory is the 'category three only' approach? Two main criticisms can be made.

The first is that it encourages an odd reversal of roles in that a blameworthy claimant will be better off, as regards contributory negligence, if it can establish that the defendant was merely liable for breach of a contractual duty of care (or the breach of a strict contractual duty) and was not also liable for the tort of negligence. In other words, as far as contributory negligence is concerned, the claimant will be trying to show that the defendant was not also liable in the tort of negligence, while the defendant will be trying to show that it was also liable in the tort of negligence.

Secondly, it would seem that contributory negligence ought to apply as a defence to breach of contract, irrespective of whether the defendant is concurrently liable in the tort of negligence and even if the duty broken was strict. If the claimant's unreasonable conduct can sometimes result in its recovering no damages, through the principles of intervening cause or the duty to mitigate, it must be sensible for there to be a mid-position where its negligence results in a mere reduction of damages. This is most obviously so where the defendant is in breach of a contractual duty of care, for then the claimant's and the defendant's fault are both in the same range, ie there is clear negligence/blameworthiness on both sides. But the same argument applies even where there is the breach of a strict contractual duty. After all, contributory negligence is applicable to torts of strict liability.[6]

The unreported decision of the Court of Appeal in *Schering Agrochemicals Ltd v Resibel NV SA*[7] constitutes a classic illustration of the injustice that the present law can cause. The claimants manufactured and bottled certain inflammable chemicals. The defendants supplied them with equipment that heat-sealed caps on to bottles. The equipment contained a safety alarm system whereby the heat sealer would be switched off if a bottle was stationary for too long and thereby exposed to excessive heat. Two months after the equipment was operational, there was a serious fire at the claimants' premises owing to a defect in the safety system of the heat sealer. On appeal, the defendants accepted that they were in breach of a strict contractual duty in supplying equipment that was not reasonably fit for its purpose, contrary to the Sale of Goods Act 1979, s 14(3). The crucial fact, in what would otherwise have been a simple case, was that three weeks before the fire there had been an

---

6   See, eg *Cork v Kirby MacLean Ltd* [1952] 2 All ER 402; *Mullard v Ben Line Steamers Ltd* [1970] 1 WLR 1414 (breach of statutory duty).

7   (26 November 1992, unreported).

incident, observed by two of the claimants' employees and reported to a supervisor, in which the safety system did not switch off when it should have done, resulting in a small explosion in one or more of the bottles and an orange flash. The supervisor took no action in response to that report.

The Court of Appeal held that the claimants' unreasonable failure to investigate that incident (which would have revealed the defect) or to close down the bottling line pending investigations meant that no damages at all should be awarded for the loss caused by the fire: the claimants had failed in their duty to mitigate their loss or had broken the chain of causation.[8] This seems a harsh result which could have been avoided had the court been able to award damages reduced for the claimants' contributory negligence.

With the increased interest in a European Contract Code, it is noteworthy that in the *Principles of European Contract Law*,[9] edited by Lando and Beale, contributory negligence is applicable to all three categories. Article 9: 504 reads as follows: 'The non-performing party is not liable for loss suffered by the aggrieved party to the extent that the aggrieved party contributed to the non-performance or its effects.' One of the main illustrations given is a category one case.[10] Similarly Article 7.4.7 of the UNIDROIT Principles of International Commercial Contracts[11] reads:

'Where harm is due in part to an act or omission of the aggrieved party or to another event as to which that party bears the risk, the amount of damages shall be reduced to the extent that these factors have contributed to the harm, having regard to the conduct of the parties.'

Given the controversy as to whether the present law is unsatisfactory, and given that it is not open to the courts to 'amend' the LR(CN)A 1945, it is unsurprising that the Law Commission carried out a project in this area in the late 1980s and early 1990s. In its Working Paper it provisionally recommended that the 1945 Act should be reformed so that contributory negligence would apply to all three categories of case.[12] However, in its

---

8   Above, p 75.
9   (2000).
10 'A leases a computer which under the terms of the contract is to be ready for use in England where the voltage is 240v. The computer supplied is capable of operating on various voltages and, in breach of contract, is actually set for 110v. A prominent sign pasted on the screen warns the user to check the voltage setting before use. A ignores this and switches on without checking the setting. The computer is extensively damaged and repairs will cost A £1,500. The court may take the view that the loss was at least half A's fault and award only £750 damages.'
11 (1994).
12 *Contributory Negligence as a Defence in Contract*, Law Commission Working Paper No 114 (1990).

final report it instead recommended (contrary to the views of the majority of its consultees who supported its wider provisional recommendation) that contributory negligence should be extended only to category two and not also to category one.[13] What primarily worried the Law Commission in back-tracking from its provisional recommendation – and was stressed to it by some consultees – was the uncertainty that contributory negligence might cause.[14] The fear was that what are at present straightforward damages claims for breach of contract would become complex disputes as to comparative blameworthiness. This would potentially increase litigation and hamper out-of-court settlements. The recommendation to move the law marginally forward to include category two as well as category three was a pragmatic compromise which would not significantly increase uncertainty in commercial litigation.[15]

This compromise reform would have the merit of removing the reversal of role oddity referred to above: and, unlike the provisional recommendation, it would limit the risk of complicating straightforward damages claims. But it would leave in play the 'all or nothing' injustice forced upon courts in cases like *Schering*. And it should be stressed that, subsequent to the acceptance of concurrent liability in *Henderson v Merrett Syndicates Ltd*,[16] very few cases fall within category two and not category three so that the proposed reform would be largely cosmetic.[17]

Perhaps a better compromise would have been a recommendation to extend contributory negligence to category one as well as category two, while restricting to a few fixed percentages (say 25%, 50% and 75%) the

13   *Contributory Negligence as a Defence in Contract*, Law Com 219 (1993).
14   *Contributory Negligence as a Defence in Contract*, Law Com 219 (1993) paras 3.39–3.40, 4.6.
15   The Law Commission also expressed concerns that extending contributory negligence to category one might operate to the disadvantage of consumers and others in weaker bargaining positions: *Contributory Negligence as a Defence in Contract*, Law Com 219 (1993) paras 3.39–3.40, 4.6. But this argument was effectively repudiated in the Working Paper No 114 para 4.45 (e) (eg 'apportionment will improve the position of the consumer whose conduct, under the present law, is held to break the chain of causation and so results in no recovery'.) The Report, paras 4.2–4.5, also relies on what was termed a reason of principle namely that a claimant should be able to rely on the defendant fulfilling a strict obligation and should not have to take precautions against the possibility that a breach might occur. But that argument had been comprehensively answered in the Working Paper No 114 Part II by clarifying that, in deciding whether the claimant has been at fault, one must take into account the contractual context. In particular the Working Paper stressed that normally a claimant should not be regarded as being at fault in relying on the defendant to perform his (strict or reasonable care) contractual obligation and by not checking up that he has done so. Eg if C takes a car to a garage for work to be done on the brakes, C should not be regarded as being at fault if he fails to check that the work has been properly done and as a consequence has an accident.
16   [1995] 2 AC 145.
17   This appears to be the main reason why the recommended reform has not been implemented.

possible reductions for contributory negligence. It is hard to believe that such a reform would have produced the significant increase in litigation that the Law Commission feared.

7. THE DEMISE OF IMPECUNIOSITY AS A LIMITATION

The House of Lords in *Owners of Dredger Liesbosch v Owners of Steamship Edison, The Liesbosch*[18] appeared to lay down that loss resulting from the claimant's weak financial position is irrecoverable. Here the dredger, 'Liesbosch', was fouled and sunk by the negligent navigation of the 'Edison'. The owners of the 'Liesbosch' were under contract to complete work within a certain time. Although a substitute dredger could have been bought and fairly quickly adapted for use, the owners of the 'Liesbosch' could not afford to buy a substitute at once and had to hire a replacement. This was more expensive to use than a substitute dredger would have been, as it required the attendance of a tug and two barges. The House of Lords held that the claimants could recover the market price of a comparable dredger, the expenses that would have been incurred in adapting the dredger for use, and the loss on the contract between the date of the sinking and the date on which the substitute dredger could reasonably have been ready for work. But they could not recover their greater actual loss including, in particular, the hire fee and expenditure incurred in using the hire vessel, because that resulted from their impecuniosity. Lord Wright rationalised this decision on grounds of either intervening cause or remoteness. He said that the extra loss arose from the claimant's '... impecuniosity as a separate and concurrent cause, extraneous to and distinct in character from the tort', and, '... if the financial embarrassment is to be regarded as a consequence of the tort, I think it is too remote, but I prefer to regard it as an independent cause.'[19] However, since by applying normal principles of causation (and more arguably remoteness) to the facts the loss from impecuniosity should have been recoverable, it appears that Lord Wright was in reality treating impecuniosity as a reason in itself for limiting damages.

At the same time Lord Wright accepted Lord Collins' dictum in *Clippens Oil Co Ltd v Edinburgh and District Water Trustees*[20] to the effect that if a claimant failed to mitigate its loss because of impecuniosity this did not act to reduce the amount of damages it would recover, ie no

---

18 [1933] AC 449. Davies 'Economic Stringency and the Recovery of Damages' (1982) JBL 21. For detailed criticism of *The Liesbosch*, as being inconsistent with legal principle, see Coote 'Damages, the Liesbosch, and Impecuniosity' [2001] CLJ 511.

19 [1933] AC 449 at 460.

20 [1907] AC 291.

argument based on mitigation could prevent full recovery by an impecunious claimant. Lord Collins had there said, '... the wrongdoer must take his victim *talem qualem*, and if the position of the latter is aggravated because he is without the means of mitigating it, so much the worse for the wrongdoer.'[1]

The denial of recovery for loss flowing from impecuniosity seems unjustified in terms of policy. As Sir Patrick Bennett QC said at first instance in *Perry v Sidney Phillips & Son*:[2]

'I find it difficult to understand why, if you harm somebody who is a millionaire and thereby increase the damages you have to pay, or a talented musician whose hands are damaged, which also increases the damages you have to pay, when the victim is impecunious ... that fact is used via *The Edison* decision to reduce the damages.'

Moreover it is mystifying how Lord Wright could regard the whole issue as being treated differently if viewed in terms of the duty to mitigate.

It is therefore no surprise that the courts have rarely followed[3] *The Liesbosch* and have chosen instead to distinguish[4] or ignore it.[5] This has finally culminated in the decision of the House of Lords in *Lagden v O'Connor*[6] that the *Liesbosch* rule on impecuniosity should no longer be regarded as good law. All of their Lordships agreed on the removal of that rule. In Lord Hope's words:[7]

'It is not necessary for us to say that the *Liesbosch* case was wrongly decided. But it is clear that the law has moved on, and that the correct test of remoteness today is whether the loss was reasonably foreseeable. The wrongdoer must take his victim as he finds him ... This rule applies to the economic state of the victim in the same way as it applies to his physical and mental vulnerability. It requires the wrongdoer to bear the consequences if it was reasonably foreseeable that the injured party would have to

---

1   [1907] AC 291 at 303.
2   [1982] 1 All ER 1005 at 1013.
3   A rare exception was *Ramwade Ltd v W J Emson & Co Ltd* [1987] RTR 72. See the second edition of this book, pp 91–92.
4   Eg *Dodd Properties v Canterbury City Council* [1980] 1 WLR 433; *Perry v Sidney Phillips* [1982] 1 WLR 1297; *Archer v Brown* [1984] 2 All ER 267; *Mattocks v Mann* [1993] RTR 13; *Alcoa Minerals of Jamaica Inc v Herbert Broderick* [2002] 1 AC 371. See also in Australia and New Zealand respectively, *Burns v MAN Automotive (Aust) Pty Ltd* (1986) 161 CLR 653; *Attorney-General v Geothermal Produce NZ Ltd* [1987] 2 NZLR 348. See the second edition of this book, pp 90–01.
5   Eg *Muhammad Issa El Sheikh Ahmed v Ali* [1947] AC 414; *Trans Trust SPRL v Danubian Trading Co Ltd* [1952] 2 QB 297 (both contract cases). Note that there was no reason in principle why *The Liesbosch* rule should be any less applicable in contract than tort; and in purporting to reconcile the *Muhammad v Ali* case with *The Liesbosch* Lord Wright in *Monarch SS Co v A/B Karlshamns Oljefabriker* [1949] 1 All ER 1, 14, did say that ' ... the difference in result did not depend on the difference (if any) between contract and tort.' See the second edition of this book, p 89.
6   [2003] UKHL 64, [2004] 1 AC 1067. See Tettenborn 'Compensating the cash-strapped: the sinking of the *Liesbosch*' [2004] LMCLQ 135.
7   [2003] UKHL 64, [2004] 1 AC 1067, at paras 61–62.

borrow money or incur some other kind of expenditure to mitigate his damages. For these reasons I would reject [the defendant's] argument that we should apply the rule that was laid down in the *Liesbosch* case that loss due to the claimant's pre-existing impecuniosity is too remote and cannot be recovered as damages. I would hold that this rule should now be departed from.'

And in the words of Lord Walker:[8]

'In the light of the development of the law in the 70 years since the *Liesbosch* case was decided, it has in my view become apparent that Lord Wright's sharp distinction between mitigation of damage and measure ... of damage is not helpful. Nor do I think his general classification of impecuniosity as "extraneous" or "extrinsic" is consistent with the modern state of the law (although loss attributable to impecuniosity, on a claim in contract or tort, may on examination prove to be too remote). Many recent cases, both in England and in the Commonwealth, have noted that the *Liesbosch* case has been distinguished so often that its authority has been greatly attenuated ... In my view the time has now come to say that the law has moved on from Lord Wright's exposition in the *Liesbosch* case ...'

The majority of their Lordships (Lord Nicholls, Slynn and Hope) went on to hold that where a claimant, whose car has been tortiously damaged, reasonably wishes to hire a replacement car but, because of lack of funds, has no real choice other than to hire through an accident-hire scheme, he or she can recover the costs incurred in so doing. This is so even though those costs are higher (and include incidental benefits) than the normal costs of hiring a replacement car. In other words, viewed as an aspect of the duty to mitigate, an impecunious claimant will be acting reasonably in incurring the higher costs of an accident-hire scheme; whereas an affluent claimant will be acting unreasonably in incurring such high costs and will instead be compensated only for the normal hiring costs.

In practice one would expect that defendants will find it difficult to challenge a claim for the higher costs of an accident-hire scheme that have been (or will be incurred) by the claimant. But Lord Nicholls suggested that insurers and credit hire companies should be able to agree on standard inquiries to assess a claimant's impecuniosity. And as a test of impecuniosity, he suggested, '[An] inability to pay car hire charges without making sacrifices the plaintiff could not reasonably be expected to make.'[9]

The minority (Lords Scott and Walker) held that the approach in *Dimond v Lovell*[10] could not be distinguished and that therefore only the

---

8   [2003] UKHL 64, [2004] 1 AC 1067, at para 102.
9   [2003] UKHL 64, [2004] 1 AC 1067, at para 9.
10   [2002] 1 AC 384. See below, p 243, n 14.

normal hiring costs (ie the 'spot-rate' of hire) could be recovered
the higher costs of an accident-hire scheme (which includes ac
benefits).

8. TWO PRINCIPLES LIMITING COMPENSATORY DAMAGES SOLELY FOR BREACH OF CONTRACT

Apart from the five general principles limiting compensatory damages
for both torts and breach of contract, there are two principles which limit
compensatory damages solely for breach of contract.[11]

(1) No damages beyond the defendant's minimum contractual obligation

Where a contract entitles the defendant to perform in alternative ways or,
as it is sometimes expressed, the defendant has a discretion as to the
contractual benefits to be conferred on the claimant, damages are
generally assessed on the basis that the defendant would have performed
in the way most favourable to herself. As Maule J said in *Cockburn v
Alexander,*[12] 'Generally speaking, where there are several ways in which
the contract might be performed, that mode is adopted which is the least
profitable to the plaintiff and the least burthensome to the defendant';
and in *Lavarack v Woods of Colchester Ltd,*[13] Diplock LJ said, 'The first task
of the assessor of damages is to estimate as best he can what the plaintiff
would have gained ... if the defendant had fulfilled his legal obligation
and had done no more.'[14]

The cases provide a number of illustrations of the application of this
principle. As shown in *Kaye Steam Navigation Co v W & R Barnett,*[15] for
example, if in a contract for the carriage of goods by sea the cargo-
owner has the right to choose between a number of different ports for
the cargo to be unloaded, damages for its failure to provide the cargo to
the carrier will be based on the assumption that it would have chosen the

---

11 A third – the rule in *Bain v Fothergill* (1874) LR 7 HL 158 – was abolished by the Law of
Property (Miscellaneous Provisions) Act 1989, s 3. For the old law, see *Remedies for Torts and
Breach of Contract* (1st edn, 1987) pp 83–84. The emphasis on the two principles being confined
to breach of contract is not intended to exclude the possibility that the same, or an analogous,
principle might be applied in a tort claim. But no example of this has been found.
12 (1848) 6 CB 791 at 814.
13 [1967] 1 QB 278.
14 [1967] 1 QB 278 at 294.
15 (1932) 48 TLR 440. See also *Phoebus D Kyprianou Co v Wm Pim Jnr & Co* [1977] 2 Lloyd's Rep
570; *The Rijn* [1981] 2 Lloyd's Rep 267; *Spiliada Maritime Corpn v Louis Dreyfus Corpn* [1983] Com
LR 268; *Kurt A Becher GmbH v Roplak Enterprises SA, The World Navigator* [1991] 2 Lloyd's Rep 23.

most distant port for unloading. In *Re Thornett & Fehr and Yuills Ltd*,[16] it was held that in a contract for the sale of goods, where the seller has an option as to the exact quantity to be delivered (in this case, '200 tons, 5% more or less') damages for non-delivery are based on the assumption that it would have delivered the smallest quantity, ie here 190 tons. Wrongful dismissal actions provide a particularly rich source of examples.[17] So, as held in *British Guiana Credit v Da Silva*,[18] where an employee could have been dismissed with notice, but has been dismissed without notice, damages for his loss of earnings are restricted to the period of notice. Again where it is at the employer's discretion to make certain payments, no damages should be awarded for them in a wrongful dismissal action: so, in *Lavarack v Woods of Colchester Ltd*, no damages were awarded (Lord Denning dissenting) in relation to bonuses under a service contract that still had two years eight months to run; and in *Beach v Reed Corrugated Cases Ltd*[19] no damages were awarded for the fees that the employee, a director, could have been paid. Similarly in *Withers v General Theatre Corpn Ltd*,[20] an actor who had been wrongfully dismissed recovered no damages for the loss of the opportunity to enhance his reputation by appearing at a famous theatre, because the defendant had the option as to the theatres at which the claimant should appear.

A very difficult question is whether the usual principle is infringed by the courts' assessment of damages in hire-purchase agreements where the debtor repudiates the contract. As established in *Yeoman Credit v Waragowski*,[1] damages are assessed on the assumption that the debtor would have gone on to pay off the instalments, albeit without exercising his option to purchase. So the creditor is entitled to recover the unpaid balance of the hire-purchase price, less the sum fixed as the fee for exercise of the option to purchase, the proceeds of resale of goods repossessed or their value, and a discount to allow for acceleration of payment.'[2]

It can be argued that that contradicts the usual principle: as the debtor had the option to terminate the contract lawfully at any time, the creditor's damages should be restricted to those to which he would have

---

16   [1921] 1 KB 219.
17   But as shown in *Rigby v Ferodo Ltd* [1988] ICR 29 the principle has no application where the defendant has continued to employ the claimant, while underpaying him. It would contradict the facts to postulate that it would have been cheaper for the defendant to have dismissed the claimant.
18   [1965] 1 WLR 248.
19   [1956] 1 WLR 807.
20   [1933] 2 KB 536.
1   [1961] 1 WLR 1124.
2   This follows from the *Waragowski* case, as modified by *Overstone Ltd v Shipway* [1962] 1 WLR 117.

been entitled if the debtor had terminated.[3] But the difficulty is that usually in such contracts the debtor in choosing to terminate (other than for the creditor's breach) would be bound by a minimum payment clause that would dictate payment of a sum at least as great as judicially assessed damages. It follows that, unless the minimum payment clause is invalid as a penalty (even though there is no breach in issue),[4] the assessment in *Waragowski* does not normally exceed the defendant's minimum contractual obligation.

In applying the usual principle there are two qualifications that must be borne in mind. The first is that where, on the construction of the contract, the court considers that it was the parties' intention that the defendant's discretion should be exercised reasonably, damages will be assessed on the basis of the defendant's minimum *reasonable* performance. In *Abrahams v Herbert Reiach Ltd*,[5] the defendants, a firm of publishers, agreed with the claimants, authors of a series of articles on athletics, to publish the articles in a book, paying the authors 4d for every copy of the book sold. The number of copies to be printed and other details regarding the publication were left to the publishers' discretion. They refused to publish the book. In an action for breach of contract, the Court of Appeal seems to have held that damages should be assessed on the basis not that the defendants would have published the minimum number of copies that could be described as a publication, but rather that they would have printed the minimum number that was reasonable in all the circumstances. Similarly in *Paula Lee Ltd v Robert Zehil & Co Ltd*[6] the claimants, who were dress manufacturers, entered into a contract by

3 See *Financings v Baldock* [1963] 2 QB 104 at 113 (per Lord Denning MR). But the decision in *Baldock* distinguished between the creditor accepting a repudiatory breach or terminating for breach of condition (*Waragowski* damages recoverable based on unpaid instalments, *future* as well as past) and the creditor terminating under a power given by an express term (where the creditor is entitled to recover only past unpaid instalments and damages for any breach prior to termination). That difficult distinction has been applied in subsequent cases: see, eg *Charterhouse Credit Co Ltd v Tolly* [1963] 2 QB 683, *Lombard North Central plc v Butterworth* [1987] QB 527. But in the latter case the distinction was regarded as unsatisfactory because skilled draftsmen can easily sidestep it. See generally Opeskin 'Damages for Breach of Contract Terminated Under Express Terms' (1990) 106 LQR 293 (cf Treitel 'Damages on Rescission for Breach of Contract' [1987] LMCLQ 143); Goode *Hire Purchase Law and Practice* (2nd edn, 1970) pp 400–402; *McGregor on Damages* (17th edn, 2003) paras 21–012–21–016.
4 Below, pp 451–455.
5 [1922] 1 KB 477.
6 [1983] 2 All ER 390. A similar approach, based on there being a contractual obligation on an employer not to act capriciously in relation to a bonus, was taken in *Clark v BET plc* [1997] IRLR 348 and *Clark v Nomura Ltd* [2000] IRLR 766. This directly contrasts with the approach to bonuses in the *Laverack* case: see Freedland *The Personal Employment Contract* (2003) pp 223–227, 365–366. Both the *Abrahams* and *Paula Lee* cases were distinguished in *Baird Textiles Holdings Ltd v Marks & Spencer plc* [2002] 1 All ER (Comm) 737, CA, where the lack of objective criteria by which the court could assess what would be reasonable either as to the quantity of garments or price meant that the alleged contract was invalid for uncertainty. In contrast, in the *Abrahams* and *Paula Lee* cases the existence of a contract was not in doubt.

which they appointed the defendants the sole distributors for the sale of their garments in a certain territory. The defendants undertook to purchase not less than 16,000 garments each season. The defendants repudiated the contract with two seasons left to run. In an action for that breach of contract, Mustill J held that there was an implied term that the garments would be selected in a reasonable manner and that it would not have been reasonable for the defendants to select the 32,000 cheapest garments because some variation of style, size and colour would be necessary to fulfil buyers' desires. Damages should therefore be assessed, applying *Abrahams v Herbert Reiach Ltd*, in terms of that reasonable selection which would be the cheapest for the defendants to buy.

The second qualification is that, while a particular performance may be the least burdensome to the defendant when judged solely according to the contract, this may not be the basis upon which damages are assessed because the courts judge the defendant's least burdensome performance by taking all other potential losses into account. The classic expression of this was in *Lavarack v Woods of Colchester Ltd*,[7] where Diplock LJ said, '... one must not assume that he [the defendant] will cut off his nose to spite his face and so [act] as to reduce his legal obligations to the plaintiff by incurring greater loss in other respects'.[8] The decision in *Bold v Brough, Nicholson and Hall Ltd*[9] is probably best explained on this basis. There the claimant, who had been wrongfully dismissed by the defendant, claimed for the loss of pension rights. Phillimore J held that the claimant should be compensated for this loss even though the defendant had the right to terminate the pension scheme on notice because it was unlikely that it would have taken 'a step so disastrous to its relations with all its employees solely to defeat a claim by this plaintiff.'[10]

It must be emphasised that, in order for the usual principle to apply, it is necessary for the defendant to have had a choice as to how to perform. Where there is no such choice, the damages must be assessed on the basis that the defendant would have performed in the one contracted-for way. This was the point that underlay the Privy Council's decision in *Lion Nathan Ltd v C-C Bottlers Ltd*.[11] The question here related to the correct measure of damages for the defendant's breach of warranty in failing to use reasonable care in providing a profit forecast for the business that the

7   [1967] 1 QB 278.
8   [1967] 1 QB 278 at 295.
9   [1964] 1 WLR 201. See also *Commonwealth of Australia v Amann Aviation Pty Ltd* (1991) 66 ALJR 123 (in assessing reliance damages it was assumed by all their Honours, with the exception of Toohey J, that the defendants would have exercised an option to renew the contract so that there was no need for a discount for the chance of non-renewal).
10   [1964] 1 WLR 201 at 212.
11   [1996] 1 WLR 1438, PC.

defendant was selling to the claimant. In working out what price the claimant would have paid had the warranty been accurate (with the damages being awarded for the difference between that price and the higher price the claimant had actually paid) it was argued by the defendant that the court should take the highest profit forecast (and hence the highest price) within the range of possible forecasts compatible with reasonable care having been used. This was argued to be in line with the minimum obligation principle of, for example, *Lavarack* and *Paula Lee*. The Privy Council disagreed and held that the court should take the forecast which the defendant would be most likely to have given had reasonable care been used. In the absence of contrary evidence, this was taken to be the forecast that, as events subsequently turned out, was correct. Lord Hoffmann distinguished *Lavarack* and *Paula Lee* because they were concerned with predicting how the defendant would have performed outstanding contractual obligations which gave a choice of what to do. This case was different because the defendant was not entitled to choose from a range of figures. Rather it was required to make its best forecast in good faith using reasonable care. There was no reason to think that that figure would have been at the higher rather than the lower end of the range.

The rationale for giving no damages beyond the defendant's minimum contractual obligation is that that is all that the claimant is legally entitled to. Had the contract been on foot, the claimant could not have complained if the defendant had merely performed its bare contractual obligation. Had it wanted a greater legal entitlement, the claimant could have contracted for it (presumably at an increased price). But it did not do so.

In his dissenting judgment on this point in *Lavarack v Woods of Colchester Ltd*,[12] Lord Denning adopted a different approach. As we have seen, the majority held that damages should not be awarded in respect of lost bonuses. But Lord Denning would have awarded damages to the claimant for his lost chance of gaining the bonuses: '... the compensation is to be based on the probabilities of the case – on the remuneration which the plaintiff might reasonably be expected to receive – and not on the bare minimum necessary to satisfy the legal right'.[13] Lord Denning was therefore adopting a loss of the chance approach rather than the usual minimum legal obligation principle. It is hard to agree with Lord Denning on this. The rationale given in the previous paragraph for the usual principle is a sound one. Moreover, it would seem odd in the

---

12 [1967] 1 QB 278.
13 [1967] 1 QB 278 at 288.

face of a defendant who has broken a contract to be considering evidence (presumably from the claimant) as to how the defendant would have acted had it not broken the contract.

The two approaches were carefully considered recently by the Supreme Court of Canada in *Hamilton v Open Window Bakery Ltd*.[14] The claimant had a three-year contract to act as the defendant's exclusive agent for the marketing and selling of certain goods in Japan. Provided 18 months of the contract had run, it permitted termination on three months' notice. The defendant terminated, without notice, after 16 months. The trial judge, applying a loss of the chance approach, had considered how likely it was that the contract would have run its full three-year course had the defendant not terminated at 16 months. He awarded 75% of what the claimant would have earned in that full remaining period up to three years. This was overturned by the Ontario Court of Appeal whose decision was upheld by the Supreme Court. The claimant was held entitled to damages assessed on the basis that the contract would have been in force for 21 months. That was the minimum legal obligation of the defendant.

An analogous (or, on another view, the same) principle as that being discussed in this section applies where the claimant would himself have committed a repudiatory breach had the contract continued. In *The Mihalis Angelos*[15] charterers were entitled to cancel a charterparty if the ship was not ready to load by 20 July. On 17 July, when it was clear that the ship would not be ready to load by 20 July, the charterers purported to terminate the contract. It was held that they were entitled to do so and were therefore not liable in damages. But in dicta the Court of Appeal discussed what the position would have been had that termination by the charterers constituted an anticipatory repudiation which had been accepted by the owners. It was thought that the owners' damages would have been nominal because the charterers would otherwise have exercised their option to terminate on 20 July. In Edmund Davies LJ's words:

'The assumption has to be made that, had there been no anticipatory breach, the defendant would have performed his legal obligation and no more ... [I]t is beyond dispute that, on the belated arrival of the Mihalis Angelos at Haiphong, the charterers

14 (2004) 235 DLR (4th) 193. See also *Janciuk v Winerite Ltd* [1998] IRLR 63 (EAT, in a wrongful dismissal case, rejected a loss of the chance approach in favour of the traditional minimum legal obligation approach).
15 [1971] 1 QB 164. In *Commonwealth of Australia v Amann Aviation Pty Ltd* (1991) 66 ALJR 123, in assessing reliance damages it was held by the majority that the *Mihalis Angelos* principle did not affect the result because there was merely a 20% chance that the defendants would otherwise have validly cancelled the contract for the claimants' own breach: see above, p 69.

not only could have elected to cancel the charterparty, but would certainly have done so. The rights lost to the owners by reason of the assumed anticipatory breach were thus certain to be rendered valueless.'[16]

(2) The only obligation broken is to pay money

London, Chatham and Dover Rly Co v South Eastern Rly[17] has traditionally been regarded as House of Lords authority for the rule that where the only obligation broken is to pay money, no damages can be awarded and the sole remedy is the award of the agreed sum.

However, this rule has never been regarded as affecting the claimant's right to terminate the contract and sue for damages for the defendant's repudiatory breach, presumably on the ground that a repudiatory breach always goes beyond merely being the breach of an obligation to pay money. So of course, a seller of goods can sue the buyer for non-acceptance, and a wrongfully dismissed employee can sue for lost earnings. Similarly damages are recoverable for a debtor's failure to pay so many hire-purchase instalments as to constitute a repudiation of the contract.[18]

But there were two respects in which the rule did formerly disadvantage the creditor. First, he could recover no compensation for loss of the general use of the money during a delay before the agreed sum was paid: in other words he could recover no interest. Secondly, he could recover no compensation for other losses caused by not receiving the agreed sum or receiving it late.

Subsequent developments have reduced these disadvantages. As regards the first – while it remains the law that damages cannot be awarded for loss of interest – the courts' statutory power to award interest on an agreed sum has gradually been extended. By the Supreme Court Act 1981, s 35A,[19] a court has a discretion to award simple interest on an agreed sum from the date of the cause of action until the date of the judgment or payment. A deficiency of this provision is that it does not permit the courts to award compound, rather than simple, interest.[20]

---

16 [1971] 1 QB 164 at 203.
17 [1893] AC 429
18 *Yeoman Credit Ltd v Waragowski* [1961] 3 All ER 145. In addition the rule does not prevent a promisee recovering damages where the promise is to pay money to a third party: below, p 435.
19 Below, ch 14. See generally Mann 'On Interest, Compound Interest and Damages' (1985) 101 LQR 30.
20 See below, pp 348–349. The High Court of Australia in *Hungerfords v Walker* (1989) 171 CLR 125 and the Supreme Court of Canada in *Bank of America Canada v Mutual Trust Co* (2002) 211 DLR (4th) 385 have departed from the *London, Chatham and Dover Railway* case by awarding lost compound interest as damages.

Moreover, there is no power to award any interest under s 35A where the sum was paid *before proceedings started*: in *Tehno-Impex v Gebr van Weelde Scheepvartkantoor BV*[1] the Court of Appeal held that arbitrators at least could get round this, by awarding damages to compensate for the loss of the use of the money in this situation. But in *President of India v La Pintada Compania Navigacion SA*[2] the House of Lords overruled *Tehno-Impex* and applied *London, Chatham and Dover Rly*. The impact of this has been reduced, however, by the Late Payment of Commercial Debts (Interest) Act 1998 which sits alongside the Supreme Court Act 1981, s 35A. Under the 1998 Act a creditor is given an automatic right[3] to simple interest after 30 days on an unpaid commercial debt.[4]

The second disadvantage has been entirely, or almost entirely, removed by the decision in *Wadsworth v Lydall*[5] (following earlier doubts cast on it in *Trans Trust SPRL v Danubian Trading Co Ltd*).[6] When the defendant failed to pay all the agreed sum, the claimant had to take out a mortgage in order to finance a contract to purchase some land and also incurred legal costs. He was awarded damages for interest charges paid on the mortgage and for his legal costs, even though these followed from the defendant's failure to pay a sum of money. The Court of Appeal distinguished *London, Chatham and Dover Rly* on the ground that, while it prevents general damages for failure to pay a sum of money, it does not prevent special damages. The exact scope of the decision rests on what is here meant by the terms general and special damages. The Lords in the *La Pintada* case regarded them as referring to the first and second rules, respectively, in *Hadley v Baxendale*.[7] But an alternative interpretation, which is to be preferred in that it limits further the traditional rule, is that special damages refers to any loss other than the general loss of use of the money (that is, other than the loss involved in the first disadvantage) so that the second disadvantage has been removed altogether.

1   [1981] QB 648.
2   [1985] AC 104. For criticism, see Wooldridge and Insley 'The Award of Interest for the Late Payment of Debts: Orthodoxy Prevails' (1985) 4 CJQ 97.
3   But by the Late Payment of Commercial Debts (Interest) Act 1998, s 5 the interest may be remitted, wholly or in part, because of the creditor's conduct.
4   The Act applies to contracts for the supply of goods or services (other than excluded contracts) where the purchaser and supplier are each acting in the course of business. The rate of interest has been fixed at the base rate plus 8%.
5   [1981] 1 WLR 598. Approved by the House of Lords in the *La Pintada* case [1985] AC 104 at 125–127. In so far as the traditional rule rested on grounds similar to those denying damages for loss from impecuniosity, *Wadsworth* is consistent with the recent departures from *The Liesbosch* [1933] AC 449: above, pp 144–147.
6   [1952] 2 QB 297.
7   (1854) 9 Exch 341. See also *International Mineral & Chemical Corpn v Karl O Helm AG* [1986] 1 Lloyd's Rep 81 and *Hartle v Laceys* [1999] Lloyd's Rep PN 315, CA, where currency exchange losses, and compound interest and bank charges paid, were respectively held recoverable as special damages applying *Wadsworth v Lydall* and the *La Pintada* case.

The effect of these statutory and common law developments is that the effects of the *London, Chatham and Dover Railway* rule have, in practice, been almost entirely circumvented. This is to be welcomed for there is nothing in terms of policy to justify that rule. Nevertheless it is to be regretted that the House of Lords in the *La Pintada* case did not take the golden opportunity presented to rid the law of the remaining disadvantages by removing *London, Chatham and Dover Rly* altogether.[8]

---

8   See also, from a comparative perspective, Treitel *Remedies for Breach of Contract* p 205.

Chapter 7

Compensating advantages

1. INTRODUCTION

The compensatory aims require the courts to assess not only the position the claimant would have been in if the breach of contract or tort had not been committed but also its actual position as a result of the tort or breach of contract, so that damages can make up the difference. Where the claimant's actual position has been, or will be, improved by benefits acquired subsequent to and as a result of the tort or breach of contract, one might expect (in accordance with the compensatory aims) that such benefits would be taken into account – if they are ignored the claimant will be left in a better position than if the contract had been performed or if no tort had been committed. In a nutshell, one might expect 'compensating advantages'[1] to be deducted or, as it is sometimes alternatively expressed, that losses mitigated would not be compensated. But in fact compensating advantages are often not deducted. Our concern here is to indicate when this is so.

However, it is first essential to stress that to be a compensating advantage the benefit in question must arise from the breach of contract or tort; that is, the breach of contract or tort must be a cause of the benefit according to the 'but for' test of factual causation. So, for example, if the claimant is injured by the defendant's negligence but completes his or her football pools coupon as usual, and wins the pools, that benefit is not a compensating advantage since he or she would have won the pools even if there had been no tort. Upjohn J in *W L Thompson Ltd v Robinson (Gunmakers) Ltd*[2] can similarly be viewed as applying the 'but for' causation test in deciding that a subsequent gain was not a compensating advantage. The issue was whether a purchaser

---

1   Lawyers tend to use the phrase 'collateral benefits' rather than 'compensating advantages'. This is especially so where the benefit is provided from a source other than the claimant or defendant (ie from a collateral source). But the disadvantage of that term is that it may be taken to imply that the benefit is in some sense unrelated to the tort or breach of contract, when the opposite is true. The term 'compensating advantage', coined by Ogus *The Law of Damages* (1973) pp 93–94, has therefore been preferred in this book.

2   [1955] Ch 177.

who had broken his contract to buy a car should be made to pay damages for the vendor's loss of profit on the sale even though the vendor had since sold the car at the same price to someone else. It was held that, because supply exceeded demand, if the purchaser had not broken the contract the vendor would have made two profits and not one; hence the subsequent sale was not a compensating advantage and the purchaser had to pay damages for the vendor's lost profit on his sale.

Having stressed the factual causation inherent in the notion of a compensating advantage, we can now attack the question: when are compensating advantages ignored?

Leaving aside claims under the Fatal Accidents Act 1976,[3] there are two general principles of non-deduction: first, indirect compensating advantages are not deducted; and, secondly, some compensating advantages provided by third parties are not deducted. We shall look at each in turn. It can be taken that a compensating advantage that does not fall within either principle is normally deducted in accordance with the compensatory aims,[4] common examples being the expenses of performance saved by a claimant because of the defendant's breach of contract and the earnings the claimant has acquired under a new job following a wrongful dismissal or dismissal necessitated by personal injury.

2.   INDIRECT COMPENSATING ADVANTAGES ARE NOT DEDUCTED

'Directness' puts a limit on the extent to which compensating advantages are deducted on the policy ground that it is unfair that a claimant should have its damages reduced by a benefit that is far removed from the wrong and is essentially coincidental to it. Directness therefore plays an analogous but reverse role to remoteness and intervening cause; they counter a rigid adherence to the compensatory principle by limiting the claimant's damages, whereas directness here counters compensation, as strictly applied, by increasing the claimant's damages.

A useful hypothetical example, illustrating an indirect and non-deductible compensating advantage, is of a claimant who, because he has more time on his hands as a result of his wrongful dismissal or

---

3   Compensating advantages following the death are almost entirely covered by the Fatal Accidents Act 1976, s 4, ordering non-deduction. For full discussion see below, pp 307–310.

4   A good example is *Westwood v Secretary of State for Employment* [1985] AC 20. One exception is the non-deduction of the price at which goods have been resold, above the market price, in cases like *Slater v Hoyle and Smith Ltd* [1920] 2 KB 11 and *Campbell Mostyn (Provisions) Ltd v Barnett Trading Co* [1954] 1 Lloyd's Rep 65, criticised below, pp 215–216, 218.

negligently-caused injuries, fills in a winning football pools coupon, which he would otherwise not have had time to do. Even though the defendant's tort or breach of contract has been a factual cause of the claimant's pools win, that benefit should not be deducted because it was too indirectly related to the tort or breach of contract.

Turning to the cases, it is submitted that those dealing with compensating advantages provided by third parties shed little light on the directness principle since the judges have used the terminology of directness for decisions that are clearly better justified on other grounds.[5] This leaves as prime examples cases where the compensating advantages have been gained from actions taken by the claimant subsequent to the tort or breach of contract; and here the test for directness appears to turn on whether the compensating advantage derived from actions taken by the claimant *to avoid* the consequences of the wrong. In McGregor's words, '... the basic rule is that the benefit to the plaintiff, if it is to be taken into account in mitigation of damages, must arise out of the act of mitigation itself.'[6]

A leading case, albeit that the advantage was considered direct and therefore deductible, is *British Westinghouse v Underground Electric Rlys Co of London Ltd.*[7] The defendants in breach of contract supplied to the claimants turbines which were defective. The claimants subsequently replaced them with other turbines. The replacement turbines turned out to be more efficient and profitable than the old turbines would have been if non-defective. In fact the extra profit gained from the replacement turbines being more efficient amounted to more than the losses caused by the original turbines being defective. The House of Lords held that the claimants were entitled only to nominal damages for the defendants' breach of contract because their losses had been completely mitigated by the extra profit gained from the claimants' steps taken to avoid the consequences of the breach. Viscount Haldane LC said:

> 'When in the course of his business he [the plaintiff] has taken action arising out of the transaction, which action has diminished his loss, the effect in actual diminution of the loss he has suffered may be taken into account even though there was no duty on him to act.'[8]

5   Below, p 162.
6   *McGregor on Damages* (17th edn, 2003) para 7–101.
7   [1912] AC 673. See also *Erie County Natural Gas & Fuel Co Ltd v Carroll* [1911] AC 105; *Bellingham v Dhillon* [1973] QB 304; *Techno Land Improvements Ltd v British Leyland (UK) Ltd* (1979) 252 Estates Gazette 805; *Cerberus Software Ltd v Rowley* [2001] ICR 376; *Dimond v Lovell* [2002] 1 AC 384 at 402–403.
8   [1912] AC 673 at 689.

An excellent illustration of the distinction between direct and indirect compensating advantages is provided by *Lavarack v Woods of Colchester Ltd.*[9] The claimant was wrongfully dismissed from his employment with the defendants and so freed from a provision in his contract with them that he should not, without their written consent, be engaged or interested in any other business. After his dismissal the claimant took employment with a company called Martindale at a lower salary than he had earned with the defendants, acquired half the shares in the Martindale company and bought shares in a company called Ventilation. The value of both the Martindale and Ventilation shares increased. The Court of Appeal held that while his new salary and the profit from the Martindale Co shares should be deducted, the profits from the Ventilation Co shares should not be. Lord Denning said:

> 'I realise that the plaintiff was only at liberty to invest in Ventilation because his employment was terminated. But nevertheless the benefit from that investment was not a direct result of his dismissal. It was an entirely collateral benefit ... for which he need not account to his [former] employers ... [his shareholding in] Martindale stands on a little different footing ... it looks as if he was getting a concealed remuneration by a profit on his shares in the company.'[10]

In other words, while the profit on the Ventilation shares was a compensating advantage, it should not be deducted because it was too indirectly related to the breach, as it did not follow from action taken to avoid its consequences. On the other hand, the profit on the Martindale shares was more directly related, as it followed from actions taken to avoid being without employment, and could not be clearly distinguished from the claimant's salary with Martindale.

Profit on shares was also not deducted, because regarded as too indirect a compensating advantage, in *Needler Financial Services Ltd v Taber.*[11] In 1990 the financial adviser of a company negligently advised Mr Taber to transfer the deferred benefits to which he was entitled under an occupational pension scheme to a personal pension plan with a mutual life assurance society. Seven years later, because of his pension-holding,

---

9 [1967] 1 QB 278. See also *Hodge v Clifford Cowling & Co* [1990] 2 EGLR 89 (compensating advantage not deducted because the mitigating conduct, in acquiring another ship, was not connected with the wrong); *Mobil North Sea Ltd v PJ Pipe & Valve Co* [2001] 2 All ER (Comm) 289 (compensating advantage not deducted because it did not arise from an act of mitigation by the claimant but from a separate settlement agreement between the claimant and another party).

10 [1967] 1 QB 278 at 290–291.

11 [2002] 3 All ER 501. See also *Primavera v Allied Dunbar Assurance Plc* [2002] EWCA Civ 1327, [2003] PNLR 12 (increased value, five years later, of an executive retirement plan, which the claimant had been negligently advised to take out, not deducted). In both these cases the controversial decision in *Hussey v Eels* [1990] 2 QB 227, discussed below, was applied.

Mr Taber was given shares in the company to which the society had transferred its business on its demutualisation. He sold those shares for £7,815 net. In 1998, when Mr Taber was 65, he discovered that his pension was less valuable than it would have been had he not transferred it in 1990. While the advising company accepted liability in negligence to compensate Mr Taber for the difference in the value between the two pensions, it argued that the profit on shares (£7,815) should be deducted as a compensating advantage. Sir Andrew Morritt V-C disagreed. He held that the profit from demutualisation was not directly caused by the breach of duty. He said:

> 'It is true that but for the negligence of Needler Mr Taber would not have taken out the personal pension plan (PPP). It is also true that but for the PPP Mr Taber would not have received any demutualisation benefit. Even allowing for these factors the demutualisation benefit was not caused by and did not flow, as part of a continuous transaction, from the negligence. In causation terms the breach of duty gave rise to the opportunity to receive the profit but did not cause it ... The link between the negligence and the benefit was broken by all these events in the mid 1990s and later which led to the directors of the Society formulating ... the transfer of the long-term insurance business of the Society ...'[12]

A more difficult example of a compensating advantage that was not deducted is provided by *Hussey v Eels*.[13] The claimants were induced to buy a bungalow from the defendants by a negligent misrepresentation that the property had not been subject to subsidence. It was estimated that the claimants had paid £17,000 more than the bungalow was worth given its actual subsidence problems. Rather than effecting repairs or reselling straightaway, the claimants sought planning permission to replace the bungalow with two new ones. After two-and-a-half years they finally succeeded in obtaining that permission and sold the bungalow and land with planning permission for nearly £23,000 more than they had paid for it. The trial judge held that the claimants were not entitled to any damages for the negligent misrepresentation because they had fully mitigated their loss by the favourable resale. But that decision was overturned by the Court of Appeal which awarded £17,000 damages. The reasoning of Mustill LJ, giving the leading judgment, was that the resale profit was too indirect a consequence of the tort:

---

12 [2002] 3 All ER 501 at 511–512.
13 [1990] 2 QB 227. This decision was controversially applied by the majority of the Court of Appeal (Peter Gibson LJ dissenting) in *Gardner v Marsh & Parsons* [1997] 1 WLR 489: damages in respect of defects in a building were awarded against a negligent surveyor even though those defects had been repaired by the landlord at no cost to the claimant tenant. For support for Peter Gibson LJ's dissent, see Allen and Thompson 'Surveyor's Negligence and Collateral Benefits' (1998) Conv 303.

'Did the negligence which caused the damage also cause the profit, if profit there was? I do not think so. It is true that in one sense there was a causal link between the inducement of the purchase by misrepresentation and the sale two-and-a-half years later, for the sale represented a choice of one of the options with which the plaintiffs had been presented by the defendants' wrongful act. But only in that sense ... It seems to me that when the plaintiffs unlocked the development value of their land they did so for their own benefit, and not as part of a continuous transaction of which the purchase of land and bungalow was the inception.'[14]

This is controversial because, although there was a considerable time lag, the seeking and obtaining of planning permission and subsequent sale were clearly actions taken to avoid the subsidence problems. It is difficult to accept that those actions were too indirectly related. While the claimants might have been entitled to damages because of the general increase in prices over that two-and-a-half year period (ie the loss of opportunity to buy an equivalent bungalow that would have increased in value), they had not produced evidence supporting such a claim. Certainly there is no reason to think that the £17,000 bore any relationship to such price increases.

3.   SOME COMPENSATING ADVANTAGES PROVIDED BY THIRD PARTIES ARE NOT DEDUCTED

(1) General factors influencing the courts

The compensating advantages in issue here may be provided by the state in the form, for example, of social security benefits; or by an insurance company or employer by the terms of an existing contract with the claimant; or gratuitously by the claimant's relatives, friends, employer, trade union or indeed by the public at large. Usually arising in respect of personal injury, it is the deduction or non-deduction of this type of compensating advantage that has given rise to the most discussion and

14   [1990] 2 QB 227 at 241.

controversy.[15] Before looking at the details of the law, it is helpful to examine the factors that influence the courts.[16]

(i)   Traditionally, the commonest explanation offered for the non-deduction of this type of compensating advantage is that it was too indirectly related to the tort or breach of contract. For example, in relation to accident insurance it has been said that the contract of insurance, rather than the accident, was the cause of the compensating advantage.[17] The same idea is often alternatively expressed by saying that the compensating advantage is a *res inter alios acta* or is collateral,[18] although the latter term invites confusion since all compensating advantages provided by third parties are commonly labelled collateral, whether deductible or not.[19] But the essential objection to this traditional reasoning is that a compensating advantage provided in response to the consequences of a tort or breach of contract cannot realistically be said to be too indirect so as to be non-deductible under the first principle examined above. In *Parry v Cleaver*,[20] the usage of remoteness and causation in this context was criticised and overall it is clear that the terminology of cause, collateral and *res inter alios acta* is here merely a shroud for decisions really justified on other grounds.

(ii)   Much of the traditional inconsistency in this area of the law appears to stem from the courts' willingness to punish the defendant, rather than merely to compensate the claimant. Hence there is often reference to the defendant being a wrongdoer who ought to pay and who does not deserve to be benefited by the compensating advantage.[1] But, if punishment is desired, it is surely

---

15   'Unreason in the Law of Damages: The Collateral Source Rule' (1964) 77 Harv LR 741; McGregor 'Compensation Versus Punishment in Damages Awards' (1965) 28 MLR 629; Cane *Atiyah's Accidents, Compensation and the Law* (6th edn, 1999) pp 322–329; Fleming *International Encyclopaedia of Comparative Law* vol XI; Law Commission *Damages for Personal Injury: Collateral Benefits* (1997) Consultation Paper No 147; Law Commission *Damages for Personal Injury: Medical, Nursing and Other Expenses; Collateral Benefits* (1999) Report No 262; Lewis *Deducting Benefits from Damages for Personal Injury* (1999). For an economic analysis, see Posner *Economic Analysis of Law* (6th edn, 2003) p 200.

16   In Consultation Paper No 147 *Damages for Personal Injury: Collateral Benefits* (1997) paras 4.30–4.51, the Law Commission referred to the factors (ii), (iv), (v) and (vi) below as, respectively, the 'wrongdoer should not be relieved' argument, the 'paid for' argument, the 'provider's intentions' argument and the 'incentive' argument. Its conclusion, at para 4.51, was that 'it is open to debate whether the policy arguments put for non-deduction of some collateral benefits withstand close scrutiny.'

17   *Bradburn v Great Western Rly Co* (1874) LR 10 Exch 1.

18   *Parsons v BNM Laboratories Ltd* [1964] 1 QB 95 at 143; *McGregor on Damages* (17th edn, 2003) para 7–092.

19   See above, p 156, n 1.

20   [1970] AC 1.

1   Eg *Yates v Whyte* (1838) 4 Bing NC 272 at 283.

better to administer it through punitive damages, where the punishment is explicit and where the amount awarded can be fixed in accordance with the extent to which it is felt the defendant deserves punishment. Note, however, that under the present law punitive damages can only be awarded in tort within the categories laid down in *Rookes v Barnard*;[2] and, it appears, cannot be awarded for breach of contract.

(iii) Parliament has sometimes laid down whether these compensating advantages are or are not to be deducted. For example, the Social Security (Recovery of Benefits) Act 1997 basically lays down that social security benefits paid as a result of an injury, or likely to be so paid, for up to five years from the accident are to be deducted from damages for personal injury; but that the state (through the Compensation Recovery Unit) is entitled to recoup the amount of benefits paid from the tortfeasor. However, there is to be no deduction from damages for non-pecuniary loss;[3] and benefits after the five years are not to be deducted.[4]

(iv) The courts sometimes regard the fact that the claimant has paid for, and in that sense earned, the advantage as a reason for not deducting it. In *Parry v Cleaver*, for example, this was part of Lord Reid's justification for not deducting a disability pension. If this were not so, it would mean that, as events have turned out, the claimant's payments would be rendered unnecessary, since he or she would have recovered the same compensation without those payments. Put another way, the person who has been a spendthrift should not be treated as well as someone who has used his or her money to guard against the unfortunate event that has occurred.

(v) The purpose of the compensating advantage is often regarded as relevant; for example, in *Parry v Cleaver* this partly underlay Lord Reid's explanation of why gratuitous payments are not deducted. But it is questionable whether this factor does provide much real assistance. In relation to any of these compensating advantages one can say that the purpose is to benefit the claimant as opposed to relieving the wrongdoer. But the real question is whether the purpose is to overcompensate the claimant and the answer to that is generally unclear. Indeed to answer it properly

---

2   [1964] AC 1129. See below, ch 18.
3   By the Social Security (Recovery of Benefits) Act 1997, s 8, and Sch 2, recoupment shall only be against compensation for loss of earnings, cost of care and loss of mobility, and then only 'like for like.'
4   Social Security (Recovery of Benefits) Act 1997, ss 3 and 17.

would require analysing the intention of, for example, each gratuitous donor or each insured claimant, and clearly the courts do not attempt this.

(vi) A factor that has been influential in relation to gratuitous payments – and provides the best explanation for their non-deduction – is that one would not wish to discourage benevolence. In the words of Andrews CJ in *Redpath v Belfast and County Down Rly*,[5] which were approved by Lord Reid in *Parry v Cleaver*, 'I would only add that if the proposition contended for by the defendants is sound the inevitable consequence in the case of future disasters of a similar character would be that the springs of private charity would be found to be largely if not entirely dried up.'

(vii) Leaving aside an indemnity insurer's subrogation rights,[6] there is rarely any question at common law of the third party (X) recovering the value of the benefit conferred on the claimant (C) from C, assuming the compensating advantage has not been deducted, or from the defendant (D), assuming the deduction has been made.

X has no restitutionary claim against C in that he has rendered the benefit, either as a volunteer, or under a valid contractual or statutory obligation owed to the claimant. Therefore the only possibility of recovery is where there is an undertaking by C to reimburse X in the event of recovering damages. At present, that undertaking is only generally exacted by an employer providing sick pay, and significantly, in this situation, the courts do indeed appear to depart from the general approach to sick pay by not deducting it from the damages.[7] The possibility of the court itself exacting an undertaking from C to use part of the damages to reimburse X has generally not found favour, being contrary to the usual rule that damages must be awarded unconditionally.[8]

---

5   [1947] NI 167, 170.
6   Street *Principles of the Law of Damages* (1962) p 105. Property insurance is indemnity insurance, accident insurance is not. An indemnity insurer's subrogation rights ensure that the normal rule of not deducting insurance payments can apply without there being any double compensation: *Arab Bank Plc v John Wood (Commercial) Ltd* [2000] 1 WLR 857. See analogously *Bristol and West Building Society v May May & Merrimans (No 2)* [1998] 1 WLR 336.
7   *Browning v War Office* [1963] 1 QB 750 at 770; *IRC v Hambrook* [1956] 2 QB 641 at 656–657. See also *Berriello v Felixstowe Dock & Rly Co* [1989] 1 WLR 695 (payments from Italian state welfare fund held not deductible because under Italian law the state would recover from C if C recovered the same loss from D); *Cosemar SA v Marimarna Shipping Co Ltd* [1990] 2 Lloyd's Rep 323 (owners able to recover voyage expenses from time charterers even though paid by third party because, on recovery from time charterers, owners bound to reimburse third party). Cf *Design 5 v Keniston Housing Assoc* (1986) 34 BLR 92 in which it was thought that a state grant given by the Department of the Environment was non-deductible: the best explanation for that otherwise controversial view was that the grant would probably have to be repaid.
8   Below, p 183. Contra, eg is *Dennis v London Passenger Transport Board* [1948] 1 All ER 779.

Where a deduction has been made, it appears that X does not have a restitutionary claim at common law against D, even where he has provided the benefit non-voluntarily, because, as laid down in *Metropolitan Police District Receiver v Croydon Corpn*,[9] X has not discharged any liability of D, since if the damages were reduced by the compensating advantage D was not liable to pay any higher amount.

The importance of X rarely having any rights at common law against C or D is that the courts almost always regard the question of deducting these compensating advantages, as solely involving C and D, so that the choice is either to overcompensate C or to relieve D. Hence, in the leading case of *Parry v Cleaver*, there was no mention of X's rights. It can be argued that, while more expensive (for example, extra litigation would be likely),[10] it would be better to deduct these compensating advantages, other than gratuitous payments, and to allow X to recover from D the value of that benefit deducted by, for example, extending subrogation rights or reversing *Metropolitan Police v Croydon Corpn*.[11]

It is arguable that this approach to reform has now been accepted by the Legislature vis-à-vis state benefits. The basic strategy of the Social Security (Recovery of Benefits) Act 1997 is precisely for there to be full deduction of compensating benefits provided by the state (X) but for the state to be able to recoup the value of those benefits from D. This may be regarded as a rejection, within the limits of the statute, of *Metropolitan Police v Croydon Corpn*.

Having examined the factors influencing the courts, we can now look at whether particular benefits provided by third parties are deducted, not deducted or partly deducted.

(2) Social security benefits

In respect of damages for personal injury the law on the deduction of social security benefits has been transformed by the radical and complex provisions contained in the Social Security (Recovery of Benefits)

---

9   [1957] 2 QB 154. *Croydon Corpn* was distinguished, with respect unconvincingly, by Sachs J in *Land Hessen v Gray & Gerrish* (31 July 1998, unreported). See generally Burrows *The Law of Restitution* (2nd edn, 2002) pp 287–290; Goff and Jones *The Law of Restitution* (6th edn, 2002) paras 15–017–15–019.

10   For other objections, see Cane *Atiyah's Accidents Compensation and the Law* (6th edn, 1999) pp 319–322; Street *Principles of the Law of Damages* (1962) p 106.

11   While being critical of the Court of Appeal's view in *Croydon Corpn* that the tortfeasor was not enriched, the Law Commission did not recommend a new statutory right for the provider of a deductible collateral benefit to recoup its value from the tortfeasor. See Law Com No 262 *Damages for Personal Injury: Medical, Nursing and Other Expenses; Collateral Benefits* (1999) paras 10.68–10.72, 12.28–12.32.

Act 1997, accompanied by the Social Security (Recovery of Benefits) Regulations 1997.[12] The 1997 Act builds on, but significantly modifies, the state recoupment scheme first introduced in 1989. The following seven points explain the general operation of the Act.[13]

(i)   The defendant (the 'compensator') must reimburse the state for the total amount of listed social security benefits received by the claimant during the 'relevant period' in respect of the injury or disease.[14]

(ii)   The 'relevant period' is five years or, if shorter, the period to a final settlement payment from the day following the accrual of the cause of action (or, in the case of disease, from the claimant's first claim for a listed benefit).[15]

(iii)   The listed social security benefits are: disability working allowance, disablement pension payable under the Social Security Contributions and Benefits Act 1992, s 103, incapacity benefit, income support, invalidity pension and allowance, jobseeker's allowance, reduced earnings allowance, severe disablement allowance, sickness benefit, statutory sick pay, unemployability supplement, unemployment benefit, attendance allowance, care component of disability living allowance, disablement pension increase payable under the Social Security Contributions and Benefits Act 1992, ss 104 and 105, mobility allowance, mobility component of disability living allowance.[16]

(iv)   Subject to significant limitations, the compensator may deduct the amount of the listed benefits, for which he must reimburse the state,

---

12   SI 1997/2205.
13   See, generally, Lewis *Deducting Benefits from Damages for Personal Injury* (1999) Pt II.
14   Social Security (Recovery of Benefits) Act 1997, s 6. This applies, without any reduction, even if the claimant was contributorily negligent: see s 1(2)(a) referring to 'liable to any extent'. Payments under the Fatal Accidents Act 1976 are exempted from the statutory scheme: Social Security (Recovery of Benefits) Regulations 1997, SI 1997/2205, reg 2(2)(a).
15   Social Security (Recovery of Benefits) Act 1997, s 3.
16   Social Security (Recovery of Benefits) Act 1997, s 29 and Sch 2. As regards relevant social security benefits not listed in the 1997 Act the common law will apply to determine whether there should be deduction or not. *Hodgson v Trapp* [1989] AC 807 (in which, prior to the legislative recoupment regime, the House of Lords held that attendance and mobility allowance were fully deductible in assessing damages for personal injury) suggests that there should be deduction of such non-listed benefits from damages: and this is supported by *Clenshaw v Tanner* [2002] EWCA Civ 1848 in which housing benefit (which is not listed in the 1997 Act) was deducted from the claimant's loss of earnings. See also *Ballantine v Newalls Insulation Co Ltd* [2001] ICR 25, CA (payment made under Pneumoconiosis etc (Workers' Compensation) Act 1979 deducted in full from damages for personal injury, applying *Hodgson v Trapp*).

from the compensation payable to the claimant.[17] The significant limitations are as follows. First, a benefit can only be deducted 'like for like'; that is, against an equivalent head of compensation.[18] For example, a benefit listed as being paid in respect of lost earnings can only be deducted from compensation for lost earnings and not from compensation for cost of care. Secondly, the heads of compensation from which there can be deduction are loss of earnings, cost of care, and loss of mobility (all during the 'relevant period').[19] There can therefore be no deduction from damages for pain, suffering, and loss of amenity. These limitations mean that, in contrast to the earlier recoupment scheme, a compensator is liable to reimburse the state in respect of a social security benefit even though that benefit may not be deductible from the damages payable. This marks an important theoretical shift because while, arguably, the original scheme could have been entirely explained on the basis that the state's recoupment was in respect of relieving a liability of the defendant's the new scheme goes beyond that and in effect holds the defendant liable for the pure economic loss caused to the state by the tort.[20]

(v) A central feature of the administration of the scheme is a certificate of recoverable benefits furnished to the compensator by the Secretary of State (ie by the Compensation Recovery Unit).[1]

(vi) The compensator is not liable to reimburse the state for listed benefits payable after five years: such benefits are not to be deducted from damages.[2] This is unfortunate. There is no good policy reason not to apply the basic principle that compensation dictates deduction: punishment is not justified, the claimant has not directly paid for such benefits, and there is no question of deduction discouraging private benevolence. The Pearson Commission

---

17 Social Security (Recovery of Benefits) Act 1997, s 8. The deduction is from the compensation payable after any reduction for contributory negligence (or because of other factors). Contrary to the normal principle that interest is awarded for the claimant being kept out of his money, the statutory scheme has been construed by the House of Lords as dictating that interest should be payable on the whole amount of damages irrespective of the deduction of social security benefits: *Wadey v Surrey County Council* [2000] 1 WLR 820.

18 Social Security (Recovery of Benefits) Act 1997, s 8 and Sch 2.

19 Social Security (Recovery of Benefits) Act 1997, s 8 and Sch 2. Loss of mobility is not defined but presumably refers to, eg the cost of a wheelchair.

20 See analogously the Road Traffic (NHS Charges) Act 1999 allowing the state to recover from the tortfeasor some of the costs incurred by the NHS in treating the victim of a motor accident. The 1999 Act will be replaced, and the scheme of recovery extended to cover all wrongfully caused personal injury, when the Health and Social Care (Community Health and Standards) Act 2003, Pt 3, comes into force.

1 Social Security (Recovery of Benefits) Act 1997, ss 4–5.

2 Social Security (Recovery of Benefits) Act 1997, ss 3, 17.

recommended that social security benefits should be fully deducted[3] and this is strongly supported by the reasoning of the House of Lords in *Hodgson v Trapp*[4] dealing with social security benefits prior to the legislative recoupment regime.

(vii)   In contrast to the earlier recoupment scheme, there is no exclusion for 'small payments.'[5] There is provision for regulations to be made for the disregarding of small payments but no such regulations have yet been made (or appear likely to be made).

In *Hassall v Secretary of State for Social Security*[6] it was decided by the Court of Appeal that the former recoupment scheme applied (and the same can be said of the Social Security (Recovery of Benefits) Act 1997), even though the claimant was receiving approximately the same amount of social security benefits prior to the accident. This was because the benefits paid after the accident were paid on the different basis that the claimant was no longer fit for work and were therefore clearly paid in consequence of the accident. The fact that the claimant would be left undercompensated was regarded as flowing not from a defect in the recoupment scheme but from his failure to claim damages for the loss of the non-recoupable benefits. Following this, damages for loss of non-recoupable benefits have been awarded.[7] But under the 1997 Act, it is no longer possible to deduct benefits from damages for non-pecuniary loss, and as a result there is now much less scope for such an award.[8]

In the light of the Social Security (Recovery of Benefits) Act 1997, the common law approach to the deductibility of social security benefits is now largely of relevance only to claims for wrongful dismissal. The cases establish that social security benefits paid as a result of the dismissal (eg unemployment benefit) are fully deducted.[9] This is to be supported for, as has been said in relation to social security benefits above in

---

3   Pearson Report paras 467–498; cf para 494. See also the more radical argument in Cane *Atiyah's Accidents, Compensation and the Law* (6th edn, 1999) pp 326–327: 'tort damages and social security benefits ... are paid for by much the same group of people (that is, a significant section of the public), and there is no rational justification for paying double compensation for the same loss at the expense of the same group.'

4   [1989] AC 807. See above, n 4.

5   The half-deduction for five years of certain social security benefits laid down in the Law Reform (Personal Injuries) Act 1948, s 2(1) no longer has any application, even to damages of £2,500 or less. By Social Security (Recovery of Benefits) Act 1997, s 33 and Sch 3, the Law Reform (Personal Injuries) Act 1948, s 2(1) is repealed.

6   [1995] 1 WLR 812, CA.

7   *Neal v Bingle* [1998] QB 466, CA.

8   Lewis *Deducting Benefits from Damages for Personal Injury* (1999) pp 219–222.

9   *Parsons v BNM Laboratories Ltd* [1964] 1 QB 95; *Westwood v Secretary of State for Employment* [1985] AC 20. See also *Chan v Hackney LBC* [1997] ICR 1014 (EAT deducted invalidity benefit in assessing compensation for loss of earnings for race discrimination).

criticising non-deduction after five years, there is no good policy reason not to apply the basic principle that compensation dictates deduction.

(3) Non-state payments

In an important speech in *Hussain v New Taplow Paper Mills Ltd*[10] (which concerned the deductibility of sick pay paid under an employer's health insurance scheme), Lord Bridge summarised the law on the deductibility of non-state benefits in personal injury cases. He clarified that the basic rule is that 'prima facie the only recoverable loss is the net loss.'[11] He then went on to explain that there are two well-established exceptions. First, money from an insurance policy paid for by the claimant and, secondly, money received from the benevolence of a third party. It is helpful to look at each of these two exceptions in turn before turning to benefits that are deducted in line with the prima facie rule.

As regards insurance,[12] it was held in *Bradburn v Great Western Rly Co*[13] that sums received under an accident insurance policy, paid for by the claimant, should not be deducted. More recently, in *Parry v Cleaver*,[14] the House of Lords decided, by a three–two majority, that sums received under a disability pension scheme should also not be deducted (in assessing damages for loss of earnings).[15] In essence this rested on the view that such a pension scheme is more akin to insurance than to wages and hence, in accordance with *Bradburn*, no deduction should be made. Lord Reid said:

> 'As regards moneys coming to the plaintiff under a contract of insurance, I think that the real and substantial reason for disregarding them is that the plaintiff has bought them and that it would be unjust and unreasonable to hold that the money which he prudently spent on premiums and the benefit from it should enure to the benefit of the tortfeasor ... Then I ask – why should it make any difference that he insured by arrangement with his employer rather than with an insurance company?'[16]

---

10   [1988] AC 514. See also his very similar subsequent comments in *Hodgson v Trapp* [1989] AC 807 (which concerned state benefits: see above p 166, n 16) and *Hunt v Severs* [1994] 2 AC 350 (which concerned gratuitous care).

11   [1988] AC 514 at 527.

12   The insurance exception does not produce double recovery in respect of indemnity insurance, as opposed to non-indemnity insurance, because of an indemnity insurer's subrogation rights: see above, p 164, n 6.

13   (1874) LR 10 Exch 1.

14   [1970] AC 1.

15   The question as to whether a pension (whether a disability or retirement pension) should be deducted from damages *for loss of pension* is more complex. In *Parry v Cleaver* [1970] AC 1 it was held that the pension should be deducted after normal retirement age in the assessment of damages for lost retirement pension. See also *Auty v National Coal Board* [1985] 1 All ER 930; *West v Versil Ltd* (1996) Times, 31 August; *Longden v British Coal Corpn* [1998] AC 653, HL.

16   [1970] AC 1 at 14.

But while the analogy drawn between the disability pension and accident insurance is justified, the controversial issue is whether accident insurance payments should be non-deductible. It is arguable that *Bradburn* is right on this because a claimant who has paid for benefits in the event of misfortune has earned those benefits over and above full damages from a defendant.[17]

In *Smoker v London Fire and Civil Defence Authority*[18] the House of Lords held that the non-deduction principle of *Parry v Cleaver* remained good law (subsequent to the *Hussain* case) and was applicable even where the employer operating the disablement pension scheme was the tortfeasor. And in *Hopkins v Norcross plc*[19] the same principles were applied by the Court of Appeal in holding that a retirement pension was not to be deducted in assessing damages for a wrongful dismissal.

Gratuitous payments are not deducted.[20] Non-deduction here is fully supported by *Parry v Cleaver* where Lord Reid said:

'It would be revolting to the ordinary man's sense of justice and therefore contrary to public policy, that the sufferer should have his damages reduced, so that he would gain nothing from the benevolence of his friends or relatives or the public at large, and that the only gainer would be the wrongdoer.'[1]

At a deeper level, as suggested earlier,[2] the best explanation for this non-deduction is that the courts do not want to discourage benevolence.

But, if that is the correct justification, gratuitous payments *made by the tortfeasor* should normally be deducted. This was accepted by the Court of Appeal in *Williams v BOC Gases Ltd*,[3] where the defendant employer had made an *ex gratia* payment to its employee, the claimant, which was expressed to be 'an advance against damages that may be awarded to you in respect of any claim you may have against the company.' After referring to Lord Bridge's approach in *Hussain* (and other cases), Brooke LJ said the following:[4]

'The "benevolence" exception is limited in terms to gifts arising from the benevolence of third parties, and does not cover benevolent gifts made by the wrongdoer himself,

---

17 For a contrary argument – that the claimant was not paying for overcompensation – see Law Commission Consultation Paper No 147 *Damages for Personal Injury: Collateral Benefits* (1997) para 4.40. See also below, pp 173–174.
18 [1991] 2 AC 502.
19 [1994] ICR 11.
20 *Redpath v Belfast & County Down Rly* [1947] NI 167 (public appeal). See also *Liffen v Watson* [1940] 1 KB 556 (charitable gifts in kind, in the shape of housing, food or clothing, ignored in assessing damages).
1   [1970] AC 1 at 14.
2   See above, p 164.
3   [2000] PIQR Q253. Obiter dicta to this effect of Lloyd LJ in *Hussain v New Taplow Paper Mills Ltd* [1987] 1 All ER 417 at 428, was approved.
4   [2000] PIQR at Q261.

for which allowance ought prima facie to be made against any compensation he might have to pay. Neither of the justifications for the benevolence exception apply to the tortfeasor. Deductibility will encourage him to make benevolent payments in future to injured employees, rather than the reverse. And it certainly cannot be said that in making the gift, his intention was to benefit the plaintiff rather than to relieve himself of liability *pro tanto*: he would have been happy to achieve both purposes at once. *A fortiori* in a case in which he said in terms, at the time he made the gift, that it was to be treated as an advance against any damages he might have to pay.'

In *Williams*, the apparently contrary decision of the Court of Appeal in *McCamley v Cammell Laird Shipbuilders Ltd*[5] – where money from an accident insurance policy taken out by the defendant employer for employees was held non-deductible on the supposed application of the benevolence exception – was said to be a case that should be confined to its own facts.

Subsequently the Court of Appeal in *Gaca v Pirelli General plc*[6] approved *Williams* and, in an excellent decision, took the opportunity formally to overrule *McCamley* on the ground that it was inconsistent with, for example, Lord Bridge's reasoning in the House of Lords in *Hussain v New Taplow Paper Mills*.[7] In *Gaca*, the claimant was seriously injured at work in an accident for which the defendant employers were responsible. The defendants paid him an ill-health gratuity and he also received disability payments under the defendants' group accident insurance policy. The Court of Appeal held that the benevolence exception to the 'net loss' principle did not apply to either of those two types of payment because they were provided by the tortfeasor.[8] They should therefore be deducted in assessing damages. Not to deduct gratuitous payments where made by the tortfeasor would tend to discourage benevolence by the tortfeasor, which would be contrary to the purpose of the exception. In any event, the payments made under the group insurance policy were not paid by benevolence. The exception was concerned with payments made out of sympathy or charity whereas these payments were arranged, and made, in order to promote good working relations between the employers and employees. This decision constitutes a long overdue and welcome clarification of the law on the benevolence exception generally and on benevolence provided by tortfeasors specifically.

---

5   [1990] 1 WLR 963.
6   [2004] EWCA Civ 373, [2004] 3 All ER 348.
7   [1988] AC 514.
8   Dyson LJ pointed out that, of course, the position would be different if the tortfeasor has spelt out explicitly that ex gratia payments are not to be deducted from any damages.

Wages, salary and sick pay are generally deducted in assessing damages for loss of earnings[9] and rightly so, for there is here no reason not to apply the 'compensation dictates deduction' (or 'net loss') principle. In *Hussain v New Taplow Paper Mills Ltd*[10] the injured claimant was entitled under his contract of employment to full sick pay for 13 weeks and thereafter to half pay under his employers' permanent health insurance scheme. The House of Lords held that payments under the scheme should be deducted in assessing damages for loss of earnings. They were indistinguishable from the sick pay paid during the first 13 weeks and were the antithesis of the pension in *Parry v Cleaver* which was payable only after employment ceased. Moreover it was the employers, not the claimant, who had paid the insurance premiums under the scheme. Lord Bridge said:

> 'It positively offends my sense of justice that a plaintiff, who has certainly paid no insurance premiums as such, should receive full wages during a period of incapacity to work from two different sources, his employer and the tortfeasor. It would seem to me still more unjust and anomalous where, as here, the employer and the tortfeasor are one and the same.'[11]

The same approach was taken in *Page v Sheerness Steel Plc*,[12] where the claimant was entitled to half pay for life under a permanent health insurance policy taken out and paid for by his employers. This was deducted in assessing his loss of earnings. Similarly in *Gaca v Pirelli General plc*[13] the Court of Appeal held that the payments made to the injured employee under the employers' group personal accident insurance policy did not fall within the 'insurance exception' to the general principle of deducting compensating advantages because the premiums were paid by the employers and not by the claimant employee.

An exception to the deduction of sick pay is where the claimant is under an obligation to refund the sick pay to his employer in the event of recovering full damages. In such a situation the courts do not make a deduction, and this seems a sensible way of both compensating the claimant and reimbursing his employer.[14]

---

9   *Parry v Cleaver* [1970] AC 1; *Turner v Ministry of Defence* (1969) 113 Sol Jo 585.
10   [1988] AC 514.
11   [1988] AC 514 at 532.
12   [1999] 1 AC 345, HL.
13   [2004] EWCA Civ 373, [2004] 3 All ER 348.
14   Above, p 164, n 7.

In accordance with the general principle of deduction, where the claimant has been made redundant as a result of his injuries and has received a redundancy payment that payment is deducted.[15]

The Law Commission completed a Report in 1999 which included detailed consideration of the common law on compensating advantages in personal injury cases. In its earlier Consultation Paper, the Law Commission put forward several options (including leaving the law unchanged) on which it sought the views of consultees.[16] The most radical option for reform was, in effect, to deduct all compensating advantages from damages meeting the same loss including charitable payments, personal accident insurance and disablement pensions. A second, still radical, option was to deduct all compensating advantages from damages meeting the same loss except charitable payments. A third, and less radical, option was to leave the present law as it is, except that disablement pensions would be deducted: it was argued that this would remove the greatest anomaly in the present law, namely that if a person is paid long-term sick pay that will be deducted from damages for loss of earnings, but if he or she is paid a disablement pension that will not be deducted.

The Law Commission indicated that there are strong arguments for favouring greater deduction of compensating advantages than is achieved under the present law. First, the basic notion that damages are to compensate the claimant, and not to punish the defendant, indicates that prima facie compensating advantages should be deducted. That is, compensation equals deduction. Secondly, to deduct compensating advantages would reduce damages and would therefore reduce the cost of the tort system without unduly prejudicing victims, who will be fully compensated in any event. Thirdly, the main policy reasons for non-deduction of, say, insurance payments that have been put by judges – in particular Lord Reid in *Parry v Cleaver*[17] – may not withstand close scrutiny. For example, to the argument that deduction would act as a disincentive for parties to take out insurance, it can be counter-argued that it is unlikely that the law is known about by those who are about to take out insurance and, even if it were, deduction would not act as a real disincentive because a prudent person would take out insurance anyway. In particular, it would guarantee payment even where the injury is not caused by a legal wrong. Similarly, to the argument that non-deduction

---

15   *Colledge v Bass Mitchells & Butlers Ltd* [1988] 1 All ER 536. See also *Wilson v National Coal Board* 1981 SLT 67, HL (Sc). Cf *Mills v Hassall* [1983] ICR 330 where the claimant would have been made redundant irrespective of his injury.
16   Consultation Paper No 147, paras 4.79–4.105.
17   [1970] AC 1.

ensures that the claimant receives back what he or she has paid for, one can equally well argue that the claimant has not paid for double recovery but has rather paid to ensure that he or she receives full compensation, including in situations where there would be no legal claim for compensation.

In its Report,[18] the Law Commission felt unable to make any recommendation for statutory reform of the law on compensating advantages in personal injury cases. No single suggested option received majority support from its consultees and, when it came to working out the details of even the limited reform of reversing *Parry v Cleaver* and equating disablement pensions with long-term sick pay, severe difficulties were encountered in trying to distinguish disablement pensions from some types of insurance. The overall message to emerge was that, while the present common law in this difficult area may not be perfect, it has reached satisfactory compromises that are difficult to improve upon.

18 *Damages for Personal Injury: Medical, Nursing and Other Expenses; Collateral Benefits* (1999) Report No 262.

Chapter 8

Form of compensatory damages, date for assessment, taxation

1. THE FORM OF COMPENSATORY DAMAGES

(1) Once-and-for-all assessment: the general rule and its exceptions

(a) The general rule

The general rule can be expressed as follows: a court must assess in a lump sum all past, present and future loss resulting from the particular tort or breach of contract being sued for, because no damages can be later given for a cause of action on which judgment has already been given. The classic authority is *Fitter v Veal*,[1] where the claimant had been awarded £11 damages against the defendant in an action for assault and battery. His injuries proved to be more serious than at first thought and he had to undergo an operation on his skull. It was held that he could not recover for this further loss in a new action.

Naturally, this rule does not prevent a different cause of action later being brought, and in deciding what amounts to a different cause of action it should be remembered that a single act may give rise to more than one cause of action. A leading case is *Brunsden v Humphrey*,[2] which involved a road accident injuring the claimant and damaging his vehicle. It was held that the claimant had two separate causes of action, one for his personal injury and another for his property damage.

---

1 (1701) 12 Mod Rep 542. For more recent examples, see *Buckland v Palmer* [1984] 1 WLR 1109; *Burke v Tower Hamlets HA* (1989) Times, 10 August.
2 (1884) 14 QBD 141. See also *Darley Main Colliery Co v Mitchell* (1886) 11 App Cas 127; *O'Sullivan v Williams* [1992] 3 All ER 385. The decision in *Brunsden* has been criticised in eg *Talbot v Berkshire CC* [1993] 4 All ER 9; cf *The Indian Endurance* [1993] AC 410 at 420 (per Lord Goff). For continuing wrongs (even apparently where the defendant commits no further acts) a fresh cause of action accrues *de die in diem* and hence future loss is irrecoverable (at common law) as being caused by a future rather than an already committed tort or breach of contract: eg *Battishill v Reed* (1856) 18 CB 696. In *Deeny v Gooda Walker Ltd* [1995] 4 All ER 289 Phillips J held that the special features of the Lloyd's litigation meant that, as an exception to the general once-and-for-all rule, names at Lloyd's were entitled to contractual and tortious damages for past losses and could later claim damages for anticipated losses.

(b) Arguments for and against the once-and-for-all rule

The purpose of the once-and-for-all rule is to prevent continual litigation. But it carries with it the problem of the court having to make an assessment of future loss, which must necessarily involve guesswork and usually produces inaccuracy. As Lord Scarman said in *Lim Poh Choo v Camden and Islington Area Health Authority*,[3] 'Knowledge of the future being denied to mankind, so much of the award as is to be attributed to future loss and suffering ... will almost surely be wrong. There is really only one certainty: the future will prove the award to be either too high or too low.' While an assessment of compensatory damages generally involves some speculation in judging what position the claimant would have been in if no tort or breach of contract had been committed, to have to assess once-and-for-all what position the claimant will from now on be in requires additional speculation about the uncertain.

For personal injury and death, future loss is often an important head of assessment, and it is here that the question of whether the once-and-for-all rule should be departed from to allow the award of periodic payments has been hotly debated over several decades.[4] The difficulties of assessing the future are particularly obvious in this field – common questions that arise, for example, are whether further operations will be necessary, whether brain damage will lead to epilepsy, when the claimant will die or when he will be fit to return to work. In all such instances, reviewable periodic payments would make the courts' task easier and would enable them to put the claimant more closely into the position he would have been in if the tort or breach of contract had not been committed.

A rather different criticism of the once-and-for-all rule in relation to future pecuniary loss following on personal injury or death is that the lump sum award, which is intended to be sufficient to provide for the claimant's pecuniary needs over the years, may be quickly and foolishly dissipated and may hence not fulfil its purpose. Periodic payments would overcome this. Moreover, periodic payments correspond more closely than does a lump sum to the continuing loss of income, for which the damages are generally intended to compensate.

In *Wells v Wells*,[5] Lord Steyn went so far as to say the following:

'[T]here is a major structural flaw in the present system. It is the inflexibility of the lump sum system which requires an assessment once and for all of future pecuniary losses ... The solution is relatively straightforward. The court ought to be given the

---

3   [1980] AC 174 at 183.
4   See, eg *Report on Personal Injury Litigation – Assessment of Damages* (1973) Law Commission Report No 56, paras 231–244; Pearson Commission Report vol 1, ch 14.
5   [1999] 1 AC 345 at 384.

power of its own motion to make an award for periodic payments rather than a lump sum in appropriate cases ... Except perhaps for the distaste of personal injury lawyers for change to a familiar system, I can think of no substantial argument to the contrary.'

However, with respect, it is misleading to think that the arguments are all one way. The finality produced by the once-and-for-all rule enables the defendant and his or her insurers to be certain where they stand and minimises judicial expense and time. Furthermore, a once-and-for-all award contains no disincentive for the claimant to recover from an injury, puts an end to any 'compensation neurosis' (which is a recognised psychiatric illness), rules out any difficulties produced by the defendant's (or his or her insurer's) subsequent insolvency, and renders unnecessary continued investigation of the claimant's condition and lifestyle, sometimes possible only by intrusive 'spying'. The precise extent to which one would allow reviewability is particularly problematic. Finally, if both claimants and defendants prefer lump sums, giving the courts the power to award periodic payments may not constitute much of a change in practice given that the parties will be free to settle out of court.

(c) Provisional damages

The first relatively minor break with lump sums was the introduction in 1982, implementing the Law Commission's recommendation of 1973, of provisional damages.[6] By the Supreme Court Act 1981, s 32A (as inserted by the Administration of Justice Act 1982, s 6) and the Civil Procedure Rules, Pt 41, the High Court has power to award provisional damages in actions:

'for damages for personal injuries in which there is proved or admitted to be a chance that at some definite or indefinite time in the future the injured person will, as the result of the act or omission which gave rise to the cause of action, develop some serious disease or suffer some serious deterioration in his physical or mental condition.'[7]

In such a case the court is able to assess the damages on the assumption that the injured person will not develop the disease or suffer the deterioration but then to award further damages at a future date if the risk should in fact materialise.[8] However, the power can only be used if

---

6   *Report on Personal Litigation – Assessment of Damages* (1973), Law Com No 56. Cf the Pearson Commission's recommendation, vol 1, ch 14, favouring reviewable periodic payments for future pecuniary loss in cases of serious or lasting injury or death.
7   Supreme Court Act 1981, s 32A(1).
8   Supreme Court Act 1981, s 32A(2).

the particulars of claim include a claim for provisional damages.[9] The provisional order must specify the disease or type of deterioration as to which an application for further damages may be made and will normally specify the period within which such application must be made, although the period may be extended on an application by the claimant.[10] Only one application for further damages may be entertained in relation to each disease or type of deterioration specified in the provisional order.[11] In the leading reported case of *Willson v Ministry of Defence*[12] provisional damages were refused on the ground that 'serious deterioration' refers to a clear and severable event rather than an ordinary continuing deterioration, as in a typical osteo-arthritic case. It was further said by Scott Baker J that the Supreme Court Act 1981, s 32A is concerned with a 'measurable rather than a fanciful' chance.[13]

Provisional damages mark an important theoretical break with the once-and-for-all lump sum system. However, they represent only a small departure from the traditional approach and are very different from a system of reviewable periodic payments. In practice, most claimants do not claim provisional damages. That is, they choose to forgo the possibility of higher damages in the long term, by taking what at trial is a higher award under the traditional once-and-for-all approach.

(d) Structured settlements

Although a development in relation to out-of-court settlements of personal injury and death cases, rather than awards made by the courts, it is important here to mention the modern phenomenon of the 'structured settlement'.[14] Under such a settlement, the defendant's insurer purchases an annuity for the claimant. It was accepted in an agreement between the Inland Revenue and the Association of British Insurers in 1987 that the payments received by the claimant from the annuity are tax free (ie they are treated as capital not income). Under a structured settlement, the defendant therefore has to pay less to produce the same (or a greater) stream of money for the claimant (the rate of discount, which presumably includes the defendant's insurer's costs as well as the tax saving, appears to be normally about 10% to 15%). Such

---

9   CPR 21.2. Examples have so far been rare: but see *Cronin v Redbridge London Borough Council* (1987) Times, 20 May.
10   CPR 21.2. For provisional damages ordered without trial (ie following a settlement), see also *Hurditch v Sheffield HA* [1989] QB 562.
11   CPR 41.3.
12   [1991] 1 All ER 638.
13   [1991] 1 All ER 638 at 642.
14   See generally Lewis *Structured Settlements: The Law and Practice* (1993); Law Commission *Structured Settlements and Interim and Provisional Damages* Report No 224 (1994) Pt III.

a settlement is also in the interests of claimants, who are guaranteed a stream of 'income', and of the state, which is saved having to support those who squander lump sums of damages. A stream of 'income' is also more true to the aim of compensation than is a lump sum.

Structured settlements relate to future pecuniary loss only: non-pecuniary loss and past pecuniary loss is paid in the usual form of a lump sum. Flexibility is possible in the sense that part of the future pecuniary loss can be paid in a lump sum or into a contingency fund to deal with unforeseen events; and more than one annuity can be bought depending on the claimant's likely future needs. Most annuities are index-linked and precise estimation of the claimant's life expectancy is not necessary; but otherwise structured settlements are as prone to inaccuracy as a lump sum for they are not reviewable. Although an annuity would normally cease on the claimant's death, it is usual to incorporate a guaranteed minimum time period of payments so that, as under the lump sum system, dependants would be guaranteed a (windfall) sum in the event of the claimant's unexpected death.

Self-financing structured settlements (ie not involving insurers) have also been entered into by public sector defendants, such as NHS trusts.

The fear that an insurer backing a structured settlement might go bankrupt, or that a public sector body behind a self-financing structure might cease to exist, led to provisions in the Damages Act 1996 providing protection to claimants in those situations. By the Damages Act 1996, s 4, the claimant is provided with complete protection under the Policyholders Protection Scheme if an insurer backing a structured settlement goes bankrupt. The Administration of Justice Act 1982, s 6 provides analogous protection for public sector structured settlements by allowing the Crown to provide a guarantee so that the claimant will be protected if the public sector body behind the settlement ceases to exist.[15]

It is important to appreciate, however, that (prior to the coming into effect of the Courts Act 2003, ss 100–101) the courts have no power to impose a structured settlement. But court approval might be required for such a settlement because of, for example, the claimant's disability or

---

15 From a day to be appointed, the Damages Act 1996, ss 4 and 6 will be amended by the Courts Act 2003, s 101 so that analogous protections will be ensured under the new scheme of (reviewable) periodical payments.

infancy;[16] and by the Damages Act 1996, s 2 a court may make an order for personal injury damages to be in the form of periodical payments if both parties consent.[17]

(e) **The new regime of (reviewable) periodical payments**

Building on the out-of-court development of structured settlements, a fundamental departure from lump sums will be introduced by the Courts Act 2003, ss 100–101 (amending the Damages Act 1996)[18] and accompanying Civil Procedure Rules and delegated legislation. In respect of damages for future pecuniary loss in respect of personal injury or death, the courts will be empowered (and will be required to consider whether) to make an order that the damages are to take the form of periodical payments.[19] Moreover, it will be possible for the periodical payments order to be made variable so that it can be reviewed by the courts.[20]

The Courts Act 2003, ss 100–101 will, therefore, give the courts, for the first time, the power to order (reviewable) periodical payments. This new regime follows a consultation paper issued by the Lord Chancellor's Department in March 2002, which set out the arguments for and against (reviewable) periodical payments that we have looked at above.[1] It is clear that a particularly influential 'political' factor was that, in respect of litigation against the National Health Service, periodical payments are more attractive to the NHS (at least in the short term) than having to find large capital sums.[2]

However, before such an order will be able to be made, a court will have to be satisfied that the continuity of payment is reasonably secure. Other than in respect of public sector defendants, this will essentially be so where the defendant's insurer purchases an annuity as under a structured settlement. Protection for claimants in the event of an insurer's insolvency or a public body's non-existence will be provided by the Damages Act 1996, ss 4 and 6, as amended by the Courts Act 2003, s 101.

---

16   As in *Kelly v Dawes* (1990) Times, 27 September.
17   From a day to be appointed, a new Damages Act 1996, s 2 will be substituted by the Courts Act 2003, s 100.
18   At the time of writing, no date has been appointed for these provisions of the Courts Act 2003 to be brought into force. The expectation is that they will be brought into force in late 2004.
19   Damages Act 1996, s 2(1), as substituted by the Courts Act 2003, s 100.
20   Damages Act 1996, s 2B, as substituted by the Courts Act 2003, s 100; and draft Damages (Variation of Periodical Payments) Order 2004.
1   See above, pp 176–177.
2   The Explanatory Notes to the Act make this clear.

Of particular interest are the provisions that will enable the variation of periodical payments. The extent to which periodical payments will be able to be reviewed is the most difficult and controversial aspect of this reform. The Government appears to have taken a very conservative approach. The reviewability provisions in the draft delegated legislation[3] closely match those on 'provisional damages'. Assuming that that draft order becomes law, the original court will be able to make a variable order but only to deal with the development of some serious disease or the suffering of some serious deterioration or significant improvement in the claimant's condition. Moreover, only one application to vary a variable order will be able to be made in respect of each specified disease or type of deterioration or improvement.

(f) Interim payments

Although not concerned with the problems of predicting the future – and not contradicting the general rule that damages *after trial* must be awarded once-and-for-all – it is convenient here to mention interim payments. This is because they constitute an exception to the general rule that damages are awarded once-and-for-all: obviously they do not prevent further damages being awarded at trial for the same cause of action.

In accordance with the Civil Procedure Rules 1998,[4] made under the Supreme Court Act 1981, s 32, and the County Courts Act 1984, s 50, the claimant may apply for an interim payment of the damages which the defendant may be held liable to pay him or for his benefit. By CPR 25.7(2), no order may be made in a personal injury action unless the defendant is insured in respect of the claim;[5] or unless the defendant's liability will be met by an insurer under the Road Traffic Act 1988, s 151 or by an insurer acting under the Motor Insurers Bureau Agreement or by the Motor Insurers Bureau where it is acting itself; or unless the defendant is a public body. The court may order an interim payment of such amount as it thinks just, not exceeding a reasonable proportion of the damages which it considers are likely to be recovered by the claimant,[6] after taking into account any contributory negligence

---

3   Draft Damages (Variation of Periodical Payments) Order 2004.
4   CPR 25.6–25.9.
5   In non-personal injury cases the means of the defendant have traditionally been relevant albeit not decisive: *Schott Kem Ltd v Bentley* [1991] 1 QB 61, CA.
6   This involves an estimate of the damages that are likely to be recovered. But the court's investigation should not turn into a long investigation of the issues in dispute; rather a broad approach should be taken: *Newport (Essex) Engineering Co v Press and Shear Machinery Co (1981)* (1984) 24 BLR 71, CA.

and any counterclaim. Before making an order, however, CPR 25.7(1) lays down that the court must be satisfied that one of the three following conditions is fulfilled:

(i)   that the defendant has admitted liability;
(ii) that the claimant has obtained judgment against the defendant for damages to be assessed;[7] or
(iii) that if the action proceeded to trial the claimant would obtain judgment against the defendant (or, in a claim for personal injury, where there is more than one defendant, against at least one of the defendants even if the court has not yet determined which of them is liable)[8] for substantial damages.[9]

By CPR 25.9, the fact that an order for an interim payment has been made must not be disclosed to the court at trial until all questions of liability and quantum of damages have been determined, unless the defendant agrees. By CPR 25.8, in giving final judgment the court may make any order with respect to the interim payment that proves to be necessary by way of adjustment and, in particular, if the interim payment exceeds the amount for which the defendant is held liable, may order repayment of the appropriate amount, plus interest,[10] by the claimant.

The policy behind interim payments is that, if he or she so wishes, the claimant should be relieved of immediate financial worries where there is a strong case on liability.[11]

7   An interim payment can be ordered even though an appeal is pending: *Halvanon Insurance Co v Central Reinsurance Corpn* [1984] 2 Lloyd's Rep 420.
8   In a non-personal injury claim, the condition must be satisfied in respect of each defendant. Interim payments comprising different fractions of the total amount thought to be 'just' may be ordered against the different defendants provided the claimant does not overall recover more than the just amount (which, in the case of damages, cannot exceed a reasonable proportion of the damages likely to be recovered): *Schott Kem Ltd v Bentley* [1991] 1 QB 61, CA.
9   The court must be satisfied of this applying the civil standard of proof: *Shearson Lehman Brothers Inc v Maclaine, Watson & Co Ltd* [1987] 1 WLR 480 at 489, CA. The necessary standard is not met – and hence no interim payment can be awarded – where summary judgment has been refused and *unconditional* leave to defend has been given: *British and Commonwealth Holdings plc v Quadrex Holdings Inc* [1989] QB 842, CA; *Andrews v Schooling* [1991] 1 WLR 783, CA.
10 *Mercers Co v New Hampshire Insurance Co* [1991] 1 WLR 1173. But the decision that the interim sum should be repaid was reversed on appeal: [1992] 1 WLR 792, CA. Interest (or other profit) gained by the claimant from the use of the interim payment is to be ignored in deciding on the final sum of damages to be paid applying the principle that it is irrelevant what the claimant does with his 'damages': *Parry v North West Surrey Health Authority* (2000) Times, 5 January.
11 Winn Committee Report (1968) Cmnd 3091, paras 71–110.

(2) Damages must be awarded unconditionally

The leading case is *Banbury v Bank of Montreal*,[12] where the defendant was held liable for negligently advising the claimant to invest in certain securities. The jury's verdict on damages was 'for £25,000 and all securities to be returned to the defendant bank.' The finding of liability was overturned by the House of Lords, but three of their Lordships considered that in any event the award was improper because of the condition attached. Similarly, in *Patel v Hooper & Jackson*[13] the Court of Appeal overturned an award of damages against a negligent surveyor where the damages were 'to be reduced by £14,200 in the event of the plaintiffs electing to treat the endowment policy as their own free standing long-term investment.' In the words of Nourse LJ, 'the powers of the court in a case of this kind are confined to making a once and for all award of damages.'[14]

The main reason for having this principle is that it brings finality to litigation. Another possible explanation is the inappropriateness of sanctions in the event that the claimant fails to comply with a condition imposed on him. But in some personal injury cases involving gratuitous nursing services rendered or expenses incurred by a relative, or gratuitous payments made by an employer, damages have been made conditional on the claimant paying them over to,[15] or holding them on trust for,[16] the relative or employer. Unfortunately, despite the convenience of these techniques in this sort of case, the force of these decisions is diminished by there having been no discussion of the principle against unconditional awards.

2. THE DATE FOR THE ASSESSMENT OF COMPENSATORY DAMAGES

This heading, although commonly used, is rather ambiguous and in order to understand the issues involved, it is helpful to distinguish two questions raised by it. Is there a time after which the court assessing damages is barred from taking into account events that have already occurred? Which value of money, property or services do the courts apply in assessing damages?

---

12 [1918] AC 626.
13 [1999] 1 WLR 1792.
14 [1999] 1 WLR 1792 at 1800.
15 Eg *Dennis v London Passenger Transport Board* [1948] 1 All ER 779; *Schneider v Eisovitch* [1960] 2 QB 430.
16 Eg *Cunningham v Harrison* [1973] QB 942; *Hunt v Severs* [1994] 2 AC 350.

(1) Is there a time after which the court assessing damages is barred from taking into account events that have already occurred?

As regards a court of first instance the answer to this question is in the negative; a trial judge can take into account evidence of all events that occur *prior to the date of judgment.* One of the clearest judicial statements on this is that of Lord Macnaughten in *Bwllfa and Merthyr Dare Steam Collieries Ltd v Pontypridd Waterworks Co,*[17] albeit that he was there dealing with an arbitrator's assessment of statutory compensation. He said:

> '... the arbitrator's duty is to determine the amount of compensation payable. In order to enable him to come to a just and true conclusion, it is his duty ... to avail himself of all information at hand at the time of making his award which may be laid before him. Why should he listen to conjecture on a matter which has become an accomplished fact?'[18]

For contractual pecuniary loss relevant events commonly arising subsequent to breach but prior to judgment include payments that the claimant has had to make to a third party because of the breach, or subsequent 'mitigation' of a loss, for example by obtaining another job having been wrongfully dismissed. In the field of personal injuries, illustrations include a deterioration of the claimant's medical condition after the initial injury, a wage-rise in the job that the claimant would have been in but for his injuries, and the death of the injured person (in a claim by the estate).

By CPR 52.11 the Court of Appeal (and by analogy the House of Lords) will not receive evidence which was not before the lower court 'unless it orders otherwise'. The appellate court therefore has the power to admit evidence of events occurring since the trial (as well as evidence of events prior to the trial).[19] But so as not to undermine finality in litigation, some restraint is exercised in using this power. As regards evidence of events occurring since trial, Lord Wilberforce laid down a few guidelines in *Mulholland v Mitchell:*[20]

> 'Negatively, fresh evidence ought not to be admitted when it bears upon matters falling within the field or area of uncertainty, in which the trial judge's estimate has previously been made. Positively, it may be admitted if some basic assumptions, common to both sides have clearly been falsified by subsequent events, particularly, if this has happened

---

17   [1903] AC 426.
18   [1903] AC 426 at 431.
19   The leading case in relation to the admission of fresh evidence of events prior to trial remains *Ladd v Marshall* [1954] 1 WLR 1489. See, since the Civil Procedure Rules 1998, *Hertfordshire Investments Ltd v Bubb* [2000] 1 WLR 2318.
20   [1971] AC 666.

by the act of the defendant.[1] Positively, too, it may be expected that courts will allow fresh evidence where to refuse it would affront common sense, or a sense of justice. All these are only non-exhaustive indications ...'[2]

A good example of where fresh evidence was admitted was *Lim Poh Choo v Camden and Islington Area Health Authority*.[3] There the trial judge had assessed damages on the assumption that the claimant would be looked after abroad by her mother but, since then, her mother had become ill and the claimant had been transferred to a nursing home in England. The House of Lords admitted such fresh evidence, so that the cost of future care was reassessed. Lord Scarman's comments are of interest. He said:

> 'The device of granting the parties leave to adduce fresh evidence at the appellate stages of litigation can, as in the present case, mitigate the injustices of a lump sum system by enabling the appellate courts to bring the award into line with what has happened since trial. But it is an unsatisfactory makeshift, and of dubious value in any case where the new facts are themselves in issue.'[4]

(2) Which value of money, property or services do the courts apply in assessing damages?

It is this question that is usually in mind when one refers to the date for the assessment of damages. The traditional general rule has been stated in one of two ways. Either that damages are assessed (that is the value is taken) at the date of the loss for which the damages are being awarded, or at the date of the accrual of the cause of action. So in *Philips v Ward*[5] Denning LJ said, 'The general principle of English law is that damages must be assessed as at the date when the damage occurs',[6] whereas in *Dodd Properties (Kent) v Canterbury City Council*[7] Donaldson LJ commented that '... the general rule is that damages fall to be assessed as at the date when the cause of action arose'.[8] The two normally correspond but where they do not, for example, as regards pecuniary losses in personal injury cases, the former seems to be the more accurate.

---

1   Eg *Murphy v Stone-Wallwork (Charlton) Ltd* [1969] 1 WLR 1023.
2   [1971] AC 666 at 679–680.
3   [1980] AC 174. See also *Curwen v James* [1963] 1 WLR 748; *Jenkins v Richard Thomas and Baldwin Ltd* [1966] 1 WLR 476; *Perry v Sidney Phillips & Son* [1982] 1 WLR 1297; cf *Hunt v Severs* [1993] 4 All ER 180, CA.
4   [1980] AC 174 at 183.
5   [1956] 1 WLR 471.
6   [1956] 1 WLR 471 at 474.
7   [1980] 1 WLR 433.
8   [1980] 1 WLR 433 at 457.

However, the modern trend, triggered by high inflation and a decline in the external value of sterling, has been to recognise exceptions to the rule. Indeed the exceptions are such that it is now arguable that assessment at the date of loss no longer represents the general rule. In examining the details of the law it is convenient to consider separately changes in the value of property or services or in the internal value of money and changes in the external value of money.

(a) Changes in the value of property or services or in the internal value of money

In the late 1960s and the 1970s, the major relevant factor shaping the law here was the dramatic fall in the internal value of money because of high inflation. But of course the value of property or services may additionally fluctuate because of ordinary market movements.

Looking first at non-pecuniary loss, it would seem that until fairly recently the traditional general rule applied, so that any internal fall in the value of money between loss and judgment was ignored. So, for example, in *Bishop v Cunard White Star Co Ltd v The Queen Mary*,[9] Hodson J did not think that the conventional figure of £200 laid down for loss of expectation of life in *Benham v Gambling*[10] should be altered despite the fall in the value of the pound since that decision and since the accident in the case. But the courts' approach has since changed. In *Yorkshire Electricity Board v Naylor*,[11] the conventional figure for loss of expectation of life was raised to £500 because of inflation. That head of loss has now been abolished but the same approach is shown in the application of the tariff system for loss of amenity and pain and suffering. There are several judicial statements recognising this. In *Mitchell v Mulholland (No 2)*[12] Widgery LJ said:

'No one doubts that an award of damages must reflect the value of the pound sterling at the date of the award and conventional sums attributed to, say the loss of an eye, have been adjusted in recent years on that account. Inflation which has reduced the value of money at the date of the award must, thus, be taken into account.'[13]

Again, in *Walker v John McLean & Sons Ltd*,[14] where the issue was the level of damages for non-pecuniary loss because of paraplegia, Cumming-Bruce LJ said:

9   [1950] P 240.
10 [1941] AC 157.
11 [1968] AC 529.
12 [1972] 1 QB 65.
13 [1972] 1 QB 65 at 83.
14 [1979] 1 WLR 760.

'We cannot distinguish any principle recognised in the law of damages which suggests that damages for non-pecuniary loss are in this regard different from damages for pecuniary loss. And in the case of damages for future pecuniary loss the award is assessed by reference to the value of money at the date of trial, and not some other lower sum calculated by reference to an earlier and higher value of the pound.'[15]

In *Wright v British Railways Board*[16] Lord Diplock, in deciding that interest on personal injury non-pecuniary loss should be kept at a low rate, regarded the judges as having a duty to assess damages for such loss '... in the money of the day at the date of the trial.'[17] Finally, in *Heil v Rankin*[18] the Court of Appeal said that, having reset the appropriate level of award for pain, suffering, and loss of amenity in personal injury cases, the standard approach of '[a]ppropriate guideline cases updated by the RPI [retail prices index] should be used to find the appropriate level of award.'[19] It rejected an argument that the more accurate way of updating for inflation was to apply the GDP (gross domestic product) or average earnings index.[20]

Although there is no express authority, it can be assumed that awards for other non-pecuniary loss, such as mental distress, similarly reflect the value of money at the date of judgment, rather than any earlier value. Analogously, the Lord Chancellor has used his discretion to keep the sum for bereavement under the Fatal Accidents Act 1976 (at present £10,000)[1] in line with inflation.

All such adjustments are necessary in order that the claimant be fully compensated for the loss he has suffered. Although money can never be perfect compensation for non-pecuniary loss, it is the best that the law can offer. If £X was the right compensation for a particular non-pecuniary loss, when £1 was worth 10% more than at the date of trial, it must be right to award £X + 10% for that loss at the later time.

Turning to pecuniary loss, past recurring pecuniary loss, such as loss of earnings and medical expenses in personal injury cases, is assessed, applying the general rule, according to the value of money at the date of the loss. So if £50 was spent on medical expenses, £50 will be awarded, irrespective of whether £50 is worth less at the date of judgment than at

---

15 [1979] 1 WLR 760 at 765.
16 [1983] 2 AC 773. See also *Cookson v Knowles* [1977] QB 913 at 921, CA; *Dodd Properties v Canterbury City Council* [1980] 1 All ER 928 at 939; *Housecroft* v *Burnett* [1986] 1 All ER 332 at 337.
17 [1983] 2 AC 773 at 782.
18 [2001] QB 272.
19 [2001] QB 272 at 312.
20 See also favouring continuation of updating by use of the RPI, the Law Commission Report, *Damages for Personal Injury: Non-Pecuniary Loss*, Law Com No 257 (1999) paras 3.171–3.176.
1 The sum was most recently raised from £7,500 to £10,000 by the Damages for Bereavement (Variation of Sum) Order 2002, SI 2002/644.

the date when spent. Future pecuniary loss has to be assessed according to the value of money at the date of judgment since there is no sound basis for choosing any other date. The question of whether future inflation is taken into account in assessing personal injury damages for future pecuniary loss is discussed in chapter 10 below.[2]

In relation to other pecuniary loss, the application of the traditional rule is shown, for example, in the prima facie rules for assessing damages under the Sale of Goods Act 1979, which take the market value of the goods at the date of the breach of contract, and by cases such as *General and Finance Facilities Ltd v Cooks Cars (Romford) Ltd*[3] and *Chubb Cash Ltd v John Crilley & Son*,[4] which show that for conversion, the value of the goods is generally to be assessed at the time of the conversion. On the other hand in several cases the traditional rule has been departed from.

In *Wroth v Tyler*,[5] for example, Megarry J was concerned to assess damages given in lieu of specific performance[6] for the breach of a contract to sell a bungalow. Applying the usual formula of market price minus contract price, the question arose whether the market price should be that at the date of the breach (£7,500) or that at the date of judgment (£11,500). Megarry J considered that where damages were being given in lieu of specific performance the usual date of breach rule did not necessarily apply, and here, since the claimants in view of their lack of funds could not have been expected to mitigate their loss by going into the market, the market price at the date of judgment was chosen. Furthermore, Megarry J indicated in dicta that even for ordinary common law damages the date of breach rule might not be inflexible.

In *Radford v De Froberville*[7] the defendant in breach of contract failed to build a wall. In assessing the claimant's damages one issue was the date at which the cost of building a wall should be assessed. Oliver J considered that the decision in *Wroth v Tyler* was equally applicable to ordinary common law damages, and indeed went so far as to say that '... the proper approach is to assess the damages at the date of the hearing unless it can be said that the plaintiff ought reasonably to have mitigated by seeking an alternative performance at an earlier date.'[8] Ultimately, however, Oliver J did not reach a decision as to which date was

---

2   Below, p 283.
3   [1963] 1 WLR 644.
4   [1983] 1 WLR 599. See also, eg *BBMB Finance (Hong Kong) Ltd v Eda Holdings Ltd* [1990] 1 WLR 409. See generally Tettenborn 'Conversion Damages Clarified' (1991) NLJ 452.
5   [1974] Ch 30.
6   Ie equitable damages; see below, ch 16.
7   [1977] 1 WLR 1262.
8   [1977] 1 WLR 1262 at 1286.

appropriate because there was insufficient evidence to enable him to decide whether the claimant should have mitigated earlier.

This move in favour of fixing the date for assessment more flexibly, so as to accord with when the claimant ought reasonably to have, or has, mitigated his loss has been authoritatively confirmed by the House of Lords in *Johnson v Agnew*,[9] where it was the vendor of land who was claimant in a situation where mortgagees had sold the land off at a low value subsequent to the date of breach. The vendor had initially obtained an order for specific performance but the defendant purchaser had delayed in complying with the order with the consequence that the vendor could not pay off his mortgage and his mortgagee became entitled to sell off his land. The vendor therefore now sought damages for the purchaser's breach of contract. Having emphasised that damages in lieu of specific performance and ordinary common law damages should be assessed on the same basis, Lord Wilberforce went on to say the following:

'The general principle for the assessment of damages is compensatory, ie that the innocent party is to be placed, so far as money can do it, in the same position as if the contract had been performed. Where the contract is one of sale, this principle normally leads to assessment of damages as at the date of breach – a principle recognised and embodied in s 51 of the Sale of Goods Act 1893. But this is not an absolute rule; if to follow it would give rise to injustice, the court has power to fix such other date as may be appropriate in the circumstances. In cases where a breach of contract for sale has occurred, and the innocent party reasonably continues to try to have the contract completed, it would to me appear more logical and just rather than tie him to the date of the original breach to assess damages as at the date when otherwise than by his default the contract is lost.'[10]

Accordingly, it was decided that the market value of the land should be assessed not at the date of the purchaser's original breach but rather when the vendor's reasonable attempts to have the contract enforced failed: ie when the mortgagees, as they were entitled to do, contracted to sell the land to another party hence making it impossible for the claimant vendor to comply with his side of the contract.

Johnson v Agnew was applied, and its approach very clearly summarised, in *Suleman v Shahsavari*.[11] This concerned actions by a prospective

---

9   [1980] AC 367.
10   [1980] AC 367 at 401.
11   [1988] 1 WLR 1181. This decision was applied in *Habton Farms v Nimmo* [2003] EWCA Civ 68, [2004] QB 1: in assessing a seller's damages (for breach of an agent's warranty of authority) the majority correctly refused to deduct from the agreed purchase price the value of the horse – which had died in the seller's possession four weeks after the failed sale – because the seller had not failed in its duty to mitigate by failing to resell the horse before it died.

purchaser of a house against the vendors for specific performance or, in the event of the contract for purchase being held invalid, against the vendors' solicitor for damages for breach of a warranty that he had authority to bind the vendors. Andrew Park QC, sitting as a deputy judge of the High Court, held that the contract was invalid because the vendors' solicitor had had no authority to sign the contract on their behalf. Specific performance against the vendors was therefore denied. The question then arose whether the damages for the solicitor's breach of warranty of authority should be calculated according to the difference between the contract price and the market price on the completion date (£9,500 plus interest) or the difference between the contract price and the market price at the date of judgment, nearly two-and-a-half years later, which was £29,500. On a straightforward application of *Johnson v Agnew* the judge awarded £29,500.

Again in *Naughton v O'Callaghan*[12] Waller J relied on *Johnson v Agnew* in awarding damages (for a negligent misrepresentation and breach of a contractual warranty) calculated according to the price paid for a horse (26,000 guineas) minus its value (£1,500) nearly two years later after it had proved a failure on the racecourse and hence lost most of its value. The claimants would not have bought the horse but for the vendor's misrepresentation as to its pedigree and had they discovered the error straightaway they would have sold the horse at its then value. Moreover, and in line with the crucial importance to the date of assessment of the duty to mitigate, it is clear that the claimants could not reasonably have mitigated their loss until they discovered the error nearly two years after purchase.

Similarly in *Smith New Court Securities Ltd v Scrimgeour Vickers (Asset Management) Ltd*,[13] in an action for deceit, the claimant was held entitled to the difference in value between the contract price paid for shares and the price for which the claimant had sold them several months later. As the share price had plummeted, that difference was far higher at the date of resale than at the date when the claimant had bought the shares. The House of Lords stressed that assessment at the later date was necessary to give the claimant full compensation; that the flexibility introduced by cases such as *Johnson v Agnew* would often allow assessment for the tort of deceit at a date later than that of the original transaction (which was

---

12   [1990] 3 All ER 191. Although this decision seems correct, it is arguable that, applying the controversial *SAAMCO* principle – see above, pp 109–122 – damages might be restricted to the difference between the horse's value had the representation been true and its then actual value (ie £26,000 – £23,500 = £3,500).

13   [1997] AC 254.

'only prima facie the right date');[14] and that here the claimant had not acted unreasonably in holding onto the shares for several months and then reselling them.

In *Dodd Properties v Canterbury City Council*[15] a similar approach was adopted in relation to the time at which the cost of repairing damaged property should be assessed in an action for tortious negligence or nuisance. Having said that the general rule was that the cost of repairs should be assessed at the date of the tort, the Court of Appeal went on to emphasise that this was not an inflexible rule, and that here the cost of repairs should be assessed at the date of the hearing. The reason for preferring this later date was that, having regard to all the circumstances and in particular the claimant's impecuniosity, it was the date when it was first reasonable for the claimant to have undertaken the repairs.

The same decision was reached in the closely analogous case of *Alcoa Minerals of Jamaica Inc v Herbert Broderick*.[16] In the light of *Johnson v Agnew*[17] it was held that the normal rule of assessment at the date of the cause of action could be departed from. Here the cost of repairing property damaged because of the defendant's nuisance (which had increased dramatically because of inflation in Jamaica) was assessed as at the date of the first instance judgment because the claimant, who could not afford to pay for the repairs, had acted reasonably in waiting for that judgment. The claimant needed to be sure that the defendant would pay or be liable before he carried out the repairs.

It should further be noted that apart from these important departures from the traditional general rule, the earlier decision in *Sachs v Miklos*,[18] while leaving the date of conversion as the date for assessing the value of the chattel, apparently accepted that subsequent increases in the market value of the converted chattel could be recovered as consequential loss. The defendant, having gratuitously stored the claimant's goods from 1940 to 1943, twice wrote to the claimant requesting their removal. Receiving no reply he sold them for £15. In 1946 the claimant demanded the goods. The defendant tendered the £15 but the market value, having risen to £115, the claimant sought, and was seemingly held able to recover, the extra £100 as consequential damages for conversion

---

14   [1997] AC 254 at 284 (per Lord Steyn).
15   [1980] 1 WLR 433. See also *Forster v Silvermere Golf & Equestrian Centre Ltd* (1981) 42 P & CR 255 (breach of contract).
16   [2002] 1 AC 371, PC; see above, p 145, n 4.
17   [1980] AC 367.
18   [1948] 2 KB 23. See also *Empresa Exportadora De Azucar v Industria Azucarera Nacional, The Playa Larga* [1983] 2 Lloyd's Rep 171, 181; *IBL Ltd v Coussens* [1991] 2 All ER 133 (conversion damages for value of cars – under what would previously have been an action for detinue – to be assessed at a date fixed flexibly, although prima facie at the date of judgment).

(on the assumption that he had never received the letters). In essence this again was a departure from the general rule albeit by a different route.

Waddams criticises the modern more flexible approach and considers that it would be preferable to stick more rigidly to assessment at (or shortly after) the date of the loss.[19] He offers several arguments in support: postponement of assessment hampers desirable finality to litigation; it encourages the claimant to be inefficient; interest awarded on the damages acts as an adequate counter to inflation; and assessment at an early date tends to reduce the total cost of litigation. But finality of litigation in the sense, seemingly intended, of litigation not going on beyond trial is no more achieved by a date of loss than a date of trial assessment; and the second argument is countered by the fact that the courts would consider that a claimant who had unreasonably delayed allowing values to rise could have mitigated earlier, and its damages would therefore be assessed at that earlier date.[20] While it is true that interest rates do reflect inflation, so that assessment of damages at an early date plus full interest will often achieve much the same result as assessment at a later date plus reduced or no interest until that date,[1] interest rates reflect price rises only very roughly and clearly they are not attuned to fluctuations (whether up or down) in the value of particular property. Finally, although rigid adherence to the date of loss rule may save litigation costs, because that approach is clear and simple (but without empirical data the extent of the cost-saving is unclear) this is at the expense of effecting true compensation. Tossing a coin is the cheapest way of deciding a dispute but it hardly represents justice.

The above discussion on pecuniary loss has assumed that it is advantageous for the claimant to have damages assessed at a later date than that of loss. But what if it is disadvantageous? Say, for example, the claimant is a buyer and that the value of property has fallen since the date of the vendor's breach; or that the defendant has converted the claimant's goods, which have since fallen in value. In these situations, assessment at the date of the breach of contract or conversion would be more advantageous to the claimant than assessment at a later date. Although the few cases on this[2] assess damages at the date of loss, they do predate the recent developments. It is submitted that logical symmetry, avoidance of overcompensation, and adherence to the duty to

---

19   'The Date for the Assessment of Damages' (1981) 97 LQR 445; *The Law of Damages* (3rd edn, 1997) paras 1.650–1.1100, 7.60–7.70.
20   As in *Malhotra v Choudhury* [1980] Ch 52.
1   For the relationship between date for assessment and interest, see below, pp 352–354.
2   *Aronson v Mologa Holzindustrie A/G Leningrad* (1927) 32 Com Cas 276; *Solloway v McLaughlin* [1938] AC 247.

mitigate dictate that the same flexibility should be adopted as where assessment at a later date is to the claimant's advantage. Waddams again disagrees and in particular focuses on a situation where the claimant buyer or owner of converted goods may wish to establish that he would have mitigated against a fall in the value of the property by, for example, selling off the goods at an early date. He writes, 'The cost of inquiry into how the plaintiff would have used his property had the defendant not deprived the plaintiff of it outweighs the cost of overcompensation ...'[3] Once more therefore Waddams is expressing a preference for rough-and-ready often inaccurate compensation produced by rigid adherence to the date of loss rule as against the true compensation produced by the more flexible approach, on the ground that the former is much cheaper, albeit that no empirical data is offered to indicate the extent of the cost-saving.

(b) Changes in the external value of money – foreign money liabilities

It should be stressed at the outset that the law here applies to the award of an agreed sum,[4] as well as to damages. Indeed the important legal change made in 1975 was initially concerned solely with the former remedy. In order to provide a coherent exposition, the law will be looked at as a whole, rather than simply examining the damages aspect of it.

The traditional assessment date rule meant that the conversion into sterling of agreed sums payable or damages calculable in foreign money was made according to the rates applicable at the time of the loss.[5] Also of relevance in understanding this area of the law was the rule that a money judgment had to be expressed in sterling.[6] The Law Commission[7] has referred to these two rules taken together as the sterling-breach-date rule, although sterling-loss-date is, strictly speaking, more accurate.

The problem with that rule was that, where the value of sterling had changed in relation to the relevant foreign currency between the date of loss and the date of judgment, the claimant was left under- or over-compensated. This began to bother the courts when sterling weakened as a currency, so that claimants were being undercompensated.[8] An example will make this clearer. Say D owes C 1,000 units of foreign

---

3   *The Law of Damages* (3rd edn, 1997) para 1.660.
4   Below, ch 19.
5   Eg *Di Fernando v Simon, Smits & Co* [1920] 3 KB 409 (contractual damages); *SS Celia (Owners) v SS Volturno (Owners)* [1921] 2 AC 544 (tort damages); *Tomkinson v First Pennsylvania Banking and Trusts Co* [1961] AC 1007 (agreed sum).
6   Eg *Manners v Pearson & Son* [1898] 1 Ch 581 at 587.
7   Report No 124 *Private International Law – Foreign Money Liabilities* (1983) Cmnd 9064.
8   As Briggs has written in *The Conflict of Laws* (2002) at p 37, 'This [rule] began to imperil the role of England as a centre for commercial litigation once the currency began to devalue.'

currency and at the date of loss those units are worth £100 (ie £1 = 10 units) but at the date of judgment they are worth £200 (ie £1 = 5 units). In other words, the value of sterling has declined. Clearly if C is given only £100 it is undercompensated. But assessment at the date of loss will overcompensate C if the value of sterling has increased. Say the units at the date of judgment are worth £50 (ie £1 = 20 units). By being given £100 C is overcompensated.

Given this defect with conversion at the date of loss, what were the alternatives? One obvious alternative was to convert at the date of judgment. But this would leave injustice where the value of sterling changed between judgment and actual payment of the agreed sum or damages. The ideal solution was therefore for conversion to be made at the rates prevailing at the date of payment. But the rule that judgment had to be in sterling was here a stumbling-block, for it was very difficult to see how one could have the judgment expressed in sterling, while converting into sterling at the date of payment. On the other hand, if judgments could be expressed in foreign currency this would free the way for the ideal solution of conversion into sterling at the date of payment: ie the order could then be for the defendant to pay the claimant X units of the foreign currency or the sterling equivalent at the time of payment. It should be stressed that for two reasons to allow judgment in a foreign currency would not prevent the need for a conversion date rule: first, English execution necessarily yields value in sterling; secondly, there seems no reason why a defendant should not have the option of satisfying an English court's judgment in sterling.

Miliangos v George Frank (Textiles) Ltd[9] is the classic case in which the House of Lords departed from the 'sterling-breach-date' rule and held that for some foreign agreed sums a judgment can be expressed in foreign currency, and that conversion into sterling can be made at the date of payment, meaning the date of actual payment or, if earlier, the date on which the court authorises enforcement of the judgment. The facts concerned the non-payment of a contract price for yarn. The money of account (ie the currency by which the debtor's obligation was measured) and the money of payment (ie the currency in which the payment was to be tendered) was Swiss francs, and the proper law of the contract was Swiss. The defendants were ordered to pay in Swiss francs or the equivalent in sterling at the time of payment.

Lord Wilberforce explained that because of the instability of sterling:

'... instead of a situation in which changes of relative value occurring between the "breach date" and the date of judgment or payment being the exception, so that a rule

9   [1976] AC 443.

which did not provide for this case could be generally fair, this situation is now the rule. So the search for a formula to deal with it becomes urgent in the interest of justice.'[10]

But Lord Wilberforce confined his departure from the long-established rule to agreed sums: 'In my opinion, it should be open for future discussion whether the rule applying to money obligations, which can be a simple rule should apply as regards claims for damages for breach of contract or for a tort.'[11] However, the policy underlying *Miliangos* does not differ whether one is talking of agreed sums or damages, and in *Services Europe Atlantique Sud v Stockholms Rederiaktiebolag SVEA, The Folias*[12] and *The Despina R,*[13] *Miliangos* was extended to claims for contractual and tortious damages respectively. It is therefore now clear law that a foreign currency liability should be expressed in foreign currency and that the date for conversion into sterling is the date of payment.

Having said that, there were some comments made by Lord Goff in the House of Lords in *The Texaco Melbourne*[14] that are, at first sight, puzzling. The case applied *The Folias* with the central question being whether the appropriate currency for contractual damages for breach of a contract for the carriage of oil between two Ghanaian ports was the US dollar or the Ghanaian cedi. This made a huge difference to the claimants because the Ghanaian currency had collapsed catastrophically since the breach of contract and, by the time of trial, it was worth less than 1% (against the US dollar) of what it had been worth at the date of breach. The House of Lords decided that, nevertheless, the appropriate currency – the currency in which the claimants felt their loss – was Ghanaian cedis essentially because this was the currency in which they carried on their business and was the currency they would have received for reselling the fuel oil. That decision was plainly correct. But, in the course of his speech, Lord Goff said the following:

'We have at all times to bear in mind that fluctuations in the relevant currency between the date of breach and the date of judgment are not taken into account. The award of damages is assessed as at the date of breach ... Delay between the date of breach and the date of judgment is compensated for by an award of interest ... But, as I have said, no account is taken of fluctuations in the relevant currency as against other currencies between the date of breach and the date of judgment.'[15]

---

10 [1976] AC 443 at 463.
11 [1976] AC 443 at 468.
12 [1979] AC 685.
13 [1979] AC 685.
14 *A-G of the Republic of Ghana v Texaco Overseas Tankships Ltd, The Texaco Melbourne* [1994] I Lloyd's Rep 473; noted by Knott 'The Currency of Damages in Contract' [1994] LMCLQ 311.
15 [1994] 1 Lloyd's Rep 473 at 476.

At first sight, this passage may be thought to contradict the departure in *Miliangos* from the sterling-breach-date rule. But that is not so.[16] The point flowing from *Miliangos* about conversion at the date of payment not breach meant that any conversion from Ghanaian cedis to sterling would be made according to the value of sterling at the date of judgment or payment not the date of breach. Rather what Lord Goff was concerned with was that, in deciding the amount of damages, expressed in Ghanaian cedis, the court should take the value of the oil at the date of the breach of contract in accordance with the normal (albeit, as we have seen, not inflexible) rule for the date of assessing the value of goods.

It is important to realise that, although the *Miliangos* reform was triggered by claimants being undercompensated where sterling had declined in value since the date of loss, it was not solely concerned with preventing undercompensation. Rather it was concerned that judgment should be expressed in the most appropriate currency, whether this was to the benefit or detriment of the claimant in comparison with the sterling-breach-date rule. Thus in *Miliangos* Lord Wilberforce explained: 'The creditor has no concern with pounds sterling: for him what matters is that a Swiss franc *for good or ill* should remain a Swiss franc.'[17] And in *The Despina R*, he said:

'To fix such a plaintiff with sterling commits him to the risk of changes in the value of a currency with which he has no connection; to award him a sum in the (appropriate) currency ... gives him exactly what he has lost and commits him only to the risk of changes in the value of that currency.'[18]

It follows that where the appropriate foreign currency loses value in relation to sterling, the claimant should not be able to resort to the sterling-breach-date rule. This point has been firmly expressed by the Law Commission:

'Although there is little authority on the point it is clear that to allow the plaintiff to seek judgment in sterling in the case of a foreign-currency claim would be contrary to the principle in *Miliangos* ... [therefore] a plaintiff should not be able to obtain judgment in sterling in the case of the enforcement of a claim which ought properly to be expressed in a foreign currency.'[19]

However, the Law Commission has accepted that, where the claimant can show that it would have converted the appropriate foreign currency into sterling, and thereby reaped the benefit of the increase in sterling's

---

16   See *McGregor on Damages* (17th edn, 2003) paras 16–043–16–045.
17   [1976] AC 443 at 466 (italics inserted).
18   [1979] AC 685 at 697.
19   Report No 124, para 3.9. See also para 2.5.

value, it should be able to recover damages for such exchange losses, subject to remoteness.[20] This was the basis of the Law Commission's interpretation of the difficult case of *Ozalid Group (Export) Ltd v African Continental Bank Ltd.*[1] Here the defendant had delayed in paying a contract price of US dollars to the claimants. By exchange control regulations the claimants were obliged to convert US dollars into sterling and would have done so if the money had been paid. During the period of delay sterling rose in value against the dollar. The claimants sought the difference in value between sterling at the time payment should have been made and when it was made. Donaldson J held that the claimants were entitled to that amount.

The Law Commission's interpretation of the decision was that damages were being awarded for non-remote exchange losses consequent on the defendant's delay in making payment. This was therefore an example of the *Wadsworth v Lydall*[2] 'special damages' exception to the *London, Chatham & Dover Rly Co v South Eastern Rly Co*[3] rule that no damages can be awarded for breach of an obligation to pay money. But an alternative interpretation was that the appropriate currency was not US dollars at all but was sterling; and that where a claimant's loss was really suffered in sterling rather than a foreign currency – and that sterling loss was not too remote – conversion according to the sterling-breach-date rule was appropriate.

Both interpretations seem acceptable: indeed they are simply different legal analyses of the same ideas. The crucial common point is that the claimant does not have a free choice to have the sterling-breach-date rule applied; rather it must have suffered a non-remote loss of sterling.

Some commentators criticise the *Miliangos* reform. Waddams, for example, suggests that it neglects the fact that many claimants can perfectly well mitigate against a decline in sterling.[4] But surely there is nothing in *Miliangos* to undermine normal mitigation principles so that, if the defendant can show a failure to mitigate, the claimant would not be entitled to full loss assessed according to *Miliangos*. More forceful are the arguments first, that introducing flexibility as against the certainty of the sterling-breach-date rule is paid for by higher litigation costs; and secondly, that the injustice to claimants of the sterling-breach-date rule has been overstated, since interest rates will generally increase in

---

20 Report No 124, paras 2.34–2.35, 3.58–3.61.
1   [1979] 2 Lloyd's Rep 231; Cf *International Minerals & Chemical Corpn v Karl O Helm AG* [1986] 1 Lloyd's Rep 81 at 105.
2   [1981] 1 WLR 598. Above, pp 153–155, esp n 7.
3   [1893] AC 429.
4   *The Law of Damages* (3rd edn, 1997) paras 7.250–7.300.

response to a decline in the currency's value; hence the sterling-breach-date rule plus interest at sterling rates will produce much the same result as expressing judgment in foreign currency, converted at the date of payment, plus interest at the rate for that foreign currency.[5] In similar vein, Waddams argues that, as regards an increase in the home currency's value, it is better to risk overcompensation than to encourage costly investigation of how the claimant would have used the foreign currency.[6] Analogous arguments have been considered earlier[7] and again it is submitted that the courts are right to effect true compensation rather than favouring a less costly approach (and the extent of the cost-saving is unclear) of rough-and-ready justice.

Finally, while not concerning the date for assessment as such, it is convenient to consider briefly two further questions of central importance. When is sterling considered a less appropriate currency than a foreign currency? And where more than one foreign currency is involved, which is the more appropriate foreign currency? The answers given by English law[8] can be indicated in five points.

(i)   For the judgment to be expressed in foreign currency the loss in question must be pecuniary loss. As laid down in *Hoffman v Sofaer*[9] non-pecuniary loss, such as pain and suffering and loss of amenity in a personal injury action, does not raise foreign currency problems; rather such a loss is calculated and expressed in sterling whatever the claimant's nationality or wherever the injury or loss occurred.

(ii)   In *Miliangos*, Lord Wilberforce confined departure from the sterling-breach-date rule to where the proper law of the contract was

---

5   Bowles and Whelan 'Law Commission Working Paper No 80, Private International Law Foreign Money Liabilities' (1982) 45 MLR 434 at 442, 444. For the relationship between foreign currency judgments and interest, see below, p 354.
6   *The Law of Damages* (3rd edn, 1997) paras 7.180–7.200.
7   See above, p 192.
8   If one applies the traditional approach in the conflict of laws, English law, as the *lex fori*, presumably applies to determine the appropriate currency in which judgment can be expressed because that is an issue concerning 'procedure'. That is so, irrespective of the law applicable to the contract or tort (or other cause of action) in question. But for breach of contract that approach may have been affected by the obscurely-worded Contracts (Applicable) Law Act 1990, Sch 1, Art 10(1)(c) which lays down that the law applicable to a contract shall govern 'within the limits of the powers conferred on the court by its procedural law, the consequences of breach, including the assessment of damages in so far as it is governed by rules of law.' In working out what is the money of account or payment (see above, p 194 for explanation of these terms) see Art 10(1)(a) and Art 10(2). See also, for non-contractual causes of action, the proposed Rome II Regulation, Article 11. For criticism of the traditional *lex fori* approach as regards remedies, see Briggs 'Conflict of Laws and Commercial Remedies' in *Commercial Remedies* (eds Burrows and Peel, 2003) pp 271–286.
9   [1982] 1 WLR 1350.

foreign, but in subsequent cases *Miliangos* has been applied to contracts whose proper law was English.[10]

(iii)   As regards agreed sums where the money of account and payment are of the same foreign money, as in *Miliangos* itself, it is clearly appropriate for judgment to be expressed in that foreign currency. Lord Wilberforce confined departure from the old approach to this situation, but in *Veflings Rederi A/S v President of India, The Bellami*,[11] Donaldson J at first instance held that where the money of payment and account are of different countries, and even if the money of payment is English, judgment can be expressed in the currency of the money of account.

(iv)   As laid down in *The Folias*,[12] for contract damages, unless there is a 'currency of the contract' – that is, an appropriate currency expressly laid down in the contract – the appropriate currency will be that in which the loss was felt or which most truly expresses the claimant's loss. This may or may not be the currency in which the loss first and immediately arose and depends on ordinary principles of proof and remoteness.

(v)   A similar approach to that adopted in *The Folias* was applied for tort damages in *The Despina R.*[13] The only main difference is that with no contract in play, the currency of the contract is obviously not a possibility.

3. TAXATION

The question here is, in assessing damages for the gains that the claimant has been prevented from making by the defendant's tort or breach of contract, do the courts deduct income tax[14] that the claimant would have paid on those gains?

10   *Barclays Bank International Ltd v Levin Bros (Bradford) Ltd* [1977] QB 270; *Federal Commerce and Navigation Co v Tradax Export, The Maratha Envoy* [1977] QB 324; *Veflings Rederi A/S a President of India* [1979] 1 WLR 59; *The Folias* [1979] AC 685.

11   [1978] 1 WLR 982. On appeal CA held that US dollar was money of account and payment: [1979] 1 WLR 59.

12   Followed in, eg *President of India v Taygetos Shipping Co SA, The Agenor* [1985] 1 Lloyd's Rep 155 (cf *President of India v Lips Maritime Corpn* [1985] 2 Lloyd's Rep 180 at 187–188 per Staughton J, [1988] AC 395, 426, HL); *Société Française Bunge SA v Belcan NV, The Federal Huron* [1985] 3 All ER 378; *Metaalhandel JA Magnus BV v Ardfields Transport Ltd* [1988] 1 Lloyd's Rep 197; *A-G of the Republic of Ghana v Texaco Overseas Tankships Ltd, The Texaco Melbourne* [1994] 1 Lloyd's Rep 473.

13   Followed in *The Lash Atlantico* [1987] 2 Lloyd's Rep 114; *The Transoceanica Francesca and Nicos V* [1987] 2 Lloyd's Rep 155.

14   This includes corporation tax which is a tax on a company's 'income'. For discussion of capital gains tax, explaining why it does not in practice raise problems in relation to damages, see *McGregor on Damages* (17th edn, 2003) paras 14–062–14–076.

(1) The *Gourley* principle

Applying the usual compensatory aims it would seem that tax that would have been paid on the gains should be deducted since, if liabilities which the claimant would have otherwise incurred are ignored, he will be put into a better position than he would have been if the contract had been performed or the tort not committed.

However, until 1955, it was considered that, other than in Fatal Accidents Act actions,[15] tax considerations should be ignored. But in that year in the now famous case of *British Transport Commission v Gourley*,[16] the House of Lords held that, in assessing damages in a personal injuries action for loss of earnings, the tax which the claimant would have paid if he had been working for those earnings must be deducted. In Lord Goddard's words:

> 'I cannot see on what principle of justice the defendants should be called upon to pay [the plaintiff] more than he would have received, if he had remained able to carry out his duties ... Damages which have to be paid for personal injuries are not punitive, still less are they a reward. They are simply compensation.'[17]

The *Gourley* principle has since been applied to actions for wrongful dismissal,[18] for trespass and conversion[19] and for libel,[20] and it can therefore be regarded as a general principle in assessing compensatory damages.

In *Gourley* itself, however, it was emphasised that the deduction should apply only if the damages themselves were not to be taxed, on the basis that otherwise the claimant would be taxed twice.[1] This has created particular difficulties in wrongful dismissal actions, where awards of damages of less than a certain amount, at present £30,000, are exempt from income tax, whereas awards over that amount are taxable. The approach traditionally adopted is that where the award (not having applied *Gourley*) is less than £30,000, *Gourley* must then be applied to reduce the damages, but that where the award of damages (not having applied *Gourley*) is greater than £30,000, *Gourley* must be applied to £30,000 of it but not to the excess.[2] But more recently, Sheen J in *Shove v*

---

15   *Zinovieff v British Transport Commission* (1954) Times, 1 April.
16   [1956] AC 185.
17   [1956] AC 185 at 207–208.
18   *Beach & Reed Corrugated Cases Ltd* [1956] 1 WLR 807.
19   *Hall & Co Ltd v Pearlberg* [1956] 1 WLR 244.
20   *Rubber Improvement Ltd v Daily Telegraph Ltd* [1964] AC 234.
1   There was therefore no *Gourley* deduction in *Deeny v Gooda Walker Ltd* [1996] 1 WLR 426, HL (names at Lloyd's bringing claims in the tort of negligence for pure economic loss).
2   *Parsons v BNM Laboratories Ltd* [1964] 1 QB 95, and particularly *Bold v Brough, Nicholson & Hall Ltd* [1964] 1 WLR 201.

Downs Surgical plc[3] adopted a more satisfactory approach. He took the view that whether the damages are themselves to be taxed or not, one should apply *Gourley* to work out first the claimant's loss, net of tax. The damages award is then the sum, taking into account the tax to be paid on the damages, which ensures that the claimant receives that amount of net loss. So on the facts of the case the claimant's net loss, applying *Gourley* was £60,729. To ensure that the claimant recovered that loss, given that the damages were themselves taxable, the claimant was awarded £83,477.

A similarly welcome move towards greater accuracy, in preference to the application of a blunt rule of there being no *Gourley* deduction if the damages are themselves taxable, was taken by Judge Humphrey Lloyd QC in *Amstrad plc v Seagate Technology Inc.*[4] Contractual damages were being awarded for loss of profits from the sale of some 67,500 computers. The corporation tax on the damages when received would be at a rate of 31%. But the corporation tax on the profits, had they been received at the proper time, would have been at rates of 33%–35%. A *Gourley* deduction was made so as to ensure that the claimants were not overcompensated by the lowering of the tax rate. Although the difference in rates was small in percentage terms, in real terms the difference was some £3.4 million. That is, the damages were subject to £3.4 million less tax than the lost profits would have been.

(2) Is the *Gourley* principle satisfactory?

It should not be thought that the *Gourley* principle has been accepted as satisfactory by everyone. On the contrary, there has been a good deal of criticism of it and the Canadian courts,[5] for example, have refused to follow it.

Apart from the clearly unsatisfactory punitive view that the defendant does not deserve to be benefited by a reduction in damages, three main arguments have been put against deducting tax.[6] First, it means that judges and practitioners, who are not tax experts, are required to argue and decide complex questions of how much tax the claimant would have paid, and on the *Shove* approach, what grossed-up amount is now needed to ensure that the claimant is compensated for his loss net of tax. But if

---

3 [1984] 1 All ER 7. See also *Stewart v Glentaggart* 1963 SLT 119.
4 (1998) 86 BLR 34.
5 *R v Jennings* (1966) 57 DLR (2d) 644; *Cunningham v Wheeler* (1994) 113 DLR (4th) 1, 21–3. See also *North Island Wholesale Groceries Ltd v Hewin* [1982] 2 NZLR 176. But in *Australia Atlas Tiles v Briers* (1978) 144 CLR 202, which had rejected *Gourley*, was overturned by *Cullen v Trappell* (1980) 146 CLR 1.
6 Ogus *The Law of Damages* (1973) pp 113–115.

Gourley has justice on its side, such an argument of impracticality can hardly be regarded as a good reason for not applying it. Moreover, there has been little evidence post-*Gourley* of lawyers being unable to cope with its consequences, and nowadays there is, in any event, greater legal education in tax matters.

Secondly, *Gourley* means that the Inland Revenue loses tax revenue that it would otherwise have gained. But as this was also true pre-*Gourley* it is not an argument against *Gourley* in itself but is rather an argument for legislation to be introduced ordering tax to be paid on all damages awards.[7] In any case, the point does not necessarily hold true; for example, a defendant employer may have replaced the injured or dismissed claimant employee.

A third argument is that without further adjustment *Gourley* would leave the claimant undercompensated. Damages awards are reduced where the claimant would not otherwise have had a capital sum to invest. But if he does invest the damages he will have to pay tax on the investment income. The pre-*Gourley* approach was a rough-and-ready way of taking this tax liability into account. So Waddams writes:

'The Canadian rule of ignoring income tax is ... justified as a short-cut to the complex and uncertain process of deducting first, the tax that the plaintiff would have had to pay on his income, and then adding back the tax the plaintiff will presumably have to pay on the income from the investment of the award.'[8]

But the objection to this short-cut is that it cannot hope to be as accurate as applying *Gourley* and also taking account of the presumed tax payable on the investment income. That standard rate tax will be paid on investment income is assumed in the fixing of the appropriate multiplier for assessing future pecuniary loss. In *Hodgson v Trapp*[9] the House of Lords in overruling *Thomas v Wignall*[10] held that, normally, there should be no increase in the multiplier to take account of higher rate tax payable on the investment income from large awards (ie there should be no '*Gourley* in reverse' as Lord Reid termed it in *Taylor v O'Connor*).[11] The main reasons given for this were the uncertainty of future higher tax rates and that it would be rare for the investment income from damages for future pecuniary loss alone to attract higher rate tax. But, as clarified by Lord Steyn in *Wells v Wells*,[12] Lord Oliver's speech in *Hodgson v Trapp* is

---

7   This is strongly advocated by Bishop and Kay 'Taxation and Damages: the Rule in Gourley's Case' (1987) 103 LQR 211.
8   *The Law of Damages* (3rd edn, 1997) para 3.980.
9   [1989] AC 807.
10 [1987] QB 1098.
11 [1971] AC 115 at 129.
12 [1999] 1 AC 345 at 388.

best interpreted as accepting that there will be exceptional cases in which the courts may accept that a lower discount rate should be applied, and hence a higher multiplier chosen, where it is likely that higher rate tax will be payable on the income from a large award.

It is submitted, therefore, that *Gourley* should remain good law. There is little force in objections put to it and, despite the greater complexity involved in the assessment of damages, the *Gourley* principle adheres to the compensatory aims and is fully justified.

Section two

Damages for the different types of loss

Chapter 9

Pecuniary loss (except consequent on personal injury, death or loss of reputation)

Breach of contract damages are normally sought and awarded for this type of loss. It is therefore not surprising that there is a host of different ways of analysing and subdividing it. Here the approach adopted will be to divide between basic pecuniary loss, which will be primarily concentrated on, and which focuses on the benefit to which the claimant was contractually entitled and of which he has been wholly or partially deprived by the defendant's breach, and additional pecuniary loss.[1]

On the other hand, for torts, where the central focus is on wrongful interference rather than a failure to benefit, it has been considered more helpful to adopt a division which gives some flavour of the interference in question. This type of tortious pecuniary loss is therefore examined under three heads:[2] damage to property, including destruction; wrongful interference with goods or land, other than causing property damage; and pure economic loss.[3]

1.   BREACH OF CONTRACT – BASIC PECUNIARY LOSS

(1) The content of the promise

It is crucial to keep constantly in mind what the defendant contractually promised, so as not to put the claimant in a better or worse economic position than if the contract had been performed.

---

1   This is similar to Farnsworth's analysis in 'Legal Remedies for Breach of Contract' (1970) 70 Col LR 1145, 1160–1175. See also the distinction between basic or normal, and consequential, pecuniary loss drawn in *McGregor on Damages* (17th edn, 2003) paras 1–035–1–040, 2–002–2–039.
2   Other examples of such pecuniary loss are the expenses of gaining release from a false imprisonment in *Prichet v Boevey* (1833) 1 Cr & M 775, and the legal costs of defending a malicious prosecution in *Savile v Roberts* (1699) 1 Ld Raym 374 and *Berry v British Transport Commission* [1962] 1 QB 306.
3   A specialised issue, which is not discussed below, is whether a company and a shareholder in that company can both recover for economic loss caused by a breach of duty (whether in contract or tort) to both the company and the shareholder. The leading case is *Johnson v Gore Wood & Co* [2002] 2 AC 1, HL. See also Mitchell 'Shareholders' Claims for Reflective Loss' (2004) 120 LQR 457.

A good illustration of how easy it is to drift away from the basic compensatory principle is where a surveyor contracts to survey a house for a prospective house purchaser. Subject to any express term, the surveyor will be taken to have promised contractually to use reasonable care in making the survey. He will not be taken to have warranted either that the house is worth any particular price or that it is free from any defects other than those reported. It follows that if in reliance on the survey the purchaser goes ahead and buys the house and it transpires that the survey was made in breach of contract, because the surveyor did not report reasonably discoverable defects, the aim of damages will be to put the claimant into as good a position as if reasonable care had been used in making the survey and the report; they are not aimed at putting the claimant into any (other) warranted position. There are two possible positions the claimant may argue that he would have been in if reasonable care had been used in making the survey and report. Either he would not have bought the house at all or he would have bought it but for less than he paid. Applying the former, the claimant's basic loss will be the purchase price paid minus the house's actual value. Applying the latter, the basic loss will be the same if one assumes that the claimant would have paid the actual value of the house. Alternatively, the court might take the cost of repairs as a convenient starting point for the deduction in price the purchaser would actually have made from the purchase price if he had known of the defects.

The principles have been clearly and correctly applied by the Court of Appeal in cases such as *Perry v Sidney Phillips & Son*[4] and *Watts v Morrow*[5] but in other cases concerning negligent surveys the court's failure to reason from the basic compensatory principle is shown not so much by wrong decisions but rather by statements suggesting that damages are to be calculated according to the warranted value or condition of the property minus its actual value.[6]

One might argue that the effect of the controversial *SAAMCO* principle is that the house purchaser could not recover more than the difference between the value of the house, had the report been accurate, and its actual value. But even if that were the law (and it has been argued above that the *SAAMCO* principle is flawed)[7] it is submitted that one should regard *SAAMCO* as a restriction (because of the 'scope of the

4   [1982] 1 WLR 1297.
5   [1991] 1 WLR 1421. See similarly *Swingcastle Ltd v Alastair Gibson (a firm)* [1991] 2 AC 223; *Gardner v Marsh & Parsons* [1997] 1 WLR 489; *Patel v Hooper & Jackson* [1999] 1 WLR 1792.
6   Eg *Philips v Ward* [1956] 1 WLR 471 at 473; *Simple Simon Catering Ltd v Binstock Miller & Co* (1973) 117 Sol Jo 529.
7   Above, pp 109–122.

duty') on the damages that would otherwise be awarded applying the compensatory aim. One must first apply the compensatory aim correctly by bearing in mind what the defendant contractually promised.

Another good illustration of the need to keep constantly in mind what the defendant contractually promised – so as to avoid awarding an erroneous measure of compensatory damages – is provided by breach of an agent's warranty of authority. This occurs where an agent, who does not have its principal's authority (for example, to conclude a contract), contractually warrants to the claimant that it does have that authority. If the claimant sues for breach of the agent's contractual warranty of authority, the aim, bearing in mind the contractual promise, must be to put the claimant into as good a position as if the agent did have the principal's authority. And if the agent did have that authority, the claimant would, for example, have had a valid contract with the principal so that the damages against the agent must ultimately be based on the claimant's position had there been a valid contract between the principal and the claimant.[8]

(2) Difference in value or cost of cure

There is often a choice between awarding the difference in value or the cost of cure. The former directly awards the claimant the financial advantage it has lost by being deprived, partially or wholly, of the benefit to which it was contractually entitled. The cost of cure, on the other hand, seeks to award the claimant the additional financial sacrifice it would have to incur to put itself into as good a position as if it had received the benefit to which it was contractually entitled.

In many situations the difference in value is in practice the only possible measure because no replacement benefit is available at any cost: for example, the party in breach may alone be capable of performing the contract or the delay may have made the performance impossible. Where both are possible measures, which will be awarded is a central question of interest and will be constantly referred to when looking at examples of the measures of basic pecuniary loss applied. But it is useful here to point to three of the factors that should and do influence the courts in making this choice. First, the claimant's duty to mitigate means that it will recover the cost of cure where it has, or ought to have, incurred that cost in reasonably seeking to minimise its losses. Secondly, the fact that the claimant has cured or intends to cure may be a decisive

---

8   For a recent careful application of these principles, see *Habton Farms v Nimmo* [2003] EWCA Civ 68, [2004] QB 1.

factor favouring the cost of cure. Thirdly, the claimant's purpose for wanting performance may be relevant; so if the claimant wanted performance primarily to reap economic gain, the difference in value will fully compensate the claimant; that is, it will obtain the intended profits. But if performance was wanted for other reasons (eg for pleasure), difference in value will not, or not as fully, compensate the claimant.

It is important to note that this long-standing choice in the law of contract damages (which also applies in analogous areas of tort damages)[9] has recently been the subject of academic and judicial scrutiny. Unfortunately this scrutiny has, with respect, been somewhat confused and confusing.

The cornerstone of this recent debate was an article by Brian Coote entitled 'Contract Damages, *Ruxley* and the Performance Interest'.[10] In it, Coote took Friedmann's terminology of 'performance interest', which Friedmann had himself regarded as merely synonymous with 'expectation interest',[11] and used it as a label to describe 'cost of cure' damages. Performance interest damages were contrasted with 'difference in value' damages which Coote saw as 'mere compensation for the economic consequences of breach'[12] or as being 'to compensate for the loss of the economic benefits of performance.'[13] Coote then suggested that there has been a tendency in the law of damages for the 'performance interest' to be subordinated to the 'compensation approach'.[14]

It is submitted that Coote's new terminology is unhelpful. Both 'difference in value' and 'cost of cure' are concerned to compensate the claimant by putting him or her into as good a position as if the contract had been performed. Both are measures of pecuniary loss. The one is concerned with the loss of financial advantage, the other with the cost (ie the out of pocket loss) that the claimant must now incur. It is erroneous to treat only difference in value as compensating pecuniary loss. The overall interest normally protected by contractual damages is usefully labelled the expectation interest or performance interest. It is at a lower, more specific, level that one must then go on to choose, in protecting that expectation/performance interest, between difference in value or cost of cure.

9   See below, pp 232, 248.
10 [1997] CLJ 537.
11 Friedmann 'The Performance Interest in Contract Damages' (1995) 111 LQR 628: see above, p 37.
12 [1997] CLJ 537, 557.
13 [1997] CLJ 537 at 544.
14 [1997] CLJ 537 at, eg 547, 569–570.

Moreover, it is misleading to indicate that English law has been more committed to 'difference in value' than 'cost of cure'. As we shall see throughout this chapter, various factors have influenced the courts in deciding between those two measures. Neither is dominant over the other.

Coote's arguments are, arguably, more powerful insofar as he argues that 'cost of cure' (using that traditional terminology) should be even more widely favoured than it traditionally has been. In particular, he would favour 'downgrading' the importance attached to the claimant's intention to cure in favour of a single 'reasonableness' test albeit that he would clothe the reasonable person with the needs and tastes of the actual promisee.[15] Coote argues that in contracts made for the benefit of third parties, this approach would lead to 'cost of cure' damages being naturally recoverable by the contracting party as his own 'loss', irrespective of whether that party has cured or intends to cure.[16]

As we shall see, that approach apparently found favour with Lords Goff and Millett (dissenting) and, to an extent, Lord Browne-Wilkinson in *Alfred McAlpine Construction Ltd v Panatown Ltd*,[17] which concerned a construction contract for a third party's benefit. But, with respect, it is an approach that is fraught with difficulty. The traditional reliance on the claimant's intention to effect cure makes good sense in avoiding overcompensation of the claimant; and in the context of a contract for the benefit of a third party it also avoids unacceptable double liability to both the contracting party and the third party.[18] We shall return to these matters when discussing the *Panatown* case.

(3) The general formulae for assessing basic pecuniary loss

From what has already been said it can readily be seen that, taking into account the advantages as well as the disadvantages resulting from the breach, the claimant's basic pecuniary loss can be represented as follows: the value to the claimant of the benefit it should have received (minus the value of any benefits gained under the contract or that have, or ought to have, been gained as a result of the breach) minus the cost it has, or ought to have, avoided as a result of the breach; *or* the cost required to

---

15 [1997] CLJ 537 at 563, 570.
16 [1997] CLJ 537 at pp 549–552.
17 [2001] 1 AC 518: see below, pp 226–229.
18 McKendrick 'The Common Law at Work: The Saga of *Alfred McAlpine Construction Ltd v Panatown Ltd*' (2003) OUCLJ 145, 175, agrees that the intention to cure is a critical factor. But, with respect, intention to cure shows the need for (an actual or anticipated) financial loss which contradicts McKendrick's general argument (on which see also McKendrick 'Breach of Contract and the Meaning of Loss' (1999) 52 CLP 37) similar to Coote's, that the courts should not be so concerned about financial loss.

put the claimant into as good a position as if it had received the benefit minus the cost it has, or ought to have, avoided as a result of the breach; put shortly, *difference in value minus cost avoided* or *cost of cure minus cost avoided*.

The beauty of such formulae is that they can be applied whatever the nature of the benefit contracted for: that is, whether it comprised the delivery of goods, the transfer of land, the rendering of services, or the payment of money.

(4) Examples of the measures of basic pecuniary loss applied

These examples show the above general formulae in operation in respect of two of the most common types of contract – contracts for the sale of goods (examples (a)–(g))[19] and contracts for the building or repairing of real property (examples (h)–(j)).

(a) Breach by seller failing to deliver goods wanted for resale

The buyer's duty to mitigate generally dictates that it should buy substitute goods in the market so as to make its resale profit. Therefore, as laid down in the Sale of Goods Act 1979, s 51(3), the generally appropriate measure is market price at time fixed for delivery minus contract price, with the market price here referring to the market buying price.[20] This is a cost of cure rather than a difference in value measure, with the contract price, assuming unpaid or recovered, being deducted as a cost avoided.

A higher resale price (that is, the price at which the buyer has contracted to sell the goods) clearly does not displace the market price, since it does not affect the buyer's duty to mitigate. More controversial is a lower resale price. Several cases indicate that this should also be ignored. The leading one is *William Bros Ltd v Agius Ltd*[1] where the

---

19   Analogous rules apply in relation to contracts for the carriage of goods. See, eg *Rodocanachi v Milburn* (1886) 18 QBD 67, *Coastal (Bermuda) Petroleum Ltd v VTT Vulcan Petroleum SA (No 2), The Marine Star (No 2)* [1994] 2 Lloyd's Rep 629 (non-delivery of goods by carrier); *The Heron II* [1969] 1 AC 350; *The Pegase* [1981] 1 Lloyd's Rep 175 (late delivery of goods by carrier). Note also *White Arrow Express Ltd v Lamey's Distribution Ltd* (1995) 15 Tr LR 69, CA in which an inferior delivery service was provided than that contracted for: it was held that the claimant was entitled as damages to the difference between the market value of the services it had contracted for minus the market value of the services obtained but, as the claimant had produced no evidence of that difference in value (nor evidence of any other loss), nominal damages only were awarded.

20   Ogus *The Law of Damages* (1973) p 324.

1   [1914] AC 510. In relation to carriage contracts, the classic case laying down that one should ignore resale prices, whether higher or lower than the market price, is *Rodocanachi v Milburn* (1886) 18 QBD 67, CA. Lord Esher MR said, at 77, '[T]he value is to be taken independently of any circumstances peculiar to the plaintiff.'

defendant contracted to sell coal to the claimant at 16s 3d per ton. The claimant agreed to resell the coal to a third party for 19s per ton. The defendant failed to deliver. The market price at the date of breach was 23s 6d. The claimant was awarded damages of 7s 3d per ton, that is 23s 6d minus 16s 3d. The defendant's argument that the damages should have been only 2s 9d per ton, that is 19s minus 16s 3d, was rejected. Although some commentators support this decision,[2] it would seem that ignoring the resale wrongly overcompensated the claimant. True, it is often reasonable, given the claimant's potential liability to the sub-buyer, to buy at a higher market price. But on the facts the claimant had not done so and there was no question of liability on the resale contract. Nor is it satisfactory to say that, if the contract had been performed, other goods could still have been bought to fulfil the resale leaving the claimant free to sell the goods that should have been delivered by the defendant at the market selling price; for those other goods would still have to be bought at the higher market price and resold at the lower resale price, thereby producing an identical loss. So, it is submitted that a lower resale price should displace the market buying price, except where the claimant has reasonably bought substitute goods to fulfil the resale, in which case damages should be the price paid for the substitutes minus the original contract price.

Where the claimant cannot mitigate by buying substitute goods in the market, it is entitled to a difference in value measure. A good example is *Re R & H Hall and W H Pim, Jr & Co's Arbitration.*[3] The claimants could not mitigate because they had contracted to resell the specific cargo of grain, and no other, to be delivered by the defendant. They were held entitled, subject to remoteness, to the actual resale price, which was higher than the market price, minus the contract price.

(b) Breach by seller failing to deliver goods wanted for use

The buyer's duty to mitigate means that it should generally buy substitute goods in the market so as to make its user profit and again, therefore, as laid down in the Sale of Goods Act 1979, s 51(3), the generally appropriate measure is market buying price at time fixed for delivery minus contract price. However, where the buyer cannot so mitigate and

2   Eg Waddams *The Law of Damages* (3rd edn, 1997) paras 1.30–1.40, 1.1940, and more generally Simon and Novack 'Limiting the Buyers' Market Damages to Lost Profits: A Challenge to the Enforceability of Market Contracts' (1979) 92 Harv LR 1395.
3   (1928) 139 LT 50. However, Viscount Haldane's judgment is misleading on remoteness; see Goode *Commercial Law* (2nd edn, 1995) p 414. See also *Coastal (Bermuda) Petroleum Ltd v VTT Vulcan Petroleum SA (No 2), The Marine Star (No 2)* [1994] 2 Lloyd's Rep 629 (lost resale profits awarded as damages for breach of contract of carriage by carrier's non-delivery where no available market).

cannot mitigate in other ways, for example by having substitute goods manufactured and adapted,[4] it will generally be awarded its lost user profit as the difference in value measure.[5]

Exceptionally, a buyer is awarded the market resale price of goods (minus the contract price if unpaid or recovered). This will be so where the cost of replacing the goods exceeds that resale value, the claimant has no intention of replacing the goods, and there is no obvious lost user profit. In *Sealace Shipping Co Ltd v Oceanvoice Ltd, The Alecos M*[6] the defendants contracted to sell a ship, including its spare parts, to the claimants. However, when it was delivered, the defendants failed to deliver also its spare propeller. The arbitrator awarded $1,100 for that breach on the grounds that the claimants were not interested in buying a replacement spare propeller (which would cost $121,000) and that, as there was no commercial market in second-hand propellers, the resale value of a propeller was its scrap value of $1,100. Steyn J disagreed and awarded $121,000 but the Court of Appeal allowed an appeal by the defendants and restored the lower award made by the arbitrator.

(c) **Breach by seller delivering defective goods wanted for resale**[7]

While one can imagine situations[8] in which the duty to mitigate would dictate that the buyer should render the goods non-defective before reselling, hence entitling it to the cost of cure, a difference in value measure is here generally applied. As laid down in the Sale of Goods Act 1979, s 53(3) the buyer is generally awarded the market price that the goods would have had if of the contracted-for quality, less the market price of the goods actually delivered and it is clear that the market price here refers to the market selling price.[9] The contract price is not deducted because it is payable by the buyer and is therefore not a cost avoided.

Resale prices here seem relevant in two senses. First, if prior to the breach the buyer had made a resale contract of the goods, one would expect the resale selling price to displace the market selling price of the goods had they been of contracted-for quality. Secondly, if after breach the buyer had sold the goods, one would expect the resale price to

---

4   See, by analogy, *Hall Ltd v Barclay* [1937] 3 All ER 620; below, pp 249–250.
5   See, by analogy, *Cullinane v British Rema Manufacturing Co Ltd* [1954] 1 QB 292.
6   [1991] 1 Lloyd's Rep 120. The decision seems correct but it is criticised by Treitel 'Damages for Non-Delivery' (1991) 107 LQR 364.
7   It is assumed here and in examples (d)–(f) that the buyer has reasonably accepted the goods. If not, the damages are assessed as for non-delivery.
8   Eg where the cost of cure is much lower than the difference in market value.
9   Ogus *The Law of Damages* (1973) p 324.

displace the market selling price of the goods actually delivered if the former was higher. But in *Slater v Hoyle and Smith Ltd*,[10] where a resale concluded prior to breach had been carried through after breach, resale prices were considered irrelevant, whether prior or subsequent, and the claimant was held entitled to the normal measure under the Sale of Goods Act 1979, s 53(3). The claimant bought cotton cloth from the defendant to fulfil a contract of sale already made. The cloth delivered was of inferior quality than warranted, although the claimant was able to use it as intended to fulfil his sub-contract and received the full contract price from the sub-buyer. The price paid by the sub-buyer was greater than the market selling price of the cloth delivered but less than the market selling price of the cloth as warranted. The defendant contended that the claimant's damages should be nominal because the resale contract price concluded prior to breach minus the resale contract price received subsequent to breach amounted to nil. But the Court of Appeal rejected this, considered cases like *Williams Bros v Agius Ltd*[11] to be correct, and awarded the claimant damages assessed according to s 53(3). Again while some commentators support this approach,[12] it is submitted that it cannot be justified on compensatory reasoning and leaves the claimant in a better position than if the contract had been properly performed.

There is strong support in *Bence Graphics Int Ltd v Fasson UK Ltd*[13] for the view that *Slater v Hoyle and Smith Ltd* was incorrect to disregard the resale price. Here the defendants supplied vinyl film to the claimants for £564,328.54. As the defendants knew, this film was to be used, and was so used, by the claimants to manufacture many thousands of 'decals' (that is, self-adhesive transfers) for use in identifying bulk containers. The decals were sold to various customers who owned bulk containers. The film supplied was defective so that some decals became illegible more quickly than they should have done. The essential question at issue was whether, applying the Sale of Goods Act 1979, s 53(3), the claimants were entitled to £564,328.54 as the difference between the market price of the film as it should have been and as it was; or were the claimants merely entitled to damages indemnifying them for the (apparently relatively minor) claims against them by their customers consequent on the decals being defective. The majority (Thorpe LJ dissenting) held that the latter was the appropriate measure. Contrary to *Slater v Hoyle and*

---

10 [1920] 2 KB 11.
11 [1914] AC 510.
12 Eg Waddams *The Law of Damages* (3rd edn, 1997) paras 1.2570–1.2580.
13 [1998] QB 87. See also *McGregor on Damages* (17th edn, 2003), paras 7–146, 20–064. For the contrary view, that the majority in the *Bence* case was incorrect, see Treitel *The Law of Contract* (11th edn, 2003) pp 950–951; Treitel 'Damages for Breach of Warranty of Quality' (1997) 113 LQR 188.

Smith Ltd, the sales by the claimants to their customers should not be ignored. They meant that the claimants had not suffered a loss from being unable to sell on the film. Auld LJ, in an enlightened judgment, boldly said that the *Slater* case should be reconsidered not least because it awarded a buyer more than the evidence clearly showed he had lost. Otton LJ preferred to distinguish the *Slater* case on the grounds – rather unconvincing as he himself seemed inclined to recognise – that in that case, in contrast to *Bence*, the same goods were sub-sold without any manufacturing process and the defendant sellers did not know of the particular sub-sale.

(d) Breach by seller delivering defective goods wanted for use

While one can imagine situations[14] where the duty to mitigate would dictate that the buyer should render the goods non-defective, hence entitling it to the cost of cure, a difference in value measure is here generally applied whereby the buyer is normally entitled to its lost user profit. For example, in *Cullinane v British Rema Manufacturing Co Ltd*,[15] the defendants sold and delivered to the claimant a clay pulverising machine warranting that it would process clay at six tons per hour. In fact it could process clay at only two tons per hour. The claimant sought damages, inter alia,[16] for his lost user profit and throughout the judgments it was taken for granted that the buyer was so entitled.[17] Jenkins LJ said:

> 'The plant having been supplied in contemplation by both parties that it should be used by the plaintiff in the commercial production of pulverised clay, the case is one in which the plaintiff can claim as damages for the breach of warranty, the loss of the profit he can show that he would have made if the plant had been as warranted.'[18]

(e) Breach by seller making late delivery of goods wanted for resale

A difference in value formula is generally applied whereby, as laid down in *Elbinger Aktiengesellschaft v Armstrong*,[19] the claimant is entitled to the

---

14 Eg where the cost of cure is much lower than the lost user profits.
15 [1954] 1 QB 292. See also *Gull v Saunders* (1913) 17 CLR 82.
16 The claimant also claimed damages for some of his wasted expenses. The majority (Morris LJ dissenting) refused these. But this seems wrong since the profits awarded were not gross; see Ogus *The Law of Damages* (1973) pp 352–354; Macleod 'Damages: Reliance or Expectancy Interest' [1970] JBL 19.
17 [1954] 1 QB 292 at 303, 308, 316.
18 [1954] 1 QB 292 at 308.
19 (1874) LR 9 QB 473. See, analogously, *The Heron II* [1969] 1 AC 350 (damages for late delivery by a carrier).

market selling price at the time when the goods should have been delivered minus the market selling price at the time when they were actually delivered.

As regards resale prices, in *Wertheim v Chicoutimi Pulp Co*[20] a resale after breach was taken into account but a resale prior to breach was not; ie the higher resale price received subsequent to breach displaced the market selling price of the goods when actually delivered but the lower resale price concluded prior to breach did not displace the market selling price of the goods at the time when they should have been delivered. The case concerned a contract for the sale of a number of tons of wood pulp. Applying the normal measure of market selling price at the time when the goods should have been delivered (70s per ton) minus the market selling price when actually delivered (42s 6d), the claimant would have been entitled to damages of 27s 6d per ton. However, the Privy Council awarded damages of 5s per ton on the ground that the claimants had subsequently resold the same goods at 65s per ton (ie 70s minus 65s). It would seem, however, that the Privy Council was taking an unsatisfactory mid-position. Either the *Slater v Hoyle and Smith Ltd*[1] approach of ignoring resale prices applies, in which case the claimants should have been entitled to 27s 6d per ton or, and preferably, resale prices of goods both prior and subsequent to breach are taken into account – in which case the claimants should have been entitled to merely nominal damages (ie 65s minus 65s).[2]

(f) Breach by seller making late delivery of goods wanted for use

A difference in value measure is here generally applied, whereby the buyer is normally entitled to its lost user profit. An illustration of this is provided by one of the classic cases on remoteness, *Victoria Laundry (Windsor) Ltd v Newman Industries*,[3] where the claimants were awarded damages for loss of their ordinary (but not exceptional) user profit following the defendants' breach of contract in delivering five months late a boiler to be used in the claimants' business.

---

20 [1911] AC 301. See, analogously, *The Pegase* [1981] 1 Lloyd's Rep 175 (lost resale profit awarded as damages where late delivery of goods by carrier and no available market).
1   [1920] 2 KB 11.
2   This is also the approach preferred by *McGregor on Damages* (17th edn, 2003) para 7–142.
3   [1949] 2 KB 528.

(g) **Breach by buyer refusing to accept the goods**

The duty to mitigate generally dictates that the seller should sell the goods to another buyer. Therefore, as laid down by the Sale of Goods Act 1979, s 50(3), the general measure is the contract price minus the market price at the date of breach.

This is a difference in value measure – the contract price represents the value to the claimant of the defendant's performance as it should have been and the market price is the market selling price[4] and represents the benefit the seller has or ought to have gained by selling the goods to another buyer.

If the seller resells the goods at a price higher than the market selling price, one would expect that this resale price – being the benefit gained – would displace the market selling price as the sum deducted from the contract price. Unfortunately, in *Campbell Mostyn (Provisions) Ltd v Barnett Trading Co*[5] (as analogously in relation to a buyer's damages for non- or defective delivery) it was held that the resale price should be ignored. The defendants had refused to accept 350 cases of tinned ham, which they had contracted to buy from the claimants. The claimants were awarded damages of the contract price minus the market price at the date of breach, even though they had subsequently sold the goods at or above the contract price. This approach leaves a claimant in a better position than if the contract had been performed and therefore unjustifiably runs contrary to the avowed compensatory goal.

Where the seller cannot mitigate by selling in the market – for example, where supply exceeds demand – the Sale of Goods Act 1979, s 50(3) does not apply, and the claimant will instead be basically entitled to its loss of profit on that sale (ie contract price minus cost avoided) without any deduction of the market selling price.[6] This is shown by *W L Thompson Ltd v Robinson (Gunmakers) Ltd*[7] in which there was a contract to sell a Vanguard car. The supply of those cars exceeded the demand and therefore when the buyer refused to take the car the seller was held entitled to his loss of profit on the sale even though there was no difference between the contract price and the market selling price at the date of breach. A particularly clear analysis of *Thompson v Robinson* was made by Jenkins LJ in *Charter v Sullivan*.[8] There, because demand

---

4   Ogus *The Law of Damages* (1973) p 324.
5   [1954] 1 Lloyd's Rep 65.
6   See similarly US Uniform Commercial Code, s 2–708(2); Goetz and Scott 'Measuring Sellers' Damages: The Lost-Profits Puzzle' (1979) 31 Stan LR 323.
7   [1955] Ch 177. Above, pp 156–157.
8   [1957] 2 QB 117.

exceeded supply, *Thompson v Robinson* was distinguished and s 50(3) applied entitling the seller of a Hillman Minx car to merely nominal damages. Jenkins LJ said:

'The number of sales he [the plaintiff] can effect and consequently the amount of profit he makes, will be governed, according to the state of the trade, either by the number of cars he is able to obtain from the manufacturers or by the number of purchasers he is able to find. In the former case demand exceeds supply, so that the default of one purchaser involves him in no loss, for he sells the same number of cars as he would have sold if that purchaser had not defaulted. In the latter case, supply exceeds demand so that the default of one purchaser may be said to have lost him one sale ...'[9]

and later he went on to say:

'Upjohn J's decision in favour of the plaintiff dealers in *Thompson's* case was essentially based on the admitted fact that the supply of the cars in question exceeded the demand and his judgment leaves no room for doubt that if the demand had exceeded the supply, his decision would have been the other way.'[10]

It should further be added that, as laid down in *Lazenby Garages Ltd v Wright*,[11] *Thompson v Robinson* cannot be applied to sales of second-hand cars, because one cannot say of such cars that supply exceeds demand, or that a subsequent sale does not mitigate the seller's loss of profit. As Lord Denning said, '... it is entirely different in the case of a second-hand car. Each second-hand car is different from the next, even though it is the same make.'[12]

(h) Breach by builder refusing to carry out work or carrying it out defectively

One obvious possibility is that the owner will here be awarded the difference in value (ie difference in market selling price) between his property as it should have been if the contract had been performed and its actual value.[13] However, the cost of cure, ie the cost of engaging someone to complete the work, is often awarded instead. This may be because the cost of cure is less than the difference in the property's value and hence the owner's duty to mitigate dictates that he should recover only the cost of cure. But even where the cost of cure greatly exceeds the

---

9 [1957] 2 QB 117 at 124–125.
10 [1957] 2 QB 117 at 130.
11 [1976] 1 WLR 459.
12 [1976] 1 WLR 459 at 462.
13 Where the owner intended to use the property to make a profit, the difference in value measure could alternatively (at least in theory) refer to his loss of user profits.

difference in the property's value, the owner has been held entitled to that cost provided he has cured or intends to cure. Three main cases repay examination.[14]

In *Tito v Waddell (No 2)*,[15] a British company mining for phosphate on Ocean Island, a small island in the Pacific, had contractually promised to restore the land mined by replanting trees but had failed to do so. One of the questions that arose was whether the islanders would be entitled as damages to the cost of cure (ie the cost of replanting the land) which ran into thousands of pounds, or merely to the difference in value between the land as it was and as it would be if replanted, which at most ran to a few hundred pounds. Megarry V-C thought that the fundamental issue was whether the claimant had already cured or intended to cure. If so, the higher cost of cure would be awarded. He said, '... if the plaintiff establishes that the contractual work has been or will be done, then in all normal circumstances, it seems to me that he has shown that the cost of doing it is, or is part of, his loss and is recoverable as damages.'[16] Of course, where the court is basing itself on the claimant's intention to cure it cannot be absolutely sure that this is what the claimant will do but Megarry V-C thought that probable intention would be sufficient. He further suggested that in cases of doubt the court might be satisfied if the claimant gave an undertaking to do the work;[17] but such an undertaking might produce problems of enforcement and satellite litigation and was subsequently rejected as an idea by the House of Lords in *Ruxley Electronics and Construction Ltd v Forsyth*.[18] On the facts of *Tito v Waddell* it was held that there was not a sufficiently clear intention on the part of the islanders to use the damages to replant Ocean Island. In particular this was because they were now living on a different island. Damages based on the lower difference in the property's value were therefore awarded.

In *Radford v De Froberville*[19] the claimant had sold a plot of land to the defendant on terms, inter alia, that the defendant would erect a wall on

---

14   See also, eg *Dean v Ainley* [1987] 1 WLR 1729, CA; *Alfred McAlpine Construction Ltd v Panatown Ltd* [2001] 1 AC 518 (*per* Lords Goff and Millett), discussed below at pp 227–228. There has been much academic discussion of this situation: eg Farnsworth 'Legal Remedies for Breach of Contract' (1970) 70 Col LR 1145, 1167–1175; Tettenborn 'Damages for Breach of Positive Covenants' (1978) 42 Conv 366; Harris, Ogus and Phillips 'Contract Remedies and the Consumer Surplus' (1979) 95 LQR 581, 589–594, 601–603; Marschall 'Wilfulness: A Crucial Factor in Choosing Remedies for Breach of Contract' (1982) 24 Ariz LR 733; Muris 'Cost of Completion or Diminution in Market Value: the Relevance of Subjective Value' (1983) 12 J Legal Studies 379; Beale *Remedies for Breach of Contract* (1980) pp 173–177.
15   [1977] Ch 106 at 328–338.
16   [1977] Ch 106 at 333.
17   Cf above, p 183.
18   [1996] AC 344. See below, pp 221–222
19   [1977] 1 WLR 1262. See also *Mertens v Home Freeholds Co* [1921] 2 KB 526.

the plot so as to divide it from the claimant's land. The defendant had failed to do so. One question was whether the claimant was entitled to damages assessed according to the cost of cure (ie the cost of building a wall on his land), which at the time of trial would have cost £3,400 and at the time of breach £1,200, or according to the difference in the land's value with and without the wall, which was almost nil. Oliver J, applying *Tito v Waddell (No 2)*, held that the claimant was entitled to the cost of cure. He said, 'In the instant case, I am entirely satisfied that the plaintiff genuinely wants this work done, and that he intends to expend any damages awarded on carrying it out.'[20]

In the leading case of *Ruxley Electronics and Construction Ltd v Forsyth*[1] the claimant contracted to have a swimming pool built with the depth at the deep end of 7ft 6ins. When built the pool was in fact only 6ft 9ins at the deep end. Nevertheless, it was still perfectly safe for swimming and diving so that the difference in resale value of the property was not affected by the admitted breach of contract. To increase the depth of the pool to the agreed depth would cost £21,460 (nearly a third of the total price of the pool). Overturning the Court of Appeal, the House of Lords refused to award the claimant the cost of cure of £21,560; that would be unreasonable, because of the contrast with the nil difference in value. Moreover the first instance judge had found that the claimant had no intention to use the damages to rebuild the pool. But rather than awarding the claimant no damages at all for the breach the House of Lords upheld the first instance judge's award of damages of £2,500 for loss of amenity. Although there has been disagreement as to the basis of such damages,[2] it appears that they fall within the well-recognised category of damages for mental distress where the predominant object of the contract is mental satisfaction. Mr Forsyth's diving was not as pleasurable as it would have been had the pool been of the depth contracted for.[3]

The House of Lords took account both of reasonableness and the claimant's intentions. On the facts, both pointed in the same direction: the claimant did not intend to have the pool rebuilt and it was thought unreasonable (given the disparity with the difference in value) to have

---

20 [1977] 1 WLR 1262 at 1284. *In Minscombe Properties Ltd v Sir Alfred McAlpine & Son Ltd* (1986) 279 Estates Gazette 759 an intention to effect the cure was held sufficient even though it was conditional on obtaining planning permission.
1 [1996] AC 344.
2 See O'Sullivan 'Loss and Gain at Greater Depth: The Implications of the *Ruxley* Decision' in *Failure of Contracts* (1997) (ed Rose) pp 1, 14–16; Burrows and Peel *Commercial Remedies* (2003) p 25.
3 This was clearly Lord Lloyd's approach: see [1996] AC 344, 363 at 373–374. Staughton LJ's judgment in the Court of Appeal sets out the judge's indication that Mr Forsyth's pleasure in diving was affected: see [1994] 1 WLR 650 at 654. See below, p 326.

done so. The same is true of *Tito v Waddell*. Where 'reasonableness' and 'intention' point in different directions, it is submitted that the 'intention' test is the more important.[4] Indeed the best approach is that the courts will award a higher cost of cure if the claimant intends to effect the cure unless effecting the cure would be contrary to the claimant's standard duty to mitigate his or her loss. So had Mr Forsyth already rebuilt the pool to the specified depth, or had he intended to do so, he should have been entitled to the cost of cure of £21,560. For a consumer to expend money to ensure that a swimming pool is of the depth he contracted for (because, for example, as on these facts, he is a tall man who wants to feel entirely comfortable when diving) should not be regarded as contrary to his duty to mitigate. In contrast, Mr Forsyth would have been acting contrary to his duty to mitigate if he had been a property speculator, who was intending to sell the property, and yet insisted on rebuilding the pool to the required depth even though that made no difference to the property's value.

It is sometimes suggested that this emphasis on the claimant's intention is unacceptable because it runs counter to the rule that the courts are not concerned with the use to which damages are put. This is a misleading objection. In assessing damages, the courts commonly have to assess the likely future costs of the claimant on the assumption that damages will cover those costs (for example, damages for the cost of care in a personal injury claim). The true rule is that, once awarded, the courts are not concerned with how the damages are used. That is, the damages are not clawed back if the claimant chooses to spend them inappropriately. But nothing that is here being said about the importance of the claimant's 'intention' in a case like *Ruxley* contradicts that 'no claw-back' rule.

Earlier cases support the 'intention' approach. For example, while the Landlord and Tenant Act 1927, s 18 lays down that, for a tenant's breach of a covenant to repair, the measure of damages is the extent by which the market value of the reversion at the end of the lease is diminished by the want of repair, cases like *Smiley v Townshend*[5] and *Haviland v Long*[6] have awarded the cost of repairs that have been or are intended to be carried out, albeit under the pretence that the cost of repair represented the diminution in value. In *Haviland v Long* Denning LJ said:

---

4   This derives strong support from Lord Lloyd's speech: [1996] AC 344 at 372–373. But note that one interpretation of the minority's reasoning in *Alfred McAlpine Construction Ltd v Panatown Ltd* [2001] 1 AC 518 is that intention is downplayed and a higher cost of cure is presumptively to be awarded unless that is unreasonable: see below, p 228.
5   [1950] 2 KB 311.
6   [1952] 2 QB 80.

'The measure of damage is the extent by which the market value of the reversion at the end of the lease was diminished by the want of repair. That depends on whether the repairs are going to be done or not. In cases where they have been or are going to be done the cost of repair is usually the measure of damage ...'[7]

Clearly the danger of this approach, where the claimant has not yet effected cure, is that he may not use the damages as he appears to intend, and will thereby end up with a windfall. But the main alternative of awarding difference in value if the cost of cure is far higher and therefore deemed to be unreasonable or, in the language used in the US, 'economically wasteful',[8] fails to compensate a claimant fully, wherever he has contracted for a purpose not reflected in the objective market value, ie this often fails to recognise properly the 'consumer surplus'[9] such as the claimant's interest in privacy in *Radford* or pleasure in diving in *Ruxley*. For this reason the reliance on the claimant's intention seems preferable. However, it should be reiterated that where the claimant wanted the contractual performance solely to make a profit (so that the difference in value can fully compensate him) and the cost of cure is far higher than the difference in value, the standard duty to mitigate should override the claimant's intention to effect cure and the lower difference in value only should be awarded.

It finally remains to consider three further approaches that have been advocated for this situation where the cost of cure far exceeds the difference in value.

The first is to award damages according to the cost the defendant has saved by not performing. These damages are restitutionary, not compensatory, and are discussed in chapter 17.[10]

The second is to award a figure representing what the claimant would have accepted to release the defendant from his contractual obligation or, similarly, the alteration to the price that, at the time of contracting, the claimant would have accepted for the relevant contractual obligation to have been omitted.[11] This approach was specifically rejected in *Tito v Waddell* and often it is a mere fiction to pretend that damages can here be assessed according to what the parties would themselves have agreed. Even if it is realistic to imagine that the claimant would have accepted a price for releasing the defendant, there will be serious difficulties in sensibly fixing that price.

---

7   [1952] 2 QB 80 at 84.
8   Eg *Peevyhouse v Garland Coal Mining Co* 382 P 2d 109 (1962).
9   Harris, Ogus and Phillips 'Contract Remedies and the Consumer Surplus' (1979) 95 LQR 581.
10 Below, pp 395–407.
11 Beale *Remedies for Breach of Contract* (1980) p 177.

The third is akin to the second but removes the fiction by simply asserting that a reasonable sum, in between the cost of cure and difference in value, should be awarded.[12] But this has no clear basis in principle and would leave uncertain how the reasonable sum should be fixed. Indeed it may simply disguise a desire to reverse the defendant's wrongful enrichment. If so this should be stated openly. It would also mean that this approach merges with the first mentioned above.

(i) Breach by builder in carrying out work late

There are no authorities on the measure of damages in this situation, but presumably the owner is entitled to either the value (market selling price) of the property at the time the work should have been completed minus its value at the time the work was actually completed, or if it intended to use the property for profit, the loss of user profit in the interim period of delay.

(j) Breach by owner refusing to allow work to proceed

There are again no cases on the measure of damages in this situation.[13] However, applying the general difference in value formula (and assuming no other profitable work has or should have been taken on in the time now left free) the builder should be entitled to the contract price minus the cost avoided because of the breach. So, for example, if a house owner has contracted with a builder for the building of an extension for £2,000 payable on completion, and it will cost the builder £800 for materials and £1,000 on labour to complete the job, and the owner repudiates when the job is three-quarters of the way through, the builder will be basically entitled to damages of £1,550, ie contract price (£2,000) minus cost avoided (£200 + £250).[14]

(5) Contracts for the benefit of third parties

Subject to exceptions, perhaps most importantly now the Contracts (Rights of Third Parties) Act 1999, the doctrine of privity prevents

---

12 See, eg Farnsworth 'Legal Remedies for Breach of Contract' (1970) 70 Columbia LR 1145, 1175.

13 For an analogous example, outside the building context, see *Western Web Offset Printers Ltd v Independent Media Ltd* [1995] 37 LS Gaz R 24, CA. In breach of contract, the owners of a newspaper cancelled an order for printing with the claimants which had 48 weeks still to run. The claimants were, reasonably, unable to find other orders to fill that gap. They were held entitled to the gross profits lost on the contract minus the costs of paper and printing which had been saved. Overhead costs were not deducted because these had not been saved.

14 Simplistically this assumes that the builder at the time of breach has used three-quarters of the required materials and labour.

actions for breach of contract by third parties. But what is the measure of damages if the promisee chooses to sue on a contract made for another's benefit?

Applying the normal expectation principle, the claimant is entitled to be put into as good a position as *it* would have been if the contract had been performed; ie the relevant loss is the claimant's not the third party's. This has been accepted as the generally correct approach and Lord Denning's reasoning to the contrary in *Jackson v Horizon Holidays Ltd*[15] (allowing the promisee to recover the third party's loss) has been rejected.[16]

However – and again as the authorities have made clear – this does not mean (even putting to one side the possibility of specific performance[17] and looking just at damages) that the promisee is necessarily restricted to nominal damages.[18] On the contrary, one would expect that in many contracts made for a third party's benefit, the defendant's failure to benefit the third party will constitute a substantial pecuniary loss to the promisee.[19] This may be, for example, because the promisee required the defendant to pay the third party in order to pay off a debt owed by the promisee to the third party. Or the promisee may have stood to gain from the use to be made by the third party of the promised benefit. And, by analogy to the cases allowing a cost of cure in excess of a difference in value,[20] the claimant should be entitled to substantial damages (measured by the cost of cure) where it has subsequently conferred the benefit on the third party or intends to do so.[1]

Moreover, the courts have recognised an important exception to the general rule (that the promisee recovers for its own loss not the third party's).[2] Developed from *The Albazero*[3] through *Linden Gardens Trust Ltd v*

---

15 [1975] 1 WLR 1468.
16 *Woodar Investment Development Ltd v Wimpey Construction UK Ltd* [1980] 1 WLR 277. See also *Coulls v Bagot's Executor and Trustee Co Ltd* [1967] ALR 385 at 410–411 (per Windeyer J); *Beswick v Beswick* [1968] AC 58, HL; *White v Jones* [1995] 2 AC 207, HL.
17 As was ordered in *Beswick v Beswick* [1968] AC 58: see below, pp 469–470.
18 See the first two cases cited above in n 16; and Lord Pearce's judgment in *Beswick v Beswick* [1968] AC 58.
19 This leaves aside the additional possibility of mental distress damages being awarded on the ground that the predominant object of the contract is the claimant's mental satisfaction: below, pp 325–327. One rationalisation of *Jackson* given in *Woodar* was that the damages were purely for the claimant's mental distress.
20 See, eg above, pp 219–223.
1   Briggs 'Privity Problems in Damages for Breach of Contract' (1981) NLJ 343.
2   Another exception is that a 'trustee' (B) suing for breach of a contract by A to create a trust in favour of a 'beneficiary' (C), can recover substantial damages as C's loss. In *St Albans City and District Council v International Computers Ltd* [1996] 4 All ER 481, the Court of Appeal drew an analogy between a local authority, recovering contractual damages for the loss suffered by its inhabitants, and a trustee.
3   *Albacruz v Albazero* [1977] AC 774, HL.

Lenesta Sludge Disposals Ltd[4] to *Darlington BC v Wiltshier Northern Ltd*[5] it has been laid down that a promisee can recover a third party's loss on a contract relating to property (whether goods or land) where it was contemplated that the property in question would be transferred to the third party or where it was otherwise contemplated that loss in respect of that property would be suffered by the third party. Having recovered the damages the promisee is then bound to account for them to the third party.

The rationale of this exception is that, on the assumption that the third party cannot itself sue, the exception prevents a defeating of the parties' intentions where it was clearly anticipated that the real loss would be suffered by the third party rather than the promisee. The exception prevents damages disappearing down a 'black-hole' where the promisee can sue but has suffered no loss and the third party who has suffered the loss cannot sue.

The scope of this exception (the so-called *Albazero* exception) came before the House of Lords in the controversial and difficult case of *Alfred McAlpine Construction Ltd v Panatown Ltd*.[6] Panatown entered into a construction contract with McAlpine for McAlpine to design and construct an office building on land owned by Unex Investment Properties Ltd (UIPL). The building was defective and delayed and Panatown sought damages for the cost of repair, loss of use and delay. These losses were actually suffered by UIPL not by Panatown so that, at least on the face of it, the claim was by a promisee to recover damages suffered by a third party. It should be noted that Panatown was in the same group of companies – the Unex Group – as UIPL; and that the reason the contract was made with Panatown rather than UIPL was as a means of avoiding value added tax.

Judge Thornton QC, as official referee, had held that Panatown could recover only nominal and not substantial damages. The Court of Appeal had overturned that and, by extending the *Albazero* exception to the normal rule that a promisee can recover only its own loss, had held that Panatown was entitled to substantial damages for UIPL's loss. By a three–two majority, the House of Lords restored Judge Thornton's decision. Panatown was not here entitled to substantial damages.

The approach of the majority (Lords Clyde, Jauncey and Browne-Wilkinson) was to accept the *Albazero* exception while holding that it did not here apply because UIPL was not merely a third party beneficiary of

---

4   [1994] 1 AC 85, HL.
5   [1995] 1 WLR 68, CA.
6   [2001] 1 AC 518, HL. For the author's full analysis of this case, see Burrows 'No Damages for a Third Party's Loss' (2001) OUCLJ 107.

the main construction contract but had also been given a direct contractual right against the promisor. That is, UIPL had been given a contractual warranty comprising a duty of care deed which gave UIPL direct contractual rights against McAlpine for breach of the latter's contractual duty of care. In Lord Clyde's words, 'the express provision of the direct remedy for the third party is fatal to the application of *The Albazero* exception.'[7] And according to Lord Browne-Wilkinson, 'If the contractual arrangements between the parties in fact provide the third party with a direct remedy against the wrongdoer the whole rationale of [the *Albazero*] rule disappears.'[8]

The difficulty with this is that the direct contractual right given to UIPL was not co-extensive with the promisee's rights under the main contract. For example, liability under the collateral warranty was for negligence and not for strict liability and, moreover, there were liquidated damages and arbitration clauses in the main contract but not in the duty of care deed. It followed that the third party might be worse off under its direct collateral contract than if the promisee sued and recovered the third party's loss under the main contract. Moreover, it appears that the purpose of the collateral warranty was to replace the tort liability that would have existed pre-*Murphy v Brentwood DC*:[9] it was surely not intended to prevent Panatown, as contracting party, recovering damages on behalf of UIPL as the known first owner of the building. It is submitted, therefore, that in this case the fact that the third party had a direct contractual right was not a good ground for excluding the *Albazero* exception.

But it is not only the decision of the majority that has proved controversial. The minority judges (Lords Goff and Millett) took a different starting point. Rather than regarding there as being a valid exception to the general rule (that the promisee recovers its own loss, not the third party's) they considered that, applying what was referred to as Lord Griffiths' 'broad ground' in the *Linden Gardens* case, the promisee is recovering its own loss in these cases. The broad ground is that a promisee itself suffers loss where services are not performed for which it has contracted even though those services are for the benefit of a third party. So here, according to the minority, Panatown was entitled to substantial damages for its own loss.

The difficulty with this is that, as Lords Clyde and Jauncey persuasively argued, it seems fictional. There is no (pecuniary) loss to the

---

7 [2001] 1 AC 518 at 532.
8 [2001] 1 AC 518 at 577.
9 [1991] 1 AC 398, HL.

promisee (other than the reliance loss constituted by the contract price paid) where the promisor has broken its contract with the promisee to render services to a third party. To award substantial damages to the promisee would therefore overcompensate the promisee (or, to put it another way, would give the promisee a windfall). In contrast, there would be a true loss to the promisee if the promisee had paid for the 'cost of cure' or intended to do so. But on the facts Panatown had not itself carried out the repairs nor did it intend to do so. Even if one were to say that the minority's speeches are best interpreted[10] as loosening the normal requirements for the recovery of a higher 'cost of cure' (as against a lower or nil difference in value) – so that, for example, a higher 'cost of cure' will be awarded, irrespective of the claimant's intention to cure, unless the defendant satisfies the court that such an award would be unreasonable – this could not account for the fact that damages for loss of use and delay were also claimed (and regarded as recoverable by the minority) even though they would not be covered by the 'cost of cure'.

A further problem with the minority's reasoning is that, on the face of it, it produces problems of double liability. If one says that the repair cost is the promisee's own loss, irrespective of whether it incurs that cost, and that it does not need to account for those damages to the third party, then in a situation, as on the facts of this case, where the third party also has direct contractual rights, it is hard to see how one can avoid saying that both the promisee and the third party are entitled to the repair costs. Admittedly Lords Goff and Millett suggested ways round this although, with respect, neither is entirely convincing.

Although problematic,[11] the reasoning of Lords Goff and Millett cannot simply be dismissed as being merely a minority view. This is not only because of the stature of Lords Goff and Millett. It is also because Lord Browne-Wilkinson, while agreeing with the majority's decision, was prepared to assume that the 'broad ground' was correct and disagreed with Lords Goff and Millett only because he thought that the broad ground was inapplicable where, as on these facts, the third party had been given a direct contractual right against the promisor.

---

10   This interpretation is consistent with the approach of Coote 'Contract Damages, *Ruxley*, and the Performance Interest' [1997] CLJ 537 which appeared to be especially influential on Lord Goff. See above, pp 210–211.

11   See also above, p 211. For somewhat similar (but more detailed) criticisms of the reasoning of Lords Goff and Millett, see Unberath *Transferred Loss* (2003) pp 59–82. For views supporting, or sympathetic to, the reasoning of Lords Goff and Millett, see Coote 'The Performance Interest, *Panatown* and the Problem of Loss' (2001) 117 LQR 81; and McKendrick 'The Common Law at Work: The Saga of *Alfred McAlpine Construction Ltd v Panatown Ltd*' (2003) OUCLJ 145 (although McKendrick ultimately regards the 'intention to cure' as critical: see above, p 211, n 18).

In summary, therefore, *McAlpine v Panatown* raises several difficult issues. It is submitted that, contrary to the reasoning of all their Lordships, the *Albazero* exception should have been applied so that Panatown should have been entitled to substantial damages for which it was bound to account to UIPL.

A final question in relation to contracts for the benefit of third parties concerns the *third party's* measure of damages where, under an exception to privity, the third party has a right to sue the promisor. For example, in relation to assignment the general rule has been that, as an assignee takes 'subject to equities,' an assignee cannot recover more from the debtor than the assignor could have done had there been no assignment.[12] Say, for example, a building is sold at full value along with an assignment to the purchaser of claims in contract or tort in relation to the building. The building turns out to need repairs as a result of a breach of the builder's contract with the assignor (whether that breach is prior, or subsequent, to the sale to the assignee) or of a tort (damaging the building prior to the sale). The assignee pays for the repairs. It might be argued that the assignor in that situation has suffered no loss so that, applying the governing principle that the assignee cannot recover more than the assignor, the assignee has no substantial claim. If correct, '... the claim to damages would disappear ... into some legal black hole, so that the wrongdoer escaped scot-free.'[13] Acceptance of the argument would also nullify the purpose of the governing principle which is to avoid prejudice to the debtor and not to allow the debtor to escape liability. Perhaps not surprisingly, therefore, that argument was directly rejected by the House of Lords in a Scottish delict case.[14] And the problem has been circumvented in England by the recognition of the *Albazero* exception. That is, where the *Albazero* exception applies, the contracting party (the assignor) is entitled to substantial damages for the loss suffered by the third party (the asssignee): by the same token, where the third party (the assignee) is itself suing, an award of substantial damages to the assignee does not infringe the principle that the assignee cannot recover more than the assignor.

Similar questions may arise where third parties are given rights to sue under the Contracts (Rights of Third Parties) Act 1999.[15] In contrast to assignment, the Act is not based on the third party taking over the

---

12 *Chitty on Contracts* (29th edn, 2004) paras 19–073–19–075.
13 *GUS Property Management Ltd v Littlewoods Mail Order Stores Ltd* 1982 SLT 533, 538 (per Lord Keith).
14 *GUS Property Management Ltd v Littlewoods Mail Order Stores Ltd* 1982 SLT 533.
15 See Stevens 'The Contracts (Rights of Third Parties) Act 1999' (2004) 120 LQR 292, 301–302.

promisee's rights. Rather both the promisee and the third party are regarded as having separate rights to sue and as suffering separate losses. But to avoid injustice to the promisor one could not always simply award the third party damages for its own loss without taking into account the position as between the promisor and the promisee. In particular, it may be unfair to the promisor on an unexecuted contract to award the third party its own full loss without taking into account the promisee's own saved cost of performance. It would appear, therefore, that in construing the Contracts (Rights of Third Parties) Act 1999, s 1(5),[16] the third party's damages should be assessed in an analogous, but not necessarily identical, way to those of the promisee.

2. BREACH OF CONTRACT – ADDITIONAL PECUNIARY LOSS

To put the claimant into as good a position as if the contract had been performed, all other pecuniary loss caused to the claimant by the defendant's breach and not ruled out by limiting principles, such as remoteness and the duty to mitigate, must be added to the basic measures of pecuniary loss so far discussed (unless already covered by the basic measure).

Loss of user profit may be an additional pecuniary loss: for example, where the claimant is basically awarded the costs of replacing and adapting goods, it is also entitled to any interim loss of user profit. Additional pecuniary loss may also comprise – albeit fairly rarely – damage to or destruction of the claimant's property. So, for example, in *Harbutt's Plasticine Ltd v Wayne Tank and Pump Co Ltd*[17] the defendant's breach of contract in installing an unsuitable heating system and insulating the pipes with unsafe material led to the claimant's factory burning down. Such damage to property is directly analogous to tortious damage to property and it has therefore been considered preferable to discuss the few contract cases in that tort subsection.[18]

But the commonest form of additional pecuniary loss is expenses caused by the breach, other than those that have been awarded within a

---

16 Contracts (Rights of Third Parties) Act 1999, s 1(5), reads: 'For the purpose of exercising his right to enforce a term of the contract, there shall be available to the third party any remedy that would have been available to him in an action for breach of contract if he had been a party to the contract (and the rules relating to damages, injunctions, specific performance and other relief shall apply accordingly).'
17 [1970] 1 QB 447. See also *Bacon v Cooper (Metals) Ltd* [1982] 1 All ER 397.
18 Below, pp 232–248.

cost of cure measure.[19] These expenses are referred to in the US Uniform Commercial Code as giving rise to 'incidental damages'. By the Uniform Commercial Code, s 2–710 a seller's incidental damages include 'any commercially reasonable charges, expenses or commissions incurred in stopping delivery, in the transportation, care and custody of the goods after the buyer's breach, in connection with return or resale of the goods or otherwise resulting from the breach.' By the Uniform Commercial Code, s 2–715 a buyer's incidental damages include '... expenses reasonably incurred in inspection, receipt, transportation and care and custody of goods rightfully rejected, any commercially reasonable charges, expenses or commissions in connection with effecting cover and any other reasonable expense incident to the delay or other breach.' Two common examples following a seller's breach are compensation paid to a sub-buyer and the costs incurred in defending a sub-buyer's claim. *Henry Kendall & Sons v William Lillico & Sons Ltd*[20] provides an example of the former. The buyer bought groundnut extractions from the seller, which were then used for making a poultry food, that the buyer sold to a game farm. The groundnut extractions were contaminated and many of the game farm's poultry died or grew up stunted. The buyer was liable to pay damages to the game farm but it successfully claimed compensation in respect of those damages from the seller. An example of the latter is the award in *Hammond & Co v Bussey*.[1] There the claimants bought coal from the defendants and resold it with the same description to X who used it for steamships. The defendants knew that it was the claimants' business to supply coal to steamships. The coal delivered by the defendants was, however, not of the warranted quality. The defendants admitted responsibility in respect of the claimants' liability to pay damages to X, but disputed that they should also have to pay damages for the claimants' legal costs in defending X's action against the claimants. The Court of Appeal held, however, that the defendants were liable to pay such damages, because not only were those costs not too remote, but also the claimants had not failed in their

---

19 One can regard expenses *wasted* because of breach as an additional loss. But in directly protecting the expectation interest (as opposed to the reliance interest – above, ch 5) such expenses are only recoverable if the basic measure has been calculated according to net rather than gross difference in value. Since the basic measure can always therefore take wasted expenses into account it seems unnecessarily complex to consider them separately here. But for claims framed in this way, see *Hydraulic Engineering Co Ltd v McHaffie, Goslett & Co* (1878) 4 QBD 670; *Cullinane v British Rema Manufacturing Co Ltd* [1954] 1 QB 292.

20 [1969] 2 AC 31. See also *Re Hall Ltd and Pim* (1928) 139 LT 50. As made clear in, eg *Total Liban SA v Vitol Energy SA* [2001] QB 643 (where defective gasoline was being sold to, and sub-sold by, the claimant) the seller is liable in damages even before the buyer has paid compensation to the sub-buyer: the incurring of a legal liability (to the sub-buyer) is itself a compensatable loss.

1   (1887) 20 QBD 79. See also *Agius v Great Western Colliery Co* [1899] 1 QB 413.

duty to mitigate by defending X's action, since the defect in the coal was discoverable only by X's using the coal and not by mere inspection, and hence there was some doubt as to X's claim.

3.   TORTS – DAMAGE TO PROPERTY, INCLUDING DESTRUCTION

This section is concerned with where the defendant's tort (such as trespass to land or goods, negligence, nuisance or conversion)[2] has caused damage to the claimant's existing property, whether real or personal. Cases where damage to property is an additional pecuniary loss consequent on a breach of contract will also be considered.[3] Whether for torts or breach of contract, the general compensatory aims dictate that the claimant should be put into as good a position as if its property had not been damaged. This was emphasised in relation to tortious damage to a ship in *The Liesbosch*,[4] where Lord Wright said:

'... the owners of the vessel are entitled to what is called *restitutio in integrum* which means that they should recover such sum as will replace them, as far as can be done by compensation in money, in the same position as if the loss had not been inflicted on them ...'[5]

A basic choice is generally presented between awarding diminution in value of the property or cost of cure. The former compensates the claimant for its loss of financial advantage in being deprived of its property, while the latter compensates for the cost of putting the claimant into as good a position as if its property had not been damaged. This choice is analogous to that presented in assessing compensation for tortious interference with goods by misappropriation or loss and in assessing basic pecuniary loss for breach of contract (the damaged property corresponds to a deprivation of the contractual benefit). The decision therefore similarly rests on factors such as the claimant's duty to mitigate, whether it intends to cure, and for what purpose it owned the property.

---

2   In respect of goods the relevant torts come within the Torts (Interference with Goods) Act 1977. Liability under the Consumer Protection Act 1987, Pt I extends, under s 5, to property damage subject to restrictions (eg that the property is for private use and that the damages exceed £275).
3   Above, p 230.
4   [1933] AC 449.
5   [1933] AC 449 at 459.

The details of the law are best examined by dividing between damage to real and personal property. Separate consideration will also be afforded to the so-called 'betterment' question.

(1) Damage to real property

The diminution in value of real property is normally assessed by taking the difference between the market selling price of the damaged and undamaged property, while the cost of cure normally comprises the cost of repair or, as a more appropriate term where a building has been destroyed, the cost of reinstatement. The cost of cure might alternatively comprise the market cost of buying or building replacement property elsewhere, minus the selling value of the claimant's damaged property, but in view of the nature of real property, this is rarely a realistic option in practice.[6]

A useful dictum on the choice between diminution in value and cost of cure is Donaldson LJ's in *Dodd Properties v Canterbury City Council*,[7] a case where the claimant's building had been damaged by the defendants' pile-driving. In an action for negligence and nuisance, the defendants conceded that they were liable for the cost of repairs. Donaldson LJ, however, took the opportunity to explain the law on damages for property damage. Having said that there are two possible measures he went on:

> 'The first is to take the capital value of the property in an undamaged state and to compare it with its value in a damaged state. The second is to take the cost of repair or reinstatement. Which is appropriate will depend on a number of factors, such as the plaintiff's future intentions as to the use of the property and the reasonableness of those intentions. If he reasonably intends to sell the property in its damaged state, clearly the diminution in capital value is the true measure of damages. If he reasonably intends to continue to occupy it and to repair the damage, clearly the cost of repairs is the true measure. And there may be in-between situations.'[8]

There have been several cases in which a decision between the two measures has had to be made. In *Hollebone v Midhurst and Fernhurst Builders Ltd*[9] the claimant's dwelling house had been damaged by fire due

---

6   An exception, on unusual facts, was *Ward v Cannock Chase District Council* [1985] 3 All ER 537, 561–563. See also *Dominion Mosaics and Tile Co Ltd v Trafalgar Trucking Co Ltd* [1990] 2 All ER 246.
7   [1980] 1 WLR 433.
8   [1980] 1 WLR 433 at 456–457.
9   [1968] 1 Lloyd's Rep 38. See also *Heath v Keys* (1984) Times, 28 May. Analogously, an owner of land is entitled to damages for the cost of abating a nuisance: *Delaware Mansions Ltd v Westminster City Council* [2001] UKHL 55, [2001] 4 All ER 737; *Abbahall Ltd v Smee* [2002] EWCA Civ 1831, [2003] 1 All ER 465.

to the admitted negligence of the defendant. The claimant was awarded the cost of repairs (£18,991 5s 8d) rather than the difference between the value of the house in its undamaged and damaged state (£14,850). This was an undoubtedly correct decision as the claimant had already carried out the repairs and it was reasonable for him to have done so given that he owned the house for living in. Similarly in *Harbutt's Plasticine Ltd v Wayne Tank and Pump Co Ltd*,[10] the claimants' factory was burnt down as a result of the defendant's breach of contract. The claimants were awarded the cost of building and equipping a new factory (£146,581) rather than the diminution in value (£116,785). Again the claimants had already had the factory rebuilt and, given that the factory was owned for business, it was not only reasonable to do so but, as stressed by the Court of Appeal, necessary in order to keep their business going.

The cost of reinstatement was also preferred, though subject to an important qualification, in *Ward v Cannock Chase District Council*.[11] Here the defendant council's negligence in failing to maintain their houses in a particular terrace had led, through the activities of vandals, to the destruction of the claimant's two houses where he had been living with his large family. Scott J held that the cost of reinstatement should be awarded, provided that the claimant could obtain planning permission to rebuild the houses. If not, and if permission was also refused to convert another of the claimant's houses nearby,[12] he should instead be awarded the diminution in value of the properties.

Again in *Dominion Mosaics and Tile Co Ltd v Trafalgar Trucking Co Ltd*,[13] in which the claimants' business premises had been burnt down because of the defendants' negligence, the Court of Appeal followed *Harbutt's Plasticine* and awarded a cost of cure measure (albeit the cost of leasing property elsewhere rather than the cost of reinstatement). Salient points were that the claimants had leased other property, that it was reasonable for them to do so to mitigate their loss of use, and that the cost of the lease was significantly less than the cost of rebuilding. The claimants were awarded £390,000, as the cost of the lease, even though the diminution in the value of the site was estimated at merely £60,000.

10   [1970] 1 QB 447.
11   [1985] 3 All ER 537.
12   Above, n 6. The issue was being tried as a preliminary question of law: had Scott J been awarding damages he could not have left open the question of planning permission because of the rule that damages must be awarded unconditionally (above, p 183).
13   [1990] 2 All ER 246.

Contrasting with those four decisions is *CR Taylor (Wholesale) Ltd v Hepworths Ltd*,[14] where the claimants' disused billiard hall was destroyed by fire. The cost of reinstating it was agreed at £28,957. The diminution in value of the site was notionally £2,500, although in the event of sale for redevelopment this would be completely offset by the beneficial effect of the fire in saving the expense of clearing the site. May J held that the diminution in value measure should here be preferred (and hence no damages were awarded under this head). This was because the site and billiard hall were owned by the claimants as an investment, which in time would be sold off for redevelopment. The claimants had no intention, prior or subsequent to the fire, of rebuilding the billiard hall.

A further issue, that arose at first instance in the *Dodd Properties* case,[15] is what exactly is meant by repair (or reinstatement). Cantley J said:

> 'The plaintiffs are entitled to the reasonable cost of doing reasonable work of restoration and repair. They are, of course, not bound to accept a shoddy job or put up with an inferior building for the sake of saving the defendants expense. But I do not consider that they are entitled to insist on complete and meticulous restoration when a reasonable building owner would be content with the less extensive work which produces a result which does not diminish to any or any significant extent the appearance, life or utility of the building, and when there is also a vast difference in the cost of such work and the cost of meticulous restoration.'[16]

Applying this, the lower cost of non-meticulous repair was awarded and there was no appeal against this. So, in other words, while generally repair or reinstatement means to produce as close a restoration to the original condition as is reasonably possible, it will mean a lesser restoration where this will serve the claimant's purposes just as well and will cost far less.

What happens where repairs (or reinstatement) have been carried out but a third party has paid for them? This raises the issue of how compensating advantages are dealt with.[17] In line with the general approach adopted in personal injury cases, the coherent position is that, assuming the compensating advantage is sufficiently direct, it should prima facie be deducted. But there are two well-recognised exceptions to this, namely benevolence and insurance.[18] The issue arose in the context

---

14 [1977] 1 WLR 659. See also *Jones v Gooday* (1841) 8 M & W 146; *Moss v Christchurch RDC* [1925] 2 KB 750; *Munnelly v Calcon Ltd* [1978] IR 387; *Farmer Giles Ltd v Wessex Water Authority* [1988] 2 EGLR 189.
15 [1980] 1 WLR 433.
16 [1980] 1 WLR 433 at 441.
17 See generally above, ch 7.
18 See above, pp 169–170.

of tortious damage to real property in *Jones v Stroud BC*.[19] The cost of repairs to a house, consequent on a local authority's negligent inspection, was awarded to the claimant even though he had not paid for the repairs. Rather the repairs had been paid for by the claimant's company which had not invoiced him for them. Neill LJ made a sweeping statement to the effect that who paid for the repairs was irrelevant.[20] With respect, that is too wide. But the actual decision may have been justified on the ground that the third party here was in effect acting out of benevolence in not invoicing the claimant and therefore fell within one of the two recognised exceptions to deduction. This was in line with Neill LJ's reliance on the statement in *The Endeavour*,[1] a damaged ship case, where it was said, 'If somebody out of kindness were to repair the injury and make no charge for it, the wrongdoer would not be entitled to refuse to pay as part of the damages the cost of the repairs to the owner.'

Finally, in addition to the diminution in value or cost of cure all other pecuniary losses resulting from the property damage should be recoverable subject to the usual limiting principles, such as remoteness and mitigation. So, for example, in *Grosvenor Hotel Co v Hamilton*,[2] the claimants' expenses in moving their hotel business from the damaged property were recovered: and in the *Dodd Properties* case[3] the claimants were awarded the potential loss of profits on their car business for the time during which the repairs would be carried out.

(2) Damage to goods

As in relation to damage to real property there is a basic choice between, on the one hand, awarding the diminution in value of the property – normally the market selling price of the goods as undamaged minus, if the goods are still in existence, their market selling price as damaged – and, on the other hand, the cost of cure, comprising the cost of replacing or, if possible, repairing the goods.[4]

But damage to goods does differ from damage to land or buildings in that here the cost of replacement is often a realistic cost of cure measure. Indeed it is convenient to distinguish between the destruction of goods (including 'constructive total loss') where the cost of replacement *is* the cost of cure measure, repair being out of the question, and mere damage to goods, where both cost of replacement and cost of repair are potential

---

19 [1986] 1 WLR 1141, CA. See also above, pp 225–229 and below, pp 241–243.
20 [1986] 1 WLR 1141 at 1150–1151.
1   (1890) 6 Asp MC 511 at 512.
2   [1894] 2 QB 836.
3   [1980] 1 All ER 928. See also *Rust v Victoria Graving Dock Co* (1887) 36 Ch D 113.
4   For what is meant by replacement or repair, see above, p 235.

cost of cure measures. Although most of the cases concern ships, it has been said on several occasions that the same principles of assessment apply to all goods.[5]

(a) Destruction of goods

Although the measure of damages chosen has sometimes been obscured by the courts' ambiguous references to damages being assessed according to the value of the chattel, early cases generally seemed to prefer the market selling price (ie diminution in value), while more modern cases have generally preferred the market replacement cost (ie cost of cure). In either case, if anything is left of the chattel, its salvage value (ie market selling price in its present condition) must be deducted.[6]

Illustrative of the earlier cases is *The Clyde*,[7] in which the market selling price was applied. In Dr Lushington's words, 'It is the market price which the Court looks to, and nothing else, as the value of the property. It is an old saying, "the worth of a thing is the price it will bring." '[8] But for goods owned for use rather than sale (such as ships) this is generally a less appropriate measure than the market replacement cost, which was awarded in *The Liesbosch*.[9] There the claimants were using their dredger 'The Liesbosch' to carry out work at Patras harbour, when it was sunk owing to the defendants' negligence. The claimants were awarded, inter alia, the market price of a replacement dredger, and the costs of adapting it for their use and of transporting it to Patras.

It is now clear, however, that whatever has been the historical preference, the choice between the market selling price and the market replacement cost turns, in relation to the tortious destruction of goods, on the same factors that we have looked at in relation to, for example, damage to real property and breach of a building contract. Relevant factors therefore include the claimant's duty to mitigate (and hence the reasonableness of a claim for the higher sum), whether the claimant intends to replace the goods, and for what purpose the goods were owned.

---

5   Eg *The Hebridean Coast* [1961] AC 545 at 562 (per Devlin LJ).
6   See, eg *The Fortunity* [1961] 1 WLR 351.
7   (1856) Sw 23.
8   (1856) Sw 23 at 25.
9   [1933] AC 449. See also *Clyde Navigation Trustees v Bowring SS* (1929) 34 Ll L Rep 319; *Jones v Port of London Authority* [1954] 1 Lloyd's Rep 489; *Dominion Mosaics and Tile Co Ltd v Trafalgar Trucking Co Ltd* [1990] 2 All ER 246 (paternoster machines).

So in *The Maersk Colombo*,[10] where the claimants' crane had been demolished by the defendants' negligence, it was decided by the Court of Appeal that the claimants were entitled as damages to the resale value of the crane (£665,000) and not its replacement value (£2,359,484). The replacement value was so much higher because a second-hand crane would have had to be modified in the US and transported from there to Southampton. The crucial factor in determining that that higher sum should not be awarded was that the claimants, prior to the accident, had already ordered a larger crane to replace the one demolished and therefore had no intention, after the accident, of buying another crane to replace the demolished one. In an excellent leading judgment, Clarke LJ analysed the main contract and tort cases on the question of difference in value or cost of care and explained that, in deciding between them, the important factors included reasonableness and intention. In rejecting an argument that there are distinct rules applying to tortious destruction of goods, he said, 'In my opinion a similar approach applies to the measure of damages for the tortious destruction of chattels as it applies to the measure of damages for both the tortious destruction of real property and for breach of contract in circumstances such as those in *Ruxley*.'[11]

Where damages are based on the chattel's market selling price at the time of destruction, additional damages for loss of use should not be recoverable: this theory of assessment rests on the assumption that the claimant could have otherwise sold his chattel at the time of destruction and clearly he could not both have sold it and used it. As Lord Wright said in *The Liesbosch*:

> 'The value of prospective freights cannot simply be added to the market value but ought to be taken into account in order to ascertain the total value for purposes of assessing the damage, since if it is merely added to the market value of a free ship, the owner will be getting pro tanto his damages twice over. The vessel cannot be earning in the open market, while fulfilling the pending charter or charters.'[12]

However, these principles have not always been correctly adhered to and in some cases loss of profit on the voyage the ship was on,[13] or even on

---

10　[2001] EWCA Civ 717, [2001] 2 Lloyd's Rep 275. This was followed in *Ali Reza-Delta Transport Co Ltd v United Arab Shipping Co* [2003] EWCA Civ 86, [2003] 2 Lloyd's Rep 450: damages were based on the market selling price (of similar goods in Saudi Arabia where they had been tortiously destroyed) rather than the replacement costs; there was no evidence that the claimants had replaced, or would replace, the destroyed goods.
11　[2001] EWCA Civ 717, [2001] 2 Lloyd's Rep 275, at para 43.
12　[1933] AC 449 at 464.
13　*The Llanover* [1947] P 80.

all other engagements already fixed,[14] has been awarded in addition to the market selling price at the date of the destruction.

On the other hand, where damages are based on the cost of replacement, damages for loss of use during the period until use could be made of the replacement are and should be recoverable subject to the usual limiting principles. As Street wrote, 'The rationale of ... claims for loss of profits is that they are allowable for that period which would elapse before a replacement is procurable.'[15] So in *The Liesbosch*[16] the House of Lords held that additional damages should be awarded for the loss of user profit for the period between the dredger's sinking and the time at which the substitute dredger could reasonably have been available for use in Patras. In Lord Wright's words, 'The true rule seems to be that the measure of damages in such cases is the value of the ship to her owner as a going concern at the time and place of loss.'[17] He then regarded the combination of replacement costs and loss of user profit, as opposed to the market selling price, as representing that value.

The other most obvious consequential losses that are prima facie recoverable are the reasonable hiring charges of a substitute chattel in the interim period before the replacement chattel can be used.[18] These costs will often mitigate any loss of use and, indeed, where they ought to have been incurred to mitigate such loss of use, they will presumably be awarded instead of damages for loss of use.

(b) Mere damage to goods

No case has been traced in which diminution in value (ie market selling price as undamaged minus market selling price as damaged) has here been awarded although if the goods were owned for sale rather than use and the repair or replacement costs are a lot higher, the diminution in selling price should be the preferred measure.[19]

---

14 *The Philadelphia* [1917] P 101; *The Fortunity* [1961] 1 WLR 351 (cf Hudson in *Interests in Goods* (eds Palmer & McKendrick) (2nd edn, 1998) p 834, fn 16 who appears to construe the latter case as having awarded the cost of replacement rather than the market selling price).

15 *Principles of the Law of Damages* (1962) p 195. See, generally, Knott 'Loss of Profit Caused by the Total Loss of a Ship: its Relationship to Value and Interest' [1993] LMCLQ 502.

16 [1933] AC 449.

17 [1933] AC 449 at 464.

18 But such costs were not recoverable in *The Liesbosch*, because they flowed from impecuniosity – see above, pp 144–147. See also *Moore v DER Ltd* [1971] 3 All ER 517, where no replacement cost was being awarded.

19 At first sight, it might be thought that *Derby Resources AG v Blue Corinth Marine Co Ltd, The Athenian Harmony* [1998] 2 Lloyd's Rep 410 is such an example. But on closer inspection – see especially at pp 417, 419 – the market value of sound (ie uncontaminated) kerosene was regarded as the market buying price of such kerosene so that the damages (against a carrier for negligent damage to goods) were assessed using a replacement cost (ie cost of cure) measure.

Under the cost of cure, there is a decision to be made here between awarding the replacement cost (minus the market selling price of the damaged chattel) and the cost of repairs.[20] Two pairs of cases may be contrasted to illustrate the courts' approach.

In *O'Grady v Westminster Scaffolding Ltd*,[1] the claimant's MG car was damaged by the defendant's admitted negligence. The claimant repaired the car at a cost of £253 and also incurred costs of about £208 in hiring a substitute car in the interim. The defendant argued that the claimant should have written the car off and replaced it which, according to the defendant, would have cost him about £145, ie market price of replacement (£180) minus scrap value of MG (£35). But Edmund Davies J held that the claimant was entitled to damages based on the cost of repair (plus hiring charges) because he had acted reasonably in carrying out the repairs; this was particularly because the car, lovingly named 'Hortensia' by the claimant, was his pride and joy, which he had spent a lot of time and effort maintaining and it could not really be replaced.

On the other hand in *Darbishire v Warran*[2] the claimant, who had repaired his car for £192 (plus hiring charges) preferring to keep a car he knew to be reliable and suitable for his needs, was restricted to damages based on the market cost of a replacement, namely £85 (plus hiring charges). The Court of Appeal held that the claimant had failed to take reasonable steps to mitigate his loss by buying a replacement and *O'Grady v Westminster Scaffolding* was distinguished on the ground that there, unlike here, the car in question was unique.

Another contrasting pair of cases concerns damaged ships. In *Italian State Rlys v Minnehaha*[3] the claimants' ship was damaged. They had it repaired for about £37,000 (and had also incurred some relatively minor consequential expenses during the repairing period). It was decided that the value of the ship when repaired, which it was assumed equalled the market cost of replacement, was £53,000. Its value, that is its market selling price, in its damaged condition had been £20,000. The Court of Appeal held that the claimants were only entitled to the replacement cost minus market selling price, which equalled £33,000. It had been unreasonable to incur the greater expense of repair, for the claimants had failed to establish that there was anything particularly special about the ship. Instead they should have sold it off in its damaged state. Lord Sterndale MR said, '... unless there is some circumstance to justify

---

20 For what is meant by replacement or repair, see above, p 235.
1   [1962] 2 Lloyd's Rep 238.
2   [1963] 1 WLR 1067.
3   (1921) 6 Ll L Rep 12.

whether the claimant intends to do so – and reasonableness. But where it is known that the claimant has not, and will not, incur the costs of repair (or has not, and will not, incur hire charges) those costs do not constitute a loss to the claimant. It is a fiction to pretend that the claimant has suffered such a loss.

On the facts of the case, the payment by the third party of the repair costs was not too indirect – on the contrary, it was in direct response to the tort – and did not fall within the benevolence and insurance exceptions to the deduction of compensating advantages. This was because the third party was not acting out of benevolence; and it paid for the repairs under an unenforceable consumer credit agreement with the claimant (and not a valid insurance contract). Moreover, as Gray J stressed at first instance, there was no good specific policy reason to ignore the compensating advantage provided by the third party in this situation. Finally, as we have seen,[13] while the wide reasoning in *Jones v Stroud DC* cannot be supported, the actual decision may have been correct because the facts may have fallen within the well-established benevolence exception to non-deduction: the claimant's own company had incurred the expense but had not invoiced him for it.

In addition to the cost of repair or replacement, all other pecuniary losses resulting from the property damage are recoverable, subject to the usual limiting principles like remoteness and mitigation. So, as already briefly mentioned, in *O'Grady v Westminster Scaffolding Ltd*,[14] damages were awarded for the charges of hiring a car while the claimant's car was being repaired, as they were in *Darbishire v Warran*[15] – although this was presumably on the basis that the claimant would have had to incur such charges even if he had bought a replacement.

Are reasonable hiring charges recoverable by the claimant even where a hire car has been supplied without any cost to the claimant? For example, the car may have been supplied by the claimant's insurers

---

13   Above, pp 235–236.
14   [1962] 2 Lloyd's Rep 238. See also *Giles v Thompson* [1994] 1 AC 142, HL (claimant able to recover because legally liable to pay hire costs albeit not yet paid). In *Dimond v Lovell* [2002] 1 AC 384 at 402–403 there was obiter dicta to the effect that, if the hiring charges had been recoverable (it was decided that they were not) one should deduct the cost of additional services, over and above the hiring of the car, that were provided as part of the hiring package. In other words, the 'spot-rate' of hire and not the higher costs of an accident-hire scheme were recoverable. But in *Lagden v O'Connor* [2003] UKHL 64, [2004] 1 AC 1067, it was decided that an impecunious claimant could recover those higher costs: see above, p 146. In *Burdis v Livsey* [2002] EWCA Civ 510, [2003] QB 36, it was clarified that the claimant could only recover for the costs of hiring (a Vauxhall Vectra) actually incurred even though higher hire charges (for a replacement sports car) might reasonably have been incurred. For the position where, without the claimant being at fault, the period of hiring is extended see above, p 126, n 8.
15   [1963] 1 WLR 1067.

under an unenforceable insurance contract or by a company providing replacement cars under what transpire to be unenforceable consumer credit agreements. In these situations, the claimant has no legal liability to pay for the hire car. Initially the view taken in *McAll v Brooks*[16] was that the reasonable hiring costs were still recoverable. Just as in the personal injury case of *Donnelly v Joyce*[17] the claimant could recover the costs of nursing care even though gratuitously rendered by a third party, so the claimant could recover the costs of hire even though those costs were borne by a third party. But that approach was departed from by the House of Lords in *Dimond v Lovell*.[18] The earlier approach was said to be based on an approach in personal injury cases that had been departed from in *Hunt v Severs*[19] where the House of Lords recognised that the loss was the third party's and not the claimant's. To ignore the fact that the costs were being borne by the third party and not the claimant could only be justified if there was an exception to the deduction of compensating advantages. But neither of the well-recognised exceptions (of benevolence or insurance) applied here. In Lord Hoffmann's words, 'The only way ... in which Mrs Dimond could recover damages for the notional cost of hiring a car which she actually had for free is if your Lordships were willing to create another exception to the rule against double recovery. I can see no basis for doing so.'[20] As we have seen, it is difficult to understand how the later decision of the Court of Appeal in *Burdis v Livsey*[1] (dealing with hire, rather than repair, costs) can be reconciled with their Lordships' decision in *Dimond v Lovell*.

Loss of user profit for the period while the goods are being repaired or replaced is also recoverable.[2] But if the chattel would have been operating at a loss during that period no such damages should be awarded.[3]

Particularly interesting are the cases allowing damages for loss of use where non-profit-earning ships have been damaged. In *The Greta Holme*,[4] for example, the damage was to a dredging boat owned by a harbour authority for removing silt from the sea bed and in *The Mediana*[5] the damage was to a harbour authority's light-ship. In addition to the cost of

16 [1984] RTR 99, CA.
17 [1974] QB 454, CA. See below, p 277.
18 [2002] 1 AC 384, HL.
19 [1994] 2 AC 350, HL. See below, p 277.
20 [2002] 1 AC 384 at 400.
1 [2002] EWCA Civ 510, [2003] QB 36. See above, pp 241–243.
2 *The Argentino* (1889) 14 App Cas 519; *The World Beauty* [1970] P 144.
3 *The Bodlewell* [1907] P 286.
4 [1897] AC 596. See also *The Marpessa* [1907] AC 241; *Admiralty Comrs v SS Susquehana* [1926] AC 655; *The Hebridean Coast* [1961] AC 545.
5 [1900] AC 113. See also *Birmingham Corpn v Sowsbery* [1970] RTR 84.

repairing these service ships the claimants were held entitled to damages for the loss of their use. In the latter case, this was held to be so even though the claimants always maintained a substitute light-ship as cover in the event of damage to the main ship. The justification for such damages for loss of use is not at all obvious. In *The Mediana* Lord Halsbury LC drew an analogy with tortious misappropriation: '… supposing a person took away a chair out of my room and kept it for 12 months, could anybody say you had a right to diminish the damages by showing I did not usually sit on that chair, or that there were plenty of other chairs in the room?'[6] That analogy is misleading. In misappropriation cases the justification for damages can be said to be either that they compensate for the loss of the fee that the claimant would have charged if he had been approached by the defendant or, perhaps more realistically, that they reverse the defendant's wrongful enrichment.[7] But in the case of damage to chattels those justifications are not in play. Furthermore, even though the claimants would have been entitled to damages to compensate for the additional costs of hiring a temporary replacement if incurred, they clearly could not be said to have suffered that loss where not incurred. Nor had the claimants suffered a loss in terms of the depreciation of the ships or the costs incurred (for example, the crew's wages) during repair or replacement, because there would have been that depreciation and those costs would have been incurred even if the ships had not been damaged.

Reflecting these problems of justification is the difficulty of how to assess damages for loss of use in this type of case. In *The Marpessa*[8] the House of Lords held that damages should be assessed according to the costs of working and maintaining the dredger that would have been incurred, plus its depreciation, during the period of repairs. In *The Hebridean Coast*[9] the House of Lords awarded a reasonable rate of interest on the value of the ship, as if it had been invested as capital money for the repair period, plus a sum of depreciation. A further possibility would be to award what it would have cost to hire a temporary replacement.[10]

Overall the approach of the courts in these cases cannot be supported. References to loss of use merely serve to obscure the truth that no

---

6   [1900] AC 113 at 117.
7   Below, ch 17.
8   [1907] AC 241. *Birmingham Corpn v Sowsbery* [1970] RTR 84.
9   [1961] AC 545. *Admiralty Comrs v SS Chekiang* [1926] AC 637.
10 Suggested in *The Bodlewell* [1907] P 286 at 292 (per Bargrave Deane J).

pecuniary (or non-pecuniary)[11] loss had been suffered by the claimants. This was particularly clear in *The Mediana* where there was a cover ship. No damages should therefore have been awarded under this head in these cases and the claimants should have been confined to recovering the cost of repair or replacement.

(3) The betterment question

The courts have sometimes been criticised[12] for purportedly leaving the claimant overcompensated by not deducting from the full repair or replacement cost of property damaged or destroyed by the defendant's tort or breach of contract an amount for 'betterment'; that is, for the fact that the replacement or repaired property is in a better condition than the property before it was damaged or destroyed. So, for example, in *The Gazelle*[13] the claimant's ship was damaged in a collision with the defendant's ship caused by the defendant's negligence. In the claimant's action for damages for the costs of repairing his ship and replacing items destroyed, the assessors of the damages had deducted one-third from those costs because the claimant was getting new for old. But Dr Lushington overruled this. He said, '… if that party derives incidentally a greater benefit than mere indemnification, it arises only from the impossibility of otherwise effecting such indemnification without exposing him to some loss of burden, which the law will not place upon him.'[14] Again, in *Harbutt's Plasticine Ltd v Wayne Tank and Pump Co Ltd*[15] where the claimants' factory was burnt down as a result of the defendants' breach of contract, it was held that the claimants were entitled to the cost of building and equipping a new factory and that no deduction would be made for the fact that the new factory would be better than the old one. Similarly in *Bacon v Cooper (Metals) Ltd*,[16] where the defendants were in breach of contract in supplying the claimants with the wrong kind of scrap metal which then broke the rotor of the claimants' fragmentiser, the claimants were held entitled to the hire-purchase cost of a new rotor and no deduction was made for the fact that

---

11 But where the owner is an individual, damages for loss of use may be justifiable as compensating for non-pecuniary loss, ie physical inconvenience or mental distress. In *Alexander v Rolls Royce Motor Cars Ltd* [1996] RTR 95, CA, damages for loss of use of a Rolls Royce car were refused because the claimant had other cars and there was no evidence of inconvenience or loss of enjoyment while repairs to the car were being carried out (or awaited).

12 Ogus *The Law of Damages* (1973) p 134.

13 (1844) 2 Wm Rob 279.

14 (1844) 2 Wm Rob 279 at 281.

15 [1970] 1 QB 447. See also *Hollebone v Midhurst and Fernhurst Builders Ltd* [1968] 1 Lloyd's Rep 38; *Dominion Mosaics and Tile Co Ltd v Trafalgar Trucking Co* [1990] 2 All ER 246.

16 [1982] 1 All ER 397.

the new rotor had an expected life of seven years, whereas the old rotor had had only three and three-quarter years' expected life left.

But it is submitted that these cases do not contradict the compensatory principle because it is not at all clear that the betterment represented a real benefit to the claimant. In *The Gazelle* and *Harbutt's Plasticine* the claimant would only realise a gain from the betterment if the ship and factory respectively were to be sold, and there was little likelihood of that. Similarly in *Bacon v Cooper* there was no certainty that having a new rotor would benefit the claimant more than the old one since by the time the old rotor would have worn out, the fragmentiser itself might have become outmoded. So these cases should not be read as an unjustifiable commitment to not deducting for a true benefit; and where the claimant has clearly benefited from the new for old – and it should probably be for the defendant to show this – an appropriate deduction should be made. That this will be so is supported by Cantley J's view in *Bacon v Cooper* that it would be absurd to allow the full cost of replacing a rotor that had only a few days of useful life left.

This principled approach now derives strong support from the Court of Appeal in *Voaden v Champion, The Baltic Surveyor*.[17] The claimant's pontoon had been sunk and lost by reason of the defendant's negligence. At first instance Colman J had awarded £16,000 in respect of the pontoon on the basis that a replacement would have cost £60,000 and had a life of 30 years but the old pontoon only had 8 years of life left in it. He therefore awarded 8/30ths of £60,000. That deduction for 'betterment' was upheld by the Court of Appeal as being correct in principle (albeit that Colman J's view that this approach only applied to where one was concerned with replacement rather than repair was doubted). Provided the new for old constituted a true (pecuniary) benefit to the claimant, it should be deducted. Having examined cases such as *The Gazelle, Harbutt's Plasticine* and *Bacon v Cooper*, Rix LJ said:[18]

> 'I suspect ... that the true principle is that in the relevant cases[19] the betterment has conferred no corresponding advantage on the claimant. Take the ordinary case of the repair of some part of a machine. Where only a new part can be fitted or is available, the betterment is likely to be purely nominal: for unless it can be posited that the machine will outlast the life left in the damaged part just before it was damaged, the betterment gives the claimant no advantage; and in most cases any such benefit is likely to be entirely speculative. So in the case of replacement buildings: the building may be new, but buildings are such potentially long-lived objects that the mere newness

---

17 [2002] EWCA Civ 89, [2002] 1 Lloyd's Rep 623.
18 [2002] EWCA Civ 89, [2002] 1 Lloyd's Rep 623 at para 85.
19 Ie where betterment appeared to be ignored.

of a building may be entirely by the way ... Even where the replacement is of a moderately bigger size ... in the absence of any reason for thinking that the bigger size is of direct benefit to the claimant, he has merely mitigated as best he can. If, however, it were to be shown that the bigger size (or some other aspect of betterment) were of real pecuniary advantage to the claimant, as where, for instance, he was able to sublet the 20 per cent extra floor space he had obtained in his replacement building, I do not see why that should not have to be taken into account. It is after all a basic principle that where mitigation has brought measurable benefits to a claimant, he must give credit for them ...'

4.   TORTS – WRONGFUL INTERFERENCE WITH GOODS OR LAND, OTHER THAN CAUSING PROPERTY DAMAGE

(1) Goods

Wrongful interference with the claimant's goods, without causing property damage, comprises misappropriation or loss of those goods whether by conversion[20] trespass to goods or negligence.[1]

In aiming to put the claimant into as good a position as it would have been in if no misappropriation or loss had occurred, as the general compensatory aim dictates, then where the goods have been permanently misappropriated or lost the courts are generally content to say simply that damages are assessed according to the value of the goods.[2] But this is a rather ambiguous phrase. For example, even if there is a market for the goods there may be a variation between the market selling and buying prices. Indeed there is often a basic choice between directly awarding the claimant its lost financial advantage from not having the goods (diminution in value) and, on the other hand, awarding it the costs of acquiring substitute goods (cost of cure). This choice is analogous to that presented in assessing compensation for damage to goods and in assessing basic pecuniary loss for breach of contract (the lost property corresponds to a deprivation of the contractual benefit).

---

20 Conversion was extended and detinue abolished by the Torts (Interference with Goods) Act 1977, s 2.
1   See above, p 232, n 2.
2   Eg *Re Simms* [1934] Ch 1; *Caxton Publishing Co Ltd v Sutherland Publishing Co* [1939] AC 178 at 192 (per Lord Roche). The relevant date for assessing the value has been in issue in several conversion cases: see above, pp 188, 191–192. For the damages recoverable by those with a limited interest in the goods, see *McGregor on Damages* (17th edn, 2003) paras 33–048–33–062; eg the creditor under a hire-purchase agreement is restricted to the unpaid instalments if lower than the goods' value: *Wickham Holdings Ltd v Brooke House Motors Ltd* [1967] 1 WLR 295; *Chubb Cash Ltd v John Crilley & Son* [1983] 1 WLR 599.

It is also noteworthy that in some of the leading cases the defendant had contracted to deliver the goods in question to the claimant, and the claimant's action in conversion (property in the goods having passed) was therefore alternative to that for breach of contract for non-delivery. Subject to differences in limiting principles, like remoteness and contributory negligence, the damages do not differ according to which action is chosen.

So the claimant's duty to mitigate means that normally the value of the goods is the market buying price of replacements. However, if there is no such market and if the claimant's purpose in having the goods was to sell them, the goods' value will be represented by the profit that would have been made on sale, ie by the market selling price or the actual resale price. The market selling price was awarded in *The Arpad*.[3] There the claimants had bought a quantity of wheat and had resold it at 36s 6d a quarter. The market price had since fallen considerably. The defendant shipowners failed to deliver some 47 tons. In an action for conversion (and breach of contract) the claimants were awarded damages only for the market selling price of the 47 tons at the time fixed for delivery, ie 23s 6d per ton, on the ground that the actual resale price was too remote. On the other hand, in *France v Gaudet*[4] the actual resale price was awarded in a situation where the defendant had failed to deliver champagne. It is submitted that the latter decision is to be preferred since if there is no market for buying replacements, as in these two cases, an award of the actual resale price puts the claimant more closely into the position it would have been in if the goods had not been misappropriated or lost; moreover it is hard to see why the resale loss was regarded as too remote in *The Arpad*.[5] Significantly, Scrutton LJ dissented in that case although it appears that his willingness to take account of the actual resale price was confined to where, as on these facts, there was no available market at the port of discharge.

Where the claimant's purpose in having the goods was for use, and there is no market for buying replacements, the claimant is likely to be awarded the cost of manufacturing a replacement plus adaptation costs. This was awarded, for example, in *J and E Hall Ltd v Barclay*,[6] where the defendant converted the claimant's machinery and there was no market

---

3   [1934] P 189.
4   (1871) LR 6 QB 199.
5   But the analogous decisions ignoring resales in *William Bros Ltd v Agius* [1914] AC 510 and *Rodocanachi v Milburn* (1886) 18 QBD 67 were applied: see above, pp 212–213.
6   [1937] 3 All ER 620.

for buying such machinery. Where the claimant cannot even mitigate by replacement manufacture he will presumably be awarded his lost user profits.

In addition to the diminution in value or cost of cure, all other pecuniary losses resulting from the misappropriation or loss of the goods should be recoverable, subject to the usual limiting principles. So, most obviously, where the claimant is having replacement goods manufactured, any loss of interim user profit or any charge reasonably incurred in hiring a temporary replacement should be recoverable.

Where the claimant gets his goods back he will still be entitled to some damages for having been temporarily deprived of them. So, for example, in *Hillesden Securities Ltd v Ryjak Ltd*,[7] where the claimant's car had been returned at the commencement of the trial, the claimant was awarded damages under the Torts (Interference with Goods) Act 1977, s 3 for the temporary loss of use based on the commercial hire fee that it would otherwise have gained during the weeks between the date of the conversion and the date of the car's return. *Strand Electric and Engineering Co Ltd v Brisford Entertainments Ltd*[8] was followed. There the defendants had wrongfully detained the claimants' electrical theatrical equipment. In a detinue action, the defendants were ordered to return the goods or pay their value (at the time of judgment) and additionally the claimants were awarded damages assessed according to a reasonable hiring charge for the period until judgment. The trial judge found, however, that the claimants would not themselves have realised the full hire during that period. Therefore the decision may be best viewed as compensating the claimants for loss of the fee that they would have charged the defendants for legitimate use of their goods or, as Denning LJ but not the majority preferred, as reversing the defendants' wrongful enrichment rather than compensating the claimants' loss of use.[9]

In *Saleslease Ltd v Davis*[10] the claimant recovered an MOT testing machine that had been wrongfully detained by the defendant. On its return, the claimant sold the machine for its market value. But during the period of wrongful detention, the claimant had lost an unusual opportunity to lease the machine to a third party. That lease would have allegedly given the claimant £8,194 more than the market selling price of

7   [1983] 1 WLR 959.
8   [1952] 2 QB 246.
9   Below, pp 379–380.
10   [1999] 1 WLR 1664.

the machine. The majority of the Court of Appeal (Walker and Butler-Sloss LJJ) held that, applying *The Arpad*[11] and *The Wagon Mound*[12] tests of remoteness, that loss could not have been reasonably anticipated by the defendant and was too remote. Nominal damages only could be recovered for the tortious conversion. Schiemann LJ, dissenting, thought that the defendant had been put on notice by the claimant of the potential unusual loss if it persisted with the detention and that the loss claimed was, therefore, not too remote and was recoverable. It is submitted that Schiemann LJ's dissenting judgment is to be preferred. Applying *The Wagon Mound*, the claimant had given the defendant clear notice of the particular loss that it would suffer by a continuation of the conversion. But, in any event, one might argue that the continued conversion was dishonest and that, applying the enlightened view of Lord Nicholls in *Kuwait Airways Corpn v Iraqi Airways Co (Nos 4 & 5)*,[13] the relevant remoteness test should have been that of directness rather than reasonable foreseeability.

(2) Land

Wrongful interference with land is mainly covered by the torts of trespass and nuisance. Normally a claimant is concerned with a temporary loss of use of his land, either because of wrongful occupation or use (and here the damages are often referred to as 'mesne profits')[14] or because the defendant's activities off the land have prevented the claimant using the land as desired.

Damages for the temporary loss of use of land attempt to compensate the claimant's lost user profit (a diminution in value measure). This will often comprise the rent or fee which would have been obtained if the defendant had not wrongfully interfered. For example, in *Hall & Co Ltd v Pearlberg*,[15] where the defendant had wrongfully occupied the claimants' two farms, the claimants were awarded, inter alia, £650 damages for trespass, representing the one year's rent that they would otherwise have been able to charge an incoming tenant. In other cases damages have been given for the loss of custom caused by the defendant's wrongful interference. For example in *Fritz v Hobson*[16] damages were awarded for the claimant's loss of custom caused by the defendant's nuisance in carrying on building operations which prevented free access along a

---

11 [1934] P 189.
12 [1961] AC 388.
13 [2002] UKHL 19, [2002] 2 AC 883. See above, p 82.
14 Eg *Clifton Securities Ltd* v *Huntley* [1948] 2 All ER 283; *Morris v Tarrant* [1971] 2 QB 143.
15 [1956] 1 WLR 244.
16 (1880) 14 Ch D 542.

public passage to the claimant's shop. Similarly in *Andreae v Selfridge & Co Ltd*[17] damages were awarded, inter alia, for the claimant's loss of hotel custom attributable to those building operations of the defendant which constituted a nuisance. Of course the loss of user profit is only recoverable to the extent that it does not infringe limiting principles, like remoteness and the duty to mitigate.

Sometimes, however, damages are based on what is regarded as a reasonable rent or fee irrespective of whether the claimant would have otherwise acquired that sum by letting to a third party.[18] Those damages can only sensibly be regarded as compensating loss of use if it is realistic to think that the claimant would have charged the defendant that sum for legitimate use of the land. The damages can alternatively be viewed as reversing the defendant's wrongful enrichment, and in some cases this seems the only realistic analysis.[19]

Where a claimant has been and *will be* prevented from using his land or using it as desired (that is, the deprivation is permanent) – for example, where no injunction is granted to restrain smells or noise or to remove buildings blocking lights – equitable damages (in lieu of an injunction) will normally be measured by the diminution in the market selling price of the land.[20] But in *Bracewell v Appleby*,[1] *Carr-Saunders v Dick McNeil Associates Ltd*,[2] and *Jaggard v Sawyer*[3] the courts have assessed damages according to what would have been a fair sum for the claimants to have accepted for granting the defendants, in the first and third case, a right of way and, in the second case, a right to obstruct light. In the first two cases the judges spoke of the damages being awarded for the claimant's 'loss of amenity'.[4] But in *Bracewell v Appleby* Graham J's emphasis on the profits the defendant had made from building his home (which was accessible

---

17 [1938] Ch 1.
18 Eg *Whitwham v Westminster, Brymbo, Coal & Coke Co* [1896] 1 Ch 894; *Swordheath Properties Ltd v Tabet* [1979] 1 WLR 285.
19 Below, pp 380–383.
20 Eg *Griffith v Clay & Sons Ltd* [1912] 2 Ch 291. For equitable damages, see below, ch 16.
1   [1975] Ch 408.
2   [1986] 1 WLR 922.
3   [1995] 1 WLR 269. See also *Severn Trent Water Ltd v Barnes* [2004] EWCA Civ 570 where damages of £610 were upheld as compensating the claimant's loss of opportunity to negotiate compensation in a case where the defendant had trespassed under a corner of the claimant's land by laying a water pipe. Of particular interest was the CA's rejection of the trial judge's additional award of £1,560 'restitutionary damages', based on the gains made by the defendant in using the pipe, on the reasoning that that overlapped with, or was inconsistent with, the compensatory award. For an analysis of the quantum of equitable damages in trespass (and breach of restrictive covenant) cases, in which the author tends to assume a compensatory rather than a restitutionary approach, see Halpern 'Damages in Lieu of an Injunction: How Much?' (2001) Conv 453.
4   [1975] Ch 408 at 420, [1986] 1 WLR 922 at 931.

only by using the claimant's road) makes it preferable to regard the damages in that case as restitutionary, reversing the defendant's wrongful enrichment.[5]

5. TORTS – PURE ECONOMIC LOSS

The term 'pure economic loss' is well-known in the realm of tortious negligence where it refers to economic loss that is not consequent on physical damage. Physical damage most obviously comprises personal injury or property damage but its 'spirit' also includes death, damage to reputation and wrongful interference with goods or land (apart from property damage). Hence, for our purposes, pure economic loss will be taken to comprise economic loss not consequent on any of the above kinds of 'physical damage'.

In looking at compensatory damages for pure economic loss it is convenient to divide between four general heads of tortious liability: misrepresentation; wrongful infringement of intellectual property rights; wrongful interference with business or contract; acts or omissions under the tort of negligence.

It is important to realise that the recovery of damages for pure economic loss was, until 40 years ago, severely restricted in that, other than for infringement of intellectual property rights, there was no liability for negligently inflicted pure economic loss; deceit and the torts concerning interference with contract or business require intentional or reckless conduct. But this restriction has been eased, initially by the development of the tort of negligent misrepresentation allowing the recovery of pure economic loss in *Hedley Byrne & Co Ltd v Heller & Partners Ltd*[6] and later by the recognition that, in some limited situations, a defendant can be liable in the tort of negligence for acts or omissions causing pure economic loss.

(1) Misrepresentation

A misrepresentation is the basis of a cause of action in tort where made fraudulently, as in the tort of deceit, or negligently, as in the tort of negligent misrepresentation. Similarly a negligent misrepresentation

---

5 Below, p 382.
6 [1964] AC 465. In *Caparo Industries Plc v Dickman* [1990] 2 AC 605 it was held that no duty of care was owed by auditors of a company to investors in that company who had relied on the auditors' accounts in making their investments. It was stressed by the House of Lords that liability for misrepresentation under *Hedley Byrne* required the representation to be claimant-specific and purpose-specific.

inducing the making of a contract between the parties is a statutory tort under s 2(1) of the Misrepresentation Act 1967.

(a) What is the aim of the damages?

Most discussion regarding damages for tortious misrepresentation has centred on what the compensatory principle here requires. As the tort consists of fraudulently or negligently making a false statement misleading the claimant, the aim should be to put the claimant into as good a position as if no statement misleading it had been made. Although the contrary has sometimes been suggested,[7] the aim is not and should not be to put the claimant into as good a position as it would have been in if the statement had been true, for this would go beyond the essence of the tort. The claimant's reliance, and not expectation, interest is therefore being protected.[8]

Damages for tortious misrepresentation are therefore fundamentally distinct from damages for breach of contract, where the claimant's expectations are fulfilled by putting it into as good a position as if the contract had been performed. At a deeper level the distinction between the two rests on the difference between lying and breaking one's promise, with the latter, unlike the former, generally comprising the breaking of a positive rather than a negative obligation. It is hence essential to distinguish between mere representations, where the sole action is for tortious misrepresentation, and warranties, where the claimant can sue for breach of contract; or, to put it another way, between statements merely inducing the making of a contract and the terms of the contract.

A number of cases show that the aim of damages for tortious misrepresentation is indeed to put the claimant into as good a position as if no statement had been made, rather than as if the statement had been true. For fraudulent misrepresentation an important case is *Doyle v Olby (Ironmongers) Ltd*.[9] The claimant had bought a business from the defendant company. He was induced to do so by various fraudulent misrepresentations. The critical one was that the trade of the business was 'all over the counter', when in fact half of it was obtained by a traveller going out to canvass customers. The judges, particularly Lord Denning, indicated that there is a difference between damages for the tort of deceit and for breach of contract. Lord Denning said:

---

7   As we have seen above at pp 109–122, the *SAAMCO* principle is flawed in its insistence that damages for breach of an obligation to use reasonable care in making a statement should be restricted by the position the claimant would have been in had the statement been true.

8   See above, pp 34, 68–69.

9   [1969] 2 QB 158. See also *East v Maurer* [1991] 1 WLR 461, below, p 260.

'It appears therefore that the plaintiff's counsel submitted and the judge accepted that the proper measure of damages was the "cost of making good the representation" or what came to the same thing, "the reduction in value of the goodwill" due to the misrepresentation. In so doing, he treated the misrepresentation as if it were a contractual promise, that is, as if there were a contractual term to the effect, "The trade is all over the counter. There is no need to employ a traveller." I think it was the wrong measure. Damages for fraud and conspiracy are assessed differently from damages for breach of contract ... On principle, the distinction seems to be this: in contract, the defendant has made a promise and broken it. The object of damages is to put the plaintiff in as good a position as far as money can do it, as if the promise had been performed. In fraud, the defendant has been guilty of a deliberate wrong by inducing the plaintiff to act to his detriment. The object of damages is to compensate the plaintiff for all the loss he has suffered, so far again, as money can do it.'[10]

Winn and Sachs LJJ agreed with Lord Denning, and Winn LJ specifically approved the passages in the 12th edition of *Mayne and McGregor on Damages*[11] which emphasised that damages for deceit aim to put the claimant into the position he would have been in if no statement had been made. The learned authors there relied, as Lord Denning did in *Doyle v Olby*, on cases such as *McConnel v Wright*[12] and *Clark v Urquhart*[13] which had established that, when the claimant is induced to buy shares by a fraudulent misrepresentation, the measure of damages is not the value of the shares if the representation had been true less their actual value but rather the purchase price paid less their actual value.

Doyle v Olby was approved and applied in the leading case of *Smith New Court Securities Ltd v Scrimgeour Vickers (Asset Management) Ltd*.[14] The claimant bought shares in F Inc that were pledged to the defendant bank. In reliance on false representations by representatives of the bank that there were rival bids close to the price offered by the claimant, the claimant went ahead and bought the shares at 82.25p per share at a total price of £23,141. A couple of months later, F Inc revealed that it had been the victim of a massive fraud and its share price dropped dramatically. The claimant sold the shares over several months at prices of between 30p and 40p for £11,788 (at a loss of £11,353). In an action for the tort of deceit, it was held by the House of Lords, approving *Doyle v Olby*, that the claimant was entitled to be put into as good a position as if no false representations had been made; that the claimant was not restricted to the loss as assessed at the date of the transaction; and that all direct

10 [1969] 2 QB 158 at 166–167.
11 (12th edn, 1961) paras 955 ff.
12 [1903] 1 Ch 546.
13 [1930] AC 28.
14 [1997] AC 254.

consequential loss, even if not reasonably foreseeable, was recoverable. The claimant was therefore held entitled to damages for the difference between the contract price and the amount actually realised by the sale of the shares (ie its full loss of £11,353).

Doyle v Olby was also applied but, it is submitted, the wrong result reached in the earlier case of *Smith Kline & French Laboratories Ltd v Long*.[15] The claimant was induced by the deceit of the defendant, the managing director of Swift Exports Ltd, to sell to Swift 16,800 packs of tablets at a price of £56.66 per pack. The fraudulent misrepresentation was to the effect that Swift would sell the tablets in Central Africa. In fact they were sold in Holland. Swift paid all but £157,028 of the agreed contract price but then became insolvent. Whitford J dismissed the claim on the ground that the claimant had suffered no loss as a result of the fraud. The Court of Appeal reversed that decision and awarded £157,028.

That award would only have been correct if the claimant would have sold the tablets at the same price to someone else had it not been induced to sell to Swift. Yet the claimant conceded that it could have supplied whatever quantity of tablets was needed to meet demand (and that it could be assumed that the tablets had cost nothing to produce). It should have followed that the contract with Swift could not be treated as having deprived the claimant of the opportunity to sell those tablets (at the same price) to someone else: and that there was no true analogy with cases on wrongful interference with goods which have awarded damages based on the value of the goods.[16]

Moving on to the tort of negligent misrepresentation, as established in *Hedley Byrne & Co v Heller & Partners Ltd*,[17] *Esso Petroleum Co Ltd v Mardon*[18] shows the application of the same principle. Here a tenant was induced to take a lease of a petrol station from an oil company by a statement made by an experienced salesman on the company's behalf, as to the potential throughput of petrol at that station. The Court of Appeal held that the defendant was liable, inter alia, for its salesman's pre-contractual negligent misrepresentation. As regards the damages, Lord Denning said:

> 'Mr Mardon is not to be compensated for "loss of a bargain". He was given no bargain that the throughput would amount to 200,000 gallons a year. He is only to be compensated for having been induced to enter into a contract which turned out to be disastrous for him. Whether it be called breach of warranty or negligent misstatement, its effect was not to warrant the throughput, but only to induce him to enter into the contract. So the damages in either case are to be measured by the loss he suffered ... It

---

15   [1989] 1 WLR 1.
16   Above, pp 248–251.
17   [1964] AC 465.
18   [1976] QB 801.

is to be measured in a similar way as the loss due to a personal injury. You should look into the future so as to forecast what would have been likely to happen if he had never entered into the contract; and contrast it with his position as it now is, as a result of entering into it.'[19]

Shaw LJ agreed with Lord Denning over these principles, and while Ormrod LJ did not clearly adopt this approach his comments on the computation of damages are consistent with it.

Similarly in *Box v Midland Bank Ltd*,[20] which concerned a negligent misrepresentation made by a bank's employee regarding the claimant's chances of getting a large loan from the bank, Lloyd J had the following to say on the question of how to assess the damages:

'The damages claimed amount to just under £250,000 but a very large part of that represents the gains that the plaintiff would have made if the Manitoban contract had been successfully carried through and the Churchman Newton group saved. Once the claim in contract had been abandoned, Mr Box could not hope to recover for loss of his bargain and [his counsel] rightly abandoned that part of the claim. Instead he says that Mr Box is entitled to be put in the position he would have been in if the negligent misstatement had not been made. That always involves questions of the greatest difficulty. It was difficult in *Doyle v Olby*; it was difficult in *Esso v Mardon*; it is even more difficult here.'[1]

Applying this principle Lloyd J ultimately assessed damages at £5,000.

With regard to statutory liability under the Misrepresentation Act 1967, s 2(1), it is also now clear (contrary to early cases suggesting that the claimant should be put into as good a position as if the representation had been true)[2] that the basic principle is to put the claimant into the position it would have been in if no statement has been made. In *F & B Entertainments Ltd v Leisure Enterprises Ltd*,[3] Walton J ordered an inquiry as to damages under s 2(1) saying that, 'The measure of damages, quite clearly, is the same as those in an action for damages for deceit.'[4] In *André & Cie SA v Ets Michel Blanc & Fils*[5] Ackner J similarly said of s 2(1), 'To my mind, the subsection puts the victim of the innocent misrepresentation in the same position, relative to his claim for damages, as the victim of the fraudulent misrepresentation. To his claim,

19   [1976] QB 801 at 820–821.
20   [1979] 2 Lloyd's Rep 391. See also *Naughton v O'Callaghan* [1990] 3 All ER 191 at 196–198.
1   [1979] 2 Lloyd's Rep 391 at 399.
2   *Gosling v Anderson* (1972) 223 Estates Gazette 1743; *Davis & Co (Wines) Ltd v Afa-Minerva (EMI) Ltd* [1974] 2 Lloyd's Rep 27; *Watts v Spence* [1976] Ch 165.
3   (1976) 240 Estates Gazette 455.
4   (1976) 240 Estates Gazette 455 at 461.
5   [1977] 2 Lloyd's Rep 166.

the measure of damages appropriate to claims in tort has to be applied'.[6] In *McNally v Welltrade International Ltd*,[7] Sir Douglas Franks QC, in assessing damages under s 2(1) applied *Doyle v Olby* and said, 'The plaintiff's position before the inducement should be compared with his position at the end of the transaction.'[8] And in *Cemp Properties (UK) Ltd v Dentsply Research & Development Corpn*,[9] in which the Court of Appeal awarded damages under s 2(1) to a purchaser of land, Bingham LJ regarded it as 'the cardinal rule of damages in this field that the plaintiff should be put in the same financial position as if the misrepresentation had not been made.' Furthermore Balcombe LJ in *Royscot Trust Ltd v Rogerson*[10] expressly disapproved the early cases describing them as 'initial aberrations' and said, '[I]t is difficult to see how the measure of damages under [s 2(1)] could be other than the tortious measure and ... that is now generally accepted.'

This must be correct. As has been explained above, it follows from the very nature of the wrong of misrepresentation. Moreover, it would be irrational to award the claimant the expectation measure under the Misrepresentation Act 1967, s 2(1) when it is confined to being put into as good a position as if no statement had been made under the very similar tort of negligent misrepresentation and under the more blameworthy tort of deceit.

It follows from the above reasoning that damages that can be awarded for even a purely innocent misrepresentation in lieu of rescission under the Misrepresentation Act 1967, s 2(2)[11] should not go beyond putting the claimant into as good a position as if no statement had been made.[12]

6   [1977] 2 Lloyd's Rep 166 at 181.
7   [1978] IRLR 497.
8   [1978] IRLR 497 at 499.
9   [1991] 2 EGLR 197 at 201.
10 [1991] 2 QB 297 at 304–305. See also *Chesneau v Interhome Ltd* [1983] CLY 988, *Sharneyford Supplies Ltd v Edge* [1987] Ch 305 at 323 (per Balcombe LJ); *Naughton v O'Callaghan* [1990] 3 All ER 191 at 196–198; *Gran Gelato Ltd v Richcliff (Group) Ltd* [1992] Ch 560 at 574–575.
11 The discretion to award damages in lieu of rescission is dependent on rescission otherwise being available and not being barred by one of the standard bars to rescission, such as *restitutio in integrum* being impossible: *Government of Zanzibar v British Aerospace (Lancaster House) Ltd* [2000] 1 WLR 2333. This is because the purpose of the Misrepresentation Act 1967, s 2(2) is not to add to the misrepresentee's remedies but to give the courts a discretion to cut back the remedy of rescission where the misrepresentation has been trivial and rescission would cause undue hardship to the misrepresentor.
12 See generally *William Sindall plc v Cambridgeshire CC* [1994] 1 WLR 1016: in obiter dicta the Court of Appeal indicated that, whether recoverable under the Misrepresentation Act 1967, s 2(1) or not, loss due to the sharp fall in the market value of the land subsequent to its purchase by the claimant could not be included within damages under the Misrepresentation Act 1967, s 2(2).

(b) Expenses caused and gains forgone

To put the claimant into as good a position as if no representation had been made it can recover damages for all the expenses caused by and gains forgone because of the misrepresentation, subject to the usual limiting principles.

Dealing first with expenses caused, a useful example is *Richardson v Silvester*.[13] The defendant inserted in a newspaper an advert for the letting of a farm which, as he knew, he had no power to let. In reliance on the advert the claimant incurred expenses by himself inspecting the property and in employing other persons to inspect and value it. It was held that the claimant had an action for deceit enabling him to recover his expenses.

Where the expenses take the form of a contract price paid under a contract induced by a misrepresentation, the damages are assessed according to the contract price paid minus the value of what has been received under the contract. This is well illustrated by cases where the misrepresentation induced the purchase of shares. So, for example, in *Smith New Court Securities Ltd v Scrimgeour Vickers (Asset Management) Ltd*,[14] as we have seen, the claimant was awarded damages of the difference between the price paid for shares (£23,141) and the price at which they were sold (£11,788). And in the earlier case of *Archer v Brown*[15] the purchase price of £30,000 was recovered as damages because the claimant received no shares in return, the defendant having already sold them to someone else. The claimant also received damages of £13,528 in respect of the interest payable on a bank loan taken out to buy the shares. Similarly in *Naughton v O'Callaghan*,[16] in which the claimants had been induced to buy a horse by a negligent misrepresentation as to its true pedigree, the damages awarded were the difference between the price paid (26,000 guineas) and the horse's value nearly two years later when the misrepresentation was discovered and the horse had proved a failure on the racecourse (£1,500); plus £9,820 expenses incurred in training and keeping the horse.

A more complex illustration of damages based on expenses caused minus benefits accruing is provided by *Doyle v Olby*.[17] The expenses amounted to £12,500, and comprised the purchase of business and stock (£9,500) and interest on a loan and overdraft plus rates (£3,000). The benefits amounted to £7,000 and comprised the sale of the business and

---

13   (1873) LR 9 QB 34.
14   [1997] AC 254. See also, eg *McConnel v Wright* [1903] 1 Ch 546; *Clark v Urquhart* [1930] AC 28.
15   [1985] QB 401.
16   [1990] 3 All ER 191. See also above, p 190.
17   [1969] 2 QB 158.

stock (£4,300) and salary and living accommodation (£2,700). The damages awarded were therefore £5,500 (£12,500 minus £7,000).

Turning to gains forgone, there are relatively few examples. One is *Burrows v Rhodes*,[18] where the claimant joined a private army invading the South African Republic in reliance on the defendant's fraudulent misrepresentations that protection was needed for women and children, that the invasion would be reinforced by other lawful troops, and that the plan had the sanction of HM Government. It was held that the claimant had a good action in deceit enabling him to recover, inter alia, his loss of earnings while involved in the invasion. Another example is *East v Maurer*,[19] in which the claimant had been induced to buy a hair salon by the vendor's fraudulent misrepresentation that he would not be continuing to run a competing salon. In an action for deceit, the claimant was awarded not only the price paid minus the selling price, plus the trading losses, plus the expenses incurred in buying and selling and carrying out improvements, but also £10,000 for profits forgone. It was explained by the Court of Appeal (in reducing the sum that had been awarded under the last head by the trial judge) that the recoverable profits forgone were what the claimant might have been expected to make in another similar hairdressing business and not the profits that would have been made in this particular business had the vendor's representation been true. The latter could only have been justified in an action for breach of a contractual warranty.

A final and particularly interesting example of the recovery of gains foregone is provided by *Clef Acquitaine SARL v Laporte Materials (Barrow) Ltd*.[20] The claimant had entered into two profitable distributorship contracts with the defendant. The defendant had induced the claimant to agree to the particular terms by a fraudulent misrepresentation. Had that fraudulent misrepresentation not been made, the claimant would have entered into the contracts with the defendant on more favourable terms and would have made greater profits than it in fact did make. In an action for deceit, it was held by the Court of Appeal that the claimant was entitled to those gains foregone (that is, the greater profits lost). It was no bar to awarding damages for those lost profits that the claimant had still entered into profitable, rather than loss-making, contracts with the defendant.

18 [1899] 1 QB 816.
19 [1991] 1 WLR 461.
20 [2001] QB 488.

(2) Wrongful infringement of intellectual property rights[1]

The torts concerned with the wrongful infringement of intellectual property rights are the infringement of a trade mark, patent, design, performer's property right, or copyright and passing-off.[2] To put the claimant into as good a position as if there had been no wrongful infringement it can recover damages for all the expenses caused by and gains forgone because of the infringement, subject to the usual limiting principles.

There are no clear examples of cases in which expenses caused by the defendant's infringement of the claimant's intellectual property rights have been compensated. However, in *A-G Spalding Bros v A W Gamage Ltd*[3] the defendants had sold some of the claimants' old and discarded footballs as their new goods and in a passing-off action the claimants were awarded damages, inter alia, for what it would have cost to counter-advertise. It clearly follows that if they had incurred expenses in counter-advertising these would have been recoverable.

In contrast there have been numerous cases compensating for the claimant's lost profits. The profits that have most commonly been lost have been from the reduction in sales of goods or materials as a result of the defendant's unlawful competition.[4] The assessment of those lost profits is often very difficult and the courts frequently resort to rough estimation. Certainly it cannot simply be assumed that the sales made by the defendant from selling infringing goods or materials correspond to the claimant's lost sales, that is, that there is equivalence between the diversion of customers from the claimant and the customers buying from the defendant.[5] In particular one is concerned only with profits lost from

---

1 See Brown 'Damages and Account of Profits in Trademark, Trade Secrets, Copyright and Patent Law' (1977) 3 Auck Univ LR 188.

2 A non-negligent wrongdoer is not liable for damages (but may be subject to an injunction) for infringement of a patent or copyright or performers' property right or primary infringement of a design right: see the Patents Act 1977, s 62(1); the Copyright, Designs and Patents Act 1988, ss 97(1), 191J(1), 233(1). In contrast, damages (and an injunction) may be awarded for the common law torts of infringement of a trade mark and passing off on a strict liability basis: *Gillette UK Ltd v Edenwest Ltd* [1994] RPC 279. The standard of liability applied in respect of an account of profits for the intellectual property torts is even more inconsistent as between the different torts: see below, pp 385–386.

3 (1918) 35 RPC 101.

4 *United Horse-Shoe and Nail Co Ltd v Stewart & Co* (1888) 13 App Cas 401 (patent infringement); *Draper v Trist* [1939] 3 All ER 513 (passing-off); *Aktiebolaget Manus v Fullwood & Bland Ltd* (1954) 71 RPC 243, 250 (infringement of trademark); *Catnic Components Ltd v Hill & Smith Ltd* [1983] FSR 512 (patent infringement); *Gerber Garment Technology Inc v Lectra Systems Ltd* [1997] RPC 443 (patent infringement). In *Sutherland Publishing Co Ltd v Caxton Publishing Co Ltd* [1936] Ch 323 at 336, Lord Wright said that for copyright infringement, 'The measure of damages is the depreciation caused by the infringement to the value of the copyright, as a chose in action.' Taking this approach the lost sale profits represent the depreciation in value.

5 *United Horse-Shoe and Nail Co Ltd v Stewart & Co* (1888) 13 App Cas 401. But there was taken to be this equivalence in *American Braided Wire Co v Thomson* (1890) 44 Ch D 274.

(that is, factually caused by) the infringement and not the profit that would in any event have been lost because of lawful competition. Furthermore the defendant's profits may have resulted from special exertions which the claimant would not have undertaken.

Some lost sale profits may also have been the result of the claimant lowering its prices to counter the defendant's unlawful competition. Damages for such losses were awarded in the patent infringement case of *American Braided Wire Co v Thomson*,[6] but were denied in *United Horse-Shoe and Nail Co Ltd v Stewart*[7] on the ground that the claimants would have lowered their prices irrespective of the patent infringement.

However, the claimant may not have lost sales profits; rather it may have lost the profits from licensing its intellectual property. This loss is assessed by determining the lump sum or royalties the claimant would have received for granting a licence to the defendant. A detailed examination of the assessment of such damages was made by the House of Lords in *General Tire Co v Firestone Tyre Co Ltd*,[8] an infringement of patent case. Ultimately damages were assessed on the basis of a royalty rate of 3/8th of a US cent, the Lords holding that there was sufficient evidence indicating that this 'going rate' (that is the rate at which other licences for the patent had been granted) was the rate for which the claimants would have granted the patent licence to the defendants. Lord Wilberforce did, however, stress that:

> 'Before a "going rate" of royalty can be taken as the basis on which an infringer should be held liable, it must be shown that the circumstances in which the going rate was paid are the same as or at least comparable with those in which the patentee and the infringer are assumed to strike their bargain.'[9]

In *Watson, Laidlaw & Co v Pott, Cassels & Williamson*,[10] an infringement of patent case, Lord Shaw suggested that even where the claimant can show neither loss of sales profit, because, for example, it could not have sold patented machines in the particular area where the defendant has sold them, nor loss of licensing profit, because it would not have granted a patent licence, it can still recover substantial damages. Lord Shaw drew an analogy with taking someone's horse, using it and returning it in the same condition, and said:

6 (1890) 44 Ch D 274. *Alexander v Henry* (1895) 12 RPC 360 (infringement of trademark); *Gerber Garment Technology Inc v Lectra Systems Ltd* [1997] RPC 443 (patent infringement).
7 (1888) 13 App Cas 401.
8 [1975] 1 WLR 819. *Meters Ltd v Metropolitan Gas Meters Ltd* (1911) 28 RPC 157 at 164–165 (patent infringement); *Scovin-Bradford v Valpoint Properties Ltd* [1971] Ch 1007 (infringement of copyright); *Catnic Components Ltd v Hill & Smith Ltd* [1983] FSR 512 (patent infringement); *Irvine v Talksport Ltd* [2003] EWCA Civ 423, [2003] 2 All ER (Comm) 141 (passing-off).
9 [1975] 1 WLR 819 at 825.
10 (1914) 31 RPC 104.

'Each of the infringements was an actionable wrong, and although it may have been committed in a range of business or of territory which the patentee might not have reached, he is entitled to hire or royalty in respect of each unauthorised use of his property. Otherwise, the remedy might fall unjustly short of the wrong.'[11]

However, it is difficult to view this approach as being concerned to put the claimant into as good a position as if no tort had been committed, and it looks rather as if it is based on reversing the defendant's wrongful enrichment, with the royalties representing either the expense the defendant saved in not having to acquire an equivalent patent licence or a fair proportion of the defendant's profits.[12] However, in the *General Tire* case the House of Lords disapproved a similar sort of approach adopted by the Court of Appeal in that case, Lord Wilberforce saying:

'Given that the respondents were not claiming an account of profits, the consequence of departing from the conception of loss can only be to discover a *tertium quid* defined, it seems, by reference to what the infringer ought fairly to have paid. But there is no warrant for this on authority or principle.'[13]

(3) Wrongful interference with business or contract

Wrongful interference with the claimant's business or contract is the basis of several torts, for example, inducing breach of contract, intimidation, interference by unlawful means, conspiracy and injurious falsehood. To put the claimant into as good a position as if there had been no such interference it can recover damages for all the expenses caused by and gains forgone because of the interference, subject to the usual limiting principles.

As regards expenses caused, *British Motor Trade Association v Salvadori*[14] provides a good example. The claimant trade association, in an attempt to keep down the price of certain cars, required all purchasers of those cars to covenant not to resell within 12 months. The defendants with the intention of breaking the system induced certain purchasers to break the covenant. In an action for inducing breach of contract and conspiracy

---

11 (1914) 31 RPC 104 at 120.
12 Below, pp 379–384.
13 [1975] 1 WLR 819 at 833.
14 [1949] Ch 556.

Roxburgh J held that the claimants could recover, inter alia, the expenses incurred in 'unravelling and detecting the unlawful machinations of the defendants.'[15]

But where the defendant has interfered with the claimant's business or contract, the claimant is usually primarily concerned to recover damages for the profit lost as a result of such interference. So, for example, in *Goldsoll v Goldman*[16] the defendant induced an employee of the claimant to break his contract with the claimant by setting up a rival jewellery business close to the claimant's. In an action for inducing breach of contract damages were awarded for the claimant's general loss of business.

Less commonly the gains forgone may comprise a loss of earnings. In *Morgan v Fry*[17] the claimant lockman had been dismissed by his employers under pressure from the defendant. In an action for intimidation the claimant was at first instance awarded the earnings he would have made as a lockman (and it was assumed that he would not have continued in that job for more than another five years) minus his present wages working in a different job.

It should be noted that damages awarded for tortious interference with contract will not necessarily be the same as for breach of that contract. In particular, principles like remoteness and contributory negligence do not apply in the same way.

(4) Acts or omissions under the tort of negligence

The courts over the last 30 or so years have struggled to decide on the extent to which pure economic loss caused by negligent acts or omissions is recoverable in the tort of negligence. At times wider liability has been favoured but, more recently, the courts have returned to a narrower approach, in which the traditional fears of an indeterminate liability to an indeterminate number and of undermining contractual terms have

---

15 [1949] Ch 556 at 569. This case was distinguished in *Admiral Management Services Ltd v Para-Protect Ltd* [2002 EWHC 233 (Ch), [2002] 1 WLR 2722, where no extra expenses had been incurred by the claimant in investigating the torts; rather the employees carrying out the investigation work had simply been paid the salaries that the claimant would have paid them in any event.

16 [1914] 2 Ch 603. See also *Admiral Management Services Ltd v Para-Protect Ltd* [2002] EWHC 233 (Ch), [2002] 1 WLR 2722: loss of revenue recoverable in principle but no evidence of this provided. Stanley Burnton J also indicated (and see further, in support of this, *Pearson v Sanders Witherspoon* [2000] PNLR 110, CA, a solicitor's negligence case, and *Standard Chartered Bank v Pakistan National Shipping Corpn* [2001] EWCA Civ 55, [2001] 1 All ER (Comm) 822, paras 48–49, a deceit case) that 'damages for management time', caused by the tort, accepted in principle by Forbes J in *Tate & Lyle Food and Distribution Ltd v Greater London Council* [1982] 1 WLR 149, were recoverable only if there was a loss of revenue (or, presumably, extra expenditure).

17 [1968] 1 QB 521; rvsd on liability [1968] 2 QB 710.

been re-emphasised.[18] Various concepts have been utilised by the courts in trying to draw a coherent boundary of liability, for example, 'assumption of responsibility', 'reliance', 'proximity', and whether imposition of a duty of care is 'fair and reasonable'. But in truth these concepts give relatively little guidance and one tends to be forced back to incremental reasoning from the facts of past decisions.[19]

In looking at how damages should be assessed for negligently caused pure economic loss, it seems helpful to divide between (a) negligent interference with contract or business and (b) negligent performance of services beneficial to the claimant.[20]

(a) Negligent interference with contract or business

No English case has yet allowed the recovery of damages for pure economic loss caused by a negligent interference with contract or business. The situation is exemplified by the pure economic loss claim in *Spartan Steel and Alloys v Martin & Co (Contractors) Ltd*.[1] In that case, the defendants had negligently damaged an electricity cable, thereby cutting off the electricity supply to the claimants' factory for 14 hours. As a result the 'melt' then in the furnace was damaged. The claimants were able to recover damages for the damaged melt (£368) and the loss of profit that would have been made on that melt (£400), but not for the profit on four further melts (£1,767) that would have been put through the furnace if the electricity supply had not been cut off. The last head was denied because it amounted to pure economic loss.

As regards the assessment of damages, the important point is that if negligently caused pure economic loss were to be recoverable in English law in this situation, it should be seen alongside the earlier section on wrongful (intentional) interference with business or contract and damages should be assessed in basically the same way; ie in aiming to put the claimant into as good a position as if the defendant had not negligently

---

18 Important cases denying a duty of care in respect of negligent acts or omissions causing pure economic loss include *Candlewood Navigation Corpn Ltd v Mitsui OSK Lines Ltd* [1986] AC 1; *Muirhead v Industrial Tank Specialities Ltd* [1986] QB 507; *Leigh and Sillavan Ltd v Aliakmon Shipping Co Ltd* [1986] AC 785; *Murphy v Brentwood District Council* [1991] 1 AC 398.
19 For an excellent attempt to give a succinct account of this turbulent area of the law, see Rogers *Winfield & Jolowicz on Tort* (16th edn, 2002) pp 145–163.
20 For a similar division, see MacGrath 'The Recovery of Economic Loss in Negligence – an Emerging Dichotomy' (1985) OJLS 350.
1   [1973] QB 27.

interfered, expenses caused,[2] and particularly gains forgone, as claimed for in *Spartan Steel*, should be compensated in so far as not ruled out by limiting principles such as remoteness. In the same vein it should be added that this aspect of pure economic loss recovery for tortious negligence does not raise problems for the distinction between tort and contract because it is within traditional tort reasoning in imposing a negative obligation not to interfere making someone worse off rather than imposing a positive obligation to confer a benefit.

(b) Negligent performance of services beneficial to the claimant

Most of the cases on negligently inflicted pure economic loss have so far been concerned with this situation. It occurs, for example, where a professional person, such as a solicitor,[3] surveyor,[4] or an engineer,[5] fails to advise his client properly. The client has an action against him in the tort of negligence to compensate for the pure economic loss caused. Similarly in *Henderson v Merrett Syndicates Ltd*[6] Names at Lloyd's were held entitled to damages for pure economic loss in the tort of negligence against the managing agents of syndicates of which they were members.

The client will also almost always have a prima facie concurrent claim for breach of the professional's contractual duty of care[7] although in several cases the tortious claim was relied on because the contractual action was time-barred. Subject to differences in limiting principles, such as remoteness, the assessment of damages will be the same for breach of the tortious as for the breach of the contractual duty of care with the basic aim being to put the claimant into as good a position as if the defendant had performed the services using reasonable care. For example, in *Perry v Sidney Phillips & Son*,[8] if the survey had been properly carried out, the purchaser would not have bought the house or at least

---

2   An example of damages compensating for expenses caused in this context is provided by the Australian case of *Caltex Oil (Australia) Pty Ltd v Dredge 'Willemstad'* (1976) 136 CLR 529: the claimants were awarded damages compensating for the costs of transporting oil by other means when the defendants' dredger negligently damaged an underwater pipeline used, but not owned, by the claimants.

3   Eg *Midland Bank Trust Co Ltd v Hett, Stubbs & Kemp* [1979] Ch 384; *Forster v Outred & Co* [1982] 1 WLR 86.

4   Eg *Perry v Sidney Phillips & Son* [1982] 1 WLR 1297.

5   Eg *Pirelli General Cable Works Ltd v Oscar Faber & Partners* [1983] 2 AC 1.

6   [1995] 2 AC 145. See above, p 6. See also *Spring v Guardian Assurance Plc* [1995] 2 AC 296 (duty of care owed to one's former employee in writing a reference that was an essential requirement for the claimant's employment by a new employer).

7   Above, pp 5–7. In so far as the basis of the tort liability is breach of promise, it is strongly arguable that the use of tort is a pragmatic, not a principled, development designed to evade deficiencies in contract: see above, p 9.

8   [1982] 1 WLR 1297.

would not have paid more for it than its true market value. Hence damages for both breach of contract and the tort of negligence were assessed according to the purchase price of the house minus its actual market value (difference in value measure); and Lord Denning, having said that the aim of damages for breach of contract is 'to put the plaintiff in the same position as he would have been in if the contract had been properly performed' continued, 'Even if the claim be laid in tort against the surveyor, the damages should be on the same basis.'[9] It is important to realise that while one can see this as being in line with the usual compensatory aim of putting the claimant into as good a position as if no tort had been committed, the tortious obligation here is a positive one to benefit the claimant by performing the services non-negligently.

But the tortious action may also be available where the defendant is performing the services under a contract with a party other than the claimant, so that (subject to an exception applying) privity prevents the claimant suing for breach of contract.[10] The best example is *White v Jones*.[11] Here delay by a solicitor in carrying out his client's instructions to draw up a new will meant that the client died without that new will having been executed. It was held (Lord Keith and Mustill dissenting) that a duty of care was owed by the solicitor to the claimants who would have benefited under the new will. Lord Goff based his reasoning on the concept of an 'assumption of responsibility' and on there being no other satisfactory way of filling the gap whereby the person who had suffered the loss could not otherwise sue and the person who could sue had suffered no loss. Note also that the claimants were a small number of identified people and there would otherwise have been no sanction in respect of the solicitor's breach of professional duty. Another example – although it is unclear whether this still remains good law – is the controversial decision of the House of Lords in *Junior Books Ltd v Veitchi Co Ltd*.[12] Here the owners of a new factory were held able to recover damages from sub-contractors, against whom they had no

---

9   [1982] 1 WLR 1297 at 1302.

10   In so far as the basis of the tort liability is breach of promise, it is strongly arguable that the use of tort is here a pragmatic, not a principled, development designed to evade an excessively restrictive privity doctrine in contract: see above, p 9.

11   [1995] 2 AC 207. This decision approved *Ross v Caunters* [1980] Ch 297. See also the claims of the *indirect* names in *Henderson v Merrett Syndicates Ltd* [1995] 2 AC 145; and *Gorham v British Telecommunications plc* [2000] 1 WLR 2129 (duty of care owed to dependants in their own right for defendant's negligent failure to advise the deceased who had opted out of a better pension scheme than the one he had opted in to).

12   [1983] 1 AC 520. For doubts as to the reliability of this decision, see, eg *D & F Estates Ltd v Church Commissioners* [1989] AC 177 at 202 (per Lord Bridge); *The Orjula* [1995] 2 Lloyd's Rep 395 at 401 (Mance J).

contractual rights, for pure economic loss caused by the sub-contractors' negligence in laying a floor in the factory, which was defective and had started to crack.

Assuming that a defendant is held tortiously liable (and in a book on remedies this is the starting point) then, as where the parties are in a contractual relationship, the damages should be assessed according to the position the claimant would have been in if the services had been performed non-negligently. In other words, subject to differences in limiting principles, the approach should be the same as for contractual pecuniary loss. For example, in *Junior Books* the factory owner was entitled to the cost of cure – namely the cost of replacing the defective floor (ie of putting in a floor as specified in the plans) – plus loss of user profit (ie lost production) while the floor was being relaid. And in *White v Jones* the claimants were held entitled to the £9,000 each that they would have received under the amended will had the solicitor carried out his instructions properly.

Chapter 10

Personal injury losses

Personal injury includes disease and physical illness as well as cuts, bruises, broken bones and loss of limbs. Recognised psychiatric illnesses[1] are included, as also are 'symptomless' personal injuries, such as pleural plaques caused by inhaling asbestos dust.[2] Damages have also been awarded for the physical and mental effects of a rape or sexual assault.[3]

Claims for personal injury are nearly always founded on a tort (and usually the tort of negligence or breach of statutory duty) but they can also be founded on a breach of contract.[4] Subject to differences in relation to some of the limiting principles, like remoteness, the principles applied are and should be the same whether founded on tort or breach of contract.

1. CLAIMS BY THE INJURED PERSON

The general compensatory aims dictate that damages should put the claimant into as good a position as if the personal injury had not occurred. In so doing, damages are awarded for several heads of loss,

---

1   *Hinz v Berry* [1970] 2 QB 40 at 42 (morbid depression); *McLoughlin v O'Brian* [1983] 1 AC 410 at 418, 431 ('organic depression and a change of personality'); *Brice v Brown* [1984] 1 All ER 997 at 1005–1006 (hysterical personality disorder); *Alcock v Chief Constable of South Yorkshire Police* [1992] 1 AC 310 (post-traumatic stress disorder); *Walker v Northumberland County Council* [1995] 1 All ER 737 (nervous breakdown consequent on workplace stress); *Page v Smith* [1996] AC 155 (chronic fatigue syndrome); *Vernon v Bosley* [1997] 1 All ER 577 (pathological grief disorder); *Frost v Chief Constable of South Yorkshire Police* [1998] QB 254 (post-traumatic stress disorder); *Hatton v Sutherland* [2002] EWCA Civ 76, [2002] 2 All ER 1 and *Barber v Somerset County Council* [2004] UKHL 13, [2004] 2 All ER 385 (depressive illness or nervous breakdown consequent on workplace stress). See generally Law Commission *Liability for Psychiatric Illness*, Report No 249 (1998) esp Part III. See also *Malyon v Lawrence, Messer & Co* [1968] 2 Lloyd's Rep 539 (compensation neurosis).
2   *Church v Ministry of Defence* (1984) 134 NLJ 623; *Sykes v Ministry of Defence* (1984) Times, 23 March.
3   *W v Meah* [1986] 1 All ER 935; *Griffiths v Williams* (1995) Times, 24 November.
4   *Summers v Salford Corpn* [1943] AC 283; *Matthews v Kuwait Bechtel Corpn* [1959] 2 QB 57; *Kralj v McGrath* [1986] 1 All ER 54; *Berryman v London Borough of Hounslow* [1997] PIQR P83; *Giambrone v JMC Holidays Ltd (No 2)* [2004] EWCA Civ 158, [2004] 2 All ER 891.

both pecuniary and non-pecuniary. Before examining these, three introductory points should be made.

First, as laid down in *Jefford v Gee*,[5] awards must be itemised, at least into non-pecuniary loss, pre-trial pecuniary loss and future pecuniary loss. This itemisation was held to be required, because of the differing awards of interest payable or non-payable under these three heads.[6] So, as regards non-pecuniary loss, interest on damages is awarded at the rate of 2% from the date of service of the claim form to the date of trial.[7] Interest on pre-trial pecuniary loss awards is normally payable from the date of the accident until trial and the normal rate is half the average rate on the special account over that period.[8] No interest is payable on damages for future pecuniary loss.[9]

An undoubted consequence of itemisation has been an increase in the damages awarded for personal injury. Indeed in a number of cases awards of several million pounds have been made to claimants requiring constant care. But as rightly stressed in *Lim Poh Choo v Camden and Islington Area Health Authority*[10] it is no ground for appeal that the global award is too high; rather rationality dictates that a particular item of damages should be challenged.

A second point is that reference is often made to a distinction between special and general damages. The traditional view has been that 'special damages' refer to losses that are capable of substantially exact calculation, that is, pre-trial pecuniary loss; whereas 'general damages' refer to non-pecuniary loss and future pecuniary loss. However, in respect of personal injury claims, the relevant pleading rule under the Civil Procedure Rules makes no reference to special damages. Rather it simply states, 'The claimant must attach to his particulars of claim a schedule of details of any past and future expenses and losses which he claims.'[11]

Finally, the necessity for an award to be made once-and-for-all in a lump sum has been departed from in this field.[12] For example, by the Supreme Court Act 1981, s 32A, and Civil Procedure Rules, Pt 41, the courts have power to award provisional damages.

5   [1970] 2 QB 130.
6   Interest is discussed below, ch 14.
7   *Wright v British Railways Board* [1983] 2 AC 773.
8   *Jefford v Gee* [1970] 2 QB 130; *Cookson v Knowles* [1979] AC 556. As regards the special account, see below, p 351, n 7.
9   *Jefford v Gee* [1970] 2 QB 130. In Australia non-pecuniary loss is further itemised into pre-trial and future loss, with no interest being payable on the latter: see *Fire and All Risks Insurance Co Ltd v Callinan* (1978) 140 CLR 427.
10   [1980] AC 174.
11   CPR 16.4(e) and 16 PD.4.2.
12   See above, pp 175–181

(1) Non-pecuniary loss

(a) Pain, suffering and loss of amenity

In the context of damages for personal injury, the non-pecuniary losses, for which the claimant is entitled to compensation, are almost invariably referred to as pain, suffering and loss of amenity. The amount of such damages – which is not susceptible to mathematical proof and accuracy – is awarded in accordance with a tariff system whereby the courts are guided by awards made for similar personal injuries in other cases. This system has depended on the publication (in, for example, *Current Law* and Kemp & Kemp *The Quantum of Damages*) of judicial awards listed under the different types of personal injury (such as deafness, loss of thumb, loss of leg, quadriplegia) with brief details of the claimant's circumstances. The past awards must then be uplifted for inflation by taking into account changes in the retail prices index since the past award was made.[13] The tariff or bracket of damages for that injury, which the previous cases have laid down (adjusted upwards for inflation), will provide the basic award (or range of award) in the instant case; but it will be adjusted flexibly by the courts to take account of the claimant's particular circumstances. For example, the injury (or treatment) may have been accompanied by a great deal of pain in one case but not so in another. And higher awards may be made in respect of younger, rather than older, claimants because the injury (if permanent) will be suffered for longer.[14] There may also be particular deprivations brought about by the injury: for example, that the claimant who has lost a hand was a pianist;[15] that the injury prevents sexual intercourse;[16] that, as a consequence of the injury, the claimant is unlikely to marry;[17] that, because of the injury, the claimant is unable to look after a terminally-ill spouse as much as the claimant would have liked;[18] or that, as a result of the injury, the claimant will not be able to obtain as satisfying a job as he previously had.[19]

Two less common examples of 'suffering' incurred by the particular claimant, meriting a specific uplift from the damages for non-pecuniary loss that would normally be awarded for a particular injury, are

---

13 *Wright v British Railways Board* [1983] 2 AC 773; *Heil v Rankin* [2001] QB 272.
14 Cf *Rose v Ford* [1937] AC 826 where £2 only was awarded for amputation of the deceased's leg the day before she died.
15 *Moeliker v Reyrolle and Co Ltd* [1977] 1 WLR 132 (fishing).
16 *Cook v JL Kier and Co Ltd* [1970] 1 WLR 774.
17 *Hughes v McKeown* [1985] 1 WLR 963.
18 *Rourke v Barton* (1982) Times, 23 June.
19 *Hale v London Underground Ltd* [1993] PIQR Q30 (this is commonly referred to as a 'loss of congenial employment').

illustrated by: *Ichard v Frangoulis*,[20] where the claimant, injured in a motor accident while on holiday, was awarded compensation within his general damages for the loss of enjoyment of his holiday; and *Meah v McCreamer*,[1] where Woolf J included within the claimant's general damages, damages for his being imprisoned on the ground that, but for the brain damage received in a car accident for which the defendant was responsible, and his resulting personality change, the claimant would not have committed the sexual and violent crimes for which he was serving a sentence of life imprisonment.[2]

In an attempt to produce greater consistency of awards, and in generally seeking to make the judicial tariff of values more accessible, the Judicial Studies Board in 1992 produced *Guidelines for the Assessment of General Damages in Personal Injury Cases*. The sixth edition of the *Guidelines* was published in 2002. They set out, in easily understood form, the range of awards for various injuries. At present the range runs from less than £100 for minor cuts and bruises through to about £205,000 for the most serious injuries. This range takes account of the most important recent decision of *Heil v Rankin*.[3] The Court of Appeal there partly implemented a recommendation of the Law Commission[4] by uplifting on a tapered scale awards over £10,000 so that the top-end of the scale was increased from £150,000 to £200,000 (as at that date). This was on the basis that awards for more serious injuries had fallen behind what was considered fair, just and reasonable.

It is theoretically, and occasionally practically, important to clarify that the loss of amenity aspect of the award is assessed objectively in the sense that it is made irrespective of the claimant's own appreciation of her condition.[5] In contrast, pain and suffering is assessed subjectively so that if the claimant is not capable of experiencing the pain or suffering no damages will be awarded for them.

---

20   [1977] 2 All ER 461.
1   [1985] 1 All ER 367.
2   But in *Meah v McCreamer (No 2)* [1986] 1 All ER 943 Meah was refused damages, indemnifying him against his liability to victims of his sex attacks, on the grounds of remoteness and public policy. There seems no satisfactory distinction between the two cases.
3   [2001] QB 272. For an excellent case-note, see Barmes 'Damages for Pain and Suffering and Loss of Amenity: Is This Enough?' (2000) 116 LQR 548. For a different view, see Lewis 'Increasing the Price of Pain: Damages, The Law Commission and *Heil v Rankin*' (2001) 64 MLR 100.
4   *Damages for Personal Injury: Non-Pecuniary Loss*, Report No 257 (1999) esp para 3.110. For criticism of the Law Commission's approach, see Harris, Campbell and Halson *Remedies in Contract and Tort* (2nd edn, 2002) pp 375–376.
5   See, generally, Ogus 'Damages for Lost Amenities: For a Foot, a Feeling or a Function?' (1972) 35 MLR 1.

Hence a majority of the Court of Appeal in *Wise v Kaye*[6] and of the House of Lords in *West & Son Ltd v Shephard*[7] upheld a loss of amenity award of £15,000, and a loss of amenity and pain and suffering award of £17,500 respectively, for claimants who had been very seriously injured and brain damaged and were totally, or almost totally, incapable of appreciating their loss. Similarly, in *Lim Poh Choo v Camden and Islington Area Health Authority*[8] the House of Lords refused to overrule *West v Shephard* and upheld an award of £20,000 under loss of amenity and pain and suffering for the claimant's brain damage even though she was largely unaware of her deprivation. As Lord Morris said in *West v Shephard*:

'An unconscious person will be spared pain and suffering and will not experience the mental anguish which may result from knowledge of what has in life been lost or from knowledge that life has been shortened. The fact of unconsciousness is therefore relevant in respect of and will eliminate those heads or elements of damages which can only exist by being felt or thought or experienced. The fact of unconsciousness does not, however, eliminate the actuality of the deprivations of the ordinary experiences and amenities of life which may be the inevitable result of some physical injury.'[9]

Such an approach has been criticised[10] and there were strong dissenting judgments by Diplock LJ in *Wise v Kaye* and by Lords Devlin and Reid in *West & Son Ltd v Shephard*.[11] A main line of criticism is that for loss of amenity the courts should be seeking to compensate for the claimant's distress or loss of happiness and hence where the claimant cannot feel any distress or unhappiness no damages should be awarded under this head. In other words, critics of these decisions are mainly advocating what has been referred to above[12] as the alternative view of non-pecuniary loss, by which all such loss is ultimately viewed in terms of distress or of loss of happiness. This contrasts with the traditional judicial approach by which the heads of loss of amenity, loss of reputation and physical inconvenience are regarded as analogous to proprietary losses, and as losses over and above any distress caused.

---

6   [1962] 1 QB 638.
7   [1964] AC 326. Also see *Andrews v Freeborough* [1967] 1 QB 1.
8   [1980] AC 174.
9   [1964] AC 326 at 349.
10 See *Skelton v Collins* (1966) 115 CLR 94; *Knutson v Farr* (1984) 12 DLR (4th) 658; and Pearson Commission Report Vol I, paras 393–398. The Law Commission in *Damages for Personal Injury: Non-Pecuniary Loss*, Report No 257 (1999) paras 2.8–2.24 explained that, while it had initially favoured reversing *Wise v Kaye* and *West v Shephard*, the majority of its consultees were against this and it therefore made no recommendation for such a change.
11 Illogically these minority judges still thought that some damages should be awarded for loss of amenity to an unconscious claimant.
12 Above, pp 30–31.

Where the claimant's expectation of life has been reduced by the injury an objective fixed sum, additional to loss of amenity and pain and suffering, used to be awarded for 'loss of expectation of life'. This was abolished by the Administration of Justice Act 1982, s 1(1)(a), although by s 1(1) (b) the courts are ordered to take into account in assessing damages for the claimant's pain and suffering, '… any suffering caused or likely to be caused to him by awareness that his expectation of life has been reduced.'

(b) Should there be a threshold for the recovery of damages for non-pecuniary loss?

The Pearson Commission recommended that no damages should be awarded for non-pecuniary loss suffered during the first three months after the injury.[13] Its reasoning was, first, that the primary concern of the tort system should be with compensating pecuniary loss and, secondly, that excluding such damages would save the system a great deal of expense.

But that recommendation has not been implemented; and when the Law Commission revisited the question of whether there should be a threshold for the recovery of damages for non-pecuniary loss, it came out firmly against such an idea.[14] It gave several main reasons for this. First, even if the tort system is too expensive, there are better ways to reduce costs (especially through procedural reforms) than interfering with basic common law principles. Secondly, a threshold might encourage potential claimants to exaggerate or prolong their symptoms in order to cross the threshold. Thirdly, since minor injuries typically cause little or no pecuniary loss, to refuse damages for non-pecuniary loss would lead to some wrongs going unremedied. Fourthly, the Pearson Commission's recommendation had to be seen in the context of its view that the role of the tort system should be as a mere supplement to no-fault compensation provided by the state. Fifthly, an exclusion of damages for non-pecuniary loss in the first three months after the accident would in many cases exclude compensation when a victim's pain is at its worst. Finally, a large majority of its consultees (93%), who responded on this issue, agreed with the Law Commission's provisional view that no such threshold should be introduced.

---

13 Report, paras 362, 382–389.
14 *Damages for Personal Injury: Non-Pecuniary Loss,* Report No 257 (1999) paras 2.25–2.28.

(2) Pecuniary loss

(a) **The different types of recoverable pecuniary loss**

The claimant is entitled to recover his or her *loss of net earnings*.[15] To calculate the net earnings, one deducts from the loss of gross earnings, the tax,[16] national insurance contributions[17] and pension payments[18] that would have been paid from the gross earnings. In principle, the expenses involved in earning, which have been saved (eg the costs of travelling to work), should be deducted, although in general this appears not to be the practice.[19]

The injured claimant may alternatively (or additionally) be awarded damages for being *handicapped in the labour market*. These are often described as '*Smith v Manchester Corpn* damages', that being the leading case.[20] The loss primarily in mind is that, as a result of the injury, the claimant may find it more difficult to find another equally-well-paid job if he or she loses the present one. This head of damages has most commonly been used where a working claimant is still in the same job despite the injury. But it has also been used, for example, for the situation where the range of future jobs open to a child has been narrowed because of the injury.[1]

As a result of the injury, the claimant may have suffered a *loss of pension rights*: that is, the claimant may have lost all rights to a pension or may be entitled merely to a lower pension. *Lim Poh Choo v Camden and Islington Area Health Authority*[2] and *Auty v National Coal Board*,[3] for example, show that the claimant is entitled to damages for this loss. The courts appear to put a present value on it by taking the price an insurance company would demand for a pension providing equivalent rights to those lost.

---

15 Loss of earnings includes all classes of earnings whether, eg wages or professional fees or partnership profits (on which see *Ward v Newalls Insulation Co Ltd* [1998] 1 WLR 1722). Benefits in kind (eg a company car) are included alongside earnings: see, eg *Kennedy v Bryan* (1984) Times, 3 May. Illegality may rule out a claim for loss of earnings: *Hewison v Meridian Shipping PTE* [2002] EWCA Civ 1821, [2003] PIQR P252.
16 *British Transport Commission v Gourley* [1956] AC 185. See above, ch 8.
17 *Cooper v Firth Brown Ltd* [1963] 1 WLR 418.
18 *Dews v National Coal Board* [1988] AC 1.
19 *Dews v National Coal Board* [1988] AC 1 at 12–13.
20 (1974) 17 KIR 1. See also, eg *Moeliker v Reyrolle & Co Ltd* [1977] 1 All ER 9.
1 *Mitchell v Liverpool Area Health Authority* (1985) Times, 17 June.
2 [1980] AC 174.
3 [1985] 1 All ER 930. See also *Dews v National Coal Board* [1988] AC 1 (where there was no loss of pension); *Longden v British Coal Corpn* [1998] AC 653.

The claimant can also recover all *medical, nursing and hospital expenses* which have been, or will be, reasonably incurred.[4] It follows that if the claimant does not incur these expenses because he makes use of the NHS, he cannot recover what he would have had to pay if he had had private treatment.[5] So as not to overcompensate, ordinary living expenses saved are deducted from the cost of staying in a private hospital or home;[6] and by the Administration of Justice Act 1982, s 5, any saving to the claimant, which is or will be attributable to his maintenance by the NHS, is to be set off against his loss of earnings.[7] In *Rialas v Mitchell*[8] it was held that, where the claimant continues to live at home, the fact that it would be much cheaper to provide medical and nursing expenses in a private institution does not prevent the full recovery of such expenses. By the Law Reform (Personal Injuries) Act 1948, s 2(4), the possibility that the claimant could have avoided expenses by using the facilities of the NHS is to be disregarded. The Pearson Commission recommended the repeal of s 2(4) so that private medical expenses should be recoverable only if it was reasonable on medical grounds for the claimant to incur them.[9] But private treatment may offer advantages which are more than merely medical in nature (eg speed and comfort) and it is hard to see how it can ever be unreasonable for a claimant to opt for it. In any event, a merit of s 2(4) is that it avoids the courts having to make difficult and invidious comparisons between the respective merits of NHS and private care. For these reasons, the Law Commission has more recently recommended that s 2(4) should not be repealed or amended.[10]

---

4   These include the costs of applicances, eg a wheelchair. In *Briody v St Helens and Knowsley Health Authority* [2001] EWCA Civ 1010, [2002] QB 856, where the claimant had been deprived of her womb because of the defendant's negligence and therefore could not have children, it was held that surrogacy costs would be unreasonably incurred and were therefore irrecoverable. But this was confined to the facts where the child would not be genetically linked to the claimant (ie where neither the baby nor the pregnancy would be hers).

5   *Cunningham v Harrison* [1973] QB 942; *Lim Poh Choo v Camden and Islington Area Health Authority* [1980] AC 174.

6   *Shearman v Folland* [1950] 2 KB 43; *Lim Poh Choo v Camden and Islington Area Health Authority* [1980] AC 174.

7   Administration of Justice Act 1982, s 5 was enacted following the Pearson Commission's recommendation, paras 510–512, that *Daish v Wauton* [1972] 2 QB 262 should be reversed. As the section requires the set off to be against loss of earnings, there can be no set off where the claimant has suffered no loss of earnings. The policy behind restricting the scope of the set off was presumably that it would not be deducting like from like to allow the set off against damages for non-pecuniary loss.

8   (1984) 128 Sol Jo 704.

9   Report, para 342.

10   *Damages for Personal Injury: Medical, Nursing and Other Expenses; Collateral Benefits*, Report No 262 (1999) paras 3.1–3.18.

There is a valid claim for nursing expenses even though the services have been rendered gratuitously by a third party.[11] In *Donnelly v Joyce*[12] the Court of Appeal attempted to fit this within the normal principle that one is compensating the claimant's loss, by regarding the claimant's loss not as the incurring of nursing expenses but rather as the need for care. There was no legal obligation on the claimant to reimburse the third party but it was considered essential that sufficient should be awarded to allow the claimant to pay the third party reasonable recompense, including making up for any lost wages, the commercial rate of nursing services providing the ceiling. However, in *Hunt v Severs*[13] the House of Lords recognised that, in reality, it was not the claimant but the gratuitous carer who suffered the loss. Damages could be recovered in respect of the services rendered but the claimant must hold them on trust for the third party.[14] In *Hunt v Severs* itself, the gratuitous carer was also the tortfeasor; no damages for the care were recoverable, since the defendant would otherwise have been paying damages only for those damages to be returnable to the defendant under the trust.

In Part III of its Report, *Damages for Personal Injury: Medical, Nursing and Other Expenses; Collateral Benefits,*[15] the Law Commission approved the adoption of the view in *Hunt v Severs* that the loss is the carer's, not the claimant's. However, it recommended that the actual decision in the case should be reversed by legislation for several reasons. First, it was undesirable either to encourage the making of contracts with friends and relatives for the provision of care, or to provoke arguments as to whether or not a particular contract should be seen as a sham. Secondly, there should be no disincentive to accept care from the person in the best position to provide it, particularly as an increased liability in damages would usually arise if the claimant adopted the alternative of engaging professional care rather than relying on the care provided by the tortfeasor. Thirdly, the situation in which the gratuitous carer was only partially liable for the claimant's injuries presented problems. The Law Commission also rejected the use of a trust to ensure recompense for the

---

11 Provided more than *de minimis*, there is no lower threshold of seriousness that needs to be crossed before gratuitous nursing care can be compensated: see *Giambrone v JMC Holidays Ltd (No 2)* [2004] EWCA Civ 158, [2004] 2 All ER 891.

12 [1974] QB 454. See also, eg *Housecroft v Burnett* [1986] 1 All ER 332, CA.

13 [1994] 2 AC 350. See Matthews and Lunney 'A Tortfeasor's Lot is not a Happy One?' (1995) 58 MLR 395; Hoyano 'The Dutiful Tortfeasor in the House of Lords' (1995) Tort L Rev 63. *Hunt v Severs* was rejected by the High Court of Australia in *Kars v Kars* (1996) 71 AJLR 107, the approach in *Donnelly v Joyce* [1974] QB 454 being preferred.

14 This was the view of Lord Denning in *Cunningham v Harrison* [1973] QB 942.

15 Law Commission Report No 262 (1999). The report has been criticised, for compounding existing errors of legal classification, by Degeling 'Carers' Claims: Unjust Enrichment and Tort' [2000] RLR 172.

gratuitous carer, preferring a personal liability on the claimant to account to the third party as regards damages for past (but not future) care. For future care it considered that the damages should be paid to the claimant without any duty to pay across to the carer, whether through a trust or personal liability.

Hunt v Severs was distinguished by the Court of Appeal in *Hardwick v Hudson*,[16] in which the injured claimant's wife provided gratuitous clerical services to his business. No damages were awarded in respect of those services. This was because the policy considerations favouring recompense for a gratuitous carer (such as encouraging effective and economical care) did not apply to the provision of those services, and the decision not to contract for them had been commercially motivated.

It was also recognised in *Hunt v Severs*[17] that *visiting costs* reasonably incurred by third parties in gratuitously visiting the claimant in hospital are recoverable by the claimant and are held on trust for the third party. In other words, they are treated in a similar way to nursing services. Correspondingly, the Law Commission has recommended that the claimant should be under merely a personal obligation to account for the damages awarded in respect of past visits to the claimant and under no legal liability at all to the visitor in respect of damages awarded for future visits.[18] The main question in *Walker v Mullen*[19] was whether the claimant could recover damages in respect of his father's lost earnings, where his father had not gone back to his job in Jordan so as to be with his wife and the claimant while the latter was in hospital. Comyn J reluctantly refused such damages on the ground that the loss was too remote. But surely that type of loss was foreseeable; and the father's loss of earnings was reasonably incurred. Nevertheless, taking the view that the loss in these sorts of cases is really the third party's, and hence that allowing the claimant to recover is highly exceptional, the decision is perhaps justified as confining recovery to a narrow range of claims.

The claimant can further recover the *cost of buying, fitting out and moving to special accommodation*. But the capital cost of a new house (as opposed to the cost of the capital) is not awarded since the claimant still has that capital in the form of the house.[20] In *Roberts v Johnstone*[1] it was laid down that the claimant can recover 2% per annum of the capital cost of the

16   [1999] 1 WLR 1770.
17   [1994] 2 AC 350, 356–357.
18   Law Commission Report No 262, para 3.68.
19   (1984) Times, 19 January.
20   *George v Pinnock* [1973] 1 WLR 118; *Cunningham v Harrison* [1973] QB 942; *Moriarty v McCarthy* [1978] 1 WLR 155; *Roberts v Johnstone* [1989] QB 878.
1   [1989] QB 878.

purchase as the cost of the capital. More recently, in *Wells v Wells*[2] the House of Lords decided that the appropriate interest rate, for the purposes of applying *Roberts v Johnstone*, is that on index-linked government stock (ILGS) and for the time being that rate was regarded as being 3%. As we shall see below, the appropriate discount rate in assessing future pecuniary loss has subsequently been reduced by the Lord Chancellor, acting under the powers conferred on him by the Damages Act 1996, s 1, to 2.5%. Presumably that is therefore also now the figure to be applied in respect of *Roberts v Johnstone*.

A claimant can also recover for *loss of ability to do work in and around the home*, such as housekeeping, gardening and carrying out repairs. Unfortunately, in the leading case of *Daly v General Steam Navigation Co Ltd*[3] the Court of Appeal appeared to adopt an inconsistent approach to whether this was a pecuniary loss depending on whether one was concerned with past or future loss. That is, for the future, loss of housekeeping capacity was considered to be a pecuniary loss, irrespective of whether any expenses in employing someone else to do the work would be incurred and irrespective of whether a third party would gratuitously carry out the work. In contrast, it was held that such a loss was only a recoverable pecuniary loss for the past where the claimant had actually employed someone or where a third party, in this case the husband, had given up earnings so as to carry out the housekeeping work. Otherwise it was thought that past loss of housekeeping capacity should be regarded as a non-pecuniary loss, which was recoverable at least where the claimant had struggled on with her housekeeping despite her injury. But this approach seems hopelessly inconsistent: it criticises the artificiality of regarding the 'housewife' as having always suffered a past pecuniary loss in respect of housekeeping incapacity, while applying that artificiality to the future.

It is submitted therefore that the correct compensatory principles are as follows[4] (assuming that, in line with the nursing services cases, the claimant can recover for a third party's loss in gratuitously carrying out the housekeeping): the claimant may herself suffer a recoverable pecuniary loss by incurring the expense of employing someone to carry out her housekeeping work; even if not, she can recover a third party's

---

2   [1999] 1 AC 345.
3   [1981] 1 WLR 120. See also *Hoffman v Sofaer* [1982] 1 WLR 1350, 1355–1356 (recovery in respect of 'do-it-yourself' work around the home); *Lowe v Guise* [2002] EWCA Civ 197, [2002] QB 1369 (recovery for the fact that the injury prevented the claimant carrying out as many hours as before of gratuitous care for his disabled brother, the difference being made up by his mother).
4   This was supported by the Law Commission which made a recommendation to the same effect in Report No 262 (1999) para 3.91.

loss where a third party gratuitously carries out that work, especially if the third party suffers a loss of earnings;[5] the claimant is entitled to damages for loss of housekeeping capacity as a non-pecuniary loss, at the very least where she struggles on with the housekeeping despite her injury; these principles are just as applicable to the past as to the future.

Most other pecuniary losses consequent on the injury are recoverable, provided they are not too remote or do not infringe the duty to mitigate. An exception is loss consequent on a divorce caused by the personal injury. Departing from earlier authority,[6] the Court of Appeal in *Pritchard v JH Cobden Ltd*[7] held that, even though a divorce has foreseeably resulted from the claimant's injury, pecuniary 'loss' on that divorce is irrecoverable. There were three main grounds for this decision. The first was that where the financial consequences of a divorce have not yet been decided on in the Family Division, a judge in a personal injury action would be placed in the invidious position of having to make an assessment of the outcome of those proceedings. Secondly, it was thought that to allow compensation for this sort of loss would produce 'infinite regress' because, in deciding on the orders to be made after divorce, the potential assets of the parties, including any claims for damages, are taken into account in making those orders. Finally, talk of loss on divorce was in any case thought inapt on the ground that the financial consequences of a divorce are based on a distribution of the parties' assets taking into account various factors.

The Law Commission looked in detail at the arguments for and against the decision in *Pritchard v Cobden*.[8] In recommending that the law should not be reformed on this issue, the Law Commission stressed that, apart from the objections referred to by the Court of Appeal, there are real difficulties in establishing whether an injury did cause a divorce. Moreover, this might require distressing and distasteful inquiries into the personal lives of the married couple. Nor rationally could one confine such recovery only to the breakdown of marriage; if allowed for divorce, one ought rationally to extend recovery to pecuniary (and non-pecuniary) losses consequent on the breakdown, because of the injury, of any personal relationship.

---

5   Applying *Hunt v Severs* [1994] 2 AC 350 by analogy, the claimant would be bound to hold such damages on trust for the third party at least as regards damages for past loss. The Law Commission in Report No 262 (1999), para 3.91, recommended that the claimant should be under a personal liability to account for damages, awarded in respect of past work, to the person (including the tortfeasor) who performed the work; but no legal obligation should be imposed in respect of damages awarded for work to be done in the future.
6   *Jones v Jones* [1985] QB 704. See also *Oakley v Walker* (1977) 121 Sol Jo 619.
7   [1988] Fam 22.
8   Law Commission Report No 262 (1999) Part IV.

(b) Calculating damages for pecuniary loss

Having identified the different types of recoverable pecuniary loss, we can now turn to the question of how damages for those pecuniary losses are calculated.

The calculation of damages for pre-trial pecuniary loss is relatively straightforward. It is essentially merely a question of adding together the expenses that the claimant has incurred; or multiplying the claimant's pre-injury monthly earnings by the number of months during which the claimant could not work. The latter calculation clearly depends upon the assumption that, but for the injury, the claimant would have continued to earn at the same rate. If this assumption is not justified (for example, because the claimant would have been promoted and had higher earnings)[9] an adjustment must be made.

The calculation of damages for future pecuniary loss is more complex. Elements of uncertainty inevitably enter into the calculation, such as the claimant's life expectancy, and what would have happened to the claimant had he or she not been injured. The standard method of assessment (the so-called 'multiplier' method) is to multiply the assessed net annual loss by a multiplier. The starting point for the multiplier is the number of years during which the loss is likely to endure and thus, in a claim for loss of future earnings, the remaining period that the claimant would have worked. This figure is then reduced to take account of the fact that the claimant receives a lump sum which can be invested. There may then be a further (normally small)[10] reduction for the 'contingencies of life' other than mortality (for example, because the claimant might in any event have been unemployed or sick). The basis of the award is that the total sum will be exhausted at the end of the period contemplated; that during the period the claimant will draw upon both the income derived from the investment of the sum awarded and the capital; and that the income and withdrawals of capital will produce a stream of payments equal to the claimant's lost earnings or cost of care (or other loss in question). The courts conventionally used multipliers based on a discount of about 4.5%. But in *Wells v Wells*,[11] the House of Lords held that this was incorrect and that the claimant was entitled to be treated as risk-averse. It was therefore appropriate that the (relatively low) rate of interest on Index-Linked Government Stock (ILGS) should be taken as the appropriate discount rate for calculating multipliers. At the time of

---

9 See, eg *Anderson v Davis* [1993] PIQR Q87.
10 In *Herring v Ministry of Defence* [2003] EWCA Civ 528, [2004] 1 All ER 44 Potter LJ said that the level of reduction for contingencies traditionally applied by the judiciary has been too high.
11 [1999] 1 AC 345.

the decision, the ILGS rate was 3% (net of tax) and this was therefore laid down as the appropriate basis for multipliers for the time being. This meant that significant higher multipliers would be used than where the discount rate was 4.5%. As we shall see shortly, the discount rate has since been reduced further to 2.5%.

After a long fight to overcome judicial reluctance to actuarial evidence, it was also laid down in *Wells v Wells* that it is appropriate in working out the correct multiplier to make use of the 'Ogden Tables'. Over 20 years earlier, Oliver LJ had famously said in *Auty v National Coal Board*[12] that in this context, '... the predictions of an actuary can be only a little more likely to be accurate (and will almost certainly be less entertaining) than those of an astrologer.' Commentators long criticised this approach[13] and in 1982 a joint working party of lawyers and actuaries was set up, under the chairmanship of Sir Michael Ogden QC, to produce tables specifically geared to the assessment of damages for future pecuniary loss in personal injury and death actions. A fourth edition of the Ogden Tables, as they have become known, was published in 2000.[14] The Ogden Tables give actuarially-accurate multipliers, applying various discount rates, according to the age of the claimant at the date of the trial. The acceptance of the Ogden Tables was spelt out by Lord Lloyd in *Wells v Wells*.[15] He said,

'I do not suggest that the judge should be a slave to the tables. There may well be special factors in particular cases. But the tables should now be regarded as the starting-point, rather than a check. A judge should be slow to depart from the relevant actuarial multiplier on impressionistic grounds, or by reference to "a spread of multipliers in comparable cases" especially when the multipliers were fixed before actuarial tables were widely used.'

The standard multipliers assume that standard rate tax will be paid on the investment income but, according to the controversial decision of the

---

12 [1985] 1 All ER 930 at 939.
13 Eg Prevett 'Actuarial Assessment of Damages: The Thalidomide Case' (1972) 35 MLR 140, 257.
14 *Actuarial Tables for Use in Personal Injury and Fatal Accident Cases* (4th edn, 2000). A 5th edn is expected in October 2004.
15 [1999] 1 AC 345 at 379. The Civil Evidence Act 1995, s 10, if and when it is brought into force, provides that the Ogden Tables are admissible in evidence and may be proved by production of a Queen's Printer's copy. In the light of *Wells v Wells*, it would appear that this has already been accepted by the courts. The tables were designed for use in personal injury and fatal accident cases. But in *Kingston Upon Hull City Council v Dunnachie (No 3)* [2003] IRLR 843 the Employment Appeal Tribunal held that, in rare cases, where there was established to be a career-long loss, it would be appropriate to use the Ogden Tables in calculating loss of future earnings in a claim for unfair dismissal.

House of Lords in *Hodgson v Trapp*,[16] there should normally be no further uplift of the multiplier to account for any higher rate tax that the claimant has to pay.

There is no adjustment made for future inflation. Now that the discount rate is essentially based on ILGS rates this follows inevitably (ie the ILGS rate automatically takes into account inflation). But even prior to the adoption of ILGS rates the courts took the same approach of making no adjustment for inflation on the reasoning that either it was too speculative to estimate what any future rate of inflation would be or that sensible investment of the damages could, to a large extent, counter the effect of inflation.[17]

Under the Damages Act 1996, s 1, the Lord Chancellor was given power to set the discount rate to be applied in assessing damages for personal injury and death (subject to a party showing that a different rate is more appropriate in the case in question). By the Damages (Personal Injury) Order 2001[18] he exercised that power to set a discount rate of 2.5%. This was therefore a reduction of 0.5% from the rate laid down in *Wells v Wells*.

The primary reason for a reduction was that the rate of return on ILGS had fallen. The net average yield figure for the three years prior to the making of the order in 2001 appears to have been just above 2%. This had led to pressure from, eg the Ogden Working Party, for the Lord Chancellor to set a rate of 2% (so that multipliers would be higher than where the discount rate was 3%) in line with the principles set out in *Wells v Wells*.

In setting a rate of 2.5%, the Lord Chancellor saw himself as basically applying the principles set out in *Wells v Wells* and updating the rate in the light of the changed ILGS rates.[19] But he also took into account in preferring 2.5% to 2%, three further reasons, the last two of which cut against the principles in *Wells*. The first further reason was that, in his view, the ILGS yields appeared to have been artificially low in recent years (that is, in the three years prior to June 2001). Secondly, the Court of Protection, even after *Wells v Wells*, had continued to invest, on behalf of claimants, in multi-asset portfolios which enabled them to achieve a real rate of return at 2.5% or above, without their being unduly exposed to risk in the equity markets. Thirdly, the Lord Chancellor thought it

---

16 [1989] AC 807; see above, pp 202–203. See also *Wells v Wells* [1999] 1 AC 345 at 388.
17 *Cookson v Knowles* [1979] AC 556, esp at 577; *Lim Poh Choo v Camden and Islington Area Health Authority* [1980] AC 174, esp at 193; *Auty v National Coal Board* [1985] 1 All ER 930.
18 SI 2001/2301.
19 *Setting the Discount Rate, Lord Chancellor's Reasons* 27 July 2001 (www.lcd.gov.uk/civil/discount.htm).

likely that real claimants who sought investment advice would not be advised to invest solely or even primarily in ILGS but rather in a mixed portfolio.

Although, by the Damages Act 1996, s 1(2), a court may apply a different rate from that set if it is 'more appropriate in the case in question,' in *Warriner v Warriner*[20] the Court of Appeal held that regard should be had to the reasons given by the Lord Chancellor for setting the 2.5% rate and that a departure should be made only if the case fell outside the categories considered by him. It was said that, in the interests of certainty, a departure from the rate set would therefore probably be rare. In the instant case, there was nothing unusual justifying a lower rate than 2.5%.

In *Cooke v United Bristol Health Care*,[1] the Court of Appeal rejected a different line of attack by the claimants on the conventional method for assessing future pecuniary loss. The claimants wanted to adduce evidence that the cost of care, and indeed earnings, had increased, and could be expected to increase, at a substantially higher rate than the retail prices index.[2] Claimants, it was argued, are therefore being undercompensated by the conventional method, especially where there are high future costs of care. The claimants sought to argue that, to prevent such undercompensation, there should be adjustments to the multiplicands. But the Court of Appeal refused to allow such evidence to be adduced on the basis that, in reality, the claimants were arguing for a departure from the 2.5% discount rate for multipliers set by the Lord Chancellor; and in line with *Warriner v Warriner* such a departure was thought to be unjustified. Although not mentioned by the Court of Appeal, it is perhaps worth adding, as a further reason for rejecting the claimant's arguments that, in adopting the ILGS rate in *Wells v Wells*, the House of Lords assumed that it is the retail prices index that is the correct measure of inflation; and this is also the index used for updating awards for non-pecuniary loss in personal injury cases.[3]

---

20   [2002] EWCA Civ 81, [2002] 1 WLR 1703.
1   [2003] EWCA Civ 1370, [2004] PIQR Q2. See also *Page v Plymouth Hospital NHS Trust* [2004] EWHC 1154, [2004] 3 All ER 367: claim for damages for the costs of investment advice and fund management charges was rejected as inconsistent with the assumption of ILGS investment and as being another attempt indirectly to depart from the 2.5% discount rate. This is also supported by the Law Commission, *Damages for Personal Injury: Medical, Nursing and Other Expenses; Collateral Benefits* Report No 262 (1999) paras 5.11–5.15.
2   For the view that, in comparison to the 'labour market' approach in the US, the traditional English approach to calculating loss of future earnings undercompensates claimants (principally because it underestimates the earnings growth claimants would have enjoyed if not injured and overestimates the earnings of claimants after injury) see Lewis, McNabb, Robinson and Wass 'Court Awards of Damages for Loss of Future Earnings: An Empirical Study and an Alternative Method of Calculation' (2002) 29 Journal of Law and Society 406.
3   See above, p 187.

It follows that the 2.5% discount rate is very unlikely to be departed from by the courts. Applying a discount rate of 2.5%, the basic multiplier[4] for calculating loss of future earnings for a male who is 16 years old (at the date of trial) and who would have worked until 65 but will now not be able to do so, is 27.76; for a 30-year-old male it is 22.80.[5] Applying a discount rate of 2.5%, the basic multiplier for calculating the cost of care for life of a male who is 16 years old (at the date of trial) is 31.60; for a 30-year-old-male it is 28.22.[6]

In calculating loss of future earnings, the multiplier applicable to an injured young woman has sometimes in the past been reduced to take account of the workless years, that she would in any event have had, bringing up a family.[7] But this was then largely balanced out by an award for loss of marriage prospects as a pecuniary loss: ie the loss of the economic support, during the years raising a family, of the never-to-be-husband.[8] Not surprisingly, therefore, in *Hughes v McKeown*[9] Leonard J took the simpler approach of making no deduction from the multiplier while also making no award for loss of marriage prospects (as a pecuniary loss). This approach was approved by the Court of Appeal in *Housecroft v Burnett*[10] provided that there was a reasonable equivalence between the loss of earnings of the woman and the economic support that a husband would have given. There might be no such equivalence, for example, where the woman was a particularly high earner. However, one might argue that, in the light of changes in working practices, attitudes and maternity rights, the old (pre-*Hughes v McKeown*) approach would, in any event, now be considered inaccurate and inappropriate.

In so far as a multiplier approach is used,[11] low multipliers are applied in respect of young children, since they might never have become wage earners. For example, in *Croke v Wiseman*,[12] where the claimant was aged seven at trial and was expected to live until 40, a multiplier of five was applied for loss of future lifetime earnings. As there was no present loss of earnings in that case, it was held acceptable to take the national average earnings during early working years as the multiplicand (or the basis for working out the multiplicand).

4   This figure is then subject to a further (normally small) reduction for the 'contingencies of life' other than mortality.
5   Ogden Tables (4th edn, 2000) Table 25.
6   Ogden Tables (4th edn, 2000) Table 19.
7   *Harris v Harris* [1973] 1 Lloyd's Rep 445, CA; *Moriarty v McCarthy* [1978] 1 WLR 155.
8   [1973] 1 Lloyd's Rep 445, CA.
9   [1985] 1 WLR 963.
10 [1986] 1 All ER 332.
11 Cf *Joyce v Yeomans* [1981] 1 WLR 549; see below, pp 287–288.
12 [1982] 1 WLR 71. See Davies 'Damages for Severely Injured Children' (1982) 45 MLR 333.

Where the injury has reduced the number of years which the claimant is expected to live, the multiplier and hence the damages are calculated according to his life expectancy prior to the accident, with a deduction for the living expenses which he would have incurred during those 'lost years' that he will no longer live through. That damages can be recovered for the 'lost years' was laid down by the House of Lords in *Pickett v British Rail Engineering Ltd*,[13] overruling *Oliver v Ashman*.[14]

What is the reason for allowing a lost years claim when the claimant will not himself be alive to suffer any financial deprivation? The formal answer is to say that, by analogy to, for example, *Wise v Kaye*,[15] the claimant's subjective enjoyment of his earnings is irrelevant. He has still *objectively* suffered a loss. An alternative explanation therefore is that a lost years claim is granted not so much because the claimant has lost out, but rather because his dependants will otherwise lose out. This is highlighted, as in *Pickett*, where the victim dies from his injuries having settled or obtained judgment, thus preventing any Fatal Accidents Act claim by his dependants.[16] But this alternative explanation can only be valid so long as the claimant has dependants. In any event it is rather confusing to represent the loss as the claimant's, if it is in reality the dependants'. As such, the main problem could be better solved, without relying on lost years awards, if dependants under the Fatal Accidents Act could be awarded damages even though the victim had settled or obtained judgment. But this would not prevent the dependants losing out if the claimant were to live on but with his life expectancy and earnings reduced. So perhaps the best solution of all, albeit a rather radical one, would be to abolish the lost years award, and for legislation to be passed allowing dependants a claim for pecuniary loss where the person on whom they are dependent has been injured as well as where he has been killed.

No award for the lost years is likely to be made where the claimant is a young child. So for example, in *Connolly v Camden and Islington Area Health Authority*[17] a four-year-old with over 20 years' life expectancy was given nothing for the lost years; nor was the seven-year-old with a life expectancy of 40 in *Croke v Wiseman*.[18] On a formal level, the justification for such decisions is that to assess the value of the lost years claim in respect of young children involves too much speculation. On a deeper

---

13   [1980] AC 136.
14   [1962] 2 QB 210.
15   [1962] 1 QB 638.
16   Below, p 298. See also *McCann v Sheppard* [1973] 2 All ER 881.
17   [1981] 3 All ER 250.
18   [1982] 1 WLR 71.

level, as stressed particularly by Griffiths LJ in *Croke v Wiseman*, they are justified by the fact that where a child's injuries render it unlikely that there will ever be any dependants, the policy reason for awarding the lost years damages is non-existent.

How the deductible living expenses in a lost years claim are to be calculated has given rise to controversy which reflects the tension between the formal objective reason and the alternative policy justification for the lost years award. In some first instance decisions[19] it was held that the same approach should be adopted as where calculating damages under the Fatal Accidents Act 1976, ie living expenses are what the claimant would have spent *exclusively* on himself (the theory being that the dependants would have benefited from the rest of the claimant's money). But these decisions were overruled in *Harris v Empress Motors Ltd*[20] where the Court of Appeal considered that one should deduct as living expenses what the claimant would have spent in maintaining himself at the standard of living appropriate to his case (the theory being that he would have the rest of his income free to spend as he wished). In contrast to an assessment under the Fatal Accidents Act 1976, a pro rata amount of his family expenditure, eg expenditure on housing, heat, light should therefore be deducted. This decision takes the objective approach. On the alternative view, as the justification for allowing the claimant damages for the lost years is to benefit his dependants, who are the ones who will otherwise lose out, calculation of the living expenses should be on the same basis as under the Fatal Accidents Act 1976.[1]

In *Housecroft v Burnett*,[2] where a 16-year-old girl was very badly injured, the Court of Appeal considered that a simpler way to proceed than deducting notional living expenses from notional earnings, and multiplying by the lost years multiplier, was to add one or half to the multiplier for the lost years and then to multiply the full multiplicand with no living expenses deduction.

Finally, it should be noted that a multiplier approach is not always appropriate for calculating future pecuniary loss. For example, '*Smith v Manchester Corpn* damages'[3] are normally assessed without first trying to fix a multiplicand.[4] Similarly, in assessing the loss of future earnings of an injured child, the courts have occasionally preferred to estimate

---

19   Eg *Benson v Biggs Wall & Co Ltd* [1982] 3 All ER 300; *Clay v Pooler* [1982] 3 All ER 570.
20   [1983] 1 WLR 65.
1   Evans and Stanton 'Valuing the Lost Years' (1984) 134 NLJ 515.
2   [1986] 1 All ER 332.
3   See above, p 275.
4   See generally *McGregor on Damages* (17th edn, 2003) para 35–079.

directly in a lump sum the loss of earnings without the use of a multiplicand.[5] These are situations where the assessment is particularly speculative and where the more precise multiplier approach may, therefore, be thought inappropriate.

(3) Compensating advantages provided by third parties in response to the personal injury ('collateral' benefits)

The important question of whether these benefits should be deducted in assessing the damages has been fully dealt with in chapter 7.[6]

(4) Addendum – damages for wrongful birth[7]

'Wrongful birth' claims are made where a child, who was originally unwanted, has been born as a result of a doctor's or health authority's civil wrong (be it the tort of negligence or breach of contract). Although the losses are not quite the same as personal injury losses, they are sufficiently similar to be included as an addendum to personal injury.

Until recently, the approach in this area was to apply the general compensatory principle and to permit recovery of all pecuniary and non-pecuniary loss suffered by the parents as a result of the wrongful birth, subject to the usual restrictions like remoteness and mitigation. So, for example, in *Emeh v Kensington Area Health Authority*,[8] where a sterilisation operation had been performed negligently, the mother was awarded damages for the pain and suffering and loss of amenity of having and looking after the child, who had congenital abnormalities, plus the pecuniary loss of maintaining her. Similarly in *Thake v Maurice*[9] the defendant surgeon had failed to warn the claimants, in breach of his contractual and tortious duty of care, that the vasectomy operation would not be a 100% guarantee against pregnancy. Consequently the mother had not sought an abortion at an early stage. The parents were awarded damages for their pecuniary loss (loss of earnings and the cost of the child's upkeep) and ante-natal pain and suffering, subject to a deduction from the latter for the fact that the pain and suffering of an abortion had not been suffered. But post-natal non-pecuniary loss (ie the

---

5　*Joyce v Yeomans* [1981] 1 WLR 549, CA.
6　Above, pp 161–174.
7　See generally Taylor 'Compensation for Unwanted Children' (1985) 15 Fam Law 147; Symmons 'Policy Factors in Actions for Wrongful Birth' (1987) 50 MLR 269; Stewart 'Damages for the Birth of a Child' (1995) 40 JLSS 298.
8　[1985] QB 1012.
9　[1986] QB 644. See also *Gold v Haringey Health Authority* [1988] QB 481; *Benarr v Kettering Health Authority* [1988] NLJR 179; *Salih v Enfield Health Authority* [1991] 3 All ER 400; *Allen v Bloomsbury Health Authority* [1993] 1 All ER 651; *Fish v Wilcox* (1993) 13 BMLR 134.

time and trouble in bringing up the child) was not claimed, and was in any event non-recoverable since it had been fully mitigated by the joy of a having a (healthy) child.

However, the scope of damages recoverable in a 'wrongful birth' claim was considerably narrowed by the House of Lords in *McFarlane v Tayside Health Board*,[10] a failed vasectomy case. A surgeon negligently advised a husband and wife that the vasectomy had rendered the husband infertile; the couple ceased to use contraceptives and the wife became pregnant, giving birth to a healthy child. The House of Lords held (Lord Millett dissenting on this point) that the mother's non-pecuniary and pecuniary losses directly consequent on the pregnancy and giving birth were recoverable; they were regarded as equivalent to personal injury losses. But all their Lordships were in agreement that the parents could not recover for their economic loss in maintaining the child, which was regarded as pure economic loss. Lords Slynn, Steyn and Hope saw the issue as one of liability, rather than the extent of liability, and held that no duty of care was owed to the parents as regards the pure economic loss because, in line with the standard approach to that sort of loss, it was not fair, just and reasonable for there to be such a duty. Lord Steyn, in particular, relied on what he termed considerations of distributive, rather than corrective, justice; that is, 'on the just distribution of burdens and losses among members of a society.'[11] And in determining that just distribution, Lord Steyn thought it relevant that, in his opinion, popular morality would be against holding the doctor or hospital liable for the costs of bringing up a child.

Two main matters were left unresolved by their Lordships in *McFarlane*. The first and more important was whether the position would be any different if the child was disabled. The previously leading case of *Emeh v Kensington Area Health Authority* concerned a disabled child. That decision was not expressly overruled and Lord Steyn specifically left open what the position would be in such a case. The second, more conceptual, point is what the position would be if the parents could sue for breach of contract. Lord Steyn expressly confined his views to claims in delict or tort; and certainly in respect of breach of contract one could not regard the issue as going to liability rather than the extent of liability.

It was not long before the question of the disabled child came before the appellate courts. In *Parkinson v St James and Seacroft University Hospital*

---

10 [2000] 2 AC 59. This was a Scottish case, but their Lordships made it clear that on this issue the same law should apply in both England and Scotland. By a four–three majority, the High Court of Australia in *Cattanach v Melchior* (2003) 77 AJLR 1312 went the other way from *McFarlane* and awarded the costs of maintaining the child.

11 [2000] 2 AC 59 at 82.

NHS Trust[12] a negligent sterilisation operation led to the birth of a disabled child. The Court of Appeal took a mid-position. The mother was awarded damages for the upbringing costs attributable to the disability. It was held that such damages had not been ruled out by *McFarlane*. On the other hand, damages for the costs which would be incurred in bringing up any child (healthy or disabled) were disallowed. Those damages, it was held, had been ruled out by *McFarlane* and to this extent, *Emeh*, in which all the costs of bringing up a disabled child were held recoverable, had been impliedly overruled by *McFarlane*.

But that is not the end of the story. On the contrary, a further factual twist – the birth of a healthy child, following a negligently conducted sterilisation operation, to a disabled mother – brought the whole question back to a seven-man House of Lords in *Rees v Darlington Memorial Hospital NHS Trust*.[13] All their Lordships decided that *McFarlane* had been correctly decided and should basically be followed. By a four-three majority (Lords Bingham, Nicholls, Millett and Scott in the majority, Lords Steyn, Hope and Hutton dissenting) it was then decided that the majority of the Court of Appeal in the instant case had been incorrect, as being inconsistent with *McFarlane*, to award damages to the mother for the additional upbringing costs attributable to the mother's disability.[14] On the other hand, a 'gloss' (as it was termed by Lords Bingham and Nicholls)[15] was placed on *McFarlane* by the majority in holding that a conventional sum of £15,000 should be awarded to the mother (or jointly to the parents) where there has been an unwanted birth attributable to a civil wrong. Such a conventional sum is to be awarded irrespective of whether the child or the parents are healthy or disabled. Although Lord Bingham at one point said that this conventional award 'would not be, and would not be intended to be, compensatory,'[16] he had earlier spoken of 'the real loss ... [of being] denied ... the opportunity to live her life in the way that she wished and planned' and that there should be 'a conventional award to mark the injury and loss.'[17] And in Lord Millett's words, '[T]he parents have lost the opportunity to live

---

12　[2001] EWCA Civ 530, [2002] QB 266. See also *Rand v East Dorset Health Authority* (2000) 50 BMLR 39; *Hardman v Amin* [2000] Lloyd's Med Rep 448; *Lee v Taunton and Somerset NHS Trust* [2001] 1 FLR 419; *Groom v Selby* [2001] EWCA Civ 1522, [2002] PIQR P201; Quick 'Damages for Wrongful Conception' (2002) Tort LR 5.

13　[2003] UKHL 52, [2004] 1 AC 309.

14　In a powerful dissenting judgment in the Court of Appeal [2002] EWCA Civ 88, [2002] 2 All ER 177, paras 53–54, Waller LJ pointed to some of the anomalies that might be thought to arise from 'picking out' the disabled mother; eg the contrast between the rich, very well assisted, disabled mother and the poor, unassisted, healthy mother.

15　[2003] UKHL 52, [2004] 1 AC 309 at paras 7 and 17.

16　[2003] UKHL 52, [2004] 1 AC 309 at para 8.

17　[2003] UKHL 52, [2004] 1 AC 309 at para 8.

their lives in the way that they wished and planned to do. The loss of this opportunity, whether characterised as a right or a freedom, is a proper subject for compensation by way of damages.'[18] Similarly, Lord Scott referred to *Farley v Skinner*[19] – a leading contractual case on mental distress – and spoke of the award as compensating the mother for being deprived of her expected benefit. It is submitted, therefore, that the conventional sum is best viewed as an award to compensate for non-pecuniary loss, namely a mother's mental distress consequent on having her lifestyle plans disrupted. Admittedly, a *fixed* conventional award – as opposed to a bracket of awards – for non-pecuniary loss is unusual but it is the approach used for bereavement damages under the Fatal Accidents Act 1976 and it is the approach that used to be applied to non-pecuniary loss of expectation of life.

Although three of the majority would have overruled *Parkinson*, Lord Millett explicitly left open whether *Parkinson* had been correctly decided.[20] Without a majority for or against that decision, it technically remains good law. Applying the majority's approach, therefore, in a wrongful birth case, a mother is entitled to all pecuniary and non-pecuniary loss directly attributable to the pregnancy and giving birth *and* a conventional sum of £15,000 for disruption of planned lifestyle. In so far as *Parkinson* remains good law, where the child is disabled, a mother will additionally be entitled to the upbringing costs attributable to the disability.

While agreeing that *McFarlane* was correctly decided, the minority judges (Lords Steyn, Hope and Hutton) disagreed with the majority's 'gloss' on it and would have upheld not only *Parkinson* but also the majority of the Court of Appeal's decision in *Rees* that the extra upbringing costs attributable to the mother's disability were recoverable.

In conclusion, the approach of the majority of their Lordships in *Rees* has much to commend it. It represents a fair and relatively clear answer to an intractable problem, albeit that it is unfortunate that there was no majority either way on *Parkinson*. Moreover, it should be appreciated – as Lord Hope explained with great clarity in his dissenting speech – that the conventional award is unique because, in contrast to damages for personal injury and death, it compensates mental distress in a situation where, for reasons of legal policy, the courts have decided that pecuniary loss is non-compensatable.[1] To place non-pecuniary loss above pecuniary

---

18 [2003] UKHL 52, [2004] 1 AC 309 at para 123.
19 [2001] UKHL 49, [2002] 2 AC 732.
20 [2003] UKHL 52, [2004] 1 AC 309 at para 112.
1   [2003] UKHL 52, [2004] 1 AC 309 at para 73.

loss is certainly odd. To that extent, it is clear that the majority have adopted a pragmatic compromise rather than a principled solution.

Although not involving a wrongful birth, the controversial decision in *Kralj v McGrath*[2] can also be conveniently mentioned here. The defendant doctor's negligence during the birth of one of the claimant's twins had caused the baby's death. The claimant wanted three children and hence would have to undergo another pregnancy and workless years which would not have been necessary had that baby not died. Inter alia, Woolf J awarded the claimant mother damages for the non-pecuniary and pecuniary loss of another pregnancy and childbirth and the pecuniary loss of initial workless years looking after another child. But the force of this decision is diminished because the only objection to those damages that was examined in the judgment was remoteness and there was no discussion of the fact that this claim was entirely novel and that the loss could not really be regarded as consequent on the personal injury to the mother. If followed to its logical conclusion the decision would mean that a mother whose baby is killed by the defendant's negligent driving should also be awarded damages for the non-pecuniary and pecuniary loss of pregnancy and workless years if she will want to have another child to replace the one lost. Yet such damages are presumably irrecoverable in a claim under the Fatal Accidents Act 1976 where the most the mother would be awarded would be £10,000 bereavement damages (plus any funeral expenses incurred).

2.   CLAIMS BY THE DECEASED'S ESTATE

The Law Reform (Miscellaneous Provisions) Act 1934, s 1(1), provides that on the death of any person all causes of action vested in him, subject to certain exceptions,[3] survive for the benefit of his estate. The most important consequence of this, and the one with which we are here concerned, is that the deceased's action for personal injury survives for the benefit of his estate. It should be stressed that the action brought by the estate is not for death caused by the defendant. The defendant may or may not have been responsible for the deceased's death. Rather the action is for the deceased's personal injury caused by the defendant.[4]

---

2   [1986] 1 All ER 54. See also *Kerby v Redbridge Health Authority* [1993] 4 Med LR 178 (damages awarded for the non-pecuniary rigours of an additional pregnancy).
3   Ie defamation (Law Reform (Miscellaneous Provisions) Act 1934, s 1(1)) and the right to bereavement damages (Law Reform (Miscellaneous Provisions) Act 1934, s 1(1A) as inserted by Administration of Justice Act 1982, s 4(1)).
4   Ogus *The Law of Damages* (1973) p 116.

Thus the estate can be awarded damages for all the deceased's recoverable loss,[5] both non-pecuniary and pecuniary, but only until the time of her death, applying the normal principle that all events up to trial are taken into account. So in *Rose v Ford*,[6] *Murray v Shuter*[7] and *Andrews v Freeborough*[8] damages for the deceased's loss of amenity were awarded, and in the first two of these cases for his pain and suffering: in *Murray v Shuter* damages for the deceased's loss of earnings were recovered and in *Rose v Ford* for the medical expenses he had incurred.

It has sometimes been argued that a damages claim for non-pecuniary loss should not survive for the benefit of the deceased's estate, as such loss is personal to the deceased. But while the estate clearly cannot itself suffer any non-pecuniary loss, there is still good reason for allowing the estate's claim in that the deceased died without having recovered the compensation for non-pecuniary loss to which he was entitled and which would have enured to the estate's benefit. Not surprisingly, therefore, the Law Commission recommended that there should be no change to the law on the survival of damages for non-pecuniary loss.[9] Indeed the Law Commission was strengthened in its view by the fact that Scottish law, which had excluded damages for non-pecuniary loss from survival actions between 1976 and 1992, was brought back into line with English law on this issue by the Damages (Scotland) Act 1993.[10]

In one respect, however, the principles governing compensatory[11] damages for the deceased's estate differ from those governing the injured claimant's damages. By the Administration of Justice Act 1982, s 4(2), amending the Law Reform (Miscellaneous Provisions) Act 1934, s 1(2), no damages may be awarded for loss of income in respect of any period after the death of the injured person; that is, the claim for loss of earnings in the 'lost years' does not survive for the benefit of the estate and *Gammell v Wilson*[12] is thereby overruled. This is a sensible reform.[13] Other than on a formal 'objective' view, the justification for allowing a

---

5   Ie subject to the usual principles, eg contributory negligence. Interest can also be awarded
     according to the usual principles.
6   [1937] AC 826
7   [1976] QB 972.
8   [1967] 1 QB 1.
9   *Damages for Personal Injury: Non-Pecuniary Loss*, Report No 257 (1999) paras 2.59–2.64.
10 Amending the Damages (Scotland) Act 1976.
11 Exemplary damages cannot be claimed by the estate – Law Reform (Miscellaneous Provisions)
     Act 1934, s 1(2).
12 [1982] AC 27.
13 Cf Cane and Harris 'Administration of Justice Act 1982, section 4(2): a Lesson in How Not to
     Reform the Law' (1983) 46 MLR 478. They criticise the reform, inter alia, because if the
     victim dies other than from his injuries the estate, and hence dependants, will lose out. But
     factual causation principles (see *Jobling v Associated Dairies Ltd* [1982] AC 794) dictate that they
     should lose out because they would have done so if there had been no wrong.

lost years claim is that the claimant's dependants will otherwise lose out. But where the victim has already died from his injuries prior to trial, the dependants are satisfactorily compensated by their Fatal Accidents Act claim and to allow his estate also to claim damages for the lost years potentially benefits persons other than his dependants, who take under his estate, thus providing a 'windfall' to those whom the lost years claim is not intended to benefit. Similarly, to allow the lost years claim to survive means that potentially the defendant may have to pay large damages both under the 1934 and 1976 Acts. Section 4(2) removes such problems.[14] It should also be realised that an effect of this reform is that where the deceased dies instantly, no claim for damages for personal injury survives for the benefit of his estate.[15]

Where 'provisional damages' have been awarded under the Supreme Court Act 1981, s 32A,[16] does the right of the injured claimant to return to court for further damages survive for the benefit of his estate? And is it caught by the 'lost years' bar? Tentative dicta of the Court of Appeal in *Middleton v Elliott Turbomachinery Ltd*[17] suggest that the claim is treated as if a judgment for damages to be assessed. Consequently in assessing those damages the court would be able to take account of the worsening of the claimant's condition, including death caused by that condition. The position has been clarified by the Damages Act 1996, s 3. This implicitly accepts that the claim for further damages does survive. But by the Damages Act 1996, s 3(4) no award of further damages made after the death is to include any amount for loss of income in respect of any period after the death (ie the 'lost years' bar applies).

By the Law Reform (Miscellaneous Provisions) Act 1934, s 1(2)(c), where the deceased's death has been caused by the act or omission which gives rise to the cause of action, damages recoverable by the estate 'shall be calculated without reference to any loss or gain to his estate consequent on his death, except that a sum in respect of funeral expenses may be included'. The main part of this is intended to emphasise that,

---

14 Waddams 'Damages for Wrongful Death: Has Lord Campbell's Act Outlived its Usefulness?' (1984) 47 MLR 437 explores the alternative method of solving the overlap problem; ie to repeal the Fatal Accidents Act, to allow the lost years claim to survive and to allow dependants to recover from the estate. See also *Gammell v Wilson* [1982] AC 27 at 80–81 (per Lord Scarman). In *Claims for Wrongful Death*, Report No 263 (1999) paras 3.1–3.2, the Law Commission rejected Waddams' approach principally because the Fatal Accidents Act and survival claims may cover two different sets of losses. To abolish the former could therefore leave dependants undercompensated.

15 Furthermore, in *Hicks v Chief Constable of the South Yorkshire Police* [1992] 1 All ER 690, CA, affirmed [1992] 2 All ER 65, HL, it was held that where injury, pain and suffering are in reality part of the death itself, albeit endured for a very short time before death, no damages are recoverable.

16 Above, pp 177–178.

17 (1990) Times, 29 October.

even where the defendant has been responsible for the death, the estate can recover only what the deceased himself could have recovered and hence neither loss, such as cessation of an annuity, nor gain, such as an insurance payment consequent on the death, is of any relevance. However, where the defendant has been responsible for the death, the courts are empowered to award the estate funeral expenses incurred. This is exceptional in that it does not represent the survival of a claim the deceased would have had.

Chapter 11

Losses on death

At common law no action could be brought for loss suffered through the killing of another. But this was altered by the Fatal Accidents Acts 1846–1959, now the Fatal Accidents Act 1976 (FAA 1976) (as amended by the Administration of Justice Act 1982, s 3) which gives a statutory action '… if death is caused by any wrongful act, neglect or default …'[1] Most such statutory actions are founded on a tort by the defendant but the basis may be breach of contract.[2]

1. DEPENDANTS

As laid down in FAA 1976, s 1(2) the action under the 1976 Act is for the benefit of the dependants of the deceased (subject to a narrower restriction on who can be awarded bereavement damages). By FAA 1976, s 1(3) 'dependant' means wife, husband, child, grandchild, father, mother, grandparent, brother, sister, uncle, aunt, or (as regards the last four) their issue, or, as inserted by the Administration of Justice Act 1982, ascendant beyond grandparent, descendant beyond grandchild, former husband or wife,[3] person treated by the deceased as a child of the family or parent, or person living with the deceased as husband or wife immediately prior to the death and for at least two years before.[4] Under FAA 1976, s 1(5) the above list includes in-laws, half-brothers and sisters, and stepchildren. By FAA 1976, s 2(1) 'The action shall be brought by and in the name of the executor or administrator of the deceased', but by FAA 1976, s 2(2), where there is no such personal representative, or no action is brought by him within six months, the action may be brought by

---

1 Special statutory regimes differing from FAA 1976 (eg under the International Transport Conventions Act 1983) are not examined here.
2 *Grein v Imperial Airways Ltd* [1937] 1 KB 50.
3 Including under a marriage that has been annulled or declared void: FAA 1976, s 1(4).
4 In *Pounder v London Underground Ltd* [1995] PIQR P217 it was held that a brief absence from the home during the two-year period prior to death did not give rise to a break in continuity in the context of a ten-year relationship.

and in the name of all or any of the persons for whose benefit a personal representative could have brought it. Although the loss and damages must ultimately be separately assessed for each dependant, the usual practice is first to determine the total liability of the defendant and then to apportion the damages between the dependants. By FAA 1976, s 2(3) only one action may be brought in respect of the death.[5]

This approach of limiting actions to a restricted range of claimants is presumably based on the desire to discourage frivolous claims and to refuse recognition to 'illicit' relationships. But it would seem preferable if anyone who could establish a non-business pecuniary loss resulting from the death were entitled to recover, subject to usual limiting principles like remoteness and the duty to mitigate. Judges are well able to decide whether a real loss has been suffered and the very fact that the list has had to be extended shows its potential arbitrariness. Nor should the deceased's non-conformity to usual family relationships deprive his or her factual dependants of compensation. As such, the most glaring injustice produced by the present list is that same-sex couples who have lived together for many years are unable to claim for loss of dependency (although this will to some extent be ameliorated if, and when, the Civil Partnership Bill 2004 becomes law).[6] These criticisms are reflected in the Court of Appeal's judgment in *Shepherd v The Post Office*[7] where it was said that a simpler approach would be a provision to the effect that any person who could show a relationship of dependence on the deceased should be entitled to make a claim. In similar vein, the Law Commission in its report, *Claims for Wrongful Death*,[8] has recommended that there should be added to the present list a generally-worded class of claimant whereby any other individual who 'was being wholly or partly maintained by the deceased immediately before the death or who would, but for the death, have been so maintained' would be able to bring an action. And a person shall be treated as being wholly or partly

---

5 'Action' is, by the Human Rights Act 1998, ss 3(1) and 6(1), to be interpreted as 'served process' so that the existence of a previous unserved writ does not bar a new claim brought within the limitation period: *Cachia v Faluyi* [2001] EWCA Civ 998, [2001] 1 WLR 1966.
6 Civil Partnership Bill 2004, cl 80 amends FAA 1976, s 1(3) (and consequentially makes amendments to ss 1(4) and 1(5) as well) by giving same-sex couples, who choose to register as civil partners, the same rights under FAA 1976 as married couples.
7 (1995) Times, 15 June.
8 Law Commission Report No 263 (1999) para 7.7 and Draft Bill, cl 1. For an argument that the restrictive nature of the present list is contrary to the Human Rights Act 1998, see Davis, Gumbel and Witcomb 'A Question of Dependency' (2001) 151 NLJ 997. But while in *Ghaidan v Godin-Mendoza* [2004] UKHL 30, [2004] 3 WLR 113, 'living as the husband or wife' of another in the Rent Act 1977, Sch 1 was interpreted, by reason of the Human Rights Act 1998, as including same-sex couples, it is hard to see what Convention right, and hence bar against discrimination, is triggered by there being a limited list of those who can claim damages for another's death.

maintained by another if that person 'otherwise than for full valuable consideration, was making a substantial contribution in money or money's worth towards his reasonable needs.'

2.   ACTIONABILITY BY INJURED PERSON

By FAA 1976, s 1(1), an action can only succeed if the wrongful act, neglect or default which caused the death '... is such as would (if death had not ensued) have entitled the person injured to maintain an action and recover damages in respect thereof ...' Therefore if the deceased was killed entirely through his own fault, if the defendant had validly excluded all liability to the deceased, if the deceased's action had become time-barred before his death, or if the deceased had settled his claim or obtained judgment against the defendant,[9] the dependants will have no action. Similarly by FAA 1976, s 5, where the deceased was contributorily negligent in relation to his death, and hence his damages would have been reduced by a certain amount under the Law Reform (Contributory Negligence) Act 1945, the damages recoverable by the dependants under the 1976 Act are to be reduced to a proportionate extent.[10]

By the Damages Act 1996, s 3, an award of provisional damages does not operate as a bar to an action in respect of the injured person's death under FAA 1976: but such part of the provisional damages or further damages awarded before the injured person's death, as was intended to compensate him for pecuniary loss in a period which in the event falls after his death, shall be taken into account in assessing the amount of any loss of support suffered by dependants.

---

9   It was this that produced the injustice to the dependants of denying the 'lost years' claim to an injured claimant, who then died from his injuries: see above, p 286. In *Jameson v Central Electricity Generating Board* [2000] 1 AC 455, HL, a settlement, satisfying a claim against one joint and several tortfeasor, on its true construction extinguished the cause of action (so that no action could be brought under FAA 1976) against the other joint and several tortfeasor.

10   In accordance with normal principle a dependant who has been contributorily negligent in relation to his tortious loss (ie was partly responsible for the death) should have his damages reduced. See *Mulholland v McCrea* [1961] NI 135.

3. THE THREE HEADS OF RECOVERABLE LOSS

(1) The first head – pecuniary loss attributable to the non-business relationship between deceased and dependant

(a) **Pecuniary loss**

This most obviously refers to the loss of support from the deceased's earnings.[11] But it is important to realise that it also includes the loss of a mother's or wife's 'services'.[12] So in *Berry v Humm & Co*,[13] a husband was able to recover damages for the loss of his wife's housekeeping 'services' which she had performed gratuitously.[14] Similarly, in *Hay v Hughes*,[15] children were able to recover damages for the loss of their mother's 'services' calculated according to the cost of engaging a housekeeper or nanny, even though on the facts this expense was not incurred because the children's grandmother was looking after them gratuitously. In *Regan v Williamson*,[16] Watkins J stressed that a mother's 'services' should be widely interpreted to take into account the fact that a mother is not just a housekeeper; on the other hand he reluctantly accepted that no damages could be given simply for the loss of a mother's love and care for this was not a pecuniary loss. As laid down in *Spittle v Bunney*,[17] a deduction must be made from the notional commercial cost of a full-time nanny (which was taken to be the net wages a nanny would receive rather than the expense of engaging her) because older children do not require the same looking-after as young children. In *Mehmet v Perry*,[18] the loss to the family of the deceased's 'services' as wife and mother was mainly calculated according to the wages lost by the father by giving up work to look after the children. And, as established in *Stanley v Saddique*,[19] lower damages should be awarded if the mother was unreliable and unlikely to have looked after the child properly.

---

11 It can also include loss of support from the deceased's future retirement pension, as in *Auty v National Coal Board* [1985] 1 WLR 784; and a loss of support because of a reduction in state benefits consequent on the death, as in *Cox v Hockenhull* [2000] 1 WLR 750.

12 See, analogously, *Clay v Pooler* [1982] 3 All ER 570 compensating for the loss of a husband and father's services as a handyman around the house.

13 [1915] 1 KB 627.

14 This has not been affected by the Administration of Justice Act 1982, s 2 abolishing the action for loss of the wife's services.

15 [1975] QB 790. See below, p 308.

16 [1976] 1 WLR 305.

17 [1988] 1 WLR 847.

18 [1977] 2 All ER 529. See also *Cresswell v Eaton* [1991] 1 WLR 1113 (value of mother's services based on wages given up by children's aunt to look after them).

19 [1992] QB 1.

(b) **Business pecuniary loss**

The pecuniary loss caused to the dependant by the deceased's death is not recoverable if it flows from the business relationship between them;[20] business pecuniary loss is clearly outside the Act's scope for otherwise there would be no sense in the restriction of claims to dependants which excludes, for example, an employer's claim for the pecuniary loss caused by the wrongful death of his employee. So in *Burgess v Florence Nightingale Hospital For Gentlewomen*[1] a husband could not recover damages for his loss of income as a dancer resulting from the death of his dancing-partner wife. Similarly in *Malyon v Plummer*[2] a wife who had been employed by her husband could not recover that part of her lost salary, which represented a true commercial payment for her services.

(c) **Proof of loss**

In accordance with general principle there will be no award if the loss is entirely speculative or if there is no 'reasonable expectation of pecuniary benefit as of right, or otherwise, from the continuance of the life'.[3] So in *Barnett v Cohen*[4] the parent of a four-year-old child was held to have no cause of action under this head and in *Davies v Taylor*,[5] where a wife had deserted her husband five weeks before his death and he had instructed a solicitor to begin divorce proceedings, she was held to have no action as she had failed to prove that there was a significant prospect of reconciliation with her husband and hence a reasonable expectation of pecuniary benefit. On the other hand, in *Taff Vale Rly Co v Jenkins*,[6] a parent recovered damages under the Act when his 16-year-old daughter died having almost completed her unpaid dressmaking apprenticeship and in *Kandalla v British Airways Board*[7] the elderly parents of two young women doctors were awarded damages on proof that the doctors had intended to flee from Iraq (where they had been working) to England, where they would have supported their parents.

20　A further restriction is where the deceased's earnings were illegally made: *Burns v Edman* [1970] 2 QB 541; *Hunter v Butler* [1996] RTR 396.
1　[1955] 1 QB 349.
2　[1964] 1 QB 330.
3　*Franklin v South Eastern Rly Co* (1858) 3 H & N 211 at 213–214. Above, p 62.
4　[1921] 2 KB 461.
5　[1974] AC 207.
6　[1913] AC 1.
7　[1981] QB 158.

(d) Multiplier method

As with future pecuniary loss for personal injury, the calculation of damages for loss of dependency is not easy. Again the courts' approach is generally[8] to use the multiplier method.

In this context, the multiplier method is used to assess all the pecuniary loss and not merely the post-trial pecuniary loss. In *Cookson v Knowles*[9] the House of Lords laid down that the dependants' pecuniary loss prior to trial should be assessed separately from that after the trial. This is essentially because the former is less speculative and because no interest is to be paid on the future loss but is payable on the pre-trial loss, normally from the date of death until the time of trial at half the average rate on the special account over that period.[10] In *Graham v Dodds*[11] it was clarified that that itemisation does not mean that the multiplier method should be abandoned for pre-trial loss. Rather the multiplier should continue to be calculated from the date of death (rather than from the date of trial) on the basis that, in contrast to a personal injury case, there can be no certainty even that the deceased would have survived until trial. So if, for example, the multiplier is fourteen, and four years have elapsed between death and trial, the pre-trial loss will be calculated using a multiplier of four and the post-trial loss, using a multiplier of ten. But a separate pre-trial and post-trial *multiplicand* is generally appropriate to take account of facts known at trial: eg the rate of wages for the job that the deceased had.[12]

In the light of the House of Lords' decision in *Wells v Wells*,[13] it is strongly arguable that, contrary to the approach in *Cookson v Knowles* and *Graham v Dodds*, the multiplier should be calculated from the date of trial. Although *Wells v Wells* was itself a personal injury case, it is clear that its approach was intended to apply to fatal accident claims as well. So the relevant discount rate for assessing the multiplier should be based on ILGS (Index Linked Government Stock) rates; and, more generally, a sound actuarial approach should be taken using the Ogden Tables as a starting point. But as the Law Commission pointed out, it is difficult to see how the Ogden Tables can be properly used where one is calculating a multiplier from the date of death rather than from trial.[14] The fourth edition of the Ogden Tables was produced with this criticism by the Law

---

8   But this might not be appropriate, for example, where there is as yet no dependency.
9   [1979] AC 556.
10 For discussion, see below, pp 349–352.
11 [1983] 1 WLR 808.
12 See especially Lord Fraser's speech in *Cookson v Knowles* [1979] AC 556 at 575–576.
13 [1999] 1 AC 345.
14 *Claims for Wrongful Death*, Law Com No 263 (1999) paras 4.1–4.23.

Commission in mind. It argued that, in the light of *Wells v Wells*, multipliers for post-trial pecuniary loss should be calculated from the date of death. In contrast, pre-trial loss should be calculated in much the same straightforward way as pre-trial loss in personal injury cases, with the qualification that there would need to be a general discount for the uncertainty as to whether the deceased would have lived to trial. The difficulties of the present approach are illustrated by *Corbett v Barking, Havering & Brentwood Health Authority*,[15] where there had been a long delay between death and trial (11½ years). Controversially, the Court of Appeal (Ralph Gibson LJ dissenting) held that it did not contradict *Graham v Dodds* to increase the normal multiplier, calculated from the date of the death, to take into account the known fact that the child dependant had survived to the age of 11½. In *White v ESAB Group (UK) Ltd*[16] Nelson J, in the light of the views of the Law Commission and the Ogden Working Party, would have preferred to calculate the multiplier from the date of trial, but held himself precluded from doing so by *Cookson v Knowles* and *Graham v Dodds*. In his view, those decisions had not been expressly or impliedly overruled by *Wells v Wells*. The decision in the *Corbett* case was held not to be applicable since, in contrast to that case, there were, in this case, no unusual significant facts that had arisen between the date of death and the trial. In *H v S*[17] the Court of Appeal approved Nelson J's refusal to depart from the traditional 'date of death' approach.

Under the present multiplier method, therefore, the *multiplicands* will be the pre-trial and post-trial annual pecuniary loss to the dependant calculated by, for example, deducting from the deceased's notional annual net[18] earnings his living expenses; and living expenses here means expenses for the deceased's own purposes exclusively.[19] There is then an adjustment to take account, for example, of the prospects of promotion that the deceased had.

But one has to be careful not to include what may at first sight appear to be a loss but on closer analysis turns out not to be. Two cases can be used to illustrate this. In *Auty v National Coal Board*[20] one of the claimants was a widow claiming under FAA 1976. She claimed as part of her loss of dependency the lost chance of gaining a widow's 'death-after-retirement' pension, and argued that the widow's 'death-in-service'

---

15 [1991] 2 QB 408.
16 [2002] PIQR Q6.
17 [2002] EWCA Civ 792, [2003] QB 965 at para 36.
18 Eg tax is deducted – *Zinovieff v British Transport Commission* (1954) Times, 1 April; *British Transport Commission v Gourley* [1956] AC 185.
19 *Harris v Empress Motors Ltd* [1984] 1 WLR 212 at 216–217; *Crabtree v Wilson* [1993] PIQR Q24.
20 [1985] 1 WLR 784.

pension that she was actually receiving was non-deductible under FAA 1976, s 4(1) (not then amended though the same argument would hold under the new wording). The Court of Appeal rejected this argument and held that, as she was only ever entitled to one or other pension and was receiving one, it was false to say that she had lost the chance of gaining the other. As Waller LJ said, '... she cannot claim for loss of an opportunity to obtain a widow's pension because she is already in receipt of a widow's pension.'[1]

Again in *Malone v Rowan*[2] Russell J held that in assessing a widow's pecuniary loss on the death of her husband the courts should not take into account that the couple planned to have a family so that, on giving up work, the wife's pecuniary dependency on her husband would have increased from the position at his death. Russell J was reluctant to so hold and did so only because he felt bound by the unreported Court of Appeal decision in *Higgs v Drinkwater*. But it is submitted that the decisions are correct and that Russell J's reluctance was ill-founded: for the increase in dependency that would have occurred was offset by the change of circumstances brought about by the death, namely that the claimant would now not suffer a loss of earnings in giving birth to and bringing up the deceased's children.

There is also some confusion on the authorities as to whether the dependant's (typically a widow's) own earning capacity should be taken into account to reduce the pecuniary loss.[3] Applying the duty to mitigate plus the principle that direct compensating advantages should be deducted, subject to a good policy reason to the contrary (like not discouraging private benevolence), earning capacity should be taken into account provided first, it is sufficiently likely that the dependant will work or it is reasonable for her to do so; secondly, she would not have worked but for the death; and thirdly it is reasonable to suppose that her earnings would have reduced the pecuniary benefit from the deceased had he lived.

The starting point for the *multiplier* is the estimated number of years (taking into account, for example, the deceased's and dependant's life expectancies) from the date of death that the dependant would have received the deceased's pecuniary support. When the deceased was unmarried and supporting his parents account must also be taken of the possibility of the deceased's marriage.[4]

---

1   [1985] 1 WLR 784 at 799.
2   [1984] 3 All ER 402. See Jones 'Calculating the Widow's Dependency' (1985) 101 LQR 20.
3   *Howitt v Heads* [1973] QB 64 (ignored); *Cookson v Knowles* [1977] QB 913 (taken into account). Presumably FAA 1976, s 4 is irrelevant to this sort of 'benefit'.
4   *Dolbey v Goodwin* [1955] 2 All ER 166.

The starting figure is then adjusted. In particular, there is a reduction because the claimant is receiving a capital sum now, which he can invest, rather than periodical payments over the years. A further small reduction may also be made for the contingencies of life, other than mortality, such as the deceased's possible unemployment. The aim is to award a capital sum, which when invested will produce an income in terms of interest and withdrawals of capital, equal to the dependant's lost income over the period intended to be covered (ie the period of dependency).[5] In *Wells v Wells*[6] the House of Lords held that the appropriate discount rate (ie the rate of return on investing the capital sum) for calculating personal injury multipliers should be based on the ILGS rate. Although fatal accident multipliers were not expressly mentioned, it is clear that the reasoning was equally applicable to them. In line with the principles laid down in that decision, and with other factors that he considered relevant, the Lord Chancellor has set a discount rate of 2.5% under the power conferred on him by the Damages Act 1996, s 1(2). That rate applies to fatal accident as well as personal injury cases.

Applying a discount rate of 2.5%, the multiplier (from death) for calculating loss of dependency in respect of a wife, who was 30 years old at the death and was dependent on her 30-year-old deceased husband, is about 23.[7]

In *Owen v Martin*[8] it was held that the prospects of a divorce between a claimant widow and the deceased are to be taken into account in assessing the widow's damages. And FAA 1976, s 3(4), as amended by the Administration of Justice Act 1982, lays down that in the case of a claim by a cohabitee, the court must take into account '... the fact that the dependant had no enforceable right to financial support by the deceased as a result of their living together.' This is presumably designed to impress upon the courts that there is even less certainty of continued future support in the case of cohabitees than in the case of married couples, particularly since legal obligations of support continue after the breakdown of marriage. But both *Owen v Martin* and s 3(4) have been criticised by the Law Commission primarily because it was thought

---

5   *Taylor v O'Connor* [1971] AC 115; *Cookson v Knowles* [1979] AC 556 at 576–577; *Robertson v Lestrange* [1985] 1 All ER 950 at 955–958. Analogously to the assessment of damages for future pecuniary loss consequent on personal injury, there is no adjustment for future inflation nor, normally, for higher rate tax payable by the claimant on the investment income: see above, pp 202–203, 282–283.

6   [1999] 1 AC 345.

7   Ogden Tables (4th edn, 2000) Table 25. As we have seen – see above, pp 301–302 – the Ogden Working Party itself proposed a different approach so that multipliers and the Ogden Tables would be used for only post-trial pecuniary loss based on the age the deceased would have been at trial.

8   [1992] PIQR Q151.

distasteful for judges to reach speculative conclusions about intimate aspects of people's lives. It was therefore recommended[9] that s 3(4) should be repealed and replaced by a provision to the effect that the prospect of breakdown in the relationship between the deceased and his or her partner should not be taken into account (although the fact of such a breakdown would continue to be relevant); and that, overruling *Owen v Martin*, the prospect of divorce or breakdown in the relationship between the deceased and his or her spouse should not be taken into account when assessing damages for the purposes of any claim under FAA 1976 unless the couple were no longer living together at the time of death, or one of the couple had petitioned for divorce, judicial separation or nullity.

By FAA 1976, s 3(3), as amended by the Administration of Justice Act 1982, in assessing a widow's claim in respect of her husband's death, 'there shall not be taken into account the re-marriage of the widow or her prospects of re-marriage'. Parliament introduced this provision to put a stop to the degrading judicial 'guessing game' of assessing a widow's prospects of re-marriage. But this is at the expense of not deducting what is a direct compensating advantage and the effect can be grotesque; eg a widow who marries a multi-millionaire, even prior to trial, is still entitled to a large sum of damages in respect of the death of her former husband. Certainly there is no good reason why a marriage that has already taken place should not be taken into account, since no guessing is then required. It should further be noted that the provision applies only to a widow's claim and therefore a mother's prospects of re-marriage must still be taken into account in assessing a child's claim. Similarly, where the claim is brought by a 'common-law wife' her prospects of marriage are to be taken into account. In addition, a widower's prospects of remarriage are relevant. All in all it is hard to dissent from Atiyah's view that this law reform 'must be one of the most irrational ... ever passed by Parliament'.[10]

Not surprisingly, the Law Commission has recommended that FAA 1976, s 3(3) should be repealed.[11] Nevertheless it saw force in the argument that assessing the prospects of a widow or widower remarrying or entering into a relationship of financially supportive cohabitation

---

9   *Claims for Wrongful Death*, Law Commission Report No 263 (1999) paras 4.54–4.71; Draft Bill, cl 4.

10 *Atiyah's Accidents Compensation and the Law* (6th edn) p 113.

11 *Claims for Wrongful Death*, Law Commission Report No 263 (1999) paras 4.27–4.53; Draft Bill, cl 4. For earlier recommendations for reform, see *Report on Personal Injury Litigation – Assessment of Damages*, Law Commission Report No 56 (1973) paras 251–252; and *Royal Commission on Civil Liability and Compensation for Personal Injury* (chaired by Lord Pearson) (1978) paras 409–412, 414. See also *De Sales v Ingrilli* (2002) 212 CLR 338, High Court of Australia.

would involve distressing and distasteful inquiries that should be avoided. It therefore recommended a new provision[12] to the effect that, unless a person is engaged to be married at the time of trial, the prospect that he or she will marry, remarry or enter into financially supportive cohabitation with a new partner, should not be taken into account when assessing any claim for damages under FAA 1976. In contrast, the fact of a marriage and, as appears to be the present law, the fact of financially supportive cohabitation should be taken into account.

(2) The second head – damages for bereavement

By FAA 1976, s 1A, as inserted by the Administration of Justice Act 1982, damages for death are to be awarded for the mental distress, eg the sorrow, grief, and loss of society and enjoyment, consequent on the death.[13] Called 'damages for bereavement', a fixed sum, of at present £10,000,[14] can by FAA 1976, s 1A(2), be claimed for the benefit:

'(a)   of the wife or husband of the deceased; and

(b)   where the deceased was a minor who was never married –

   (i)   of his parents, if he was legitimate;[15] and

   (ii)   of his mother, if he was illegitimate.'

This rightly brought English law into line with most other countries, although not all have a fixed award, nor restrict so severely those entitled to claim.

If, and when, the Civil Partnership Bill 2004 becomes law, those same-sex couples who choose to register as civil partners will have the same right to bereavement damages as married couples.[16]

In its Report *Claims for Wrongful Death*, the Law Commission recommended that the list of those who can claim bereavement damages should be widened (so as to include parent, child, sibling, fiancé(e) and

---

12   *Claims for Wrongful Death*, Law Commission Report No 263 (1999) paras 4.27–4.53 and Draft Bill, cl 4.

13   For cases denying such damages prior to the Administration of Justice Act 1982, see *Franklin v South Eastern Rly Co* (1858) 3 H & N 211; *Davies v Powell Duffryn Associated Collieries Ltd* [1942] AC 601 at 617.

14   The Lord Chancellor's power to alter the amount, most recently exercised by the Damages for Bereavement (Variation of Sum) Order 2002, SI 2002/644, is conferred by FAA 1976, s 1A(5). In principle interest should be payable as for personal injury non-pecuniary loss: ie 2% from the date of the service of the claim form until trial. In practice it has been awarded at the full special account rate from the date of death until trial: Kemp and Kemp *The Quantum of Damages* paras 16–031–16–032.

15   By FAA 1976, s 1A(4) if both parents claim, the fixed sum is to be divided equally between them.

16   Civil Partnership Bill 2004, cl 80 amends FAA 1976, s 1A(2)(a) by inserting 'civil partner' and also amends FAA 1976, s 1A(2)(b) by inserting 'or a civil partner' after 'was never married.'

co-habitee of the deceased) but that there should be a maximum payable of £30,000 in respect of any one death.[17]

(3) The third head – funeral expenses

By FAA 1976, s 3(5), as amended by the Administration of Justice Act 1982, 'If the dependants have incurred funeral expenses in respect of the deceased, damages may be awarded in respect of those expenses.' Case law has established that, to be recoverable, the expenses must have been reasonably incurred in all the circumstances, including the deceased's station in life, religion and racial origin.[18]

4.   FATAL ACCIDENTS ACT 1976, SECTION 4

By FAA 1976, s 4, inserted by the Administration of Justice Act 1982, 'In assessing damages in respect of a person's death in an action under this Act, the benefits which have accrued or will or may accrue to any person from his estate or otherwise as a result of his death shall be disregarded.'

Under the former FAA 1976, s 4(1) any benefit – defined to mean social security benefit, or payment by a trade union or friendly society – insurance money, pension or gratuity was not to be deducted. This was criticised by the Law Commission[19] and the Pearson Commission[20] for not also ordering the non-deduction of benefits derived from the deceased's estate; the benefits in mind being the acceleration and certainty of the inheritance of the deceased's property and awards for non-pecuniary loss[1] under the Law Reform (Miscellaneous Provisions) Act 1934. The new s 4 was passed in response to that criticism. This is unfortunate since that criticism lacked force. Compensation dictates the deduction of compensating advantages, the benefits in mind arise directly from the death, and there is no question of deduction discouraging benevolence or undermining the deceased's prudent spending of money in providing for his dependants after death.

The new FAA 1976, s 4 (as well as the old s 4(1)) is also inconsistent with the approach advocated in chapter 7 for compensating advantages rendered by third parties in response to the consequences of a tort or

---

17   Law Commission No 263 (1999) Part VI.
18   *Gammell v Wilson* [1982] AC 27, CA where the funeral expenses were held to include the cost of a gravestone. Although in this case these damages were being awarded under the Law Reform (Miscellaneous Provisions) Act 1934, s 1(2)(c), the same would apply under FAA 1976.
19   Report no 56, paras 254–256.
20   Report, paras 537–539.
1   Below, pp 310–311.

breach of contract.[2] According to that, while life assurance payments, gratuitous payments and probably pensions should continue not to be deducted, social security benefits should be deducted. This was a further reform of s 4(1) recommended by the Pearson Commission[3] and there seems no good reason why the provisions for the recoupment of social security benefits contained in the Social Security (Recovery of Benefits) Act 1997[4] have not been made applicable to damages under FAA 1976.

A further difficulty is the actual wording of FAA 1976, s 4. For the natural interpretation of 'benefits [accruing] ... as a result of his death' is that all compensating advantages (that is, all benefits factually caused by the death applying the 'but for' test) are covered. But if so, a widow's remarriage or her earnings from starting work after the death or gratuitous services rendered by a relative may all be benefits accruing as a result of the death and therefore non-deductible under the Act. Yet s 4 was clearly not intended to introduce such a wide reform.[5] Indeed if it had been, FAA 1976, s 3(3) ordering remarriage to be ignored in assessing a widow's damages would now be unnecessary and criticism of that provision for not also applying to a child's claim, and for not being matched by an equivalent provision regarding a widower's remarriage, would now be unfounded.

Of course the way out of this difficulty is to take a narrow interpretation of FAA 1976, s 4. Indeed, somewhat ironically, the same narrow construction has often been taken at common law – a good example being *Hay v Hughes*[6] concerning gratuitous services rendered by a relative – in deciding that benefits did not result from the death and were therefore *non-deductible* under the general principle of *deduction* laid down in *Davies v Powell Duffryn Associated Collieries Ltd*.[7] But it seems clear that the narrow interpretation taken in cases like *Hay v Hughes* is artificial and that the decisions were really justified on policy grounds such as not discouraging private benevolence. Yet now that s 4 has used similar wording, that artificial narrow construction must live on if the section is not to have a far wider effect than intended.

This exact dilemma has surfaced in the apparently contradictory interpretations of FAA 1976, s 4 taken in two Court of Appeal decisions.

---

2   Above, pp 161–174.
3   Report, paras 480–483.
4   Above, pp 165–168. For a recommendation that the scheme of the Social Security (Recovery of Benefits) Act 1997 should be expanded so as to apply to benefits received by a claimant under the FAA 1976, see *Claims for Wrongful Death* Law Commission Report No 263 (1999) paras 5.56–5.69.
5   See, eg 428 HL Official Report (5th series) col 28.
6   [1975] QB 790. See also, eg *Peacock v Amusement Equipment Co Ltd* [1954] 2 QB 347.
7   [1942] AC 601.

In *Stanley v Saddique*[8] it was held that, in assessing a child's damages for the death of his mother, the advantages to the child from the father's marriage to a woman who provided excellent motherly services to the child (and better care than the child's natural mother would have provided had she lived) were benefits accruing as a result of the death under s 4 and were to be disregarded. Section 4 was not to be given a narrow interpretation. In contrast the majority of the Court of Appeal in *Hayden v Hayden*[9] (McCowan LJ dissenting) decided that, where the tortfeasor was the father of the infant claimant and had given up his paid work to look after the claimant, the value of his services was not a benefit accruing as a result of the death under s 4 and was to be deducted in assessing the claimant's damages for the death of her mother.

The Divisional Court followed *Stanley v Saddique* in *R v Criminal Injuries Compensation Board, ex p K*.[10] This case concerned the assessment of compensation under the old Criminal Injuries Compensation Scheme for children whose mother had been murdered and who had then been well looked after by their uncle and aunt. On a judicial review application, it was held that the gratuitous services of the uncle and aunt fell to be disregarded under s 4. *Hayden v Hayden* was distinguished as a case on its special facts, namely that the provider of the gratuitous services was the tortfeasor who was only carrying out his parental duty.

Stanley v Saddique was also applied but with an important additional qualification in *H v S*.[11] The mother of infant children had been killed. Their father, who was not the tortfeasor, and had not previously provided them with any care or support, cared for them thereafter. The Court of Appeal held that the father's care and support was a benefit accruing as a result of the death and that, applying FAA 1976, s 4, it should therefore be disregarded in assessing damages. However, it was also held that *Hunt v Severs*[12] – the leading personal injury case on gratuitous services – should be applied to this Fatal Accidents Act claim. The Fatal Accident Act damages in respect of the lost gratuitous services were therefore here given only on the basis that they would be used to reimburse the

---

8   [1992] QB 1. For more straightforward applications of FAA 1976, s 4 leading to the non-deduction of benefits, see, eg *Pidduck v Eastern Scottish Omnibuses Ltd* [1990] 1 WLR 993 (widow's pension); *Wood v Bentall Simplex Ltd* [1992] PIQR P332 (inheritance of the deceased's assets).

9   [1992] 1 WLR 986. FAA 1976, s 4 was not discussed in *Watson v Willmott* [1991] 1 QB 140 where a child's loss of dependency was treated as the difference between the pecuniary support that the claimant's natural father (as bread-winner) would have provided and that provided by his adoptive father.

10 [1999] QB 1131.

11 [2002] EWCA Civ 792, [2002] 3 WLR 1179.

12 [1994] 2 AC 350. See above, p 277.

voluntary carer (the father) for his services; and they were therefore to be held on a trust for the carer, which the court could enforce.

In addition to recommending the integration of the central reasoning in *Hunt v Severs* into the Fatal Accidents Act regime[13] – along the lines now applied in *H v S* – the Law Commission has recommended the replacement of FAA 1976, s 4 by a new provision making clearer which benefits are, and are not, to be deducted.[14] This would be far preferable to the current rule of complete non-deduction, which depends for its intended effect on a narrow and questionable interpretation of 'benefits [accruing] … as a result of his death'.

5.   THE RELATIONSHIP BETWEEN ACTIONS UNDER THE LAW REFORM (MISCELLANEOUS PROVISIONS) ACT 1934 AND THE FATAL ACCIDENTS ACT 1976 WHERE THE WRONG HAS CAUSED DEATH

It seems appropriate finally to clarify this relationship because, where the defendant's tort or breach of contract has caused death, an action may be brought under both the Law Reform (Miscellaneous Provisions) Act 1934 and FAA 1976 and the two are commonly combined. The former is for the benefit of the deceased's estate and the latter for the benefit of her dependants. Usually, however, a person benefiting from the estate and hence from the 1934 Act will also be a dependant under the FAA 1976. The former law, embodied in *Davies v Powell Duffryn Associated Collieries Ltd*, was that an award made or likely to be made under the 1934 Act to a dependant was to be deducted from the Fatal Accidents Act damages, although not vice versa. But as held in *Murray v Shuter*[15] an award under the 1934 Act for pre-death loss of earnings (and analogous reasoning applied to awards for other pre-death pecuniary loss) should not be deducted because the dependants would have benefited from those earnings. In other words such an award compensates the dependants for their pre-death loss consequent on the deceased's injury and does not constitute a compensating advantage. Under the old law therefore it was, in any event, only awards for non-pecuniary loss (and, while they lasted, 'lost years' earnings awards) that were deducted. The

---

13   *Claims for Wrongful Death*, Law Commission Report No 263 (1999) paras 5.47–5.55; Draft Bill, cl 3.
14   *Claims for Wrongful Death*, Law Commission Report No 263 (1999) paras 5.21–5.46; Draft Bill, cl 5.
15   [1976] QB 972.

new FAA 1976, s 4 now means that even non-pecuniary loss awards under the 1934 Act are not to be deducted.

Thus where the death is not instantaneous the action under the Law Reform (Miscellaneous Provisions) Act 1934 enables the estate to recover damages for the deceased's pre-death personal injury losses, both pecuniary and non-pecuniary (plus any property damage), while the action under FAA 1976 enables dependants to recover their pecuniary loss as a result of the death and a spouse or parent(s) to recover damages for bereavement. Damages to cover the funeral expenses may be awarded under either Act[16] depending on whether incurred by the estate or by the dependants (though clearly the courts would not award them twice over). On the other hand, where the death is instantaneous and there has been no property damage, there is no point bringing an action under the 1934 Act, other than where the estate (and not a dependant) has incurred the funeral expenses.

16   The relevant provision in the Law Reform (Miscellaneous Provisions) Act 1934 is s 1(2)(c). The relevant provision in the FAA 1976 is s 3(5): see above, p 307.

Chapter 12

Loss of reputation

Loss of reputation is a non-pecuniary loss, which is traditionally regarded as distinct from mental distress in that it deals with society's feelings towards the claimant, rather than with the claimant's own feelings. But often, particularly in defamation cases where the award of damages is made by a jury, mental distress consequent on loss of reputation is not clearly separated from the award for loss of reputation itself. Indeed on a preferable view, alternative to that traditionally taken by the courts, all non-pecuniary loss, including loss of reputation, is ultimately regarded as a loss only in terms of the distress or loss of happiness caused to the claimant.[1] However, where a claimant complains of a loss of reputation he is generally concerned not only about loss of reputation itself, but also and often primarily about the pecuniary loss flowing from it and both will be considered.

In order to put the claimant into as good a position as if the tort or breach of contract had not occurred, as the general compensatory aims dictate, damages should be awarded, subject to the usual limiting principles, wherever loss of reputation and consequential pecuniary loss result from a tort or breach of contract. But the courts have taken a more restrictive approach especially where the claimant is suing for breach of contract.

1.   WHEN ARE DAMAGES AWARDED FOR LOSS OF REPUTATION?

(1) Breach of contract

Addis v Gramophone Co Ltd[2] is the leading authority for the rule that no damages can be given for loss of reputation for breach of contract. In

---

1   See above, pp 30–31. On this view too, only a person and not, eg a company, would be able to recover for loss of reputation as a non-pecuniary loss: a company would be solely concerned with the pecuniary loss flowing from a loss of reputation.
2   [1909] AC 488.

that case the House of Lords held that in the claimant's action for wrongful dismissal he should be confined to damages for his direct pecuniary loss, such as loss of salary, and should not be compensated for any loss of his reputation or for the fact that the dismissal might make it more difficult for him to get another job. So the decision appears to deny damages both for loss of reputation in itself – ie as a non-pecuniary loss – and for the pecuniary loss flowing from it. Lord Atkinson said:

> 'I can conceive nothing more objectionable and embarrassing in litigation than trying in effect an action of libel or slander as a matter of aggravation in an action for illegal dismissal, the defendant being permitted, as he must in justice be permitted, to traverse the defamatory sense, rely on privilege, or raise every point which he could raise in an independent action brought for the alleged libel or slander itself.'[3]

Yet in many cases subsequent to *Addis,* while damages for loss of reputation in itself have continued to be denied – for example, in *Groom v Crocker*[4] damages were held irrecoverable for any loss of the claimant's reputation as a careful driver, caused by his defendant solicitor's breach of contract in wrongfully admitting that the claimant had been negligent in his driving – pecuniary loss flowing from loss of reputation has been held recoverable. This distinction was particularly clearly applied in *Aerial Advertising Co v Batchelors Peas Ltd.*[5] There the defendants had contracted with the claimants to advertise their peas by trailers from a plane. In breach of contract the claimants flew the plane with the advertising trailers over a city centre during minutes of silence in armistice services. The public was horrified and the defendants' sales dropped. Atkinson J held that, while following *Groom v Crocker* the defendants were not entitled to damages for loss of reputation in itself, they were entitled to damages for loss of sales following on that loss of reputation.

There are several groups of cases in which damages for pecuniary loss flowing from loss of reputation have been awarded for breach of contract.

First, where the defendant's breach comprises a refusal to allow an actor's appearance or to publish an author's book, the actor or author has been held able to recover for the lost income flowing from the loss of the chance to enhance his reputation or, as it is often termed, the 'loss of publicity'. The leading cases are *Marbé v George Edwardes (Daley's Theatre) Ltd*[6] and *Herbert Clayton v Oliver,*[7] which concerned actors, and

---

3   [1909] AC 488 at 496.
4   [1939] 1 KB 194. *Bailey v Bullock* [1950] 2 All ER 1167.
5   [1938] 2 All ER 788.
6   [1928] 1 KB 269.
7   [1930] AC 209.

Tolnay v Criterion Film Productions Ltd[8] and *Joseph v National Magazine Co*[9] concerning authors. In *Withers v General Theatre Corpn Ltd*[10] the Court of Appeal stressed that while an actor can recover income lost from the loss of a chance to enhance his reputation he cannot recover that lost from damage to his existing reputation. This distinction is not only very difficult to justify in terms of policy but also in *Marbé v George Edwardes* the Court of Appeal had earlier specifically said that damages could be given for lost income flowing from damage to the actor's existing reputation.[11] Since *Marbé* was later applied by the House of Lords in *Herbert Clayton v Oliver*, and since it seems preferable in principle, it is submitted that the *Withers* distinction should be regarded as incorrect.

Secondly, where the breach of contract comprises a mismanagement of advertising, the claimant can recover for pecuniary loss flowing from the loss of reputation. This is particularly well illustrated by the *Aerial Advertising v Batchelors Peas* case. Similarly in *Marcus v Myers and Davis*,[12] where the defendant in breach of contract failed to insert an advert in a newspaper, the claimant was awarded damages for loss of business. Although loss of reputation was not mentioned, the loss of business can be regarded as analogous to pecuniary loss flowing from the loss of a chance to enhance one's reputation.

Thirdly, where a bank in breach of contract refuses to honour the claimant trader's cheque, as in *Rolin v Steward*,[13] or fails to supervise the claimant's business as agreed so that the claimant goes bankrupt, as in *Wilson v United Counties Bank Ltd*,[14] the claimant can recover damages for the pecuniary loss flowing from the damage to his credit and reputation.

Fourthly, where in breach of contract the defendant supplies goods or provides services that are not of the standard required by the claimant's customers, the claimant can recover damages for the pecuniary loss flowing from the loss of reputation. In *Anglo-Continental Holidays Ltd v Typaldos Lines (London) Ltd*,[15] travel agents were awarded damages for loss of goodwill when the shipowner, with whom they had arranged a cruise, substituted a smaller less attractive ship and a less satisfactory timetable of ports of call. Similarly in *GKN Centrax Gears Ltd v Matbro Ltd*,[16] where the claimants had supplied defective drive axles for fork-lift trucks that

---

8   [1936] 2 All ER 1625.
9   [1959] Ch 14.
10   [1933] 2 KB 536.
11   [1928] 1 KB 269 at 281, 288.
12   (1895) 11 TLR 327.
13   (1854) 14 CB 595. See also, eg *Kpohraror v Woolwich Building Society* [1996] 4 All ER 119: above, pp 85–86.
14   [1920] AC 102.
15   [1967] 2 Lloyd's Rep 61.
16   [1976] 2 Lloyd's Rep 555.

the defendants had then sold to their customers, the defendants, on their counterclaim, were awarded damages for the loss of repeat orders. Somewhat similar is *Foaminol Laboratories v British Artid Plastics Ltd*[17] where the claimants, who were putting a sun-tan cream on the market in attractive containers, had secured the co-operation of certain editors of ladies' magazines. The claimants had ordered 10,000 of the containers from the defendants who, however, failed to deliver most of them. Hallett J held that damages for loss of profit flowing from the loss of future co-operation with the editors could in theory be recovered, although here they would not be because the pecuniary loss was, first, too speculative and, secondly, too remote. Neither of these grounds of denial is convincing and in the *GKN Centrax* case Lord Denning doubted the actual decision in this case.[18]

The courts have therefore been prepared to compensate pecuniary loss flowing from loss of reputation. Indeed, in terms of policy there is no good reason why those four groups should be regarded as exhaustive: whatever one may say about loss of reputation as a non-pecuniary loss there is no convincing argument for leaving the claimant undercompensated by refusing to recognise this kind of pecuniary loss. As Hallett J said in *Foaminol*, '… if pecuniary loss be established, the mere fact that the pecuniary loss is brought about by the loss of reputation caused by a breach of contract is not sufficient to preclude the plaintiffs from recovering in respect of that pecuniary loss'.[19]

That that is a correct statement of the law has been authoritatively established in the leading modern case of *Malik v Bank of Credit and Commerce International SA*.[20] Former employees of the corrupt bank, BCCI, claimed damages from the bank for loss of reputation: that is, they sought compensation (so-called 'stigma damages') for their handicap in the labour market flowing from the dishonesty stigma that attached to employees of BCCI. It was laid down by the House of Lords that damages are recoverable for the pecuniary loss of reputation flowing from the employer's breach of the implied term not to undermine the employee's trust and confidence. Lord Nicholls specifically cited with approval Hallett J's statement in *Foaminol* set out above. The *Addis* case was departed from albeit that it was recognised that, on the facts of *Malik*, the relevant loss of reputation did not flow from the wrongful nature of the dismissal but rather from a breach of the implied term of mutual trust and confidence.

17 [1941] 2 All ER 393.
18 [1976] 2 Lloyd's Rep 555 at 573.
19 [1941] 2 All ER 393 at 400.
20 [1998] AC 20.

One might have thought that *Malik* had cleared the way for there to be a departure from *Addis*, allowing damages for financial loss consequent on a loss of reputation, even where the claim is for wrongful dismissal. But in *Johnson v Unisys Ltd*[1] (which did not directly concern a loss of reputation) the House of Lords decided that statute prevented them departing from *Addis* in a case where the claimant alleged that the manner of his (wrongful) dismissal had caused him a psychiatric illness which made it impossible for him to find another job. In the realm of wrongful dismissal, there has been, since 1971, a special statutory compensation scheme for unfair dismissal. It is now contained in the Employment Rights Act 1996. Their Lordships reasoned that to allow employees to recover damages for pecuniary loss (or indeed for non-pecuniary loss) beyond the salary that they were owed, and were not paid, for the notice period would conflict with that statutory compensation scheme. In particular, had the claimant sued for unfair dismissal, the statutory maximum sum that he could have recovered was £11,000 whereas he was here claiming damages for loss of earnings of £400,000. In the words of Lord Nicholls,[2]

> '[A] common law right embracing the manner in which an employee is dismissed cannot satisfactorily co-exist with the statutory right not to be unfairly dismissed. A newly developed common law right of this nature, covering the same ground as the statutory right, would fly in the face of the limits Parliament has already prescribed on matters such as the classes of employees who have the benefit of the statutory right, the amount of compensation payable and the short time limits for making claims. It would also defeat the intention of Parliament that claims of this nature should be decided by specialist tribunals, not the ordinary courts of law.'

Lord Steyn dissented from the other Law Lords on this reasoning and agreed with the decision only because he thought that the psychiatric illness was too remote.[3] It should be emphasised that none of their Lordships supported the decision in *Addis* as such. The reasoning was rather that common law principle – allowing pecuniary loss consequent on a psychiatric illness (or a loss of reputation) caused by a breach of contract – should not be applied to a wrongful dismissal because of the clash with the unfair dismissal legislation.

---

1   [2001] UKHL 13, [2003] 1 AC 518. The *Unisys* case was distinguished by the House of Lords, without reopening its correctness, in *Eastwood v Magnox Electric plc* [2004] UKHL 35, [2004] 3 WLR 322.
2   [2001] UKHL 13, [2003] 1 AC 518 at para 2.
3   In *Eastwood v Magnox Electric plc* [2004] UKHL 35, [2004] 3 WLR 322, Lord Steyn, in powerful obiter dicta, gave several reasons for doubting the approach of the majority in the *Unisys* case.

What about the continued denial of damages for loss of reputation in itself, that is, as a non-pecuniary loss? This was not in issue in the *Malik* case and is closely linked to the question of whether, and when, mental distress damages can be awarded for breach of contract. While less crucial than the denial of pecuniary loss consequent on a loss of reputation, the blanket refusal of damages for non-pecuniary loss of reputation is unjustified. Adherence to full compensation dictates recovery, and although proof of this loss may be difficult, as may assessing damages, these are not reasons for a blanket refusal, particularly given the judicial willingness to compensate other types of non-pecuniary loss. Nor, if allowed, is there any reason to think that the courts would be swamped with claims. Furthermore, Lord Atkinson in *Addis* was misguided in fearing that the intricacies of defamation law would be incorporated into breach of contract claims, for the simple reason that the issue here concerns damages, not liability. Defences of privilege, truth and so on, are thus irrelevant. It is therefore to be hoped that, just as the courts (with the exception of a claim for wrongful dismissal) have departed from *Addis* as regards pecuniary loss consequent on loss of reputation, and as regards mental distress,[4] they will also feel able to depart from it as regards damages for loss of reputation in itself.

(2) Torts

Although the term 'loss of reputation' is often not referred to, and although the damages are generally not itemised, loss of reputation in itself, and pecuniary loss flowing from it, are both recoverable for some torts.

The tort of defamation, for example, largely exists in order to protect reputations, and damages there can compensate for both the non-pecuniary and pecuniary loss caused.[5] In *McCarey v Associated Newspapers Ltd*,[6] for example, £9,000 damages had been awarded by the jury in a libel action. The Court of Appeal overturned this as being too high; no punitive damages could here be awarded, and as the claimant had not proved any consequent pecuniary loss, he should be restricted to general loss of reputation as a non-pecuniary loss, plus mental distress damages for grief and annoyance. The judgments do recognise, however,

---

4 Below, pp 324–333.
5 There is some doubt whether loss of reputation in itself is recoverable for slander actionable only on proof of damage. But once liability is established it would seem that it is: *Dixon v Smith* (1860) 5 H & N 450.
6 [1965] 2 QB 86.

that pecuniary loss flowing from the loss of reputation, as well as the non-pecuniary loss itself, can be compensated. Diplock LJ said, for example:

> 'Under head (1) – that is to say, the consequences of the attitude adopted towards the plaintiff by other persons – it may be possible to prove pecuniary loss, such as loss of practice or employment, or inability to obtain fresh appointment … But the major consequences under head (1) may be purely social and lie in the attitude adopted towards the plaintiff by persons with whom he comes into social or professional contact.'[7]

Damages for loss of reputation and for consequential pecuniary losses have further been awarded for false imprisonment[8] and have been recognised to be recoverable for malicious prosecution.[9]

In other cases damages for pecuniary loss consequent on loss of reputation have been awarded without any question being raised as to compensating the non-pecuniary loss.[10] For example, damages have been held recoverable where goods infringing the claimant's intellectual property rights are so inferior to the claimant's that his reputation was diminished and sales were lost.[11] And in *Mulvaine v Joseph*,[12] where a professional golfer was injured in a car accident, his damages for negligence included compensation for the lost opportunity to enhance his golfing prestige by competing in a number of European tournaments.

In contrast it was held by the Court of Appeal in *Lonrho plc v Fayed (No 5)*[13] that, while consequential pecuniary loss is recoverable for lawful means conspiracy, loss of reputation itself is not. And, although this is essentially an issue going to liability rather than damages, there is no liability in the tort of negligence for inflicting a loss of reputation (that is not consequent on the claimant's personal injury).[14]

---

7   [1965] 2 QB 86 at 108.
8   *Childs v Lewis* (1924) 40 TLR 870; *Walter v Alltools Ltd* (1944) 61 TLR 39; *White v Metropolitan Police Comr* (1982) Times, 24 April.
9   *Savile v Roberts* (1699) 1 Ld Raym 374; *Childs v Lewis* (1924) 40 TLR 870; *Clark v Chief Constable of Cleveland Constabulary* [1999] 21 LS Gaz R 38.
10   In addition to the cases cited below, see *GWK Ltd v Dunlop Rubber Co Ltd* (1926) 42 TLR 593 (inducing breach of contract); *E Worsley & Co Ltd v Cooper* [1939] 1 All ER 290 (injurious falsehood).
11   *Sykes v Sykes* (1824) 3 B & C 541 (passing-off). See similarly *AG Spalding & Bros v Gamage Ltd* (1918) 35 RPC 101 (passing-off).
12   (1968) 112 Sol Jo 927.
13   [1993] 1 WLR 1489. Cf *Pratt v British Medical Association* [1919] 1 KB 244, 282 (unlawful means conspiracy).
14   See, eg *Calveley v Chief Constable of Merseyside* [1989] AC 1228 at 1238, where Lord Bridge said, speaking of the type of injury protected by the tort of negligence, 'The submission that "anxiety, vexation and injury to reputation may constitute such an injury" needs only to be stated to be seen to be unsustainable.'

So, to summarise, assuming a tort has been established and one is simply concerned with the question of damages, there appear to be no particular restrictions on tortious recovery for pecuniary loss consequent on a loss of reputation; but, for some torts, damages for loss of reputation in itself are irrecoverable. This latter restriction can be criticised for the same reasons as have been put forward above in relation to the denial of compensation for non-pecuniary loss of reputation caused by breach of contract.

2. ASSESSING DAMAGES FOR LOSS OF REPUTATION

Pecuniary loss consequent on loss of reputation generally comprises lost earnings – as, for example, in *McCarey v Associated Newspapers Ltd* or *Marbé v George Edwardes* – or lost profits, as in the *Aerial Advertising* or *Anglo-Continental Holidays* cases. It is usually not possible to offer precise proof of those losses, although of course the more precise the proof the less the court (be it judge or jury) needs to resort to educated guesswork.

Loss of reputation in itself is, like all non-pecuniary losses, very difficult to assess and all that the courts can aim for is a fair and reasonable sum and some degree of uniformity between awards. Clearly the greater the loss of reputation the greater the damages should be, and in order to prove anything other than general loss of reputation a claimant would presumably need to bring evidence to indicate the difference between his present and former reputations. It is submitted that one of the best statements relating to the assessment of damages for loss of reputation is that of Diplock LJ in *McCarey v Associated Newspapers Ltd*,[15] where he made the point that there should be some degree of uniformity not only between loss of reputation damages but also between damages for all non-pecuniary losses. He said:

'In putting a money value on these kinds of injury, as the law requires damage-awarding tribunals to do, they are being required to attempt to equate the incommensurable. As in the case of damages for physical injuries, it is impossible to say that any answer looked at in isolation is right, or that any answer is wrong. But justice is not justice if it is arbitrary or whimsical, if what is awarded to one plaintiff for an injury bears no relation at all to what is awarded to another plaintiff for an injury of the same kind, or, I would add, if what is awarded for one kind of injury shows a wrong scale of values when compared with what is awarded for injuries of a different kind which are also incommensurable with pounds, shillings and pence.'[16]

15 [1965] 2 QB 86. See also *Coyne v Citizen Finance Ltd* (1991) 172 CLR 211 at 221 (per Mason CJ and Deane J dissenting).
16 [1965] 2 QB 86 at 108.

And he later went on:

> 'If, as I have said, figures much lower than that awarded in this case are the proper compensation for the loss of an eye or limb, or for other life-long disabling injuries, a sum of £9,000 as compensation for this injury ... is a figure that no reasonable jury, applying correct principles which included a proper scale of value, could have reached.'[17]

Although that approach, of seeking consistency with personal injury awards, was for many years rejected[18] – primarily because damages for defamation are normally decided by juries and it was felt inappropriate for juries to be referred to awards in personal injury cases – it was approved by the Court of Appeal in *John v MGN Ltd.*[19] In substituting a figure of £35,000 compensatory damages for the 'excessive' £75,000 damages awarded by the jury,[20] the Court of Appeal laid down that in defamation cases the scale of awards for non-pecuniary loss in personal injury cases could be drawn to the attention of juries and that the level of an appropriate award could be indicated by the judge.[1] In Sir Thomas Bingham MR's words:

> 'It is in our view offensive to public opinion, and rightly so, that a defamation plaintiff should recover damages for injury to reputation greater, perhaps by a significant factor, than if that same plaintiff had been rendered a helpless cripple or an insensate vegetable.'[2]

Nevertheless the Master of the Rolls was anxious to assert that, at root, the decision was one for the jury not the judge or the Court of Appeal. He said:

> 'The jury must of course make up their own mind and must be directed to do so. They will not be bound by the submission of counsel or the indication of the judge. If the jury make an award outside the upper or lower bounds of any bracket indicated and

---

17   [1965] 2 QB 86 at 110.
18   See, eg *Cassell & Co Ltd v Broome* [1972] AC 1027 at 1070; *Blackshaw v Lord* [1984] QB 1; *Sutcliffe v Pressdram Ltd* [1991] 1 QB 153; *Rantzen v Mirror Group Newspapers Ltd* [1994] QB 670.
19   [1997] QB 586.
20   The Court of Appeal's power to substitute a figure for that of the jury is conferred by the Courts and Legal Services Act 1990, s 8: see also CPR Sch 1 r 59.11. Formerly, where damages were excessive or inadequate, the Court of Appeal merely had power to order a new trial.
1   This was in line with the majority of the High Court of Australia in *Carson v John Fairfax & Sons Ltd* (1993) 178 CLR 44. It was also the position advocated in the second edition of this book, at p 228.
2   [1997] QB 586 at 614.

such award is the subject of appeal, real weight must be given to the possibility that their judgment is to be preferred to that of the judge.'[3]

One might argue that, having gone so far, it would be preferable to go one step further and to remove the assessment of damages from juries in defamation (and indeed all other) cases. Under the present law, by the Supreme Court Act 1981, s 69 and the County Courts Act 1984, s 66, there is a right to jury trial in claims for libel, slander, malicious prosecution, false imprisonment or where there is a charge of fraud.[4] Otherwise trial is by judge alone, unless the court exercises its discretion to order trial by jury.

The unpredictability of, and inconsistency between, jury awards tends to undermine the essential justice of like cases being treated alike. This, plus the expense and length of a jury trial, explains why jury assessment has declined since the middle of the twentieth century. In *Ward v James*[5] the Court of Appeal held that personal injury cases should almost always be tried by a judge and this was confirmed and strengthened in *H v Ministry of Defence*,[6] where the Court of Appeal reversed a decision to order trial by jury in a case where a major part of the claimant's penis had been amputated. Lord Donaldson MR said, '[T]rial by jury is normally inappropriate for any personal injury action in so far as the jury is required to assess compensatory damages, because the assessment of such damages must be based upon or have regard to conventional scales of damages.'[7]

In Part IV of its Report on *Damages for Personal Injury: Non-Pecuniary Loss*,[8] the Law Commission recommended that the assessment of damages for all actions, except defamation, should always be a matter for a judge not a jury. Defamation was excluded not because judge-assessment was inappropriate or because a split of function between judge (deciding quantum) and jury (deciding liability) would be unworkable, but rather because it was thought that the future of defamation actions needed to be looked at as a whole once recent

3   [1997] QB 586 at 616. In *Kiam v MGN Ltd* [2002] EWCA Civ 43, [2003] QB 281, it was held (by a majority) that the 'proper award' is 'the highest award which the jury could reasonably have thought necessary', and that the jury's award should not be disturbed unless it substantially exceeds that sum. The bracket suggested by the judge was £40,000 to £80,000 and the jury awarded £105,000; this was not 'out of all proportion to what could sensibly have been thought appropriate' given the deference to be shown to jury awards in defamation cases. Guidance on the use of brackets in directing juries was also given.
4   But there is no right to jury trial where 'the court is of the opinion that the trial requires any prolonged examination of documents or accounts or any scientific or local investigation which cannot conveniently be made with a jury': Supreme Court Act 1981, s 69(1).
5   [1966] 1 QB 273.
6   [1991] 2 QB 103.
7   [1991] 2 QB 103 at 112.
8   Law Commission No 257 (1999).

changes made by the Defamation Act 1996 had bedded down.[9] It was further noted that in New South Wales, the Defamation Amendment Act 1994 had not only removed the jury assessment of damages for defamation but had also provided that the judge not the jury should determine whether any defence was available. The Law Commission was also constrained in what it could recommend because the radical solution of removing the right to jury trial in defamation cases altogether – which was earlier recommended by the Faulks Committee on Defamation[10] – was beyond the scope of its enquiry.

For the present, where one of the parties exercises its right to have a jury trial, juries will continue to assess damages. But, following *John v MGN Ltd*, juries in defamation cases will be assisted by being told of the scale of awards for non-pecuniary loss in personal injury cases and by the bracket which the judge considers appropriate.

9   Law Commission No 257 (1999) paras 4.14–4.23.
10   Report (1975) Cmnd 5909, ch 17.

Chapter 13

Mental distress or physical inconvenience (except consequent on personal injury or death)[1]

Mental distress covers, for example, disappointment, worry, anxiety, fear, upset and annoyance. On the traditional approach taken by the courts, mental distress, along with 'pain and suffering' consequent on a personal injury and 'bereavement,' compensated under the Fatal Accidents Act 1976, are the heads of non-pecuniary loss covering the claimant's loss of happiness and distress in contrast to the other 'objective' non-pecuniary losses (such as 'loss of amenity' consequent on a personal injury and 'loss of reputation'). On an alternative and preferable view,[2] all non-pecuniary loss is regarded as ultimately dealing with distress or loss of happiness and 'mental distress' is seen as a residual head for distress not falling within any of the other heads.

Traditionally, and especially in the contract realm, physical inconvenience has been regarded as distinct from mental distress and as an objective loss analogous to loss of amenity in a personal injuries claim. But even leaving aside the point made at the end of the previous paragraph, the distinction between mental distress and physical inconvenience has become less important as the courts have become more willing to award mental distress damages for breach of contract. In particular, as we shall see, a now well-recognised category of recovery for non-pecuniary loss in contract is physical inconvenience and mental distress directly consequent on it. It has therefore been thought more helpful to look at physical inconvenience alongside mental distress in this chapter rather than separating it out into a different chapter.

It should be emphasised that mental distress has to be distinguished from a psychiatric illness, such as depression or post-traumatic stress

---

1   For damages for pain and suffering consequent on personal injury and for bereavement see above, pp 271–274, 306–307. Damages for loss of amenity in a personal injury case will usually include some damages for physical inconvenience.
2   See above, pp 30–31.

disorder. The law regards psychiatric illness as a type of personal injury[3] and the restrictions on damages for mental distress do not apply to damages for psychiatric illness.[4]

In order to put the claimant into as good a position as if the tort or breach of contract had not occurred, as the general compensatory aims dictate, damages for mental distress or physical inconvenience should be awarded, subject to the usual limiting principles, whenever mental distress or physical inconvenience result from a tort of breach of contract. Traditionally, however, the courts have been reluctant to award mental distress damages, particularly for breach of contract, and despite recent developments they are still sometimes irrecoverable for both torts and breach of contract.

1.   WHEN ARE DAMAGES AWARDED FOR MENTAL DISTRESS OR PHYSICAL INCONVENIENCE?

(1) Breach of contract[5]

Traditionally *Addis v Gramophone Co Ltd*[6] was regarded as barring any damages for mental distress in an action for breach of contract. There the claimant had been wrongfully dismissed. The House of Lords confined damages to his direct pecuniary loss and refused to award any damages for the injury to the claimant's feelings following the 'harsh and humiliating manner'[7] in which he had been treated. Similarly in *Groom v Crocker*,[8] in which a solicitor in breach of contract had wrongly admitted negligent driving on the part of the claimant, the claimant's action for damages for the humiliation of being branded a negligent driver was denied and *Addis* applied. Further illustrations of the traditional denial of damages for mental distress are provided by cases on physical inconvenience, which drew a distinction between recoverable damages for physical inconvenience and non-recoverable damages for mental distress. For example, in *Hobbs v London and South Western Rly Co*[9] Mellor J said 'For the mere inconvenience, such as annoyance and loss of temper

3   See above, p 269, n 1.
4   So, for example in *Hatton v Sutherland* [2002] EWCA Civ 76, [2002] 2 All ER 1 and *Barber v Somerset County Council* [2004] UKHL 13, [2004] 1 WLR 1089, which are leading cases on psychiatric illness consequent on stress at work, there was no mention of the leading case on contractual damages for mental distress of *Addis v Gramophone Co Ltd* [1909] AC 488.
5   See generally Veitch 'Sentimental Damages in Contract' (1977) 16 UWOLR 227. For a comparative account, see Treitel *Remedies for Breach of Contract* pp 194–201.
6   [1909] AC 488.
7   [1909] AC 488 at 493 (per Lord Atkinson).
8   [1939] 1 KB 194.
9   (1875) LR 10 QB 111.

or vexation ... you cannot recover damages. That is purely sentimental and not a case where the word inconvenience, as I here use it, would apply.'[10]

This traditional denial was departed from by the Court of Appeal in *Jarvis v Swan's Tours*,[11] where the claimant was compensated for his disappointment at not getting as good a holiday as he had contracted for. Since then, mental distress damages have been awarded in many cases, primarily but not only for ruined holidays. But Lord Denning said that mental distress damages were recoverable only in a 'proper case'; and the Court of Appeal in *Watts v Morrow*,[12] as confirmed and expanded by the House of Lords in *Farley v Skinner*,[13] has clarified that there are only two exceptional categories of case where mental distress damages are recoverable. In Bingham LJ's words, neatly summarising the position, in *Watts v Morrow*:[14]

'A contract-breaker is not in general liable for any distress, frustration, anxiety, displeasure, vexation, tension or aggravation which his breach of contract may cause to the innocent party. The rule is not, I think founded on the assumption that such reactions are not foreseeable, which they surely are or may be, but on considerations of policy. But the rule is not absolute. Where the very object of a contract is to provide pleasure, relaxation, peace of mind or freedom from molestation, damages will be awarded if the fruit of the contract is not provided or if the contrary result is procured instead. If the law did not cater for this exceptional category of case it would be defective. A contract to survey the condition of a house for a prospective purchaser does not, however, fall within this exceptional category. In cases not falling within this exceptional category, damages are in my view recoverable for physical inconvenience and discomfort caused by the breach and mental suffering directly related to that inconvenience and discomfort.'

The first category, therefore, is where the very, or predominant, object of the contract, from the claimant's point of view, was to obtain mental satisfaction, whether enjoyment or relief from distress. The ruined holiday cases, such as *Jarvis v Swan's Tours* and *Jackson v Horizon Holidays*[15] most obviously fall within this. So does *Heywood v Wellers*,[16] where the defendant solicitors, in breach of their contractual duty of care, had

---

10 (1875) LR 10 QB 111 at 122. Also see *Bailey v Bullock* [1950] 2 All ER 1167.
11 [1973] QB 233.
12 [1991] 1 WLR 1421.
13 [2001] UKHL 49, [2002] 2 AC 732.
14 [1991] 1 WLR 1421 at 1445.
15 [1975] 1 WLR 1468. See also *Hunt v Hourmont* [1983] CLY 983.
16 [1976] QB 446. See also *McLeish v Amoo-Gottfried & Co* (1993) 137 Sol Jo LB 204. Cf *Dickinson v Jones Alexander & Co* [1990] Fam Law 137 (which is controversial because the wife's mental distress consequent on the negligent handling of her *financial* claims surely fell outside this first category).

failed to gain an injunction to stop molestation of the claimant by her former boyfriend. She was awarded damages for the mental distress resulting from being further molested. The same principle can also be said to underpin the influential Scottish case of *Diesen v Samson*[17] in which mental distress damages were awarded for the defender's breach of contract in failing to appear at a wedding to take photographs. Although not everyone agrees about this,[18] it is submitted that the decision of the House of Lords in *Ruxley Electronics and Construction Ltd v Forsyth*[19] also falls within this category. The damages of £2,500 for so-called 'loss of amenity' are best rationalised as flowing from the fact that the claimant's primary object in specifying the particular depth of the deep end of a swimming pool was mental satisfaction. That is, damages were being given for Mr Forsyth's loss of pleasure in diving into a deep pool rather than diving into a merely safe pool.[20]

In *Farley v Skinner*,[1] the House of Lords examined the width of this first category and decided that it extended to where *an important object* of the contract was mental satisfaction or freedom from distress even though that was not the very, or predominant, object. The claimant was considering buying a house 15 miles from Gatwick Airport. He engaged the defendant to survey the property and specifically asked him to investigate whether the property was affected by aircraft noise. After buying the property and moving in, the claimant discovered that aircraft bound for Gatwick flew directly over, or nearly over, the house and that the noise substantially affected the property and was 'a confounded nuisance.' Nevertheless he decided not to sell. Moreover, he was found to have suffered no financial loss in that he had paid the market value of the property where that value took into account the aircraft noise. Nevertheless he sought mental distress damages because his enjoyment of the property was detrimentally affected. The House of Lords upheld the first instance judge's award of £10,000 because an important object of the contract, albeit not the very object of the contract, was peace of mind in relation to the aircraft noise. No doubt the major point of the survey contract was to help ensure that he claimant paid the right price for the property. But given that he had made an express request for the aircraft noise to be investigated, it was an important object of the contract for him to be satisfied as to the aircraft noise.

---

17   1971 SLT 49. See also *Reed v Madon* [1989] 2 All ER 431 (contract for exclusive burial rights).
18   See above, p 221, n 2.
19   [1996] AC 344.
20   See above, p 221, n 3.
1   [2001] UKHL 49, [2002] 2 AC 732.

It is significant that an express specific request was made in this case. This enables the concept of 'an important object of the contract being mental satisfaction' to be narrowly construed. Without that controlling feature, there would be a danger that this first category has been expanded to cover most consumer contracts; for one can say that mental satisfaction is an important object of most consumer contracts even if not the predominant object. For example, the purchaser of a new kitchen or a person who contracts for a standard house survey or even a person who pays for financial advice has mental satisfaction and peace of mind as an important object of the contract. Yet it is clear that the House of Lords did not intend the concept of an important object to be so widely construed given that it treated an ordinary surveying contract as not falling within this category.

A case that was held to fall within the first category, as expanded by *Farley v Skinner*, was *Hamilton Jones v David & Snape*.[2] Here a claim was brought against solicitors in contract and tort for having negligently failed to renew 'agency notifications' of the risk of the claimant's twin sons being taken out of England by her former husband. The children had been taken to Tunisia and, as a consequence, the mother had lost custody of them. Neuberger J held that the claimant was entitled to £20,000 mental distress damages for breach of contract (and concurrently for the tort of negligence). While the primary object of the contract between the claimant and her solicitors was the welfare of the children, an important factor was to ensure, so far as possible, that the claimant retained custody of the children for her own pleasure and peace of mind. Applying the approach to the first category taken in *Farley v Skinner*, damages for the mental distress consequent on losing custody of her children were therefore recoverable.

A second situation in which mental distress damages can be awarded is where the claimant's mental distress is directly consequent on physical inconvenience caused by the defendant's breach of contract. That damages for the physical inconvenience itself can be awarded has long been established.

In *Burton v Pinkerton*,[3] for example, a sailor left a ship at a foreign port, when in breach of his contract of employment, the captain of the ship decided to take it into war. The sailor was able to recover damages for the non-remote physical inconvenience caused by the captain's breach of contract. Similarly in *Hobbs v London and South Western Rly Co*,[4] a man and

2   [2003] EWHC 3147 (Ch), [2004] 1 All ER 657.
3   (1867) LR 2 Exch 340.
4   (1875) LR 10 QB 111.

his family were set down at the wrong station by the defendant railway company in breach of contract. As it was late at night, there was no available transport or accommodation and so, despite rain, they had to walk five miles home. They were able to recover damages for that physical inconvenience. Again damages have long been awarded for the physical inconvenience of living in a house requiring repairs (including the inconvenience while the repairs are carried out) when the house would not have been bought, or at least not in that condition, but for a breach of the contractual duty of care by the purchaser's surveyor or solicitor.[5] A solicitor was also held liable for physical inconvenience damages in *Bailey v Bullock*[6] where he had delayed in bringing an action for possession of a house. As a result the claimant and his family were forced to live in one room of his parents-in-law's small house. A final example is *Perera v Vandiyar*,[7] where the defendant landlord, in an attempt to evict the claimant tenant, cut off the supply of gas and electricity to his flat, leaving the claimant without alternative means of heat or light. After two days' discomfort, the claimant left with his wife and child to stay with friends for five days until the gas and electricity supply were restored. The claimant was awarded physical inconvenience damages for breach by the landlord of his tenancy agreement.

But, more recently, the courts have clarified that damages for mental distress directly consequent on the physical inconvenience are also recoverable. For example, in *Perry v Sidney Phillips & Son*[8] the claimant bought a house on the faith of a survey report prepared by the defendants, a firm of chartered surveyors. The report had been negligently made, in breach of the defendants' contractual and tortious duty of care, and did not mention several serious defects including a leaking roof and a septic tank which produced an offensive smell. The claimant was held entitled to mental distress damages for the 'anxiety, worry and distress'[9] caused and this mental distress is best viewed as

---

5　Eg *Hill v Debenhams Tewson & Chinnock* (1958) 171 Estates Gazette 835; *Moss v Heckingbottom* (1958) 172 Estates Gazette 207; *Hipkiss v Gaydon* [1961] CLY 9042 (where the defendant was the vendor-builder); *Sinclair v Bowden* (1962) 183 Estates Gazette 95; *Collard v Saunders* [1971] CLY 11161. *Piper v Daybell Court-Cooper & Co* (1969) 210 Estates Gazette 1047 and *Trask v Clark & Sons* [1980] CLY 2588 are analogous (lack of privacy).

6　[1950] 2 All ER 1167.

7　[1953] 1 WLR 672.

8　[1982] 1 WLR 1297. See also *McCall v Abelesz* [1976] QB 585 (landlord's breach of tenancy agreement); *Buckley v Lane Herdman & Co* [1977] CLY 3143, *Wapshott v Davis Donovan & Co* [1996] PNLR 361 (both concerning breach by a solicitor); *Calabar Properties Ltd v Stitcher* [1984] 1 WLR 287, *Lubren v London Borough of Lambeth* (1988) 20 HLR 165, *Wallace v Manchester CC* (1998) 30 HLR 1111 (all concerning breach of landlord's repairing obligations); *Cross v David Martin & Mortimer* [1989] 1 EGLR 154, *Bigg v Howard Son & Gooch* [1990] 1 EGLR 173 (both concerning surveyors' breach).

9　[1982] 1 WLR 1297 at 1303 (per Lord Denning).

directly consequent on the physical inconvenience of having to live in a house that was in a poor condition; for having emphasised that the mental distress here was recoverable because reasonably foreseeable, Lord Denning, with whom Oliver LJ apparently agreed, went on to cite with approval that part of the judgment at first instance where no clear distinction was drawn between physical inconvenience and mental distress consequent on it. Sir Patrick Bennett QC had there said:

> 'I think it was reasonably foreseeable that, if Mr Perry bought the house in such a condition that he was exposed to the incursion of water, the anxiety resulting from the question of when the repairs should be done and the odour and smell from the defective septic water tank would cause him distress and discomfort which I have gathered together under the term "vexation"... In my view, the plaintiff is entitled ... to damages for such discomfort, distress and the like ...'[10]

Furthermore, Kerr LJ, in upholding the trial judge's decision on damages for vexation and inconvenience, emphasised that those damages were recoverable because, '... the physical consequences of the breach were all foreseeable at the time.'[11]

Similarly in *Watts v Morrow*[12] a husband and wife were each awarded £750 for the physical inconvenience and directly related mental distress of living (at weekends) in a house undergoing extensive repairs. The repairs were necessitated by defects that had been negligently omitted from the defendant's survey report upon which the claimants had relied in buying the house. As we have seen, Bingham LJ clarified that, in addition to the first exceptional category considered above, damages are 'recoverable for physical inconvenience and discomfort caused by the breach and mental suffering directly related to that inconvenience and discomfort.'[13] Damages were therefore awarded within this second category whereas they could not have been awarded within the first category (the contract being for an ordinary house survey).

In *Farley v Skinner*,[14] the facts of which we have considered above, the House of Lords held that mental distress damages could be awarded within this second category as well as within the first. Aircraft noise causes 'physical inconvenience' because that term should be interpreted in a wide sense to include all matters detrimentally affecting sight,

---

10 [1982] 1 All ER 1005 at 1016–1017.
11 [1982] 1 WLR 1297 at 1307.
12 [1991] 1 WLR 1421. See also *Patel v Hooper & Jackson* [1999] 1 WLR 1792, CA (damages of £2,000 each for the relative discomfort of having to live in less desirable rented accommodation until the uninhabitable house bought as a result of the defendant's negligent survey could be sold).
13 [1991] 1 WLR 1421 at 1445. See above, p 325.
14 [2001] UKHL 49, [2002] 2 AC 732.

hearing, smell or touch. In Lord Scott's words, '[I]f the cause of the inconvenience or discomfort is a sensory (sight, touch, hearing, smell etc) experience, damages can, subject to the remoteness rules, be recovered.'[15]

Beyond the two exceptional categories, mental distress damages remain irrecoverable for breach of contract.

For example, in *Bliss v South East Thames Regional Health Authority*,[16] the defendant health authority in breach of contract had suspended the claimant, a consultant surgeon, on the unfounded grounds that he was mentally unfit for his job. At first instance, Farquharson J awarded £2,000 mental distress damages. This was overturned by the Court of Appeal, which held that, until altered by the House of Lords, *Addis* largely remains good law.

In *Hayes v James & Charles Dodd*,[17] the claimants were a husband and wife in the motor car repair business and they bought a yard and workshop on the faith of their solicitors' advice that there was a right of access to the rear of the workshop. This was untrue. The yard and workshop were therefore useless for the claimants' business plans and they were forced to sell them. In an action against the solicitors for breach of their contractual duty of care the claimants were awarded £92,000 for their pecuniary losses. But the Court of Appeal overturned Hirst J's award of £1,500 each for mental distress (largely comprising the anxiety and vexation of the dispute itself). *Bliss* was applied and it was stressed that mental distress damages were inappropriate where the contract was merely a commercial one entered into with a view to profit. Reflecting a widely-held fear that, unless heavily restricted, mental distress damages would feature in almost every award of contractual damages, Staughton LJ said:

> 'I would not view with enthusiasm the prospect that every shipowner in the Commercial Court, having successfully claimed for unpaid freight or demurrage, would be able to add a claim for mental distress suffered while he was waiting for his money.'[18]

In *Johnson v Gore Wood & Co*,[19] which involved claims for professional negligence against the defendant solicitors in connection with the purchase of land by the claimant and the claimant's company, the

---

15   [2001] UKHL 49, [2002] 2 AC 732 at para 85.
16   [1985] IRLR 308. In addition to the cases denying mental distress damages discussed in the text below, see *Rae v Yorkshire Bank plc* [1988] BTLC 35 (dishonouring of cheque); *O'Laoire v Jackel International Ltd (No 2)* [1991] ICR 718 (wrongful dismissal); *Branchett v Beaney* [1992] 3 All ER 910 (breach of covenant of quiet enjoyment).
17   [1990] 2 All ER 815.
18   [1990] 2 All ER 815 at 823.
19   [2002] 2 AC 1.

claimant sought damages for the mental distress and anxiety, and for the financial embarrassment and deterioration in his family relationships, caused by the protracted litigation. Although the case primarily concerned other issues, the House of Lords (Lord Cooke dissenting)[20] struck out the claim for damages for non-financial loss. This was on the basis that *Addis* largely remains good law and the facts of this case did not fall within the two exceptional categories recognised in *Watts v Morrow*.[1]

It should also be noted that, in relation to the facts of *Addis* itself, which concerned a wrongful dismissal, the House of Lords in *Johnson v Unisys Ltd*[2] has held that, whatever the normal position at common law, wrongful dismissal is a special case because of the need to avoid undermining the statutory regime of unfair dismissal (which, for example, includes a statutory cap on compensation of, at present, £55,000).[3] In other words, there is a special reason for denying mental distress damages for wrongful dismissal.[4]

It is submitted, therefore, that the present law on the recoverability of mental distress damages in contract is relatively clear. Outside the two exceptional categories, each of which has been 'loosened' somewhat by the House of Lords in *Farley v Skinner*,[5] mental distress damages are irrecoverable.

---

20   While agreeing that damages for the mental distress and anxiety were irrecoverable, Lord Cooke dissented because he thought that damages for the financial embarrassment and deterioration in family relationships could be recovered as being akin to physical inconvenience and discomfort within the second category in *Watts v Morrow*. He was also anxious to assert that he doubted the correctness of *Addis* in laying down that mental distress damages are irrecoverable for wrongful dismissal.

1   [1991] 1 WLR 1421.

2   [2001] UKHL 13, [2003] 1 AC 518. See above, p 316. The *Unisys* case was distinguished, without reopening its correctness, in *Eastwood v Magnox Electric plc* [2004] UKHL 35, [2004] 3 WLR 322.

3   Employment Rights (Increase of Limits) Order 2003, SI 2003/3038. Compensation for unfair dismissal is awarded by employment tribunals under the Employment Rights Act 1996, ss 112(4), 117(3)(a), 118–27. Prior to *Johnson v Unisys Ltd* it had been decided by the National Industrial Relations Court in *Norton Tool Co Ltd v Tewson* [1972] ICR 501 that the loss compensated for unfair dismissal was limited to pecuniary loss: this has recently been approved as still good law, so that there can be no unfair dismissal compensation for injured feelings (or psychiatric illness), by the House of Lords in *Dunnachie v Kingston-upon-Hull County Council* [2004] UKHL 36, [2004] 3 WLR 310.

4   As shown by the facts of *Unisys* case itself, the *Unisys* bar to damages for mental distress for wrongful dismissal applies also to bar damages for psychiatric illness. For the drawing of the line between wrongful dismissal and a breach of the employment contract (including causing psychiatric illness) that is sufficiently distinct from wrongful dismissal as to fall outside the *Unisys* bar to damages, see *Eastwood v Magnox Electric plc* [2004] UKHL 35, [2004] 3 WLR 322: the House of Lords there pointed to the unsatisfactory but, as the majority saw it, unavoidable consequences of its own decision in *Unisys* and called for legislative reform to be considered as a matter of urgency.

5   [2001] UKHL 49, [2002] 2 AC 732.

In *Farley v Skinner* Lord Scott put forward a rather different approach.[6] Part of his reasoning was to distinguish between loss of expected mental benefits and mental distress as a consequential loss. With respect, this is an unworkable distinction (not least because where one has lost a mental benefit, there is an inevitable consequential suffering of mental distress) and required Lord Scott to adopt forced classifications of past cases.[7] But ultimately, the essential thrust of his approach appears to be that mental distress (but, peculiarly, with the apparent exception of disappointment) should be recoverable if not too remote. While, as we shall see in a moment, this reliance on remoteness has much to commend it as a matter of principle and policy, it is plainly inconsistent with past cases. Indeed it was specifically rejected by the Court of Appeal in *Bliss v South East Thames Regional Health Authority*;[8] and in his classic statement in *Watts v Morrow* Bingham LJ emphasised that the law on mental distress damages was concerned to place restrictions over and above the normal restriction of remoteness. If remoteness is the test, surely *Bliss*, *Hayes v Dodd* and *Johnson v Gore Wood* – and many other cases – would have been decided differently.

Having said that, a strong argument can be made (supporting the general thrust of Lord Scott's speech) that English courts should be more willing to award mental distress damages than they presently are. For while the first exceptional category perhaps presents the strongest claim for such relief, since mental distress damages there reflect the 'consumer surplus'[9] (namely the particular value to the claimant of the contractual performance over and above its objective market value), the compensatory principle indicates that mental distress caused by the breach of contract should always be compensated, subject to the usual limiting principles, such as remoteness. After all, the confusion between punitive and mental distress damages has been clearly exposed in cases

---

6   For a more favourable view of Lord Scott's speech than that taken here, see Capper 'Damages for Distress and Disappointment – Problem Solved?' (2002) 118 LQR 193. See also McKendrick and Graham 'The sky's the limit: contractual damages for non-pecuniary loss' [2002] LMCLQ 161.

7   Eg he regarded *Hobbs v London and South Western Rly Co* (1875) LR 10 QB 111 as a loss of expected benefit case but *Heywood v Wellers* [1976] QB 446 as a consequential mental distress case.

8   [1985] IRLR 308. This overruled *Cox v Philips Industries Ltd* [1976] 1 WLR 638 in which Lawson J had said, at p 644, that there was '… no reason in principle why, if a situation arises which within the contemplation of the parties would have given rise to vexation, distress and general disappointment and frustration, the person who is injured by a contractual breach, should not be compensated in damages for that breach.' For a similar approach to Lawson J's see the excellent dissenting judgment of Thomas J in the New Zealand Court of Appeal in *Bloxham v Robinson* (1996) 7 TCLR 122.

9   Harris, Ogus and Phillips 'Contract Remedies and the Consumer Surplus' (1979) 95 LQR 581.

like *Rookes v Barnard*[10] and, while assessing damages is difficult for mental distress, it is no more difficult than for other non-pecuniary losses. Similarly, the fact that mental distress is difficult to prove should not deter the courts, since applying normal principle if the claimant cannot establish that he or she has suffered mental distress that is not *de minimis*, he or she should recover no damages. Although it has been suggested that parties to commercial contracts accept the risk of mental distress consequent on a breach of contract,[11] it is hard to see why this should be thought to be so. While parties plainly accept the strains and stresses of commercial life, it is hard to see why they are regarded as accepting the risk of mental distress consequent on contract-breaking any more than they accept the risk of financial loss consequent on contract-breaking. If the risks of 'losses' consequent on contract-breaking were truly accepted, no damages at all would be payable. Certainly in many other jurisdictions there has been a greater willingness to award mental distress damages.[12] Finally it should be realised that, even if mental distress damages were freely available, it would not be correct to imagine that they would figure in almost every contractual damages claim, for often the claimant is not a human person but is a company which is incapable of experiencing mental distress.[13]

(2) Torts

Looking first at physical inconvenience, it appears that, as in contract so in tort, damages for physical inconvenience have long been recoverable and are not subject to special restrictions. Moreover, in contrast to the position taken until recently in contract, it would seem that in tort cases damages for mental distress consequent on physical inconvenience have not been separated out as being irrecoverable.

So, while usually not classified under the head of physical inconvenience, damages for the tort of false imprisonment must always include some compensation for the claimant's physical inconvenience. The same must generally be true for nuisance. In *Bone v Seale*,[14] for example, two owners of neighbouring property were awarded damages

---

10 [1964] AC 1129.
11 Cf Lord Cooke's statement in *Johnson v Gore Wood & Co* [2002] 2 AC 1 at 49: 'Contract-breaking is treated as an incident of commercial life which players in the game are expected to meet with mental fortitude.'
12 For Canadian cases, see Waddams *The Law of Damages* (3rd edn, 1997) paras 3.1310–3.1450. For the US, see Chmiel 'Recovery for Mental Suffering from Breach of Contract' (1957) 32 Notre Dame LR 482; Second Restatement of Contracts, s 353.
13 Contra is *Messenger Newspapers Group Ltd v National Graphical Association* [1984] IRLR 397.
14 [1975] 1 WLR 797.

for the 'inconvenience, discomfort and annoyance'[15] caused by the smells from the defendant's pig farm which constituted a nuisance; and in *Hunter v Canary Wharf Ltd*[16] Lord Goff said, 'If a nuisance should occur, then the spouse who has an interest in the property can ... recover any damages in respect of the discomfort or inconvenience caused by the nuisance'. In *Mafo v Adams*,[17] damages for physical inconvenience were expressly awarded to a tenant in an action for deceit against his landlord, who had induced him to leave protected premises, and in *Millington v Duffy*[18] a tenant was awarded damages for inconvenience and distress primarily for trespass to land, his landlord having wrongfully evicted him. In *Saunders v Edwards*[19] damages for inconvenience and disappointment were awarded to the tenants of a flat who had been induced to buy the lease by the defendant vendor's fraudulent misrepresentation that it included the roof terrace. And in *Perry v Sidney Phillips & Son*[20] and *Watts v Morrow*[1] damages for the physical inconvenience (and consequent distress) of living in a house with defects (or while repairs were being made to remedy those defects) that had been negligently omitted from the defendant surveyor's report were awarded in an action brought for both the tort of negligence and breach of contract. Finally in *Ward v Cannock Chase District Council*[2] damages were awarded for the discomfort and consequent distress of living initially in a house with a hole in the roof and later in overcrowded temporary accommodation, all of which was caused by the defendants' tortious negligence in leaving neighbouring houses derelict.

Turning to mental distress, that is not consequent on physical inconvenience, the law has traditionally been more favourable to the distressed claimant in tort than in contract. So there has been compensation, often under the head of 'aggravated damages',[3] for

---

15   [1975] 1 WLR 797 at 804.
16   [1997] AC 655, 694. See similarly the references to 'damages for loss of amenity value' (per Lord Lloyd, at 696); 'compensation for the diminution in the amenity value of the property during the period for which the nuisance persisted' (per Lord Hoffmann, at 706): damages for 'loss of amenity' (per Lord Hope, at 724). But, as their Lordships recognised, because the landowner alone has the right to sue in private nuisance, the discomfort and inconvenience of others living at the property is irrelevant except in so far as it affects the landowner's own enjoyment of his land.
17   [1970] 1 QB 548.
18   (1984) 17 HLR 232.
19   [1987] 1 WLR 1116.
20   [1982] 1 WLR 1297. See also, eg *Roberts v J Hampson & Co* [1990] 1 WLR 94 (compensation for disruption of having to live with wife's mother consequent on negligence of surveyor engaged by building society).
1   [1991] 1 WLR 1421. See also *Patel v Hooper & Jackson* [1999] 1 WLR 1792: above, p 329, n 12.
2   [1986] Ch 546.
3   Below, p 339.

mental distress caused by torts such as false imprisonment,[4] malicious prosecution,[5] assault and battery,[6] defamation,[7] nuisance[8] trespass to land,[9] deceit,[10] and even trespass to goods.[11] The Copyright, Designs and Patents Act 1988, s 97(2) (formerly the Copyright Act 1956, s 17(3)) appears to empower the award of mental distress damages for copyright infringement, although there has as yet been no case clearly awarding such damages.[12] The Sex Discrimination Act 1975,[13] the Race Relations Act 1976,[14] and the Disability Discrimination Act 1995[15] empower the courts (or, in the employment field, employment tribunals)[16] to award damages (or, in the employment field, compensation) for 'injured feelings' where the claimant sues for breach of statutory duty laid down in Pt III

---

4 Eg *Walter v Alltools Ltd* (1944) 61 TLR 39; *White v Metropolitan Police Comr* (1982) Times, 24 April; *Thompson v Metropolitan Police Comr* [1998] QB 498; *Metropolitan Police Comr v Gerald* (1998) Times, 26 June.

5 Eg *Savile v Roberts* (1698) 1 Ld Raym 374; *White v Metropolitan Police Comr*, ibid; *Thompson v Metropolitan Police Comr*, ibid; *Metropolitan Police Comr v Gerald*, ibid.

6 Eg *White v Metropolitan Police Comr*, ibid; *Ballard v Metropolitan Police Comr* (1983) 133 NLJ 1133; *Barbara v Home Office* (1984) 134 NLJ 888; *George v Metropolitan Police Comr* (1984) Times, 31 March; *W v Meah* [1986] 1 All ER 935; *Griffiths v Williams* (1995) Times, 24 November; *Appleton v Garrett* [1996] PIQR P1; *Metropolitan Police Comr v Gerald*, ibid.

7 Eg *McCarey v Associated Newspapers Ltd* [1965] 2 QB 86 (libel); *Khodaparast v Shad* [2000] 1 All ER 545 (malicious falsehood).

8 Eg *Bone v Seale* [1975] 1 WLR 797; *Dunton v Dover District Council* (1977) 76 LGR 87. The damages for 'loss of amenity' in *Carr-Saunders v Dick McNeil Associates Ltd* [1986] 1 WLR 922 presumably also included some compensation for mental distress. But private nuisance does not protect against interference with television reception caused by a building: *Hunter v Canary Wharf Ltd* [1997] AC 655.

9 In *Drane v Evangelou* [1978] 1 WLR 455 and *McMillan v Singh* (1984) 17 HLR 120 aggravated damages were awarded to a tenant for his landlord's trespass to land (or nuisance) in wrongfully evicting him. In the former, the Court of Appeal emphasised the worry and stress of being deprived of a roof over one's head and, in the latter, Sir John Arnold stressed also the tenant's outrage at the landlord's actions. See also *Merest v Harvey* (1814) 5 Taunt 442; *Millington v Duffy* (1984) 17 HLR 232; *Guppys (Bridport) Ltd v Brookling and James* (1984) 269 Estates Gazette 846 at 942; *Ashgar v Ahmed* (1984) 17 HLR 25. See also, somewhat analogously, the award of mental distress damages for breach of the statutory duty not to infringe exclusive burial rights in *Reed v Madon* [1989] 2 All ER 431.

10 *Archer v Brown* [1984] 2 All ER 267 (Peter Pain J here used both the terminology of 'injured feelings' and 'aggravated damages'); *Saunders v Edwards* [1987] 2 All ER 651.

11 *Owen and Smith v Reo Motors (Britain) Ltd* (1934) 151 LT 274. See also *Piper v Darling* (1940) 67 Ll L Rep 419 – sentimental value taken into account in fixing the value of the claimant's yacht, destroyed by the defendant's negligence.

12 But see *Nichols Advanced Vehicle Systems Inc v Rees and Oliver* [1979] RPC 127. As to whether s 97(2) authorises punitive damages, see below, ch 18.

13 Sex Discrimination Act 1975, s 66(4).

14 Race Relations Act 1976, s 57(4).

15 Disability Discrimination Act 1995, s 25(2).

16 Sex Discrimination Act 1975, s 65(1); Race Relations Act 1976, s 56(1); Disability Discrimination Act 1995, s 8(4). 'Industrial tribunals' were renamed 'employment tribunals' by the Employment Rights (Dispute Resolution) Act 1998, s 1.

(or, in the employment field, in Pt II) of those Acts.[17] And under the Protection from Harassment Act 1997 a claimant who suffers a course of conduct[18] which amounts to harassment (which is defined to include 'causing the person alarm or distress')[19] may be awarded damages for, among other things, 'any anxiety caused by the harassment.'[20]

It has also been accepted that damages for mental distress may be awarded under the Human Rights Act 1998 for the infringement by a public authority of a person's Convention rights.[1]

However – and although one can strongly argue (analogously to the arguments put forward in respect of breach of contract) that, once liability in tort has been established and one is purely concerned with damages, the law should always be willing to award damages for mental distress subject to the usual limitations such as remoteness – the above decisions do not mean that damages for mental distress are now always recoverable in tort.[2] Most importantly, although this is usually an issue going to liability rather than damages, there is no liability in the tort of negligence[3] for the infliction of mental distress (not consequent on death[4]

---

17   See, eg *Alexander v Home Office* [1988] 2 All ER 118, *Deane v Ealing London Borough Council* [1993] ICR 329, *Armitage, Marsden and HM Prison Service v Johnson* [1997] ICR 275 (racial discrimination); *Vento v Chief Constable of West Yorkshire Police (No 2)* [2002] EWCA Civ 1871, [2003] IRLR 102 (sex discrimination). In these cases, aggravated damages were awarded as well as compensation for injured feelings. See further below, p 339.

18   Protection from Harassment Act 1997, s 1(1).

19   Protection from Harassment Act 1997, s 8(3).

20   Protection from Harassment Act 1997, s 8(2).

1   *R (on the application of Bernard) v Enfield London Borough Council* [2002] EWHC 2282 (Admin), [2003] HRLR 4; *R (on the application of KB) v Mental Health Review Tribunal* [2003] EWHC 193 (Admin), [2003] 2 All ER 209. But in the latter case, which concerned infringement of a mental patient's right to speedy determination of whether correctly detained, Stanley Burnton J held that to be compensatable the distress had to be of sufficient intensity to justify an award. For his view that breach of a Convention right might trigger aggravated damages, see [2003] EWHC 193 (Admin) at para 50.

2   In addition to the restriction discussed below in this paragraph, see *Lonrho plc v Fayed (No 5)* [1993] 1 WLR 1489 (no damages for injured feelings for lawful means conspiracy).

3   For the denial of mental distress damages for a tort other than negligence, see the denial of damages for fear for oneself, in respect of liability for animals, in *Behrens v Bertram Mills Circus Ltd* [1957] 2 QB 1. The claimant was in a booth when an elephant went out of control and knocked the booth over, terrifying the claimant. Devlin J, at 28, said that damages could not be given '… infringing the general principle embedded in the common law that suffering caused by grief, fear, anguish and the like is not assessable.' Note also that there is no liability under *Wilkinson v Downton* [1897] 2 QB 57 for even intentionally inflicted mental distress (as opposed to psychiatric illness): *Wong v Parkside Health NHS Trust* [2001] EWCA Civ 1721, [2003] 3 All ER 932. Cf *Hunter v Canary Wharf Ltd* [1997] AC 655 at 707 (per Lord Hoffmann); *Wainwright v Home Office* [2003] UKHL 53, [2003] 3 WLR 1137, paras 41–47 (per Lord Hoffmann). See Trindade 'The Intentional Infliction of Purely Mental Distress' (1986) 6 OJLS 219; Mullany and Handford *Tort Liability for Psychiatric Damage* (1993) pp 297–307.

4   Bereavement damages may be awarded to a spouse or parent of the deceased under the Fatal Accidents Act 1976: see above, p 306.

or the claimant's personal injury[5] as opposed to a recognisable psychiatric illness. In *McLoughlin v O'Brian*,[6] Lord Bridge said, '[T]he first hurdle which a plaintiff claiming damages of the kind in question must surmount is to establish that he is suffering, not merely grief, distress or any other normal emotion, but a positive psychiatric illness.' In *Hicks v Chief Constable of the South Yorkshire Police*[7] Lord Bridge said, 'Those trapped in the crush at Hillsborough who were fortunate enough to escape without injury have no claim in respect of the distress they suffered in what must have been a truly terrifying experience.' It follows that fear of impending death felt by the victim of a fatal injury before that injury is inflicted cannot by itself give rise to a cause of action which survives for the benefit of the victim's estate. Again in *Page v Smith*,[8] Lord Jauncey said, 'The ordinary emotions of anxiety, fear, grief or transient shock are not conditions for which the law gives compensation.' Finally in *White v Chief Constable of the South Yorkshire Police*[9] Lord Hoffmann said, '[A] "recognised psychiatric illness" ... is distinguished from shock, fear, anxiety or grief which are regarded as normal consequences of a distressing event and for which damages are not awarded.'

However, it should be added here that the extension of tortious negligence to the negligent performance of services causing pure economic loss, and the acceptance of concurrent liability,[10] presumably means that mental distress damages are recoverable in the tort action provided they would be recoverable in that situation for breach of

---

5   See also, alongside but distinct from personal injury, the conventional sum of £15,000 awarded for 'wrongful birth' in *Rees v Darlington Memorial Hospital NHS Trust* [2003] UKHL 52, [2004] 1 AC 309, discussed above at p 290–292.

6   [1983] 1 AC 410 at 431. In addition to the cases cited below, see *Hinz v Berry* [1970] 2 QB 40, 42; *Calveley v Chief Constable of the Merseyside Police* [1989] AC 1228, 1238; *F v Wirral Metropolitan Borough Council* [1991] Fam 69, esp at 104 (mother had no claim in negligence against a local authority for the mental distress of 'losing' her child to long-term foster parents); *Alcock v Chief Constable of South Yorkshire Police* [1992] 1 AC 310 at 401, 409–10, 416; *Kerby v Redbridge Health Authority* [1994] PIQR Q1 (no damages recoverable for 'dashed hopes' of claimant in respect of death of new-born baby caused by defendants' negligence); *Reilly and Reilly v Merseyside Regional Health Authority* [1995] 6 Med LR 246 (claustrophobia and fear suffered when trapped in a lift for over an hour did not give rise to a cause of action). Cf *Whitmore v Euroways Express Coaches Ltd* (1984) Times, 4 May in which a wife was awarded damages, against a holiday coach firm for negligent driving, for the 'ordinary shock', falling short of a recognised psychiatric illness, suffered at seeing her husband's injuries both at the time of the accident and in the weeks afterwards; and in *Robinson v St Helens Metropolitan Borough Council* [2002] EWCA Civ 1099, [2003] PIQR P128 (and see also *Adams v Bracknell Forest Borough Council* [2004] UKHL 29, [2004] 3 WLR 89) emotional or psychological harm, falling short of a recognised psychiatric illness, caused by a negligent failure to diagnose dyslexia, was held to be actionable (and to constitute personal injury for the purposes of the Limitation Act 1980).

7   [1992] 2 All ER 65 at 69.

8   [1996] AC 155 at 171.

9   [1999] 2 AC 455 at 501.

10 See above, pp 5–7.

contract. In other words, mental distress damages will be recoverable provided one can show that an important object of the services was to provide mental satisfaction or freedom from distress, or that the mental distress is directly consequent on physical inconvenience. This is illustrated by one of the leading cases on the recovery of mental distress damages in contract, *Perry v Sidney Phillips & Son*,[11] where the claim was alternatively framed in the tort of negligence. Similarly in *Hamilton Jones v David & Snape*,[12] where a claim for a solicitor's negligence was brought in contract and tort, Neuberger J held that, while there was no claim for the mental distress of losing the custody of a child in the tort of negligence standing alone, that did not prevent such an award in contract or, apparently, concurrently in tort. After referring to the reasoning of the Court of Appeal in *Verderame v Commercial Union Assurance Co plc*,[13] to the effect that there could be no liability in the tort of negligence for mental distress where there would have been no such liability had there been a contract (because the *Watts v Morrow* exception did not apply), Neuberger J said the following:[14]

> '[I]f a head of claim, in a case such as this, is recoverable in contract, the fact that it may not normally be recoverable in tort should not prevent it being recoverable in contract. The logic of the reasoning in *Verderame* suggests, if anything, that the approach to damages in tort in a case such as this is governed by the approach to damages in contract.'

But outside a contractual relationship, to expand liability in the tort of negligence to cover mere mental distress would be highly controversial[15] for that would be to expand enormously the scope of that tort and would raise legitimate fears of 'opening the floodgates of litigation.' One can also argue that mere mental distress is a transient and less significant type of harm than personal injury, property damage or economic loss and that, for that reason, one should not expand liability in the tort of negligence to cover it.[16]

---

11 [1982] 1 WLR 1297. See also *Wood v Law Society* (1995) Times, 2 March; *Johnson v Gore Wood & Co* [2002] 2 AC 1 at 49 (per Lord Cooke).
12 [2003] EWHC 3147 (Ch), [2004] 1 All ER 657.
13 [1992] BCLC 793, 803.
14 [2003] EWHC 3147 (Ch), [2004] 1 All ER 657, at para 51.
15 But some jurisdictions in the US have expanded the tort of negligence to cover severe mental distress: see Mullany and Handford, *Tort Liability for Psychiatric Damage* (1993) pp 48–49; Law Commission Consultation Paper No 137 (1995), *Liability for Psychiatric Illness* pp 115–116. In principle, French law, through Article 1382, protects against negligently caused mental distress (as 'dommage moral').
16 For discussion, see Mullany and Handford *Tort Liability for Psychiatric Damage* (1993) pp 43–45, 56–58.

A final word is merited on 'aggravated damages'.[17] In *Rookes v Barnard*[18] those damages were stressed to be compensatory – albeit compensating for mental distress – and not punitive. But the confusion between the two lingers on. For example, it has been held that aggravated damages cannot be awarded for the tort of negligence or breach of contract:[19] but it is hard to see the justification for this once one accepts that aggravated damages are not punitive and that mental distress damages can sometimes be awarded for breach of contract (and concurrently in the tort of negligence). This continued confusion is not surprising given that aggravated damages are regarded as a sub-category of mental distress damages to be awarded only where the defendant's behaviour has been particularly reprehensible.[20] Now that mental distress damages are more freely recoverable this link to the especially bad conduct of the defendant seems unhelpful and unnecessary. All confusion would be avoided by abandoning the notion of aggravated damages and by referring only to damages for mental distress or 'damages for injured feelings'. This approach has been supported by the Law Commission. In its Report on *Aggravated, Exemplary and Restitutionary Damages*[1] it recommended that, wherever possible, the label 'damages for mental distress' should be used instead of the misleading phrase 'aggravated damages'; and that legislation should provide that so-called 'aggravated damages' are awarded to compensate for mental distress and must not be intended to punish.[2]

2.   ASSESSING DAMAGES FOR MENTAL DISTRESS OR PHYSICAL INCONVENIENCE

As with all non-pecuniary losses the aim must be to award a fair and reasonable sum, which is in line with other awards for mental distress or

---

17 See, generally, Law Commission Report No 247 (1997) *Aggravated, Exemplary and Restitutionary Damages* Part II.
18 [1964] AC 1129.
19 *Kralj v McGrath* [1986] 1 All ER 54, approved in *AB v South West Water Services Ltd* [1993] QB 507, CA; *Levi v Gordon*, 12 November 1992 (unreported CA). See also the clear confusion in *Messenger Newspapers Group Ltd v National Graphical Association* [1984] IRLR 397.
20 The Law Commission in its Report No 247, paras 2.18–2.20, referred to this as the 'exceptional conduct' requirement. It follows that a court may combine aggravated damages with (ordinary) mental distress damages: see, eg *Appleton v Garrett* [1996] PIQR P1; and the discrimination cases referred to above at p 336, n 17. For judicial criticism of this combination (because one is simply dealing with the one type of damages, namely mental distress damages) see *Joyce v Sengupta* [1993] 1 All ER 897, 908; *McConnell v Police Authority for Northern Ireland* [1997] IRLR 625, 629; *Gbaja-Biamila v DHL International (UK) Ltd* [2000] ICR 730 at para 32.
1   Law Com No 247 (1997). See also the last three cases referred to in n 20 above.
2   Law Com No 247 (1997), para 2.42 and Draft Bill, cl 13.

physical inconvenience. It would also be sensible to maintain 'external consistency', most obviously with damages for non-pecuniary loss in personal injury cases.

In *Thompson v Metropolitan Police Comr*[3] the Court of Appeal held that an analogy should be drawn with personal injury damages in assessing compensatory damages for false imprisonment and malicious prosecution. Lord Woolf MR said that this was even more apt than in defamation cases where, as we have seen in the previous chapter, it was decided in *John v MGN Ltd*[4] that the scale of damages for non-pecuniary loss in personal injury cases was thought relevant. In Lord Woolf's words in *Thompson*, '[W]here what is being calculated is the proper compensation for loss of liberty or the damaging effect of a malicious prosecution the analogy with personal injuries is closer than it is in the case of defamation. The compensation is for something which is akin to pain and suffering.'[5] Lord Woolf went on to lay down some specific figures as part of the guidance to be given to juries in assessing damages in cases of false imprisonment and malicious prosecution. What was said is, of course, equally helpful in a case where a judge alone is assessing damages. Lord Woolf said:

> 'In a straightforward case of wrongful arrest and imprisonment the starting point is likely to be about £500 for the first hour during which the plaintiff has been deprived of his or her liberty. After the first hour an additional sum is to be awarded, but that sum should be on a reducing scale so as to keep the damages proportionate with those payable in personal injury cases and because the plaintiff is entitled to have a higher rate of compensation for the initial shock of being arrested. As a guideline we consider, for example, that a plaintiff who has been wrongly kept in custody for 24 hours should for this alone normally be regarded as entitled to an award of about £3,000. For subsequent days the daily rate will be on a progressively reducing scale … In the case of malicious prosecution the figure should start at about £2,000 and for prosecution continuing for as long as two years, the case being taken to the Crown Court, an award of about £10,000 could be appropriate.'[6]

---

3   [1998] QB 498.
4   [1997] QB 586. See above, p 320.
5   [1998] QB 498 at 512.
6   [1998] QB 498 at 515. In *Clark v Chief Constable of Cleveland Constabulary* [1999] 21 LS Gaz R 38, CA, a jury's award of £500 for malicious prosecution was increased to £2,000 in line with *Thompson*. In *R v Governor of Brockhill Prison, ex p Evans (No 2)* [1999] QB 1043, the Court of Appeal increased damages from £2,500 to £5,000 for false imprisonment (where the wrongful imprisonment was for 59 days but was as a result of a mistake). See also *R (on the application of Bernard) v Enfield London Borough Council* [2002] EWHC 2282 (Admin), [2003] HRLR 4 where a local authority had failed, in breach of the Human Rights Convention Art 8, to provide suitable accommodation to a severely disabled wife and her carer husband so that they had to live in deplorable conditions for about 20 months. The damages awarded under the Human Rights Act 1998 were £8,000 to the wife and £2,000 to the husband. The awards in *R (on the*

To these 'basic' compensatory damages could then be added aggravated damages where appropriate. These would rarely be less than £1,000 or greater than double the basic damages.

One can argue that, having gone so far in guiding juries as to the correct quantum of damages in cases of false imprisonment and malicious prosecution, the logical next step would be to remove the assessment of damages from juries. Indeed this is what the Law Commission has recommended. In Part IV of its Report on *Damages for Personal Injury: Non-Pecuniary Loss*[7] its recommendation was that the assessment of damages for all actions (except defamation) should always be a matter for a judge not a jury.

In *Vento v Chief Constable of West Yorkshire (No 2)*[8] the Court of Appeal emphasised the need for some consistency with awards for non-pecuniary awards in personal injury cases in deciding the appropriate level of compensation for injured feelings in sex and race discrimination cases. This was also a point made by Smith J in *Armitage, Marsden and HM Prison Service v Johnson*[9] in her statement of principles for the assessment of such damages in discrimination cases, which was approved by the Court of Appeal in *Vento*. The Court of Appeal went on to lay down a tariff for injured feelings in discrimination cases with a top band of £15,000–£25,000 for the most serious cases, £5,000–£15,000 for serious cases and £500–£5,000 for less serious cases. Additional sums could be awarded for aggravated damages (and for psychiatric illness) although the overall global sum must be in line with conventional wisdom on levels of compensation for non-pecuniary loss generally. On the facts of *Vento*, which was a very serious case of persistent sexual discrimination against a female police officer, the Court of Appeal reduced the sums awarded by the Employment Tribunal and the Employment Appeal Tribunal to £18,000 for injured feelings plus £5,000 aggravated damages (and £9,000 for psychiatric damage).[10] In the *Armitage* case, the Employment Appeal Tribunal had upheld an award of £21,000 for injured feelings

---

application of *KB*) *v Mental Health Review Tribunal* [2003] EWHC 193 (Admin), [2003] 2 All ER 209 to claimants for breach of their Convention rights (under Art 5(4)) to a speedy determination of whether they should continue to be detained under powers conferred by the Mental Health Act 1983 ranged from £750 to £4,000.

7   Law Commission No 257 (1999). See above, pp 321–322.
8   [2002] EWCA Civ 1871, [2003] IRLR 102.
9   1997] ICR 275.
10 The *Vento* tariff has also been applied by the EAT, outside sex and race discrimination, to discrimination against trade union members (contrary to the Trade Union and Labour Relation (Consolidation) Act 1992, s 146) in *London Borough of Hackney v Adams* [2003] IRLR 402; and to discrimination against 'whistle-blowers' (contrary to the Employment Rights Act 1996, s 47B) in *Virgo Fidelis Senior School v Boyle* [2004] IRLR 268. In the latter case, a separate award of £10,000 aggravated damages was also made.

plus £7,500 aggravated damages in a case of very serious race discrimination which had gone on over a period of 18 months.

The move in these cases to try to ensure greater consistency, both 'internally' between awards for injured feelings for discrimination and 'externally' with awards for non-pecuniary loss, is to be welcomed. But there are two points of concern. The first is the separation out of aggravated damages from the tariff for injured feelings. It would have been preferable to have absorbed aggravated damages within the tariff. Secondly, the tariff does appear high. More specifically, it is hard to see why damages for injured feelings in a discrimination case should exceed those awarded for moderate or minor general psychiatric damage in a personal injury case, where the bracket (in the 2002 edition of the *Guidelines for the Assessment of General Damages in Personal Injury Cases*)[11] is £750–£10,000.

As regards the tort of private nuisance, the majority of the Court of Appeal in *Bone v Seale*,[12] in assessing 'loss of amenity'[13] damages for 'inconvenience, discomfort and annoyance'[14] caused by offensive smells from a pig farm, drew an analogy with assessing damages for loss of amenity in a personal injury action. But in *Hunter v Canary Wharf Ltd*[15] Lord Hoffmann disagreed with this. Yet, while the fact that the tort of private nuisance is actionable only by a person with an interest in the land means that one has to be careful not to compensate others without such an interest, it surely cannot be right to have the quantum of damages for 'loss of amenity' in nuisance exceeding damages for non-pecuniary loss for a serious personal injury. There should be some consistency between all awards for non-pecuniary loss.

In respect of discomfort and inconvenience consequent on a landlord's breach of repairing obligations, the Court of Appeal in *Wallace v Manchester City Council*[16] assumed, without deciding, that there was an unofficial tariff of £1,000–£2,750 per annum (as at July 1998).

In general, the courts have not regarded mental distress (or physical inconvenience) as that serious (although of course the worse the distress or inconvenience the higher the damages should be) and have often

---

11 Produced by the Judicial Studies Board. The 2002 edition was the sixth.
12 [1975] 1 WLR 797.
13 [1975] 1 WLR 797 at 803.
14 [1975] 1 WLR 797 at 804.
15 [1997] AC 655, 706.
16 (1998) 30 HLR 1111. The Court of Appeal suggested that a judge should cross-check the award by reference to the rent payable for the duration of the landlord's breach of obligation so as to give proper consideration to the period of breach and the nature of the property. That the award should be directly related to the rent payable – because the award relates to the tenant not getting proper value for the rent – was confirmed in *Shine v English Churches Housing Group* [2004] EWCA Civ 434.

stressed that awards should be kept at a moderate level.[17] To give some other miscellaneous examples of awards that have been mentioned earlier in this chapter, £750 was awarded to each of the two claimants for the physical inconvenience and consequent distress of living in a house that was in a poor condition in *Watts v Morrow*; £2,500 'loss of amenity' damages was awarded in *Ruxley Electronics and Construction Ltd v Forsyth* for the lost pleasure of diving and swimming in a deeper pool; and £10,000 was awarded for the disturbance from aircraft noise in *Farley v Skinner* albeit that the House of Lords recognised that this was at the very top end of what could possibly be regarded as appropriate.[18]

---

17 Eg *Perry v Sidney Phillips & Son* [1982] 1 WLR 1297; *Archer v Brown* [1985] QB 401; *Watts v Morrow* [1991] 1 WLR 1421; *Farley v Skinner* [2001] UKHL 49, [2002] 2 AC 732.

18 Cf *Dennis v Ministry of Defence* [2003] EWHC 793 (QB), [2003] NLJR 634, where £50,000 was awarded for long-term loss of amenity caused by aircraft noise. See below, p 519.

Section three

Miscellaneous issues relevant to compensatory damages

Chapter 14

Awards of interest on damages

1. INTRODUCTION

When damages have been awarded then as a 'judgment debt' they automatically carry interest until paid under the Judgments Act 1838.[1] But what we are here concerned with is whether the court will award interest on damages (that is, whether at judgment a sum of interest will be ordered to be paid forthwith along with the damages) and if so, how much interest will be awarded.[2]

Prior to 1934 the courts had no power to award interest on damages, but this has subsequently been altered by statute, the law now being contained in the Supreme Court Act 1981, s 35A.[3] By s 35A(1), the High Court has discretion to award simple interest on damages;[4] and by the Supreme Court Act 1981, s 35A(2) the High Court must award simple interest on damages for personal injuries or death (exceeding £200) unless satisfied that there are 'special reasons' why it should not do so.

2. WHY SHOULD INTEREST BE AWARDED?

The answer to this is typified by Robert Goff J's statement in *BP Exploration Co (Libya) Ltd v Hunt (No 2)*:[5] 'The fundamental principle is that

---

1   Since 1 April 1993, the rate of interest on judgment debts has been 8%: Judgment Debts (Rate of Interest) Order 1993, SI 1993/564. Where, eg there is a split trial, the judgment debt rate of interest runs from the damages judgment and not from the liability judgment: *Thomas v Bunn* [1991] 1 AC 362.
2   Interest (and its rate and period) may be provided for by a contract term, but it is being assumed here that there is no such term.
3   Inserted by the Administration of Justice Act 1982, Sch 1. Analogous provisions are contained in the County Courts Act 1984, s 69. Generally speaking, the same principles apply to interest on an agreed sum.
4   Supreme Court Act 1981, s 35A does not allow interest to be awarded on 'damages' paid (under a settlement) before the commencement of proceedings: *IM Properties plc v Cape & Dalgleish* [1999] QB 297, CA. For the analogous position on debts paid before the commencement of proceedings, see above, p 154.
5   [1982] 1 All ER 925 at 974. See also *Jefford v Gee* [1970] 2 QB 130 at 146; *Tate & Lyle Food and Distribution Ltd v Greater London Council* [1981] 3 All ER 716 at 722; *Wentworth v Wiltshire County Council* [1993] 2 All ER 256 at 269.

interest is not awarded as punishment but simply because the plaintiff has been deprived of the use of the money which was due to him.' The money due to the claimant comprises either the money that the claimant would have had but for the defendant's wrong, or, where the wrongful loss was not of money, the damages themselves which it is felt the defendant should have paid to compensate the loss as soon as it occurred. In commercial cases it is then generally assumed that as a result of being deprived of that money the claimant has had to borrow it, whereas in non-commercial cases the assumption is simply that the claimant has lost the interest from investing that money.[6]

However, one should note that under the Civil Procedure Rules, CPR 36.21, the courts may award interest at an enhanced rate[7] as a sanction against a defendant for having refused an offer by the claimant which the claimant then 'beats' at trial.[8]

3.   SIMPLE INTEREST ONLY

The Supreme Court Act 1981, s 35A empowers a court to award simple interest only. In some circumstances, especially in commercial cases, the claimant's loss will be best reflected in the compound interest rate at which it has had to borrow replacement funds or at which it has had to forgo lending, or otherwise investing, the funds. To confine the interest to simple interest may therefore leave the commercial claimant undercompensated. And, as we have seen in chapter 6, this deficiency[9] cannot be met by awarding damages because of the rule in *London, Chatham and Dover Rly Co v South Eastern Rly*.[10]

Moreover, arbitrators have been given the power to award compound interest by the Arbitration Act 1996, s 49. And there is power in equity to

---

6   For this distinction see especially *Tate & Lyle Food and Distribution Ltd v Greater London Council* [1981] 3 All ER 716 at 722–723.
7   The rate must not exceed 10% above base rate.
8   *Civil Procedure* (2004) para 3.1.6 indicates, more generally, that the courts may exercise their discretion as to the period and rate of interest as a sanction for delay in the conduct of the litigation.
9   For criticism see Mann 'On Interest, Compound Interest and Damages' (1985) 101 LQR 30, 42–46: Bowles and Whelan 'Law Commission Working Paper No 80, Private International Law Foreign Money Liabilities' (1986) 64 CBR 142; Law Commission *Pre-Judgment Interest on Debts and Damages*, Law Commission Report No 287 (2004) esp paras 4.1–4.38
10   [1893] AC 429. See above, pp 153–155.

award compound interest, albeit that it appears that this equitable jurisdiction is restricted to where necessary to strip away gains made by breach of fiduciary duty or fraud.[11]

The Law Commission has recently recommended a reform of the Supreme Court Act 1981, s 35A (and the County Courts Act 1984, s 69) so that the courts would be permitted to award compound, rather than just simple, interest.[12] It recommended that there should be a rebuttable presumption that awards of £15,000 or more would attract compound interest whereas sums of less than £15,000 would attract simple interest. The Commission further recommended that tables should be published by the Court Service so as to make it easy to calculate compound interest at a particular rate. It is to be hoped that these eminently sensible recommendations will be legislatively implemented without delay.

4. WHEN DO THE COURTS AWARD INTEREST?

As regards personal injury and death, the statute leaves no discretion – interest must be awarded subject to special reasons. But in *Jefford v Gee*[13] and *Cookson v Knowles*[14] it has been held that the different types of loss must be itemised, since no interest is payable on damages for future pecuniary loss for the reason that that loss has not yet been suffered and hence the claimant has not been deprived of the use of money due to him.

Outside the realm of personal injury and death, the courts are generally willing to exercise their discretion to award interest on damages for pecuniary loss:[15] but interest on damages for non-pecuniary loss is denied. So in an action for deceit in *Saunders v Edwards*[16] the Court of Appeal refused to award interest (even at the low 2% rate used in personal injury cases)[17] on damages for inconvenience and disappointment. This denial was thought to be correct in principle because in Bingham LJ's words, 'the damages [cannot] be realistically seen as having accrued due to the plaintiff at a certain time in the past

---

11 *President of India v La Pintada Compania* [1985] AC 104, HL; *Westdeutsche Landesbank Girozentrale v Islington London Borough Council* [1996] AC 669, HL. See below, pp 633–634.
12 *Pre-Judgment Interest on Debts and Damages*, Law Commission Report No 287 (2004).
13 [1970] 2 QB 130.
14 [1979] AC 556.
15 In *Metal Box Ltd v Currys Ltd* [1988] 1 WLR 175 interest was awarded on damages for loss of goods that were not income-producing. But in *Giles v Thompson* [1994] 1 AC 142, HL, interest on damages for the costs of hiring a replacement car was denied because the claimant was not obliged to pay these costs until judgment so that she was not 'kept out of' any money while the claim was being litigated.
16 [1987] 1 WLR 1116. See also *Holtham v Metropolitan Police Comr* (1987) Times, 28 November.
17 Below, pp 352–353.

and as having thereafter been wrongly withheld from him.'[18] It was also pointed out that no interest has traditionally been awarded on damages for non-pecuniary loss in defamation cases. The inconsistency with the approach to non-pecuniary loss in personal injury cases was put to one side as a product of the statutory requirement of awarding interest in such cases.

5.   FOR WHAT PERIOD IS INTEREST PAYABLE?

Under the statute, the courts have the discretion to choose the period for which interest is payable, although the maximum is between the date when the cause of action arose and the date of judgment (or the date of payment in respect of a sum paid before judgment). The date *to which* interest is payable causes little difficulty and is almost always fixed as the date of judgment or trial. More interesting is the date *from which* interest is payable. This was carefully examined by Robert Goff J in *BP Exploration v Hunt (No 2)*,[19] albeit in the context of an award under the Law Reform (Frustrated Contracts) Act 1943 rather than an award of damages. His conclusion was that the general rule is that interest runs from the date of loss, but that there are three main exceptions to this. The first is where it would be unfair on the defendant to make it pay interest from the date of loss: for example, '... if the defendant neither knew, nor reasonably could have been expected to know, that the plaintiff was likely to make a claim, and so was in no position to tender payment, or even to make provision for payment if the money should be found due.'[20] The second is where the claimant's conduct is such that it should not have interest awarded from the date of loss: for example, where it has unreasonably delayed in pursuing its claim.[1] Finally interest will not be awarded from the date of loss where it would otherwise be unjust in all the circumstances of the case to do so. The most obvious example of this is that, as laid down in *Jefford v Gee*,[2] interest on damages for non-pecuniary loss in a personal injury action is payable from the date of the service of the claim form until trial, the reasoning being that, as the loss is spread over a long period of time, it is more just to award interest from when the damages were first formally demanded.

---

18   [1987] 1 WLR 1116 at 1135.
19   [1982] 1 All ER 925.
20   [1982] 1 All ER 925 at 975. See *Allied London Investments Ltd v Hambro Life Assurance Ltd* [1985] 1 EGLR 45; *Kuwait Airways Corpn v Kuwait Insurance Co SAK (No 2)* [2000] 1 All ER (Comm) 972; *Quorum A/S v Schramm (No 2)* [2002] 2 All ER (Comm) 179.
1   See *Quorum A/S v Schramm (No 2)* [2002] 2 All ER (Comm) 179.
2   [1970] 2 QB 130.

It should further be noted that interest on damages for pre-trial pecuniary loss in personal injury and Fatal Accident Act cases is normally payable from the date of the accident or death until trial, as laid down in *Jefford v Gee* and *Cookson v Knowles*[3] respectively. But this is not an exception to the date of loss rule. Rather it represents half of a formula, considered more fully below, designed as a rough substitute for detailed calculations of the interest on each pecuniary loss from the date it was suffered.

6. WHAT IS THE RATE OF INTEREST?

In commercial cases, where the focus is generally on the claimant having to borrow replacement money, the courts usually take the average clearing bank base rate plus 1%, this being the borrowing rate for big companies.[4] Smaller less prestigious companies may be awarded more, corresponding to the higher borrowing rate charged to them[5]

In personal injury and death cases (and commercial cases where it is unrealistic to think that the claimant has had to borrow) the focus is on the lost interest from investment. So for personal injury non-pecuniary loss[6] interest is payable at a fixed rate of 2%, as is examined further below. For pre-trial pecuniary loss, interest on the whole amount of loss is normally payable from the date of the accident or death until trial at half the average rate on the special account[7] over that period.[8] This represents a rough substitute for awarding interest on each pecuniary loss for the period from when it was suffered until trial at the full average rate (on the special account) over that period. As recognised in *Dexter v Courtaulds Ltd*,[9] it may be more appropriate in exceptional cases, for example where all the loss has been incurred years before trial, to award interest on the whole amount of loss for a period from half-way through the time when the loss was suffered until trial at the full average rate (on

---

3   [1979] AC 556.
4   *BP Exploration v Hunt (No 2)* [1982] 1 All ER 925; *Tate & Lyle Food and Distribution Ltd v Greater London Council* [1981] 3 All ER 716; *International Military Services Ltd v Capital & Counties plc* [1982] 1 WLR 575; *Polish SS Co v Atlantic Maritime Co* [1985] QB 41; *Metal Box Ltd v Currys Ltd* [1988] 1 WLR 175; *Shearson Lehman Hutton Inc v Maclaine Watson & Co Ltd (No 2)* [1990] 3 All ER 723; *Kuwait Airways Corpn v Kuwait Insurance Co SAK (No 2)* [2000] 1 All ER (Comm) 972.
5   *Catnic Components Ltd v Hill & Smith Ltd* [1983] FSR 512.
6   For interest on bereavement damages, see above, p 306, n 14.
7   The special account (sometimes referred to as the special investment account) is an investment account used for court funds: see Court Funds Rules 1987, SI 1987/821. It was formerly called the short-term investment account. Since 1 February 2002, the rate of interest on the special account has been 6%: see *Civil Procedure* (2004) 6A-171.
8   *Jefford v Gee* [1970] 2 QB 130; *Cookson v Knowles* [1979] AC 556.
9   [1984] 1 WLR 372.

the special account) over that period. But, as stressed, it would be for the claimant to plead and prove that such an alternative method of calculation is more appropriate than the normal method.

7.   THE RELATIONSHIP BETWEEN THE DATE FOR ASSESSMENT OF DAMAGES AND INTEREST

(1) Liabilities other than foreign currency liabilities

Traditionally the date for assessing damages, ie the date at which the value of money, goods or services is assessed, is the date of loss. But more recently, particularly in response to inflation, the courts have assessed damages at a later date.[10] What effect does this have on the award of interest?

The main judicial discussion of this has been in relation to non-pecuniary loss in personal injury actions. One view is that since interest rates contain a large inflationary element (an element to preserve the real value of money) it would overcompensate the claimant to award both damages assessed according to the internal value of sterling at the date of judgment plus full interest on those damages from the date of service of the claim form. Put another way, in times of high inflation an investor cannot generally expect to do much more than maintain the real value of its money; an award of interest designed to compensate for the claimant being kept out of money to which it is entitled should therefore not be given if damages are already based on the real value of money. This lay behind the decision of the Court of Appeal in *Cookson v Knowles*:[11] since damages for non-pecuniary loss, in contrast to, for example, damages for pre-trial loss of earnings, are now based on the value of money at the time of judgment, it was held that no interest should be awarded on them. But in *Pickett v British Rail Engineering Ltd*[12] the House of Lords overruled this and considered that a clear distinction could be drawn between maintaining the real value of money, to which interest was thought to be irrelevant, and being kept out of money, which was the reason for an award of interest. Lord Wilberforce said:

> 'Increase for inflation is designed to preserve the "real" value of money, interest to compensate for being kept out of that "real" value. The one has no relation to the

---

10 See above, pp 186–193.
11 [1977] QB 913, CA.
12 [1980] AC 136.

other. If the damages claimed remained nominally the same ... because there was no inflation, interest would normally be given. The same should follow if damages remain in real terms the same.'[13]

In *Birkett v Hayes*,[14] while he accepted that *Pickett* meant that some interest must be awarded on the non-pecuniary losses, Lord Denning considered in the spirit of his approach in *Cookson v Knowles* that a low rate of interest of 2% was appropriate and this was agreed with by the two other judges. Eveleigh LJ said that, where interest rates have a large inflationary element:

'... it cannot be right to apply such interest rates to an award which already takes into account the need for preserving the value of money. We must look for some other rate of interest.'[15]

This low 2% rate of interest was confirmed as correct by the House of Lords in *Wright v British Railways Board*.[16]

Although the rate for awarding interest was not in issue in *Wells v Wells*,[17] one might argue that their Lordships' preference for the rate of return on Index Linked Government Stock (ILGS), as the most accurate indicator of the rate of interest on a low-risk investment, means that the ILGS rate (which was taken to be 3% in *Wells v Wells*) should be the rate of interest applied to damages for non-pecuniary loss. But this argument was rejected by the Court of Appeal in *Lawrence v Chief Constable of Staffordshire*.[18] May LJ said that there was no reason why the guideline rate for calculating future pecuniary loss should be the same as the guideline rate of interest on damages for non-pecuniary loss. This was, not least, because damages for non-pecuniary loss take account of inflation up until the date of judgment. In any event, 'since general damages in personal injury cases are awarded on amounts which are conventional, and since an award of interest is discretionary, a rigid mathematical approach to the calculation of interest is less appropriate than in an actuarial calculation of future loss.'[19]

There has been little other discussion of the effects on interest of assessing damages at a date later than the date of loss.[20] But the clear message from the above cases is that wherever damages are assessed at a

13 [1980] AC 136 at 151.
14 [1982] 1 WLR 816.
15 [1982] 1 WLR 816 at 822.
16 [1983] 2 AC 773.
17 [1999] 1 AC 345.
18 [2000] PIQR Q349.
19 [2000] PIQR Q349 at para 26.
20 But see dictum in *Perry v Sidney Phillips & Son* [1982] 1 WLR 1297 at 1302.

date later than the date of loss, the courts must be careful not to award interest at a rate which will overcompensate the claimant.

(2) Foreign currency liabilities

Under the former sterling-breach-date rule, interest was awarded on an agreed sum or damages at sterling rates. But what effect has the reversal of that rule in *Miliangos v George Frank (Textiles) Ltd*[1] had on the award of interest?

In *Shell Tankers (UK) Ltd v Astro Comino Armadora SA, The Pacific Colocotronis*[2] the Court of Appeal held that, where *Miliangos* applies and judgment is expressed in a foreign currency, interest should be awarded, prima facie, at the rate applicable to that currency. Judgment had there been expressed in US dollars and the rate of interest applied was therefore the dollar rather than the sterling rate. This approach should be supported as effecting true compensation; for example if sterling has declined in value, then since interest rates generally increase in response to a decline in the value of currency, it would usually overcompensate the claimant to express judgment in foreign currency (with a conversion into sterling at the date of payment) and then to award interest at the sterling rate.[3]

---

1   [1976] AC 443. Above, pp 193–199.
2   [1981] 2 Lloyd's Rep 40 at 45, 77. See also *Miliangos v George Frank (No 2)* [1976] 2 Lloyd's Rep 434.
3   For similar reasons the courts have also been given a wide discretion to award a different interest rate, than the usual fixed rate, on judgment debts expressed in a foreign currency: see Private International Law (Miscellaneous Provisions) Act 1995, Pt I.

Chapter 15

Limitation periods

1. INTRODUCTION

Although, strictly speaking, the law of limitation is separate from the law of remedies, the two are closely connected. Moreover, it has been said to be '... trite law that the English Limitation Acts bar the remedy and not the right.'[1] It has therefore been thought helpful to include here a very brief outline of limitation periods for claims for damages, albeit with the warning that this chapter does not attempt to deal with all the details of the law.[2]

For the purposes of limitation, no distinction has been drawn between compensatory and non-compensatory damages. So, for example, the limitation period for punitive damages for a tort is the same as for compensatory damages. Indeed, although there are significant departures from this, the Limitation Act 1980 basically fixes the limitation periods according to the cause of action (breach of contract or tort) rather than the remedy.

2. THE NORMAL TIME LIMITS

By the Limitation Act 1980, s 5, 'An action founded on simple contract shall not be brought after the expiration of six years from the date on which the cause of action accrued.' By s 8(1), 'An action upon a specialty shall not be brought after the expiration of twelve years from the date on which the cause of action accrued.' The reason for this difference is not obvious but perhaps it relates to a contract by deed being easy to prove.

---

1   *Ronex Properties Ltd v John Laing Construction Ltd* [1982] 3 WLR 875 at 879 (per Donaldson LJ). But this is not always the case; see, eg the Limitation Act 1980, s 11A(3).
2   For detailed accounts, see, eg McGee *Limitation of Actions* (4th edn, 2002); *Clerk and Lindsell on Torts* (18th edn, 2000) ch 35; *Chitty on Contracts* (28th edn, 1999) ch 29. See also the extensive reforms recommended by the Law Commission in Report No 270 *Limitation of Actions* (2001).

The date of the cause of action accruing for breach of contract, and hence the date from which the six or twelve years run, is the date of the breach of contract.[3]

By the Limitation Act 1980, s 2, 'An action founded on tort shall not be brought after the expiration of six years from the date on which the cause of action accrued.' The date of the cause of action accruing for torts, and hence the date from which the six years run, is the date of the tort.[4]

One issue of particular practical importance stems from the expansion of the tort of negligence to cover pure economic loss (in certain situations) combined with the acceptance of concurrent liability between tortious negligence and breach of contract: for these developments mean that, for example, where a professional person has negligently performed services beneficial to his claimant client causing pure economic loss, the latter is now generally given a longer period in which to sue for the tort of negligence (time running from the date of damage) rather than for breach of contract (time running from the date of breach).[5] It is debatable whether there should be this difference: if this expansion of negligence is based on recognising a negligent breach of promise as a tort,[6] it would perhaps be preferable to hold that, as for breach of contract, so for such a negligence action, time runs from the date of the breach of duty.[7]

3.   THE MAIN EXCEPTIONS TO THE NORMAL TIME LIMITS[8]

(1)   Damages for personal injury and death

The law on limitation periods for damages for personal injury and death is now contained in the Limitation Act 1980, ss 11–14, which contain the

---

3   The same periods apply to an action for an agreed sum: below, ch 19.
4   Where there is more than one conversion of the same chattel time runs from the date of the original conversion: Limitation Act 1980, s 3(1). For patent infringement the action can accrue before proceedings can be instituted; *Sevcon Ltd v Lucas CAV Ltd* [1986] 2 All ER 104.
5   See, eg *Midland Bank Trust Co Ltd v Hett, Stubbs & Kemp* [1979] Ch 384.
6   Above, pp 7–9.
7   For the opposite solution (that the contractual action should run from the date of the damage) see Cooke 'Tort and Contract' in *Essays on Contract* (ed Finn, 1987) ch 8.
8   Special provisions of the Limitation Act 1980 deal with the defendant's fraud or deliberate concealment or the claimant's mistake (s 32) and the claimant's disability (s 28). See also s 4A, introduced by the Defamation Act 1996, reducing the basic period for defamation actions to

basic time limits, and s 33 of that Act, which gives the courts a discretion to disapply the basic time limits. One exception, as controversially laid down by the House of Lords in *Stubbings v Webb*,[9] is that a personal injury claim, based on trespass to the person as the cause of action, falls outside s 11 and within the normal six-year period of s 2.

(a) Basic time limits for personal injury – s 11

Where the action is brought by the injured person the limitation period, as laid down in the Limitation Act 1980, s 11(4), is three years from either the date on which the cause of action accrued or, if later, the date of knowledge of the person injured.

By the Limitation Act 1980, s 14(1), the date of knowledge means the date on which the person first had knowledge (including constructive knowledge as dealt with by s 14(3)) of all the following facts: that the injury was significant (as defined in s 11(2)); that the injury was attributable in whole or in part to the act or omission which is alleged to constitute negligence, nuisance or breach of duty; the identity of the defendant; and if it is alleged that the act or omission was that of a person other than the defendant, the identity of that person and the additional facts supporting the bringing of an action against the defendant.

Where the estate is bringing the action under the Law Reform (Miscellaneous Provisions) Act 1934 the limitation period laid down in the Limitation Act 1980, s 11(5), is three years from the date of death or the date of the personal representative's knowledge, whichever is the later. Section 14(1) again applies to define the date of knowledge. It should also be remembered that a precondition of a claim by the estate is that there is a valid personal injury action surviving. Hence no action can be brought if the deceased was himself time-barred.

(b) Basic time limits for death – s 12

By the Limitation Act 1980, s 12(2), the limitation period for a claim under the Fatal Accidents Act 1976 is three years from either the date of death or the date of knowledge of the person for whose benefit the action is brought, whichever is the later. The date of knowledge is again defined by s 14(1).

one year (although, by s 32A, this is subject to the court's discretion to disapply that period); and s 11 A which, inter alia, imposes a three-year basic period and a ten-year long-stop for actions under the Consumer Protection Act 1987, Pt 1. Other special limitation periods for damages claims are laid down in, eg the Maritime Conventions Act 1911, s 8 and the Carriage by Air Act 1961, Sch 1, Art 29.

9   [1993] AC 498. See Rogers 'Limitation and Intentional Torts' (1993) NLJ 258.

By the Fatal Accidents Act 1976, s 1(1), an action can only succeed if the deceased would himself have been entitled to damages. Hence, if the deceased's action was time-barred, no Fatal Accidents Act claim lies, and this is reiterated in the Limitation Act 1980, s 12(1).

(c) The discretion to disapply the basic time limits for personal injury and death – s 33

In a novel development, the Limitation Act 1980, s 33(1) gives a court the discretion to disapply the basic time limits under ss 11 and 12 if equitable to do so having regard to the prejudice to the claimant of sticking to the limits and the prejudice to the defendant of extending them. In exercising this discretion the courts, by s 33(3), are to have particular regard to certain factors, such as the length of and reason for delay by the claimant, the extent to which the cogency of evidence will be impaired, and the defendant's conduct after the cause of action arose.

The discretion is also applicable vis-à-vis a deceased's action (with, by the Limitation Act 1980, s 33(5), references to the 'plaintiff' in s 33(3) being replaced by references to the deceased) so that a claim under the Law Reform Act 1934 or the Fatal Accidents Act 1976 can succeed even though the basic time limits would have barred the deceased's action.

There have been many legal decisions dealing with the Limitation Act 1980, s 33 discretion. One controversial issue is whether that discretion is unfettered. In *Firman v Ellis*[10] the Court of Appeal thought that it was, but in no less than three cases[11] the House of Lords accepted that there is one restriction in that, other than in exceptional circumstances, there is no discretion under s 33 to allow an action to proceed where an earlier action had been commenced within the basic time limits but had been discontinued by the claimant's choice or by failing to serve the claim form on time or had been struck out because of the claimant's delay. The reasoning put forward for this is that it is not the time limits under ss 11 and 12 which have prejudiced the claimant but rather the claimant's own conduct. But this is unconvincing, since the claimant's conduct is only prejudicial given the time limits. Moreover, it seems rather anomalous that delay subsequent to issuing the claim form does not allow the courts to exercise their discretion under s 33, whereas delay prior to issuing the claim form does. Lord Diplock purported to explain this in *Thompson v Brown* when he said:

---

10 [1978] QB 886.
11 *Walkley v Precision Forgings Ltd* [1979] 1 WLR 606; *Thompson v Brown* [1981] 1 WLR 744; *Deerness v Keeble & Son Ltd* [1983] 2 Lloyd's Rep 260.

'It may seem anomalous that a defendant should be better off where, unknown to him, a writ has been issued but not served, than he would be if the writ had not been issued at all; but this is a consequence of the greater anomaly, too well established for this House to abolish that, for the purposes of a limitation period, an action is brought when a writ is issued ... and not when it is brought to the knowledge of the defendant by service on him.'[12]

But this is hardly a justification and it is submitted that it would be preferable to regard the Limitation Act 1980, s 33 discretion as not being fettered in this way.[13]

(2) Damages for latent damage (other than personal injury) in the tort of negligence

By definition, latent damage occurs, and hence for the tort of negligence the cause of action begins to run, at a time when the claimant has no reasonable opportunity of knowing of the damage. Indeed the normal time period may have run out before the claimant ever had a reasonable opportunity to discover the damage. While for latent personal injury this problem was solved by the provisions examined above, the expansion of the tort of negligence in the 1970s led to a revival of concern over latent damage this time particularly (although not exclusively)[14] in relation to negligently constructed or designed buildings.

In *Sparham-Souter v Town and Country Developments*[15] the Court of Appeal, in seeking to do justice to claimants, held that the cause of action accrued, and hence time began to run, only when the claimant discovered or ought to have discovered the damage (or possibly the defect). But this decision was overruled by the House of Lords in *Pirelli General Cable Works Ltd v Oscar Faber and Partners*,[16] which said that, by analogy to the common law rule for personal injury, time begins to run only from when damage to the building occurs, whether reasonably

---

12 [1981] 1 WLR 744 at 752–753.
13 In *Shapland v Palmer* [1999] 1 WLR 2068, 2073, Simon Brown LJ commented that the authorities showed 'a marked unwillingness on the court's part to apply the *Walkley* case unless it is plainly indistinguishable.'
14 The problem has also arisen in claims against, eg negligent solicitors or surveyors: eg *Forster v Outred & Co* [1982] 1 WLR 86; *D W Moore & Co Ltd v Ferrier* [1988] 1 WLR 267; *Lee v Thompson* [1989] 2 EGLR 151; *Bell v Peter Browne & Co* [1990] 2 QB 495; *Knapp v Ecclesiastical Insurance Group* [1998] PNLR 172; *Byrne v Hall Pain & Foster* [1999] 1 WLR 1849; *McCarroll v Statham Gill Davies* [2002] EWCA Civ 425, [2003] PNLR 25.
15 [1976] QB 858.
16 [1983] 2 AC 1. *Pirelli* has not been followed in New Zealand: *Invercargill City Council v Hamlin* [1996] AC 624, PC.

discoverable or not. However, the House of Lords recognised the injustice that such an approach can cause to claimants and called for legislative reform.

The overruling of *Anns v Merton London BC*[17] in *Murphy v Brentwood District Council*[18] has cast doubt on whether there is any liability in the tort of negligence for defective buildings, other than for negligent misstatements under *Hedley Byrne & Co Ltd v Heller & Partners Ltd*.[19] Mysteriously the Lords in *Murphy* approved *Pirelli* as falling within the *Hedley Byrne* principle.[20] What can be said with certainty is that, irrespective of whether the cause of action recognised in *Pirelli* survives, *Pirelli* remains valid in so far as it laid down that a cause of action in negligence accrues at the date of the damage and not the date of discoverability.

The calls in *Pirelli* for legislative reform were soon answered. Following the proposals of the Law Reform Committee[1] the Latent Damage Act 1986 was enacted, amending the Limitation Act 1980 in respect of negligently-caused latent damage (other than personal injury).[2] By the Limitation Act 1980, s 14A(4)(a) the normal six-year limit running from the date of the cause of action (ie the *Pirelli* approach) remains but is now subject to two crucial qualifications: first, by s 14A(4)(b) and (5) a claimant can bring an action within three years from the date when he first had the knowledge required for bringing an action, including constructive knowledge (as dealt with by s 14A(10)); and secondly, by s 14B there is an absolute long-stop bar to actions 15 years from the date of the (alleged) negligent act or omission causing the relevant damage.

These provisions appear to achieve a measure of fairness for both claimants and defendants: by the 15-year long-stop defendants are protected against actions being brought scores of years after their negligence, such actions being not only hard to defend but rendering insurance difficult and expensive; and on the other hand, in most situations, the discoverability qualification will allow a claimant to get to know of and hence to bring an action for the damage before the 15-year absolute limit expires. Of course, if *Murphy* has largely eradicated liability

17 [1978] AC 728.
18 [1991] AC 398.
19 [1964] AC 465.
20 For an excellent discussion of this and other related problems thrown up by *Murphy*, see McKendrick '*Pirelli* Re-Examined' (1991) 11 Legal Studies 326. See also *Nitrigin Eireann Teoranta v Inco Alloys Ltd* [1992] 1 All ER 854; *Lancashire and Cheshire Association of Baptist Churches Inc v Howard & Seddon Partnership* [1993] 3 All ER 467.
1 24th Report Latent Damage Cmnd 9390.
2 Negligence here means the tort of negligence and not breach of a contractual duty of care: *Iron Trade Mutual Insurance Co Ltd v J K Buckenham Ltd* [1990] 1 All ER 808; *Société Commerciale de Réassurance v ERAS (International) Ltd* [1992] 2 All ER 82n.

in the tort of negligence for defective buildings, the scope of the Latent Damage Act 1986 has been correspondingly cut back (leaving it as merely applying to other forms of latent economic loss).

(3) Equitable damages[3]

It would appear that the question of what is the limitation period for equitable damages (for a tort or breach of contract) has never been dealt with in the cases.[4] By the Limitation Act 1980, s 36(1), none of the statutory time limits applies directly to specific performance, injunctions or 'other equitable relief'. As such, the most obvious view is that whether equitable damages are time-barred or not depends in turn on whether the specific performance or injunction, in lieu of or in addition to which the damages are potentially being given, would be barred under the laches doctrine. Alternatively one might consider that, as equitable damages are so similar to common law damages, the statutory limitation periods for common law damages should apply by analogy. Indeed there is express provision in s 36(1) for the statutory limitation periods to be applied by analogy to equitable relief; but only '... in like manner as the corresponding time limit under any enactment repealed by the Limitation Act 1939 was applied before 1940' and this would not appear to cover equitable damages. In terms of policy it would certainly seem that, if actions for common law damages are basically acceptable before but not after six years, the same should apply to equitable damages. But given that equitable damages rest on the power to award specific performance or an injunction, the former 'most obvious' view is more likely to prove acceptable.[5]

---

3   For equitable (compensatory) damages generally, see ch 16. For equitable (restitutionary) damages, see below, p 367 and pp 379–384.
4   For limitation periods for equitable remedies for equitable wrongs, see below, pp 634–635.
5   This is, in effect, the position that the Law Commission arrived at in recommending that, while the standard limitation period should apply to equitable remedies for torts or breach of contract, the discretion to refuse an equitable remedy (including equitable damages) because of the claimant's laches should still apply. See Law Commission Report No 270 *Limitation of Actions* (2001) paras 4.268–4.278 and Draft Bill, cl 34(2).

Chapter 16

Equitable (compensatory) damages

1. WHEN MAY EQUITABLE DAMAGES BE AWARDED?

Prior to 1858 there was probably some power, albeit very restricted, to award damages in equity in addition to specific performance.[1] But this is of merely historical interest, because by the Chancery Amendment Act 1858, s 2 (Lord Cairns's Act) the Court of Chancery was given power to award damages in addition to or in substitution for an injunction or specific performance. This power to award equitable damages is now vested in the courts by the Supreme Court Act 1981, s 50. As regards damages in addition, the power is self-explanatory – whenever an injunction or specific performance is granted, damages can be added. But when may damages in lieu be awarded?

By the Supreme Court Act 1981, s 50, this will depend on whether the court 'has jurisdiction to entertain an application for an injunction or specific performance.' But there is difficulty in deciding when this is satisfied. The traditional approach has been to decide whether the particular reason for denying specific performance or the injunction is jurisdictional or discretionary and only if it is the latter can damages in lieu be awarded. For example, in *Price v Strange*[2] the Court of Appeal in dicta considered that the want of mutuality bar to specific performance was discretionary so that damages in lieu could have been awarded had specific performance been refused. Both Buckley and Goff LJJ also thought that the denial of specific performance in contracts for the sale of non-unique goods was jurisdictional, but they disagreed as to whether the personal service bar was jurisdictional or discretionary, Buckley LJ thinking that it was the former and Goff LJ that it was the latter. This disagreement tends to support the view that, given that the bars to specific performance are nowadays rarely absolute,[3] the approach of categorising them as either jurisdictional or discretionary is unhelpful.

---

1   *Todd v Gee* (1810) 17 Ves 273.
2   [1978] Ch 337. See also *Jaggard v Sawyer* [1995] 1 WLR 269, 285 (per Millett LJ).
3   Below, ch 20

A simpler and preferable approach to the Supreme Court Act 1981, s 50 – and one which can equally well justify past decisions – is to ask whether the claimant had an arguable case for specific performance or an injunction at the time the claim was brought; if so, equitable damages can be awarded.[4] In *Ferguson v Wilson*,[5] for example, specific performance of a contract for the allotment of shares to the claimant had been refused because, as the shares had already been allotted to third parties (in fact that had been done prior to the claim being brought) compliance would be impossible. It was further held that no equitable damages could be awarded and this can be best justified by saying that the claimant had no arguable case for specific performance at the time the claim was brought. On the other hand, in *Miller v Jackson*,[6] where the Court of Appeal refused an injunction but granted damages in lieu, the claimant clearly had an arguable case for an injunction – indeed Geoffrey Lane LJ dissented and considered that an injunction should be granted.

Two further points are noteworthy. First, it has traditionally been thought that the Supreme Court Act 1981, s 50 does not allow the award of equitable damages in the unusual case where the claimant would have been granted specific performance or an injunction had he claimed it but he has made no such claim (since he wants damages in lieu).[7] Secondly, the fact that a court has power to award equitable damages does not mean that it will necessarily use that power. For example, where a claimant's conduct has debarred him from specific relief, the court may refuse him even damages in lieu.[8]

2. WHEN ARE EQUITABLE DAMAGES MORE ADVANTAGEOUS THAN COMMON LAW DAMAGES?

As the Supreme Court 1981, s 49, embodying the fusion provisions of the Judicature Acts 1873–1875, allows the claimant to combine a claim for common law damages with an action for specific performance or an injunction, equitable damages generally offer no advantage to a

---

4   There is also jurisdiction where specific performance was ordered but has since been abandoned because of the defendant's non-compliance: eg *Biggins v Minton* [1977] 1 WLR 701; *Malhotra v Choudhury* (1980] Ch 52
5   (1866) 2 Ch App 77. See also *Proctor v Bayley* (1889) 42 Ch D 390.
6   [1977] QB 966.
7   *Horsler v Zorro* [1975] Ch 302. Also see Jones 'Restitution of Benefits Obtained in Breach of Another's Confidence' (1970) 86 LQR 463, 491. Contra is Albery 'Mr Cyprian Williams' Great Heresy' (1975) 91 LQR 337, 352–353.
8   See below, p 572. For delay barring equitable damages, see above, p 361.

claimant. This is particularly so since *Johnson v Agnew*[9] in which it was clearly laid down, following doubts in, for example, *Wroth v Tyler*,[10] that the assessment of equitable damages – and in this case the particular dispute concerned the time for assessing market value – is no different to that for common law damages.[11]

However, there remains one major advantage:[12] equitable damages may be awarded even though there is no cause of action at common law and hence no possible award of common law damages. A number of illustrations can be given of the application of this advantage in relation to torts and breach of contract.

(i) In *Eastwood v Lever*[13] it was first recognised that a third party can be awarded damages in addition to or in lieu of an injunction, available under the *Tulk v Moxhay*[14] principle, for the breach of a restrictive covenant concerning land, although he would have no cause of action at common law because of the privity of contract rule.[15] A more recent instance of this is *Wrotham Park Estate Co v Parkside Homes Ltd*[16] where houses had been built by the defendants in breach of a restrictive covenant. While Brightman J refused to grant a mandatory injunction to demolish them, he did award substantial damages in lieu.

(ii) In *Hasham v Zenab*[17] it was held by the Privy Council that while an anticipatory breach that has not been accepted gives rise to no cause of action at common law, specific performance can be ordered. It had to follow that equitable damages could be awarded in this situation, even though common law damages could not, and this has since been confirmed by the decision in *Oakacre Ltd v Claire Cleaners (Holdings) Ltd*.[18]

(iii) In the classic case of *Leeds Industrial Co-operative Society v Slack*[19] it was held by the House of Lords that damages can be awarded in lieu of a *quia timet* injunction, which is an injunction to prevent a threatened wrong where no wrong has yet been committed. So on the facts damages were held recoverable in lieu of a *quia timet* injunction preventing the

---

9 [1980] AC 367. See also *Surrey CC v Bredero Homes Ltd* [1993] 1 WLR 1361; *Jaggard v Sawyer* [1995] 1 WLR 269.

10 [1974] Ch 30.

11 So the law discussed in chs 2–14 applies analogously to equitable damages. See also *Malhotra v Choudhury* [1980] Ch 52 (the duty to mitigate, *Bain v Fothergill* restriction).

12 A minor advantage is that equitable damages may be awarded even though not claimed: *Betts v Neilson* (1863) 3 Ch App 429 at 441.

13 (1863) 4 De GJ & Sm 114.

14 (1848) 18 LJ Ch 83.

15 It is conceivable that the third party would now have a claim for common law damages under the Contracts (Rights of Third Parties) Act 1999.

16 [1974] 1 WLR 798. See below, p 398.

17 [1960] AC 316.

18 [1982] Ch 197.

19 [1924] AC 851. See also *Hooper v Rogers* [1975] Ch 43 (damages in lieu of *quia timet* mandatory injunction).

defendant constructing buildings which, when complete, would have obstructed the claimant's ancient lights but as yet were causing no obstruction. Similarly, in respect of continuing torts or a continuing breach of contract equitable damages in lieu of even an ordinary (ie not a *quia timet*) injunction are more advantageous than common law damages in compensating for an anticipated rather than just an accrued cause of action. Common law damages, in contrast, compensate only for loss (whether past or prospective) caused by a tort or breach of contract that has already been committed.[20] The explanation for this is that, as equitable damages are a substitute for an injunction or specific performance, and as those specific remedies can be granted to prevent an anticipated tort or breach of contract, equitable damages can instead be awarded in respect of the anticipated cause of action. As Sir Thomas Bingham MR said in *Jaggard v Sawyer:*[1]

'[Lord Cairns' Act] also enabled the Chancery Court to award damages instead of granting an injunction to restrain unlawful conduct in the future. Such damages can only have been intended to compensate the plaintiff for future unlawful conduct, the commission of which, in the absence of any injunction, the court must have contemplated as likely to occur.'

So, for example, in *Bracewell v Appleby*[2] and *Jaggard v Sawyer,*[3] where damages were awarded in lieu of an injunction to prevent defendants continuing to trespass by using the claimant's road to reach their houses, there was no question of the equitable compensatory damages being assessed only for loss caused by past, as opposed to future, acts of trespass.

Although reversed on liability by the House of Lords,[4] there was an interesting recent discussion at first instance of this power to award equitable damages in *Marcic v Thames Water Utilities Ltd (No 2).*[5] The claimant owned property that was regularly subject to flooding. In an action against the defendant, a sewerage undertaker, the claimant sought damages and a mandatory injunction ordering the defendant to implement a scheme to stop the flooding. Judge Richard Havery QC held that the defendant was not liable in the tort of nuisance but was liable – it was this aspect of his decision that was held to be incorrect by the House of Lords – for the wrong of infringing the claimant's

---

20 Above, p 175, n 2.
1   [1995] 1 WLR 269 at 276–277.
2   [1975] Ch 408. See also above pp 252–253.
3   [1995] 1 WLR 269. In this case there was held to be both a continuing trespass and breach of a restrictive covenant.
4   [2003] UKHL 66, [2004] 2 AC 42.
5   [2002] 2 WLR 1000.

convention rights under the Human Rights Act 1998, s 6. However, he refused a mandatory injunction on the ground that this would require supervision by the court. As regards damages, he held that these should be awarded for both past and future wrongs. The claimant was therefore entitled to the difference between the value his property would have had if rendered non-susceptible to wrongful flooding minus its actual value. As regards the damages for future flooding caused by the future wrongs, these were being awarded in substitution for the mandatory injunction. The judge was satisfied that the defendant would commit the future wrongs because they intended not to carry out works necessary to remedy the flooding. Pressed with the argument that he should follow the common law and refuse equitable damages for the future wrongs, Judge Havery QC said, 'The common law would not afford the claimant just satisfaction. He would have to bring onerous proceedings from time to time to enforce his rights. Nor would he be able to recover any diminution in the value of his property caused by the prospect of future wrongs.'[6] In awarding equitable damages for future wrongs, he also rejected a novel argument that this would be contrary to the jurisprudence on the European Convention on Human Rights.

Lord Upjohn's much-discussed statement in the classic mandatory injunctions case of *Redland Bricks Ltd v Morris*[7] – that Lord Cairns's Act had nothing to do with the case – plainly seems wrong. Damages could have been awarded in lieu of a mandatory injunction to restore the support to the claimant's land, albeit that on the facts it was arguably preferable to leave the claimant to bring fresh proceedings should a new cause of action arise, since the probability of further landslips and their likely extent were both in doubt, and the claimant could not carry out effective preventive work on his own land.

In all these situations the normal compensatory aims of putting the claimant into as good a position as if no tort or breach of contract had been committed must of course be modified to include the aim of putting the claimant into as good a position as if the threatened or continuing tort or breach of contract were not to be committed or continued.

---

6   [2002] 2 WLR 1000 at 1008.
7   [1970] AC 652. Below, pp 537–538. Jolowicz 'Damages in Equity – A Study of Lord Cairns' Act' (1975) 34 CLJ 224, 242–5; Pettit 'Lord Cairns' Act in the County Court: A Supplementary Note' (1977) 36 CLJ 369.

3. NON-COMPENSATORY EQUITABLE DAMAGES

In all that has been said above, the assumption has been that the equitable damages in question are compensatory. But it is clear that, just as common law damages may sometimes be restitutionary (concerned to remove the wrongdoer's gain) rather than compensatory, so may equitable damages. Indeed most (but not all) of the examples of restitutionary damages for torts and breach of restrictive covenants have concerned equitable damages awarded in substitution for an injunction. These are considered in chapter 17 below.

There has been no case in which equitable punitive damages have been awarded. It is conceivable that a case might fall within the *Rookes v Barnard*[8] categories permitting punitive damages and yet only equitable (and not common law) damages are available. But as regards anticipated wrongs it may be thought unattractive to punish a defendant in advance of the wrong having been committed. The most likely possibility for the award of equitable punitive damages is for accrued equitable wrongs (such as breach of confidence). This is considered in chapter 24 below.

8   [1964] AC 1129.

Part two

Restitution and punishment

Chapter 17

Restitutionary remedies (for torts and breach of contract)

1. INTRODUCTION

(1) Restitution for wrongs

In *Lipkin Gorman v Karpnale Ltd*[1] it was finally authoritatively accepted by the House of Lords that there is an English law of restitution based on reversing unjust enrichment.[2] In this book we are concerned with only a part of the law of restitution, namely restitutionary remedies – that is, remedies reversing enrichments – for a tort or breach of contract (or, in chapter 24, for an equitable wrong).

Where the restitution is not based on a wrong, the claimant must establish that the defendant has been unjustly enriched 'at the claimant's expense' with the latter phrase meaning 'by subtraction from the claimant'. The claimant's payment of money, or rendering of services, to the defendant by mistake or under duress, or subject to a condition being fulfilled that has not been, are examples of unjust enrichment by subtraction which, subject to defences, will trigger restitution. But where the unjust enrichment is 'at the claimant's expense' in the sense of 'by the defendant committing a wrong to the claimant', the law of restitution is concerned with the wrong as the cause of action not the unjust enrichment. Hence the central distinction drawn in the law of restitution between restitution for wrongs and unjust enrichment by subtraction. In this chapter, we are solely concerned with restitution for wrongs where the wrong is a tort or breach of contract.[3]

---

1 [1991] 2 AC 548.
2 See generally Goff and Jones *The Law of Restitution* (6th edn, 2002); Birks *An Introduction to the Law of Restitution* (revsd edn, 1989) hereinafter cited as *Introduction*; Burrows *The Law of Restitution* (2nd edn, 2002); Virgo *The Principles of the Law of Restitution* (1999).
3 Apart from the relevant chapters in the works cited in the previous note, see generally Jackman 'Restitution for Wrongs' [1989] CLJ 302; Birks 'Civil Wrongs: A New World' (*Butterworths Lectures 1990–91*); Law Commission Report No 247 (1997) *Aggravated, Exemplary and Restitutionary Damages* Pt III; Edelman *Gain-Based Damages* (2002). For discussion of the problems of multiple defendants and multiple claimants in respect of restitution for wrongs, see Burrows 'Reforming Non-Compensatory Damages' in *The Search for Principle* (eds Swadling and Jones, 1999) pp 295, 307–310.

It is worth adding here that many[4] have argued that the central distinction referred to in the last paragraph is so fundamental that the two sides of it should be seen as two separate subjects rather than as two parts of one subject. That is, the law of restitution should be confined – and renamed as the law of unjust enrichment – to where the cause of action is an unjust enrichment not a tort or breach of contract or other wrong.

As will become apparent the main restitutionary remedies in issue in this chapter are an account of profits, an award of money in an action for money had and received and restitutionary damages.[5]

(2) Alternative analysis

What complicates this chapter's concern solely with restitution for wrongs (whether by a tort or breach of contract) is that in some situations where a claim for restitution could be based on a tort or breach of contract, there is an alternative claim that does not rely on the wrong and rather is based on an unjust enrichment by subtraction. This 'alternative analysis' is best understood by reference to an example. Say the defendant has induced the claimant to give her £25 by a deliberate misrepresentation of fact. Irrespective of establishing the tort of deceit, the claimant has a good reason for a restitutionary remedy based on an unjust enrichment by subtraction; namely he has paid £25 to the defendant under an induced mistake of fact which taints the validity of the shift in wealth. The fact that the defendant has deliberately lied causing the claimant loss is irrelevant to that.

It follows that, where a wrong does result in an enrichment by subtraction, the fact that there may be some restriction, preventing restitutionary remedies based on the wrong, will not necessarily rule out restitutionary remedies for unjust enrichment by subtraction, and vice versa. It also follows that, where attention is being focused solely on restitution for wrongs as in this chapter, some care must be taken not to include cases based instead on unjust enrichment by subtraction.

---

4   See, most importantly, Birks 'Misnomer' in *Restitution: Past, Present and Future* (eds Cornish, Nolan, O'Sullivan and Virgo, 1998) pp 1–29; *Unjust Enrichment* (2003) esp p 63.
5   For the form of damages, including restitutionary damages, see above, ch 8. For (pre-judgment) interest on restitutionary remedies, see Burrows *The Law of Restitution* (2nd edn, 2002) pp 53–56. For limitation periods for restitution for torts or breach of contract, see pp 552–554 of the same title.

(3) The enrichment

By committing a tort or breach of contract, a defendant may either acquire a positive benefit, which in general terms can be described as a *profit*, or it may merely be negatively benefited, by *saving expense* that it would otherwise have incurred. But whichever sort of benefit is in question, it is a precondition of restitution – as analogously for compensation – that the tort or breach of contract was a factual cause of the benefit: if the defendant would have made that profit or saved that expense irrespective of the wrong (applying a 'but for' test) there is here no justification for a restitutionary remedy.

Since profits commonly result from various causes, of which the wrong may be just one, the courts may prefer to award merely a fair proportion of the profits gained by the wrong, rather than all those profits.[6] This may be regarded as analogous to the desire to limit compensatory damages for loss, on grounds such as remoteness or intervening cause. The sort of factors that one would expect would influence the courts in deciding whether to award merely a fair proportion of the profits, and if so, what would amount to a fair proportion, are the skill and effort the defendant has expended to make the profits, the blameworthiness of the wrong and, perhaps, the maintenance of some sense of proportion between the benefit acquired and the claimant's loss or lack of it.

The expense the defendant has saved by a breach of contract generally comprises what the defendant would have had to spend to complete its promised performance (minus any part of the contract price now lost). For torts, the expense saved will commonly comprise what the defendant would have had to pay to acquire a substitute for the property it has tortiously used or, in some cases, the fee that the claimant would have charged, if the defendant had negotiated with the claimant for legitimate use of the property. The latter can alternatively be viewed as the fee the claimant has lost because of the defendant's tort; that is, in some cases, but by no means all, an alternative compensatory analysis can be taken.[7]

---

6   See, generally, on the quantum of restitution for wrongs, Friedmann 'Restitution for Wrongs: The Measure of Recovery' (2001) 79 Texas LR 1879.
7   Sharpe and Waddams 'Damages for Lost Opportunity to Bargain' (1982) 2 OJLS 290 go too far by in effect arguing that a compensatory analysis can always be taken in property interference cases.

(4) Edelman's thesis

Dr Edelman in his excellent book *Gain-Based Damages*[8] has put forward the novel thesis that so-called restitution for wrongs in fact embodies two different remedial measures which should be kept distinct. The first is the reversal of a wrongful transfer of value from a claimant to a defendant. He terms this measure 'restitutionary damages'. The second is the stripping away of profits made by the defendant committing a wrong to the claimant. He calls this measure 'disgorgement damages'. The importance of this distinction, according to Edelman, is that the former rests on corrective justice, is analogous to unjust enrichment by subtraction, is relatively uncontroversial and should be available for every type of wrong. The latter, in contrast, is designed to deter a wrong where compensatory damages are inadequate to do so. Disgorgement damages are, and should therefore be, restricted to two main circumstances. First, where a wrong is committed cynically with a view to making material gain and the profit made exceeds the compensation payable; and, secondly, for breach of fiduciary duty (an equitable wrong) in order to protect the institution of trust inherent in the fiduciary relationship.

There is a great deal to admire in Edelman's work. But one difficulty with it is that, on what appears to be the present law, a rigid line between restitution and disgorgement for a wrong does not sit well with the range of factors and range of measures that courts seem to apply. Gain-based measures awarded have ranged from stripping away all profits to stripping away some profits through to thinking in terms of 'expense saved' rather than 'profit'. Similarly, allowances for skill and labour have sometimes been granted. The state of mind of the wrongdoer appears sometimes to be a relevant factor. While clear principle is to be preferred to wide discretion, it is not obvious that this diversity of factors and measures is satisfactorily explained by Edelman's sharp distinction albeit that he purports to do so by treating that range of factors as being relevant to 'disgorgement damages' through the concepts of legal causation and remoteness.[9]

Another difficulty is that in all (or almost all) examples of what Edelman calls 'restitutionary damages' for a wrong, there is an identical claim for compensatory damages for the wrong (because the gain is matched by the claimant's loss); and in all the examples, there appears to be an alternative claim for restitution based not on the wrong but on unjust enrichment by subtraction. With this in mind, it is hard to isolate any cases – upon which Edelman's thesis is dependent – where the cause

8   (2002).
9   Edelman *Gain-Based Damages* (2002) pp 73–76.

of action was the wrong and yet the measure was (in his terminology) 'restitutionary damages' rather than being compensatory damages (or 'disgorgement damages').

A final difficulty[10] is that, even after *Attorney-General v Blake*,[11] Edelman's thesis is particularly hard to reconcile with the law on restitution for breach of contract. The most natural interpretation of Lord Nicholls' speech is that, contrary to Edelman's general thesis,[12] restrictive criteria should apply wherever, for a breach of contract, one is awarding an account of profits or damages concerned to remove some of the defendant's gain. In other words, both so-called 'disgorgement damages' and 'restitutionary damages' are exceptional remedies for breach of contract and available only where compensatory damages, specific performance and injunctions, are inadequate.

2. RESTITUTION FOR TORTS[13]

(1) Introduction

We are here concerned with remedies that reverse gains because the defendant has acquired them by committing a tort against the claimant. This is often what is meant by 'waiver of tort', that is, the claimant sues on the tort but seeks a restitutionary remedy rather than usual compensatory damages. But it can be argued that 'waiver of tort' also refers to where the claimant ignores the tort, and bases its claim for restitution on the cause of action of unjust enrichment by subtraction. It should further be realised that the judicial usage of 'waiver of tort' appears to be confined to where the restitutionary remedy in issue is the award of money had and received (or one of the other 'quasi-contractual' remedies, like a *quantum meruit*) rather than being an account of profits or restitutionary damages. The term 'waiver of tort' is therefore ambiguous and unhelpful and should be avoided wherever possible.

---

10 For a normative difficulty, see Burrows *The Law of Restitution* (2nd edn, 2002) p 461.
11 [2001] 1 AC 268. See below, pp 401–407.
12 But for a different interpretation, tending to support Edelman's thesis, see para 24 of the judgment of Mance LJ in *Experience Hendrix LLC v PPX Enterprises Inc* [2003] EWCA Civ 323, [2003] 1 All ER (Comm) 830. For Edelman's analysis of that case, see his note '*Attorney-General v Blake* Revisited' [2003] RLR 101.
13 See generally Teller 'Restitution as an Alternative Remedy for a Tort' (1956) 2 NY Law Forum 40; York 'Extension of Restitutional Remedies in the Tort Field' (1957) 4 UCLALR 499; Hodder 'Profiting from Tortious Use of Property: A Reply to the Lost Bargain Theory' (1984) 42 UT Fac LR 105; Beatson *The Use and Abuse of Unjust Enrichment* (1991) pp 206–243.

It is also convenient to stress at this initial stage that rescission of a contract for misrepresentation where enrichments gained are reversed,[14] is better viewed as based on unjust enrichment by subtraction, rather than a tort; that is, the reason for the remedy is essentially that the benefit has been rendered non-voluntarily because of induced mistake.[15] This non-wrong analysis is supported by the facts that first, rescission for misrepresentation is similar to that for undue influence, duress, mistake and non-disclosure, where there is no tort (or wrong as such) involved; secondly, rescission was available for non-fraudulent misrepresentation, before the development of the tort of negligent misrepresentation or the passing of the Misrepresentation Act 1967; thirdly, rescission is an available remedy for a purely innocent misrepresentation which is not treated as a tort (or other wrong); and fourthly, for the torts involved, whether deceit, negligent misrepresentation or under the Misrepresentation Act 1967, it is necessary to show damage resulting from the misrepresentation, that is, the torts are actionable only on proof of damage, whereas no damage needs to be proved for rescission.[16]

(2) Why should a claimant want a restitutionary remedy for a tort, rather than compensatory damages?

The main and most obvious advantage is that the claimant may obtain more by restitution than compensation, since the gain the defendant has made by the tort may exceed the loss caused to the claimant by the tort.

But there may be other advantages in that a common law rule or a statutory provision may be regarded as barring compensatory damages but not a restitutionary remedy for the tort. Birks has argued that there can only be an evasion of a bar where it is the remedy (compensation) and not the cause of action (tort) that is barred.[17] But whether illogical or not, the courts in the past have been willing to allow at least some restitutionary remedies for torts to evade bars on 'tort actions'. The major example concerned the *actio personalis* rule, or what was left of it in the Law Reform (Miscellaneous Provisions) Act 1934, s 1(3), whereby there was a six-month limitation period for 'tort actions' against a wrongdoer's personal representatives; for while this was regarded as

---

14 Rescission may simply be concerned to allow escape from a contract. For the same reasons as those in the text such rescission is best viewed as not being a remedy for a tort and hence as being outside this book's scope.

15 Birks *Introduction* pp 167–171; Burrows *The Law of Restitution* (2nd edn, 2002) pp 171–178.

16 *Street on Torts* (11th edn, 2003) pp 133–134.

17 Birks *Introduction* p 347. Cf Burrows *The Law of Restitution* (2nd edn, 2002) pp 26–27.

barring tortious compensatory damages, it was considered not to be a bar to restitutionary remedies, at least if an award of money had and received or an account of profits.[18]

It is worth adding as a postscript that, now that the Proceedings Against Estates Act 1970 has finally removed any trace of the unjust *actio personalis* rule, it is unlikely that the courts will see any reason to allow restitutionary remedies for a tort to avoid the six-year limitation period applicable to tortious compensatory damages.[19] Certainly nothing in the Limitation Act 1980 contradicts this. An award of money had and received is not mentioned and no distinction is drawn between compensatory and restitutionary damages. Moreover by the Limitation Act 1980, s 23 an action for an account of profits '... shall not be brought after the expiration of any time limit under the Act which is applicable to the claim which is the basis of the duty to account', which does appear to mean that if the basis is tort, tort limitation periods should apply.

(3) When are restitutionary remedies available for torts?

There are a number of cases which are most naturally analysed as awarding restitution for a tort rather than the more usual compensatory damages.[20] These cases will be examined by dividing them according to whether the remedy given for the tort was money had and received, restitutionary damages, or an account of profits.

(a) Money had and received

An award of money had and received is automatically restitutionary: ie by its very nature it is looking at the defendant's receipt and not just the claimant's loss (if any). It is submitted, therefore, that it would be sufficient in proving that restitution may be awarded for a tort to point to cases in which this remedy has been awarded *for* a tort. But if the defendant's gain correlates to the claimant's loss, as is usually the case with this remedy in unjust enrichment by subtraction, there is the

---

18 *Chesworth v Farrar* [1967] 1 QB 407, and reasoning in *Phillips v Homfray* (1883) 24 Ch D 439.
19 Burrows *The Law of Restitution* (2nd edn, 2002) p 553.
20 For influential cases in the US see, eg *Federal Sugar Refining Co v US Sugar Equalisation Bd* 286 F 575 (1920) (profits from inducing breach of contract); *Edwards v Lee's Administrators* 96 SW 2d 1028 (1936) (account of profits for trespass to land); *Raven Red Ash Coal Co v Ball* 39 SE 2d 231 (1946) (value of use of land); *Olwell v Nye and Nissen Co* 26 Wash 2d 282 (1946) (reasonable value of use/expense saved by conversion of egg-washing machine). Cf *Hart v EP Dutton & Co Inc* 93 NYS 2d 871 (1949) (refusing restitution for libel). See generally Palmer *Law of Restitution* (1978) Vol I, pp 49–140, 157–166.

conceivable re-interpretation that one is concerned with the well-established principle of compensating for wrongful loss. It follows that the best proof lies in the fact that in several cases awarding money had and received it is at least strained to regard the measure of recovery as corresponding to the claimant's loss and it is more natural, either in the light of the amount awarded or the court's reasoning or both, to regard the measure as solely concerned to strip the tortfeasor of some or all of the gains made by the tort.

First, there are the cases of *Lamine v Dorrell*[1] and *Chesworth v Farrar*[2] on the tort of conversion. In the former, the defendant had wrongfully converted the claimant's Irish debentures by selling them off. It was held that the claimant could recover the actual sale price of the debentures. No investigation was made as to whether that sale had been at the market price. Had the claim been for compensatory damages the normal measure would have been the value of the goods assessed according to the market price at the date of the tort. It must be admitted, however, that the actual reasoning in the case weakens its authority as an example of restitution for the tort because, in justifying the measure, Holt CJ relied on an idea of 'extinctive ratification' agency reasoning which was later disapproved by the House of Lords in *United Australia Ltd v Barclays Bank Ltd.*[3]

In *Chesworth v Farrar* the deceased landlord had wrongfully converted, by selling off, property belonging to his tenant. The tenant successfully recovered the sale price of the goods from the deceased's administrators without any investigation of their value at the date of conversion. The central issue in the case concerned whether the claim was time-barred by the statutory remnant of the *actio personalis* rule laying down a six-month limitation period for an action in tort where the tortfeasor had died. In holding that it was not so time-barred Edmund Davies J reasoned that that limitation period only applied to an action for damages for the tort and not to a quasi-contractual or, as we would now say, restitutionary, remedy. In an important passage he said:

> 'A person upon whom a tort has been committed has at times a choice of alternative remedies, even though it is a *sine qua non* regarding each that he must establish that a tort has been committed. He may sue to recover damages for the tort, or he may waive the tort and sue in quasi-contract to recover the benefit received by the wrongdoer.'[4]

---

1   (1701) 2 Ld Raym 1216.
2   [1967] 1 QB 407.
3   [1941] AC 1.
4   [1967] 1 QB 407 at 417.

Turning to the tort of trespass to goods, in *Oughton v Seppings*[5] a sheriff's officer in executing a writ of *fieri facias* against a Mr Winslove had seized a horse belonging to the claimant. That horse had subsequently been sold by the sheriff and the proceeds of sale paid to the officer. Again, without any investigation of the loss to the claimant, it was held that he could recover the sale proceeds from the officer in an action for money had and received.

Finally, there is *Powell v Rees*[6] which concerned the tort of trespass to land by the extraction of coal from the claimant's land. The claimant was held able to evade the *actio personalis* bar by suing the deceased tortfeasor's estate in an action for money had and received to recover the sale proceeds of the coal. But this case is somewhat weaker than the above three in that Lord Denman CJ did not seem concerned by the lack of direct evidence of the sale price and also indicated that a compensatory award would have yielded the same sum.

(b) Restitutionary damages

The suggestion that damages can be restitutionary will appear to many as a heresy, since it is generally taken for granted that, other than punitive or nominal or contemptuous damages, damages are concerned to compensate the claimant. However, in some cases, the decision and the reasoning indicate that the damages are better or equally-well viewed as restitutionary, reversing the defendant's wrongful enrichment.[7]

(i) Wrongful interference with goods

In *Strand Electric Engineering Co Ltd v Brisford Entertainments Ltd*,[8] the Court of Appeal awarded damages for the then tort of detinue assessed according to a reasonable hiring charge for the period that the defendant had wrongly kept and used theatre equipment. Denning LJ made it plain that he regarded the damages as restitutionary reversing the wrongful benefit acquired by the defendant:

'If a wrongdoer has made use of goods for his own purposes, then he must pay a reasonable hire for them, even though the owner has in fact suffered no loss. It may be

---

5 (1830) 1 B & Ad 241.
6 (1837) 7 Ad & El 426.
7 In addition to the cases below, see dicta of Lord Shaw in *Watson, Laidlaw & Co Ltd v Pott, Cassels & Williamson* (1914) 31 RPC 104, 120: above, p 263. The measure of damages laid down for the statutory tort of unlawful eviction under the Housing Act 1988, ss 27–28 also appears to be restitutionary: *see Jones v Miah* (1992) 24 HLR 578 at 587, 592; *Melville v Bruton* (1997) 29 HLR 319; *King v Jackson* (1998) 30 HLR 541. There is also a natural restitutionary interpretation of the Copyright, Designs and Patents Act 1988, s 97(2).
8 [1952] 2 QB 246.

that the owner would not have used the goods himself, or that he had a substitute readily available, which he used without extra cost to himself. Nevertheless the owner is entitled to a reasonable hire ... The claim for a hiring charge is therefore not based on the loss to the plaintiff, but on the fact that the defendant has used the goods for his own purposes. It is an action against him because he has had the benefit of the goods. It resembles therefore, an action for restitution, rather than an action of tort.'[9]

On Denning LJ's analysis therefore, the damages awarded are best viewed as reversing the expense the defendant saved in not having to hire alternative equipment, or in not paying to the claimant the fee it would have charged if the defendant had negotiated with it for legitimate hire of the goods. Any actual profits the defendant had made from using the equipment were apparently not considered relevant, although Denning LJ said that he could imagine cases where the '... owner might be entitled to the actual profits made by the wrongdoer by the use of the chattel.'[10]

While there are passages in the majority's judgments which support Denning LJ's approach, Somervell and Romer LJJ overall preferred to fit their decision within the normal conception of damages compensating the claimant's loss.[11] This is an equally acceptable approach for even if the claimant would not have hired out the equipment for the full period at the full rate to someone else, as the trial judge had found, it may be realistic to say that it suffered a loss in that it was not paid the fee it would have charged the defendant for its legitimately retaining the goods. Indeed, as we have just observed, on the opposite restitutionary approach, the saving of *that* expense, represents one possible explanation of the reasonable hiring charge measure.

(ii) Trespass to land

Lord Denning, sitting as a single judge in *Penarth Dock Engineering Co Ltd v Pounds*,[12] again adopted a restitutionary approach to the assessment of damages, where the defendants were trespassers in the claimants' dock by failing to remove their pontoon. It was clear that the claimants would not have made any gain by letting out the dock to a third party during that period; nor could it be said that they had suffered a loss, in that they had not been paid the fee they would have charged the defendants for legitimately using the dock, for the claimants were desperately trying to have the defendants remove their pontoon and would not have accepted

---

9   [1952] 2 QB 246 at 254–255.
10 [1952] 2 QB 246 at 255.
11 See similarly, *Hillesden Securities Ltd v Ryjak Ltd* [1983] 1 WLR 959.
12 [1963] 1 Lloyd's Rep 359.

a price for the defendants to have continued using the dock legitimately. But relying on *Whitwham v Westminster, Brymbo, Coal & Coke Co*[13] and his own judgment in *Strand Electric*, Lord Denning awarded damages reversing the benefit the defendants had acquired by use of the dock:

> '... the Penarth company would not seem to have suffered any damage to speak of. They have not to pay any extra rent to the British Transport Commission. The dock is no use to them: they would not have made any money out of it. But ... in a case of this kind ... the test of the measure of damages is not what the plaintiffs have lost, but what benefit the defendant has obtained by having the use of the berth.'[14]

Damages were assessed at £32 5s a week. This was apparently based on the evidence that £37 10s a week was what the defendants would have had to pay for an alternative dock of that kind. Why there was some reduction is not made clear but perhaps the claimants' berth was inferior to the alternatives, or involved the defendants in some expense which the alternatives did not, so that to award the full £37 10s would have gone beyond reversing the defendants' benefit.

Whitwham v Westminster, Brymbo, Coal & Coke Co, which Lord Denning relied on in *Strand Electric* and *Penarth Dock*, concerned trespass by the defendants' tipping of soil from their colliery on to part of the claimants' land. The judgments tended to the view that the damages awarded were compensatory. Presumably this was on the assumption that the damages covered the loss the claimants had suffered by not renting out that part of the land, or by the non-payment of the fee the claimants would have charged for the tipping if they had been approached. But the former seems unrealistic, since it was most unlikely that the claimants would have otherwise rented out that part of the land to a third party. Moreover there are passages which support Lord Denning's restitutionary interpretation. For example, Lindley LJ said, '... if one person has without leave of another been using that other's land for his own purposes, he ought to pay for such user.'[15] On a restitutionary analysis the damages could be said to represent either a fair proportion of the profits made by the defendants, or the expense they had saved by not having to dispose of the spoil elsewhere, or, if regarded as realistic, the saving of the fee the claimants would have charged them for legitimate tipping.

Again in *Swordheath Properties Ltd v Tabet*[16] damages for trespass by tenants remaining in premises after they should have left were assessed

---

13   [1896] 2 Ch 538.
14   [1963] 1 Lloyd's Rep 359 at 361–362.
15   [1896] 2 Ch 538 at 541–542.
16   [1979] 1 WLR 285.

according to the ordinary letting value of the property. The Court of Appeal regarded it as irrelevant whether the claimants would have used the property or not and *Whitwham* and *Penarth Dock* were relied on. Megaw LJ said:

> '... the plaintiff ... is entitled, without bringing evidence that he could or would have let the property to someone else in the absence of the trespassing defendant, to have as damages for the trespass the value of the property as it would fairly be calculated: and in the absence of anything special in the particular circumstances it would be the ordinary letting value of the property that would determine the amount of damages.'[17]

Such damages could only be compensatory, if it was realistic to assume that the claimants would have allowed the defendants to stay on at that rent if they had approached them. But on a restitutionary analysis, while the saving of that expense is one possible explanation of the damages, the alternative is that they represented the expense the defendants had saved in not having to rent alternative property of that type.

In *Bracewell v Appleby*,[18] where the courts refused an injunction to prevent the defendant continuing to trespass by using the claimants' road to reach his newly-built house, damages in lieu (ie equitable damages) were granted, assessed according to what would have been a fair sum for the claimants to have accepted for granting the defendant a right of way over the road, albeit that the claimants would probably not have been willing to grant the right of way. Such a fair sum can be viewed as compensating the claimants for their 'loss of amenity and increased user'[19] or, on a restitutionary approach, as representing a fair proportion of the profits made by the trespass. The latter seems the preferable analysis since in assessing the fair sum Graham J considered it important to take into account the profits the defendant had made on the house. Ultimately damages of £2,000 out of a notional profit of £5,000 were awarded.

Finally, and perhaps most importantly, in *Ministry of Defence v Ashman*,[20] in which a tenant had wrongfully ignored a notice to quit RAF accommodation because she and her children had nowhere else to go, a majority of the Court of Appeal (Kennedy and Hoffmann LJJ) accepted that the claimant landlord was entitled to restitutionary damages for the

---

17   [1979] 1 WLR 285 at 288.
18   [1975] Ch 408.
19   [1975] Ch 408 at 420.
20   (1993) 66 P & CR 195. See also *Ministry of Defence v Thompson* [1993] 2 EGLR 107; *Gondall v Dillon Newsagents Ltd* [2001] RLR 221. See generally Cooke 'Trespass, Mesne Profits and Restitution' (1994) 110 LQR 420. Cf *Inverugie Investments Ltd v Hackett* [1995] 1 WLR 713, PC.

trespass. The *Swordheath* and *Penarth Dock* cases were relied on: and it was held that the damages should be assessed according to what it would have cost the tenant to rent alternative local authority accommodation had any been available. Hoffmann LJ said:

'A person entitled to possession of land can make a claim against a person who has been in occupation without his consent on two alternative bases. The first is for the loss which he has suffered in consequence of the defendant's trespass. This is the normal measure of damages in the law of tort. The second is the value of the benefit which the occupier has received. This is a claim for restitution. The two bases of claim are mutually exclusive and the plaintiff must elect before judgment which of them he wishes to pursue. These principles are not only fair but, as Kennedy LJ demonstrated, also well established by authority.

It is true that in earlier cases it has not been expressly stated that a claim for mesne profit for trespass can be a claim for restitution. Nowadays I do not see why we should not call a spade a spade. In this case the Ministry of Defence elected for the restitutionary remedy.'[1]

The purpose of this exercise has been to bring to light cases where the decision and reasoning indicate that the damages are better, or equally-well, viewed as restitutionary rather than compensatory. But it should be added that in two trespass to land cases, *Jaggard v Sawyer*[2] and *Severn Trent Water Ltd v Barnes*,[3] influential Court of Appeal judges (Sir Thomas Bingham MR and Millett LJ in the former case, and Potter LJ in the latter) have emphatically supported a compensatory analysis whereby the damages have been viewed as compensating for the loss of the reasonable fee that could have been negotiated for the right in question.

(iii) Nuisance

The hypothetical bargain approach adopted in *Bracewell v Appleby* was further applied in assessing damages in lieu of a mandatory injunction in *Carr-Saunders v Dick McNeil Associates Ltd*,[4] where the defendants were liable in nuisance for having erected extra storeys to their buildings which interfered with the claimant's light. Most significantly for present purposes Millett J said that he was 'entitled to take account of ... the amount of profit which the defendants would look to in the development of their site.'[5] This may have indicated his willingness to adopt a restitutionary analysis. However, since no evidence of profit was

1 (1993) 66 P & CR 195, 200–201.
2 [1995] 1 WLR 269. See above, p 252.
3 [2004] EWCA Civ 570. See above, p 252, n 3.
4 [1986] 2 All ER 888.
5 [1986] 2 All ER 888 at 896.

available, the damages awarded are most naturally viewed as compensating for the claimant's loss of use and amenity rather than reversing profit. Only if in reality the claimant would have been willing to accept a fee to allow that building had the defendants approached him are the damages explicable as restitutionary, for the damages could then be regarded as either compensating for the lost fee or as reversing the expense the defendants had saved in not paying that fee.

(c) Account of profits

This is an equitable remedy by which the defendant is required to draw up an account of, and then to pay the amount of, the net profits it has acquired by particular wrongful conduct. The remedy's label 'account of profits' is therefore shorthand for 'account and award of profits'. The contrast with compensatory damages was clearly stressed in the typically superb judgment of Windeyer J in the Australian infringement of trade mark case, *Colbeam Palmer Ltd* v *Stock Affiliates Pty Ltd*:[6]

> 'The distinction between an account of profits and damages is that by the former the infringer is required to give up his ill-gotten gains to the party whose rights he has infringed; by the latter he is required to compensate the party wronged for the loss he has suffered. The two computations can obviously yield different results, for a plaintiff's loss is not to be measured by the defendant's gain, or a defendant's gain by the plaintiff's loss. Either may be greater, or less, than the other. If a plaintiff elects to take an inquiry as to damages the loss to him of profits which he might have made may be a substantial element of his claim ... But what a plaintiff might have made had the defendant not invaded his rights is by no means the same thing as what the defendant did make by doing so.'

As yet, an account of profits is only available for a tort if the tort involves an infringement of intellectual property rights, whether by the infringement of a patent,[7] copyright,[8] design right,[9] performer's property right,[10] or trade mark,[11] or passing off.[12] Confinement of this equitable remedy to those torts is explicable historically because they have their roots in equity. But this is not a policy justification and it can be argued

---

6   (1968) 122 CLR 25 at 32.
7   Patents Act 1977, s 61(1)(d), *Siddell v Vickers* (1892) 9 RPC 152. Presumably design infringement is analogous.
8   Copyright, Designs and Patents Act 1988, s 96(2); *Delfe v Delamotte* (1857) 3 K & J 581; *Potton Ltd v Yorkclose Ltd* [1990] FSR 11.
9   Copyright, Designs and Patents Act 1988, s 229(2).
10 Copyright, Designs and Patents Act 1988, s 191I(2).
11 *Edelsten v Edelsten* (1863) 1 De GJ & SM 185; *Slazenger & Sons v Spalding & Bros* [1910] 1 Ch 257.
12 *Lever v Goodwin* (1887) 36 Ch D 1; *My Kinda Town Ltd v Soll* [1982] FSR 147; revsd on liability [1983] RPC 407.

that the role of an account of profits should be expanded to reverse gains made by any dishonestly-committed tort.

Originally the courts would only award an account of profits if ancillary to an injunction. For example, in *Smith v London and South Western Rly Co*[13] and *Price's Patent Candle Co Ltd v Bauwen's Patent Candle Co Ltd*[14] it was held that no account of profits could be awarded because, as there would be no further patent infringement, there was no justification for an injunction. But while it is generally the case that an account of profits is awarded in addition to an injunction, this is no longer a requirement. Presumably as with an injunction traditional equitable defences concerning the claimant's conduct, such as clean hands and acquiescence, will apply as bars to an account of profits.

There are four remaining issues of importance:

(i) Innocent wrongdoing

There is an interesting difference between these torts as to whether an account of profits will be refused because the defendant was an innocent wrongdoer. So by the Patents Act 1977, s 62(1), in proceedings for patent infringement, it is a defence to a claim for an account of profits or indeed damages (but not an injunction) that the defendant was not aware, and had no reasonable grounds for supposing, that the patent existed. In other words, a negligence standard is laid down for an account of profits (and damages).

At common law, an account of profits may be ordered for the torts of passing off[15] or infringement of trade mark[16] although it appears that dishonesty is here a pre-condition of an account of profits[17] (albeit not of a claim for damages).[18] Windeyer J explained this as follows in *Colbeam Palmer Ltd v Stock Affiliates Pty Ltd*:[19]

'By [the account of profits] a defendant is made to account for, and is then stripped of profits he has made which it would be unconscionable that he retain. These are profits made by him dishonestly, that is by knowingly infringing the rights of the proprietor of the trade mark.'

---

13 (1854) Kay 408.
14 (1858) 4 K & J 727.
15 *Lever v Goodwin* (1887) 36 Ch D 1; *AG Spalding & Bros v AW Gamage Ltd* (1915) 84 LJ Ch 449; *My Kinda Town Ltd v Soll* [1982] FSR 147, reversed on liability [1983] RPC 407.
16 *Edelsten v Edelsten* (1863) 1 De GJ & Sm 185; *Slazenger & Sons v Spalding & Bros* [1910] 1 Ch 257; *Colbeam Palmer Ltd v Stock Affiliates Pty Ltd* (1968) 122 CLR 25. Cf Trade Marks Act 1994, s 14(2): 'In an action for infringement [of a registered trade mark] all such relief by way of damages, injunctions, accounts or otherwise is available to him as is available in respect of the infringement of any other property right.'
17 *Colbeam Palmer Ltd v Stock Affiliates Pty Ltd* (1968) 122 CLR 25.
18 *Gillette UK Ltd v Edenwest Ltd* [1994] RPC 279.
19 (1968) 122 CLR 25 at 34.

But in contrast to the above are the Copyright, Designs and Patents Act 1988, ss 97(1), 233(1) and 191J(1) whereby, for infringement of copyright, a primary infringement of a design right and infringement of a performer's property right respectively, it is a defence to damages *but not to an account of profits* that the defendant did not know and had no reason to believe that copyright or the design right or performer's property right subsisted in the work to which the action relates. In other words, an account of profits is awarded on a strict liability basis.

There is no justification for such a difference of approach and the inconsistency should be removed. Whether this should be by adopting the standard of dishonest wrongdoing, as for the common law torts, or negligence, as for patent infringement, or strict liability, as for copyright, primary design infringement and infringement of performer's property right, is a difficult policy issue which ultimately rests on the justification for applying restitution as a mid-position between compensation and punishment.

(ii) Account of which profits?

The courts' approach shows a veiled awareness that the wrong must have been a factual cause of the profits for which the account is ordered. Slade J recently affirmed the central principle in the following classic statement in *My Kinda Town Ltd v Soll*,[20] where the defendants were alleged to be liable for passing off by using a name similar to the claimants' for their own chain of restaurants:

> 'The purpose of ordering an account of profits in favour of a successful plaintiff in a passing off case is not to inflict punishment on the defendant. It is to prevent an unjust enrichment of the defendant by compelling him to surrender those ... parts of the profits, actually made by him which were improperly made and nothing beyond this.'

It followed that, as the alleged tort comprised confusing the public into thinking the defendants' restaurants were the claimants', the profits to be accounted for were only those additional profits caused by that confusion, and not all the profits made by the defendants from those restaurants.[1]

Again, in relation to infringement of a trade mark, it is not all the profits from the sale of infringing goods that are gained by the infringement and

---

20 [1982] FSR 147 at 156; revsd on liability [1983] RPC 407. See also *Potton Ltd v Yorkclose Ltd* [1990] FSR 11.

1   *Lever v Goodwin* (1887) 36 Ch D 1, where the amount of profits included sales to non-confused customers, was distinguished on the unconvincing ground that the sales there were to middlemen.

must be accounted for: rather it is only those made because the goods were sold under the trade mark. As Windeyer J said in *Colbeam Palmer v Stock Affiliates Pty Ltd*[2] 'The profit for which the infringer of a trade mark must account is thus not the profit he made from selling the article itself but ... the profit made from selling it under the trade mark.'

Similarly, as Lord Watson pointed out in dicta in *United Horse-Shoe & Nail Co Ltd v Stewart & Co*,[3] it 'would be unreasonable to give the patentee profits which were not earned by the use of his invention.' So where the patent infringement comprises using a particular means of manufacturing goods, but there are other means, the profits to be accounted for are those made by using that particular means; that is, as suggested in *Siddell v Vickers*,[4] one should compare the profits actually made with those that would have been made if the next most likely means of manufacture had been adopted.

In *Celanese International Corpn v BP Chemicals Ltd*[5] Laddie J controversially held that, in assessing the sum to be awarded under an account of profits for patent infringement, no sum could be awarded if no profits (but instead losses) were made (even though the losses would have been greater but for the infringement); and while he thought causation was important, so that the profits must be ones made by the infringement, Laddie J peculiarly thought it inappropriate to consider what profits the defendant would have made had it adopted the most likely non-infringing method of production.

It can also be argued that, beyond applying factual cause, a court should restrict an account of profits to a fair proportion of the profits made by the wrong to take account, for example, of the skill and effort expended by the defendant to make the profit. But as yet there has been no such restriction,[6] perhaps because the wrongdoing in issue has generally been intentional.

(iii) Difficulty of an account of profits

A point emphasised in many of the cases, particularly those of the nineteenth century, in which an account of profits has been ordered is the difficulty of working out the profits the defendant has wrongfully acquired. For example, in *Price's Patent Candle Co Ltd v Bauwen's Patent*

---

2   (1968) 122 CLR 25 at 37.
3   (1888) 13 App Cas 401 at 412–413.
4   (1892) 9 RPC 152.
5   [1999] RPC 203.
6   But see in support, Robert Goff J's dicta in *Redwood Music Ltd v Chappell & Co Ltd* [1982] RPC 109 at 132 (innocent copyright infringement).

Candle Co Ltd[7] Sir Page Wood V-C said, '... the questions involved in taking accounts of the particular instances in which patents have been infringed, and of the profits thereby made, are questions of great nicety and difficulty and never tend to any satisfactory result.'[8] But particularly where all profits on the manufacture and sale of certain goods have to be accounted for, it is hard to see why this is regarded as that difficult. Even where only some of the profits from sales of goods have to be accounted for, it is not clear why it is thought more difficult to work out the profits the defendant has made from his wrong, than it is to calculate compensatory damages for, for example, the profits the claimant has lost as a result of the wrong.

Perhaps the explanation for this emphasis on difficulty is that traditionally the courts have taken the view that an account of profits requires a very precise calculation of the relevant profits, with an actual account having to be drawn up, showing gains and losses, whereas it has been accepted that damages can be calculated in a rough and ready manner. But there is no reason why an account of profits should not also be roughly rather than precisely calculated and in support of this are Slade J's comments in *My Kinda Town Ltd v Soll:*[9]

> '... the general intention of the Court in making the order [of an account of profits] ... has been to achieve a fair apportionment, so that neither party will have what justly belongs to the other. What will be required on the inquiry, if it has to be pursued, will not be mathematical exactness, but only a reasonable approximation.'

It may be that such recognition that an account of profits does not require absolute exactness will open the way for a greater use of this remedy which traditionally, because of the precision thought to be required, has rarely been claimed in preference to damages.

(iv) Account of profits and damages

It has been laid down that a claimant cannot both be awarded damages and an account of profits.[10] In *Neilson v Betts*[11] Lord Westbury explained the rule on the ground that, 'The two things are hardly reconcilable, for

---

7   (1858) 4 K & J 727.
8   (1858) 4 K & J 727 at 730. See also *Crosley v Derby Gas Light Co* (1838) 3 My & Cr 428; *Siddell v Vickers* (1892) 9 RPC 152.
9   [1982] FSR 147 at 159. See also *Potton Ltd v Yorkclose Ltd* [1990] FSR 11.
10 *Neilson v Betts* (1871) LR 5 HL 1; *De Vitre v Betts* (1873) LR 6 HL 319; Patents Act 1977, s 61(2); *Colbeam Palmer Ltd v Stock Affiliates Pty Ltd* (1968) 122 CLR 25. *Island Records Ltd v Tring International plc* [1996] 1 WLR 1256, noted by Birks 'Inconsistency Between Compensation and Restitution' (1996) 112 LQR 375; *Spring Form Inc v Toy Brokers Ltd* [2002] FSR 276, noted by Bently and Mitchell 'Combining Money Awards for Patent Infringement' [2003] RLR 79. See analogously *United Australia Ltd v Barclays Bank Ltd* [1941] AC 1 in which it was accepted that a

if you take an account of profits you condone the infringement.' But this reasoning is unconvincing, and it has been restrictively interpreted in *Codex Corpn v Racal-Milgo Ltd*,[12] where the actual decision was that the taking of an account of profits for infringement of patent does not amount to a 'franking' of the defendant's products so as to prevent future actions for patent infringement. Indeed Lord Westbury's view is reminiscent of the argument rejected in *United Australia Ltd v Barclays Bank Ltd*[13] that, having 'waived the tort' and sued for an action for money had and received, the claimant cannot switch to claiming damages for conversion if judgment on that prior action is unsatisfied.

Although that reasoning is unconvincing, the rule that a claimant cannot be awarded both compensation and restitution for a wrong may be thought to be justified on the basis that it prevents double recovery or 'inconsistency'.[14] For example, if D, by committing a tort against C has made a net gain of £2,000 and by the same tort has caused loss to C of £5,000, the effect of requiring D to pay C £7,000 would be that C is neither just compensated for its loss nor is D just stripped of its wrongly acquired gain. An award of £7,000 would therefore appear to be inconsistent with either of the remedial purposes being pursued and would constitute double recovery.

On the other hand, there would appear to be no objection to a combination of compensation and restitution provided one takes account of the other. So the correct award of £5,000 in the above example *could* be justified as an award of restitution (£2,000) plus partial compensation (£3,000).

At present the law requires a claimant to make an election or choice between these so-called 'inconsistent' remedies. That election need not be made until judgment and even then it can be changed if the judgment is unsatisfied.[15]

A requirement of election between 'inconsistent' remedies saves the court from having to become embroiled in the issue of the extent to which an award of both restitution and compensation would entail 'double recovery'. It may also remove the risk of defendants being

---

claimant cannot recover both compensatory damages and an award of money had and received for a tort. See also on breach of fiduciary duty *Mahesan S/O Thambiah v Malaysian Government Officers Co-operative Housing Society* [1979] AC 374; *Tang Min Sit v Capacious Investments Ltd* [1996] AC 514. See generally Tilbury *Civil Remedies* (1990) paras 2015, 2027. See also above, pp 14–16.
11 (1871) LR 5 HL 1 at 22.
12 [1984] FSR 87.
13 [1941] AC 1.
14 See above, pp 14–16.
15 *United Australia Ltd v Barclays Bank Ltd* [1914] AC 1; *Tang Min Sit v Capacious Investments Ltd* [1996] AC 514.

pressurised into paying inappropriate measures of recovery. The disadvantage of requiring an election is that it is conceivable that a claimant may be deprived of its full entitlement by making an inappropriate election although normally a claimant will make the right choice by electing the remedy which, on the facts, yields the higher measure of recovery. The chance of injustice to claimants (by choosing a lower measure) has been further reduced by the decision in *Island Records Ltd v Tring International Plc*[16] to the effect that a claimant is entitled to defer election until after an inquiry as to the amount of profits.

(d) Three significant anti-restitution cases?

Three Court of Appeal decisions stand as possible obstacles to the full or wide acceptance of restitution as a remedial measure for a tort. In *Phillips v Homfray*[17] the deceased had trespassed by using roads and passages under the claimants' land to transport coal. In an earlier action the claimants had won a judgment for 'damages' to be assessed against the then living tortfeasor.[18] After his death, the question at issue was whether the claimants could treat the judgment for damages for use of their land as one for a restitutionary remedy which would survive against the deceased's executors despite the *actio personalis* rule. The majority held not on the ground that for a restitutionary remedy, at least one that is to survive against the deceased's executors, it is necessary for the gain made by the tortfeasor to comprise the claimant's property or the proceeds of that property. On the facts that was not so: the deceased had gained by saving himself the expense of not paying the claimant for using the underground roads or alternatively by not paying for other methods of transporting the coal. Baggallay LJ, in a powerful dissenting judgment, could not see why the type of benefit should matter. He said:

> 'I feel bound to say that I cannot appreciate the reasons upon which it is insisted that although executors are bound to account for any accretions to the property of their testator derived directly form his wrongful act, they are not liable for the amount or value of any other benefit which may be derived by his estate from or by reason of such wrongful act.'[19]

This case can be, and has been, analysed in many different ways. Goff and Jones in the first three editions of their *The Law of Restitution* regarded it as an unfortunate decision on restitution for the tort of trespass to land which should be overruled. They wrote, 'In our view the

---

16 [1996] 1 WLR 1256.
17 (1883) 24 Ch D 439.
18 (1871) 6 Ch App 770.
19 (1883) 24 Ch D 439 at 471–472.

principle of Baggallay LJ's dissent should be adopted and *Phillips v Homfray* overruled.'[20] Underpinning this view was that, while the issue in point was whether an action could be brought against the deceased's executors, and was therefore bound up with the *actio personalis* rule which no longer applies, the reasoning appeared to be also directed to claims against the wrongdoer himself. For example, Bowen LJ said:

> 'The true test to be applied in the present case is whether the plaintiffs' claim against the deceased … belongs to the category of actions *ex delicto* or whether any form of action against the executors of the deceased, or *the deceased man in his lifetime*, can be based upon any implied contract or duty.'[1]

Birks has argued that the case presents no obstacle to restitution for wrongdoing because, given the *actio personalis* bar to tort actions then existing, the case could only be concerned with the cause of action of unjust enrichment by subtraction and not restitution for wrongs.[2] But while it would be *possible* to analyse the decision as concerned purely with unjust enrichment by subtraction, the judgments seemed principally geared towards enrichment by wrongdoing.

On another view, favoured more recently by Goff and Jones[3] and in a forceful article by Swadling, while the decision does deal with restitution for wrongs, it should be regarded as posing no difficulty for the modern law because of the abolition of the *actio personalis* rule. Swadling persuasively contends that, taking into account the earlier 1871 decision (which he calls *Phillips v Homfray (No 1)*), the 1883 decision (which he calls *Phillips v Homfray No 2)*) was not denying that a court can award restitution for negative benefits against a living trespasser.[4] He writes:

> '*Phillips & Homfray (No 2)* is not the anti-restitutionary case it is painted to be. It should not be overruled, or banished to a dark corner of our law, but instead set out in lights. It is a decision concerned only with the operation of the maxim *actio personalis moritur cum persona*, and therefore tells us nothing of the restitutionary liability of living wrongdoers. And when read in conjunction with *Phillips v Homfray (No 1)*, it is in fact authority *against* the very proposition for which it is said to stand, namely, that a restitutionary claim in respect of the wrong of trespass to land yields only positive benefits, for in the first stage of the litigation Stuart V-C at first instance, and

---

20 Goff and Jones *The Law of Restitution* (3rd edn, 1986) p 611.
1 (1883) 24 Ch D 439 at 460–461 (author's italics).
2 *An Introduction to the Law of Restitution* (revised edn 1989) p 323.
3 Goff and Jones *The Law of Restitution* (6th edn, 2002) para 36–003: the reasoning 'may have been then valid but … can no longer be supported'. See also Hedley 'Unjust enrichment as the basis of Restitution – an overworked concept' (1985) 5 LS 56, 64; Gummow 'Unjust Enrichment, Restitution and Proprietary Remedies, in *Essays on Restitution* (ed Finn, 1990) pp 60–67.
4 'The Myth of *Phillips v Homfray*' in *The Search for Principle* (eds Swadling and Jones, 1999) pp 277–294.

> Lord Hatherley LC on appeal, allowed a restitutionary claim for expense saved by the
> then living defendants ... The only thing which needs to be buried is the myth in
> *Phillips v Homfray*, not the decision itself.'[5]

Even if one treats *Phillips v Homfray* as a problem case it must not be
forgotten that it was not totally anti-restitution in that it indisputably did
recognise that restitution could be given for a tort where the gain
comprised the claimant's property or its proceeds.[6] It was therefore
implicit in the majority's reasoning that the first part of the 'damages' to
be assessed for the value of the coal taken (which the Court of Appeal in
the later *Phillips v Homfray* appeal[7] construed as being for an equitable
account of profits so that no interest could be added) was maintainable
against the deceased's executors despite the *actio personalis* rule.

Moreover, it is noteworthy that the decision has had no impact outside
actions for money had and received: the granting of an account of
profits for intellectual property torts accepted at common law and in
statutes and, more directly, the restitutionary damages cases, such as
Penarth Dock v Pounds and *Bracewell v Appleby*, conflict with, while ignoring,
the *Phillips v Homfray* restriction.

A second problematic Court of Appeal case is *Stoke-on-Trent City Council
v W & J Wass Ltd*.[8] The defendants had deliberately committed the tort
of nuisance by operating a market within a distance infringing the
claimant's proprietary market right. The claimant was granted an
injunction to restrain further infringement of its right. On the question of
damages it was accepted by the claimant that it had not suffered any loss,
in the sense of loss of custom. But at first instance Peter Gibson J
awarded damages on the basis of an appropriate licence fee that the
claimant could have charged the defendant for lawful operation of its
market: that is, he awarded damages applying the 'hypothetical bargain'
approach of *Bracewell v Appleby*. On the facts this could have constituted a
compensatory measure because the claimant might well have granted
such a licence. Alternatively those damages could have been
restitutionary, stripping the defendant of some of the profits made.

In contrast the Court of Appeal restricted the claimant to nominal
damages. The damages cases considered above were distinguished on,
with respect, unconvincing grounds. Most alarming was that the whole
question was approached as if only compensatory damages could be

---

5   *The Search for Principle* (eds Swadling and Jones, 1999) p 294.
6   Taking account of all the stages of the litigation, Birks regards the case as 'indisputably
     authority in favour of the proposition that an account does lie for the profits of a trespass':
     'Civil Wrongs: A New World' (*Butterworths Lectures 1990–91*) pp 64–67.
7   [1892] 1 Ch 465.
8   [1988] 1 WLR 1406.

awarded. It was only at the very end of Nourse LJ's judgment that there was any reference to restitution. He said:

> 'It is possible that the English law of tort, more especially of the so-called "proprietary torts" will in due course make a more deliberate move towards recovery based not on loss suffered by the plaintiff but on the unjust enrichment of the defendant – see Goff and Jones *The Law of Restitution* (3rd edn), pp 612–614. But I do not think that that process can begin in this case and I doubt whether it can begin at all at this level of decision.'[9]

The contrast to Lord Denning's judgment in *Penarth Dock*, at first instance, could not be more clear. It should have been plain that restitution for a tort is not a novel concept beyond the reach of the Court of Appeal. Moreover, this was not only a proprietary tort case but one where the tort was committed cynically. The case for restitution was therefore particularly strong.

In the final case of the problematic trio, *Halifax Building Society v Thomas*,[10] the defendant fraudulently misrepresented his identity and creditworthiness to obtain a loan from the claimant to finance the purchase of a flat. The loan was secured by a mortgage over the flat. When the defendant defaulted on the repayments, the claimant exercised its right to sell off the flat. The proceeds of sale exceeded the loan. The claimant sought a declaration that it was entitled to keep all the proceeds of sale (ie including the surplus of £10,504.90 plus interest) as restitution for the tort of deceit. If made out, such a restitutionary claim would have defeated the Crown's competing claim to confiscate the surplus in execution of a criminal confiscation order made when the defendant was found guilty of conspiring to obtain mortgage advances by deception.

The Court of Appeal held that the claimant was not entitled to restitution (whether personal or proprietary) for the tort of deceit. The primary reasoning was that this was not a proprietary tort case. Nor did it involve a breach of fiduciary duty. Moreover, the claimant had affirmed the mortgage and had recovered all that, as a secured creditor, it was contractually entitled to under the loan agreement.

One may interpret this case as a significant block on restitution for a personal, non-proprietary tort. But especially in the light of *Attorney-General v Blake*,[11] which awarded an account of profits for a 'non-proprietary' breach of contract, the case is best interpreted narrowly as being dependent on the criminal convictions and confiscation order.

---

9 [1988] 1 WLR 1406 at 1415.
10 [1996] Ch 217.
11 [2001] 1 AC 268. See below, pp 401–407.

They ensured that the defendant would not profit from his wrong and there was therefore no work needing to be done by the civil law of restitution.

(e) Conclusion

It is submitted, therefore, that the three significant anti-restitution cases can largely be put to one side and that the main picture emerging from the cases is that, at least for proprietary torts, restitution (reversing some, or all, of the defendant's wrongful gains) is an available remedial response. That is, taking all three types of restitutionary remedy together (award of money had and received, account of profits, restitutionary damages) the torts for which restitution have been awarded have involved interference with the claimant's property, whether that property be real or personal or intellectual. The cases therefore reveal a judicial desire firmly to deter even innocent interference with the claimant's property; that is, merely to compensate for any loss caused appears to be regarded as insufficient to deter that interference. This seems sensible. Applying Jackman's theory, restitution is justified as a means of deterring harm to the 'facilitative institution' of private property.[12]

A subsidiary feature exhibited in a few of the account of profits cases (eg for passing off and infringement of trade mark) is that the tort must be committed intentionally if restitution is to be awarded. It can be strongly argued that this category should be expanded[13] so that restitution should be awarded to reverse gains made by, eg intentionally inducing a breach of contract or an intentional libel.[14] This is particularly so, if the courts can rid themselves of the former emphasis on an account of profits being mathematically exact. Indeed punitive damages can be awarded for these torts under the category of cynically exploiting wrongdoing to make a profit[15] and, since stripping the defendant of its unjust profits by restitution is less drastic than punishment,[16] it is arguable that restitution should follow on the reasoning that the greater should include the lesser. This is supported by the Law Commission. Irrespective of any other power to award restitution for torts (eg for proprietary torts) the Commission has

---

12 'Restitution for Wrongs' [1989] CLJ 302.
13 See Birks *Introduction* pp 326–327.
14 Street also gave examples for the tort of battery in *Principles of the Law of Damages* p 254.
15 Below, pp 413–416.
16 *Cassell & Co Ltd v Broome* [1972] AC 1027 at 1130 (per Lord Diplock); Ashworth *Sentencing and Penal Policy* (1983) p 294.

recommended that a claimant may be awarded restitutionary damages for any tort if the defendant's conduct shows a deliberate and outrageous disregard of the claimant's rights.[17]

3. RESTITUTION FOR BREACH OF CONTRACT[18]

(1) Restitution for breach of contract and unjust enrichment by subtraction

We are here concerned with remedies that reverse gains because the defendant has acquired them by breach of a contract with the claimant.

It is initially important to stress that remedies, such as the recovery of money had and received for total failure of consideration and a *quantum meruit*, which an innocent party can claim once it has validly terminated a contract for breach, are better viewed as based on unjust enrichment by subtraction, rather than being remedies for breach of contract.[19] Three main features of the law support this view. First, the claimant must have validly terminated the contract, before it can claim these remedies. If the remedies were simply for breach of contract, there would be no need for this; whereas on the view that the cause of action is unjust enrichment by subtraction this is readily explicable on the ground that it is only where the contract is terminated that the direct shift of wealth from the claimant to the defendant is invalidated. Indeed traditionally there has been a further restriction on the recovery of money in there must have been a total rather then merely a partial failure of consideration.[20]

Secondly, even though no breach is involved, the same restitutionary remedies governed by the same, or very similar, principles are available where the contract is unenforceable (for example, for lack of formality) or is void (for example, for uncertainty) or is merely anticipated. Prior to the

---

17 Law Commission Report No 247 *Aggravated, Exemplary and Restitutionary Damages* (1997) para 3.51 and Draft Bill, cl 12.
18 See generally Jones 'The Recovery of Benefits Gained From a Breach of Contract' (1983) 99 LQR 443; Farnsworth 'Your Loss or My Gain? The Dilemma of the Disgorgement Principle in Breach of Contract' (1985) 94 Yale LJ 1339; Birks 'Restitutionary Damages for Breach of Contract: *Snepp* and the Fusion of Law and Equity' [1987] LMCLQ 128; Stoljar 'Restitutionary Relief for Breach of Contract' (1989) 2 JCL 1; O'Dair 'Restitutionary Damages for Breach of Contract and The Theory of Efficient Breach: Some Reflections' (1993) 46(2) CLP 113; Weinrib 'Punishment and Disgorgement as Contract Remedies' (2003) 78 Chicago-Kent LR 55; Palmer *Law of Restitution* Vol I, pp 437–452; Beatson *The Use and Abuse of Unjust Enrichment* pp 15–17.
19 Birks *Introduction* p 334; 'Restitution and the Freedom of Contract' (1983) 36 CLP 141, 149 ff.
20 The requirement that the failure of consideration be total has come under attack both in decisions and from commentators: see Burrows *The Law of Restitution* (2nd edn, 2002) pp 327–331, 333–336.

Law Reform (Frustrated Contracts) Act 1943 this was also true of the remedies available where the contract was frustrated.

Thirdly, it is no restriction on the recovery of money paid in an action for money had and received that the defendant had made a good bargain. Say, for example, the claimant contracts to buy a car from the defendant for £900 and pays £100 in advance; the defendant fails to deliver the car: the market price is £700: the claimant can recover £100 in an action for money had and received.[1] This cannot be sensibly explained if the recovery is regarded as a restitutionary remedy *for* the breach of contract: for the breach cannot be regarded as a cause of the defendant's gain, since if there had been no breach, the defendant would still have made that gain from the contract. The same may also be the law regarding the claimant's *quantum meruit* claim. Certainly in *Lodder v Slowey*[2] on appeal from New Zealand, the Privy Council in assessing the claimant's *quantum meruit* considered it irrelevant that the defendant might have made a good bargain so that he would have retained some part of that gain if he had not broken the contract. Again, this aspect of the law is readily explicable if one regards such restitutionary remedies as reversing an unjust enrichment by subtraction rather than being remedies for breach of contract; for if the basis is not breach of contract, but rather an invalidation of the shift of wealth from the claimant to the defendant, there is no necessary reason why the value of the defendant's contractual counter-performance should be regarded as relevant.[3]

But if the remedies just discussed are not restitutionary remedies for breach of contract, does the law ever award restitution *for* breach of contract?

(2) The law, and analysis, prior to *Blake*

The traditional view, prior to *Attorney-General v Blake*,[4] was that there can be no restitution *for* breach of contract. So, for example, in the Scottish case of *Teacher v Calder*,[5] the defendant financier broke a contract to invest £15,000 in the claimant's timber business, and instead invested the same sum in a distillery. It was held that the claimant's damages were to

---

1   *Wilkinson v Lloyd* (1845) 7 QB 27.
2   [1904] AC 442. See also *Boomer v Muir* 24 P 2d 570 (1933).
3   This is not to deny that there may be other good reasons for thinking *Lodder v Slowey* incorrect: eg it can be strongly argued that, given 'subjective devaluation', the contract price should often be relevant to unjust enrichment by subtraction in assessing the services' value to the defendant.
4   [2001] 1 AC 268.
5   (1899) 1 F 39.

compensate for the loss to his business and were not concerned with a disgorgement of the much higher profits the defendant had gained from the distillery investment.

The same view applied in England. As Megarry V-C said in *Tito v Waddell (No 2)*:[6]

'... It is fundamental to all questions of damages that they are to compensate the plaintiff for his loss or injury by putting him as nearly as possible in the same position as he would have been in had he not suffered the wrong. The question is not one of making the defendant disgorge what he has saved by committing the wrong, but one of compensating the plaintiff.'

So in that case it was irrelevant that the defendants had saved themselves considerable expense by not replanting Ocean Island as they had covenanted to do. The claimant's loss was alone considered relevant, and as the islanders no longer intended to replant the island, and were therefore not entitled to the cost of cure, a small sum of damages for the trivial difference in value of the land was awarded.[7] It is important to stress that while the cost of cure may, in some cases, be equivalent to the expense saved, there is no necessary correlation between the two: for example, where cheaper materials have been used in building, the cost of replacing them is likely to be far greater than the expense the defendant saved. In a nutshell, cost of cure damages are indisputably compensatory and not restitutionary.

Similarly, in *Surrey CC v Bredero Homes Ltd*[8] the Court of Appeal refused to award restitutionary damages for a breach of contract whether assessed according to the full profits made by the breach by the contract-breaker or according to the expense saved by the contract-breaker in not seeking a release from its contractual undertaking. The claimant councils had sold two adjoining parcels of land to the defendant for the development of a housing estate. The defendant covenanted to develop the land in accordance with the scheme approved by the claimants. In breach of that covenant it built more houses on the site than under the approved scheme thereby making extra profit. Although aware of the breach, the claimants did not seek an injunction or specific performance but waited until the defendant had sold all the houses on the estate and then sought damages. Nominal damages only were awarded on the ground that the claimants had suffered no loss and

6   [1977] Ch 106 at 332.
7   An interim sum, which it was argued the claimants would have accepted for releasing the defendants from their obligation, was also rejected, [1977] Ch 106 at 319: see above, p 223.
8   [1993] 1 WLR 1361. See O'Dair 'Remedies for Breach of Contract: A Wrong Turn' [1993] RLR 31; Burrows 'No Restitutionary Damages for Breach of Contract' [1993] LMCLQ 453.

restitutionary damages were inappropriate because this was an action for ordinary common law damages for breach of contract: it did not involve either a tort or an invasion of proprietary rights or equitable damages.

The one clear exception – a 'solitary beacon' as Lord Nicholls referred to it in *Attorney-General v Blake*[9] – was the decision in *Wrotham Park Estate Co v Parkside Homes Ltd*.[10] The defendants had built a number of houses on land in breach of a restrictive covenant enforceable in equity by the claimant neighbouring landowner. Brightman J refused an injunction ordering the demolition of the houses but held that, although the claimant's land had not been diminished in value, the defendants were liable to pay substantial damages assessed using the 'hypothetical bargain' approach. That is, he asked what would have been a reasonable contract price for the claimant to have accepted for relaxation of the covenant. In working out the price, the major factor taken into account was the defendants' profits from the housing development. That emphasis on the defendants' profits, in addition to Brightman J's acceptance that it was artificial to pretend that the claimant would ever have relaxed the covenant, means that the damages are most naturally viewed as restitutionary, stripping the defendants of part (5%) of their profits, not compensatory. It is therefore not at all surprising that the authorities relied on by Brightman J were those examined above under restitution for a tort: *Whitwham v Westminster Brymbo Coal and Coke Co,* Denning LJ's judgment in *Strand Electric Engineering Co v Brisford Entertainments,* and *Penarth Dock Engineering Co Ltd v Pounds*.[11]

Looked at alongside the tort cases *Wrotham Park* can be easily justified. Not only was the breach apparently cynical but it also constituted a 'proprietary' wrong. Breach of a restrictive covenant, albeit an action for breach of contract, is enforceable by third parties, contrary to normal privity restrictions, and is closely akin to a 'proprietary tort'.

Was the traditional denial of restitution for breach of contract satisfactory? Several commentators argued that it was not. For example, Jones wrote, 'It is difficult to accept the justice of the result of such cases as *Tito v Waddell (No 2)*, where the defendant had saved himself considerable expense from failing to execute his promise but where the plaintiff's damages were trivial because he had suffered no "loss".'[12] Jones cited the Louisiana case of *City of New Orleans v Fireman's Charitable*

---

9   [2001] 1 AC 268 at 283.
10   [1974] 1 WLR 798. See also, subsequent to *Attorney-General v Blake*, the award of restitutionary damages for breach of a restrictive covenant, assessed applying the 'hypothetical bargain' approach, in *AMEC Developments Ltd v Jury's Hotel Management (UK) Ltd* (2000) 82 P & CR 286.
11   Brightman J also relied on Lord Shaw's dicta in the *Watson* case: above, pp 263, 379, n 7.
12   'The Recovery of Benefits Gained from a Breach of Contract' (1983) 99 LQR 443 at 459.

Association[13] as a further striking example of injustice. The defendant had contracted with the claimant to provide a fire-fighting service over a number of years and had received the full contract price. After the expiry of the contract, the claimant discovered that the defendant had not had available the number of men or horses or the footage of pipe promised under the contract. As the claimant had suffered no loss – for example, there was no averment that the defendant had failed to extinguish any fires because of the breach – no substantial damages were recovered, despite the fact that the defendant had saved itself over $40,000 by the breach of contract.

Birks, too, applying a cynical wrongdoing test, argued that restitution should be more widely available as a remedy for breach of contract.[14] As an example of cynical wrongdoing he pointed to *Tito v Waddell (No 2)*[15] as a case in which restitutionary damages, rather than nominal or a small sum of compensatory damages, should have been awarded. It was also a theme of Birks' work that sometimes the label 'breach of fiduciary duty' is merely acting as a mask for what are in reality already examples of restitution for breach of contract.[16]

Some expansion of restitution was also advocated by Beatson.[17] He saw restitution as 'in reality a monetised form of specific performance'. This is because if a person knows he will be stripped of his profits from breach there is no advantage for him in breaking the contract. Restitution is therefore justified in the rare cases where specific performance is available (or would have been available were it not now too late for such an order); most obviously where damages are inadequate. This theory has the attraction of building on existing principles of contract law. However, on closer inspection it is far from clear that one would want to apply principles of specific performance to restitution. For example, would general bars to specific performance, such as the bar to specific performance in contracts of personal service or the severe hardship bar, apply also to rule out restitution? And how would the theory apply to negative contractual promises where the prohibitory injunction is the primary remedy and damages are generally

---

13   9 So 486 (1891).
14   'Restitutionary Damages for Breach of Contract: Snepp and the Fusion of Law and Equity' [1987] LMCLQ 421.
15   [1977] Ch 106.
16   Birks relied on *Reading v Attorney-General* [1951] AC 507; *Reid-Newfoundland Co v Anglo-American Telegraph Ltd* [1912] AC 555; *Lake v Bayliss* [1974] 1 WLR 1073; and the dissenting judgment of Deane J in *Hospital Products Ltd v United States Surgical Corpn* (1985) 156 CLR 41.
17   *The Use and Abuse of Unjust Enrichment* (1991) pp 15–17. See similarly Maddaugh and McCamus *The Law of Restitution* (1st edn, 1990) pp 432–438 tentatively favouring restitution where compensatory damages are inadequate and yet equitable relief is not available.

regarded as inadequate? It would be odd if restitution were widely available for the breach of negative but not positive promises.

In contrast, Jackman suggested that there may be no need for restitution to protect the facilitative institution of contract because protection is sufficiently afforded by the standard award of expectation damages.[18] In other words, one of the justifications for awarding expectation damages is to protect the institution of contract. On his view, *Wrotham Park* was a rare and acceptable exception because it was not a pure contract case. Breach of a restrictive covenant constitutes the infringement of a proprietary right and falls to be treated like a 'proprietary tort'.

Support for the denial of restitution is also derived from the 'efficient breach' theory that it is more economically efficient to allow breach of contract than to deter it, as restitution would prima facie do.[19] But this sort of argument has been considered in detail and rejected elsewhere in this book,[20] and here it is sufficient to point out that restitutionary damages will not necessarily deter the defendant from an efficient breach – namely one where the profits to be made from breach exceed the claimant's expectation loss – because it will be in both parties' interests to negotiate the defendant's release from the contract. Say D contracts to make a machine part for C for £10,000, which C values at £13,000. X offers D £15,000 for that part. The fact that C may be entitled to restitution of say £5,000 for breach, would not deter the efficient result of D delivering the part to X, because it is in C's interest to accept between £3,000 and £5,000 to release D from the contract (because if D sticks to the contract, C will make only £3,000) and in D's interest to pay up to £5,000 to C to be released to transfer the part to X.

---

18 'Restitution for Wrongs' [1989] CLJ 302, 318–321. However, at the end of his analysis of breach of contract he very tentatively suggests that his secondary principle of the moral quality of the wrongdoing might justify restitution for cynical breach.
19 For this general theory, see Posner *Economic Analysis of Law* (6th edn, 2003) pp 118–126, 131–132. See also below, pp 472, n 11, 473, n 14.
20 Below, pp 473–475.

(3) *Attorney-General v Blake* and its aftermath

All previous writings and case law on restitution for breach of contract must now be read in the light of the fascinating and controversial decision of the House of Lords in *Attorney-General v Blake.*[1]

The notorious spy, George Blake, had written his autobiography in 1989. The publishers had agreed to pay him, as an advance against royalties, three sums of £50,000 on signing the contract, delivery of the manuscript and on publication. They had paid him £60,000 so that £90,000 was still owing. The Crown sought to stop him being paid that £90,000 and for that sum, instead, to be paid to the Crown. Their claims were brought in both public and private law. The Court of Appeal had upheld Sir Richard Scott V-C's decision at first instance that Blake was not acting in breach of fiduciary duty in publishing the book because there was no fiduciary duty owed by an ex-employee to the Crown. There was also no question of a breach of confidence claim succeeding because, by the time of publication, the information in the book was in the public domain and no longer confidential. But the Court of Appeal had decided that a public law claim should succeed: the Attorney-General, as an extension of his power to obtain injunctions in aid of the criminal law in furtherance of the public interest, was entitled to an order for payment so as to prevent Blake receiving money from his breach of the Official Secrets Act 1989.

The House of Lords firmly rejected that novel public law order on the ground that, without any established private law claim, it constituted a criminal confiscatory order that had not been expressly authorised by Parliament. Nevertheless the House of Lords (Lord Hobhouse dissenting) found in favour of the Crown not in public law but by revisiting *obiter dicta* of the Court of Appeal in relation to whether the Crown was entitled to the private law remedy of 'restitutionary damages' for breach of contract.

The argument that succeeded was based on the fact that, while there was no cause of action for breach of fiduciary duty or for breach of confidence, there was a cause of action for breach of contract. Blake had expressly undertaken at the beginning of his employment not to publish, during or after his employment with the Secret Service, any official

---

1 [2001] 1 AC 268. For a useful casenote see Fox 'Restitutionary Damages to Deter Breach of Contract' [2001] CLJ 33. See generally McKendrick 'Breach of Contract, Restitution for Wrongs, and Punishment' in *Commercial Remedies* (eds Burrows and Peel) ch 10. For a very hostile view of restitutionary damages for breach of contract, see Campbell and Harris 'In Defence of Breach: a Critique of Restitution and the Performance Interest' (2002) 22 Legal Studies 208 and Campbell and Wylie 'Ain't No Telling (Which Circumstances Are Exceptional)' [2003] CLJ 605.

information gained by him as a result of that employment. And, although the normal remedy for breach of contract is damages, compensating the claimant, this was regarded as an exceptional case where an account of profits, aimed at a disgorgement of the gains made from the breach of contract, could, and should, be awarded.

Lord Nicholls, giving the leading speech, elegantly drew together the cases awarding restitution for, for example, proprietary torts, intellectual property torts, and breach of fiduciary duty, and concluded that there was no good reason in principle why an account of profits (or as one might otherwise term it, although Lord Nicholls did not like this term,[2] 'restitutionary damages') should not be awarded for breach of contract. However, as to when such an order would be made, his Lordship's speech is rather thin on detail and relies heavily on this being at the discretion of the court. He stressed that an award would be exceptional and should only be made where the standard remedies for breach of contract of compensatory damages or specific performance or an injunction were inadequate. He said:

> 'An account of profits will be appropriate only in exceptional circumstances. Normally the remedies of damages, specific performance and injunction, coupled with the characterisation of some contractual obligations as fiduciary, will provide an adequate response to a breach of contract. It will be only in exceptional cases, where those remedies are inadequate, that any question of accounting for profits will arise. No fixed rules can be prescribed. The court will have regard to all the circumstances, including the subject matter of the contract, the purpose of the contractual provision which has been breached, the circumstances in which the breach occurred, the consequences of the breach and the circumstances in which relief is being sought. A useful general guide, although not exhaustive, is whether the plaintiff had a legitimate interest in preventing the defendant's profit-making activity and, hence, in depriving him of his profit.'[3]

Later in his speech his Lordship said that three facts which, individually, would *not* constitute a good reason for ordering an account of profits are:

> 'the fact that the breach was cynical and deliberate; the fact that the breach enabled the defendant to enter into a more profitable contract elsewhere; and the fact that by entering into a new and more profitable contract the defendant put it out of his power to perform his contract with the plaintiff.'[4]

---

2   See also, eg Doyle and Wright 'Restitutionary Damages – The Unnecessary Remedy?' (2001) 25 MULR 1.

3   [2001] 1 AC 268 at 285.

4   [2001] 1 AC 268 at 286.

It is obvious that phrases like 'inadequacy'[5] and 'legitimate interest' are open-ended and import a wide degree of judicial discretion. They could be used to justify an account of profits in a wide or a narrow range of cases. The crucial point, therefore, is that the House of Lords regarded restitution as an exceptional remedy reserved for rare cases. However, we must then ask, how exceptional and how rare?

The *Blake* case itself was unusual. What Blake had done came very close to being, but was not quite, a breach of fiduciary duty and a breach of confidence. Moreover, the courts had no sympathy with a notorious traitor whose book profits would to some extent have derived from his crime of breaking the Official Secrets Act. One might therefore be tempted to dismiss this case as so exceptional that it is a 'one-off' that will not be repeated. That would be a mistake. It is submitted that there will be a limited range of cases where an account of profits or restitutionary damages will be awarded for a breach of contract. Certainly after *Blake* one must bear this in mind as a possibility whenever one is concerned with remedies for breach of contract. So, for example, although perhaps not formally overruled, it is clear that the House of Lords did not like the decision in *Surrey County Council v Bredero*.[6] If similar facts were to reoccur after *Blake*, the defendant would surely be held liable to the claimant to account for some or all of the profits made from building the extra houses.[7] Although the loss to the claimant from the breach may have been minimal, *Blake* means that the claimant need not be limited to nominal damages. Again, one may draw on cases, which have traditionally been rationalised on the basis of a breach of fiduciary duty but which Lord Nicholls indicated are, in substance, examples of an account of profits being granted for breach of contract. For example, in *Reid-Newfoundland Co v Anglo-American Telegraph Co Ltd*[8] the defendant company agreed not to transmit any commercial messages over a particular telegraph wire except for the claimant. The Privy Council held the defendant liable to account for the profits made in breach of that

---

5   It is noteworthy that the inadequacy referred to is in respect of specific remedies as well as damages. But if compensatory damages are considered inadequate, and profits have been made from a past breach, it is likely to be rare for an injunction or specific performance to be 'adequate' (given that they can only ensure that there is no future or continuing breach).

6   [1993] 1 WLR 1361. See above, pp 397–398.

7   This derives support from *Lane v O'Brien Homes Ltd* [2004] EWHC 303 (QB) where the defendant developer built four houses, instead of three, in breach of a collateral contract with the claimant seller of the land. Applying the *Wrotham Park* case, David Clarke J upheld an award of damages of £150,000 based on the defendant's estimated profit from building the extra house of £280,000.

8   [1912] AC 555. See also *Lake v Bayliss* [1974] 1 WLR 1073 (breach of a contract to sell land); and *CMS Dolphin Ltd v Simonet* [2001] 2 BCLC 704 in which Lawrence Collins J said that, had an account of profits for breach of fiduciary duty not been available, he would have awarded an account of profits for breach of the contractual duty of fidelity in line with *Blake*.

agreement. Similarly, Lord Nicholls indicated that the award of damages in *British Motor Trade Association v Gilbert*,[9] for breach of a covenant not to resell a car within a certain period of time, was in reality concerned to strip the defendant of the profits he had made by breaking that covenant.

Again, although in a difficult passage Lord Nicholls seemed to regard this as rather different,[10] restitutionary damages could provide a satisfactory solution to the 'skimped performance' situation exemplified by *Tito v Waddell*.[11] After *Blake*, it would be possible to award the claimant the cost the defendant saved by the breach of contract.

In contrast, it is unlikely that, where the assessment of expectation damages is straightforward, the courts would wish to strip away the gains made by a defendant breaking one contract in order to enter into another more lucrative contract. Indeed, as we have seen, Lord Nicholls expressly said that such a fact alone would not justify an account of profits. To lock parties into less profitable contracts would be inconsistent with the general approach in English law whereby specific performance is not the primary remedy for breach of contract.

That *Blake* was far from being a one-off has been shown by *Esso Petroleum Co Ltd v Niad*[12] in which Sir Andrew Morritt V-C decided that the claimants were entitled, at their election, to compensatory damages or an account of profits or a 'restitutionary remedy' for breach of contract. Niad, who owned a petrol station, had entered into a pricing agreement (called 'Pricewatch') with Esso who supplied Niad with petrol. In breach of that agreement, Niad charged higher prices to its customers than had been agreed. This in turn meant that Niad was given 'price support' by Esso to which Niad was not entitled: that is, Niad paid less to Esso for its petrol than it would have done had Esso known that Niad was over-charging its customers. Applying *Blake*, Morritt V-C held that Esso was here entitled to an account of profits aimed at stripping away the gains Niad had made from breaking the contract. Compensatory damages were inadequate because it was almost impossible for Esso to establish that sales had been lost as a result of the breach by Niad. The breach undermined the whole Pricewatch scheme that Esso had agreed

---

9   [1951] 2 All ER 641.

10   [2001] 1 AC 268 at 286. Lord Nicholls indicated that 'expense saved' is not within the scope of an account of profits as ordinarily understood. He suggested that 'skimped performance' should lead to damages based on the difference between the price paid and the value of the services received or contracted-for. It is unclear whether he had in mind expectation (or reliance) damages for breach of contract; or restitution for (partial) failure of consideration subject to counter-restitution.

11   See above, p 397.

12   [2001] All ER (D) 324 (Nov). See also the comments of the Supreme Court of Canada in *Bank of America Canada v Mutual Trust Co* [2002] SCC 43 to the effect that restitutionary damages for breach of contract can be awarded but not where this would discourage efficient breach.

with all retailers in the area. Esso had complained to Niad on several occasions. And Esso had a legitimate interest in preventing Niad from profiting from its breach. Alternatively Morritt V-C said that Esso was entitled to a 'restitutionary remedy' for the amount of the price support that, in breach of contract, it had obtained from Esso.

Although the distinction between an account of profits and the so-called 'restitutionary remedy' is a difficult one to draw on these facts (ie it is not clear what the difference is between the two) the great importance of the case is that it shows *Blake* being applied to a commercial contract far removed from the peculiar facts of *Blake* itself.

The most important case on this issue since *Blake* has been *Experience Hendrix LLC v PPX Enterprises Inc.*[13] This case followed from a settlement in 1973 of a dispute between the rock star Jimi Hendrix and the defendant record company. By the terms of that contractual settlement, it was agreed that certain master tapes could be used for recording purposes by the defendant but that the rest should be delivered up to Jimi Hendrix. In breach of that contract, the defendant used master tapes that should have been delivered up. The claimant, the estate of Jimi Hendrix, sought damages or an account of profits for that breach of contract. *Attorney-General v Blake* was in part applied and in part distinguished.

Blake was applied in holding that the claimant was entitled to damages based not on compensating the claimant's loss but on what was a reasonable sum taking into account the gains made by the defendant from its use of the forbidden master tapes. Although the Court of Appeal was not required to assess that reasonable sum, Mance LJ, with whom Peter Gibson LJ and Hooper J agreed, thought that one-third of the defendant's royalties on the retail selling price of records made from the forbidden tapes would probably be an appropriate reasonable sum. Although there are passages where the judges slipped into referring to these damages as 'compensation', the better view is that they are restitutionary (not compensatory) damages concerned to strip some of the defendant's profits. This is in line not only with counsel for the claimant's starting-point that the claimant was not seeking compensation for loss because that was too speculative to assess but also with the acceptance that the claimant would not have agreed to the defendant's use of those master tapes.[14] It is also consistent with the judges' emphasis on the profits made by the defendant in fixing the reasonable sum and

---

13   [2003] EWCA Civ 323, [2003] 1 All ER (Comm) 830. For a helpful case-note, see Graham 'Restitutionary Damages: The Anvil Struck' (2004) 120 LQR 26.
14   See esp Peter Gibson LJ in [2003] EWCA Civ 323, [2003] 1 All ER (Comm) 830 at para 57.

with their regarding themselves as applying *Wrotham Park Estates v Parkside Homes*. So, it is submitted that, to the extent that restitutionary not compensatory damages were awarded, *Blake* was being applied. As Mance LJ said, '[I]f Lord Nicholls' general guide is a useful starting point in respect of an account of profits, it must be all the more so in respect of the lesser claim to a reasonable sum taking account of the defendant's profitable infringement.'[15] And in the words of Peter Gibson LJ:

> 'In my judgment, because (1) there has been a deliberate breach by PPX of its contractual obligations for its own reward, (2) the claimant would have difficulty in establishing financial loss therefrom, and (3) the claimant has a legitimate interest in preventing PPX's profit-making activity carried out in breach of PPX's contractual obligations, the present case is a suitable one (as envisaged by Lord Nicholls) in which damages for breach of contract may be measured by the benefits gained by the wrongdoer from the beach. To avoid injustice I would require PPX to make a reasonable payment in respect of the benefit it has gained.'[16]

But *Blake* was also distinguished in the sense that an account of profits, stripping the defendant of *all* its gains made from the breach of contract, was not awarded. The Court of Appeal stressed that the facts of this case were not so exceptional as those in *Blake*. In particular, although the defendant knew it was doing something which it had contracted not to do and to which the claimant would not have consented, the defendant was not close to being a fiduciary to the claimant and no issue analogous to national security was involved. The relationship was a straightforward commercial one. The Court of Appeal also referred to *Esso v Niad Petroleum* without disapproval but distinguished that decision – which involved a commercial relationship – on the ground that the contractual obligation broken had been central to the claimant's whole mode of operation and integrity which was not the position on the facts of this case.

In conclusion, it is tentatively suggested, in the light of *Blake* and subsequent cases, that an account of profits or restitutionary damages are an appropriate remedy for a breach of contract where two factors are present. First, the breach of contract must be cynical, deliberately calculated to make gains. It is this that triggers the courts' wish to deter the breach by stripping the gains. The breach was cynical in *Blake*, *Esso v Niad Petroleum* and *Experience Hendrix LLC v PPX Enterprises Inc*. The same can be said, although restitution was refused, of the earlier cases of *Tito v Waddell* and *Surrey County Council v Bredero Homes*. But, as Lord Nicholls

---

15   [2003] EWCA Civ 323, [2003] 1 All ER (Comm) 830 at para 35.
16   [2003] EWCA Civ 323, [2003] 1 All ER (Comm) 830 at para 58.

stressed, this is not a sufficient condition. This is because there are many cynical breaches (for example, where a party to a commercial contract of sale breaks it in order to enter into a more lucrative contract with someone else) that the law does not wish to deter.[17] The second factor that must also be present, therefore, is that normal compensatory damages are 'inadequate' in the sense that difficulties of assessment, or bars to the recovery of certain types of damages, mean that compensatory damages will not put the claimant into as good a position as if the contract had been performed. In other words, compensatory damages will not properly protect the claimant's contractual expectations. In cases like *Surrey County Council v Bredero Homes* and *Tito v Waddell* and *Blake* the claimants had non-financial expectations which would not be protected by compensatory damages; their interests were in protecting the environment or in protecting national security. And in *Esso v Niad* and *Experience Hendrix*, while the claimants entered into the contract for financial reasons, the assessment of damages compensating their financial losses would be highly problematic and prone to error.

Having decided that restitution is to be awarded, the courts then have a discretion (although clear principles should, in time, develop) as to the quantum of that restitution.[18] They may strip all the defendant's gains made by the breach of contract or merely a proportion.[19] Relevant factors in exercising that discretion will be the degree of skill and time the defendant has expended in securing the profit and also the degree of moral blameworthiness attached to the particular cynical breach. The mechanisms open to the court to exercise this discretion on quantum are either the making of an allowance for skill and effort in the context of a claim for an account of profits; or the fixing of a reasonable sum (that the parties would supposedly have agreed to in a 'hypothetical bargain') in respect of restitutionary damages.

---

17 See, eg *AB Corpn v CD Company, The Sine Nomine* [2002] 1 Lloyd's Rep 805 in which an account of profits was refused by arbitrators for the withdrawal, and use of, a ship in breach of a charterparty.
18 See above, p 374.
19 This may be reflected by an 'expense saved' award of restitutionary damages.

Chapter 18

Punitive damages

Punitive or exemplary damages are damages whose purpose is to punish
the defendant for his or her wrongful conduct.[1] In *Broome v Cassell*[2]
Lord Hailsham said that he preferred the term 'exemplary damages' to
'punitive damages' as better expressing the policy of the law. English
courts have subsequently followed Lord Hailsham's preference. But in its
Report on this area in 1997,[3] the Law Commission recommended that
the pre-*Broome v Cassell* terminology of 'punitive damages' was clearer
and more straightforward and did not accept that this label deflected
attention from the deterrence and disapproval aims of such damages. As
the Law Commission said, 'When one uses the term "punishment" in the
criminal law, one does not thereby indicate that deterrence is not an
important aim.'[4] Although nothing of substantive importance should
turn on which label is adopted, the Law Commission's approach is
persuasive and the term 'punitive damages' is therefore preferred in this
chapter and book.

The fascinating and crucial question of policy is whether punitive
damages are justified but, before examining that, we must look at the
details of the present law.

1. ARE PUNITIVE DAMAGES AWARDED FOR BREACH
OF CONTRACT?

As laid down in *Addis v Gramophone Co Ltd*,[5] no punitive damages can be
awarded for breach of contract. There the claimant had been wrongfully

---

1   See generally Law Commission Report No 247 (1997) *Aggravated, Exemplary and Restitutionary
    Damages*. Of the law on compensatory damages examined above in Part One, the form of
    damages and foreign currency awards (ch 8), awards of interest (ch 14) and limitation periods
    (ch 15) are also relevant to punitive damages.
2   [1972] AC 1027 at 1073.
3   *Aggravated, Exemplary and Restitutionary Damages* (1997) Report No 247, para 5.39.
4   *Aggravated, Exemplary and Restitutionary Damages* (1997) Report No 247, para 5.39.
5   [1909] AC 488.

dismissed. The House of Lords restricted damages to his pecuniary loss and refused to award any damages for the harsh manner in which he had been treated.

The same approach has been applied in several subsequent cases. In *Perera v Vandiyar*,[6] for example, the claimant was the tenant of the defendant's flat and in an attempt to get rid of him, the defendant cut off the supply of gas and electricity to the flat, leaving the claimant without alternative means of heat or light. A week later the gas and electricity supply was restored as a result of an interlocutory judgment granted by the county court, and the tenant was able to return. In an action for damages for breach of the defendant's covenant of quiet enjoyment the trial judge awarded inter alia, £25 punitive damages, but the Court of Appeal overturned this; since damages were here being given for breach of contract (and indeed no tort had been committed) no punitive damages could be awarded. Similarly in *Kenny v Preen*,[7] which also involved the breach by a landlord of his covenant of quiet enjoyment, punitive damages were refused, Pearson LJ saying, 'As the claim was only in contract and not tort, punitive or exemplary damages could not be properly awarded.'[8]

On the other hand in *McMillan v Singh*,[9] where again a landlord evicted a tenant, punitive damages of £250 were awarded. Although parts of Sir John Arnold's judgment seem to indicate that those damages were being given for breach of the covenant of quiet enjoyment, they are better viewed as being given for the tort of trespass or nuisance. This was not only because of his reliance solely on tort cases, but also because no mention was made of the traditional rule barring such damages for breach of contract.

Three relatively recent developments suggest that the rule in *Addis* that punitive damages can never be awarded for breach of contract may require reconsideration in the near future.

The first was the decision of the House of Lords in *Attorney-General v Blake*[10] to the effect that restitution, through an account of profits, can be awarded, albeit exceptionally, for breach of contract. This has been fully discussed in the previous chapter. Although punishment is a more extreme remedial response to a wrong than restitution, the importance of

6   [1953] 1 WLR 672.
7   [1963] 1 QB 499.
8   [1963] 1 QB 499 at 513. Stephenson LJ cited these words in *Guppys (Bridport) Ltd v Brookling and James* (1984) 269 Estates Gazette 846 at 942. See also *Drane v Evangelou* [1978] 1 WLR 455.
9   (1985) 17 HLR 120. See also *Warner v Clark* (1984) 134 NLJ 763 (CA dubiously finding a tort justification – inducing breach of contract – for punitive damages awarded at trial for breach of contract).
10 [2001] 1 AC 268.

Blake for punitive damages is its recognition that, exceptionally, a substantial monetary remedy that is non-compensatory is appropriate for a breach of contract.

Secondly, there has been the decision of the House of Lords in *Kuddus v Chief Constable of Leicestershire Constabulary*[11] removing the former 'cause of action' restriction on punitive damages for torts. This is discussed below. Although their Lordships did not mention breach of contract, the removal of the 'cause of action' test for torts clearly leads on to the question whether it is satisfactory to rule out punitive damages because the cause of action is breach of contract rather than tort.

Thirdly, as is discussed below, punitive damages have recently been awarded for the first time in Canada for breach of contract by the Supreme Court in *Whiten v Pilot Insurance Co.*[12]

2.   WHEN ARE PUNITIVE DAMAGES AWARDED FOR TORTS?

(1) The three categories

The situations in which punitive damages can be awarded for torts were laid down in Lord Devlin's classic speech in *Rookes v Barnard.*[13] The case concerned the tort of intimidation, and at first instance Sachs J had ruled that punitive damages could be awarded. The House of Lords overturned that ruling.

The general tenor of Lord Devlin's speech, with which the other Law Lords agreed, was that awarding punitive damages tends to confuse unsatisfactorily the role of the civil and criminal law and that, while precedent and statute prevent their judicial abolition, the ambit of punitive damages should be restricted. Having extensively reviewed the relevant authorities, and having stressed that aggravated damages are compensatory and should therefore not be confused, as they often have been, with punitive damages,[14] Lord Devlin laid down the three sole categories in which punitive damages can be awarded: first, where there is '... oppressive or unconstitutional action by the servants of the government';[15] secondly, where 'the defendant's conduct has been calculated by him to make a profit for himself which may well exceed the

---

11   [2001] UKHL 29, [2002] 2 AC 122. See below, pp 417–418.
12   [2003] SCC 18. See below, p 429.
13   [1964] AC 1129
14   Above, p 339.
15   [1964] AC 1129 at 1226.

compensation payable to the plaintiff';[16] and thirdly, where expressly authorised by statute. As the facts of this case did not fall within any of these categories, Lord Devlin concluded that no punitive damages should have been awarded. Lord Devlin's speech was later confirmed by the House of Lords in *Cassell & Co Ltd v Broome*[17] following an attempt by the Court of Appeal in the case to outflank that restrictive approach. It is therefore now beyond argument that, applying the present law, for a claimant to be awarded punitive damages the tortious conduct must fall within one of the three categories. That, of course, is not the same as saying that the three categories are justified. It is submitted that they are not, as will be explained later when considering reform.[18]

(a) 'Oppressive, arbitrary or unconstitutional actions by servants of the government'

In *Cassell v Broome* it was made clear that 'servants of the government' is to be widely construed. As Lord Diplock said, 'It would embrace all persons purporting to exercise powers of government, central or local, conferred upon them by statute or at common law by virtue of the official status or employment which they hold.'[19] But the defendant must be exercising governmental power and in *AB v South West Water Services Ltd*[20] it was felt that that constituted a different idea in this context than in relation to whether a decision can be judicially reviewed or whether a body is an emanation of the state for the purposes of European Community law. The actions of a nationalised corporation in contaminating drinking water and failing to warn the public properly of this were therefore held not to fall within the first category.

In *Rookes v Barnard* Lord Devlin instanced three eighteenth-century cases within this category. The best known are the two concerning the printing of the *North Briton*.[1] In *Wilks v Wood*[2] the claimant's house in which it was alleged that the paper had been printed was searched under an illegal general warrant issued by the Secretary of State. In the claimant's action for trespass, it was held that punitive damages could be

---

16 [1964] AC 1129.
17 [1972] AC 1027
18 See below, p 424.
19 [1972] AC 1027 at 1130.
20 [1993] QB 507, overruled on other grounds by *Kuddus v Chief Constable of Leicestershire Constabulary* [2001] UKHL 29, [2002] 2 AC 122. See also *Virgo Fidelis Senior School v Boyle* [2004] IRLR 268, EAT (school governors not acting as servants of government). Cf *Bradford City Metropolitan Council v Arora* [1991] 2 QB 507 where the public/private divide drawn for judicial review purposes was also rejected but so as to *award* punitive damages.
1 The third was *Benson v Frederick* (1766) 3 Burr 1845.
2 (1763) Lofft 1.

awarded. Similarly, in *Huckle v Money*[3] the claimant was held entitled to punitive damages for false imprisonment, having been detained for six hours by a King's Messenger on suspicion of having printed the *North Briton*.

But until relatively recently this first category was otherwise more or less devoid of examples and one could be forgiven for regarding it as something of a dead letter. The 1980s, however, saw a dramatic turnabout, with this category finding its sharpest ever cutting-edge in actions against the police. So in *White v Metropolitan Police Comr*[4] (which was one of the few cases in which Lord Devlin's first category was actually referred to) £20,000 punitive damages were awarded to each of two claimants for false imprisonment, assault and malicious prosecution by several police officers. In *George v Metropolitan Police Comr*[5] £2,000 punitive damages were awarded for trespass and assault where police officers had unlawfully searched the claimant's house looking for her son and had kicked and hit her. In *Connor v Chief Constable of Cambridgeshire*[6] there was an award of £500 punitive damages for 'assault' where a police officer had without justification hit the claimant over the head with his truncheon in the course of crowd trouble outside the entrance to a football ground and had persisted in a baseless defence to the claimant's action. And in *Makanjuola v Metropolitan Police Comr*[7] punitive damages of £2,000 were awarded for trespass to the person and intimidation where a police officer had sexually assaulted the claimant. Significantly this rebirth of the first category coincided with increased public criticism of the police, and a widespread belief that police powers are often abused at the expense of civil liberties.

Significant cases in the 1990s, falling within this first category, included *Treadaway v Chief Constable of West Midlands*[8] where, in addition to £10,000 compensatory damages, £40,000 punitive damages were awarded to the claimant who had had a confession extracted from him by police officers placing a bin bag over his head; and *Thompson v Metropolitan Police Comr*[9] where, as we shall see, £15,000 punitive damages

---

3   (1763) 2 Wils 205.
4   (1982) Times, 24 April. This and the two following cases (but not the third where vicarious liability was denied) also show that vicarious liability may apply where punitive damages are being claimed, presumably on the ground that the employer deserves punishment and can best prevent future misconduct. See Atiyah *Vicarious Liability* (1967) pp 433–437; Law Commission Report No 247 (1997) paras 4.102–4.105, 5.209–5.230.
5   (1984) Times, 31 March.
6   (1984) Times, 11 April. See also *Holden v Chief Constable of Lancashire* [1987] QB 380.
7   (1989) Times, 8 August.
8   (1994) Times, October 25.
9   [1998] QB 498: see below, p 422.

was substituted by the Court of Appeal for a jury award of £200,000 for false imprisonment and assault by the police.

(b) 'The defendant's conduct has been calculated by him to make a profit for himself which may well exceed the compensation payable to the plaintiff'

This category, which until the 1980s was the only really important one of the three, was the focus of attention in *Cassell v Broome*.[10] The claimant, a distinguished retired naval officer, brought an action for libel against two publishers of a book presented as an authentic account of a war-time disaster when a British convoy had been destroyed. The jury had awarded the claimant £15,000 compensatory damages and £25,000 punitive damages. The defendants appealed against the award of punitive damages, but the House of Lords upheld it as falling within Lord Devlin's second category. In construing Lord Devlin's words it was held that while, on the one hand, the fact that the tortious act was committed in the course of carrying on a profit-making business is not sufficient to bring a case within the second category, on the other hand it is not necessary for the defendant actually to have calculated in arithmetical form that the profit to be made from the tort would exceed the damages and costs to which he would make himself liable. Indeed, as Lord Hailsham said, 'The defendant may calculate that the plaintiff will not sue at all.'[11] So, according to his Lordship, what is required is:

'(i) knowledge that what is proposed to be done is against the law or a reckless disregard whether what is proposed to be done is illegal or legal and (ii) a decision to carry on doing it because the prospects of material advantage outweigh the prospects of material loss.'[12]

In the words of Lord Morris:

'The situation contemplated is where someone faces up to the possibility of having to pay damages for doing something which may be held to have been wrong but where nevertheless he deliberately carried out his plan because he thinks it will work out satisfactorily for him. He is prepared to hurt somebody because he thinks he may well gain by so doing even allowing for the risk that he may be made to pay damages.'[13]

---

10 [1972] AC 1027. See also *Manson v Associated Newspapers Ltd* [1965] 1 WLR 1038; *John v Mirror Group Newspapers Ltd* [1997] QB 586.
11 [1972] AC 1027 at 1079.
12 [1972] AC 1027.
13 [1972] AC 1027 at 1094.

Applying these approaches to the facts, punitive damages were justified because there was clear evidence that the defendants, in the knowledge that they might be defaming the claimant, were still prepared to sell the book in its sensational form.

A crucial additional point made by Lord Diplock is that damages under this second category are not concerned merely to reverse the defendant's unjust enrichment. He said:

'It ... may be a blunt instrument to prevent unjust enrichment by unlawful acts. But to restrict the damages recoverable to the gain made by the defendant if it exceeded the loss caused to the plaintiff, would leave a defendant contemplating an unlawful act with the certainty that he had nothing to lose to balance against the chance that the plaintiff might never sue him, or if he did, might fail in the hazards of litigation. It is only if there is a prospect that the damages may exceed the defendant's gain that the social purpose of this category is achieved – to teach a wrongdoer that tort does not pay.'[14]

Apart from libel, the main use of this second category has been in actions by tenants against landlords for wrongful harassment or eviction founded on the torts of trespass or nuisance. In *Drane v Evangelou*,[15] for example, the jury had awarded £1,000 damages for the landlord's wrongful eviction of his tenant, and the Court of Appeal held that this award was justified as including some punitive damages[16] for the tort of trespass under the second category. Both Lord Denning and Goff LJ cited that part of Lord Devlin's judgment where he said:

'This category is not confined to moneymaking in the strict sense. It extends to cases in which the defendant is seeking to gain at the expense of the plaintiff some object – perhaps some property which he covets – which either he could not obtain at all or not obtain except at a price greater than he wants to put down.'[17]

And Lord Denning said:

'... this category includes cases of unlawful eviction of a tenant. The landlord seeks to gain possession at the expense of the tenant, so as to keep or get a rent higher than that awarded by the rent tribunal, or to get possession from a tenant who is protected by the Rent Acts.'[18]

---

14 [1972] AC 1027 at 1130.
15 [1978] 2 All ER 437. See also *Devonshire and Smith v Jenkins* [1979] LAG Bull 114; *McMillan v Singh* (1985) 17 HLR 120; *Millington v Duffy* (1984) 17 HLR 232; *Asghar v Ahmed* (1985) 17 HLR 25; *Ramdath v Daley* [1993] 1 EGLR 82 (also illustrating the point that there can be no punitive damages under this category where the defendant is acting for another's benefit).
16 Confusingly Lord Denning appears to use the term 'exemplary damages' to describe an award of both compensatory and exemplary damages.
17 [1964] AC 1129 at 1227.
18 [1978] 1 WLR 455 at 459.

Similarly in *Guppys (Bridport) Ltd v Brookling and James*[19] landlords had set about converting a building occupied by tenants into self-contained flats. They had no intention of offering alternative accommodation to the tenants and wanted to be rid of them as soon as possible. During the building work they removed all the internal sanitary and washing facilities, discontinued the supply of water to the external toilets and cut off the electricity. The trial judge awarded £1,000 'exemplary damages' to each of the two claimant tenants. The Court of Appeal upheld this as awarded not for the tort of trespass, which was here difficult to make out, but rather for the tort of nuisance. The case fell within Lord Devlin's second category as the claimants were content to ignore the rights of the tenants in order to pursue their own profit-seeking alterations. It should be added, however, that the trial judge and the Court of Appeal were almost certainly accepting that part of the £1,000 included compensatory damages: if so, to refer to it all as 'exemplary damages' was unnecessarily confusing.[20]

Analogously, in *Design Progression Ltd v Thurloe Properties Ltd*[1] punitive damages were awarded against a landlord for breach of its statutory duty under the Landlord and Tenant Act 1988, s 1(3) in failing to give a decision, within a reasonable time, on a tenant's application for a licence to assign. Peter Smith J explained that, following the removal of the cause of action test in *Kuddus v Chief Constable of Leicestershire Constabulary*,[2] it was possible for punitive damages to be awarded for breach of statutory duty under the 1988 Act. And here the facts fell within the second category in *Rookes v Barnard* because the landlord had behaved in a cynical way designed to frustrate the tenant's legitimate expectation of being able to assign the premises. The landlord's aim had been to force the tenant out of the premises and then to be able itself to rent the premises out at a higher rent. In addition to compensatory damages (the amount of which was not fixed but appeared to be approximately £111,000), the judge awarded £25,000 punitive damages. He made clear that this went beyond any profit that the landlord had actually made and was designed to deter similar conduct by the landlord in the future and to mark the court's disapproval of its past conduct.[3]

Finally punitive damages have occasionally been awarded under this second category for tortious interference with the claimant's business.

---

19 (1983) 269 Estates Gazette 846.
20 See also above, n 16.
1   [2004] EWHC 324 (Ch), [2004] 10 EG 184 (CS).
2   [2001] UKHL 29, [2002] 2 AC 122. See below, pp 417–418.
3   Although not mentioned by the judge, the breach of statutory duty can be classified as a statutory tort.

The case Lord Devlin principally relied on within his second category –
Bell v Midland Rly Co[4] – can be regarded as an early example of this.
There the defendants had wrongfully prevented trains running to the
claimant's wharf so as to divert trade to themselves. A jury award of
£1,000 was upheld, Willes J saying:

> '... if ever there was a case in which the jury were warranted in awarding exemplary
> damages, this is that case. The defendants have committed a grievous wrong ... for the
> purpose of destroying the plaintiff's business and securing gain for themselves.'[5]

More controversially in *Messenger Newspaper Group Ltd v National Graphical
Association*[6] punitive damages were awarded against a trade union under
the second category for the torts of interference with business by
unlawful means, intimidation and public and private nuisance, committed in the course of a dispute over the claimants' refusal to operate a
closed shop. But this is hard to justify given that the defendants were not
directly seeking any material gain from their conduct. Nor does Caulfield
J satisfactorily overcome the objection, considered below, that the NGA
had already been heavily fined for its conduct, so that the award of
punitive damages amounted to double punishment.

(c) Express authorisation by statute

In *Rookes v Barnard* Lord Devlin mentioned the Reserve and Auxiliary
Forces (Protection of Civilian Interests) Act 1951, s 13(2), as a statutory
provision expressly authorising punitive damages. There are no other
clear examples. Most discussion has centred on whether what was
formerly the Copyright Act 1956, s 17(3), and is now the Copyright,
Designs and Patents Act 1988, s 97(2), authorises punitive damages.

Prior to *Rookes v Barnard* the Court of Appeal in *Williams v Settle*[7] held
that punitive damages could be awarded for breach of copyright either at
common law or as authorised by what is now the Copyright, Designs and
Patents Act 1988, s 97(2). There the defendant, a professional
photographer, following the murder of the claimant's father-in-law, sold
to the Press certain photographs taken by him at the claimant's wedding
which were then published in two national newspapers. Punitive
damages of £1,000 were awarded in the claimant's action for breach of
copyright. However, in *Rookes v Barnard* Lord Devlin left open whether

---

4   (1861) 10 CBNS 287.
5   (1861) 10 CBNS 287 at 307.
6   [1984] IRLR 397, noted Jones and Morris 'Picketing, The Closed Shop, and Enforcement of
    the Employment Acts' (1985) 14 ILJ 46. See also *Warner v Islip* (1984) 134 NLJ 763 (inducing
    breach of contract).
7   [1960] 1 WLR 1072.

punitive damages can be awarded under what is now the Copyright, Designs and Patents Act 1988, s 97(2)[8] and said that the decision in *Williams v Settle* was more easily justified as an example of aggravated rather than punitive damages.[9] In *Cassell v Broome* Lord Hailsham agreed with Lord Devlin that the question was an open one,[10] but Lord Kilbrandon considered that what is now s 97(2) did not authorise punitive damages.[11] Similarly, in *Beloff v Pressdram Ltd*[12] Ungoed-Thomas J considered that, since the subsection is directed to providing 'effective relief' for the claimant, it empowers the award of purely compensatory and not punitive damages. Again in *Redrow Homes Ltd v Bett Brothers plc*,[13] Lord Clyde suggested, without having to decide, that additional damages under s 97(2) were 'more probably' aggravated rather than punitive damages.[14] It should be clarified that, after the decision in *Kuddus v Chief Constable of Leicestershire Constabulary*[15] – which, as we shall see below, has removed the cause of action test for punitive damages – there is no bar to awarding punitive damages for the statutory tort of breach of copyright irrespective of s 97(2). But for claimants, the advantage of establishing that s 97(2) does authorise punitive damages is that it would obviate the need to show that the facts fall within one of Lord Devlin's (other) two categories (most obviously, the cynical profit-making category).

(2) Restrictions beyond the three categories

Punitive damages will not necessarily be awarded just because the case falls within one of the three categories. After discussing the demise of a former restriction, we discuss six restrictions beyond the need for the case to fall within one of the three categories.

(a) Demise of the 'cause of action test'

Prior to the decision of the House of Lords in *Kuddus v Chief Constable of Leicestershire Constabulary*[16] the most important additional restriction was

---

8   [1964] AC 1129 at 1225.
9   [1964] AC 1129 at 1229.
10 [1972] AC 1027 at 1080.
11 [1972] AC 1027 at 1134.
12 [1973] 1 All ER 241 at 265. But the words 'effective relief' in the Copyright Act 1956, s 17(3) have not been repeated in the Copyright, Designs and Patents Act 1988, s 97(2).
13 [1999] 1 AC 197, HL (Sc). The decision of their Lordships was that, as a matter of statutory interpretation, additional damages under the Copyright, Designs and Patents Act 1988, s 97(2) could not be added to an account of profits as opposed to an award of damages.
14 In *Nichols Advanced Vehicle Systems Inc v Rees* [1979] RPC 127 it was held that damages should be awarded under what is now the Copyright, Designs and Patents Act 1988, s 97(2) but without clarifying whether punitive or not. See also *ZYX Music GmbH v King* [1995] 3 All ER 1.
15 [2001] UKHL 29, [2002] 2 AC 122.
16 [2001] UKHL 29, [2002] 2 AC 122.

the 'cause of action test', which had been laid down by the Court of Appeal in *AB v South West Water Services Ltd*.[17] It was decided in the latter case that *Cassell v Broome* required that the tort be one for which punitive damages had been awarded prior to *Rookes v Barnard* in 1964. This was thought to be the view not only of Lords Hailsham and Diplock but also of Lords Wilberforce and Kilbrandon and, possibly, Lord Reid and therefore of the majority of the seven Law Lords sitting in that case.[18] There could therefore be no award of punitive damages for the tort of public nuisance in supplying contaminated drinking water to inhabitants of Camelford, Cornwall, since public nuisance was not a tort for which punitive damages had been awarded prior to *Rookes v Barnard*. The result of the decision was that punitive damages were only available for malicious prosecution, false imprisonment, assault and battery, defamation, trespass to land or to goods, private nuisance and tortious interference with business. Other torts, such as negligence, deceit, misfeasance in public office and unlawful discrimination, failed the cause of action test and did not qualify for the award of punitive damages.

In *Kuddus* the House of Lords held unanimously that the cause of action test should be removed. It was noted that the need to search through old authorities to find a pre-1964 award of punitive damages for a particular tort was unfortunate, especially as, since aggravated and punitive damages have only been clearly distinguished since *Rookes v Barnard* itself, it may well be difficult to determine the characterisation of an award of damages in an older case. Argument was not heard on the wider question of whether punitive damages should be retained at all, although three of their Lordships expressed their opinion on the subject.[19]

The demise of the cause of action test in *Kuddus* means that, subject to what is said below about Euro-torts and infringement of human rights, punitive damages can now be awarded for any tort (provided the facts fall within one of the three categories of *Rookes v Barnard*).

17 [1993] 1 All ER 609. The state of the law had previously been uncertain: see, inter alia, *Cassell v Broome* [1972] AC 1027 at 1076, 1130–1131 (Lords Hailsham and Diplock); *Mafo v Adams* [1970] 1 QB 548; *Metall & Rohstoff AG v Acli Metals (London) Ltd* [1984] 1 Lloyd's Rep 598 at 612 (Purchas LJ); *Archer v Brown* [1984] 2 All ER 267 at 281 (Peter Pain J); *Morton-Norwich Products v Intercen (No 2)* [1981] FSR 337; *Catnic Components v Hill & Smith Ltd* [1983] FSR 512; *Bradford City Metropolitan Council v Arora* [1991] 3 All ER 545 (where the point was not taken).
18 In *Kuddus* Lords Slynn, Mackay and Hutton found that *Cassell v Broome* did not support the cause of action test, whereas Lords Nicholls and Scott held that the interpretation of that case adopted in *AB v South West Water Services Ltd* was correct.
19 Lords Nicholls and Hutton favoured their retention; Lord Scott took the opposite view. For discussion of this issue see below, pp 424–429.

(b) Euro-torts?

It is an unresolved issue whether punitive damages can be awarded for a Euro-tort (eg for breach of a directly effective EU directive).[20] The main judicial analysis of this was in *R v Secretary of State for Transport, ex p Factortame (No 5)*[1] where the availability of punitive damages was denied. But an important part of the Divisional Court's reasoning was that this denial would not discriminate against claimants for Euro-torts, in comparison to claimants under English domestic law, because punitive damages could not be awarded for an analogous breach of statutory duty under English domestic law: applying the 'cause of action' test, punitive damages could not be awarded for breach of a post-1964 statute (and had not been expressly authorised by the European Communities Act 1972). Since that decision the 'cause of action' test has been abolished by the House of Lords in *Kuddus v Chief Constable of Leicestershire Constabulary*.[2] This has therefore undermined that part of the Divisional Court's reasoning. But this does not necessarily mean that the Divisional Court would have reached a different conclusion. The judgment is hostile in general terms to punitive damages in this context and stressed that, as no other EU state has punitive damages, uniformity within the EU supported the view that such damages were not available.[3] The Law Commission considered that the arguments for and against 'seem finely balanced.'[4] But if English domestic law would award punitive damages for an analogous tort, the 'non-discrimination' principle may be thought more important than uniformity in the EU. If that is so, then subsequent to the *Kuddus* case, punitive damages should be available for Euro-torts.

(c) Proposed Rome II Regulation, Article 24

The Rome II Regulation, which (assuming enacted) will come into force on 1 January 2005, lays down the private international 'choice of law' rules within the EU for non-contractual obligations. By the Rome II Regulation, Article 24, 'The application of a provision of the law designated by this Regulation which has the effect of causing non-compensatory damages, such as exemplary or punitive damages, to be awarded shall be contrary to Community public policy.' This means that, if English law is being applied by reason of a 'choice of law' rule laid

---

20 For the term 'Euro-tort', see above, p 19.
1   [1997] Eu LR 475. On appeal, there was no discussion of punitive, as opposed to compensatory, damages: [2000] 1 AC 524, HL.
2   [2001] UKHL 29, [2002] 2 AC 122.
3   See similarly Rome II Regulation, Article 24 which is discussed in the text below.
4   Law Commission Report No 247 *Aggravated, Exemplary and Restitutionary Damages* (1997) para 5.69.

down by the Rome II Regulation, the English law allowing the award of punitive damages shall not be applied.

The precise genesis of this provision is not entirely clear. But it reflects the general hostility within the EU to punitive damages. One should note, however, that its wording is sufficiently wide to rule out, in a case where a non-contractual conflict of laws arises within the EU, not only punitive damages but also restitutionary damages (and arguably an account of profits).

(d) Infringement of human rights

If a claim is brought for infringement of a Convention right under the Human Rights Act 1998, it appears that no punitive damages are to be awarded even if the facts fall within one of the *Rookes v Barnard* categories (most obviously category one). This is because the Human Rights Act 1998, s 8(3) refers to the award being necessary to afford 'just satisfaction' to the claimant, which appears to be a reference to compensation alone. Moreover, by s 8(4) the courts are required to take into account in deciding whether to award damages the principles applied by the European Court of Human Rights; and the Strasbourg court has never awarded punitive damages. That this is the correct interpretation of the Human Rights Act 1998 – that no punitive damages can be awarded under that Act – has been supported in obiter dicta of Stanley Burton J in *R (KB) v Mental Health Review Tribunal*[5] and the Court of Appeal in *Anufrijeva v London Borough of Southwark.*[6]

(e) Double punishment

As laid down in *Devonshire and Smith v Jenkins*[7] and *Archer v Brown*[8] where a defendant has already been punished by the criminal law in respect of the facts upon which the claimant now founds his tortious action, no punitive damages should be awarded since a person should not be punished twice for the same offence. In the first of these cases the defendant had already been fined and, in the second, imprisoned for the conduct in question.

---

5   [2003] EWHC 193 (Admin), [2003] 2 All ER 209.
6   [2003] EWCA Civ 1406, [2004] 1 All ER 833, at para 55.
7   [1979] LAG Bulletin 114, CA.
8   [1985] QB 401 (tort of deceit). See also *Loomis v Rohan* (1974) 46 DLR (3d) 423; *Daniels v Thompson* [1998] 3 NZLR 22 (abrogated by what is now the Injury Prevention, Rehabilitation and Compensation Act 2001, NZ, s 319); *Gray v Motor Accident Commission* (1999) 73 AJLR 45.

(f) The claimant's conduct

In *Rookes v Barnard*[9] Lord Devlin said that the court should take into account all mitigating circumstances. So most obviously, punitive damages may be refused (or reduced) if the claimant has brought the defendant's conduct upon himself. Indeed this is analogous to the principles of causation and contributory negligence applied in relation to compensatory damages. A rare example of its application is *O'Connor v Hewitson*[10] where punitive damages were refused for trespass to the person under the first category because the claimant had provoked the defendant policeman's assault. Conduct by the claimant which is not a cause of the offending behaviour is not relevant; thus, a refusal to co-operate in a complaints procedure will not affect an award of punitive damages.[11]

(g) Compensatory damages adequate

As stressed in *Rookes v Barnard*[12] and *Cassell v Broome*[13] there should be no punitive damages if it is considered that the compensatory damages awarded are adequate to punish the defendant. This has been referred to as the 'if but only if' test because Lord Devlin in *Rookes v Barnard* said that, if a case fell within one of the categories, a jury should be directed that:

> 'if, but only if, the sum which they have in mind to award as compensation (which may, of course, be a sum aggravated by the way in which the defendant has behaved to the plaintiff) is inadequate to punish him for his outrageous conduct ... then it can award some larger sum.'[14]

3. THE QUANTUM OF PUNITIVE DAMAGES

Assuming punitive damages are to be awarded (and hence under the present law we are here dealing solely with tort cases) how does the court, be it judge or jury, assess them? While Lord Devlin did stress that awards should be moderate,[15] the basic answer has traditionally been that there is almost total discretion to award whatever sum is felt necessary to punish the defendant and to set an example to others.

---

9   [1964] AC 1129 at 1228.
10   [1979] Crim LR 46. See also *Bishop v Metropolitan Police Comr* [1990] 1 LS Gaz R 30.
11   *Thompson v Metropolitan Police Comr* [1998] QB 498.
12   [1964] AC 1129 at 1228.
13   [1972] AC 1027 at 1062, 1089, 1096, 1104, 1118, 1121–1122, 1134.
14   [1964] AC 1129 at 1227–1228.
15   [1964] AC 1129 at 1227–1228.

There have, however, been two main developments in respect of a jury's assessment of punitive damages. Firstly, there have been cases in which the Court of Appeal[16] has substituted a very much lower figure for an award of punitive damages made by a jury. In *John v MGN Ltd*[17] the jury awarded £275,000 in punitive damages for defamation, which on appeal was reduced to £50,000. Similarly, in *Thompson v Metropolitan Police Comr*,[18] £15,000 was substituted for an award of £200,000 punitive damages for false imprisonment and assault. Secondly, in cases of jury assessment the judge is now encouraged to give guidance on the quantum of the punitive award, and a guideline 'tariff' is emerging. In *Thompson v Metropolitan Police Comr* the Court of Appeal stated that, in a case of false imprisonment or assault against the police, unless the figure for punitive damages is at least £5,000 the case is unlikely to be suitable for the award of such damages.[19] For a punitive award of £25,000 to be appropriate in such a case 'the conduct must be particularly deserving of condemnation', and £50,000 'should be regarded as the absolute maximum', the example given being a case where officers of at least the rank of superintendent were directly involved.[20]

However, these developments do not remove the risk of jury awards being hopelessly inconsistent with each other or with awards made by judges. Moreover, there is no convincing reason why the quantum of punitive damages should ever be decided by a jury rather than a judge even if the civil trial is by jury. After all, it is for a judge and not a jury to decide on the appropriate sentence in a criminal trial. It is therefore submitted that, as the Law Commission has recommended,[1] the assessment of punitive damages should be made the sole preserve of the judges, whose first priority should be consistency of awards.

There are three further important points on assessment. First, Lord Devlin said that the parties' means and all mitigating circumstances should be taken into account.[2] The latter most obviously refers to the claimant's own contributory blameworthy conduct, and has already been considered. The former is presumably in line with the criminal

---

16 In the exercise of its powers under the Courts and Legal Services Act 1990, s 8(2).
17 [1997] QB 586.
18 [1998] QB 498.
19 But in *Watkins v Secretary of State for the Home Department* [2004] EWCA Civ 966 it was said that a lower minimum figure of punitive damages could be appropriate for a case of malicious prosecution where there was no jury.
20 [1998] QB 498 at 517.
1   Report No 247 (1997) paras 5.44, 5.81–5.90. The Law Commission further recommended in these paragraphs that the question of whether punitive damages should be awarded should also be for the judge and not the jury.
2   [1964] AC 1129 at 1228.

sentencing principle that there is no sense in fining someone beyond what he can pay.[3] Following some debate as to whether, in vicarious liability cases, reference should be made to the means of the wrongdoer himself or only to those of the defendant employer, it was held in *Thompson v Metropolitan Police Comr*[4] that the means of the employee are irrelevant and do not limit the award against the vicariously liable employer.

Secondly, as laid down in *Cassell v Broome*,[5] where there are joint defendants punitive damages must not exceed the lowest sum that any of the defendants ought to pay; so that if damages are not justified against any one of the defendants, they should not be awarded at all. It follows that if he can identify him the claimant is best advised to sue the most blameworthy defendant alone.

Finally, where there are multiple claimants *Riches v News Group Newspapers*[6] makes clear that the total amount of punitive damages considered fair for the defendant to pay should first be decided on. Then that amount can be divided among the claimants. The Court of Appeal therefore set aside a total award of £250,000 punitive damages to ten claimants for libel because, inter alia, there had been no direction on this point by the judge and there was the possibility (and on the face of it, surely a high probability) that the jury had considered that £25,000 rather than £250,000 (£2,500 rather than £25,000 to each claimant) should be the total amount of punitive damages.

---

3   It can be argued that a defendant ought not to be able to insure against punitive damages just as he cannot insure against criminal fines. In *Lancashire County Council v Municipal Mutual Insurance Ltd* [1997] QB 897, however, it was decided that there is no public policy objection to insurance against a liability to pay punitive damages where they are awarded against a defendant on the basis of vicarious liability for another's tort. Stuart-Smith LJ also considered the issue in relation to personal liability, and suggested that insurance would be acceptable where it covers conduct which is not also criminal. The Law Commission recommended that insurance against punitive damages should never be regarded as against public policy: Report No 247 (1997) paras 5.234–5.269.

4   [1998] QB 498. But see the comments of Lord Mackay in *Kuddus v Chief Constable of Leicestershire Constabulary* [2001] UKHL 29, [2002] 2 AC 122 at para 47. The decision causes difficulty where the employer seeks contribution or an indemnity from the employee in respect of the punitive damages award. The court solved this pragmatically by holding that contribution disproportionate to the employee's means should not be ordered.

5   [1972] AC 1027 at 1063. See also *Francis v Brown* (1998) 30 HLR 143, CA (no punitive damages for unlawful eviction under the Housing Act 1998, ss 27–28 because one of the joint defendants did not merit punishment). The Law Commission has recommended that a separate assessment of punitive damages should be made against each defendant, who would be severally liable to pay it: Report No 247 (1997) paras 5.186–5.208.

6   [1986] QB 256. There are practical difficulties in deciding who are the multiple claimants on any particular facts. For the Law Commission's recommendations for dealing with those difficulties, based on the principle that 'the first past the post take all,' see Report no 247 (1997) paras 5.159–5.185.

4.   SHOULD THE LAW ON PUNITIVE DAMAGES BE REFORMED?[7]

To echo Stephenson LJ's words in the *Riches* case,[8] the law on punitive damages '… cries aloud … for parliamentary intervention'. Although the law has become less artificial following the abolition of the cause of action test, reform is still desirable. Lord Devlin's categories in *Rookes v Barnard*[9] lack satisfactory rationale in principle or policy. As regards category one, why, for example, should a private store detective who maliciously falsely imprisons an alleged shoplifter be immune from punitive damages when a police officer, who does exactly the same, is not? And as regards category two, why, for example, should it make all the difference as regards the availability of punitive damages, whether a person who attacked an old lady was paid to do so or not? In essence, the categories represent an unhappy compromise between the desire to rid the law of punitive damages altogether and the belief that precedent is too firmly entrenched to allow this.

But what form should reform take? There are two main options: the abolition of punitive damages or their retention and extension on a principled basis.

---

7   Street *Principles of the Law of Damages* (1962) pp 34–36 (arguing that an empirical study of the effectiveness of punitive damages in attaining their stated goals is a necessity in order to decide whether they should be retained or abolished); Ogus *The Law of Damages* (1973) pp 32–34; Waddams *The Law of Damages* (3rd edn, 1997) paras 11.10–11.100; Posner *Economic Analysis of Law* (6th edn, 2003) p 192; Collins *The Law of Contract* (4th edn, 2003) pp 422–427; Stone 'Double Count and Double Talk: The End of Exemplary Damages?' (1972) 46 ALJ 311; Sullivan 'Punitive Damages in the Law of Contract: The Reality and the Illusion of Legal Change' (1977) 61 Minn LR 207; Mallor and Roberts 'Punitive Damages: Towards a Principled Approach' (1980) 31 Hastings LJ 639; Owen 'The Moral Foundations of Punitive Damages' (1989) 40 Alabama LR 705; Chapman and Trebilcock 'Punitive Damages: Divergence in Search of a Rationale' (1989) 40 Alabama LR 741; Perlstein 'Crossing the Contract-Tort Boundary: An Economic Argument for the Imposition of Extracompensatory Damages for Opportunistic Breach of Contract' (1992) 58 Brooklyn LR 877; McBride 'A Case for Awarding Punitive Damages in Response to Deliberate Breaches of Contract' (1995) 24 Anglo-American LR 369; McBride 'Punitive Damages' in *Wrongs and Remedies in the Twenty-First Century* (ed Birks, 1996) pp 175–202; Ogus 'Exemplary Damages and Economic Analysis' in *The Human Face of Law: Essays in Honour of Donald Harris* (1997) pp 85–102; Edelman, *Gain-Based Damages* (2002) ch 1; Beever 'The Structure of Aggravated and Exemplary Damages' (2003) 23 OJLS 87; Weinrib 'Punishment and Disgorgement as Contract Remedies' (2003) 78 Chicago-Kent LR 55; Smith *Contract Theory* (2004) pp 417–420. For a detailed examination of the arguments, see Law Commission Report No 247 (1997) Pt V.
8   [1985] 2 All ER 845 at 850.
9   [1964] AC 1129.

(1) Arguments for the abolition of punitive damages[10]

(i) Most importantly, it is argued that punitive damages, because their primary aim is punishment, confuse the role of the criminal and the civil law and that this is unsatisfactory for several reasons. First, punishment is an extreme sanction justifiable only if a law designated as criminal has been broken. Secondly (as under present criminal proceedings), the defendant should have the benefit of more protective procedures, evidential rules and rights of appeal if punishment rather than, say, compensation is in issue. In *Cassell v Broome*[11] Lord Reid was particularly critical of jury awards of punitive damages on the ground that in criminal cases it is never left to a jury to decide the punishment. Thirdly, punishment requires a state-individual relationship rather than being for one individual to demand against another. It follows that the rightful recipient of monetary punishment should be the state, and not a claimant. Of course all this in no sense denies that the criminal courts are justified in awarding compensation or restitution to the victim of a crime, for there is no objection to less drastic remedies than punishment being ordered for a crime. The objection is to the more drastic sanction of punishment being used for civil wrongs.

(ii) It may also be contended that any useful purpose served by tortious punitive damages within Lord Devlin's categories could be achieved by other satisfactory means. For example, all the cases on actions against the police within the first category also involved crimes, and a criminal prosecution would serve equally well to punish and deter police misconduct. Even better, as many have argued, would be to introduce a new fully independent police complaints system. Similarly, within the second category there are already adequate criminal sanctions against landlords for wrongful eviction under the Protection from Eviction Act 1977.[12] Moreover, and irrespective of whether criminal punishment is felt justified, the civil law in respect of the second category can justifiably go beyond compensation by awarding restitutionary remedies stripping the defendant of her profits.[13] Compensation alone does not and need not underpin tortious or, more controversially, contractual monetary remedies;

---

10 It has also been argued that punitive damages would deter an efficient breach of contract. As discussed below, pp 473–475, this is an unsatisfactory argument given the opportunity to bargain round the remedy. Note also that punitive damages are almost unknown in civil law systems.

11 [1972] AC 1027 at 1087.

12 As amended by the Housing Act 1988.

13 Above, ch 17.

restitution, occupying a mid-position between compensation and punishment, is an acceptable remedial function for a civil wrong. Arguably, therefore, cases within the second category like *Cassell v Broome* could be satisfactorily dealt with by awarding a restitutionary remedy to the claimant. Indeed that there is dispute over the extent of even restitutionary remedies for torts could be said to make pursuit of the more drastic aim of punishment doubly surprising.

(2) Arguments for extending punitive damages on a principled basis

There are strong arguments in favour of retaining punitive damages, while removing the illogicalities in the present law by giving punitive damages an extended ambit based on principle to replace the artificial categories test. In addition to the two main arguments set out below, support for this is derived from the experience in other Commonwealth countries where punitive damages continue to be awarded for a wide range of torts.[14] Tortious punitive damages are also freely recoverable in the US.[15]

(i)   The primary argument is encapsulated in the following passage from Lord Wilberforce's judgment (dissenting on some points) in *Cassell v Broome*:

> 'It cannot lightly be taken for granted, even as a matter of theory, that the purpose of the law of tort is compensation, still less that it ought to be ... or that there is something inappropriate or illogical or anomalous in including a punitive element in civil damages, or, conversely, that the criminal law, rather than civil law, is in these cases the better instrument for conveying social disapproval, or for redressing a wrong to the social fabric, or that damages in any case can be broken down into the two separate elements. As a matter of practice English law has not committed itself to any of these theories ...'[16]

There is no logical reason why punishment should not be a response available to the civil law. Moreover, it is not intended to be, and is not, identical to criminal punishment. In particular, civil punishment can be demanded by an individual, the victim of the

---

14   *Uren v John Fairfax & Sons Pty Ltd* (1966) 117 CLR 118; *Taylor v Beere* [1982] 1 NZLR 81; Waddams *The Law of Damages* (3rd edn, 1997) paras 11.190–11.200.
15   Second Restatement of Torts, para 908.
16   [1972] AC 1027 at 1114.

wrongdoing, whereas criminal punishment is sought by or on behalf of the state; civil punishment also lacks the stigma of criminal punishment.

(ii) Even if illogical, punitive damages can serve a useful purpose. This is supported by the following passage from the speech of Lord Devlin himself:

> '... there are certain categories of case in which an award of exemplary damages can serve a useful purpose in vindicating the strength of the law and thus affording a practical justification for admitting into the civil law a principle which ought logically to belong to the criminal.'[17]

These words were echoed by Lord Nicholls in *Kuddus v Chief Constable of Leicestershire Constabulary*:

> 'From time to time cases do arise where awards of compensatory damages are perceived as inadequate to achieve a just result between the parties. The nature of the defendant's conduct calls for a further response from the courts. On occasion conscious wrongdoing by a defendant is so outrageous, his disregard of the plaintiff's rights so contumelious, that something more is needed to show that the law will not tolerate such behaviour. Without an award of exemplary damages, justice will not have been done ... [T]he underlying rationale lies in the sense of outrage which a defendant's conduct sometimes evokes, a sense not always assuaged fully by a compensatory award of damages, even when the damages are increased to reflect emotional distress.'[18]

Punitive damages represent another means of protection for the victim of wrongdoing and an additional deterrent to engaging in such conduct. Aggravated and restitutionary damages cannot cover the whole field. For instance, D may have libelled C in order to make a profit, but if any profit cannot be identified there will be no appropriate response to D's blameworthy motivation in the absence of punitive damages. Moreover, the criminal law offers incomplete protection; for example, its substantive scope does not cover all wrongs deserving of punishment.[19] In addition, the resources and priorities of the state determine whether the wrongdoer is caught

17 [1964] AC 1129 at 1226.
18 [2001] UKHL 29, [2002] 2 AC 122 at paras 63–65.
19 There may indeed be persuasive objections to criminalising certain wrongs, for example because they are not thought to warrant the stigma of criminal punishment.

and prosecuted, and this may be felt to be particularly inappropriate where the state itself has committed the wrongdoing; punitive damages have perhaps been most useful in protecting civil liberties.[20]

(3) The Law Commission's recommendations

The latter arguments persuaded the Law Commission,[1] it is submitted correctly, to recommend the retention of punitive damages and a redefinition of the cases in which they could be awarded so as to put them on a sound principled basis. In particular, it recommended that the cause of action test should be abolished (as has subsequently been brought about judicially in the *Kuddus* case)[2] and that, instead of Lord Devlin's three categories, punitive damages should be available for any civil wrong (except breach of contract) where 'the defendant's conduct shows a deliberate and outrageous disregard of the [claimant's] rights'.[3] Such a principled approach (albeit without the emphasis on 'deliberate') replacing the categories derives strong support from obiter dicta of Lord Nicholls in the *Kuddus* case.[4] It also underpins his comment in the Privy Council in *A v Bottrill*[5] that English law is 'still toiling in the chains of *Rookes v Barnard*.'

The Law Commission recommended the retention of several of the current features of the law: for example, that punitive damages should not be awarded unless other possible remedies (and the Law Commission highlighted not merely compensation but also an award of restitutionary damages) do not go far enough to punish the defendant. Other factors to guide the judge's discretion were listed, such as the harm caused or intended to the claimant, any benefit the defendant derived or intended to derive from the conduct, the nature of the right infringed and the defendant's state of mind. An important change recommended was that, in a jury trial, the judge, rather than the jury, should decide whether

---

20   See eg Lord Hutton's speech in *Kuddus v Chief Constable of Leicestershire Constabulary* [2001] UKHL 29, [2002] 2 AC 122 at paras 75–79.

1   *Aggravated, Exemplary and Restitutionary Damages*, Report No 247 (1997) Pts IV and V. At present the government has no plans to take forward the Report's proposals for legislation: Hansard (HC Debates), 9 November 1999, col 502, citing the absence of a clear consensus on the way ahead, and anticipating future judicial clarification of the position.

2   Above, pp 417–418.

3   The Law Commission thought that intention or subjective recklessness should be required (hence the inclusion of the word 'deliberate'). A different view has been taken in *A v Bottrill* [2002] UKPC 44, [2003] 1 AC 449, in which the Privy Council (by a majority) held that in New Zealand (where punitive damages are available for outrageous tortious wrongdoing) tortious negligence, which was not committed with subjective recklessness, could be outrageous so as to justify punitive damages.

4   [2001] UKHL 29, [2002] 2 AC 122 at paras 65–68.

5   [2002] UKPC 44, [2003] 1 AC 449 at para 41.

punitive damages should be awarded and their quantum.[6] This should address a major objection to punitive damages, ie that they are arbitrary and excessive.

It was not recommended that the law should be changed to allow the award of punitive damages for breach of contract.[7] It is certainly more difficult to envisage cases of breach of contract in which an award of punitive damages would be merited, particularly as the damage suffered is usually purely economic. Yet the same considerations which support the award of punitive damages in a tort case – deterrence, for example – may equally apply in an exceptional case of breach of contract. This may be illustrated by reference to the facts of *Whiten v Pilot Insurance Co*,[8] the case which clearly established that in Canada punitive damages may in certain circumstances be awarded for a breach of contract where no tortious conduct is involved. An accidental fire destroyed the claimant's home, and she claimed under the insurance policy issued to her by the defendant company. However, the defendant alleged that the claimant had started the fire deliberately and paid hardly any of the sum due under the policy. The allegation of arson was contradicted by the local fire chief and by the company's own expert investigator and initial expert; it was made in bad faith (and pursued through an eight-week trial) in order to try to force the claimant, who was in a very poor financial position, into an unfairly low settlement. This was held by the Supreme Court of Canada to justify an award of $1 million punitive damages. Although there had been no tort in addition to the breach of contract, the defendant had committed an 'actionable wrong' in breaching the duty to act in good faith which, as the other party to an insurance contract, it owed to the claimant. In such a case, punitive damages are an appropriate legal response, and it appears unduly restrictive to allow them only if a tort has also been committed.

---

6 See above, p 422, n 1.
7 For equitable wrongs, see below, pp 625–627.
8 (2002) 209 DLR (4th) 257. For a useful casenote, see Fridman 'Punitive Damages for Breach of Contract – A Canadian Innovation' (2003) 119 LQR 20. See also *Royal Bank of Canada v W Got & Associates Electric Ltd* (2000) 178 DLR (4th) 385 (punitive damages awarded for breach of contract but, on the facts, a tort had also been committed) noted by Edelman 'Exemplary Damages for Breach of Contract' (2001) 117 LQR 539.

Compelling performance or preventing (or compelling the undoing of) a wrong

Chapter 19

The award of an agreed sum

The award of an agreed sum is a remedy which protects the promisee's expectations by enforcing the defendant's contractual promise to pay a sum of money. As such, its justification ultimately rests on the morality of promise-keeping.[1] The remedy can be regarded as a hybrid, being like damages in that it is common law and monetary but like specific performance in that its function is to compel performance of a positive contractual obligation.[2]

The most important agreed sum is an agreed price (or remuneration).[3] Indeed an action for the price is the commonest claim brought for breach of contract.[4] Yet it is not afforded separate treatment in some standard works on contract, where references to it are rather uncomfortably contained in sections on damages or discharge.[5] This chapter further differs from most analyses in including liquidated damages and related sums (generally treated under damages)[6] alongside an agreed price, on the ground that they are also agreed sums awarded by the courts.[7]

To analyse the main issues raised, each of the three principal types of agreed sum will be examined in turn, after looking at some points that apply whichever type of agreed sum is in question.

---

1   Above, pp 36–37.
2   For judicial confusion – so that this remedy was incorrectly treated as if it were specific performance and hence subject to, eg a want of mutuality bar – see *Ministry of Sound (Ireland) Ltd v World Online Ltd* [2003] EWHC 2178 (Ch), [2003] 2 All ER (Comm) 823.
3   If the amount has not been expressly agreed, but there is a valid contract for goods or services, a reasonable sum is payable and is awarded in a (contractual) action for *quantum valebant*, where goods, or *quantum meruit*, where services. See the Sale of Goods Act 1979, s 8(2); Supply of Goods and Services Act 1982, s 15(1); Treitel *The Law of Contract* (11th edn, 2003) p 1061.
4   Beale *Remedies for Breach of Contract* (1980) p 144; Judicial Statistics (Annual Report) 1999 (Cm 4786). An action for an agreed price or remuneration is commonly referred to as an action in debt (although that latter concept can also extend to non-contractual liquidated demands based on unjust enrichment).
5   Eg *Cheshire, Fifoot & Furmston's Law of Contract* (14th edn, 2001) pp 685–687.
6   Eg Treitel *Law of Contract* (11th edn, 2003) pp 997–1007.
7   For a similar approach see Waddams *The Law of Damages* (3rd edn) paras 7.10–7.20, 8.10–8.30.

1.   GENERAL POINTS

The defendant must be in breach of a valid contractual obligation to pay the agreed sum. So the contract must not be void or unenforceable, and must not have been rescinded; neither must the obligation be one that has been wiped away by termination of the contract for frustration or breach.[8] Also the sum must be due. So an agreed sum payable on breach will only be awarded once that breach has occurred and an agreed sum payable on an event other than breach only when that specified event has taken place.[9] An agreed price is only regarded as due, in the absence of any express provision as to advance payment, where the claimant has completed or substantially completed what he is being paid for: for example, a seller of goods is generally not entitled to the agreed price until property in the goods has passed to the buyer, as laid down in the Sale of Goods Act 1979, s 49(1),[10] and a builder generally not until he has completed or substantially completed the stage of the building to which the payment relates.[11]

Agreed sums are normally awarded after trial of the action. However, by the Supreme Court Act 1981, s 32 and CPR 25.6–25.9, a court has power in certain circumstances to award an interim payment pre-trial in respect of an agreed sum (or indeed any other monetary sum, including damages).[12] Generally speaking, the court must be satisfied that, if the claim went to trial, the claimant would obtain judgment for a substantial amount of money (other than costs).

The law governing interest payable on an agreed sum and the limitation period for claiming agreed sums[13] has already been dealt with in chapters 14 and 15.[14]

A difficult question is whether a promisee can enforce a contractual obligation to pay a sum of money to a third party by an action for an agreed sum. In principle there seems no objection to this. The

---

8   In *Hyundai Heavy Industries Co Ltd v Papadopoulos* [1980] 1 WLR 1129, HL, and *Stocznia Gdanska SA v Latvia Shipping Co* [1998] 1 WLR 574, HL, the claimants, builders and sellers of a ship, were held able to recover an agreed sum, payable before termination for the defendant's breach, because the right to that part payment had already accrued and the defendant had no set-off for restitution (because there had been no total failure of consideration).

9   Eg in *Damon Cia Naviera SA v Hapag-Lloyd International SA, The Blankenstein* [1985] 1 All ER 475, the 10% deposit was not recoverable as a debt because it was only payable on the buyers' signing of the contract.

10   Treitel *The Law of Contract* (11th edn, 2003) pp 1014–1015 takes the view that the Sale of Goods Act 1979, s 49(1) adds a requirement to the sum being due and that this is explicable as encouraging mitigation. But see also Goode *Commercial Law* (2nd edn, 1995) pp 424–425.

11   *Hoenig v Isaacs* [1952] 2 All ER 176.

12   See above, pp 181–182.

13   But for agreed sums ('any debt or other liquidated pecuniary claim') time runs afresh from an acknowledgment or part payment – Limitation Act 1980, s 29(5).

14   For agreed sums payable in a foreign currency, see above, pp 193–199.

defendant's promise is simply being enforced albeit that, subject to exceptions, the doctrine of privity prevents an action by the third party beneficiary. Yet there is no clear support for this, nor indeed direct discussion of it, in the cases or in academic writings.[15] What has been discussed is whether the promisee can sue for an agreed sum to be paid to him, which should have been paid to a third party. The objection in that situation is that (unless on a true construction of the contract the promisee can insist on the defendant paying him rather than the third party)[16] the award of the agreed sum would no longer be specifically enforcing the defendant's promise to pay the third party. Windeyer J's dicta rejecting this idea in *Coulls v Bagot's Executor and Trustee Co Ltd*[17] therefore seems correct. If the promisee wishes to recover a monetary sum for himself he should instead sue for (unliquidated) damages.

2.   AWARD OF AN AGREED PRICE OR REMUNERATION

The main issue and one of burning controversy is whether an action for the agreed price may fail where the defendant has clearly repudiated the contract[18] but the claimant, instead of accepting the repudiation and suing for damages, has kept the contract open. For example, a builder may have gone on to complete a building even though the owner has repudiated, or a seller of goods, where property in them has passed to the buyer, may have kept the goods for the buyer even though the buyer has refused to take delivery of them.

There are two major and contradictory approaches to this issue. First, one might say that the claimant has an unfettered option to hold the contract open and recover the agreed price: that is, that the duty to mitigate never applies to an action for the agreed price[19] and that it is no bar that damages are adequate. The alternative view is that the claimant may not be entitled to hold the contract open and recover the agreed price; the duty to mitigate can apply to an action for the agreed price and, where damages are adequate to compensate a claimant for his loss, it is contrary to that duty for him to carry on with his own unwanted

---

15   However, passages in *Beswick v Beswick* [1968] AC 58 at 81, 88, 97 may be thought to suggest that the administratrix could sue for arrears to be paid *to the widow* in her personal capacity.
16   As in *Tradigrain SA v King Diamond Shipping SA, The Spiros C* [2000] 2 Lloyd's Rep 319 at 331.
17   [1967] ALR 385 at 411. Cf *Cleaver v Mutual Reserve Fund Life Association* [1892] 1 QB 147; Treitel *The Law of Contract* (11th edn, 2003) p 591.
18   The repudiation will almost always, but not necessarily, be anticipatory.
19   For a standard non-application of the duty to mitigate and mitigation to the award of agreed remuneration see, eg *Abrahams v Performing Right Society Ltd* [1995] ICR 1028, CA: 'damages', which an employer was bound to pay in lieu of notice following a dismissal, were a debt and therefore not limited by the duty to mitigate (cf *Cerberus Software Ltd v Rowley* [2001] EWCA Civ 78, [2001] IRLR 160, CA).

performance and to claim the agreed price: rather, he should accept the repudiation, claim damages and make substitute contracts.

The leading case is *White and Carter (Councils) Ltd v McGregor.*[20] The claimants supplied to local authorities litterbins on which they let advertising space. The defendants contracted to pay for the display of adverts, advertising their garage business, but later that day they repudiated the contract, which had been concluded by their sales manager contrary to the wishes of the proprietor. The claimants refused to accept the repudiation, went ahead and displayed the adverts for the three-year period of the contract and claimed the agreed price of £196 4s. The House of Lords held, by a three–two majority, that they were entitled to the agreed price. Two of the majority (Lords Hodson and Tucker) simply adopted the first of the two views examined above. The third, Lord Reid, while basically taking that view, suggested a possible qualification:

> '... it may well be that, if it can be shown that a person has no legitimate interest, financial or otherwise, in performing the contract, rather than claiming damages, he ought not to be allowed to saddle the other party with an additional burden with no benefit to himself.'[1]

But Lord Reid failed to clarify what having 'no legitimate interest' means. Presumably, though, he had a very narrow notion in mind, since despite the fact that damages would surely have been adequate for the claimants, so that they had nothing to gain by continuing performance, Lord Reid did not think it established that they had no legitimate interest in continuing. On the other hand, Lords Morton and Keith, dissenting, took the second of the two views above. Lord Keith said:

> 'I find the argument advanced for the appellants a somewhat startling one. If it is right it would seem that a man who has contracted to go to Hong Kong at his own expense and make a report, in return for remuneration of £10,000, and who, before the date fixed for the start of the journey and perhaps before he has incurred any expense, is informed by the other contracting party that he has cancelled or repudiated the contract, is entitled to set off for Hong Kong and produce his report in order to claim in debt the stipulated sum. Such a result is not, in my opinion, in accordance with principle or authority, and cuts across the rule that where one party is in breach of contract, the other must take steps to minimise the loss sustained by the breach.'[2]

---

20 [1962] AC 413.
1   [1962] AC 413 at 431.
2   [1962] AC 413 at 442.

It is interesting to contrast immediately the leading US case on this issue. In *Clark v Marsiglia*[3] a restorer of paintings, who had completed the restoration contracted for, despite an earlier repudiation of the contract by the owner, was held not to be entitled to the agreed price and was rather restricted to damages. Similarly by the Uniform Commercial Code, s 2–709(l)(b), the seller of goods may only recover their price if he is '... unable after reasonable effort to resell them at a reasonable price or the circumstances reasonably indicate that such effort will be unavailing.'[4]

White & Carter has been both attacked and defended by academics,[5] and the judicial reaction has also been mixed.[6] In *Hounslow London Borough Council v Twickenham Garden Developments Ltd*[7] Megarry J explained, as Lord Reid had himself observed, that *White & Carter* can only apply where the claimant is able to carry on with his performance without the defendant's co-operation. But it is particularly significant, and reveals an underlying antipathy towards *White & Carter*, that Megarry J included passive co-operation within this: he therefore held that *White & Carter* did not apply to the facts before him since an owner of land on which building work is being carried out is required to co-operate with the builder in that he has to allow him to enter his land.[8]

The Court of Appeal also distinguished *White & Carter* in *Attica Sea Carriers v Ferrostaal*.[9] This concerned a demise charterparty. On the assumption that the charterers were bound to repair the vessel before redelivery, it was held that, following repudiation by the charterers, the owners should have taken redelivery and were not entitled to insist on holding the contract open and receiving the agreed hire until the ship was repaired. Most radical was Lord Denning. He did not think *White & Carter* should be followed except in a case on all fours with it. 'It has no application whatever in a case where the plaintiff ought in all reason to accept the repudiation and sue for damages – provided that damages

3   1 Denio 317 (NY 1845).
4   See Atiyah, Adams and MacQueen *The Sale of Goods* (10th edn, 2001) pp 484–486.
5   Goodhart 'Measure of Damages when a Contract is Repudiated' (1962) 78 LQR 263; Neinaber 'The Effect of Anticipatory Repudiation: Principle and Policy' [1962] CLJ 213; Tabachnik 'Anticipatory Breach of Contract' [1972] CLP 149.
6   It was followed very soon after in *Anglo-African Shipping Co of New York Inc v J Mortner Ltd* [1962] 1 Lloyd's Rep 81.
7   [1971] Ch 233. See also *Finelli v Dee* (1968) 76 DLR (2d) 393 (Ont CA).
8   In dismissing an application for summary judgment, Nicholas Strauss QC in *Ministry of Sound (Ireland) Ltd v World Online Ltd* [2003] EWHC (Ch) 2178, [2003] 2 All ER (Comm) 823, held that a firm that provided packaging and distribution services for CDs supplied by the defendant could perform without the defendant's co-operation – and had done so thereby entitling it to the final payment of £200,000 – even though, for the last eighteen months of the two-year agreement, the defendant, in breach of contract, had supplied no CDs.
9   [1976] 1 Lloyd's Rep 250.

would provide an adequate remedy for any loss suffered by him.'[10] An analogy was then drawn with specific performance to emphasise, in contradiction of *White & Carter*, that, when damages are adequate, specific relief (including the action for the agreed sum) should not be granted. Lord Denning went on to emphasise that what made the claimants' refusal particularly unreasonable on these facts was that the repairs would cost four times as much as the difference in value between the repaired and unrepaired ship. The owners' refusal to accept repudiation was, therefore, doubly wasteful. Orr LJ, with whom Browne LJ concurred, while saying that he agreed with Lord Denning, distinguished *White & Carter* on the grounds that here co-operation was needed from the defendants, and the claimants had no legitimate interest in holding the contract open. Unfortunately, no explanation of these points was forthcoming. One can safely assume, however, that on the latter point the majority was also influenced by the cost of repairs being uneconomic; it was this that made the facts *of Attica* so extreme.

There were no such unusual facts in *The Odenfeld*.[11] Charterers had repudiated a charterparty but the owners had refused to accept this and had kept the vessel at their disposal. The claimants, assignees of money due under the charterparty, now claimed the agreed hire for the period in question. Kerr J distinguished *Attica Sea Carriers* and considered that it was only in extreme cases like that that *White & Carter* did not apply. In a statement resembling Lord Reid's, Kerr J said '... any fetter on the innocent party's right of election whether or not to accept a repudiation will only be applied in extreme cases, viz where damages would be an adequate remedy and where an election to keep the contract alive would be wholly unreasonable.'[12] Kerr J went on to say that on the facts of the case there was doubt about the adequacy of damages because of the difficulty in their assessment and that, since the owners had obligations to the claimants to keep the charterparty in existence, they were not acting unreasonably in refusing to accept the repudiation.

But it would seem that an important, albeit veiled, departure from *White & Carter* and *The Odenfeld* was made by Lloyd J in *Clea Shipping Corpn v Bulk Oil International Ltd*.[13] The facts were straightforward and again concerned a charterparty: the charterers had repudiated, but the owners had refused to accept this and had kept the vessel at the charterers' disposal until the expiry of the charter. The charterers in fact paid the hire for the full period, but now sought to recover it on the ground that

10   [1976] 1 Lloyd's Rep 250 at 255.
11   [1978] 2 Lloyd's Rep 357.
12   [1978] 2 Lloyd's Rep 357 at 374.
13   [1984] 1 All ER 129.

the owners should have accepted the repudiation and were restricted to damages. The arbitrator's decision in favour of the charterers was upheld by Lloyd J. After a masterly survey of the case law he said the following:

'Whether one takes Lord Reid's language which was adopted by Orr and Browne LJJ in *The Puerto Buitrago*, or Lord Denning MR's language in that case ("in all reason") or Kerr J's language in *The Odenfeld* ("wholly unreasonable ...") there comes a point at which the court will cease, on general equitable principles, to allow the innocent party to enforce his contract according to its strict legal terms. How one defines that point is obviously a matter of some difficulty for it involves drawing a line between conduct which is merely unreasonable ... and conduct which is *wholly* unreasonable. But however difficult it may be to define the point, that there *is* such a point seems to me to have been accepted ...'[14]

Applying this approach to the case before him, Lloyd J considered that the arbitrator could not be said to have been wrong to conclude that the relevant point had been reached, and hence that the owners should be restricted to damages. But ultimately, it is hard to see how this decision can be squared with *White & Carter* and *The Odenfeld*. True, Lord Reid and Kerr J recognised a point at which the claimant should accept the repudiation, but what is crucial is that that point was regarded as being reached only on extreme facts, like those in *Attica Sea Carriers*. Yet the facts in *Clea Shipping* were in no sense extreme. It would seem, therefore, that Lloyd J's decision represents a move towards the minority approach in *White & Carter* and the second of the two views set out above.

It should also be noted that in dicta Lloyd J did express tentative 'first blush' support for the view, accepted by the majority in *Attica Sea Carriers* but rejected in *The Odenfeld*, that a charterparty requires such co-operation as to fall outside *White & Carter*. Again this approach cannot be sensibly reconciled with *White & Carter*, and if adopted would similarly undermine that decision.

Recently in *Ocean Marine Navigation Ltd v Koch Carbon Inc, The Dynamic*[15] Simon J has usefully summarised the above main cases as follows:

'These cases establish the following exception to the general rule that the innocent party has an option whether or not to accept a repudiation: (i) The burden is on the *contract-breaker* to show that the innocent party has no legitimate interest in performing the contract rather than claiming damages. (ii) The burden is not discharged merely by showing that the benefit to the other party is small in comparison to the loss to the

---

14 [1984] 1 All ER 129 at 136–137.
15 [2003] EWHC 1936 (Comm), [2003] 2 Lloyd's Rep 693, para 23.

contract-breaker. (iii) The exception to the general rule applies only in extreme cases: where damages would be an adequate remedy and where an election to keep the contract alive would be unreasonable.'

Should *White & Carter* be supported, or is that decision justified? This depends on the extent to which it is felt that economic efficiency, as represented by the duty to mitigate, should counter the claimant's wish for specific enforcement of the promise to pay him money. Under *White & Carter* that wish is given overriding importance where the claimant can go ahead and fulfil his obligations. It is submitted that that is unsatisfactory. Where the claimant can be adequately compensated by damages, so that it is of no real benefit to him to carry on with his side of the contract, his wishes should be outweighed by the pure waste of his carrying on with an unwanted performance. Put shortly, where damages are adequate, economic efficiency dictates that the claimant should be required to mitigate, by stopping performance and making substitute contracts, rather than holding the contract open and claiming the agreed sum.[16] Indeed it should be realised, as clearly Lord Denning did in *Attica Sea Carriers*, that the *White & Carter* approach runs counter to the traditional approach to specific performance, where if damages are adequate, specific performance will not be granted. The importance of upholding the duty to mitigate, which is the primary argument used in chapter 20 to support the traditional subsidiary role of specific performance,[17] is therefore equally valuable for criticising *White & Carter*.

3.   AWARD OF AN AGREED SUM PAYABLE ON BREACH – LIQUIDATED DAMAGES[18]

(1) The distinction between liquidated damages and penalties

Although the award of liquidated damages is conventionally treated as an aspect of contractual damages, it is in reality the same type of judicial remedy as the award of an agreed price, in that it is a common law monetary remedy which specifically enforces the defendant's promise to pay a sum of money. Where it differs fundamentally from the award of an agreed price is that the promise enforced represents the parties' agreed remedy for the (primary) breach of contract, and the important question is whether the courts should uphold what the parties have

16   The same argument has been used to criticise the damages principle – analogous to *White & Carter*, but arising only where the repudiation is anticipatory – that there is no duty to mitigate unless the claimant chooses to accept an anticipatory repudiation. See above, p 128.

17   Below, pp 472–475.

18   For a comparative account, see Treitel *Remedies for Breach of Contract* (1988) pp 208–234.

themselves agreed should be paid for breach rather than assessing what should be paid according to the usual principles of damages. Although strictly speaking this question is concerned with the validity of the promise, rather than the judicial remedy itself, examination of it is essential to understand what is meant by an award of liquidated damages. Moreover, it must be relevant to one's general understanding of damages to know whether the courts do award such an agreed sum, rather than damages assessed according to the usual principles.

The short answer is that the courts will award the agreed sum if it is liquidated damages; but if it is a penalty, the promise to pay is invalid and the courts will instead award normal (unliquidated) damages.[19] Wherein lies the difference? Liquidated damages are a sum which represents a genuine pre-estimate of the loss caused by the breach, that is, of what is needed to put the claimant[20] into as good a position as if the contract had been performed. A penalty, on the other hand, is a sum which is greater than such a genuine pre-estimate, and is inserted to punish the other party in the event of breach and to pressurise him into carrying out his contractual obligations. The distinction was emphasised in Lord Dunedin's classic speech in *Dunlop Pneumatic Tyre Co Ltd v New Garage & Motor Co Ltd*,[1] which in addition laid down several principles that are relevant in deciding whether a sum is liquidated damages or a penalty.[2] These will now be examined although some are perhaps so obvious as hardly to merit repetition.

(i) The parties' use of the words 'penalty' or 'liquidated damages' does not conclusively decide the issue.

(ii) One must judge the issue according to the circumstances at the time the contract was made and not at the time of breach.

(iii) The sum will be held to be a penalty if it is 'extravagant and unconscionable in amount in comparison with the greatest loss that could conceivably be proved to have followed from the breach.' So,

---

19 Under the Unfair Terms in Consumer Contracts Regulations 1999, SI 1999/2083, one of the examples of a term, in Sch 2, para 1(e), that may be unfair is one 'requiring any consumer who fails to fulfil his obligation to pay a disproportionately high sum in compensation.' In respect of sums payable on breach, it is likely that this will be construed so as to be consistent with the present law on liquidated damages and penalties.

20 Or a third party in a situation where the law allows the promisee to recover a third party's loss: see above, pp 224–229.

1 [1915] AC 79.

2 [1915] AC 79 at 87–88. In *Lordsvale Finance plc v Bank of Zambia* [1996] QB 752 a small percentage increase in the interest payable, imposed prospectively on a borrower who had defaulted in repayment, was upheld as not being a penalty. This was because, although not directly a genuine pre-estimate of loss, the increase was commercially justified as the borrower now posed an increased risk: moreover unlike a penalty, the increase was not primarily designed to deter the borrower from breach.

for example, if a contract to carry out building work worth £100 provided that the builder should pay £50,000 if he failed to do the work, this would be a penalty.

(iv) 'It will be held to be a penalty if the breach consists only in not paying a sum of money, and the sum stipulated is a sum greater than the sum which ought to have been paid.' According to this, a clause making a debtor liable to pay £200, if he fails to pay £150 on the due day would be penal. But this point is clearly open to criticism in that a creditor's obligations may mean that his loss exceeds the sum due and the sum stipulated could very well, therefore, be a genuine pre-estimate of loss.

(v) 'There is a presumption (but no more) that it is a penalty when "a single lump sum is made payable by way of compensation, on the occurrence of one or more or all of several events, some of which may occasion serious and others but trifling damage".'[3]

(vi) 'It is no obstacle to the sum stipulated being a genuine pre-estimate of damage that the consequences of the breach are such as to make precise pre-estimation almost an impossibility. On the contrary, that is just the situation when it is probable that the pre-estimated damage was the true bargain between the parties.'

In the case itself, the defendants bought tyres from the claimants under an agreement that they would neither tamper with the manufacturer's markings on the tyres, nor sell the tyres to the public below list price, nor sell them to persons whose supplies the claimants had decided to suspend, nor exhibit or export them without the claimants' consent. £5 was made payable for every tyre 'sold or offered' in breach of the agreement. The House of Lords held that this sum was liquidated damages. Although there were several ways in which tyres could be 'sold or offered' in breach of the agreement, the presumption in principle (v) was rebutted because the loss likely to result from any such breach was difficult to assess and £5 represented a genuine attempt to do so.

In *Philips Hong Kong Ltd v Attorney-General of Hong Kong*[4] Lord Woolf, giving the judgment of the Privy Council upholding as liquidated damages a clause in a road construction contract, considered that the courts should not be too zealous in knocking down clauses as penal. '[W]hat the parties have agreed should normally be upheld.'[5] More specifically it was stressed that a clause can be a genuine pre-estimate of loss even though hypothetical situations could be presented in which the

3   Citing from *Elphinstone v Monkland Iron & Coal Co* (1886) 11 App Cas 332 at 342.
4   (1993) 61 BLR 41.
5   (1993) 61 BLR 41 at 59.

claimant's actual loss would be substantially lower. To hold otherwise would be to render it very difficult to draw up valid liquidated damages clauses in complex commercial contracts. Moreover it was thought acceptable to take account of the fact that, as it happened, the actual loss was not much greater than the agreed damages. Although the matter must be judged as at the date the contract was made, what actually happened 'can provide valuable evidence as to what could reasonably be expected to be the loss at the time the contract was made.'[6]

Hire-purchase and conditional sale agreements are a particularly rich source of illustrations of agreed sums payable on breach.[7] In *Bridge v Campbell Discount Co Ltd*,[8] for example, there was a minimum payment clause in the hire-purchase agreement whereby if the debtor was in breach of contract (or chose to terminate lawfully the contract) he should return the goods to the creditor and make up the payments already paid to two-thirds of the hire-purchase price. This sum was expressed to be 'compensation for depreciation'. The debtor, having made several payments, refused to pay any more and returned the car. The House of Lords, having held that he was in breach of contract, decided that the sum payable under the minimum payment clause was penal and irrecoverable because it did not represent a genuine pre-estimate of loss. In particular, the amount stated could not be regarded as compensation for depreciation because, in Lord Radcliffe's words, the clause:

'... produces the result, absurd in its own terms, that the estimated amount of depreciation becomes progressively less the longer the vehicle is used under the hire. This is because the sum agreed upon diminishes as the total of cash payments increases. It is a sliding scale of compensation but a scale that slides in the wrong direction ...'[9]

On the other hand, in *Wadham Stringer Finance Ltd v Meaney*[10] an accelerated payments clause in a conditional sale agreement – whereby on default of payment in two or more monthly instalments, the creditor was entitled to call for the unpaid balance of the purchase price plus certain charges, in return for title in the car passing to the debtor – was held to be a valid liquidated damages clause. It did represent a genuine pre-estimate of the creditor's loss, given that title was to pass to the debtor.

Further very common examples of agreed sums payable on breach are the demurrage which the charterer of a vessel agrees to pay for detention

6   (1993) 61 BLR 41 at 59.
7   And of sums payable on events other than breach.
8   [1962] AC 600.
9   [1962] AC 600 at 623.
10   [1981] 1 WLR 39 at 48.

of the ship for unloading or loading beyond the lay-days and the compensation for delay provided for in building contracts.

The law on penalty clauses was extended to a clause to transfer shares, rather than to pay money, in *Jobson v Johnson*.[11] The defendant bought shares in a football club for £351,688. The purchase price was payable by an initial sum of £40,000 plus six half-yearly instalments of £51,948. The contract contained a clause that if the defendant defaulted in paying any instalment he was to transfer the shares back to the vendors for £40,000. Having paid £140,000 the defendant defaulted. The claimant, who was the assignee of the vendors, sought specific performance of the agreement for the retransfer of the shares. The Court of Appeal held that the clause for retransfer was an unenforceable penalty clause in that it was not a genuine pre-estimate of the vendors' loss. It did not matter that the clause required a transfer of property rather than a payment of money; nor that this was a rare case where equitable relief against forfeiture might *alternatively* have been sought. Dillon LJ said:

'In principle, a transaction must be just as objectionable and unconscionable in the eyes of equity if it requires a transfer of property by way of penalty on a default in paying money as if it requires a payment of an extra, or excessive, sum of money.'[12]

One might have expected that the defendant would therefore have been entitled to keep the shares, while compensating the claimant for his actual loss (ie for all the unpaid instalments plus interest). But as the claimant did not want that, the majority of the Court of Appeal instead gave him the option of insisting on either a sale of the shares by the court out of which his actual loss should be paid or an order of specific performance requiring the transfer of the shares for £40,000 if, on inquiry, that sum would not overcompensate him.

This case leads on to a question that has not so far been discussed by the judges and has barely been touched on by commentators. In the light of *Attorney-General v Blake*,[13] in which the House of Lords accepted that, in exceptional circumstances, on account of profits (or 'restitutionary damages') could be awarded for breach of contract, what is the status of a contractual clause which requires the defendant, in the event of a profitable breach, to disgorge some or all of the profits made? Clearly this is not a 'liquidated damages' clause because it neither specifies a particular sum to be paid and nor does it constitute a genuine pre-estimate of loss. On the other hand, it would seem odd to knock out such

11 [1989] 1 WLR 1026.
12 [1989] 1 WLR 1026 at 1034.
13 [2001] 1 AC 268. See above, pp 401–407.

a clause as a penalty at least in a situation where the courts would otherwise be willing to award an account of profits or restitutionary damages. Let us assume, for example, that in *Blake* itself, there had been a contractual clause to the effect that, in the event of breach, Blake would pay over all his profits from writing a book to the Crown.[14] Surely such a clause would be enforceable. In contrast, if such a clause were to be inserted in a standard commercial contract, where the courts would not be willing to award an account of profits or restitutionary damages, one might be more inclined to knock out such a clause as a penalty.

This suggests that the validity of parties' own agreed remedies will to some extent be assessed in line with the judicial remedies available. The further the parties stray from what the courts would themselves award, the more likely it is that the agreed remedy will be regarded as penal or otherwise invalid.

Finally, it should be noted that the courts' power to relieve against a forfeiture clause, requiring the forfeiture of money paid,[15] raises somewhat analogous problems to that raised by penalties and liquidated damages. The obvious difference is that the money has already been paid whereas, in relation to penalties and liquidated damages, the dispute is as to a payment that has yet to be made. This leads to the important point that the underlying cause of action is generally different because, in relation to the forfeiture of money paid, one is generally concerned with the cause of action of (autonomous) unjust enrichment rather than breach of contract. It would not therefore be appropriate in this book to deal with the forfeiture of money paid in any detail.[16] But it is important to appreciate that, after some dispute in earlier cases,[17] the Privy Council in *Workers Trust and Merchant Bank Ltd v Dojap Investments Ltd*[18] decided that a clause allowing the forfeiture of money paid could be and, on the facts, would be struck down as a 'penalty'; and, in this context, given that

---

14 Cf *R v Attorney-General for England and Wales* [2003] UKPC 22, [2003] EMLR 24, in which the Privy Council upheld the 'enforcement' by an account of profits and damages of a clause whereby a member of the SAS had promised to assign to the Crown any rights acquired (eg by writing a book) in breach of a confidentiality clause. No question of this being a 'penalty' clause was raised either in the Privy Council or in the courts below.

15 The jurisdiction to relieve against forfeiture clauses extends beyond the forfeiture of money paid. Important House of Lords cases dealing with the scope of that jurisdiction include *The Scaptrade* [1983] 2 AC 694; *Sport International Bussum BV v Inter-Footwear Ltd* [1984] 1 WLR 776; and *On Demand Information plc v Michael Gerson (Finance) plc* [2002] UKHL 13, [2003] 1 AC 368. See Treitel *The Law of Contract* (11th edn, 2003) pp 779–782; L Smith 'Relief against Forfeiture: a Restatement' [2001] CLJ 178.

16 For the details, see Treitel *The Law of Contract* (11th edn, 2003) pp 1007–1013.

17 See, eg *Stockloser v Johnson* [1954] 1 QB 476; *Galbraith v Mitchenall Estates Ltd* [1965] 2 QB 473.

18 [1993] AC 573.

deposits are generally not concerned to pre-estimate loss, the test applied to decide whether the sum to be forfeited was penal or not was one of reasonableness.

(2) Controversial issues under the present law

(a) **Actual or legally recoverable loss?**

Since an accepted important function of liquidated damages is to avoid difficulties of assessment, it must be the case that the loss that needs to be genuinely pre-estimated includes loss that is legally irrecoverable because it falls foul of the required standard of proof. But whether the loss referred to is exclusive of other legal restrictions on normal damages is unclear. In *Robophone Facilities Ltd v Blank*[19] Diplock LJ considered that liquidated damages could properly include loss that was beyond the defendant's reasonable contemplation (while a fortiori within the claimant's) and which would therefore be too remote under the principles for normal damages. And in obiter dicta in *Abrahams v Performing Right Society Ltd*,[20] Hutchison J thought that arguments about the duty to mitigate and mitigation were irrelevant to liquidated damages. On the other hand, the Law Commission provisionally thought 'that the proper yardstick by reference to which it should be determined whether the stipulated sum is a genuine pre-estimate is the damages which a court would award.'[1]

An intermediate answer is to say that it depends which legal restriction on actual loss is in issue. While there is no obvious objection to liquidated damages circumventing remoteness, or the fact that the type of loss is non-compensatable, it may well be unsatisfactory, for example, to uphold an agreed sum estimated on the assumption that the claimant will fail to mitigate for, as Beale writes, '… this would either encourage wasteful failures to mitigate or would over-compensate the wily party who both claimed the liquidated damages and mitigated.'[2]

However, it would seem unrealistic for parties to estimate, in advance, what the actual opportunities to mitigate might turn out to be or, to take another example, what the extent and relevance of the claimant's contributory negligence might be. It is submitted, therefore, that the

---

19   [1966] 1 WLR 1428.
20   [1995] ICR 1028.
1   Working Paper No 61 'Penalty Clauses and Forfeiture of Monies Paid' para 44.
2   *Remedies for Breach of Contract* (1980) p 57.

clearest and best approach is to say that the yardstick for assessing whether the damages are a genuine pre-estimate is actual, not legally recoverable, loss.[3]

It is conceivable that, as a separate policy issue, one might want to strike down, on grounds of public policy, a liquidated damages clause because it contradicts the law on, for example, the duty to mitigate or contributory negligence.[4] But if the parties have agreed that a particular sum should be payable on breach – and it is a genuine pre-estimate of actual loss – it is hard to see why one should not give effect to that agreement. This is in line with the fact that, subject to unfair terms legislation, one presumably can 'contract out' of the duty to mitigate or the law on contributory negligence.

(b) Loss greater than penalty

What if the agreed sum is a penalty, but the claimant's loss is greater than that agreed sum, so that to refuse to enforce the penalty would actually be to the claimant's advantage? Can the claimant insist on the penalty being invalid and thereby recover his actual loss? The situation is not as peculiar as may at first sight appear. For example, it is quite likely to occur when the penalty takes the form of one single agreed sum being fixed for the occurrence of several possible breaches. In *Wall v Rederiaktiebolaget Luggude*[5] it was held that charterers could disregard what was construed as a penalty clause (rather than as a liquidated damages or limitation clause) and sue for their greater actual loss. But this is rather weak authority since it is hard to see why the clause in question was penal. In *Cellulose Acetate Silk Co Ltd v Widnes Foundry Ltd*[6] the issue was expressly left open by the House of Lords, and Diplock LJ similarly regarded it as 'by no means clear' in *Robophone Facilities Ltd v Blank*.[7]

Which is the better view? On the one hand, it can be argued that, as matters are supposed to be judged at the time the contract is made, the penalty clause should be held invalid even where this is to the claimant's advantage. As against that, it can be argued that, since the refusal to enforce penalty clauses is a rare departure from freedom of contract and is designed to prevent unfairness to the defendant, there is no justification

---

3   *Commercial Remedies* (eds Burrows and Peel, 2003) p 225. But one would need to exclude legal costs from the estimate of loss because costs are recoverable in the normal way in addition to liquidated damages.
4   See, as arguably analogous, the discussion of a stipulated remedy of specific performance, below, pp 505–506.
5   [1915] 3 KB 66, approved in *Watts Watts & Co Ltd v Mitsui & Co Ltd* [1917] AC 227. See also *Jobson v Johnson* [1989] 1 WLR 1026.
6   [1933] AC 20.
7   [1966] 1 WLR 1428 at 1446.

for holding penalties invalid where there is no such unfairness. Moreover, as Hudson has forcefully pointed out,[8] since it is well-settled that where the claimant's loss is greater than the liquidated damages, he is confined to the liquidated damages,[9] to allow him to recover more than a penalty wrongly treats the claimant who has acted unfairly by inserting the penalty clause more favourably than the claimant who has acted fairly by genuinely pre-estimating the loss. It also encourages the inclusion of penalty clauses, since the claimant can take the advantage of having the clause, without suffering any disadvantage. So in this situation it does indeed seem preferable to uphold the penalty clause and, significantly, this was the view taken in the important Canadian case of *Elsley v JG Collins Ins Agencies Ltd*.[10]

(c) Liquidated damages used to limit damages[11]

While not a genuine pre-estimate of loss, a stipulated sum may be regarded as valid liquidated damages if it seeks to under-estimate and hence limit the claimant's damages. In *Cellulose Acetate Silk Co v Widnes Foundry Ltd*[12] a contract for the construction of an acetone recovery plant provided that if completion was delayed the contractor should pay 'by way of penalty the sum of £20 per working week'. The work was completed 30 weeks late and the owners suffered losses of £5,850 as a result. It was held by the House of Lords that the owners were restricted to £20 per week (that is £600) the clause being held valid albeit that its purpose was to limit rather than pre-estimate loss. It is important to realise that, while such a clause looks like a limitation clause, the House of Lords was in fact regarding it as a type of liquidated damages clause, the difference being that under a liquidated damages clause a defendant is bound to pay the agreed sum, even if the claimant's loss is less, whereas under a limitation clause, he is bound to pay only the claimant's loss up to the limit fixed. So Lord Atkin said, 'I entertain no doubt that what the parties meant was that in the event of delay the damages and the only damages were to be £20 a week, *no less and no more.*'[13] But it may be doubted whether it is sensible to take such a hybrid interpretation, and perhaps the clause ought to have been treated as an ordinary limitation clause such that the owners would only have been entitled to their loss if less than £20. Furthermore if it were regarded as an ordinary limitation

---

8   'Penalties Limiting Damages' (1974) 90 LQR 31; (1975) 91 LQR 25; (1985) 101 LQR 480.
9   *Diestal v Stevenson* [1906] 2 KB 345.
10   (1978) 83 DLR (3d) 1 at 14–15.
11   Fritz ' "Underliquidated" Damages as Limitation of Liability' (1954) 33 Tex LR 196.
12   [1933] AC 20.
13   [1933] AC 20 at 25 (author's emphasis).

clause, it would clearly fall within the Unfair Contract Terms Act 1977, whereas it must be doubted whether this is so if the hybrid construction is taken.[14] However, the hybrid view is further supported by Lord Upjohn's speech in *Suisse Atlantique Société d'Armement Maritime SA v Rotterdamsche Kolen Centrale NV*[15] where he said that, even if the demurrage clause in question represented an underestimate of loss, the sum agreed was valid liquidated damages rather than a limitation of liability.

(3) Should penalties, like liquidated damages, be valid?

The initial question is, why is it that the courts allow a claimant to recover liquidated damages, thereby ousting the judicial assessment and awarding of damages? The primary answer is that liquidated damages have a number of advantages. They make it less likely that there will be a serious dispute between the parties. They enable the defendant to know in advance what its exact liability will be. From the administration of justice angle, they save judicial time and expense in deciding what the claimant's damages should be and, from the claimant's point of view, they avoid such evils as the cost of litigation, the risk of inaccurate assessment by the courts, the need to prove one's loss according to the judicially imposed standard and probably restrictions such as remoteness and the non-recoverability of certain types of loss. Further to these advantages, the courts are not hostile to liquidated damages because they reflect the compensatory aim of judicially assessed damages: that is, they are a genuine pre-estimate of the sum needed to put the claimant into as good a position as if the contract had been performed.

In contrast, penalties run counter to the central principle that contractual damages are for compensating the claimant and not punishing the defendant. They are therefore regarded as substantively unfair. However, in other areas the courts almost always require some procedural unfairness before they will undermine the freedom of the parties to fix their own terms, and hence their refusal to enforce penalty clauses is rather exceptional. This is one of the points made by those who argue that even penalty clauses should be upheld, subject to standard factors invalidating a contract (in particular, inequality of bargaining

---

14 But in a contract with a consumer there would be significantly less difficulty in saying that such a clause falls under the Unfair Terms in Consumer Contracts Regulations 1999, SI 1999/2083, the central provisions of which are not confined to exclusion or limitation clauses.

15 [1967] 1 AC 361 at 421.

power and unconscionability).[16] Indeed this point has arguably been strengthened by the enactment of the Unfair Terms in Consumer Contracts Regulations 1999[17] which allow the courts to protect consumers against unfair terms (including penalty clauses) without the need for a special rule against penalties. Additionally, it is said that there would be important advantages in making all agreed damages clauses prima facie valid. There would be less need for judicial assessment of damages with its attendant expense and, because parties would be more certain as to the validity of an agreed damages clause, litigation costs in testing validity would be reduced and contract making would be encouraged.

On the other hand it has been argued by some adherents of 'economic analysis' that to uphold penalty clauses would encourage defendants to stick to contracts, which it would be economically efficient for them to break.[18] In other words, the 'efficient breach' theory is against upholding penalty clauses. This theory is discussed in more detail in chapter 20[19] and it will be sufficient here to give an example and to make a general criticism. Say D contracts to make a machine part for C for £10,000. If X offers D £15,000 for that part, breach by D is efficient if X values the part more than C, and inefficient if X values the part less than C. Let us assume, therefore, that C values the part at £13,000 so that efficiency dictates that D breaks the contract, pays C £3,000 damages and transfers the part to X for £15,000. The argument is that a penalty clause of, let us say, £6,000 in the contract between C and D will prevent the efficient breach, since D will no longer be better off by breaking the contract. However, the flaw in this is that it ignores the possibility of bargaining round the clause. It is in C's interests to accept between £3,000 and £5,000 to release D from the contract (because if D sticks to the contract C will make only £3,000) and in D's interest to pay up to £5,000 to C to be released to transfer the part to X. In other words, the validity of a penalty clause will only undermine efficiency where no bargaining round the clause will take place because the transaction costs are too high. As

---

16   Goetz and Scott 'Liquidated Damages, Penalties and the Just Compensation Principle' (1977) 77 Col LR 554; Kaplan 'A Critique of the Penalty Limitation on Liquidated Damages' (1977) 50 Southern Californian LR 1055; Beale *Remedies for Breach of Contract* (1980) pp 60–61; Rea 'Efficiency Implications of Penalties and Liquidated Damages' (1984) 13 JLS 147; Muir 'Stipulations for the Payment of Agreed Sums' (1985) 10 Syd LR 503; Ham 'The Rule Against Penalties in Contract: an Economic Perspective' (1990) 17 Melb ULR 649; Downes 'Rethinking Penalty Clauses' in *Wrongs and Remedies in the Twenty-First Century* (ed Birks, 1996) pp 249–269 and Chen-Wishart 'Controlling the Power to Agree Damages' in same publication, pp 271–299.
17   SI 1999/2083. See especially Sch 2, para 1 (e); above, p 441, n 19
18   Fenton 'Liquidated Damages as Prima Facie Evidence' (1975) 51 Ind LJ 189, 191.
19   Below, pp 473–475.

the transaction costs are unlikely to be high, the efficient breach theory is an unsatisfactory argument for knocking down penalty clauses. As Goetz and Scott write:

'... the existence of an overcompensation provision is never per se evidence of an efficiency impediment. Absent significant negotiation costs, the pre-stipulation of a penalty still permits ... efficient solutions in which the efficiency gains are divided between the breacher and the non-breacher in a bargained for manner.'[20]

But while the efficient breach theory seems defective, there may be some validity in the argument of Clarkson, Miller and Muris, that in many cases to uphold penalty clauses will act as an incentive for the claimant wastefully to direct resources to induce the defendant to break the contract.[1] More straightforwardly, it is submitted the strongest argument for knocking down penalty clauses is that this would contradict the traditional approach to damages according to which punitive damages are not available for breach of contract.[2] That is, while the courts should and do allow the parties to make their own assessment of compensation, it would contradict normal judicial remedies for the claimant to enforce a clause punishing the defendant for breach of contract.

It follows that this powerful argument has been weakened by the recent developments which suggest that English law might be moving towards allowing the award of punitive damages for breach of contract albeit in very exceptional cases.[3] If that were to become the law, it would be hard to justify denying validity to an agreed penalty clause between parties of equal bargaining power who have negotiated the contract in question.

4. AWARD OF AN AGREED SUM (OTHER THAN AN AGREED PRICE OR REMUNERATION) PAYABLE ON AN EVENT OTHER THAN BREACH

This sort of agreed sum occupies a position between an agreed price and an agreed sum payable on breach. Traditionally it is treated like an agreed price, so that once the event has occurred the sum can be

---

20 'Liquidated Damages, Penalties and the Just Compensation Principle' (1977) 77 Col LR 554, 568.
1 'Liquidated Damages v Penalties: Sense or Nonsense?' (1978) Wisconsin LR 351.
2 For the contrary view that there is no good reason to link the purpose of common law damages with agreed damages, see Downes 'Rethinking Penalty Clauses' in *Wrongs and Remedies in the Twenty-First Century* (ed Birks, 1996) pp 249, 265–266.
3 See above, pp 409–410.

recovered without any type of liquidated damages/penalty analysis. However, the main controversy is whether it is always sensible so to distinguish these agreed sums from those payable on breach.[4]

A colourful example is *Alder v Moore*,[5] where the defendant, a professional footballer, was injured and certified as unable to play football. Under an insurance policy the claimants paid him £500, subject to his agreement to the following term:

> 'In consideration of the above payment I hereby declare and agree that I will take no part as a playing member of any form of professional football and that in the event of infringement of this condition I will be subject to a penalty of the amount stated above.'

Four months later, the defendant began to play professional football again, and the claimants sought payment of the £500, which the defendant resisted on the ground that it was a penalty. The majority of the Court of Appeal held that the claimants were entitled to the £500. The liquidated damages/penalty distinction did not apply since the defendant had made no promise not to play football again. In any case, even if the sum was payable on breach, £500 was a genuine pre-estimate of loss and was therefore liquidated damages rather than a penalty. Devlin LJ dissented because he thought that the sum was payable on breach and was not a genuine pre-estimate of loss, but rather a penalty.

Agreed sums payable on events other than breach (as well as on breach) are particularly common in hire-purchase and conditional sale agreements. The conventional approach – that the liquidated damages/penalty distinction does not apply if the sum is payable on an event other than breach – is shown in a case such as *Associated Distributors Ltd v Hall*,[6] where the agreed sum was payable on the debtor exercising his option to terminate the contract. In *Bridge v Campbell Discount Co Ltd*,[7] however, some doubt was cast on this where the sum is payable either on breach[8] or on lawful termination by the debtor. It was held that, as on the facts, the debtor was in breach and hence the accelerated payment was payable on breach, the liquidated damages/penalty distinction was applicable in accordance with normal principles, and the sum was held

---

4   See, generally, Gullifer 'Agreed Remedies' in *Commercial Remedies* (eds Burrows and Peel, 2003) pp 191, 198–205.
5   [1961] 2 QB 57.
6   [1938] 2 KB 83.
7   [1962] AC 600.
8   It has been accepted that the law on penalty clauses applies where the creditor has terminated the contract, under an express power of termination, for a breach by the debtor even though that power extends to events other than the debtor's breach: *Cooden Engineering Co Ltd v Stanford* [1953] 1 QB 86. This was also assumed, without discussion, in *Lombard North Central plc v Butterworth* [1987] QB 527 (see above, p 149, n 3).

to be a penalty. But Lords Denning and Devlin considered that, even if the debtor had lawfully terminated the contract, so that on the facts the sum was payable on an event other than breach, the liquidated damages/penalty approach should still be applied. The reasoning behind this is that otherwise, as Lord Denning put it, 'It means that equity commits itself to this absurd paradox: it will grant relief to a man who breaks his contract but will penalise the man who keeps it.'[9]

Certainly Lord Denning's approach has much to commend it. Like agreed sums payable on breach, the purpose of agreed sums payable on an event closely allied to breach is either to pre-estimate the claimant's loss caused by the 'event' or to punish the defendant for, and hence deter him from, failure to perform. To distinguish them from agreed sums payable on breach does, therefore, produce unsatisfactory paradoxes. In line with this, the Law Commission provisionally recommended that the liquidated damages/penalty distinction should be applied to agreed sums payable on events closely allied to breach.[10]

On the other hand, it can be argued that, as the refusal to uphold penalty clauses is a somewhat unusual intrusion into freedom of contract, in that it does not rest on inequality of bargaining power, it is not sensible to extend it, particularly since to uphold an agreed sum payable on an event other than breach would not directly oust judicial compensation because there is no liability to pay unliquidated damages for an event that does not amount to a breach.

The House of Lords decision in *Export Credits Guarantee Department v Universal Oil Products Co*[11] indicates that the common law position remains that the liquidated damages/penalty distinction will not be extended at the expense of freedom of contract. To simplify the very complex facts, a Newfoundland company engaged the defendant building company to construct an oil refinery. Financing of the project was by arrangement between the Newfoundland company and a consortium of bankers. By this, the Newfoundland company were to issue promissory notes to the bankers, in return for their paying the defendants for the work as it proceeded. Payment on the promissory notes by the Newfoundland company was guaranteed by the claimants. The claimants made this guarantee in consideration of a premium paid to them by the defendants, under an agreement, which by clause 7 provided that where the Newfoundland company dishonoured promissory notes at a time when the defendants were in breach of contract the defendants would

---

9   [1962] AC 600 at 629.
10 Working Paper No 61, para 26. Lord Denning's approach is also strongly supported by Deane J, dissenting, in *AMEV-UDC Finance Ltd v Austin* (1986) 162 CLR 170 at 197–201.
11 [1983] 2 All ER 205.

reimburse the claimants for any sums paid to the bankers under the guarantee. The Newfoundland company subsequently dishonoured many promissory notes and the claimants paid the bankers £39 million under their guarantee. They then claimed £39 million from the defendants under clause 7, as the defendants had been in breach of contract at the relevant time. The defendants argued that clause 7 was invalid as a penalty clause, since it imposed an obligation to repay the claimants no matter how trivial the defendants' breach of contract and the loss caused by it.

On the facts such an argument could never hope to succeed for the simple reason that clause 7 only ever insisted on reimbursement of the claimants' payment to the bankers. So here the claimants had indeed lost the £39 million claimed, and therefore, as stressed by the House of Lords, even if a penalty/liquidated damages analysis were to be applied, the clause had to be valid as liquidated damages. The fact that the defendants would as a result be doing the work for a smaller sum than agreed, such that the Newfoundland company would ultimately benefit excessively, was of no consequence to the claimants, who could not be said to be linked to the Newfoundland company, so as to reap the benefit. The defendants were therefore held bound to pay the £39 million.

However, the House of Lords thought that the penalty/liquidated damages distinction was in any case irrelevant because the sum was to be paid on an event other than breach of a contractual obligation owed to the claimants. Lord Roskill, giving the principal speech, confirmed the lower courts' reasoning that:

> 'The clause was not a penalty clause because it provided for payment of money on the happening of a specified event other than a breach of a contractual duty owed by the contemplated payer to the contemplated payee.'[12]

This confirms the traditional common law position of confining the power to strike down terms by a penalty clause analysis. The judiciary's attitude is well summed-up in the observation of Diplock LJ in *Philip Bernstein (Successors) Ltd v Lydiate Textiles Ltd*[13] which Lord Roskill cited with approval:[14]

> 'I, for my part, am not prepared to extend the law by relieving against an obligation in a contract entered into between two parties which does not fall within the well-defined limits in which the court has in the past shown itself willing to interfere.'

---

12 [1983] 2 All ER 205 at 223.
13 Sub nom *Sterling Industrial Facilities Ltd* v *Lydiate Textiles Ltd* (1962) 106 Sol Jo 669.
14 [1983] 2 All ER 205 at 224.

It should be emphasised, however, that in order to protect consumers, statutory provisions have been enacted which do allow (or require) the courts to 'knock out' some sums payable on an event other than breach. For example, there is the Consumer Credit Act 1974, s 100 dealing with regulated hire-purchase and conditional sale agreements: where a debtor exercises its statutory right to terminate, its maximum liability, despite a higher agreed sum payable on termination (assuming he has taken reasonable care of the goods), is to pay what is needed to bring his payments up to half the purchase price, and the court can further reduce this if the creditor's loss is less.

Potentially most wide-ranging are the Unfair Terms in Consumer Contracts Regulations 1999.[15] One of the examples of a term that may be unfair is one 'requiring any consumer who fails to fulfil his obligation to pay a disproportionately high sum in compensation.' It is strongly arguable that the Regulations and that example will be construed so as to knock out some sums payable on an event other than breach.[16]

---

15   SI 1999/2083.
16   Treitel *The Law of Contract* (11th edn, 2003) pp 1006–1007. Cf above, p 441 n 19.

Chapter 20

Specific performance

1. INTRODUCTION

Specific performance is an equitable remedy which enforces a defendant's positive contractual obligations: that is, it orders the defendant to do what he or she promised to do. It is therefore a remedy protecting the claimant's expectation interest, the justification for such protection resting ultimately on the morality of promise-keeping.[1] Prohibitory injunctions also enforce contractual promises, but differ in that the promises in question are there negative. However, if what is in form a prohibitory injunction, in substance orders specific performance, or if the courts consider that in practice the injunction amounts to specific performance, it is governed by specific performance principles and is dealt with in this chapter.[2]

Strictly speaking, it is not an essential prerequisite of specific performance that the defendant is in breach of contract. Rather as Snell says: '... an action for specific performance is based on the mere existence of the contract, coupled with circumstances which make it equitable to grant a decree'.[3] But in practice, it is a breach of contract, actual or threatened,[4] that renders it 'equitable' to grant the decree.[5]

However, in contrast to damages, specific performance is not available for every breach of contract. Indeed, as in this chapter, specific

---

1 Above, pp 36–37.
2 For further discussion of indirect specific performance see below, pp 529–536.
3 *Snell's Equity* (30th edn, 2000) para 40–03.
4 *Hasham v Zenab* [1960] AC 316; Maudsley (1960) 76 LQR 200. See also *Zucker v Tyndall Holdings plc* [1992] 1 WLR 1127. The term 'threatened' is here preferred to 'anticipatory' so as to avoid the technicalities of the English doctrine of 'anticipatory breach'. According to that doctrine, an anticipatory breach does not constitute a breach unless and until it is accepted by the innocent party as terminating the contract. The better approach would be to say that an anticipatory breach is automatically a breach of contract because it constitutes a breach of the implied promise to be ready, able and willing to perform. As, on that better approach, a threatened breach of contract is itself a breach of contract, it would seem inappropriate ever to label specific performance '*quia timet*' (cf Meagher, Heydon and Leeming *Meagher Gummow and Lehane's Equity, Doctrines and Remedies* (4th edn, 2002) para 20–025). For that labelling generally, see below, pp 513, 546.
5 An exception is *Bass v Clivley* (1829) Taml 80, but it is unclear why it was there equitable to grant the order.

performance is best approached negatively, that is by examining the numerous restrictions on its availability. Positively, it then follows that if the remedy is not barred by such restrictions, a claimant who applies for it will succeed.[6]

Three other introductory points should be made. First, no order of specific performance can be made at the interim stage, where instead the appropriate remedy to enforce positive contractual obligations is the interim mandatory injunction. In so far as the availability of a final order is relevant to the grant of such an interim mandatory injunction, it is of course the principles governing specific performance that are applied.

Secondly, it is often said that, unlike damages, specific performance is a discretionary remedy. This is a misleading contrast.[7] It is misleading not only because the courts have a wide discretion (through, for example, intervening cause, remoteness and the duty to mitigate) in deciding on the losses to be compensated by compensatory damages or in deciding on whether to award, and the quantum of, restitutionary damages or punitive damages, but also because the law on specific performance is relatively clear and certain. In truth, the description 'discretionary' makes the essentially trivial point that, while there are no bars on damages, which are therefore available as of right for breach of contract (or a tort),[8] there are numerous, albeit clearly established, bars to specific performance. The same trivial contrast can be made of all common law, as against equitable, remedies for breach of contract (and torts).

Finally, a commonly-drawn contrast is between English law's regard of specific performance as a secondary remedy to damages and the allegedly reverse situation under civil law systems. What does this mean? It cannot mean that specific performance is as freely available in civil law systems as damages, for this is plainly not true. It could mean that the bars to specific performance are not as wide-ranging in civil law systems as here, but that this is so is hardly sensibly expressed by referring to specific performance as a primary remedy. It seems rather that the contrast is based on the fact that, deriving from the historical role of equitable remedies as supplementary to those of the common law, a claimant in English law will not be awarded specific performance unless he has shown that damages are inadequate whereas in civil law systems there is no such major hurdle.[9] Some recent cases indicate a weakening

---

6   In addition to the bars discussed in this chapter specific performance cannot be ordered against the Crown: Crown Proceedings Act 1947, s 21(1)(a).
7   See above, pp 11–12
8   Cf damages under the Human Rights Act 1998, s 8(3), above, p 17.
9   *Co-operative Insurance Society Ltd v Argyll Stores (Holdings) Ltd* [1998] AC 1, 11 (per Lord Hoffmann).

of this bar, and it has even been argued that specific performance is now the primary remedy in England. This seems exaggerated, but a fascinating theme throughout this chapter is the recent apparent weakening not only of this, but of several other of the traditional bars, so that specific performance may be more freely available now than it was in the past.[10]

2.   THE BARS TO SPECIFIC PERFORMANCE

(1) The primary restriction – adequacy of damages

Specific performance will not be ordered unless damages (and the common law remedy of the award of an agreed sum) are inadequate. This is the major hurdle that a claimant seeking specific performance must overcome, but, even having done so, it may still fail because of one of the several other bars.

(a) Availability of substitute – uniqueness

The most important factor in determining whether damages are adequate is whether money can buy a substitute for the promised performance. Most discussion of this has been in relation to a seller's obligation under a contract of sale, where the issue has often been expressed as one of the 'uniqueness' of the subject matter.

(i) Breach of a contract to sell land

Here specific performance is almost invariably granted where it is sought,[11] the traditional reasoning being that each piece of land is unique and cannot be replaced in the market. However, specific performance is ordered even where this does not reflect reality, for example in the case of a contact for the sale of identical new houses on a housing estate. Nor is the claimant's purpose in buying the land considered relevant. In other words, it makes no difference that the purchaser bought the land for resale or long-term investment rather than

---

10   For a similar trend in the US, see Van Hecke 'Changing Emphases in Specific Performance' (1961) 40 North Carolina LR 1; Comment 'Specific Performance: A Liberalization of Equity Standards' (1964) 49 Iowa LR 1290. For a general comparative account of 'enforced performance', see Treitel *Remedies for Breach of Contract* (1988) ch 3.

11   *Sudbrook Trading Estate Ltd v Eggleton* [1983] 1 AC 444 at 478. Specific performance is also ordered of contracts to dispose of lesser interests in land: in *Verrall v Great Yarmouth Borough Council* [1981] QB 202, it was even ordered of a short-term contractual licence.

as a home.[12] The courts are therefore not confining specific performance to where the claimant places a subjective consumer value on the land over and above that reflected in the objective market price.[13] Assuming that there is no true substitute land, specific performance for the long-term investor is justified because of the acute difficulty of accurately assessing his profits. But there is no such obvious justification where the claimant was intending a quick resale, particularly where the resale contract has already been concluded. All in all, it seems clear that specific performance has simply taken over as the primary remedy for breach of an obligation to sell land, and that the adequacy of damages hurdle is in effect ignored. This is unfortunate as, for reasons later discussed, the adequacy of damages restriction rests on a sound footing.

The seller of an interest in land is also readily awarded specific performance ordering the buyer to accept title and to pay the contract price.[14] Since the seller's interest is purely monetary, damages or, where title has already passed, the remedy of the award of the agreed price would be perfectly adequate, except in a rare case where damages could not be accurately assessed. Nor is it an explanation to say that as the buyer can get specific performance, it is only just, in accord with 'affirmative mutuality',[15] for the seller to be so entitled, since no injustice would be caused by the grant of the common law remedies. In truth it seems that on this side of the contract too, the adequacy of the common law remedies is ignored and specific performance is the primary remedy.

(ii) Breach of a contract to sell goods

The Sale of Goods Act 1979, s 52 expressly gives the courts a discretion to order the specific performance of the sale of 'specific or ascertained' goods; but the courts have not interpreted this section as removing the adequacy of damages hurdle or as altering their traditional approach to it. Specific performance therefore continues not to be ordered for the sale of most goods, whether 'specific or ascertained' or not, on the ground

---

12 For discussion see Brenner 'Specific Performance of Contracts for the Sale of Land Purchased for Resale or Investment' (1978) 24 McGill LJ 513, esp 545–548; Jones and Goodhart, *Specific Performance* (2nd edn, 1996) pp 130–132; Sharpe, *Injunctions and Specific Performance* (3rd edn, 2000) paras 8.30–8.90. Cf *Semelhago v Paramadevan* (1996) 136 DLR (4th) 1, 9–11 (Supreme Court of Canada).

13 Harris, Ogus and Phillips 'Contract Remedies and the Consumer Surplus' (1979) 95 LQR 581, 588.

14 *Walker v Eastern Counties Rly Co* (1848) 6 Hare 594; *Eastern Counties Rly Co v Hawkes* (1855) 5 HL Cas 331; *Maskell v Ivory* [1970] Ch 502; *Johnson v Agnew* [1980] AC 367.

15 Sharpe *Injunctions and Specific Performance* (3rd edn, 2000) paras 7.820–7.880, 8.160.

that money enables substitutes to be bought in the market.[16] On the other hand, specific performance is ordered where the goods are unique.

Goods are most obviously unique where substitutes cannot be bought because the goods possess significant physical characteristics that very few, if any, other goods have. That the courts will order specific performance for the sale of physically unique goods is well-established. So in *Falcke v Gray*,[17] although specific performance was refused on other grounds, the court would have been prepared to order specific performance of a contract to sell two china jars on the ground that the jars were of 'unusual beauty, rarity and distinction';[18] and in *Thorn v Public Works Comrs*,[19] specific performance was ordered of a contract to sell the arch-stone, the spandrill stone and the Bramley Fall stone of the old Westminster Bridge, which had been pulled down. Again the courts are often willing to order specific performance of a contract to sell a ship, because a ship often has characteristics shared by very few, if any, other ships. So, for example, in *Behnke v Bede Shipping Co Ltd*[20] Wright J, in ordering specific performance of a contract to sell the ship *City*, said 'the *City* was of peculiar and practically unique value to the plaintiff ... A very experienced ship's valuer has said that he knew of only one other comparable ship but that may now have been sold.'[1] On the other hand, in *CN Marine Inc v Stena Line A/B and Regie Voor Maritiem Transport, The Stena Nautica (No 2)*,[2] specific performance was refused because the ship was not sufficiently different from other ships.

While there are few other cases in which the specific performance of the sale of physically unique goods has been ordered, there are analogous examples. First, there are cases where specific performance was ordered of contracts relating to such goods. In *Lingen v Simpson*,[3] for example, in breach of a contract dissolving a partnership one partner failed to release for copying a book of ornamental plates that had been used in the business. The court ordered him to release the book and, although there was no discussion of inadequacy, we can assume that damages were thought inadequate because each of the two books was physically unique. Again when in *Phillips v Lamdin*[4] the defendant, who

---

16   An extreme example is *Cohen v Roche* [1927] 1 KB 169, refusing the analogous remedy of delivery up in relation to Hepplewhite chairs.
17   (1859) 4 Drew 651.
18   (1859) 4 Drew 651 at 658.
19   (1863) 32 Beav 490.
20   [1927] 1 KB 649. See also *The Oro Chief* [1983] 2 Lloyd's Rep 509 at 521; and *Bristol Airport plc v Powdrill* [1990] Ch 744 at 759 (lease of an aircraft).
1   [1927] 1 KB 649 at 661.
2   [1982] 2 Lloyd's Rep 336.
3   (1824) 1 Sim & St 600.
4   [1949] 2 KB 33.

had contracted to sell his home to the claimant, was in breach of that contract by removing an Adam-style door from one of the rooms he was ordered to replace it. Croom-Johnson J said, 'You cannot make a new Adam door. You cannot in these times refashion a door or make a copy ... I do not see how damages can be an adequate remedy.'[5] Secondly, there are several oft-cited and particularly good examples of the analogous remedy of delivery up for wrongful detention being ordered in respect of physically unique goods, such as antiques, heirlooms and works of art.[6]

Analogously to their approach to land, the courts appear not to be concerned with the purpose for which the claimant is buying the physically unique goods. In other words, no distinction appears to be drawn between the consumer, with his non-monetary interest, and the businessman who wants the goods for profitable use or resale.[7] The same criticism can be made as in relation to land contracts: namely, that for the reseller damages are adequate, since his interest is purely monetary and, unlike the long-term investor, they can generally be readily assessed.

Will specific performance be ordered for the sale of commercially unique goods? Goods can be said to be commercially unique, a term coined by Treitel,[8] where, although the goods may not be physically unique, buying substitutes would be so difficult or would cause such delay that the claimant's business would be seriously disrupted.

Until fairly recently, no case could be confidently cited in which specific performance had been ordered on this ground,[9] although in *Behnke v Bede Shipping*, Wright J did appear to regard it as relevant that the buyer needed the ship immediately for the purposes of his business. There was also Lord Hardwicke's dictum in *Buxton v Lister*[10] that in a supply contract the close vicinity of the goods to the buyer can make damages inadequate. Furthermore in *North v Great Northern Rly Co*,[11] it was accepted that the analogous remedy of delivery up could be ordered for commercially unique goods, here 54 coal waggons; and the interim order

---

5   [1949] 2 KB 33 at 41.
6   Below, pp 578–579.
7   Eg in *Falcke v Gray* and *Thorn v Public Works Comrs*, the claimants seemed to have merely a commercial interest in the goods. Contra is Sharpe *Injunctions and Specific Performance* (3rd edn, 2000) para 8.350 citing *Cohen v Roche* [1927] 1 KB 169 and *Dowling v Betjemann* (1862) 2 John & H 544.
8   *The Law of Contract* (11th edn, 2003) p 1022; 'Specific Performance in the Sale of Goods' [1966] JBL 211.
9   But see in Australia, *Dougan v Ley* (1946) 71 CLR 142 (licensed taxi-cab).
10 (1746) 3 Atk 383 at 385. But the correctness of this was specifically doubted in *Pollard v Clayton* (1855) 1 K & J 462.
11 (1860) 2 Giff 64.

for delivery up of 500 tons of steel, made more recently in *Howard Perry Ltd v British Railways Board*,[12] can also be said to have been based on this reasoning.

But commercial uniqueness as a ground for specific performance was radically accepted in *Sky Petroleum Ltd v VIP Petroleum Ltd*.[13] Here, an interim injunction amounting to temporary specific performance was granted to enforce the supply of petrol to the claimants' filling stations, at a time when the petrol market was in such an unusual state that the claimants would be unlikely to find an alternative supply and as a result would be forced to stop trading. The reason why this is particularly radical is that petrol is not even 'specific or ascertained' goods within the Sale of Goods Act 1979, s 52. In *Re Wait*,[14] the majority of the Court of Appeal thought that the Act meant that specific performance could not be ordered of non-specific or unascertained goods and any application of commercial uniqueness to such goods was therefore clearly rejected. But in *Sky Petroleum* Goulding J adopted a different approach. He said:

> 'I come to the most serious hurdle in the way of the plaintiffs, which is the well-known doctrine that the court refuses specific performance of a contract to sell and purchase chattels not specific or ascertained ... The ratio behind the rule is, as I believe, that under the ordinary contract for the sale of non-specific goods, damages are a sufficient remedy. That to my mind, is lacking in the circumstances of the present case. The evidence suggests, and indeed it is common knowledge, that the petroleum market is in an unusual state in which a would-be buyer cannot go into the market and contract with another seller, possibly at some sacrifice as to the price. Here the defendants appear for practical purposes to be the plaintiffs' sole means of keeping their business going, and I am prepared so far to depart from the general rule as to try to preserve the position under the contract until a later date.'[15]

It is noteworthy here that the US Uniform Commercial Code, para 2.716(1) has sought to encourage acceptance of the notion of 'commercial uniqueness' in relation to goods that are not specific or ascertained. The comment to that section reads:

> 'The test of uniqueness must be made in terms of the total situation, which characterises the contract. Output and requirements contracts involving a particular or peculiarly available source or market present today the typical contractual specific

---

12   [1980] 1 WLR 1375.
13   [1974] 1 WLR 576.
14   [1927] 1 Ch 606.
15   [1974] 1 WLR 576 at 578–579.

performance situation, as contrasted with contracts for the sale of heirlooms or priceless works of art, which were usually involved in the older cases.'[16]

But while the acceptance of commercial uniqueness for non-specific goods in the *Sky Petroleum* case is important, a degree of caution must be exercised in assessing its effects. Apart from the fact that it was a first instance decision that has not yet been followed or approved, doubt has been cast on the courts' acceptance of commercial uniqueness, even in relation to specific or ascertained goods, by the Court of Appeal decision in *Société des Industries Métallurgiques SA v Bronx Engineering Co Ltd*.[17] Here it was held that an interim injunction restraining the sellers from removing certain machinery from the jurisdiction should not be granted since, even if the sellers were in breach of contract, there was no likelihood of the claimant buyers being granted specific performance at the trial, because damages were adequate. This was held to be so, even though the court accepted that the delay of nine to twelve months in obtaining substitute machinery might substantially disrupt the claimants' business. While one might try to reconcile the cases by saying, for example, that the degree of disruption threatened in *Bronx Engineering* was not as great as in *Sky Petroleum* (or the analogous *North v Great Northern Rly*) the plain truth seems to be that the Court of Appeal was here rejecting commercial as opposed to physical uniqueness. Although *Howard Perry* has since been decided, without any reference being made to *Bronx Engineering*, it is still too early to say that such a rejection will be disregarded. As yet, therefore, even if the goods are specific or ascertained, it cannot be confidently asserted that specific performance will be ordered of a contract to sell goods that are commercially unique for the buyer.

In terms of policy, commercial uniqueness should be accepted, for while theoretically damages for the substantial disruption to a business are adequate, since it is ultimately only money that the claimant is losing, in practice in this situation, an accurate assessment of the claimant's losses is so difficult that the claimant is likely to be incorrectly compensated; and this high risk of incorrect compensation is a strong justification for accepting commercial uniqueness, whether the goods in question are specific or ascertained or not. Nor, it should be added, is

---

16 Nichols 'Remedies – Specific Performance and Long Term Supply Contracts' (1976) 30 Ark LR 65. Output and requirements contracts are the major types of long-term supply contracts. Even where, in contrast to *Sky Petroleum*, there are substitute goods readily available at the time of the suppliers' breach, goods in such contracts are typically commercially unique, because the claimant is very often unsure of obtaining a substitute supply during the full contract period, and is thereby threatened with disruption to his business.

17 [1975] 1 Lloyd's Rep 465.

there any need as a matter of construction to take the restrictive exhaustive interpretation of the Sale of Goods Act 1979, s 52 adopted in *Re Wait*.

It should further be noted that our courts, in contrast again to those in the US, may not recognise sentimental uniqueness. In Treitel's words, 'It is ... uncertain whether sentimental attachment to otherwise ordinary goods makes them unique.'[18] If this is so, it represents an unfortunate failure to take into account the consumer interest, for damages do not enable a satisfactory substitute to be bought for such goods.

All the above discussion has focused on the concept of uniqueness. One must now take note, however, of the Sale and Supply of Goods to Consumers Regulations 2002,[19] which insert new ss 48A–48F into the Sale of Goods Act 1979.[20] These give a buyer, who is a consumer, a right to the repair or replacement, within a reasonable time, of goods which do not conform to the contract terms unless repair or replacement is impossible or disproportionate to a price reduction or rescission of the contract. The courts are expressly given the power to enforce this right to repair or replacement by an order of specific performance.[1] This marks an interesting move in favour of specific performance being the primary judicial remedy for consumers in this situation. The structure of the provisions militates against the courts applying the normal common law approach of denying specific performance unless damages are inadequate.[2] Rather it appears that courts should only refuse specific performance (ordering repair or replacement)[3] if repair or replacement would be impossible or disproportionate to a price reduction or rescission.[4] Given that these Regulations implement an EC Directive,[5] it is perhaps not surprising that, in the primacy afforded to specific performance, they reflect a civilian rather than a common law approach.

Finally, can specific performance ever be obtained by the vendor of goods? The Sale of Goods Act 1979 makes no provision for specific performance being granted against a buyer so as to order the taking of and paying for goods and there is little authority to suggest that a vendor

18   [1966] JBL 211, 214.
19   SI 2002/3045.
20   And the Supply of Goods and Services Act 1982, ss 11M–11S (for contracts, other than sale, where property passes).
1   Sale of Goods Act 1979, s 48E(2).
2   See Harris 'Specific Performance – A Regular Remedy for Consumers' (2003) 119 LQR 541.
3   As between the two, a court may refuse specific performance ordering repair if disproportionate to replacement and vice versa: Sale of Goods Act 1979, ss 48B(3)(b) and 48E(2).
4   Sale of Goods Act 1979, ss 48B(3)(a) and (c) and 48E(2).
5   EC Directive 1999/44/EC.

of goods can be awarded specific performance at common law.[6] Normally, as the vendor's interest is purely monetary, damages or the award of the agreed price will be adequate. However, in long-term requirements contracts, specific performance may be merited because of the difficulty in assessing the vendor's damages, particularly in view of uncertainty as to the exact quantity of goods being sold and as to the future state of the market.[7] Certainly, prohibitory injunctions are commonly granted in respect of such contracts to restrain the purchaser from buying goods other than from the vendor.[8] But as the courts in such cases have not regarded themselves as in effect ordering specific performance, it is probably misleading to regard such cases as authorities on specific performance.

(iii) Breach of a contract to sell shares or stocks

Where the shares or stocks are freely available on the market, specific performance will generally not be ordered, since damages enable substitutes to be bought. For example, in *Cud v Rutter,*[9] specific performance of a contract to sell South Sea stock was refused, Lord Parker LC saying:

'... a court of equity ought not to execute any of these contracts, but to leave them to law, where the party is to recover damages, and with the money may if he pleases buy the quantity of stock agreed to be transferred to him; for there can be no difference between one man's stock and another's.'[10]

But in the converse situation, where substitute shares are not readily available, an extreme case being where the breach deprives the claimant of a majority holding, damages are regarded as inadequate and specific performance will be ordered.[11] Generally this approach is fully justified, although one can imagine situations, for example where the purchaser has bought for a quick resale, where damages can be accurately assessed, and would be adequate.[12] A vendor of such shares has also been awarded specific performance,[13] but as with contracts for the sale of land

---

6　But see *Shell-Mex Ltd v Elton Cop Dyeing Co Ltd* (1928) 34 Com Cas 39; *Elliott v Pierson* [1948] 1 All ER 939.
7　Treitel [1966] JBL 211, 229–230.
8　Below, pp 534–535.
9　(1720) 1 P Wms 570. Also *Re Schwabacher* (1907) 98 LT 127; *Chinn v Hochstrasser* [1979] Ch 447 at 462, 470.
10　(1720) 1 P Wms 570 at 571.
11　*Duncuft v Albrecht* (1841) 12 Sim 189; *Langen and Wind Ltd v Bell* [1972] Ch 685; *Harvela Investments Ltd v Royal Trust Co of Canada* [1985] 2 All ER 966.
12　See analogously above, pp 459, 461.
13　*Odessa Tramways Co v Mendel* (1878) 8 Ch D 235.

there rarely seems any justification for this, and at root it probably rests on the unsatisfactory notion of 'affirmative mutuality'.[14]

(b) Difficulty in assessing damages

This head and the previous one (uniqueness) are inextricably linked; difficulty in assessing damages – whether in putting a value on a consumer's interest, or in calculating possible investment profit, or in putting a figure on the serious disruption to a business – lies as the root justification for specific performance, where the contractual subject matter is unique.[15] But the question now to be examined is, does difficulty in assessing damages in itself render damages inadequate?

The answer would appear to be that it does not for while there are eighteenth- and nineteenth-century cases relying on this, such as *Taylor v Neville*,[16] which concerned a contract for the sale of 800 tons of iron involving delivery in instalments over a number of years, and *Adderley v Dixon*,[17] which dealt with a contract for the sale of debts proved in bankruptcy, later cases, such as *Fothergill v Rowland*,[18] denied the relevance of the difficulty of assessing damages. Indeed this concerned an output contract, where, irrespective of any commercial uniqueness, one would have expected difficulties of assessment to be particularly problematical because not only is there the usual difficulty in long-term contracts of judging future market prices but, in addition, as with requirements contracts, one cannot state in advance the exact quantity of goods to be supplied. Yet Sir G Jessel MR said:

> 'To say that you cannot ascertain the damage in a case of breach of contract for the sale of goods, say in monthly deliveries extending over three years ... is to limit the power of ascertaining damages in a way which would rather astonish gentlemen who practise on what is called the other side of Westminster Hall. There is never considered to be any difficulty in ascertaining such a thing. Therefore I do not think it is a case in which damages could not be ascertained at law.'[19]

That the difficulty of assessing damages is irrelevant gains further and more recent support from the judgments in the *Bronx Engineering* case.[20]

---

14   Above, p 459.
15   Kronman 'Specific Performance' (1978) 45 U of Chi LR 351, 362.
16   Unreported but cited in *Buxton v Lister* (1746) 3 Atk 383.
17   (1824) 1 Sim & St 607.
18   (1873) LR 17 Eq 132. The injunction sought was regarded as amounting to specific performance – see below, pp 535–536.
19   (1873) LR 17 Eq 132 at 140.
20   [1975] 1 Lloyd's Rep 465 at 468, 469–470.

This approach is most unfortunate, for where there is grave doubt about whether damages will put the claimant into as good a position as if the contract had been performed, specific performance is prima facie a better remedy.[1] Certainly, the difficulty of assessing damages has been expressly regarded as a factor rendering damages inadequate in respect of interim prohibitory injunctions restraining defendants from selling goods other than to or through the claimant, their exclusive agent or distributor.[2] But the courts in these cases did not regard themselves as in effect ordering specific performance, and this, plus the ease with which the adequacy of damages hurdle has been traditionally overcome with regard to prohibitory injunctions restraining the breach of negative contractual obligations, probably renders it misleading to use such cases as authorities on specific performance.[3]

(c) Inability to pay the damages

The question of whether the defendant's inability to pay the damages renders them inadequate, has traditionally received surprisingly little attention in the cases. In *Re Wait*[4] though, the Court of Appeal clearly did not consider the defendant's insolvency sufficient to render damages inadequate for failure to deliver wheat, and Goulding J appeared to take the same view in *Anders Utkilens Rederi A/S v Lovisa Stevedoring Co A/B:*[5] 'Commercial life would be subjected to new and unjust hazards if the court were to decree specific performance of contracts normally sounding only in damages simply because of a party's threatened insolvency.' On the other hand, in the *Bronx Engineering* case, which in all other respects is so anti-specific performance, Lord Edmund Davies did think it relevant in relation to adequacy that the defendants would be able to pay; and in *The Oro Chief*,[6] Staughton J said in dicta that even if a ship was not unique '… it may be that in special circumstances, such as when the seller is insolvent and can pay no damages, [the buyer] will still obtain an order for specific performance.' There are also prohibitory injunction cases, expressly stating that damages are inadequate where the

---

1   Similarly it is arguable that damages are inadequate where some of the loss is irrecoverable because of a particular type (eg mental distress) or too remote. But see *The Stena Nautica (No 2)* [1982] 2 Lloyd's Rep 336 at 342 (per Parker J).
2   *Evans Marshall & Co v Bertola SA* (1973) 1 WLR 349; *Decro-Wall International SA v Practitioners in Marketing Ltd* [1971] 2 All ER 216. Below, p 535.
3   Contra is Treitel *Law of Contract* (11th edn, 2003) pp 1021–1022.
4   [1927] 1 Ch 606.
5   [1985] 2 All ER 669 at 674.
6   [1983] 2 Lloyd's Rep 509 at 521. See also *Doloret v Rothschild* (1824) 1 Sim & St 590 at 598.

defendant is unable to pay,[7] but again it is probably misleading to use them as authorities on specific performance.

In general, the former view is correct. If one focuses on a contract for the sale of goods, to allow a claimant to obtain specific performance simply because of the defendant's insolvency or imminent insolvency would, in effect, turn all unsecured creditors into secured creditors. In other words, it would undermine our present law of insolvency by entitling unsecured creditors to 'take out' particular goods from the insolvent's assets. Exceptionally, however, our insolvency system would not be undermined by such an order; for example, where the claimant is the defendant's only creditor or where the performance will not reduce the defendant's assets. In such (unusual) circumstances it is clearly right that an inability to pay damages renders them inadequate and justifies specific performance.

(d) Contractual obligation to pay money

The common law remedies, being monetary orders, are normally adequate where the breach is of a contractual obligation to pay money. However, specific performance has been ordered of a contract to pay an annuity.[8] In dicta in *Adderley v Dixon*,[9] this was justified on the ground of the difficulty of here assessing a lump sum of damages. An alternative justification, put forward in *Beswick v Beswick*,[10] is that specific performance avoids the inconvenience of bringing numerous actions to recover the agreed sum. Specific performance can also be granted to enforce the purchaser's payment obligation in a contract for the sale of

---

7   *Evans Marshall & Coy Bertola SA* [1973] 1 WLR 349; *Associated Portland Cement Manufacturers Ltd v Tiegland Shipping A/S* [1975] 1 Lloyd's Rep 581. Analogously to these see *Hodgson v Duce* (1856) 28 LTOS 155 (injunction for trespass).

8   *Ball v Coggs* (1710) 1 Bro Parl Cas 140; *Beswick v Beswick* [1968] AC 58.

9   (1824) 1 Sim & St 607.

10   [1968] AC 58 at 81, 88, 97.

land, or for the sale of shares that cannot be replaced in the market,[11] but there rarely seems any justification for here regarding the common law remedies as inadequate.[12]

(e) Contracts that can be immediately terminated

A leading case is *Sheffield Gas Consumers' Co v Harrison*,[13] where specific performance was refused of a contract to allow the claimant to join a partnership. In Sir John Romilly's words:

'... this Court will not enforce the specific performance of a contract to enter into a partnership, which, so far as the defendant is concerned, he may dissolve immediately afterwards. To specifically perform a contract of this description would be merely nugatory.'[14]

But if the order would be futile because the contract can be immediately terminated, it would seem that a fortiori damages are adequate, and that the case fails at this initial hurdle.[15]

However, one should not regard specific performance of such contracts as necessarily being ruled out, for one can imagine situations where damages are inadequate and where there is some point from the claimant's point of view in being granted specific performance even though the defendant can terminate the contract almost immediately. For example, specific performance of a contract of employment terminable at short notice may be important so as to give the claimant an extra period of employment necessary for the accrual of certain rights (eg to maternity leave or to a pension).

(f) Nominal damages and privity

In *Beswick v Beswick*[16] a coal merchant transferred his business to his nephew, who in return promised that, after his uncle's death, he would pay £5 a week to his widow. The uncle died and his widow brought an action for specific performance of the nephew's promise, suing both personally and as administratrix. The House of Lords, upholding the

---

11 Further examples are the payment obligations in a contract to take up and pay for debentures; in a contract to discharge another's debt; and in a loan agreement collateral to a specifically enforceable agreement. See Jones and Goodhart *Specific Performance* (2nd edn, 1996) pp 154–161.
12 Above, pp 459, 465–466.
13 (1853) 17 Beav 294. See also *Hercy v Birch* (1804) 9 Ves 357; *Tito v Waddell (No 2)* [1977] Ch 106 at 326–327.
14 (1853) 17 Beav 294 at 297.
15 The same reasoning applies to a contract for a lease that has already expired by trial, see *Turner v Clowes* (1869) 20 LT 214.
16 [1968] AC 58.

doctrine of privity, held that while the widow could not maintain a successful action suing personally, she could as administratrix succeed in suing for the estate's loss, though not her own personal third party loss. Crucially, however, the Lords held that as administratrix she should be granted specific performance of the nephew's promise rather than being confined to damages.

One aspect of the decision – that specific performance can be granted for failure to pay an annuity – has already been dealt with, and the wider implications of their Lordships' speeches will be considered shortly. But the decision is probably principally well known for laying down that specific performance can be granted to avoid the injustice that the privity rule can produce. The reasoning was as follows: if a party sues on a contract made for the benefit of a third party his damages, which are assessed according to his own loss, are usually going to be nominal; where this produces injustice, as here where the nephew had got the business and would end up paying almost nothing for it, nominal damages should be regarded as inadequate, enabling specific performance to be granted to enforce the defendant's promise. Only Lord Pearce thought that the administratrix could have recovered substantial damages but, if wrong on this, he too considered nominal damages 'manifestly useless'.[17] Two points should be added. First, while usually regarded as a pioneering manoeuvre around the doctrine of privity, there were earlier cases ordering specific performance of a contract for the benefit of a third party,[18] and these were relied on by the House of Lords. Secondly, the reform of the doctrine of privity by the Contracts (Rights of Third Parties) Act 1999 means that, on the facts of *Beswick v Beswick*, the third party (ie the widow in her personal capacity) would probably now have a direct right of action against the nephew.

(g) *Beswick v Beswick* – the radical interpretation

On a narrow view, *Beswick* lays down merely that damages may be inadequate, and specific performance can be ordered, for breach of a contract to pay an annuity or to benefit a third party.[19] But there is an alternative wide view of *Beswick*, which focuses on the fact that each of their Lordships at some stage described the relationship between damages and specific performance in terms other than the adequacy of damages. Thus Lord Reid, with whom Lord Guest agreed, was

---

17   [1968] AC 58 at 89.
18   *Keenan v Handley* (1864) 2 De GJ & Sm 283; *Peel v Peel* (1869) 17 WR 586; *Hohler v Aston* [1920] 2 Ch 420.
19   On this, *Beswick* was followed in *Gurtner v Circuit* [1968] 2 QB 587.

concerned with ordering specific performance to produce '... a just result'.[20] Lord Upjohn said, 'Equity will grant specific performance when damages are inadequate to meet the justice of the case.'[1] Lord Hodson talked of deciding which was the more appropriate remedy and concluded that, as there had been an unconscionable breach of faith, the equitable remedy was 'apt'.[2] Lord Pearce too said that specific performance was 'the more appropriate remedy',[3] and it is particularly significant that he cited with approval sections of Windeyer J's judgment in *Coulls v Bagot's Executor and Trustee Co Ltd*[4] including the following: 'It is ... a faulty analysis of legal obligations to say that the law treats the promisor as having a right to elect either to perform his promise or to pay damages. Rather ... the promisee has "a legal right to the performance of the contract".'[5]

The wide view is that, given such terminology, the Lords were concerned to effect a general change in the relationship between damages and specific performance so that, to use conventional terminology, damages are inadequate in a far wider range of circumstances than in the past. Indeed Lawson thought that *Beswick* could be interpreted as saying that specific performance replaces damages as the primary remedy in English law. He wrote:

'... it is not unreasonable to see in it an acknowledgement of a right to specific performance of all contracts where there is no adequate reason for the courts to refuse it. If this is so, we have already in England reached the Scottish principle that specific performance is the normal remedy for breach of contract, and a refusal of it must be justified in specific types of case or on special grounds. In other words ... the choice between specific performance and damages should in principle rest with the plaintiff, not the court ...'[6]

While *Beswick can* be given such a wide interpretation, and it is hard to interpret Lord Pearce's judgment in any other way, the courts have taken the narrow view, for they have continued to apply the adequacy of damages bar without even mentioning *Beswick*.

In *The Stena Nautica (No 2)*[7] May LJ, while not referring to *Beswick*, also preferred a different terminology than adequacy, and cited Sachs LJ's

---

20 [1968] AC 58 at 77.
1 [1968] AC 58 at 102.
2 [1968] AC 58 at 83.
3 [1968] AC 58 at 88.
4 (1967) 119 CLR 460.
5 (1967) 119 CLR 460 at 504, citing *Alley v Deschamps* (1806) 13 Ves 225 at 228.
6 *Remedies of English Law* (2nd edn, 1980) pp 223–224.
7 [1982] 2 Lloyd's Rep 336 at 346–347. Macdonald 'The Inadequacy of Adequacy: the Granting of Specific Performance' (1987) 38 NILQ 244 supports this approach. See also Goulding J in *Anders Utkilens Rederi A/S v O/Y Lovisa Stevedoring Co A/B* [1985] 2 All ER 669 at

statement in *Evans Marshall & Co v Bertola SA*[8] (a prohibitory injunction rather than a specific performance case)[9] that, 'The standard question ... are damages an adequate remedy? might perhaps, in the light of authorities of recent years, be rewritten: is it just in all the circumstances that the plaintiff should be confined to his remedy in damages?'[10] Like *Beswick*, May LJ's approach can be interpreted widely as advocating that damages will be held inadequate in a far wider set of circumstances than in the past. But again a narrow view has prevailed so that May LJ's terminology has not heralded a substantive change. Indeed May LJ himself went on to apply seemingly traditional reasoning in denying specific performance: that is, the ship in question was not unique. The majority reached the same result by the same reasoning without advocating any change of terminology.

(h) Is it satisfactory to maintain an adequacy of damages hurdle?

It is a complex policy question whether the primacy traditionally given to damages by the adequacy of damages rule is justified other than historically.[11] On the one hand, it might be said that, subject to other bars, a claimant ought to be entitled to specific performance if it so chooses, since in accordance with the morality of promise-keeping, this most closely fulfils its expectations. In particular, specific performance satisfies a consumer's non-monetary interest in performance and does not run the risk of inaccurate assessment or the defendant's inability to pay. Moreover, it saves the costs of a judicial assessment of damages.

On the other hand, a claimant entitled to specific performance has an incentive to be idle and inefficient, for while a claimant seeking damages has a duty to mitigate its loss, so that its damages will be reduced if it fails to do so, specific performance requires no reasonable steps to be taken by

674, referring to what 'good conscience' requires; and Lawrence Collins QC in *Rainbow Estates Ltd v Tokenhold Ltd* [1999] Ch 64 at 73, 'Subject to the overriding need to avoid injustice or oppression, the remedy should be available when damages are not an adequate remedy or, in the more modern formulation, when specific performance is the appropriate remedy.'

8   [1973] 1 WLR 349.
9   Below, p 535.
10 [1973] 1 WLR 349 at 379. It is unclear which 'authorities of recent years' Sachs LJ was referring to.
11 Kronman 'Specific Performance' (1978) 45 U of Chi LR 351; Schwartz 'The Case for Specific Performance' (1979) 89 Yale LJ 271; Linzer 'On the Amorality of Contract Remedies – Efficiency, Equity and the Second Restatement' (1981) 81 Col LR 111; Yorio 'In Defence of Money Damages for Breach of Contract' (1982) 82 Col LR 1365; Ulen 'The Efficiency of Specific Performance: Towards a Unified Theory of Contract Remedies' (1984) Mich LR 341; Ogus 'Remedies' in *Contract Law Today* (eds Harris and Tallon, 1989) pp 243–263; Harris, Campbell and Halson *Remedies in Contract and Tort* (2nd edn, 2002) pp 221–227; Collins *The Law of Contract* (4th edn, 2003) pp 399–405. See also Laycock *The Death of the Irreparable Injury Rule* (1991) esp ch 11.

the claimant to put itself into as good a position as if the contract had been performed. Specific performance is also more of an infringement of individual liberty in that ordering people to stick to their promises is more coercive of their behaviour than requiring them to pay damages. Similarly it may be thought relevant that the sanction to enforce specific performance is more drastic with disobedience amounting to a contempt of court, potentially punishable by imprisonment. Indeed it was one of Dawson's[12] main arguments that specific performance might be more widely used if, as in Germany, the consequences of non-compliance were less severe and more varied. A further argument against specific performance is that it potentially generates undesirable future friction between the parties. Moreover, there is the view that non-monetary remedies generally are less satisfactory than damages, since they give the claimant too much of an advantage in pre- and post-judgment bargaining.[13]

Consideration must also be given to probably the most discussed argument against specific performance, namely the economic analysis theory of 'efficient breach'.[14] The basis of this is that in a contract in which the claimant is to receive a contractual performance from the defendant in return for the payment of money, the claimant places a certain value on that contractual performance. This value most simply accords with the profits expected to be made from the performance. The free market produces economic efficiency by moving resources to those who place the highest value on them. In order to support this the law must permit and indeed encourage a defendant to break a contract where this will lead to resources passing to those who place higher values on them while at the same time discouraging breach where the claimant has a higher value use than others. The right encouragement and discouragement to breach is produced by awarding, where possible to estimate, expectation damages in preference to specific performance. An example will make this clearer.[15] Say D contracts to make a machine part

---

12 'Specific Performance in France and Germany' (1959) 57 Mich LR 495, 538.
13 Above, p 22.
14 In addition to the writings cited above, p 472, n 11, see Birmingham 'Breach of Contract, Damages Measures and Economic Efficiency' (1970) 24 Rutgers LR 273; Goetz and Scott 'Liquidated Damages, Penalties and the Just Compensation Principle' (1977) 77 Col LR 554; Farber 'Reassessing the Economic Efficiency of Compensatory Damages for Breach of Contract' (1980) 66 Va LR 1443; Macneil 'Efficient Breach of Contract: Circles in the Sky' (1982) 68 Va LR 947; Craswell 'Contract Remedies, Renegotiation and the Theory of Efficient Breach' (1988) 61 So Cal LR 629; Friedmann 'The Efficient Breach Fallacy' (1989) 18 JLS 1; Posner *Economic Analysis of Law* (6th edn, 2003) pp 118–126, 131–132; Beale *Remedies for Breach of Contract* (1980) pp 13–14, 142; Harris, Campbell and Halson *Remedies in Contract and Tort* (2nd edn, 2002) pp 5–21, esp 11–13; Smith *Contract Theory* (2004) chs 4 and 11.
15 It is assumed in all economic analysis examples that the parties are rational maximisers of value.

for C for £10,000. If X offers D £15,000 for that part, breach by D is efficient if X values the part more than C, and is inefficient if X values the part less than C. The regime of expectation damages in preference to specific performance produces the efficient result: if C values the part at more than £15,000, D will not breach, since it will have to pay C expectation damages, which together with the contract price lost, will not exceed the £15,000 offered by X; on the other hand, if C values the part at less than £15,000, D will breach, since by paying C expectation damages and transferring the part to X, it will be better off. The machine part therefore passes to whichever party, C or X, places the higher value on it.

As it stands, this theory can be challenged on the ground that even if the claimant were entitled to specific performance, this would not necessarily prevent the machine part passing to the highest value user. Indeed, according to the Coase theorem,[16] if transaction costs are absent, market forces will ensure that resources go to the person placing the highest value on them, irrespective of the initial assignment of legal rights and remedies. So in the above situation, assuming no transaction costs, D would negotiate from C a release from the specific performance so as to transfer the part to X, if X places a higher value on it than £15,000. Of course, in order to succeed in gaining a release, D will have to offer C more than the latter's expectation damages: as such, it is the distribution of wealth, but not overall efficiency, that is affected by ordering specific performance in the absence of transaction costs.

Ultimately, therefore, the efficient breach theory has to take account of the fact that in the real world there are transaction costs; and it becomes the theory either that the transaction costs of D gaining release from C are often so high as to prevent that release, so that the efficient transfer to X does not result, or that, even if the transaction costs are not so high as to prevent release, nevertheless the efficient transfer to X is more costly under specific performance than damages because of the transaction costs required.[17]

The defect of the former is that, since the parties are already known to each other, the transaction costs are unlikely to be so high as to prevent a release bargain. The latter is also flawed in that it pays insufficient attention to the costs associated with damages. Even though damages allow D to break the contract with C without bargaining for a release, D still has to pay and deciding on the amount will in itself involve

16 Above, p 20.
17 Posner *Economic Analysis of Law* (6th edn, 2003) pp 131–132; Beale *Remedies for Breach of Contract* (1980) p 14.

transaction costs, or the costs of a judicial assessment of damages, with its attendant risk of inaccurate assessment. Such costs may be greater than the transaction costs associated with specific performance. So for this form of the efficient breach theory to have force empirical data would be needed to prove that the transaction costs of specific performance outweigh the transaction (and other) costs of damages.[18]

Finally, brief mention must be made of Professor Kronman' s 'intention justification' theory,[19] that the present restrictive approach to specific performance is economically efficient, because rational parties stipulating remedies in their contracts would agree to specific performance only where the subject matter was unique. As the law is in accord with this, initial transaction costs are thereby minimised. But there seems no necessary reason why it cannot be equally plausibly argued that rational parties would stipulate specific performance in a far wider range of cases, particularly where irrespective of uniqueness, damages are difficult to assess.[20] In short, it seems that Kronman's argument could be used for and against the present primacy of damages.

In conclusion, it is submitted that damages should remain the primary remedy: especially convincing is the duty to mitigate objection to specific performance. This conclusion is strengthened by the recent improvements in damages awards from a claimant's point of view, brought about, for example, by the modification of the time for assessment and the expansion of compensation for non-pecuniary loss, such as mental distress. Having said that, there is still room for the courts to show a more realistic awareness of when damages will not put the claimant into as good a position as if the contract had been performed. As such, the decision in *Sky Petroleum*[1] must be supported. Moreover, difficulty in assessing damages should in itself be regarded as rendering damages inadequate, thereby opening the door to wider specific performance, particularly of long-term supply obligations and of obligations in which the claimant has a subjective consumer interest.

(2) The constant supervision objection

Traditionally, specific performance has not been ordered where this would require what is termed constant supervision. This is not an easily understood notion, but what it appears to mean is that, irrespective of

18 Macneil 'Efficient Breach of Contract: Circles in the Sky' (1982) 68 Va LR 947.
19 'Specific Performance' (1978) 45 U of Chi LR 351, 365–369.
20 Kronman's theory is criticised by Schwartz 'The Case for Specific Performance' (1979) 89 Yale LJ 271, 278–284.
1 [1974] 1 WLR 576.

the uncertainty bar,[2] specific performance will be denied where too much judicial time and effort would be spent in seeking compliance with the order. In the words of Lord Hoffmann in *Co-operative Insurance Society Ltd v Argyll Stores (Holdings) Ltd:*[3]

'[S]upervision would in practice take the form of rulings by the court, on applications made by the parties, as to whether there had been a breach of the order. It is the possibility of the court having to give an indefinite series of such rulings in order to ensure the execution of the order which has been regarded as undesirable.'

Such an objection clearly does not arise where there is an easy method of enforcement without the defendant's co-operation, for example by nominating a person to effect a conveyance of land. It is rather where continuous acts are required of the defendant that the objection bites. In contrast, a lump sum of damages always requires merely a single act and, as Sharpe succinctly puts it, 'enforcement is left to the administrative rather than the judicial machinery of the court'.[4]

The long-standing classic authority is *Ryan v Mutual Tontine Westminster Chambers Association.*[5] Here the lease of a service flat to the claimant lessee included an obligation on the part of the defendant lessor to provide a resident porter who would be 'constantly in attendance'. The lessor in fact appointed as resident porter someone who absented himself every weekday for several hours. The claimant brought an action claiming specific performance of that obligation. The Court of Appeal held that specific performance should be denied because this would involve constant supervision by the courts. Lord Esher MR said:

'The contract is that these services shall be performed during the whole term of the tenancy: it is therefore a long-continuing contract to be performed from day to day and under which the circumstances of non-performance might vary from day to day. I apprehend, therefore, that the execution of it would require that constant superintendence by the court, which the court in such cases has always declined to give.'[6]

In Lopes LJ's words:

'... it is clear that it is such a contract, that, in order to give effect to it by an order for specific performance, the court would have to watch over and supervise its execution.

---

2   For a clear recognition of the difference between these bars, see *Greenhill v Isle of Wight Rly Co* (1871) 23 LT 885.
3   [1998] AC 1 at 12.
4   *Injunctions and Specific Performance* (3rd edn) para 7.480.
5   [1893] 1 Ch 116.
6   [1893] 1 Ch 116 at 123.

But it is a recognised rule that the court cannot enforce a contract by compelling specific performance where the execution of the contract requires such watching over and supervision by the court.'[7]

Kay LJ also considered that the court could not here order specific performance because the case fell within the general rule that '... the court will not enforce specific performance of works, such as building works, the prosecution of which the court cannot superintend'.[8]

In addition to *Ryan*, there have been numerous cases in which the constant supervision objection to specific performance has been applied.[9] However, this has not always been so. An important example is *Wolverhampton Corpn v Emmons*,[10] where the Court of Appeal laid down that specific performance could be ordered of contracts to build, provided the order was certain, damages were inadequate and, in accordance with the contract, the defendant had already gained the land on which the work was to be done – that is, the bargain was for the claimant to transfer land to the defendant in return for the defendant building something wanted by the claimant, such as a road across the land. Traditionally this approach has been explained away by saying that it is a valid exception to the otherwise clearly established rule. But it is hard to see on what rational ground this 'exception' is based. After all, the first two conditions must always be satisfied if specific performance is to be ordered; and the fact that the defendant has already received its part of the bargain, while of relevance to mutuality, in no sense counters the constant supervision objection. Not surprisingly the third requirement has since been modified so that it is now sufficient that the defendant has possession of the land, thereby rendering it possible to carry out the work.[11] But again the possibility of complying with the order is a normal requirement of specific performance. Hence a better explanation of the *Emmons* approach than that traditionally offered is

7   [1893] 1 Ch 116 at 125.
8   [1893] 1 Ch 116 at 128.
9   *Pollard v Clayton* (1855) 1 K & J 462; *Blackett v Bates* (1865) 1 Ch App 117; *Phipps v Jackson* (1887) 56 LJ Ch 550; *Dominion Coal Co Ltd v Dominion Iron & Steel Co Ltd* [1909] AC 293; *Dowty Boulton Paul Ltd v Wolverhampton Corpn* [1971] 1 WLR 204. And see, most importantly, *Co-operative Insurance Society Ltd v Argyll Stores (Holdings) Ltd* [1998] AC 1, HL, discussed below, pp 480–481. See also *Gravesham Borough Council v British Railways Board* [1978] Ch 379, below, pp 540–541 (mandatory injunction).
10 [1901] 1 KB 515. Prior cases applying the same approach include: *Storer v Great Western Rly Co* (1842) 2 Y & C Ch Cas 48; *Wilson v Furness Rly Co* (1869) LR 9 Eq 28; *Greene v West Cheshire Rly Co* (1871) LR 13 Eq 44; *Wolverhampton & Walsall Rly Co v London and North Western Rly Co* (1873) LR 16 Eq 433; *Fortescue v Lostwithiel and Fowey Rly Co* [1894] 3 Ch 621. *Emmons* has been followed, with the modification discussed below in the text, in *Carpenters Estates Ltd v Davies* [1940] Ch 160 and most importantly *in Jeune v Queen's Cross Properties Ltd* [1974] Ch 97 applying the principles to a landlord's repair covenant, since confirmed and extended, as regards dwellings, in the Landlord and Tenant Act 1985, s 17.
11 *Carpenters Estates Ltd v Davies* [1940] Ch 160.

that at root it rests on the view that there is no validity in the constant supervision objection. Certainly this is supported by dicta of Collins LJ and Sir Archibald Smith MR in *Emmons*, the latter, for example, saying quite bluntly that he had never been able to see the force of that objection.

Whatever one's explanation of the *Emmons* approach, it has been the *general* rule that the courts have refused to order specific performance where this involves constant supervision.

More recently, however, the validity of the constant supervision objection has been directly attacked in several cases.[12] In *Giles & Co Ltd v Morris*,[13] although the actual decision did not turn on the supervision bar, Megarry V-C thought that the refusal of specific performance of contracts for personal service or involving the continuous performance of services could not '... be based on any narrow consideration such as difficulties of constant superintendence by the courts'.[14] In *Tito v Waddell* (*No 2*)[15] his criticisms were expressed even more firmly. One of the many issues raised was whether specific performance should be ordered of a contractual obligation to replant land that had been mined. While Megarry V-C ultimately refused specific performance he thought that it was no longer a valid objection that the order involved constant supervision by the court. He said:

> 'In cases of this kind, it was at one time said that an order for the specific performance of the contract would not be made if there would be difficulty in the court supervising its execution: see, for example, *Ryan v Mutual Tontine Westminster Chambers Association*. Sir Archibald Smith MR subsequently found himself unable to see the force of this objection (see *Wolverhampton Corpn v Emmons*): and after it had been discussed and questioned in *Giles v Morris*, the House of Lords disposed of it (I hope finally) in *Shiloh Spinners Ltd v Harding*.[16] The real question is whether there is a sufficient definition of what has to be done in order to comply with the order of the court.'[17]

12 In addition to the cases discussed below one can argue that two important cases on the adequacy of damages bar, *Beswick v Beswick* [1968] AC 58 and *Sky Petroleum Ltd v VIP Petroleum Ltd* [1974] 1 WLR 576, support the view that the constant supervision objection is invalid. This is because the obligations in question were specifically enforced though they involved continuous acts. Admittedly, however, there was no discussion of this objection (unless Lord Pearce had this in mind in his comments at [1968] AC 58, 90). See also *Luganda v Service Hotels Ltd* [1969] 2 Ch 209 where *Ryan* was distinguished. Note also that specific performance ordering repair (or replacement) of non-conforming goods appears to be the primary remedy for a consumer (who wants it) under the Sale of Goods Act 1979, ss 48A–48F: see above, p 464.
13 [1972] 1 WLR 307.
14 [1972] 1 WLR 307 at 318.
15 [1977] Ch 106.
16 [1973] AC 691.
17 [1977] Ch 106 at 321–323.

Megarry V-C also stressed that the courts were particularly willing to overcome such an objection where, as on the facts, the defendants had some or all of the benefit to which they were entitled under the contract; but as has been commented in relation to the *Emmons* case, it is hard to see the relevance of this in undermining the constant supervision objection. Importantly, however, Megarry V-C's reliance on *Shiloh Spinners* seems unjustified:[18] for in that case, Lord Wilberforce appeared to accept the traditional constant supervision objection to specific performance of a contract to do work and was rather stressing that the objection was irrelevant to the requested relief against forfeiture for breach of such a covenant, since all the court had to do was to satisfy itself *ex post facto* that the covenanted work had been done.

Further support for the removal of this bar is provided by *Regent International Hotels (UK) Ltd v Pageguide Ltd*[19] where the Court of Appeal granted an interim injunction, amounting to temporary specific performance, preventing the defendant company from terminating or hindering the claimants in carrying out their management of the defendant's hotel. In so doing, the constant supervision objection was apparently rejected, reliance being placed on Megarry V-C's comments in *Giles v Morris* and *Tito v Waddell (No 2)*.

Megarry V-C's comments were also cited with approval by Mervyn Davies J in *Posner v Scott-Lewis*.[20] The facts were almost identical to those in *Ryan*. The defendant landlord had broken his covenant to have a resident porter at a block of flats for the purposes of removing rubbish, opening the main door, and controlling the central heating etc. The claimant, a tenant of one of the flats, sued for and was granted specific performance ordering the defendant to employ a resident porter for those purposes. Although the actual decision did not contradict the constant supervision objection – since the defendant was not as such ordered to perform, or to ensure performance of, continuous acts but was merely ordered to employ the porter – the judge did indicate his support for the removal of that bar.

Finally, in *Rainbow Estates Ltd v Tokenhold Ltd*[1] Lawrence Collins QC, in holding that, exceptionally, a tenant's (as well as a landlord's) repairing obligation can be specifically enforced, said the following, '[T]he problems of defining the work and the need for supervision can be

---

18 This point is supported by Lord Hoffmann in *Co-operative Insurance Society Ltd v Argyll Stores (Holdings) Ltd* [1998] AC 1 at 14.
19 (1985) Times, 13 May.
20 [1987] Ch 25.
1   [1999] Ch 64.

overcome by ensuring that there is sufficient definition of what has to be done in order to comply with the order of the court.'[2]

Lest it be thought, however, that this clutch of recent cases means that the constant supervision objection will no longer be applied, we must now turn to consider the leading modern case. In *Co-operative Insurance Society Ltd v Argyll Stores (Holdings) Ltd*[3] the House of Lords reaffirmed the constant supervision objection in refusing to order specific performance of a covenant in a lease. The defendants were the lessees of the largest shopping unit in the claimants' shopping centre. Sixteen years of the thirty-five-year lease had expired when the defendants closed their supermarket. The claimants, concerned that the closure would have an adverse effect on the rest of the shopping centre, sought specific performance of the defendants' covenant to keep the premises open for retail trade during usual hours of business. This order was refused.

Lord Hoffmann, giving the leading speech, said that there had been some misunderstanding about what is meant by continued superintendence. 'It is the possibility of the court having to give an indefinite series of rulings in order to ensure the execution of the order which has been regarded as undesirable.'[4] He added that it was oppressive (and, moreover, put the claimant in an undesirably strong position) to have to run a business under the threat of proceedings for contempt. His Lordship drew a distinction between orders to carry on activities and orders to achieve results (building contracts, for example, were regarded as falling within the latter category), arguing that the possibility of repeated applications for rulings on compliance with the order which arises in the former type of case does not exist to anything like the same extent in relation to the latter type of case. His Lordship further thought that, in the case at hand, the order could not be drawn up with sufficient precision to avoid arguments over whether it was being complied with.

With respect, Lord Hoffmann's reasoning is unconvincing. In particular, it is hard to see why the order could not be drawn up with sufficient precision; and nor is it clear why the constant supervision objection should be thought valid in respect of orders to carry on activities but not orders to achieve results. This is not to say that the decision in this case was wrong. To force a defendant to carry on with a business that is losing money may well fall foul of the severe hardship bar

---

2   [1999] Ch 64 at 73.
3   [1998] AC 1.
4   [1998] AC 1 at 12.

or a separate specific bar.[5] But this should have been addressed separately rather than being confused with the constant supervision objection.

In terms of policy, it is submitted that the constant supervision objection has little to commend it. In all but a few cases, the fact that the court has ordered specific performance will be sufficient to ensure compliance. In other words in almost all cases defendants do obey these court orders. It is hardly sensible to deny the claimant the remedy because of problems which arise only occasionally. Even in a case of non-compliance or alleged non-compliance, there is no need for full judicial machinery to be invoked: for example, a person could be appointed as an officer of the court to ensure enforcement or to investigate the allegations.[6] And even if judicial time and effort are involved, it is still strongly arguable that this is outweighed by the fact that justice otherwise requires the claimant to be granted specific performance. In other words, it should be clearly understood that the constant supervision objection rests on denying a remedy to the claimant not because as between the parties it is less appropriate than damages but because the costs to society are regarded as too great. Clearly the resources to be devoted to achieving justice between the parties must have some limit, but it may be doubted whether that limit is even approached by the few problematical specific performance cases involving further judicial time and effort. This is particularly so when one bears in mind that specific performance may also save judicial time and effort, namely that involved in the often-complex task of assessing damages. Certainly it is unsatisfactory to deny justice on an unsubstantiated hunch about the costs of specific performance,[7] and in any event, it has to be explained why this area should be treated differently from, for example, family law, where the cost of continuing judicial involvement in supervising maintenance, access and custody orders is considered acceptable. In short, the policy justifications for the constant supervision objection to specific performance seem particularly weak and the attempts by some judges, but, alas, not the House of Lords, to remove this bar should therefore be supported.

---

5   Analogous mandatory injunction cases indicate that a separate bar, albeit not absolute, is where the order would require the defendant to carry on a business, requiring the continuous employment of people, especially where the business is a losing concern: *Attorney-General v Colchester Corpn* [1955] 2 QB 207; *Gravesham BC v British Railways Board* [1978] Ch 379. See below, pp 540–541.

6   Treitel *The Law of Contract* (11th edn, 2003) p 1003; Schwartz (1979) 89 Yale LJ 271, 293–294. The court could also use the power in RSC Ord 45, r 8 (see CPR Sch 1) to direct another to do the work at the defendant's expense.

7   Kronman 'Specific Performance' (1978) 45 U of the Chi LR 351, 373–374; Schwartz 'The Case for Specific Performance' (1979) 89 Yale LJ 271, 292–294.

(3) Contracts for personal service[8]

It is traditionally a well-established rule that the courts will not order specific performance of such a contract, of which the prime example is the contract of employment.[9] Assuming that damages are inadequate (and this assumption cannot be made too readily, particularly since many contracts for personal service are terminable at short notice) and that the constant supervision objection is at best very weak, what are the reasons for this rule?[10]

One general reason often given is that such a contract creates a relationship of mutual confidence and respect and that where that has broken down, it cannot be satisfactorily rebuilt by a court order: on the contrary, to force the relationship to continue is only likely to lead to friction between the parties, or at least between the employee and the employer's representative (for example, his foreman). Another reason suggested by Megarry J in *Giles & Co Ltd v Morris*[11] is that where services are of an artistic kind, like opera-singing, it would not be possible to judge whether an order of specific performance against the employee was being properly complied with:

'... if ... the singer sang flat, or sharp, or too fast, or too slowly, or too loudly, or too quietly, or resorted to a dozen of the manifestations of temperament traditionally associated with some singers ... who could say whether the imperfections of performance were natural or self-induced?'[12]

But whether such reasons are in play or not, more fundamental objections to specific performance may be suggested. From the employee's point of view specific performance would result in involuntary servitude. Thus in *De Francesco v Barnum*[13] Fry LJ said that the

---

8   This is shorthand for contract of service or contract for personal services.
9   Specific performance was refused against an employee in *Clark* v *Price* (1819) 2 Wils Ch 157; *De Francesco v Barnum* (1890) 45 Ch D 430; *Ehrman v Bartholomew* [1898] 1 Ch 671 (injunction amounting to specific performance). And against an employer in *Johnson v Shrewsbury and Birmingham Rly Co* (1853) 3 De GM & G 914; *Brett v East India and London Shipping Co Ltd* (1864) 2 Hem & M 404; *Rigby v Connol* (1880) 14 Ch D 482; *Page One Records Ltd v Britton* [1968] 1 WLR 157 (injunction amounting to specific performance).
10   It is sometimes said that repudiatory breach automatically terminates an employment contract and that this is a reason for no specific performance. But rightly this 'automatic' theory was firmly rejected in *Thomas Marshall Ltd v Guinle* [1979] Ch 227 (per Megarry V-C) because, for example, injunctions enforcing negative obligations are still available. See also *Gunton v Richmond-upon-Thames London Borough Council* [1981] Ch 448 (per Buckley LJ); *Dietman v Brent London Borough Council* [1987] ICR 737 (affd [1988] ICR 842); *Marsh v National Autistic Society* [1993] ICR 453. Indeed apparent automatic termination is a consequence of rather than a reason for there being no specific performance. Cf *Boyo v Lambeth London Borough Council* [1995] IRLR 50, CA.
11   [1972] 1 WLR 307.
12   [1972] 1 WLR 307 at 318.
13   (1890) 45 Ch D 430.

courts were afraid of turning 'contracts of service into contracts of slavery.'[14] From the employer's side the analogous rationale, seemingly implicitly accepted by the courts, is that as he has to organise and pay for the work he should have the prerogative to decide who remains employed by him.

As regards an employee being ordered to carry out a contract of service, the bar still applies in full force, being enshrined in the Trade Union and Labour Relations (Consolidation) Act 1992, s 236, which provides that:

> 'No court shall, whether by way of – a) an order for specific performance ... of a contract of employment, or b) an injunction ... restraining a breach or threatened breach of such a contract, compel an employee to do any work or attend at any place for the doing of any work.'

However, on the other side of the relationship, there have been some interesting modern developments.[15] For a full appreciation of these, private law, public (ie administrative) law, and the unfair dismissal legislation must all be examined.

(a) Private law

In *Hill v CA Parsons & Co Ltd*[16] the Court of Appeal confirmed the granting of an interim injunction which amounted to temporary specific performance of a contractual obligation to employ the claimant. The defendant employers had made a closed shop agreement with a trade union and gave the claimant one month to join that union. When he failed to do so, he was given one month's notice of termination of employment. The claimant sought an interim injunction restraining the defendants from implementing their notice of termination. The court held that the defendants were in breach of contract by giving only one month's notice, but the crucial point is that the majority held, Stamp LJ dissenting, that the interim injunction should be granted, even though this amounted to temporary specific performance of a contract for personal service. Both Lord Denning and Sachs LJ stressed that the rule barring specific performance against an employer in a contract for personal service was not absolute. Lord Denning said:

---

14 (1890) 45 Ch D 430 at 438.
15 See generally Carty 'Dismissed Employees: the Search for a More Effective Range of Remedies' (1989) 52 MLR 449; Ewing 'Remedies for Breach of the Contract of Employment' [1993] CLJ 405; Freedland *The Personal Employment Contract* (2003) pp 369–376.
16 [1972] Ch 305. See also the comments of Megarry J in *Giles v Morris* [1972] 1 WLR 307, cited with approval in dicta of Goff LJ in *Price v Strange* [1978] Ch 337 at 359–360. The actual decision in *Giles* was that the traditional rule is no bar to ordering the employer to make, rather than to perform, a contract for personal service.

'The rule is not inflexible. It permits of exceptions. The court can in a proper case grant a declaration that the relationship still subsists and an injunction to stop the master treating it as at an end ... It may be said that ... the court is indirectly enforcing specifically a contract for personal services. So be it.'[17]

The majority thought that an exception to the general rule was justified because damages were inadequate and by granting the injunction the claimant would remain an employee until the coming into effect of the Industrial Relations Act 1971 by which he would be protected if dismissed for not joining the union. Sachs LJ also stressed that there was no breakdown in mutual confidence between employer and employee. On the other hand, Stamp LJ in his dissent thought that there was no justification for departing from the rule that specific performance should not be granted in a contract for personal service.

Hill v Parsons can be and, in some cases,[18] was viewed as a 'freak' case, showing merely that there may be a very rare exception to the usual rule; after all, unfair dismissal legislation has been in force for decades, and so there is now no question of continuing employment to catch those provisions. Having said that, there are indications that the majority regarded the case as one of numerous exceptions. Lord Denning spoke of the rule as applying only in the '... ordinary course of things'[19] and Sachs LJ thought that, as there had been a recent marked trend towards '... shielding the employee', courts must be prepared to modify the traditional rule so as to conform '... to the realities of the day'.[20]

That less restrictive interpretation of *Hill v Parsons* has subsequently prevailed. For example, in *Irani v Southampton and South West Hampshire Health Authority*[1] the claimant was an ophthalmologist employed on a part-time basis by the defendants at an eye clinic. Following disagreements between the claimant and the consultant in charge of the clinic, the defendants gave the claimant six weeks' notice of dismissal. As the defendants had failed to go through the disputes procedure laid down in the claimant's contract of employment, the dismissal was in breach of contract. The claimant sought an interim injunction restraining implementation of the dismissal notice until that disputes procedure had

---

17 [1972] Ch 305 at 314–315.
18 Eg *GKN (Cwmbran) Ltd v Lloyd* [1972] ICR 214; *Sanders v Ernst A Neale Ltd* [1974] ICR 565.
19 [1972] Ch 305 at 314.
20 [1972] Ch 305 at 321.
1   [1985] ICR 590. See also *Jones v Lee and Guilding* [1980] ICR 310 (injunction amounting to temporary specific performance preventing school managers dismissing a teacher in breach of procedures established in his contract) and *Regent International Hotels (UK) Ltd v Pageguide Ltd* (1985) Times, 13 May (injunction granted amounting to temporary specific performance of a hotel management agreement: but it was doubted that this was analogous to a contract for personal service).

been complied with. This amounted to a claim for temporary specific performance of his contract of employment and, as Warner J described, the defendants had contended that:

'... there was a clear rule that the court would not grant specific performance of a contract of employment, or in general, grant an injunction to restrain breach of it and that there were no special circumstances which would justify my granting an injunction, the effect of which would compel the defendant authority to continue to employ Mr Irani ...'[2]

Warner J disagreed, applied *Hill v Parsons* and granted the interim injunction sought. Damages would plainly be inadequate at the pre-trial stage because the six weeks' notice of dismissal would probably have elapsed by trial; in any event, dismissal would make it difficult for the claimant to get another job in the Health Service. Warner J was particularly liberal in his application of the two other justifying reasons given in *Hill v Parsons*. He thought that there was still complete confidence between employer and employee in the sense that the defendants had perfect faith in the claimant's honesty, integrity and loyalty, and merely considered him an incompatible colleague of the consultant at the clinic; and the fact that the claimant was seeking protection under the disputes procedure was regarded as analogous to the protection sought by Mr Hill under the then imminent Industrial Relations Act 1971.

It should be noted, however, that the temporary specific performance granted did not extend to ordering the defendants to allow the claimant to attend work (let alone to provide work for him) albeit that this was arguably one of the defendants' contractual obligations.[3] Indeed the claimant undertook as a condition of specific performance that he would not present himself for work at any of the defendants' establishments. As such the primary obligations enforced were those of paying the claimant his full salary and retaining him on the books as an employee. It would seem that specific performance was similarly limited in *Hill v Parsons & Co Ltd*.[4]

The most important case subsequent to *Hill v Parsons* has been *Powell v Brent London BC*.[5] The claimant was appointed principal benefits officer for the defendant local authority. A few days after starting work, she was told that her appointment was invalid because there might have been a breach of the defendant's equal opportunity code of practice in appointing her. She sought an interim injunction requiring the defendant

2   [1985] ICR 590 at 597.
3   Freedland *The Personal Employment Contract* (2003) pp.129–140.
4   [1972] Ch 305 at 314 (per Lord Denning).
5   [1988] ICR 176.

to treat her as if she was properly employed as principal benefits officer and, even though that would amount to temporary specific performance, the Court of Appeal granted it. Ralph Gibson LJ, giving the leading judgment, relied on *Hill v Parsons* and especially Sachs LJ's judgment, to justify a departure from the general bar to specific performance. In an important statement of principle, he said:

> 'Having regard to the decision in *Hill v Parsons* and the long-standing general rule of practice to which *Hill v Parsons* was an exception, the court will not by injunction require an employer to let a servant continue in his employment, when the employer has sought to terminate that employment and prevent the servant carrying out his work under the contract, unless it is clear on the evidence not only that it is otherwise just to make such a requirement but also that there exists sufficient confidence on the part of the employer in the servant's ability and other necessary attributes for it to be reasonable to make the order. Sufficiency of confidence must be judged by reference to the circumstances of the case, including the nature of the work, the people with whom the work must be done and the likely effect upon the employer and the employee's operations if the employer is required by injunction to suffer the plaintiff to continue in the work.'[6]

On the facts there was held to be sufficient mutual confidence between the parties in that the claimant had been doing the job satisfactorily, and without complaint, for over four months before the hearing.

Powell has been followed – and interim injunctions, amounting to temporary specific performance, ordered – in *Hughes v London Borough of Southwark*[7] and *Wadcock v London Borough of Brent*.[8] Both concerned attempts by local authorities to reorganise the duties of social workers and, in both, an injunction was granted primarily because there was no breakdown of mutual confidence. The employees were clearly competent at their jobs.

More radical still was the decision in *Robb v Hammersmith and Fulham London Borough Council*[9] in which a director of finance was dismissed without his employers going through the disciplinary procedures required under his contract. As in *Irani*, an injunction was granted requiring the defendants to continue to employ and pay the claimant unless and until the procedure had been properly complied with (the claimant undertaking not to attend for work unless instructed to do so). Morland J accepted that the claimant had lost the trust and confidence of the defendants but regarded the important point as being that the order

---

6   [1988] ICR 176 at 194.
7   [1988] IRLR 55.
8   [1990] IRLR 223.
9   [1991] ICR 514. See also *Jones v Gwent County Council* [1992] IRLR 521.

proposed was perfectly workable. To refuse the injunction would be to allow the defendants to snap their fingers at the rights of the claimant.

Lest it be thought that, in the light of such cases, specific performance is now the rule rather than the exception, it is helpful to refer to *Alexander v Standard Telephones and Cables plc*[10] in which *Powell* and *Irani* were distinguished. The defendants had made the claimants redundant preferring to keep more skilled employees than applying a 'last in, first out' selection. Even if that action by the defendants had constituted a breach of contract, Aldous J held that there was no real prospect of an injunction being granted at trial because, in the context of the rationalisation of the workforce, the employers did not have sufficient confidence in those employees made redundant.

(b) Public law

A further battle-ground on which the bar has been attacked concerns the use of the 'public law' principle whereby certain types of public employee – commonly labelled 'office-holders' – are protected against wrongful dismissal. Traditionally it has been recognised that such a dismissal, particularly where in breach of natural justice, can be declared invalid and may be restrained by an injunction;[11] that is, an 'office' may be specifically protected by the courts.[12] This has traditionally been reconciled with the rule against specific performance by simply regarding an office-holder as not really being an 'employee' under an ordinary or 'pure' contract of personal service.

Since the late 1950s the courts have applied this 'public law' principle to an increasingly wide range of dismissed 'employees' with the result that the area of pure contracts of personal service has been narrowed.[13] But two fairly recent cases have developed this even further by intimating that the very distinction between officeholders and employees under ordinary contracts of personal service is no longer helpful.

In *Stevenson v United Road Transport Union*[14] a regional officer of a trade union was dismissed by the union's executive committee. The Court of Appeal confirmed a declaration that the dismissal was void because the committee had acted in breach of natural justice. While the case could

---

10 [1990] ICR 291. See also *Marsh v National Autistic Society* [1993] ICR 453. The traditional rule was also reaffirmed by the House of Lords in *Scandinavian Trading Tanker Co AB v Flota Petrolera Ecuatoriana, The Scaptrade* [1983] 2 AC 694 at 701.
11 On the face of it, an officer could alternatively seek a 'mandatory order', a 'prohibiting order' or a 'quashing order' under CPR Pt 54.
12 Early cases are *Willis v Childe* (1851) 13 Beav 117; *Fisher v Jackson* [1891] 2 Ch 84.
13 Eg *Vine v National Dock Labour Board* [1957] AC 488 (a registered dock-worker); *Malloch v Aberdeen Corpn* [1971] 1 WLR 1578 (a Scottish schoolmaster).
14 [1977] ICR 893.

presumably have been decided on the traditional principle that the claimant held an office, Buckley LJ giving the decision said, '... it does not much help ... to try to place the plaintiff in the category of a servant on the one hand, or an officer, on the other', and he went on to apply the following test:

> 'Where one party has a discretionary power to terminate the tenure or employment by another of an employment or an office or a post or a privilege, is that power conditional on the party invested with the power being first satisfied on a particular point which involves investigating some matter on which the other party ought in fairness to be heard or to be allowed to give his explanation or put his case? If the answer to the question is Yes, then unless, before the power purports to have been exercised, the condition has been satisfied after the other party has been given a fair opportunity of being heard or of giving his explanation or putting his case, the power will not have been well exercised.'[15]

This test was further applied in *R v BBC, ex p Lavelle*.[16] Here Woolf J held that a tape examiner, employed under what would traditionally have been regarded as an ordinary contract of personal service, had the right to be heard, and could be protected by a declaration and injunction, particularly because the employer was required to go through various disciplinary procedures before dismissal, and this took the case out of the pure master and servant category. As such disciplinary procedures are probably incorporated into the contracts of several millions of workers, this approach is clearly of great importance, although on the facts no remedy was granted since Miss Lavelle had in effect waived her rights with regard to the initial disciplinary meeting.

However, it is important to note that Woolf J did not consider Miss Lavelle's case an appropriate one for judicial review under RSC Ord 53 (now CPR Pt 54) since the BBC was exercising private and not public powers in dismissing her. Therefore the public law notions of an officer and the right to be heard were being relied on, but the procedure for reviewing the exercise of public powers was not.

Of even wider potential significance for the personal service bar was Woolf J's dictum that:

> '... the employment protection legislation has substantially changed the position at common law so far as dismissal is concerned. In appropriate circumstances the statute now provides that an industrial tribunal can order the reinstatement of an employee. It is true that the order cannot be specifically enforced. However, the existence of that power does indicate that even the ordinary contract of master and servant now has

---

15   [1977] ICR 893 at 902.
16   [1983] 1 WLR 23.

many of the attributes of an office, and the distinctions which previously existed between pure cases of master and servant and cases where a person holds an office are no longer clear.'[17]

In other words, Woolf J seemed to consider that, irrespective of the contractual incorporation of disciplinary procedures, unfair dismissal legislation has elevated ordinary employees to the status of office-holders, thereby paving the way for their specific protection on traditional principles, But this is clearly a controversial view of the impact of the unfair dismissal legislation, particularly as the legislature there shied away from providing the equivalent of full specific performance.

Perhaps not surprisingly, therefore, this dictum has not been approved since and in the leading case of *R v East Berkshire Health Authority, ex p Walsh*[18] there was an apparent back-tracking from *Stevenson* and *Lavelle*. The question arising was whether a senior nursing officer could apply for judicial review under RSC Ord 53 (now CPR Pt 54) to quash his dismissal as being in breach of natural justice. The Court of Appeal answered this in the negative on the ground that it was only if the public law officer principle applied to this claimant that he could proceed under Ord 53, and there was no such public law element in his employment, although, like *Lavelle*, there were disciplinary procedures engrafted onto the contract of employment. Without mentioning them, the approach in *Stevenson* and *Lavelle* was impliedly rejected, a narrow view of who is an officer was taken, and the reasoning sought to restore a clear distinction between public officers and private employees.

While on the one hand such a decision prevents the unfair dismissal regime being supplemented, or even by-passed, by judicial review for procedural unfairness,[19] on the other hand a clear distinction between public officers and private employees is difficult to maintain. In any event cases like *Irani* and *Powell* supplement the unfair dismissal regime irrespective of the officer principle.

It is also of interest that while insisting on a consistency between RSC Ord 53 and the officer principle, which *Lavelle* had rejected, *Walsh*, in contrast to *Lavelle*, freed the right to be heard from its public law confinement to officers. As Purchas LJ said in *Walsh*, commenting on the decision at first instance:

---

17 [1983] 1 WLR 23 at 34.
18 [1985] QB 152. See also eg *R v Home Secretary, ex p Broom* [1986] QB 198; *McClaren v Home Office* [1990] ICR 824 (judicial review unavailable for prison officers); *R v Derbyshire County Council, ex p Noble* [1990] ICR 808 (judicial review unavailable for police surgeon).
19 It is unclear whether an application for judicial review may be refused simply on the ground that proceedings before an industrial tribunal would be more appropriate: *R v Civil Service Appeal Board, ex p Bruce* [1989] ICR 171.

'The importation by direct reference or by implication into a contract of employment of the rules of natural justice does not of itself import the necessary element of public interest which would convert the case from [the pure master and servant category] into one in which there was an element of public interest created as a result of status of the individual or the protection or support of his position as a public officer. With great respect to the judge, it is this distinction which seems to have escaped him.'[20]

(c) Unfair dismissal legislation

In providing a full picture of the recent challenges to the rule against specific performance of an employer's contractual obligations, it would be a mistake to leave out of account the unfair dismissal legislation, introduced in the Industrial Relations Act 1971 and now embodied in the Employment Rights Act 1996. By the Employment Rights Act 1996, ss 113–117, an employment tribunal can order the reinstatement or reengagement of an employee who has been unfairly dismissed. Indeed these remedies are treated in the legislation as the primary remedies although in practice, and presumably for the same reasons as the traditional rule against specific performance, tribunals usually prefer to award compensation, irrespective of the employee's wishes.[1] But even where made, an order of reinstatement or reengagement is not the same as specific performance for breach of contract: an unfair dismissal is not necessarily a breach of contract, and reinstatement or reengagement does not correspond to full specific performance since non-compliance does not constitute contempt and is instead dealt with by an award of extra compensation to the employee. In other words, the legislature accepted that an employer who is prepared to pay can always get rid of an employee. However, the regime is clearly very similar to specific performance for breach, and indeed the sanction of a monetary penalty is somewhat similar to the French 'astreinte' which is there the way of enforcing specific performance.[2]

(d) Conclusion

From the above examination, and particularly in the light of *Hill v Parsons*, *Irani*, *Powell*, and *Robb*, it is safe to say that the rule barring specific performance against an employer is less absolute than it once was. But the claim should not be exaggerated. Specific performance will generally still be denied. Moreover, some of the cases carrying the attack on the traditional position have not been concerned to ensure that the employer

---

20   [1985] QB 152 at 180.
1   Davies and Freedland *Labour Law* (2nd edn, 1984) pp 493–497.
2   Nicholas *French Law of Contract* (2nd edn, 1992) pp 221–224.

allows the employee to work or provides work for him,[3] and have primarily been concerned that the correct procedures are complied with before dismissal. In short, the view still holds sway that it is an employer's prerogative to decide ultimately who remains employed by him.

As a matter of policy one might wish to challenge this view, and to support a greater move towards specific performance, which would secure more fully an employee's status.[4] But specific performance can only ever go as far as the contractual terms allow: that is, it can only ensure that dismissal is implemented without a breach of contract. As such, full security of employment can only be brought about by statute. The preference for increased compensation rather than contempt sanctions in the unfair dismissal regime shows that the legislature has as yet been prepared to travel only part way down that road.

(4) Want of mutuality[5]

Fry, in his book on specific performance first published in 1858, stated a rule of mutuality to the effect that a court will not in general order specific performance against the defendant unless from the time the contract was made he could have got specific performance against the claimant had the claimant been in breach. To use Fry's exact words, 'A contract to be specifically enforced by the court must, as a general rule, be mutual, that is to say, such that it might at the time it was entered into have been enforced by either of the parties against the other of them.'[6] Over the years many exceptions to such a rule have been recognised and indeed, on close examination, the rule has not *necessarily* been supported by any authority. This has lent support to Ames's view[7] that Fry's formulation overstated the position and that the true rule is that the defendant will not be ordered to perform unless there is adequate assurance that the claimant will in turn perform. In Ames's words, 'Equity will not compel specific performance by a defendant if after performance the common law remedy of damages will be his sole

---

3   Above, pp 485–487. The exact effect of nullifying the dismissal of an officer is unclear; but in *Chief Constable of North Wales Police v Evans* [1982] 3 All ER 141 mandamus to coerce reinstatement was refused.

4   Clark 'Unfair Dismissal and Reinstatement' (1969) 32 MLR 532; Cohen 'The Relationship of Contractual Remedies to Political and Social Status: A Preliminary Inquiry' (1982) 32 U Tor LJ 31; Brown 'Contract Remedies in a Planned Economy' in *Studies in Contract Law* (eds Reiter and Swan, 1980) pp 94, 100–107.

5   Sometimes referred to as negative mutuality, this is to be contrasted with affirmative mutuality, which is the unsound notion that specific performance will be granted to the claimant, simply because it could have been granted against him. See Sharpe *Injunctions and Specific Performance* (3rd edn, 2000) paras 7.820–7.880, 10.430–10.570.

6   *Fry on Specific Performance* (6th edn, 1921) p 219.

7   'Mutuality in Specific Performance' (1903) 3 Col LR 1.

security for the performance of the plaintiff's side of the contact.'[8] On this approach, in contrast to Fry's, there is no need to view as exceptional the fact, for example, that a vendor who acquires the property to be sold subsequent to the making of the contract can be granted specific performance against the buyer, or that a claimant who has performed personal services in return for a promised transfer of land can compel conveyance. On the other hand, like Fry's rule, Ames's will support the refusal of specific performance where the claimant's performance is to be subsequent to the defendant's and will not be specifically enforceable.[9]

The leading case is now *Price v Strange*,[10] where the Court of Appeal rejected Fry's rule. The defendant, the headlessee of some flats in a house, orally agreed to grant the claimant a new underlease of his flat in return for the claimant's promise to carry out certain repairs to the house. The claimant did half the repairs but the defendant refused to allow him to complete them, had them done at her own expense, and refused to grant the underlease. The claimant brought an action for specific performance of the promise to grant the underlease and this was granted by the Court of Appeal, subject to the claimant compensating the defendant for the expense she had incurred in having the remaining repair work done. The defendant had argued that, in accordance with Fry's rule, specific performance should not be granted because she could not from the time the contract was made have obtained specific performance against the claimant, since his obligation to repair was not specifically enforceable. But Fry's rule was held to be wrong and as on these facts there could be no risk of the claimant not performing (since the work had already been completed) specific performance was granted. As regards what the correct rule is, however, there appears to be a slight difference between the views of Goff LJ and Buckley LJ: for while the former would seemingly having applied Ames's formulation, the latter tentatively indicated that, even if the defendant could not be assured of actual performance by the claimant, specific performance might still be granted so long as damages would be an adequate remedy to the defendant for any default on the claimant's part. So Buckley LJ's formulation of the true rule was as follows:

---

8   'Mutuality in Specific Performance' (1903) 3 Col LR 1, 2–3, 12.
9   As in *Flight v Bolland* (1828) 4 Russ 298 (infant claimant); *Ogden v Fossick* (1862) 4 De GF & J 426 (claimant to employ defendant).
10 [1978] Ch 337. This was applied in *Rainbow Estates Ltd v Tokenhold Ltd* [1999] Ch 64 where Lawrence Collins QC said, at p 69, '[I]t is now clear that it does not follow from the fact that specific performance is not available to one party that it is not available to the other: want of mutuality is a discretionary, and not an absolute, bar to specific performance.'

'The court will not compel a defendant to perform his obligation specifically if it cannot at the same time ensure that any unperformed obligations of the plaintiff will be perfectly performed, unless, perhaps, damages would be an adequate remedy to the defendant for any default on the plaintiff's part.'[11]

This formulation (with 'perhaps' omitted) is to be preferred to Ames's; the defendant can have no complaints so long as it is assured of a satisfactory remedy against the claimant for any non-performance and it should not be necessary for the defendant to be assured of actual performance; after all, the risk of subsequent non-performance is one that the defendant has contractually undertaken.

Indeed even this watered-down version of mutuality may be too kind to a defendant because, rather than refusing specific performance, the courts could grant it on terms that ensure adequate monetary security to the defendant or otherwise provide an incentive for the claimant to perform. Even more radical, and yet highly persuasive, is the argument that the defendant merits no such concern at all.[12] A fortiori damages will inadequately compensate the claimant, and hence by denying him specific performance, he is, as a matter of certainty, being denied a more appropriate remedy. In contrast, mutuality protects the defendant against a mere *risk* of the claimant subsequently not performing, and that is after all a risk which the defendant accepted by entering into that contract.[13]

(5) Uncertainty

The terms must satisfy a test of certainty for there to be a valid contract. But even if this is so, and damages are therefore recoverable for breach, specific performance may still be denied where the terms are too vague to allow a clear order to be made. A good example is provided by *Joseph v National Magazine Co*,[14] where the defendants contracted to publish an

---

11   [1978] Ch 337 at 367–368.
12   Lewis 'The Present State of the Defence of Want of Mutuality in Specific Performance' (1903) 51 Univ of Penn LR 591, 625–629; Schwartz 'The Case for Specific Performance' (1979) 89 Yale LJ 271, 301–303. Durfee 'Mutuality in Specific Performance' (1921) 20 Mich LR 289 takes a mid-position: the defence is justified where the defendant's potential hardship is greater than the claimant's hardship.
13   Under the Landlord and Tenant Act 1985, s 17, specific performance can be ordered of a dwelling landlord's repairing covenant 'notwithstanding any equitable rule restricting the scope of the remedy, whether on the basis of a lack of mutuality or otherwise.' The courts also allow waiver of the defence – *Price v Strange* [1978] Ch 337 at 358, applied in *Sutton v Sutton* [1984] Ch 184. Also contrast injunctions where want of mutuality is not a defence (see Beale *Remedies for Breach of Contract* (1980) p 138), although the courts may grant an injunction on terms that the defendant can apply for dissolution if the claimant does not perform, see below, p 535, n 8.
14   [1959] Ch 14. See also *South Wales Rly Co v Wythes* (1854) 5 De GM & G 880; *Greenhill v Isle of Wight Rly (Newport Junction) Co* (1871) 23 LT 885.

article by the claimant on the subject of jade. In breach of contract, they later refused to publish it without major amendments. It was held that, while the claimant was entitled to damages, specific performance should be refused because the terms of publication were too vague to allow a clear order to be made. This is also a reason why many building contracts are not specifically enforceable: for example, damages for breach of contract to build a house of a certain value can be readily assessed, but no specific performance will be ordered without building specifications.[15]

Again, in *Co-operative Insurance Society Ltd v Argyll Stores (Holdings) Ltd*[16] one of the reasons given by the House of Lords for refusing to enforce specifically a business tenant's covenant to keep premises in a shopping centre open for retail trade was that the order could not be drawn up with sufficient precision. In Lord Hoffmann's words:

> 'The fact that the terms of a contractual obligation are sufficiently definite to escape being void for uncertainty, or to found a claim for damages ... does not necessarily mean that they will be sufficiently precise to be capable of being specifically performed ... Precision is of course a question of degree and the courts have shown themselves willing to cope with a certain degree of imprecision in cases of orders requiring the achievement of a result in which the plaintiffs' merits appeared strong; ... it is, taken alone, merely a discretionary matter to be taken into account. It is, however, a very important one.'[17]

And later he concluded, 'I do not think that the obligation [in question] can possibly be regarded as sufficiently precise to be capable of specific performance.'[18] This conclusion is a surprising one on the facts and it was bound up with their Lordships' controversial (and, with respect, incorrect) application in this case of the constant supervision objection to specific performance.

There are several reasons for this uncertainty restriction. Most obviously it is only fair to the defendant that he should know precisely what he has to do to comply with the order and avoid being held in contempt. As Lord Hoffmann said in the *Co-operative Insurance* case, 'If the terms of the court's order, reflecting the terms of the obligation, cannot be precisely drawn ... [there is an increase in] the oppression caused by the defendant having to do things under threat of proceedings for contempt.'[19] The courts too must be able to enforce an order and to

---

15   *Brace v Wehnert* (1858) 25 Beav 348.
16   [1998] AC 1. See above, pp 480–481.
17   [1998] AC 1 at 14.
18   [1998] AC 1 at 16.
19   [1998] AC 1 at 13.

judge whether there has been compliance with it. Furthermore, there may be a fear that in complying with an unclear order the defendant will perform in a way that does not match the claimant's expectations. Finally it can be argued that, as in relation to the constant supervision objection, an unclear order is likely to give rise to future disputes, which will take up judicial time and effort. In Lord Hoffmann's words in the *Co-operative Insurance* case, 'If the terms of the court's order, reflecting the terms of the obligation, cannot be precisely drawn, the possibility of wasteful litigation over compliance is increased.'[20] But this problem in itself could be overcome by appointing a court officer to deal with any subsequent dispute if and when it arises and in any case it is not a strong argument where justice otherwise requires the order.

Despite the decision in the *Co-operative Insurance* case, it is reasonable to expect that the increased willingness of courts to imply terms will, in cases of doubt, normally enable them to make clear orders of specific performance and thereby overcome the uncertainty objection. This is supported by *Sudbrook Trading Estate Ltd v Eggleton*[1] where the House of Lords held that if the agreed machinery for valuation breaks down in a contract for the sale of land a court will ascertain the fair and reasonable price, thereby rendering the contract specifically enforceable.

(6) Contracts not supported by valuable consideration

While the common law remedies are granted for breach of a contract made by deed or supported merely by nominal consideration – that is where there is no true bargain but rather a gratuitous promise – specific performance is not.[2] This is essentially what is meant by the maxim, 'Equity will not assist a volunteer.'

It is hard to see any rational reason for this distinction between the approach at common law and in equity and it is best regarded as a legacy of history. Moreover, since underlying morality justifies upholding gratuitous promises it is submitted that the common law is here to be preferred and that this bar to specific performance should be removed.

Indeed there is now some support for an undermining of this restriction. *Mountford v Scott*[3] concerned an attempt by the defendant to

---

20 [1998] AC 1 at 13.
1 [1983] 1 AC 444. In *Regent International Hotels (UK) Ltd v Pageguide Ltd* (1985) Times, 13 May, the Court of Appeal suggested that any certainty problems could be avoided by insisting on arbitration of any bona fide disputes prior to court action.
2 *Cannon v Hartley* [1949] Ch 213; *Lister v Hodgson* (1867) LR 4 Eq 30. But it would be surprising, applying usual equitable principles, if specific performance were to be refused where the promisee has detrimentally relied on the promise.
3 [1975] Ch 258 at 263. See also *Gurtner v Circuit* [1968] 2 QB 587 at 596.

withdraw an option to purchase land granted to the claimant for £1. Brightman J regarded the claimant as seeking specific performance not only of the contract to sell but also of the option contract and granted the remedy even though the consideration supporting the option was nominal. He said, 'It is not the function of equity to protect only those equitable interests which have been created for valuable consideration.'[4] However, it would be dangerous to place too much weight on this as the Court of Appeal,[5] while upholding the decision, adopted a different analysis under which the question of specific enforcement of the option did not arise; that is, it regarded the grantee of an option as being able to exercise that option, and hence create a valid contract for the sale of the land, without any need for the defendant's co-operation.

(7) Contract unfairly obtained

Specific performance may be denied where there has been procedural unfairness, whether misrepresentation, mistake induced by or known to the claimant, undue pressure, or unfair advantage taken of the defendant's weak position. So, for example, in *Walters v Morgan*[6] the defendant contracted to grant the claimant a mining lease over land which he had just bought; but specific performance was refused because the defendant had been hurried into signing the agreement in ignorance of the true value of his property. Similarly in *Webster v Cecil*[7] the defendant, due to an arithmetical error, offered his property to the claimant for £1,250 instead of £2,250. The claimant accepted this, although since his previous offer of £2,000 had been refused, he must have known of the mistake. His action for specific performance was dismissed. Furthermore, while it appears that inadequacy of consideration is not in itself a ground for refusing specific performance,[8] that is, substantive unfairness is insufficient, this will probably tip the balance against specific performance, where there is any hint of procedural unfairness.[9] Finally it should be stressed that *Tamplin v James*[10] lays down the 'modem' approach that unilateral mistake, neither known to nor induced by the claimant, is not a defence to specific performance.

---

4   [1975] Ch 258 at 262.
5   [1975] Ch 258.
6   (1861) 3 De GF & J 718.
7   (1861) 30 Beav 62. If damages were available at common law (but cf *Hartog v Colin and Shields* [1939] 3 All ER 566), there would be no advantage here in resisting specific performance, ie damages would probably be £1,000.
8   *Colliery Brown* (1788) 1 Cox Eq Cas 428.
9   *Griffith v Spratley* (1787) 1 Cox Eq Cas 383 at 389.
10   (1880) 15 Ch D 215. Contrasting with earlier cases, such as *Malins v Freeman* (1836) 2 Keen 25.

However, these days it may be doubted whether a defendant needs to rely on unfairness in obtaining the contract as a defence to specific performance; for, given the expansion of doctrines, such as duress, undue influence, misrepresentation and, though more arguably, unilateral mistake and unconscionability, the defendant will generally be able to escape from all contractual liability where there is a defence to specific performance because of procedural unfairness. For example, on the facts of *Walters v Morgan*, it may be that the defendant could now escape from the contract, and avoid all remedies for breach, by invoking unilateral mistake or unconscionability. One can argue that such assimilation is to be supported, on the ground that it is only separate historical development that has led to procedural unfairness that is sufficient to deny specific performance being insufficient to rule out damages.[11] But perhaps some distinction can be rationally defended on the basis that the reasons that justify damages retaining their primacy, under the adequacy hurdle, also justify the courts being more willing to accept wider versions of particular defences where specific performance rather than damages is being claimed.

(8) Impossibility

Specific performance will not be ordered where performance is physically impossible, for there is clearly no sense in ordering the defendant to do something on pain of contempt, which he simply cannot do. So, for example, specific performance will not be ordered against a person who has agreed to sell land which he does not own and cannot compel the owner to convey to him.[12] Similarly, where the defendant has sold property to a third party whose title is unaffected by the claimant's prior interest, the claimant will not be granted specific performance.[13] Analogous is *Wroth v Tyler*[14] where specific performance of a contract to sell a home with vacant possession was refused because it would require the defendant to embark upon uncertain litigation in an attempt to force his wife to leave the house.

Specific performance will also be refused where this would require the defendant to do something he is not lawfully competent to do. In *Warmington v Miller*,[15] for example, the defendant, a lessee of business premises, agreed to grant an underlease to the claimant, even though he

---

11 Schwartz 'The Case for Specific Performance' (1979) 89 Yale LJ 271, 300–301. Cf Sherwin 'Law and Equity in Contract Enforcement' (1991) 50 Maryland LR 253.
12 *Castle v Wilkinson* (1870) 5 Ch App 534.
13 *Ferguson v Wilson* (1866) 2 Ch App 77.
14 [1974] Ch 30.
15 [1973] QB 877.

was prohibited by his lease from sub-letting. He failed to grant the underlease but specific performance was refused because it would necessitate the defendant breaking the terms of his lease.

Sometimes in these situations, a defendant can escape from the contract and avoid all remedies for breach, by invoking doctrines such as common mistake, frustration or illegality. But those doctrines are clearly narrower than the impossibility bar to specific performance, so that a claimant may be able to recover damages if he is denied specific performance.

(9) Severe hardship

Specific performance will be refused where it would cause severe hardship to the defendant.[16] It was on this ground that in *Denne v Light*,[17] the court refused to order specific performance against the buyer of farming land which was apparently landlocked: that is, there seemed to be no right of way over surrounding land. Similarly, in *Hope v Walter*[18] it was thought unfair to a purchaser to order him to complete the sale of a house that, unknown to both parties, was being used as a brothel by the tenant. Again, in *Wroth v Tyler*[19] specific performance to order the defendant to convey title with non-vacant possession was refused because for the defendant's wife, but not the defendant, to have the right to continue to live in the house could encourage a split-up of the family.

A modern and particularly vivid example is *Patel v Ali*.[20] Here the defendant, a married Pakistani woman who could hardly speak English, had contracted to sell her home to the claimants. In the years after the contract was made, the defendant's husband was sent to prison, she bore two more children and had a leg amputated because of bone cancer. A number of friends and relatives brought her shopping and helped with household chores. However, if she was forced to move it was likely that she would lose this daily assistance. In such circumstances, Goulding J refused to order specific performance and left the claimants to their remedy of damages, even though the defendant's hardship did not exist at the time of the contract and was not in any way caused by the claimants.

---

16 Or, sometimes, to third parties, eg *Thames Guaranty Ltd v Campbell* [1985] QB 210. See Jones and Goodhart *Specific Performance* (2nd edn, 1996) pp 121–122.
17 (1857) 8 De GM & G 774. In addition to the cases cited below, see *Gravesham Borough Council v British Railways Board* [1978] Ch 379 at 405.
18 [1900] 1 Ch 257.
19 [1974] Ch 30.
20 [1984] Ch 283.

On the other hand, specific performance will not be refused simply because the defendant is in financial difficulties[1] or because, on a rising market, the defendant vendor of a house is finding it difficult to acquire alternative accommodation.[2]

Again, it is interesting to see that in many situations of 'severe hardship', the defendant can escape from the contract and avoid all remedies for breach, by invoking doctrines such as common mistake or frustration. But that in this context a clear gap is left for the refusal of specific performance alone is shown by *Patel v Ali*, and by Goulding J's comment that 'Equitable relief may ... be refused because of an unforeseen change of circumstances not amounting to legal frustration, just as it may on the ground of mistake insufficient to avoid a contract at law.'[3]

(10) The claimant's conduct[4]

(a) **Serious breach**

Specific performance will be refused if the claimant has committed a serious breach of contract. So for example, in *Australian Hardwoods Pty Ltd v Railways Comr*[5] the Privy Council refused specific performance of a contractual obligation to take steps to ensure the transfer of a sawmill licence because, inter alia, of the claimant's own breach. Similarly, a claimant will not be awarded specific performance if he himself is in breach of a time stipulation where time is of the essence.[6] But since the fusion of the common law and Chancery courts, the defendant rarely needs to rely on this defence, for a breach that is serious enough to justify refusing specific performance should and it seems does entitle the defendant to terminate the contract, rendering him no longer liable to perform. Put another way, the sort of breach necessary to bar specific performance will never be less serious than a breach justifying discharge of the contract.[7]

---

1   *Francis v Cowcliffe* (1976) 33 P & CR 368.
2   *Mountford v Scott* [1975] Ch 258.
3   [1984] Ch 283 at 288. See generally Sherwin 'Law and Equity in Contract Enforcement' (1991) 50 Maryland LR 253.
4   This refers to conduct other than in contract formation. For unfairness in formation see above, pp 496–497.
5   [1961] 1 WLR 425. In *Dyster v Randall & Sons* [1926] Ch 932 at 942–943, the breach was thought too trivial to be a bar.
6   *Steedman* v *Drinkle* [1916] 1 AC 275.
7   Farnsworth *Contracts* (3rd edn, 2004) para 12.5.

(b) He who comes to equity must come with clean hands[8]

By this maxim specific performance will be denied to a claimant whose past conduct, as revealed by the facts of the dispute, has been highly improper. Indeed, one can regard the previous head of serious breach as incorporated within clean hands, although it is more usually treated separately. As such, clean hands plays a loose and residual role. An example is *Lamare v Dixon*,[9] where the owner of some cellars had orally promised the proposed lessee, prior to the signing of the contract for a lease, that he would make the cellars dry. This he had failed to do and as a result the court refused him specific performance. More recently in *Quadrant Visual Communications Ltd v Hutchison Telephone (UK) Ltd*[10] the defendant contracted to buy the claimant's car and portable telephone business. The price to be paid depended on the number of the claimant's customers prior to the completion date. Prior to completion, the claimant increased the number of its customers through two marketing deals that involved supplying free telephones. The claimant informed the defendant of the first but not the second deal. Following breach by the defendant, the Court of Appeal upheld the trial judge's decision not to award the claimant specific performance of the agreement because the claimant had tricked the defendant and had therefore not come to equity with clean hands.

(c) He who seeks equity must do equity

This means that there will be no specific performance if the claimant is not willing and able to perform his own obligations from now on (or is otherwise not willing to do what is fair and right for the defendant). So for example, in *Chappell v Times Newspapers Ltd*,[11] employees were refused an injunction amounting to specific performance of a contract of employment because, inter alia, they could not show themselves ready and willing to perform their contracts without disruption as they were not prepared to renounce their union. Clearly this defence normally rests on similar grounds to that of want of mutuality but it differs in that the court is reacting to a clear indication of the claimant's unwillingness to counter-perform.

---

8   Generally, see Chafee 'Coming into Equity with Clean Hands' (1948–9) 47 Mich LR 877, 1065.
9   (1873) LR 6 HL 414. See also *Mason v Clarke* [1954] 1 QB 460 at 472.
10   [1993] BCLC 442.
11   [1975] 1 WLR 482.

(d) Laches

By the Limitation Act 1980, s 36(1), it appears that the usual six-year limitation period does not apply to an action for specific performance.[12] But under the doctrine of laches the remedy may be denied for unreasonable delay by the claimant in seeking it.[13] Traditionally, the classic authority was *Milward v Earl of Thanet*,[14] where Sir Richard Arden MR said that a claimant wanting specific performance had to show himself to be 'ready, desirous, prompt and eager'; and although there were always exceptional situations (for example, delay, of whatever length, did not bar an action merely to transfer the legal estate)[15] delays of more than a few months were generally considered fatal to specific performance, particularly where there was prejudice to the defendant or the subject matter was property of fluctuating value.[16]

However, *Lazard Bros & Co Ltd v Fairfield Properties Co (Mayfair) Ltd*[17] indicates that in modern times the courts are more tolerant of a claimant's delay. There specific performance of a contract for the sale of land was sought over two years after completion was due and was granted. Megarry V-C regarded *Milward v Earl of Thanet* and the idea that specific performance was a prize to be awarded to the zealous and to be denied to the indolent as the wrong approach today; and he went on to say, 'If between the plaintiff and the defendant it was just that the plaintiff should obtain the remedy, the court ought not to withhold it merely because the plaintiff has been guilty of delay.'[18] What exactly this means and hence how far the courts will grant specific performance despite lengthy delays by the claimant is left unclear; but it may be

---

12 It appears that, for specific performance, the statutory limitation periods for contract have not been applied 'by analogy' under the proviso to the Limitation Act 1980, s 36(1): *Fitzgerald v Masters* (1956) 95 CLR 420 at 428. See, generally, Beatson 'Limitation Periods and Specific Performance' in *Contemporary Issues in Commercial Law* (eds Lomnicka and Morse, 1997) pp 9–23. Under the Law Commission's proposals for reform, the standard limitation periods for breach of contract would apply to claims for specific performance, albeit that the doctrine of laches (and acquiescence) would also apply within those periods: see *Limitation of Actions*, Law Commission Report No 270 (2001) paras 4.268–4.278 and Draft Bill, cl 34.

13 Limitation Act 1980, s 36(2). This would remain the law if the Law Commission's recommendations for reforming the law on limitation were implemented. See *Limitation of Actions*, Law Commission Report No 270 (2001) paras 4.274–4.278 and Draft Bill, cl 34(2).

14 (1801) 5 Ves 720n.

15 *Sharp v Milligan* (1856) 22 Beav 606 (18 years); *Williams v Greatrex* [1957] 1 WLR 31 (10 years); *Frawley v Neill* (1999) Times, 5 April (16 years). The rationale of this exception is that, applying the maxim 'equity treats as done that which ought to be done,' a contract to transfer a legal interest in property is as good as a transfer of that interest when a party has taken possession of the property in reliance on that interest: see *Limitation of Actions*, Law Commission Report No 270 (2001) paras 4.268–4.273 and Draft Bill, cl 34(1).

16 *Pollard v Clayton* (1855) 1 K & J 462 (eleven months); *Huxham v Llewellyn* (1873) 28 LT 577 (five months); *Glasbrook v Richardson* (1874) 23 WR 51 (three and a half months).

17 (1977) 121 Sol Jo 793.

18 (1977) 121 Sol Jo 793.

expected that in the absence of additional factors, such as prejudice to the defendant, a long delay – and certainly more than a few months – will be needed to bar specific performance.

(e) Acquiescence

Although no case has been found, it has traditionally been assumed that, as with injunctions, acquiescence is a bar to specific performance:[19] that is, that a claimant will be denied specific performance where it has encouraged the defendant to believe that it has no objection to the defendant doing what amounts to a breach of contract, and the defendant has acted to his detriment in that belief.

(f) Valid termination of the contract by the claimant

Where the claimant has validly terminated the contract for the defendant's breach, it can no longer claim specific performance. This was regarded as an 'incontrovertible' principle by Lord Wilberforce in dicta in *Johnson v Agnew*[20] and he later commented, '... it is easy to see that a party who has chosen to put an end to a contract by the other party's repudiation cannot afterwards seek specific performance. This is simply because the contract is dead – what is dead is dead.'[1] An alternative way of expressing this is to say that the claimant's election bars specific performance; but the terminology and supposed doctrine of election of remedy is likely to confuse rather than to clarify the law and, at least here, it is easier to manage without it.

Sharpe has criticised the present law on the ground that it should only be where the defendant has detrimentally relied on the claimant's termination that the claimant should be prevented from going back on it.[2] But such an approach would leave the issue too uncertain, hindering the parties' plans for future action. Under the present law the parties know for sure that once the claimant has made a clear decision to terminate they are each free to ignore the contract.

Finally, it should be stressed that merely claiming damages for breach does not bar specific performance, as specific performance and damages may be mutually consistent. Rather specific performance is barred where

---

19   Meagher, Heydon and Leeming *Meagher, Gummow and Lehane's Equity Doctrines and Remedies* (4th edn, 2002) para 21–175; *Fry on Specific Performance* (6th edn, 1921) p 516.
20   [1980] AC 367 at 392.
1   [1980] AC 367 at 398.
2   Ie the full requirements of estoppel by election are required, Sharpe *Injunctions and Specific Performance* (3rd edn, 2000) paras 10.820–10.880.

the claim for damages shows that the claimant is terminating the contract, that is that he is accepting the defendant's repudiation.[3]

(11) No partial specific performance?

The principle has sometimes been applied that there can be no specific performance of only some of the defendant's obligations under a contract; so if one or more of the obligations is not specifically enforceable, there can be no specific performance of the rest. For example, in *Ryan v Mutual Tontine Westminster Chambers Association*,[4] where the court refused to order specific performance of an obligation to provide a porter who would be constantly in attendance, an alternative claim that the defendants should merely be ordered to appoint a porter was also refused; '… when the court cannot grant a specific performance of the contract as a whole it will not interfere to compel specific performance of part of a contract.'[5]

There seems to be nothing in terms of policy to justify such a bar.[6] Damages (or equitable compensation) can be added to compensate the claimant for the unperformed part, as they are where performance will be late or where land being bought does not correspond to what was promised. In any event, as it is the claimant who is seeking the order, he is clearly prepared to accept the disadvantage of part performance. Nor can the defendant validly complain if he is ordered to do part only of what he agreed.

Fortunately, it is doubtful whether this principle has ever been generally accepted, since there are numerous decisions that conflict with it. In *Lytton v Great Northern Rly Co*,[7] for example, specific performance was ordered of the defendants' contractual obligation to build a railway siding while being refused of their obligation to keep it in repair; and in *Elmore v Pirrie*[8] the defendants' obligation to purchase patent rights was specifically enforced although there could be no specific performance of their obligation to form a company to work the patents and to pay royalties to the claimants. In Kay J's words:

---

3   See *Meng Leong Development Pte Ltd v Jip Hong Trading Co Pte Ltd* [1985] AC 511.
4   [1893] 1 Ch 116. See also, eg *Merchants' Trading Co v Banner* (1871) LR 12 Eq 18.
5   [1893] 1 Ch 116 at 123 (per Lord Esher MR).
6   *Ogden v Fossick* (1862) 4 De GF & J 426 may be justified, but if so this is because of want of mutuality and not because of the 'no partial specific performance' principle relied on.
7   (1856) 2 K & J 394.
8   (1887) 57 LT 333. See also, eg *Peacock v Penson* (1848) 11 Beav 355; *Soames v Edge* (1860) John 669; *Wilkinson v Clements* (1872) 8 Ch App 96.

'Why should not the plaintiffs have damages for that part of the agreement of which the court does not grant specific performance? The court has power to order specific performance of the whole of the agreement, or part of it, with damages for the rest.'[9]

Moreover in the more recent case of *Posner v Scott-Lewis*[10] Mervyn-Davies J ordered specific performance of a landlord's covenant to appoint a resident porter at a block of flats and, although there was no discussion of the 'no partial specific performance' idea, the decision does appear to be a direct contradiction of *Ryan*.

Finally, in *Rainbow Estates Ltd v Tokenhold Ltd*[11] Lawrence Collins QC, in ordering specific performance of a tenant's repairing obligation, said the following:

'[T]he court should not be constrained by the supposed rule that the court will not enforce the defendant's obligation in part … it is by no means clear that there is such a principle, and in any event if there is such a principle, it applies where the contract is in part unenforceable … it does not mean that the court cannot in an appropriate case enforce compliance with a particular obligation such as a repairing covenant.'[12]

(12) Conclusion – the trend towards specific performance

Having completed an examination of the various bars to specific performance it is appropriate to take a brief overview of the present availability of the remedy.

In spite of some of the more radical proposals in some cases not finding favour in others, the general picture is one of a trend in favour of specific performance. Indeed in relation to no less than eight of the bars there have been recent developments favouring specific performance: adequacy of damages, constant supervision, personal service, want of mutuality, uncertainty, contracts not supported by valuable consideration, laches and, in so far as it was ever a bar, no partial specific performance. So it appears that a claimant will now find it easier than ever before to obtain specific performance.

The one major case bucking this trend is *Co-operative Insurance Society Ltd v Argyll Stores (Holdings) Ltd*;[13] as has been explained above, while the decision in that case seems correct, their Lordships' support for the constant supervision objection was misplaced.[14]

9   (1887) 57 LT 333 at 336.
10 [1987] Ch 25.
11 [1999] Ch 64.
12 [1999] Ch 64 at 73.
13 [1998] AC 1.
14 Above, pp 480–481.

Our examination of policy has further shown that, with the exception of the wide view of *Beswick v Beswick*, all such developments in favour of specific performance are either justified or at least unobjectionable. The verdict is therefore one of support for this trend.

Finally it may be asked, why has this trend occurred in recent times? Several answers may be suggested; for example, there is now, arguably, a more flexible approach to precedent; damages are particularly problematical in times of high inflation and when insolvency is common: and the courts are more willing than ever before to intervene in individuals' lives.

3. OTHER ISSUES

(1) Stipulated remedy

There are two issues here. The first, which no English case has yet dealt with, is whether a clause by which the parties indicate that specific performance should be the remedy for breach will be valid so as to ensure the granting of specific performance where it would otherwise not be available. Arguably such a clause, unlike a penalty clause, cannot be knocked down as unfair for it cannot be objectionable to insist, as at the time the contract is made, that the defendant performs as it promises. Rather such a clause, like a liquidated damages clause, has the merit of saving judicial time and expense, here in deciding between damages and specific performance. However, the courts are never keen to allow their jurisdiction to be ousted and, at the end of the day, it is likely that they would take the view that, if there are good grounds for otherwise refusing specific performance, an agreed remedy clause is not sufficient to undermine the validity of those grounds.[15]

The second issue is whether a penalty or liquidated damages clause ousts specific performance. It might be argued, for example, that the insertion of such a clause gives the defendant an option to perform or to pay agreed damages; or, more forceful still, that such a clause indicates that monetary remedies are adequate and that specific performance of the primary obligation is unwarranted. But the courts lean against a construction that would oust a judicial remedy and they have consistently taken the view that the money clause is added as security for

---

15 But see the views of Sharpe *Injunctions and Specific Performance* (3rd edn, 2000) paras 7.710–7.810. See also Macneil 'Power of Contract and Agreed Remedies' (1962) 47 Cornell LQ 495, 520–523.

performance and/or as clarifying the amount of damages the claimant will receive if suing for damages.[16] Specific performance is therefore not ousted.

(2) The flexibility of specific performance – additional damages or compensation and conditional enforcement

(a) Damages in addition to specific performance

The Supreme Court Act 1981, s 49, allows a claim for ordinary common law damages to be combined with an action for specific performance. In the same action therefore, the claimant may be awarded specific performance and, where what is ordered is not identical with what was promised,[17] damages to overcome the deficiency. For example, since specific performance seldom results in performance at the time fixed by the contract, damages for delay may be awarded along with specific performance.[18]

Equitable damages may also be awarded in addition to specific performance under the Supreme Court Act 1981, s 50, the successor to Lord Cairns's Act.[19] But since *Johnson v Agnew*[20] has assimilated the principles of assessment, additional equitable damages are only more advantageous to a claimant in the situation where they are available and common law damages are not.[1]

(b) Specific performance with compensation or abatement of purchase price[2]

Prior to the Chancery Amendment Act 1858 (Lord Cairns's Act), s 2, the Court of Chancery had at most a very limited power to award damages in addition to specific performance. This was offset to an extent by the practice of awarding to a purchaser of land that is not as promised, the equitable remedy of compensation or abatement of price along with

---

16   *Howard v Hopkyns* (1742) 2 Atk 371; *Magrane v Archbold* (1813) 1 Dow 107; *Long v Bowring* (1864) 33 Beav 585. The same approach is taken with regard to injunctions, see below, pp 536–537.
17   But no order should be made for performance of something entirely different from what was promised: see analogously *Cedar Holdings Ltd v Green* [1981] Ch 129 esp 141–143.
18   *Jaques v Millar* (1877) 6 Ch D 153. See also *Seven Seas Properties Ltd v Al-Essa* [1988] 1 WLR 1272 (specific performance granted against a vendor of land along with an order for the holding back, and retention by the parties' solicitors, of so much of the purchase price as would cover the purchaser's damages claim against the vendor for loss of a sub-sale of the land).
19   *Eg Grant v Dawkins* [1973] 1 WLR 1406.
20   [1980] AC 367.
1   As in example (i), above, p 364.
2   Harpum 'Specific Performance with Compensation as a Purchaser's Remedy – a Study in Contract and Equity' [1981] CLJ 47.

specific performance.[3] Yet purchasers and courts still respectively claim and award this additional remedy[4] despite the power the courts now have to award common law or equitable damages in addition to specific performance. The continuation of this habit is doubly surprising since, rather than offering advantages over damages, compensation seems less advantageous; for in *Rudd v Lascelles*,[5] several restrictions were placed on the power to award compensation in addition to specific performance and in, for example, *Grant v Dawkins*,[6] it was assumed that the amount of compensation, like abatement, could not exceed the purchase price. Harpum thinks that the practice '… perhaps reflects no more than the conservatism of the legal profession who have preferred to stick with the devil they have known for so long.'[7] Seemingly no one would lose anything and unnecessary duplication and complexity would be avoided if the power to award compensation or abatement of price to a purchaser of land along with specific performance was simply abolished.

(c) Conditional specific performance

To protect the defendant, and to enable the remedy to be as widely applicable as possible, specific performance may be granted on terms. The most common example occurs where the vendor of land seeks specific performance against the purchaser and there is some non-substantial defect[8] in the property; specific performance will be ordered 'with compensation', that is, subject to the vendor paying compensation to the purchaser to cover the defect.[9]

Specific performance on terms has also been commonly adopted as a means of producing a just result for both parties in cases where the defendant is able to resist specific performance because of his mistake. The claimant may be granted specific performance if it agrees to conditions reflecting the defendant's understanding of the bargain. For example, in *Baskcomb v Beckwith*,[10] the defendant purchaser had contracted to buy an area of land, without realising – the plans not making it clear – that a small plot of land nearby was to be retained by the vendor, and was not covered by restrictive covenants preventing the building of a public house. The claimant vendor was given the choice: no

---

3   *Mortlock v Buller* (1804) 10 Ves 292.
4   *Topfell Ltd v Galley Properties Ltd* [1979] 1 WLR 446 is a recent example.
5   [1900] 1 Ch 815.
6   [1973] 1 WLR 1406.
7   [1981] CLJ 47 at 51.
8   The leading case on the meaning of this is *Flight v Booth* (1834) 1 Bing NC 370, but it was actually dealing with rescission.
9   *Re Fawcett and Holmes' Contract* (1889) 42 Ch D 150; *Shepherd v Croft* [1911] 1 Ch 521.
10   (1869) LR 8 Eq 100. See also *Preston v Luck* (1884) 27 Ch D 497.

specific performance or specific performance with the restrictive covenant extended to his own retained plot.

Langen and Wind Ltd v Bell[11] shows that where the courts want to protect the defendant against a subsequent failure by the claimant to perform they may make specific performance conditional, rather than denying specific performance altogether for want of mutuality. The defendant had there contracted to transfer shares to the claimants for a price that could only be fixed in the future. The defendant was ordered to transfer the shares but as security for future payment they were to be held by the claimants' solicitors until payment.

A more unusual illustration of conditional specific performance is provided by *Price v Strange*,[12] where simply to have ordered the defendant to grant the lease to the claimant would have given the claimant a windfall, since he had promised in return to carry out the repairs which the defendant had had finished at her own expense. The claimant was therefore granted specific performance but subject to compensating the defendant for that expense.

Finally in *Harvela Investments Ltd v Royal Trust Co of Canada Ltd*[13] the House of Lords granted specific performance to a purchaser of shares on condition that it paid the vendor interest from the date fixed for completion until payment.[14] Specific performance by itself would have put the claimant into a far better position than if there had been no breach, because it would have had the use of the purchase money during the period of delay, plus taking the rise in value of the shares. Indeed irrespective of such a justification, ordinary equitable principles, generally rationalised in terms of equitable interests or constructive trusts, establish that a vendor is entitled to interest on the purchase price from the date of completion, while a purchaser is in return entitled to the interim profits from the property.[15]

(3) The effect of specific performance on termination and damages

In *Johnson v Agnew*,[16] the claimant vendor of land had obtained specific performance against the purchaser. The purchaser delayed in complying with the order, so that mortgagees of the land enforced their security by

---

11 [1972] Ch 685.
12 [1978] Ch 337.
13 [1986] AC 207.
14 For rates of interest, see above, p 351.
15 [1985] AC 207 at 236–237. See also *Re Hewitt's Contract* [1963] 1 WLR 1298; *Fry on Specific Performance* (6th edn, 1921) pp 640–641; *Emmet on Title* (19th edn, 1986) paras 7.021–7.033.
16 [1980] AC 367.

selling off the land. With specific enforcement no longer possible, the claimant now sought damages for the defendant's breach of contract. The defendant argued, first, that having obtained an order of specific performance the claimant had irrevocably forfeited his right to damages – all contractual rights had become merged in the specific performance decree;[17] and secondly, that having 'rescinded' the contract for breach, as the claimant had now done, there could in any event be no damages. The House of Lords rejected both arguments. The latter, which is beyond our immediate concern, was held to rest on an incorrect line of authority,[18] that had mistakenly regarded rescission for breach as meaning rescission *ab initio* rather than termination *in futuro*. The former was emphatically rejected, it being held that a contract remains in force after an order of specific performance so that the claimant can ask the court to dissolve the decree and revert to his rights to termination and damages.

However, the House of Lords did make one concession to the 'irrevocable election' view, namely that the claimant has no *right* to revert to termination and damages. In Lord Wilberforce's words:

'Once the matter has been placed in the hands of a court of equity ... the subsequent control of the matter will be examined according to equitable principles. The court would not make an order dissolving the decree of specific performance and terminating the contract (with recovery of damages) if to so do would be unjust, in the circumstances then existing to the other party, in this case to the purchaser.'[19]

This concession would appear to be designed to deal with the situation where it is because of the claimant's default that specific performance has not been complied with, so that had the contract been in force in the normal way, it would be the defendant rather than the claimant who would be entitled to damages.[20] Beyond this situation, there seems no justification for such a concession.[1]

---

17 The terminology of election is often used; but, as in other instances, it is confusing and unnecessary.
18 Eg *Horsler v Zorro* [1975] Ch 302.
19 [1980] AC 367 at 399. See also *Singh v Nazeer* [1979] Ch 474 esp 480–481; *GKN Distributors Ltd v Tyne Tees Fabrication Ltd* (1985) 50 P & CR 403.
20 The extent of the concession is discussed by Hetherington 'Keeping the Plaintiff out of his Contractual Remedies: the Heresies that Survive *Johnson v Agnew*' (1980) 96 LQR 403, and Jackson 'Chimeral Heresies' (1981) 97 LQR 26.
1   Hetherington, ibid, and *Meagher, Gummow & Lehane's Equity* (4th edn, 2002) para 20–265 do not think the concession is ever justified.

Chapter 21

Injunctions

1. INTRODUCTION

An injunction is an equitable remedy available for torts and breach of contract (and equitable wrongs) as well as being available in other situations outside the scope of this book.[1] The approach adopted in this chapter will be to introduce briefly in this section the three important pairs of contrasting injunctions before going on in the next sections to examine in depth the principles governing the grant of each of the main types of injunction along with the function each performs as a remedy for torts and breach of contract. Although not an injunction, the final section of this chapter is considered the most appropriate place in this book to consider the remedy of the appointment of a receiver (and manager).

Five further points can be conveniently dealt with at this stage. First, a court will sometimes accept an undertaking from the defendant in substitution for, and in the same terms as, an injunction that it would otherwise have granted.[2] Since, contrary to its non-coercive appearance, such an undertaking plays exactly the same role as an injunction, being enforceable by contempt proceedings,[3] it is hard to see the justification for this judicial practice.

Secondly, by the Crown Proceedings Act 1947, s 21(1)(a), an injunction cannot be granted against the Crown.[4] But, as explained by the House of

---

1 The Supreme Court Act 1981, s 37(1), gives the High Court power to grant an injunction 'whenever just and convenient to do so', but generally the infringement of a legal or equitable right is required – Hanbury and Martin *Modern Equity* (16th edn, 2001) pp 764–769. For treatment of situations outside torts and breach of contract (and equitable wrongs) see Sharpe *Injunctions and Specific Performance* (3rd edn, 2000) ch 3 and paras 5.190–5.540. For civil statutory injunctions backed up by specific criminal penalties for breach (separate from contempt) see, eg *R (McCann) v Crown Court at Manchester* [2002] UKHL 39, [2003] 1 AC 787 (which dealt with 'anti-social behaviour orders').
2 *Evans Marshall & Co Ltd v Bertola SA* [1973] 1 WLR 349.
3 *Camden London Borough Council v Alpenoak Ltd* [1985] NLJ Rep 1209; *Hussain v Hussain* [1986] Fam 134.
4 However, an interim injunction can be granted against the Crown to protect the claimant's directly effective EC rights: *R v Secretary of State for Transport, ex p Factortame Ltd (No 2)* [1991] 1 AC 603.

Lords in *M v Home Office*,[5] an injunction, including an interim injunction, can be granted against *an officer of the Crown* when sued in his personal capacity and, in judicial review proceedings (to which s 21 does not apply), when sued in his official capacity. Commonly a claimant will be equally satisfied with a declaration against the Crown and there is now power to award an interim declaration.[6]

Thirdly, an injunction can affect third parties: ie contempt proceedings can be brought against not only the tortfeasor or contract-breaker for failure to comply with the injunction but also against any person who frustrates the purpose of the injunction.[7]

Fourthly, it was held in *Bloomsbury Publishing Group plc v News Group Newspapers Ltd*[8] that an injunction (or an order for delivery up) can be granted against a person or persons who have not been named but merely described. There an interim injunction was granted to the claimant restraining, until the date of publication, 'the person or persons who have offered the publishers of [certain newspapers] a copy of the book Harry Potter and the Order of the Phoenix by JK Rowling' from disclosing to any person any part of the book.[9] There was no injustice to anyone in making such an order provided the description was sufficiently certain to identify those included and those who were not.

Finally, it was laid down by the Court of Appeal in *Wookey v Wookey*[10] that no injunction should be ordered against a person whose mental incapacity means that he is incapable of understanding the order; nor, in the vast majority of cases, against a minor who has no earnings from which a fine for disobedience could be paid and is too young to be sent to prison.

(1) Prohibitory and mandatory injunctions

A prohibitory injunction acts negatively, ie it orders the defendant not to do something. A mandatory injunction acts positively, ie it orders the defendant to do something. The distinction is one of substance and not one of form so that, for example, an injunction ordering the defendant

---

5 [1994] 1 AC 377.
6 CPR 25.1(1)(b).
7 *Z Ltd v A-Z and AA-LL* [1982] QB 558 (freezing injunction); *Attorney-General v Times Newspapers Ltd* [1992] 1 AC 191; *Attorney-General v Punch Ltd* [2002] UKHL 50, [2003] 1 AC 1046. But it has been held, rather surprisingly, that such contempt proceedings against third parties can be brought only in respect of interim, and not final, injunctions: *Jockey Club Ltd v Buffham* [2002] EWHC 1866 (QB), [2003] QB 462. See ATH Smith 'Third Parties and the Reach of Injunctions' [2003] CLJ 241.
8 [2003] EWHC 1205 (Ch), [2003] 1 WLR 1633.
9 Such a disclosure, prior to the publication date for the book, would constitute breach of copyright and/or breach of confidence and/or conversion.
10 [1991] Fam 121.

not to allow a particular building to remain standing on its land is a mandatory injunction, since in substance the defendant is being ordered to knock the building down. Indeed, prior to *Jackson v Normanby Brick Co*[11] the courts tended to express mandatory injunctions in such a negative form but in that case it was laid down that form should reflect substance and that a mandatory injunction should be expressed in a positive form.

But so long as in substance breach of a negative obligation is being restrained the courts apply prohibitory injunction principles even though *in practice* it is most likely that compliance will necessitate particular positive steps. For example, an injunction restraining a factory-owner from continuing to pollute a river so as to cause a nuisance to the claimant is regarded as prohibitory and governed by prohibitory injunction, rather than mandatory injunction, principles. Only on the question of whether to suspend the injunction is any weight attached to the argument that compliance may in practice force the defendant to take particular positive steps, for example, replacing the factory's existing 'waste disposal' system with a new one. The justification for this is presumably that so long as the defendant *can* comply with the injunction without positive steps, for example by not continuing with that business, one cannot be sure that in complying it will take positive steps, and certainly one cannot predict with any accuracy which particular steps it might take. Traditionally the one judicially recognised exception is in the realm of breach of contract, where specific performance generally takes over the role of the mandatory injunction: it has long been recognised that an order which the defendant can comply with only by either not working (or not carrying on business) at all or carrying out particular positive contractual obligations is regarded as indirect specific performance, and is governed by specific performance, rather than prohibitory injunction, principles. The argument later advanced in regard to that area[12] – that, as indicated in some recent cases, the exception should be extended to wherever the order is in practice likely to force the defendant to take particular positive steps – is applicable also to the distinction between prohibitory and mandatory injunctions.

---

11   [1899] 1 Ch 438.
12   Below, pp 532–533, 535–536

(2) *Quia timet*[13] injunctions and injunctions where a wrong has already been committed

In *Redland Bricks Ltd v Morris*[14] Lord Upjohn said that a '... *quia timet* action ... is an action for an injunction to prevent an apprehended legal wrong, though none has occurred at present', and Jolowicz has written that a *quia timet* injunction is granted where '... no actionable wrong has yet been committed by the defendant.'[15]

Most obviously, therefore, an injunction sought to prevent a continuing wrong is not *quia timet*. But the same can perhaps also be said of an injunction sought to prevent a *recurrence* of wrongful acts by the defendant, or a mandatory injunction sought to prevent the defendant's earlier acts causing a *further* wrong. In relation to the latter, Lord Upjohn in *Redland Bricks Ltd v Morris* treated as *quia timet* a mandatory injunction sought to compel the defendant to restore support to the claimant's land. As the land had slipped several times before, so that the same sort of wrong as that now sought to be prevented had previously been committed by the defendant against the claimant, the injunction sought should perhaps not have been regarded as *quia timet*.[16]

(3) Final and interim injunctions

A final injunction, otherwise known as a perpetual injunction, is one that is granted at the trial of the action or other hearing in which final judgment is given.[17] In contrast, an interim injunction, as normally understood,[18] is one made at an earlier stage in the proceedings and is to last only until the trial at the latest. It may be expressed to continue in force 'until the trial of this action or further order'. Or it may be expressed to continue only until a specified pre-trial date: for example, 'until 10.30am on Wednesday 25th March (or so soon thereafter as counsel may be heard) or until further order.' For the claimant the great advantage of an interim injunction is that it can be gained quickly, without having to wait for the trial.

---

13 'Since he fears'.
14 [1970] AC 652 at 644.
15 'Damages in Equity – A Study of Lord Cairns' Act' (1975) 34 CLJ 224, 244.
16 'Damages in Equity – A Study of Lord Cairns' Act' (1975) 34 CLJ 224, pp 244–245.
17 Eg summary judgment under CPR Pt 24.
18 But freezing injunctions granted after final judgment have been treated as interim because they are ancillary to a final judgment. See *Orwell Steel v Asphalt and Tarmac (UK) Ltd* [1984] 1 WLR 1097; *Hill Samuel v Littauer* [1985] NLJ Rep 57. Also see *Distributori Automatici Italia SpA v Holford General Trading Co Ltd* [1985] 3 All ER 750 (search orders made after final judgment).

2.   FINAL PROHIBITORY INJUNCTIONS[19]

(1) Torts

(a) **The present law**

A prohibitory injunction is the appropriate remedy to prevent the continuation or repetition of a tort. By it the defendant is ordered not to perform the acts that constitute the tort. While a prohibitory injunction can be granted in respect of any tort that can be continued or repeated – and has been granted, for example, to prevent trespass to the person,[20] inducing breach of contract,[1] defamation,[2] infringement of copyright,[3] infringement of patent,[4] and passing off[5] – it has mainly been sought, particularly at the final rather than interlocutory stage, to restrain torts protecting the claimant's real property rights, namely the torts of nuisance and trespass to land.

In relation to these two torts – and, despite the stress often laid on the claimant's proprietary rights, there is no reason to suppose that different principles apply to other torts – it is clear that the prohibitory injunction rather than damages is the primary remedy. In other words, the courts rarely exercise their power under the Supreme Court Act 1981, s 50, the successor to Lord Cairns's Act, to award damages in lieu of a prohibitory injunction sought to restrain the continuation or repetition of a nuisance or trespass to land; and an award of ordinary common law damages is generally not in issue, since in this context such damages are almost inevitably 'inadequate', being available to compensate only for loss caused by past torts.

The classic case indicating the primacy of the prohibitory injunction is *Shelfer v City of London Electric Lighting Co.*[6] Here an electric housing station had been built next to a pub and the vibration and noise caused by the operation of the machines generating the electricity constituted an actionable nuisance to the lessee of the pub. The trial judge had awarded

---

19   *Quia timet* prohibitory injunctions are discussed below, pp 543–546.
20   *Egan v Egan* [1975] Ch 218 (interim).
1   *Emerald Construction Co Ltd v Lowthian* [1966] 1 All ER 1013 (interim). The availability of the prohibitory injunction contrasts here with the reluctance to grant specific performance of positive obligations in the main contract.
2   *Saxby v Easterbrook* (1878) 3 CPD 339; *Bonnard v Perryman* [1891] 2 Ch 269 (interim); *Grobbelaar v News Group Newspapers Ltd* [2002] UKHL 40, [2002] 1 WLR 3024.
3   *Performing Right Society Ltd v Mitchell & Booker Ltd* [1924] 1 KB 762; *Phonographic Performance Ltd v Maitra* [1998] 1 WLR 870.
4   *Coflexip SA v Stolt Comex Seaway MS Ltd* [2001] 1 All ER 952 (note).
5   *Erven Warnink BV v J Townend & Sons (Hull) Ltd* [1979] AC 731; *British Telecommunications plc v One In A Million Ltd* [1999] 1 WLR 903; *Microsoft Corpn v Plato Technology Ltd* (1999) Times, 17 August 1999 (infringement of trade mark and passing off).
6   [1895] 1 Ch 287.

damages in lieu of the prohibitory injunction sought to restrain a further nuisance, but the Court of Appeal reversed this decision and granted the injunction. Particularly important is A L Smith LJ's judgment where he said that damages should only be awarded in lieu of an injunction:

> 'If the injury to the plaintiff's legal rights is small. And is one which is capable of being estimated in money. And is one which can be adequately compensated by a small money payment. And the case is one in which it would be oppressive to the defendant to grant an injunction.'[7]

This statement has been applied many times since, a good example being in *Kennaway v Thompson*,[8] where the Court of Appeal awarded a prohibitory injunction to limit powerboat racing, the noise from which was causing the claimant a nuisance.

The primacy of the prohibitory injunction – or, as it is often expressed, the claimant's prima facie right to a prohibitory injunction – was also stressed in the well-known case of *Pride of Derby and Derbyshire Angling Association Ltd v British Celanese Ltd*,[9] where a prohibitory injunction was granted to restrain the defendants from polluting a river with untreated sewage so as to constitute a nuisance to the claimant angling association which operated a fishery in the river. In Lord Evershed MR's words:

> 'It is, I think, well settled that if A proves that his proprietary rights are being wrongfully interfered with by B, and that B intends to continue his wrong, then A is prima facie entitled to an injunction, and he will be deprived of that remedy only if special circumstances exist, including the circumstance that damages are an adequate remedy for the wrong that he has suffered.'[10]

Similarly in the early case of *Imperial Gas Light & Coke Co v Broadbent*,[11] where a prohibitory injunction was granted to restrain the defendants from operating their gas works so as to cause a nuisance to the claimant who carried on business as a market-gardener, Lord Kingsdown said:

> '... if a plaintiff applies for an injunction to restrain a violation of a common law right ... he must establish that right at law: but when he has established his right at law, I apprehend that unless there be something special in the case, he is entitled as of course to an injunction to prevent the recurrence of the violation.'[12]

7 [1895] 1 Ch 287 at 32.
8 [1981] QB 88.
9 [1953] Ch 149.
10 [1953] Ch 149 at 181.
11 (1859) 7 HL Cas 600.
12 (1859) 7 HL Cas 600 at 612.

Finally and more recently, Lord Upjohn in dicta in *Redland Bricks v Morris*,[13] the classic authority on mandatory injunctions, confirmed that a prohibitory injunction to prevent a person withdrawing support from his neighbour's land would be granted 'as of course'.[14]

Naturally all this does not mean that damages will never be awarded instead. Clearly a prima facie right can be lost. The main ground on which this will be so[15] is that, in line with usual equitable principles, the claimant's conduct may debar him.[16]

It may also be that a prohibitory injunction will be refused where the interference with the claimant's rights is trivial, although there is inconsistency in the authorities on this point. On the one hand, A L Smith LJ's principles in *Shelfer* can be regarded as recognising that, at least where the injunction is also oppressive to the defendant (and this requirement seems to add next-to-nothing) damages in lieu should be awarded where the tortious interference is trivial. Several trespass cases also show the application of a triviality restriction.[17] In *Llandudno Urban District Council v Woods*,[18] an injunction to restrain a clergyman from trespassing by holding services on the claimant local authority's seashore was refused, Cozens Hardy J saying that the injunction was '... a formidable legal weapon which ought to be reserved for less trivial occasions'.[19] Similarly in *Behrens v Richards*,[20] having decided that the defendants, local inhabitants, were indeed trespassing on the claimant's land – an area of the Cornish coast – by crossing it to reach a beach, Buckley J refused a prohibitory injunction because the trespass was causing no real harm to the claimant. Nominal damages alone were considered sufficient. A further illustration is *Armstrong v Sheppard & Short Ltd*,[1] where the defendant was trespassing on a small strip of land at the rear of the claimant's premises by having a sewer discharging effluent there. An injunction to restrain this trespass was refused, inter alia,

---

13   [1970] AC 652.
14   [1970] AC 652 at 664. See also *Cowper v Laidler* [1903] 2 Ch 337 at 341; *Wood v Conway Corpn* [1914] 2 Ch 47; *Attorney-General v PYA Quarries Ltd* [1957] 2 QB 169; *Armstrong v Sheppard and Short Ltd* [1959] 2 QB 384.
15   Although rare, uncertainty may also be a bar, ie it must be possible to frame an order clearly specifying what the defendant must not do: *PA Thomas & Co v Mould* [1968] 2 QB 913 at 922–923.
16   Below, pp 569–575.
17   See also *Lillywhite v Trimmer* (1867) 36 LJ Ch 525 (trivial nuisance).
18   [1899] 2 Ch 705.
19   [1899] 2 Ch 705 at 710.
20   [1905] 2 Ch 614.
1   [1959] 2 QB 384. See also *Woollerton & Wilson Ltd v Richard Costain Ltd* [1970] 1 WLR 411; *League Against Cruel Sports Ltd v Scott* [1985] 2 All ER 489.

because the interference was trivial. The Court of Appeal cited the following useful passage from *Kerr on Injunctions*:[2]

> 'After the establishment of his legal rights, and of the fact of its violation, a plaintiff is generally entitled as of course to a perpetual injunction to prevent the recurrence of the wrong, unless there be something special in the circumstances of the case, such as ... where the interference with the plaintiff's rights is trivial.'

Again in *Jaggard v Sawyer*,[3] in refusing a prohibitory injunction restraining the defendants from trespassing over the claimant's road to reach their house (which also constituted a breach of covenant), the Court of Appeal considered it relevant that the harm to the claimant was minimal and that the claimant could have successfully sought an interim injunction but had not done so.

On the other hand, in granting a prohibitory injunction to restrain a trespass by the defendant's parking of vehicles on the claimant's land, the Court of Appeal in *Patel v W H Smith (Eziot) Ltd*[4] preferred the view that an injunction can be granted irrespective of the harm suffered and *Behrens v Richards* was put to one side as an exceptional case. And *Patel* was applied by Scott J in *Anchor Brewhouse Developments Ltd v Berkley House Docklands Developments Ltd*[5] in granting an injunction to restrain the defendants trespassing in the claimants' air space by their tower cranes. Scott J said:

> 'It would be possible for the law to be that the court should not grant an injunction to restrain a trifling trespass if it were shown to be reasonable and sensible that the trespass be allowed to continue for a limited period upon payment of substantial and proper damages. But I do not think it is open to me to proceed on that footing ... The authorities establish, in my view, that the plaintiffs are entitled as of course to injunctions to restrain continuing trespasses.'[6]

There is no obvious way of reconciling those two opposing views. To say that a prohibitory injunction may *exceptionally* be refused where the harm is trivial is of no real help for it is hard to see what was exceptional about a case like *Behrens v Richards*. In terms of policy, the view that triviality of harm precludes a prohibitory injunction is probably to be preferred for, as is discussed below,[7] there are strong arguments for the judiciary making a greater use of damages.

---

2   (6th edn, 1927) p 30. See also *Cowper v Laidler* [1903] 2 Ch 337 at 341.
3   [1995] 1 WLR 269.
4   [1987] 1 WLR 853.
5   [1987] 2 EGLR 173.
6   [1987] 2 EGLR 173 at 178.
7   Below, pp 522–527.

Several points concerning the primacy afforded to the prohibitory injunction merit further consideration. The first is that the courts have often stated that one reason why the prohibitory injunction should be the primary remedy is that otherwise the court would be enabling a defendant who could afford to do so to buy itself the right to commit wrongs. Typical is Lindley LJ's judgment in the *Shelfer* case in which he said, '... the Court has always protested against the notion that it ought to allow a wrong to continue simply because the wrongdoer is able and willing to pay for the injury he may inflict'.[8] In this respect, the courts show themselves to be zealous to protect individual rights, by preventing defendants – and one thinks particularly of large-scale enterprises – riding roughshod over those rights by simply working into their calculations the costs of compensating for wrongs they may commit.

Secondly, and assuming that the interference with the claimant's rights is more than trivial, the hardship that compliance with the prohibitory injunction will cause to the defendant has traditionally not been regarded as a reason to refuse it. For example, in *Pennington v Brinsop Hall Coal Co*[9] compliance with the injunction granted would involve closure of the defendant's undertaking at a cost of £190,000, whereas the claimant's loss by the nuisance was at most £100 a year. This approach contrasts sharply with the balancing of benefit and burden applied to mandatory injunctions and the 'severe hardship' bar that is a defence to specific performance.

Similarly, so long as any triviality threshold is crossed,[10] the courts are not prepared to deny a prohibitory injunction on the ground that the public interest is more important than the claimant's private interest. The *Shelfer* and *Pride of Derby* cases show this.[11] In the former the public interest in having electricity generated was not allowed to override the claimant's private interest in living in and running a public house free from undue interference by noise and vibration. Similarly in the latter case the public interest in having the town's sewage cheaply and easily disposed of was not allowed to override the claimant club's private interest in being able to fish in the river. A particularly vivid illustration is provided by *Attorney-General v Birmingham Borough Council*,[12] where counsel

---

8   [1895] 1 Ch 287 at 315–316.
9   (1877) 5 Ch D 769. See also *Redland Bricks Ltd v Morris* [1970] AC 652 at 664 (defendant's financial difficulties irrelevant to prohibitory injunctions).
10   *Llandudno Urban District Council v Woods* [1899] 2 Ch 705 and *Behrens v Richards* [1905] 2 Ch 614 are examples of the upholding of the public interest where interference was trivial.
11   The public interest in the saving of jobs was also ignored in *Pennington v Brinsop Hall Coal Co* (1877) 5 Ch D 769.
12   (1858) 4 K & J 528.

for the defendant argued, in graphic detail, that if the injunction restraining the corporation from discharging sewage into the river were granted:

'... the evil that must ensue ... would be incalculable. If the drains are stopped ... the entire sewage of the town will overflow. Birmingham will be converted into one vast cesspool, which in the course of nature, from the great elevation of the town (450 feet above sea-level) must empty itself into the Tame, only in a far more aggravated manner. The deluge of filth will cause a plague, which will not be confined to the 250,000 inhabitants of Birmingham, but will spread over the entire valley and become a national calamity ... In such cases private interests must bend to those of the country at large. The safety of the public is the highest law.'[13]

But to this Sir Page Wood V-C retorted, 'We cannot talk of that in this Court'[14] and in granting the interim prohibitory injunction sought he said, '... so far as this Court is concerned, it is a matter of almost absolute indifference whether the decision will affect a population of 250,000 or a single individual.'[15] More recently in *Kennaway v Thompson*[16] the Court of Appeal, in granting the injunction sought, followed *Shelfer* and refused to allow the public interest in having facilities for powerboat racing to override the private interest of the claimant in living in her house without excessive interference by noise from the adjoining lake.

Dennis v Ministry of Defence[17] is a rare and extreme case where the court did refuse a declaration (treated as being equivalent to an injunction) in respect of a nuisance because of the strong public interest involved. Buckley J held that the operations of RAF Wittering, where Harrier fighter pilots are trained, did constitute a private nuisance (because of the noise) to the claimant who lived nearby. But the declaration sought was refused because of the strong public interest (that is, the defence of the realm) in the continuation of training at RAF Wittering. Instead, damages of £950,000 (including £50,000 for 'loss of amenity') were awarded.

But while the courts rarely *refuse* a prohibitory injunction to restrain a continuing tort, they do often suspend or restrict its operation, and it is through this power that some account is taken of the defendant's hardship or the public interest. In Troman's words, the power '... can be seen as an uneasy compromise between the traditional fervour for the

---

13 (1858) 4 K & J 528 at 536.
14 (1858) 4 K & J 528.
15 (1858) 4 K & J 528 at 539–540.
16 [1981] QB 88.
17 [2003] EWHC 793 (QB), [2003] NLJR 634.

injunction as the appropriate remedy, and the realisation that an unlimited and immediate injunction may have undesirable effects'.[18]

So, for example, in *Pride of Derby v British Celanese*,[19] the injunction was suspended for two years; as it was by the Privy Council in *Stollmeyer v Petroleum Development Co Ltd*,[20] where the defendant's oil-drilling constituted a nuisance by polluting a stream flowing by the claimant's land, Lord Sumner saying, 'Their Lordships are of the opinion that it would not be right to enforce the injunction at once. The loss to the respondents would be out of all proportion to the appellant's gain.'[1] Again in *Halsey v Esso Petroleum Co Ltd*,[2] an injunction restraining a nuisance constituted by the noise of tankers coming and going from an oil-depot at night was suspended for six weeks. In each of these cases the suspension gave the defendants ample opportunity to sort out how best to comply with the order. A particularly controversial use of the power to suspend was made in *Woollerton and Wilson Ltd v Richard Costain Ltd*.[3] There a crane being used to construct a building was trespassing into the claimant's airspace. The claimant was granted a prohibitory injunction to restrain this trespass but Stamp J suspended its operation until the date when the building was due to be completed, the crane then being no longer needed. By so doing, the injunction was prevented from having any effect: it might just as well have been refused. Not surprisingly therefore, in *John Trenberth Ltd v National Westminster Bank Ltd*,[4] where an injunction was granted to take immediate effect to prevent the defendant entering the claimant's land to erect scaffolding for work on his own property, Walton J considered that *Woollerton* was wrongly decided. If, as seems to be the case, the triviality of the damage was influencing Stamp J to suspend the injunction, it would indeed have been preferable if he had refused the injunction on that ground and awarded damages in lieu. It should also be noted that, as one would expect, given the finding of liability, the defendant will generally be bound to pay damages for the claimant's loss during the period for which an injunction is suspended. Indeed, the suspension is likely to be made conditional on the defendant's undertaking to pay such damages.[5]

18 'Nuisance – Prevention or Payment?' [1982] CLJ 87 at 95.
19 [1953] Ch 149.
20 [1918] AC 498n.
1   [1918] AC 498n at 500.
2   [1961] 1 WLR 683.
3   [1970] 1 WLR 411.
4   (1980) 39 P & CR 104; Street (1980) Conv 308.
5   *Stollmeyer v Trinidad Lake Petroleum Co* [1918] AC 485 at 497; Ogus and Richardson 'Economics and the Environment: A Study of Private Nuisance' [1977] CLJ 284, 313–314.

Cases on nuisance by noise provide the main illustrations of the courts' imposition of restrictions on the operation of a prohibitory injunction. In *Vanderpant v Mayfair Hotel Co Ltd*,[6] for example, an injunction was granted to restrain noise from a hotel between 10.00 pm and 8.00 am; and in *Halsey v Esso Petroleum*[7] the injunction was to operate from 10.00 pm until 6.00 am. In *Dunton v Dover District Council*[8] an injunction was granted allowing a children's playground to be used by under-12s between 10.00 am and 6.30 pm. The injunction granted in *Kennaway v Thompson*[9] is notable for its particularly detailed specifications of what was and was not permitted. The injunction basically restrained 'motor boat racing, water skiing and the use of boats creating a noise of more than 75 decibels on the club's water', but this was made subject to the following restrictions:

'... the club is allowed to have, each racing season, one international event extending over three days, the first day being given over to practice and the second and third to racing. In addition, there can be two national events, each of two days, but separated from the international event and from each other by at least four weeks. Finally there can be three club events, each of one day, separated from the international and national events and each other by three weeks. Any international or national event not held can be replaced by a club event of one day.'

Additionally the club was '... not to allow more than six motor boats to be used for water skiing at any one time.'

Finally it should be realised that there have been cases that cannot be reconciled with the traditional approach affording the prohibitory injunction such primacy. In *Bracewell v Appleby*,[10] for example, Graham J refused a prohibitory injunction preventing the defendant trespassing on the claimants' private road because to grant it would in effect make the house the defendant had built 'uninhabitable and would put the claimants into an unassailable bargaining position.'[11] As we have seen, in *Dennis v Ministry of Defence*[12] a declaration (treated as equivalent to an injunction) was refused because of the public interest involved; but the public interest there involved was particularly strong because it concerned the defence of the realm and, for that reason, one should perhaps not see the decision as departing from traditional principles. A

6   [1930] 1 Ch 138.
7   [1961] 1 WLR 683.
8   (1977) 76 LGR 87.
9   [1981] QB 88 at 94–95. This was distinguished in *Tetley v Chitty* [1986] 1 All ER 663 where an unrestricted injunction was granted to restrain a nuisance by go-kart racing.
10 [1975] Ch 408.
11 [1975] Ch 408 at 416.
12 [2003] EWHC 793 (QB), [2003] NLJR 634. See above, p 519.

more obvious departure is *Miller v Jackson*,[13] where the majority of the Court of Appeal refused to grant an injunction restraining the defendant cricket club from playing cricket on a ground next to which the claimant's house had been built and into whose garden balls were quite often being hit. Cumming-Bruce LJ considered that, in granting the injunction, the trial judge had paid insufficient regard 'to the interest of the inhabitants of the village as a whole':[14] and Lord Denning, who would even have been prepared to decide that there was no actionable nuisance, was clear that the public interest dictated that no injunction should be granted. He said:

> 'The *public* interest lies in protecting the environment by preserving our playing fields in the face of mounting development, and by enabling our youth to enjoy all the benefits of outdoor games, such as cricket and football. The *private* interest lies in securing the privacy of his home and garden without intrusion or interference by anyone ... I am of opinion that that public interest should prevail over the private interest.'[15]

A different Court of Appeal in *Kennaway v Thompson*[16] refused to follow *Miller*, correctly indicating that its approach is irreconcilable with precedent as represented by *Shelfer's* case.

(b) Is the present law satisfactory?

The present law by which the claimant is nearly always able to obtain a prohibitory injunction to restrain the continuance or repetition of a tort seems uncontroversial in respect of torts protecting the claimant against personal injury or property damage. But it has been criticised in respect of the tort of nuisance,[17] and many of the arguments are equally applicable to other torts, such as trespass to land. Their central thrust is that damages should be awarded far more than they are and that prohibitory injunctions should not be granted 'as of course'. On such an approach, a decision like *Miller v Jackson* is to be welcomed. What then are the arguments for and against greater use of damages in preference to the prohibitory injunction?

---

13 [1977] QB 966.
14 [1977] QB 966 at 989.
15 [1977] QB 966 at 981–982.
16 [1981] QB 88. See also *Webster v Lord Advocate* 1984 SLT 13.
17 Ogus and Richardson 'Economics and the Environment: A Study of Private Nuisance' [1977] CLJ 284; Tromans 'Nuisance – Prevention or Payment?' [1982] CLJ 87; Rotherham 'The Allocation of Remedies in Private Nuisance: An Evaluation of the Judicial Approach to Awarding Damages in Lieu of an Injunction' (1989) 4 Canterbury LR 185; Sharpe *Injunctions and Specific Performance* (3rd edn, 2000) paras 4.60–4.580.

(i) Arguments for greater use of damages

(i)   As the courts weigh the defendant's hardship against the benefit to the claimant in deciding whether to grant a mandatory injunction, they should do the same for prohibitory injunctions. But it may be doubted whether this is a valid argument where one is dealing with a truly negative injunction. What is true, however, is that the courts sometimes regard as prohibitory, injunctions that are better viewed as mandatory, because in practice compliance will force the defendant to take particular positive steps.[18] If such injunctions were recognised as mandatory, traditional legal principle would rightly require the defendant's hardship to be considered. Beyond this, change seems unnecessary.

(ii) The courts should be prepared to refuse a prohibitory injunction where the public interest outweighs the claimant's private rights. Under the traditional approach, once any triviality threshold is crossed, the courts only take the public interest into account in suspending or restricting a prohibitory injunction. According to this argument, there is no reason why they should not go further.

(iii) The courts should be wary of awarding injunctions because, like all specific remedies, they allow the claimant too much of an advantage in pre- and post-judgment bargaining. So Tromans writes, 'The effect of an injunction may be certainty, but it is certainty achieved by tying one of the defendant's hands behind his back before negotiations begin. This is hardly likely to produce a fair or economic result.'[19]

(iv) The automatic granting of an injunction can be further criticised as absolving the claimant from any duty to mitigate its own loss. While, generally speaking, mitigation is less likely to be possible where one is dealing with negative tort obligations than positive contractual promises, there will be situations where a claimant could relatively easily take steps to avoid being harmed by the defendant's actions. Automatic injunctions remove the incentive to take such steps.

(v)   The fact that an injunction is so routinely awarded may have an unfortunate effect on the substantive law, since the courts may steer

---

18 Above, p 512.
19 [1982] CLJ 87, 105. For detailed discussion of this, see Thompson 'Injunction Negotiations: An Economic, Moral, and Legal Analysis' (1975) 27 Stan LR 1563. Also see above, p 22. In *Phonographic Performance Ltd v Maitra* [1998] 1 WLR 870 the Court of Appeal did not think it a good reason for denying a final injunction of unlimited duration to restrain copyright infringement that the claimant would use that injunction as a lever to extract payment of licence fees for past (and future) 'infringements'.

clear of finding liability, knowing of the consequent drastic remedy. As Tromans writes in the context of nuisance, '… an unwillingness to give the plaintiff anything other than the best remedy can lead to his getting no remedy at all.'[20] As examples he instances the non-liability for temporary nuisances, and the wide construction courts give to the defence of statutory authority. The latter is shown by *Allen v Gulf Oil Refining Ltd*,[1] where the House of Lords' liberal construction of a private Act of Parliament enabled the defendants to construct and operate an oil refinery without incurring any liability in nuisance to the claimants who were affected by its noise, smell and vibration. No doubt the Lords were influenced by the fact that a finding of liability would inevitably lead to an injunction and hence the potential closure of the refinery. Lord Denning's solution in the Court of Appeal awarding 'damages to cover past or future injury in lieu of an injunction'[2] seems far preferable.

(vi)   Calabresi and Melamed[3] have put forward a sophisticated economic analysis which would also seem to support a freer use of damages awards in relation to land use conflicts. According to their model, entitlements can be protected by either property or liability rules.[4] Where protection is by a property rule '… someone who wishes to remove the entitlement from its holder must buy it from him in a voluntary transaction in which the value of the entitlement is agreed upon by the seller.'[5] Protection is by a liability rule 'whenever someone may destroy the initial entitlement if he is willing to pay an objectively determined value for it.'[6]

It follows that there are four possible outcomes to a land use conflict. If D is polluting C's land, then first, C may have an entitlement to be free from pollution protected by a property rule; that is, C may be granted an injunction to restrain D's nuisance. Secondly, C may have an entitlement to be free from pollution protected by a liability rule; that is, C may be

---

20   [1982] CLJ 8 at 107.
1   [1981] AC 1001.
2   [1980] QB 156 at 169.
3   'Property Rules, Liability Rules and Inalienability: One View of the Cathedral' (1972) 85 Harv LR 1089. See also Michelman 'Pollution as a Tort: a Non-Accidental Perspective on Calabresi's Costs' (1971) 80 Yale LJ 647; Ellickson 'Alternatives to Zoning: Covenants, Nuisance Rules and Fines as Land Use Controls' (1972) 40 U Chi LR 681, esp 738–748; Rabin 'Nuisance Law: Rethinking Fundamental Assumptions' (1977) 63 Va LR 1299; Krier and Schwab 'Property Rules and Liability Rules: The Cathedral in Another Light' (1995) 70 NYU LR 440; Farnsworth 'Do Parties to Nuisance Cases Bargain After Judgment? A Glimpse Inside the Cathedral' (1999) 66 U Chi LR 373; Harris, Campbell and Halson *Remedies in Contract and Tort* (2nd edn, 2002) pp 496–519.
4   An entitlement can also be 'inalienable'.
5   (1972) 85 Harv LR 1089, 1092.
6   (1972) 85 Harv LR 1089, 1092.

merely awarded damages for D's nuisance. Thirdly, D may have an entitlement to pollute protected by a property rule; that is, D may be held not liable for nuisance, so that C can only prevent the pollution by paying D to stop it. Finally D may have an entitlement to pollute protected by a liability rule; that is, D may be free to pollute unless C pays him a judicially determined price not to: this would most obviously be achieved by a 'compensated injunction', never yet used in England,[7] whereby C would be bound to pay D the costs of D's compliance with the injunction.

In deciding which of these four to choose, Calabresi and Melamed consider that economic efficiency dictates the following results. If transaction costs are low, so that it can be expected that parties will bargain round legal rights and remedies to correct any 'errors',[8] property rules should be chosen, thereby avoiding the costs of a judicial determination of values. Whether the first or third outcome is adopted, depends on whether it is thought D or C is the cheaper cost-avoider. But where transaction costs are high, as they are likely to be in the pollution field, property rules should only be chosen if it is certain which party is the cheaper cost-avoider. No guessing should be undertaken, since the parties will not negotiate round to correct any error. If, as is likely in most pollution cases, it is uncertain who is the cheaper cost-avoider, a liability rule should be adopted; that is, the second or fourth outcome should be chosen. To decide between these two, the court should make a cost-benefit analysis, mimicking the transaction the parties would themselves have made.

So in a standard land use conflict, where transaction costs are high, and it is difficult to be certain who is the cheaper cost-avoider, this approach indicates that the claimant should be awarded damages or a compensated injunction. Clearly this contrasts with the present English judicial preference for a prohibitory injunction.

(ii) Arguments against greater use of damages

(i) From the claimant's point of view an injunction is a better remedy than damages. Damages may be very difficult to assess either because one cannot know the extent of the claimant's future loss, or because his loss is non-pecuniary comprising, for example, interference with the enjoyment of land. Moreover the defendant may be unable to pay.

---

7   But see *Spur Industries Inc v Del E Webb Development Co* 494 P 2d 700 (Ariz, 1972).
8   Coase 'The Problem of Social Cost' (1960) 3 J Law & Econ 1, above, p 20.

(ii)   To allow a defendant to continue with the wrong by paying damages sacrifices to some degree the claimant's individual rights. On one view such rights merit absolute specific protection and should not be downgraded in this way.

(iii) An injunction prevents a ruthless defendant simply including the damages in a calculated decision to ride roughshod over the claimant's rights. But this objection' could be countered to some extent by awarding restitutionary, or even punitive, damages rather than merely compensation.

(iv)   The injunction is the best remedy for protecting the environment.[9] Hence the upholding of individual rights and the public interest in environmental control coincide in favouring the injunction as against damages.

(v)   On one view it is not the function of the courts, nor are they properly equipped, to decide what the public interest demands.[10] Their role is and should be one of protecting individual rights which should not be sacrificed for social welfare goals. So, for example, the courts should never involve themselves in deciding whether it is in the public interest to keep open a nuclear power installation that is causing a nuisance by its occasional leaks of radiation. But examination of the common law shows that legal decision-making is best understood as a complex mix of principle and policy and that the courts do make decisions on where the public interest lies. So, for example, they judge the public interest in deciding whether to suspend an injunction, and sometimes even in deciding initially whether the defendant is liable. Moreover, this seems perfectly acceptable so long as the courts aim for consistency with the long-term policy goals enshrined in the common law.

(iii) Conclusion

Having weighed up the above arguments, it is submitted that there is a case for damages being awarded more readily than at present for torts involving land use conflicts.[11] However, the case for this should not be exaggerated and generally an injunction should be ordered. But where the defendant is pursuing what is in the long-term public interest, or where the claimant could easily take steps to remove the harm, equitable damages in lieu should be preferred to a prohibitory injunction. It is also

9   McLaren 'The Common Law Nuisance Actions and the Environmental Battle – Well-Tempered Swords or Broken Reeds?' (1972) 10 Osgoode Hall LJ 505, esp 547–561.
10 Dworkin *Taking Rights Seriously* (revised edn, 1978)
11 As in the US and Canada; see Tromans 'Nuisance – Prevention or Payment?' [1982] CLJ 87, 97–99.

true that the compensated injunction, whereby the claimant pays the defendant the costs of his compliance, would be a useful weapon for the English courts to add to their armoury. For while at first sight it is somewhat alarming to suggest that a claimant should pay the defendant for not infringing its rights, on closer inspection, it can be seen that this would add further remedial flexibility and would provide another sensible way of resolving the conflict between the public interest and private rights; and, after all, the claimant may well prefer a compensated injunction to no injunction at all.

(2) Breach of contract

(a) **Prohibitory injunction as primary remedy**

The prohibitory injunction is the appropriate remedy for restraining the breach[12] of a negative contractual promise – that is a promise not to do something: put another way, it enforces a negative contractual promise. It therefore belongs on the reverse side of the coin from specific performance, which enforces a positive contractual promise.

As in relation to torts, and in contrast to specific performance, the prohibitory injunction is the primary remedy as against damages for breach of a negative promise; and here, in contrast to torts, it is generally ordinary common law damages that are in issue as the alternative to the prohibitory injunction – for the breach of contract is not normally regarded as a prospective (rather than an accrued) wrong and hence common law damages are as advantageous as damages under the Supreme Court Act 1981, s 50.[13] Since common law damages must be shown to be inadequate before an injunction, being an equitable remedy, can be granted, the primacy afforded to the prohibitory injunction can be expressed by saying that, in this context, adequacy is given a very narrow meaning, so that damages are hardly ever considered adequate.

The classic 'authority' on the primacy of the prohibitory injunction is the dictum of Lord Cairns LC in *Doherty v Allman*.[14] He said:

'... if there had been a negative covenant, I apprehend, according to well-settled practice, a Court of Equity would have no discretion to exercise. If parties, for valuable consideration, with their eyes open, contract that a particular thing shall not be done, all that a Court of Equity has to do is to say, by way of injunction that which

12 Including a threatened breach.
13 But equitable damages may be the only alternative to a prohibitory injunction restraining breach of a restrictive covenant affecting land; see, eg above, p 364.
14 (1878) 3 App Cas 709 at 720. For recent examples of *Doherty* being applied see *Avon County Council v Millard* (1985) 274 Estates Gazette 1025; *Attorney-General v Barker* [1990] 3 All ER 257, 261–262 (per Nourse LJ).

the parties have already said by way of covenant, that the thing shall not be done; and in such case, the injunction does nothing more than give the sanction of the process of the Court to that which already is the contract between the parties. It is not then a question of the balance of convenience or inconvenience, or the amount of damage or of injury – it is the specific performance by the Court, of that negative bargain which the parties have made, with their eyes open, between themselves.'

To similar effect is Sir Page Wood V-C's statement in *Tipping v Eckersley*[15] that, '... if the construction of the instrument be clear and the breach clear, then it is not a question of damage but the mere circumstance of the breach of covenant affords sufficient ground for the Court to interfere by injunction.' He went on to grant an injunction whereby the defendant was not to increase the temperature of the water flowing down to the claimant's steam engine, such action constituting a breach of the defendant's covenant to allow the claimant the free use and enjoyment of the stream.

Why is there this judicial readiness to order prohibitory injunctions to restrain the breach of a negative promise, contrasting as it does with the approach to specific performance, and given that both remedies more closely protect the claimant's expectation interest than damages? Perhaps the principal reasons are that prohibitory injunctions do not as commonly contradict a claimant's duty to mitigate, and nor do they infringe individual liberty to the same extent as positive orders. Additionally, damages are often less easy to assess for breach of a negative than a positive obligation. Nor do prohibitory injunctions fall foul of the constant supervision objection that has traditionally barred specific performance. But having said all this, the present automatic grant of a prohibitory injunction for breach of contract under *Doherty v Allman* probably goes too far. The arguments examined above in relation to torts suggest that sometimes damages should be awarded in preference to a prohibitory injunction for breach of a negative promise.[16] This is particularly so where the claimant could take steps to mitigate its loss.

To say that the prohibitory injunction is the primary remedy does not of course mean that it will never be refused. Two main grounds for refusal[17] are that the claimant's conduct debars him,[18] or that the harm

---

15   (1855) 2 K & J 264 at 270.
16   A rare example of a case not following the traditional approach is *Baxter v Four Oaks Properties Ltd* [1965] Ch 816, where Cross J did not want to put the claimant into too strong a position in post-judgment bargaining.
17   Although rare, uncertainty may also be a bar: *Hampstead and Suburban Properties v Diomedous* [1969] 1 Ch 248; *Bower v Bantam Investments Ltd* [1972] 1 WLR 1120.
18   Below, pp 569–575.

suffered by the claimant is trivial.[19] But indisputably the most discussed ground for refusal is that to grant the prohibitory injunction would amount to indirect specific performance of a contractual promise for which specific performance would not be ordered. This will now be examined.

(b) Indirect specific performance

Strictly speaking this is not a ground for refusing a prohibitory injunction, but rather an argument that what appears to be a prohibitory injunction enforcing a negative obligation is in reality specific performance of a positive obligation, and should be governed by specific performance principles.

It should be emphasised straightaway that some cases provide no difficulty for it is pellucidly clear that, despite the prohibitory form in which the order is sought, in substance it amounts to specific performance. For example, an order to restrain the defendants breaking their positive contractual obligation is specific performance and not a prohibitory injunction. Again in *Sky Petroleum v VIP Petroleum Ltd*[20] and *Hill v Parsons*,[1] the injunctions respectively sought – to restrain the defendants withholding supplies of petrol to the claimant and to restrain the defendants implementing their notice of dismissal terminating the claimant's employment – were negative in form, but clearly positive in substance.

The interesting and controversial cases are those where, although in substance breach of a negative obligation is being restrained, it is arguable that compliance with the negative obligation will *in practice* force the defendant to comply with his positive obligations. The essential question is to what extent do the courts accede to this argument? Sir George Jessel MR in *Fothergill v Rowland*[2] thought that it was difficult to find any consistent judicial approach:

> 'I cannot find any distinct line laid down ... dividing ... the class of cases in which the Court, feeling that it has not the power to compel specific performance, grants an injunction to restrain the breach by the contracting party of one or more of the stipulations of the contract, and the class of cases in which it refuses to interfere.'[3]

---

19 *Harrison v Good* (1871) LR 11 Eq 338 at 352. See also *Jaggard v Sawyer* [1995] 1 WLR 269, discussed above at p 517, where a prohibitory injunction was refused which sought to prevent conduct which constituted a breach of covenant as well as a trespass.
20 [1974] 1 WLR 576.
1   [1972] Ch 305. See also *Davis v Foreman* [1894] 3 Ch 654.
2   (1873) LR 17 Eq 132.
3   (1873) LR 17 Eq 132 at 141.

It is submitted, however, that a principle has traditionally been applied, namely that a prohibitory injunction will be regarded as indirect specific performance, and subject to specific performance principles, if compliance with the order will leave the defendant with the 'choice' of either performing his positive obligations to the claimant or not being able to work or carry on any business at all. The issue has arisen with regard to two main types of contract – contracts for personal service and contracts for the sale of goods.

(i)   Contracts for personal service

Lumley v Wagner[4] is the classic case. Here Mlle Wagner undertook that for three months she would sing at Mr Lumley's theatre in Drury Lane on two nights a week and not use her talents at any other theatre without Mr Lumley's written consent. She then agreed to sing for Mr Gye at Covent Garden for more money. Lord St Leonards LC granted an injunction restraining her from singing except for Mr Lumley, and considered that this did not amount to indirect specific performance of her obligation to sing for Mr Lumley, which he recognised could not be granted. He said:

> 'It was objected that the operation of the injunction in the present case was mischievous, excluding the defendant ... from performing at any other theatre while this Court had no power to compel her to perform at Her Majesty's Theatre. It is true, that I have not the means of compelling her to sing, but she has no cause of complaint, if I compel her to abstain from the commission of an act which she has bound herself not to do ... in continuing the injunction, I disclaim doing indirectly what I cannot do directly.'[5]

This approach was followed and explained further in *Warner Bros Pictures Inc v Nelson*,[6] where the film actress Bette Davis had agreed that she would render her exclusive services as an actress to the claimants for a certain period and would not during that time render any similar services to any other person. In breach of that contract she entered into an agreement to appear for another film company. The claimants were granted an injunction restraining her for three years from appearing for any other film company. Branson J reasoned that this did not amount to indirectly ordering specific performance of her contact with the

---

4   (1852) 21 LJ Ch 898. Parks 'Equitable Relief in Contracts Involving Personal Services' (1918) 66 U of Pa LR 251; Stevens 'Involuntary Servitude by Injunction: The Doctrine of *Lumley v Wagner* Considered' (1921) 6 Cornell LQ 235; Tannenbaum 'Enforcement of Personal Service Contracts in the Entertainment Industry' (1954) 42 Cal LR 18.

5   (1852) 21 LJ Ch 898 at 902.

6   [1937] 1 KB 209. See also *William Robinson & Co Ltd v Heuer* [1898] 2 Ch 451; *Marco Productions CLJ v Pagola* [1945] KB 111.

claimants – for while the defendant was being ordered not to work as a film actress for anyone else, she was left free to work elsewhere in any other capacity. Branson J said:

'It was also urged that the difference between what the defendant can earn as a film artiste and what she might expect to earn by any other form of activity is so great that she will in effect be driven to perform her contract ... [but] no evidence was addressed to show that, if enjoined from doing the specified acts otherwise than for the plaintiffs, she will not be able to employ herself both usefully and remuneratively in other spheres of activity ... She will not be driven, although she may be tempted, to perform the contract, and the fact that she may be so tempted is no objection to the grant of an injunction.'[7]

In both these and other cases,[8] it was regarded as important that the negative promise in question was express. This is a red herring, and should not be allowed to cast confusion over the indirect specific performance discussion. As other authorities recognise,[9] so long as a clear negative promise can be made out, it should not matter whether that promise is express or implied.

Consistent with the emphasis on the freedom to take up other employment, albeit falling on the reverse side of the line, are *Whitwood Chemical Co v Hardman*,[10] *Ehrman v Bartholemew*[11] and *Rely-a-Bell Burglar & Fire Alarm Co v Eisler*.[12] In each case the injunction sought was to restrain the breach of a promise not to accept any other employment at all. Therefore, if granted, the defendant would have had only the choice of working for the claimant or remaining idle. Since this was not a real choice, a prohibitory injunction would in practice amount to specific performance and, as specific performance would not be ordered of a contract for personal service, the injunction was refused.

However, there have been cases in which the courts have taken a different approach. In *Mortimer v Beckett*,[13] for example, the defendant agreed to employ the claimant as his boxing manager, to be solely in charge of arranging the defendant's boxing contracts. When the defendant agreed to box for someone else, the claimant sought an interim injunction to restrain him; that is, to enforce his implied promise not to box for anyone else. But even though the promise only related to

7   [1937] 1 KB 209 at 219–220.
8   Eg *Mutual Reserve Fund Life Assurance v New York Insurance Co* (1896) 75 LT 528; *Mortimer v Beckett* [1920] 1 Ch 571.
9   *Wolverhampton & Walsall Rly Co v London & North Western Rly Co* (1873) LR 16 Eq 433; *Whitwood Chemicals Co v Hardman* [1891] 2 Ch 416 at 427.
10   [1891] 2 Ch 416.
11   [1898] 1 Ch 671.
12   [1926] Ch 609. See also *Kirchner & Co v Gruban* [1909] 1 Ch 413.
13   [1920] 1 Ch 571.

boxing, the injunction was refused, inter alia,[14] because it was thought that it would amount to specific performance of the defendant's personal obligations. Russell J said, 'The effect will be to force the defendant to employ a particular person as his agent, so far as his boxing engagements are concerned, and to accept the agent's services.'[15] Similarly in *Page One Records Ltd v Britton*[16] 'The Troggs' pop group employed the claimant as their sole agent and manager for five years, and agreed not to make records for anyone else during that time. In breach of that contract they then entered into an agreement to be managed by someone else. The claimant sought an interim injunction to restrain this breach. Stamp J refused to grant it because he thought that it would amount to indirect specific performance of the defendants' personal obligations:

> '... it was said in this case, that if an injunction is granted, The Troggs could without employing any other manager or agent ... seek other employment of a different nature ... I think that I can and should take judicial notice of the fact that these groups, if they are to have any great success, must have managers. As a practical matter ... I entertain no doubt that they would be compelled, if the injunction were granted, ... to continue to employ the plaintiff as their manager and agent ... I should if I granted the injunction, be enforcing a contract for personal services, in which personal services are to be performed by the plaintiff.'[17]

Clearly these cases differ factually from *Lumley* and *Warner Bros* in that it was the employee (the manager and agent) rather than the employer who was seeking the injunction. But that cannot account for the difference in result. The better view is that these cases go beyond the traditional principle in considering it insufficient that the defendant is left free to take up other employment or business. Rather it is the likelihood of his doing so that is important. This is a preferable approach requiring, as it does, a closer examination of the practical realities of the injunction. Applying it to the facts of *Warner Bros v Nelson*, a different decision would be reached, for it was most unlikely that Bette Davis would take up another occupation and abandon making films for the three-year period. On the other hand, *Lumley v Wagner* might well be decided in the same way; for as Mlle Wagner was merely being restrained from singing elsewhere for three months, it was quite likely that she would choose to do something else, or nothing, for that short period, rather than singing for the claimant.

---

14 The other, and unsatisfactory, ground was the lack of an express negative covenant.
15 [1920] 1 Ch 571 at 581.
16 [1968] 1 WLR 157.
17 [1968] 1 WLR 157 at 166–167.

Authoritative support for that preferable approach has been provided by the Court of Appeal in the leading modern case of *Warren v Mendy*,[18] in which *Page One Records v Britton* was preferred to *Warner Bros v Nelson* on grounds of 'realism and practicality'.[19] The facts – which concerned a dispute over the management of the boxer, Nigel Benn – differed from the usual restrictive covenant case in that the injunction being sought by the claimant was not against Benn for breach of contract but against another manager in a tort action for inducing breach of Benn's contract with the claimant. But the Court of Appeal felt that, as the claimant would seek an injunction against anyone who arranged to manage Benn, the same principles should be applied as if the injunction had been sought against Benn for breach of contract. The injunction was refused on the ground that to grant it would constitute indirect specific performance of Benn's contract to be exclusively managed by the claimant for the three-year contract period. While disapproving the approach in *Warner Bros v Nelson*, the Court of Appeal did not doubt the correctness of the decision in *Lumley v Wagner* given the short contract period there in issue. Nourse LJ said:

> 'Although it is impossible to state in general terms where the line between short- and long-term engagements ought to be drawn it is obvious that an injunction lasting for two years or more (the period applicable in the present case) may practically compel performance of the contract.'[20]

Three final points should be made. First, there has traditionally been some doubt as to the application of the substantive restraint of trade doctrine to the sort of negative obligations in these cases, especially given that they apply during rather than after the employment. The above discussion has assumed the substantive validity of the negative obligation but clearly if it is invalid there is no question of any remedy for breach. Secondly, it has further been assumed above that the claimant wants the defendant to perform his positive contractual obligations. Where this is not so, for example where there is a restrictive covenant to take effect after termination of the defendant's employment,[1] or where the claimant undertakes to pay the defendant and to give him his other contractual benefits even though the defendant does no work for him,[2] there is no

---

18 [1989] 1 WLR 853.
19 [1989] 1 WLR 853 at 865 (per Nourse LJ).
20 [1989] 1 WLR 853 at 865–866.
1   As in, eg *General Billposting Co Ltd v Atkinson* [1909] AC 118; *Credit Suisse Asset Management Ltd v Armstrong* [1996] ICR 882; *Rock Refrigeration Ltd v Jones* [1997] ICR 938.
2   *Evening Standard Co Ltd v Henderson* [1987] IRLR 64; *Provident Financial Group plc v Hayward* [1989] 3 All ER 298. The defendant under such an arrangement is described as being on 'garden leave'.

question of an injunction amounting to indirect specific performance. Finally, an approach adopted in the US is to grant an injunction to prevent the defendant working for a competitor of the claimant's but not otherwise.[3] So, for example, on the facts of *Lumley v Wagner* an injunction would be granted to prevent the defendant working for Mr Gye, a close rival of the claimant's, but would not be granted in respect of a theatre in, for example, northern England; the justification being that the claimant had a separate legitimate interest in preventing his audience being diverted to Gye's theatre. This has not found favour in England[4] and, while it will often arrive at the same decision as the preferred approach examined above, it fails to address sufficiently closely the problem of indirect specific performance; for to prevent the defendant working for any of the claimant's competitors may in practice leave no real choice but to work for the claimant.

(ii) *Contracts for the sale of goods*

The question of indirect specific performance has here arisen in relation to obligations not to buy one's requirements of particular goods other than from the claimant (requirements contracts), not to sell a particular output of goods other than to the claimant (output contracts) or not to distribute goods other than through the claimant (sole franchise/distributorship contracts).[5] Traditionally specific performance of the positive obligations in such contracts would not be ordered because of the supposed adequacy of damages. The personal service or constant supervision bars are also sometimes in play. But the courts have generally been willing to grant injunctions restraining breach of the above 'negative' obligations, on the ground that this does not amount to indirect specific performance. Analogously to contracts of employment the unarticulated principle appears to be that so long as the defendant is left with more of a choice than either buying from/selling to the claimant or not carrying on any business at all the injunction does not amount to indirect specific performance.

As regards requirements contracts, there are several cases granting a prohibitory injunction restraining defendants from buying petrol for their service station[6] or beer for their pub[7] other than from the claimants. But

---

3   Second Restatement of Contracts, para 367, illustration 4.
4   See especially *Marco Productions v Pagola* [1945] KB 111.
5   Again it is assumed that the obligation is not invalid under the restraint of trade doctrine.
6   Eg *Texaco Ltd v Mulberry Filling Station Ltd* [1972] 1 WLR 814.
7   Eg *Clegg v Hands* (1890) 44 Ch D 503.

the best-known authority is *Metropolitan Electric Supply Co Ltd v Ginder.*[8] An injunction was here granted restraining the defendant from breaking his promise not to take electricity from anyone but the claimant company. It was reasoned that this did not amount to forcing the defendant to take electricity from the claimants, since the defendant could, if he liked, use no energy at all or bum gas.

Donnell v Bennett[9] shows the grant of an injunction in relation to what was in effect an output contract, being to sell to the claimant all the left-overs of fish not used by the defendant in his business. Fry J granted an injunction restraining the defendant from selling those left-overs to anyone else, albeit that he was clearly not totally convinced about the purported distinction between the injunction and specific performance.

Turning to sole distributorship/franchise contracts, in *Decro-Wall International SA v Practitioners in Marketing Ltd*[10] the claimants had contracted not to sell their goods in the UK to anyone other than the defendants. The Court of Appeal held that the defendants were entitled to an injunction to restrain breach of this negative promise, albeit that Salmon LJ recognised that '… the plaintiffs cannot be compelled to continue to supply the defendants until the termination of the contract.'[11] Similarly in *Evans Marshall v Bertola SA*[12] the claimants had been appointed sole agents for the sale of the defendants' sherry in England under a long-term contract. They were granted an interim injunction restraining the defendants from breaking this contract by selling sherry other than through the claimants' agency. Sachs LJ applied *Warner Bros v Nelson* and the *Decro-Wall* case, and said, '… the specific performance of such an agreement will not be ordered, but it is no less plain that the courts will grant negative injunctions to encourage a party in breach to keep to his contract.'[13]

However, not all cases have adhered to the thin theoretical distinction being drawn between prohibitory injunctions and specific performance. The classic example is *Fothergill v Rowland*,[14] where the defendants had contracted to sell all of a particular seam of coal to the claimants. The claimants sought an injunction to prevent the defendants selling elsewhere, but this was refused on the ground that it amounted to

---

8   [1901] 2 Ch 799. This case also provides the classic example of terms being attached to an injunction to avoid any problems over want of mutuality, the condition attached being that the defendant could dissolve the injunction if the claimant failed to supply his requirements.
9   (1883) 22 Ch D 835.
10   [1971] 1 WLR 361.
11   [1971] 1 WLR 361 at 372. Ultimately no injunction was necessary since the defendants gave an undertaking in the same terms.
12   [1973] 1 WLR 349. See also *Thomas Borthwick v South Orago Freezing Co Ltd* [1978] 1 NZLR 538.
13   [1973] 1 WLR 349 at 382.
14   (1873) LR 17 Eq 132.

indirect specific performance of a contract to sell non-unique goods, for which damages were adequate. This case can be regarded as equivalent to *Page One Records* and *Warren v Mendy* in the employment context, and as taking a more realistic view of the effect of the prohibitory injunction; for surely in almost all the above cases compliance with the prohibitory injunction would render it virtually certain that the defendant would perform his positive obligations to the claimant. In practical terms specific performance was being ordered.

But there is a final twist to the tale. It has been argued in chapter 20 that, whether because of commercial uniqueness or the difficulty of assessing damages, specific performance ought to be more readily granted than in the past in respect of long-term supply contracts such as these.[15] Therefore the actual decisions in these cases, now with the exception of *Fothergill v Rowland*, are to be welcomed, but on the basis that specific performance was in effect being ordered and was justified. Some commentators[16] have indeed used these cases as authorities on specific performance but, with the exception of *Fothergill v Rowland*, this would seem misleading, given that the reasoning took the opposite view.

(c) **Stipulated remedy**[17]

What effect will be given to a contractual term that the claimant should be entitled to an injunction for breach of a negative covenant? One of the few English cases dealing with this was *Warner Bros Pictures Inc v Nelson*.[18] In Branson J's words:

> '... parties cannot contract themselves out of the law; but it assists, in all events, on the question of evidence as to the applicability of an injunction in the present case, to find the parties formally recognising that in cases of this kind injunction is a more appropriate remedy than damages.'[19]

However, it is hard to see the courts attaching any real relevance to such a clause.[20] As has been indicated, true negative obligations are enforceable by prohibitory injunction as of course and hence irrespective of the parties agreeing on that remedy; and where the prohibitory injunction would in effect amount to specific performance of a contract that would

---

15 Above, pp 461–467, 475.
16 Eg Treitel *The Law of Contract* (11th edn, 2003) p 1022.
17 See analogously above, pp 505–506.
18 [1937] 1 KB 209. The best-known case in the US is *Stokes v Moore* 262 Ala 5977 (1955).
19 [1937] 1 KB 209 at 221.
20 But see the views of Sharpe *Injunctions and Specific Performance* (3rd edn, 2000) paras 7.710–7.810, and Kyer 'A Case Study in Party Stipulation of Remedy: the NHL Standard Player's Contract' (1981) 39 U of Tor Fac LR 1.

not be directly specifically enforced it is hard to believe that the courts would allow such a clause to oust their refusal of the remedy.

A related but converse question is whether the existence of a penalty or liquidated damages clause will oust a prohibitory injunction that would otherwise be granted. Several cases show that the answer to this is in the negative,[1] and that the clause will rather be construed as indicating the amount of damages the claimant will recover if it sues for damages rather than an injunction. But in *General Accident Assurance Corpn v Noel*,[2] while this was agreed, it was held that the injunction and liquidated damages were exclusive remedies. While this must be correct as regards future loss, there seems no reason why liquidated damages for past loss and an injunction should not both be awarded, an approach adopted in the important Canadian case of *Elsley v J G Collins Insurance Agencies Ltd.*[3]

3.   FINAL MANDATORY INJUNCTIONS[4]

(1) Torts

The mandatory injunction – ordering the defendant to do something – is the appropriate remedy to remove the effects of a tort committed by the defendant; that is, it compels the defendant to undo the wrong. This function is conveniently and commonly emphasised by referring to the injunction as a mandatory restorative injunction. To give a couple of examples straightaway, in *Kelsen v Imperial Tobacco Co*,[5] the defendants were ordered to remove the advertising sign they had erected which was trespassing into the airspace above the claimant's shop; and in *Lawrence v Horton*,[6] the defendant was ordered to pull down buildings he had erected which obstructed the claimant's ancient lights. Conceivably a mandatory enforcing injunction could be granted to enforce a positive tort obligation. But given the rarity of such tort obligations, this injunction will be rare indeed, and there is no obvious example of its having been granted.

The classic discussion of the general principles governing mandatory injunctions is Lord Upjohn's speech in *Redland Bricks v Morris*[7] though his

---

1   Eg *Jones v Heavens* (1877) 4 Ch D 636; *National Provincial Bank of England v Marshall* (1888) 40 Ch D 112.
2   [1902] 1 KB 377.
3   (1978) 83 DLR (3d) 1.
4   *Quia timet* mandatory injunctions are discussed below, pp 543–546.
5   [1957] 2 QB 334.
6   (1890) 59 LJ Ch 440. See similarly *Allen v Greenwood* [1980] Ch 119.
7   [1970] AC 652.

controversial view that the injunction in issue was *quia timet*[8] means that he includes some principles that are relevant only to *quia timet* mandatory injunctions. The injunction being sought was for steps to be taken by the defendants to restore support to the claimant's land. The House of Lords discharged the mandatory injunction that had been granted – that the defendants '... do take all necessary steps to restore the support to the plaintiff's land within a period of six months' – because it left as too uncertain what the defendants were required to do. Lord Upjohn said, 'If ... it is a proper case to grant a mandatory injunction, then the court must be careful to see that the defendant knows exactly in fact what he has to do ...'[9] So uncertainty is a bar to mandatory injunctions as it is to specific performance and prohibitory injunctions. But in his espousal of the general principles, what is particularly important is that Lord Upjohn clearly accepted that a mandatory injunction is not granted as readily as a prohibitory injunction. He said, 'The grant of a mandatory injunction is, of course, entirely discretionary, and unlike a negative injunction can never be "as of course".'[10] The antipathy of the courts to positive orders is therefore shown in this area, as in relation to specific performance for breach of contract. Again, the desire not to undermine the claimant's duty to mitigate, and not to restrict unduly the defendant's freedom of action may be suggested as the root objections. There are also express indications in some cases that the argument that non-monetary remedies give the claimant too much of an advantage in pre- and post-judgment bargaining does here weigh with the courts. For example, in *Isenberg v East India House Estate Co Ltd*[11] Lord Westbury, in refusing an injunction to compel the defendant to pull down a building which interfered only slightly with the claimant's ancient lights, said that the court would not grant a mandatory injunction which would deliver 'the Defendants to the Plaintiff bound hand and foot, in order to be made subject to any extortionate demand that he may by possibility make.'[12]

So it is the case that, while the injunction may be the better remedy for the claimant, damages (in lieu) are generally regarded as sufficient and

---

8   Above, p 513.
9   [1970] AC 652 at 666. See also *Kennard v Cory Bros Co Ltd* [1922] 1 Ch 265 at 274 (per Sargant J), [1922] 2 Ch 1 at 13 (per Warrington LJ).
10 [1970] AC 652 at 665. See also *Durell v Pritchard* (1865) 1 Ch App 244 at 250, and cases on breach of contract, below, pp 541–543. It is therefore misleading to say as some judges have – eg in *Smith v Smith* (1875) LR 20 Eq 500, and *Davies v Gas Light and Coke Co* [1909] 1 Ch 708 – that the same principles govern mandatory as prohibitory injunctions.
11 (1863) 3 De GJ & Sm 263. See also *Senior v Pawson* (1866) LR 3 Eq 330.
12 (1863) 3 De GJ & Sm 263 at 273.

are the primary remedy. A fortiori, no mandatory injunction will generally be granted where the tortious interference is merely trivial.[13]

Furthermore in contrast to a prohibitory injunction, the hardship to the defendant is here a bar. So, in dicta in *Pride of Derby v British Celanese*,[14] Lord Evershed commented '... the court will not impose ... an obligation to do something which is impossible, or which cannot be enforced, or which is unlawful.' The leading authority is again *Redland Bricks v Morris*, where Lord Upjohn indicated that hardship can here be a very wide restriction since, even in contrast to specific performance, the test can be a relative one; that is, so long as the defendant has acted reasonably, albeit wrongly, the courts can weigh the burden to him against the benefit to the claimant. In Lord Upjohn's words:

> '... the amount to be expended under a mandatory order by the defendant must be balanced ... against the anticipated possible damage to the plaintiff and if, on such balance, it seems unreasonable to inflict such expenditure ... then the court must exercise its jurisdiction accordingly.'[15]

Applying this to the facts, it was held that a mandatory injunction ordering the defendants to carry out the restoration work as described by the claimant's expert, while probably overcoming the uncertainty objection so long as set out in detail, would impose an excessive burden on the defendant who had acted reasonably and should not be granted; such work might cost £35,000, while the value of the claimant's land affected by the slip was only about £1,500.

On the other hand, Lord Upjohn made plain that no sympathy will be shown for a defendant who has tried 'to steal a march' on the claimant, or who has otherwise acted 'wantonly and quite unreasonably'.[16] Indeed in this situation, the courts appear to go to the opposite extreme, and to be only too willing to grant even an interim mandatory injunction against the defendant, revealing, seemingly, a punitive approach. For

---

13 *Isenberg v East India House Estate Co Ltd* (1863) 3 De GJ & Sm 263; *Colls v Home & Colonial Stores Ltd* [1904] AC 179; *Tollemache and Cobbold Breweries Ltd v Reynolds* (1983) 268 Estates Gazette 52; *Ketley v Gooden* (1997) 73 P & CR 305. Cf *Kelsen v Imperial Tobacco Co* [1957] 2 QB 334. In *London Borough of Harrow v Donohue* [1995] 1 EGLR 257, CA, it was held that a different approach applies where the defendant has trespassed on a claimant's land by erecting a building: as a claimant in that situation is entitled to a possession order (see below, p 583), it was held that a claimant must, alternatively, have the right to choose a mandatory restorative injunction irrespective of the adequacy of damages.
14 [1953] Ch 149 at 181.
15 [1970] AC 652 at 666. See also *Kelk v Pearson* (1871) 6 Ch App 809 at 812; *National Provincial Plate Glass Insurance Co v Prudential Assurance Co* (1877) 6 Ch D 757 at 761; *Rileys v Halifax Corpn* (1907) 97 LT 278; *Sharp v Harrison* [1922] 1 Ch 502 (breach of contract). In dicta in *Gravesham Borough Council v British Railways Board* [1978] Ch 379 at 405, the benefit to *the public of* the injunction was balanced against its hardship to the defendants.
16 Ibid. See also *Colls v Home and Colonial Stores Ltd* [1904] AC 179; *Pugh v Howells* (1984) 48 P & CR 298.

example, in *Daniel v Ferguson*,[17] on receiving notice of the claimant's complaint that the building being constructed would interfere with his ancient lights, the defendant doubled his efforts to have the building completed before any court order could be made. In view of this attempt 'to steal a march', the court granted an interim mandatory injunction ordering that that part of the building, which allegedly interfered with the claimant's rights, should be pulled down.

Consideration must finally be given to the constant supervision objection, which has traditionally been regarded as a bar to mandatory injunctions.[18] As with specific performance, however, the restriction has not always found favour. In this regard *Kennard v Cory Bros & Co Ltd*,[19] the 'moving mountain' case, is instructive, for while the Court of Appeal purported to accept the constant supervision objection, it indicated a lack of genuine support for it. The defendants argued that to order them to unblock a particular drain in the remedial works built to help prevent further landslides would in effect mean that they would be recognised as having a continuing obligation to repair and maintain those remedial works. As such the constant supervision objection would be infringed. While much of the judicial discussion focused on uncertainty, rather than constant supervision itself, the court rejected the above argument and stressed that the limited nature of the order being made meant that the constant supervision objection was inapplicable. But the judges were seemingly not enamoured of that objection. Lord Sterndale MR, after citing *Ryan v Mutual Tontine Westminster Chambers Association*,[20] the classic specific performance authority on constant supervision, could not find '... any objection in principle to the imposition of such [a continuous] obligation upon a wrongdoer';[1] and in Scrutton LJ's words, '... the Court will in some cases make an order which involves future maintenance ... when and though that involves that applications from time to time may have to be made to the Court to supervise the carrying out of the order.'[2]

Moreover, even though constant supervision has traditionally been a bar to mandatory injunctions, one can strongly argue that, as some recent cases on specific performance suggest, it should no longer be so regarded. This indeed, was part of an argument considered in *Gravesham*

---

17 [1891] 2 Ch 27. See also *Von Joel v Hornsey* [1895] 2 Ch 774; *Esso Petroleum Co Ltd v Kingswood Motors Ltd* [1974] QB 142.
18 *Powell Duffryn Steam Coal Co v Taff Vale Rly Co* (1874) 9 Ch App 331; *Attorney-General v Staffordshire County Council* [1905] 1 Ch 336.
19 [1922] 2 Ch 1.
20 [1893] 1 Ch 116.
1   [1922] 2 Ch 1 at 13.
2   [1922] 2 Ch 1 at 21.

Borough Council v British Railways Board,[3] where the cause of action was probably best viewed as tortious. One question was whether a mandatory enforcing injunction should be granted, assuming breach of a common law duty to maintain ferry crossings at reasonable times over the Thames. The objection put by the defendants was that this would necessitate a series of acts requiring the continuous employment of people over a number of years in a losing business.[4] Although this is not quite the same as just the constant supervision objection, counsel for the claimants argued that as some recent cases, such as *Tito v Waddell (No 2)*,[5] had suggested that there was no longer a constant supervision objection to specific performance so, analogously, the court should be willing to grant a mandatory injunction even though this would require continuously employing people. Slade J's reaction to that argument was not entirely clear. On the one hand, in the light of the authorities, he accepted that '... it cannot be regarded, as an absolute and inflexible rule that the court will never grant an injunction requiring a person to do a series of acts requiring the continuous employment of people over a number of years.'[6] But he went on to say that he would still have refused the injunction if there had been a breach of duty inter alia because of the '... risk of potential practical difficulties in regard to enforcement arising from the grant of an injunction compelling British Rail to operate its ferry service to a particular timetable.'[7] This ultimately seems to represent an acceptance of the constant supervision objection. If so this is unfortunate; for, as discussed in relation to specific performance[8] – and despite the approval of the constant supervision objection to specific performance by the House of Lords in *Co-operative Insurance Society Ltd v Argyll Stores (Holdings) Ltd*[9] – the policy reasons for this objection are weak and calls for its removal should be supported. The better justification for the refusal of the mandatory injunction in the *Gravesham* case is that, whether as an aspect of hardship or as a separate bar, the courts will not order a defendant to carry on with a losing business.

(2) Breach of contract

At first sight, one might expect that the mandatory injunction would be the appropriate remedy to enforce a positive contractual promise – that

---

3   [1978] Ch 379.
4   See also *Attorney-General v Colchester Corpn* [1955] 2 QB 207.
5   [1977] Ch 106.
6   [1978] Ch 379 at 405.
7   [1978] Ch 379.
8   Above, p 481.
9   [1998] AC 1. Above, pp 480–481.

is, a promise to do something. But other than at the interlocutory stage,[10] this role is entirely taken over by the remedy of specific performance.[11] This leaves the mandatory restorative injunction as the appropriate remedy for removing the effects of, that is for undoing, what the defendant has done in breach of a negative contractual promise, just as it is for undoing a tort.

The leading case in the contractual sphere is *Shepherd Homes Ltd v Sandham*,[12] even though what was there being sought was an *interim* mandatory injunction to remove a fence that the claimant alleged had been erected in breach of a restrictive covenant. Ultimately the injunction was refused, Megarry J stressing that the courts are particularly reluctant to grant interim mandatory injunctions and would not do so here, where it was unclear whether a mandatory injunction would be granted at trial, and where the claimant had delayed in bringing his application.

In discussing the relevant principles – which should be the same as those for torts (set out in the previous subsection) – Megarry J contrasted *Doherty v Allman*[13] and said that a mandatory injunction was not as easy to obtain as a prohibitory injunction.[14] Put another way, damages (in lieu) are generally regarded as sufficient and are the primary remedy. As regards specific bars Megarry J preferred not to try to particularise all the grounds upon which a mandatory injunction might be refused but he said that they at least included '... the triviality of the damage to the plaintiff and the existence of a disproportion between the detriment that the injunction would inflict on the defendant, and the benefit that it would confer on the plaintiff.'[15] The former is illustrated by *Sharp v Harrison*[16] where a mandatory injunction to remove a window overlooking the claimant's property and built in breach of a restrictive covenant was refused, since little or no interference was being caused. The latter is the important 'hardship' bar, which was also clearly recognised in *Sharp v Harrison* in a passage cited with approval by Megarry J. An example of its application, coupled with a desire to uphold the public interest, is *Wrotham Park Estate Co Ltd v Parkside Homes Ltd*.[17] There a mandatory injunction ordering the defendants to

---

10 Below, pp 546–547, 564–565. Specific performance is a final remedy only.
11 Viewed from this angle, it is perhaps surprising that specific performance developed as a separate remedy, since the mandatory injunction could have fulfilled its entire role.
12 [1971] Ch 340.
13 (1878) 3 App Cas 709.
14 See also *Sharp v Harrison* [1922] 1 Ch 502.
15 [1971] Ch 340.
16 [1922] 1 Ch 502.
17 [1974] 1 WLR 798. See also *Gafford v Graham* [1999] 3 EGLR 75, CA (refusal to grant mandatory injunction to pull down riding school).

knock down a housing estate built in breach of a restrictive covenant (enforceable by the claimant in equity) was refused and damages awarded, because the court wished to avoid 'an unpardonable waste of much needed houses.'[18] By analogy to mandatory injunctions for torts and specific performance one would expect that of the bars not mentioned by Megarry J uncertainty would be the most important; it must be possible for a clear order to be made.

Of course all this does not mean that a mandatory injunction will never be granted to remove the effects of the breach of a negative promise. In *Charrington v Simons & Co Ltd*,[19] for example, the Court of Appeal granted a mandatory injunction ordering the defendant to remove a tarmac farm road the height of which contravened a restrictive covenant with the claimant; and in *Wakeham v Wood*[20] where, in flagrant disregard of a restrictive covenant (enforceable by the claimant in equity) and of the claimant's complaints, the defendant had erected a building that obscured the claimant's sea-view, the Court of Appeal distinguished *Wrotham Park*, albeit not very convincingly, and ordered the defendant to remove so much of the building as obscured the view.

4. FINAL *QUIA TIMET* INJUNCTIONS

(1) Torts

A *quia timet* injunction is granted where no wrong has yet been committed. The commonest type is a prohibitory injunction to restrain wrongful acts which the defendant has not before committed. Although there is no reason why such an injunction should not be ordered to restrain the commission of any tort, most cases concern nuisance. To give a couple of examples of such an injunction being ordered, in *Dicker v Popham Radford & Co*[1] a *quia timet* injunction was granted to restrain the defendant from continuing a building which when completed would infringe the claimant's right to light; and in *Goodhart v Hyatt*,[2] where the claimant had the right to have water pipes running through the defendant's land, a *quia timet* injunction was granted preventing the defendant from continuing with building work which would interfere with the claimant's access to the pipes.[3]

---

18 [1974] 1 WLR 798 at 811.
19 [1971] 1 WLR 598.
20 (1982) 43 P & CR 40.
1   (1890) 63 LT 379.
2   (1883) 25 Ch D 182.
3   A more recent example is *Torquay Hotel & Co Ltd v Cousins* [1969] 2 Ch 106 (interim *quia timet* injunction to prevent tort of inducing breach of contract).

Far less common is a mandatory *quia timet* injunction, ordering positive steps to be taken to prevent earlier actions causing a wrong. The example that most obviously comes to mind is the removal of support from a neighbour's land where no subsidence of that land, and hence no tort of nuisance, has yet taken place.[4] So in *Hooper v Rogers*,[5] where the defendant's work in deepening a farm-track cut out of a slope threatened the foundations of the claimant's house standing at the top of the slope, the Court of Appeal held that a mandatory *quia timet* injunction to reinstate the natural angle of the slope could have been ordered and that the trial judge had therefore had jurisdiction to award damages in lieu.

The principles examined earlier dictating whether an ordinary injunction will be granted for tort apply in just the same way where the injunction is *quia timet*. This means, most importantly, that it will be easier to obtain a prohibitory than a mandatory *quia timet* injunction.

But the crucial importance of an injunction being classified as *quia timet* is that, as against ordinary injunctions where these requirements are presumed,[6] the claimant must show that the tort is highly probable to occur and to occur imminently. As Lord Dunedin said in *Attorney-General for Canada v Ritchie Contracting and Supply Co Ltd*[7] 'it is not sufficient to say "timeo".'

As regards the first requirement Chitty J in *Attorney-General v Manchester Corpn*[8] said, 'The principle which I think may be properly and safely extracted from the *quia timet* authorities is that the plaintiff must show a strong case of probability that the apprehended mischief will, in fact, arise';[9] and as the claimant could not so establish that a smallpox hospital when built would contravene statutory regulations, no *quia timet* injunction was granted. Again in *Pattisson v Gilford*[10] a *quia timet* injunction restraining the defendant from selling, for building, land over which the claimant had shooting rights was refused because it had not been shown that building on the land would 'necessarily and inevitably'[11] interfere with those shooting rights; and in *Redland Bricks v Morris*[12] Lord Upjohn said that a mandatory *quia timet* injunction '... can only be granted where

---

4   See also *Express Newspapers plc v Mitchell* [1982] IRLR 465 (interim injunction ordering a trade union official to withdraw a strike notice that if acted on would constitute the tort of inducing breach of contract).

5   [1975] Ch 43.

6   The presumption can be rebutted: eg *Proctor v Bayley* (1889) 42 Ch D 390; *Race Relations Board v Applin* [1973] QB 815.

7   [1919] AC 999 at 1005.

8   [1893] 2 Ch 87. See also *Attorney-General v Kingston-on-Thames Corpn* (1865) 34 LJ Ch 481; *Attorney-General v Nottingham Corpn* [1904] 1 Ch 673.

9   [1893] 2 Ch 87 at 92.

10   (1874) LR 18 Eq 259.

11   (1874) LR 18 Eq 259 at 264.

12   [1970] AC 652.

the plaintiff shows a very strong probability upon the facts that grave damage will accrue to him in the future'.[13] In *Hooper v Rogers*,[14] although it was found on the facts that future damage was a proven probability, Russell LJ criticised the need to show always that the tort is highly probable to occur when he said, 'In truth, it seems to me that the degree of probability of future injury is not an absolute standard: what is to be aimed at is justice between the parties, having regard to all the relevant circumstances.'[15] It can also be argued that a *quia timet* injunction does no harm to a law-abiding defendant. But granting such injunctions too readily may unduly hamper a defendant's freedom of action and may encourage excessive litigation and it is submitted that for such reasons the present high degree of probability should be retained as a requirement.

In other cases the stress has been on the tort being very likely to occur *imminently*. In *Fletcher v Bealey*,[16] for example, the claimant sought an injunction to prevent the dumping of 'vat-waste', his fear being that noxious liquid would flow from the waste into a river thereby causing him a nuisance. Pearson J refused the injunction and said that 'imminent danger'[17] must be proved. But his decision could equally be said to rest on the fact that the tort was not sufficiently likely to occur, for he stressed that it was quite possible for the defendants to prevent liquid flowing into the river, and in any case, they might find a means of rendering that liquid innocuous. Again in *Lemos v Kennedy Leigh Development Co*,[18] the claimant's application for a *quia timet* mandatory injunction ordering the removal of his neighbour's tree roots, which he alleged would cause damage to his land, was dismissed because the apprehended danger was not imminent. Finally, in the most recent and, it is submitted, sensible discussion of this requirement in *Hooper v Rogers*,[19] Russell LJ said that it meant that the action should not be premature, and that it would not be where, as in that case (and in contrast to *Fletcher v Bealey*) no other step could be taken to avoid the damage. So although subsidence of the claimant's house, following the defendant's removal of support, might not occur for many years, it was held that a mandatory *quia timet* injunction could have been granted and hence damages in lieu were justified.

---

13 [1970] AC 652 at 665. Presumably 'grave' damage is stressed because a mandatory injunction was in issue.
14 [1975] Ch 43.
15 [1975] Ch 43 at 50.
16 (1885) 28 Ch D 688.
17 (1885) 28 Ch D 688 at 698.
18 (1961) 105 Sol Jo 178. See also *Lord Cowley v Byas* (1877) 5 Ch D 944; *Draper v British Optical Association* [1938] 1 All ER 115.
19 [1975] Ch 43.

(2) Breach of contract

The role of *quia timet* injunctions for breach of contract is unclear. This lack of clarity stems from the technicalities of the English doctrine of 'anticipatory breach'. According to that doctrine, an anticipatory breach does not constitute a breach unless and until it is accepted by the innocent party as terminating the contract. On that technical approach, an injunction to prevent a threatened breach of contract, where there has been no actual failure to perform, would class as a *quia timet* injunction.[20] But the better approach is to say that an anticipatory breach is automatically a breach of contract because it constitutes a breach of the implied promise to be ready, able and willing to perform. On that better approach, there are no *quia timet* injunctions for breach of contract because a threatened breach is itself a breach of contract.

5. INTERIM INJUNCTIONS

Interim injunctions, which may be prohibitory or mandatory, *quia timet* or not *quia timet*, are injunctions given prior to trial or other hearing in which final judgment is given, and are intended to last until the trial at the latest. Although temporary in this sense their advantage, as against final injunctions, is that they can be obtained quickly: indeed in some situations, such as where the claimant seeks to prevent a particular threatened act, it would be too late for the claimant to wait until trial.

In contrast to, for example, a freezing injunction,[1] an ordinary interim injunction is within the scope of this book, since it is not best viewed as being concerned to aid the enforcement of other remedies, that is, as being concerned to enable a final injunction to be effective. Rather it is designed to protect, where justified, the claimant's alleged rights during the inevitable delay before trial, and this is so even where an injunction at trial can effectively protect those rights from then on without an interim injunction having been granted.

So as a remedy for torts and breach of contract an interim injunction fulfils analogous functions to a final injunction, but does so more quickly. For example, an interim prohibitory injunction is the appropriate remedy pre-trial to prevent an alleged continuing or recurring tort. In one respect, however, an interim injunction plays a wider role than a final injunction; for prior to trial, an interim mandatory injunction is the

---

20 See, eg Spry *Equitable Remedies* (6th edn, 2001) pp 381–382 (and pp 77–78).
1   Below, p 568.

appropriate remedy to enforce a positive contractual obligation, whereas specific performance rather than a mandatory injunction would be granted at trial.

The fact that an interim injunction is granted at an earlier stage of proceedings means that different principles must be applied in deciding whether to grant this sort of injunction than a final injunction. In *American Cyanamid Co v Ethicon Ltd*[2] the House of Lords controversially reformulated the principles governing interim injunctions. However, in order to understand *American Cyanamid*, it is first necessary to consider briefly the law prior to it.

(1) The law prior to *American Cyanamid*

What should be stressed straightaway is that not all cases adopted the same approach to interim injunctions.[3] Nevertheless, as shown for example by the House of Lords in *Stratford & Son Ltd v Lindley*,[4] and at first instance and by the Court of Appeal in *American Cyanamid*[5] itself, a claimant generally needed to show: first, a prima facie case[6] both that the defendant was committing or was intending to commit a wrong against the claimant and (apparently) that the claimant would be entitled to a final injunction at trial for that wrong: and, secondly, that the balance of convenience favoured an interim injunction. Furthermore, given the uncertainty as to whether the granting of an injunction would turn out to have been unjustified, the court almost invariably insisted, as a condition of granting an interim injunction, that the claimant should give an undertaking to pay damages for any unjustifiable loss caused to the defendant in complying with the injunction.[7]

While the courts often talked of a prima facie case solely in relation to the defendant committing or intending to commit a wrong, it does appear to have been impliedly accepted that there must also be a prima facie case for a final injunction at trial. Certainly this is how

---

2 [1975] AC 396.
3 See, eg *Hubbard v Vosper* [1972] 2 QB 84. Interim injunctions pending appeals were also treated differently, as they still are: *Polini v Gray* (1879) 11 Ch D 741; *Orion Property Trust Ltd v Du Cane Court Ltd* [1962] 1 WLR 1085; *Erinford Properties Ltd v Cheshire County Council* [1974] Ch 261.
4 [1965] AC 269.
5 [1974] FSR 312.
6 Often a strong prima facie case was required: *Challender v Royal* (1887) 36 Ch D 425; *Smith v Grigg Ltd* [1924] 1 KB 655 at 659.
7 The principles governing such damages are discussed in *Hoffmann-La Roche & Co AG v Secretary of State for Trade and Industry* [1975] AC 295 at 361. That case principally lays down that, where seeking to enforce the law, the Crown cannot be required to give such an undertaking. The same applies to other public authorities seeking interim injunctions to enforce the law: *Kirklees Metropolitan BC v Wickes Building Supplies Ltd* [1993] AC 227.

Lord Diplock interpreted the approach of Graham J and of the Court of Appeal in *American Cyanamid*. He said that they had thought there was a rule:

> '... that the court is not entitled to take any account of the balance of convenience unless it has first been satisfied that if the case went to trial upon no other evidence than is before the court at the hearing of the application the plaintiff would be entitled to *judgment for a permanent injunction* in the same terms as the interlocutory injunction sought.'[8]

In essence then, the first requirement was that the courts undertook a 'mini-trial' of the dispute, according to the evidence and arguments then available to it.

Assessing the balance of convenience, on the other hand, required the court to do what was most just, on the assumption that it could not at the pre-trial stage decide on the merits whether an injunction was justified or not. The main factors taken into account in deciding this were whether damages would adequately compensate either party for any interim unjustifiable loss, and whether in general terms it would cause greater hardship to grant or refuse the injunction. It was also sometimes said that the courts would prefer to maintain the status quo: but this was ambiguous, since any one of several different positions could be regarded as the status quo, for example, the position at trial or the position prior to the issue of proceedings or the position prior to the alleged wrong. Moreover, there was no obvious justification for such a preference.[9]

What is perhaps particularly significant about the old law is that, at least in more recent times, it was the first mini-trial hurdle that parties regarded as the most important aspect of the interim application. As Hammond writes, 'Counsel began to use the interlocutory injunction as a means of providing a rapid and relatively cheap method of arbitration of disputes.'[10] So even where it would not be too late to challenge the interim decision at trial, cases very rarely proceeded to trial (even as regards a claim for damages) because the parties accepted what was decided regarding the prima facie case as indicative of the trial outcome and settled accordingly. Indeed it has been said that 99% of cases in which the interim injunction was sought did not proceed to trial.[11] The parties' attitude was also reflected or, more arguably, inspired by the courts' refusal to treat the two requirements as rigidly sequential steps,

---

8   [1975] AC 396 at 407 (author's italics).
9   This remains a problem post-*Cyanamid*; below, pp 552–553. See Sharpe *Injunctions and Specific Performance* (3rd edn, 2000) para 2.550.
10 'Interlocutory Injunctions: Time for a New Model?' (1980) 30 UTLJ 240, 251.
11 *Fellowes & Son v Fisher* [1976] QB 122 at 133 (per Lord Denning).

and their consequent tendency to treat the balance of convenience as subsidiary to the strength of the claimant's case. So, for example, if the claimant had established a very strong prima facie case, the judges seemed happy to ignore the balance of convenience altogether. As Prescott wrote in 1975, '... in recent times the tendency has been to adopt a more robust attitude, and to be guided more and more by the apparent strength or otherwise of the plaintiff's case as revealed by the affidavits.'[12]

(2) *American Cyanamid v Ethicon*[13]

Lord Diplock, in a speech agreed with by the other Lords, here sought to put a stop to the approach of regarding the interim application as a mini-trial. The claimants were seeking an interim *quia timet* injunction to prevent the defendants marketing in Great Britain sterile sutures which they alleged infringed their patent. At first instance Graham J granted the injunction on the basis that the claimants had made out a prima facie case, and that the balance of convenience favoured them. But on appeal this was overturned, the Court of Appeal holding that the claimants had failed to make out a prima facie case. The House of Lords restored the first instance decision but on different reasoning, which was as follows.

First, the claimant must establish that there is a serious question to be tried; in other words, that its claim is not frivolous or vexatious. But it should *not* be required to establish a prima facie case.

Secondly, assuming that it establishes that there is a serious question, the claimant must go on to show that the balance of convenience favours granting the interim injunction. In assessing this, the following sequential approach should be adopted.

(i) The court should ask whether damages would adequately compensate the claimant for its interim loss and whether the defendant could pay them. If the answer is yes, the interim injunction should not be granted.

(ii) However, if the answer is no, the court should ask whether damages payable under the claimant's undertaking would adequately compensate the defendant for its interim loss and whether the claimant could pay them. If yes, there is a strong case for the interim injunction.

---

12   (1975) 91 LQR 168, 169.
13   [1975] AC 396. Baker 'Interlocutory Injunctions – A Discussion of the New Rules' (1977) 42 Sask LR 53.

(iii) If, however, there is doubt as to the adequacy of the respective damages, the case turns on the balance of convenience generally. The main factor is whether it would cause greater hardship to grant or refuse the injunction – or as Lord Diplock phrased it, 'the extent of the uncompensatable disadvantage to each party.'[14] Where this and other considerations are evenly balanced, two factors that can be taken into account as a last resort are first, the desirability of maintaining the status quo and, secondly, the strength of one party's case being disproportionate to that of the other.

Applying this approach to the facts, an interim injunction was granted because first, it was a serious question whether the defendants were infringing a patent of the claimants so as to entitle the claimants to a final injunction at trial; and secondly, the balance of convenience favoured the grant of the interim injunction, particularly since the claimants' monopoly of the market would effectively be destroyed for ever if the interim injunction were refused.

Consideration of the parties' ability to pay damages, and the sequential structuring of the approach to the balance of convenience, with the adequacy of damages first having to be looked at and in itself possibly resolving which way the balance lies, are two changes *American Cyanamid* has made from the previous law. But the crucial change is that the claimant does not first have to establish a prima facie case. The much lower threshold of a serious question to be tried is all that needs to be satisfied, and the strength of the claimant's case is relevant only as a last resort within the balance of convenience. In Sharpe's words, '... the strength of case consideration of the traditional approach is stood on its head.'[15] The policy behind this is that the interim application should *not* serve as a mini-trial, in which the merits of the dispute are judged, since evidence is merely on affidavit, rather than being oral and subject to cross-examination. Nor are the legal arguments fully presented. The aim is to restore the interim injunction to its supposedly true function of protecting the claimant during the period of uncertainty before trial, where this is justified on the balance of convenience. In Lord Diplock's words:

> 'It is no part of the court's function at this stage of the litigation to try to resolve conflicts of evidence on affidavits as to facts on which the claim of either party may ultimately depend nor to decide difficult questions of law which call for detailed argument and mature consideration. These are matters to be dealt with at the trial.'[16]

14   [1975] AC 396 at 409.
15   *Injunctions and Specific Performance* (3rd edn, 2000) para 2.200.
16   [1975] AC 396 at 407.

Subsequent case law has further clarified the *American Cyanamid* principles.

So it was emphasised by Browne LJ in *Smith v Inner London Education Authority*[17] that the three phrases Lord Diplock used to describe the initial hurdle – 'a serious question to be tried', 'not frivolous or vexatious', 'a real prospect of succeeding at the trial'[18] – are all ways of phrasing the same test; and although a relatively easy threshold to cross, there have been cases, *Smith* being one,[19] where a claimant has been denied an interim injunction for failure to overcome it.

In very few cases has the grant or refusal of the interim injunction been decided by the adequacy of damages for either the claimant or the defendant. Even where the courts have been willing to rest their decisions on this – as in *Fosesco International v Fordath*,[20] where it was held that damages would adequately compensate the defendants and could be paid by the claimants, and *Roussel-Uclaf v GD Searle & Co*,[1] where damages were thought adequate for the claimant – they have gone on to justify their decision according to the general balance of convenience. This feature is hardly surprising. Adequacy is such an elusive concept that permissible reliance on other factors is almost always to be preferred.

Only factors concerning the parties were traditionally thought to be relevant within the balance of convenience, an approach which was consistent with that for final prohibitory injunctions, where the public interest has not been allowed to override private rights. But in *Smith v ILEA* Browne LJ, in dicta, said that where the defendant was a local authority the court should take into account the interests of the public within the balance of convenience.[2] This has also been applied even where the defendant was not a public authority. In *Roussel-Uclaf v GD Searle & Co* the detriment to the public of being deprived of a life-saving drug considered the major factor in deciding that the balance of convenience lay against the injunction; and in several industrial dispute

---

17 [1978] 1 All ER 411.
18 [1975] AC 396 at 407–408. But it may be doubted whether 'a real prospect of success' sets as low a threshold as 'a serious question to be tried': see *Cream Holdings Ltd v Banerjee* [2003] EWCA Civ 103, [2003] Ch 650, below, p 561.
19 Also, *Re Lord Cable* [1977] 1 WLR 7; *Morning Star Co-operative Society Ltd v Express Newspapers Ltd* [1979] FSR 113; *Associated British Ports v TGWU* [1989] 3 All ER 822.
20 [1975] FSR 507; *Laws v Florinplace Ltd* [1981] 1 All ER 659.
1   [1977] FSR 125.
2   See also *R v Ministry of Agriculture, ex p Monsanto* [1999] QB 1161 where the main application was for judicial review of a public authority's approval of a rival company's product and interim relief, by way of a stay of the approval, was sought pending the decision of the European Court of Justice.

cases,[3] the courts have regarded the detrimental impact of strike action on the public as a factor weighting the balance of convenience in favour of granting an interim injunction, thereby further curtailing the right to strike. It is also relevant here to mention *R v Secretary of State for Transport, ex p Factortame (No 2)*[4] in which it was held by the House of Lords that, where an interim injunction is sought to restrain the enforcement by the Secretary of State of an English statute on the grounds that it is invalid under European Community law, the public interest in the enforcement of what, on the face of it, is the law of the land requires that no injunction should normally be granted unless the claimant establishes a strong prima facie case of invalidity. In contrast to Lord Jauncey, Lord Goff, giving the leading speech, saw this approach as not affecting the initial threshold to be crossed under *Cyanamid* but as going instead to the balance of convenience.[5]

Sir John Donaldson MR in *Francome v Mirror Group Newspapers Ltd*[6] expressed preference for the term 'balance of justice' as against 'balance of convenience'; and May LJ made a similar comment in *Cayne v Global Natural Resources plc*.[7] But it is hard to see what possible advantage there would be in such a change of terminology.

What is meant by the status quo has been discussed in several cases subsequent to *American Cyanamid*. In *Fellowes v Fisher*[8] Sir John Pennycuick regarded it as the position prior to the wrong, and this was supported by Geoffrey Lane LJ in *Budget Rent A Car International Inc v Mamos Slough Ltd*.[9] In *Alfred Dunhills v Sunoptic*[10] Megaw LJ took the rather vague view that '... the relevant point in time for the purposes of the "status quo" may well vary in different cases.' Lord Diplock attempted to clarify authoritatively what is meant in *Garden Cottage Foods Ltd v Milk Marketing Board*,[11] but his approach is far from simple:

> '... the relevant status quo to which reference was made in *American Cyanamid* is the state of affairs existing during the period immediately preceding the issue of the writ claiming the permanent injunction, or if there be unreasonable delay between the

3   *Star Sea Transport Corpn of Monrovia v Slater* [1978] IRLR 507; *Beaverbrook Newspapers Ltd v Keys* [1978] ICR 582; *NWL Ltd v Woods* [1979] 1 WLR 1294; *Duport Steel Ltd v Sirs* [1980] ICR 161.
4   [1991] 1 AC 603.
5   In *R v Secretary of State for Health, ex p Imperial Tobacco Ltd* [2001] 1 WLR 127, the House of Lords left unresolved the question whether domestic law or community law applies to determine whether an interim injunction should be granted restraining the Secretary of State from making regulations to implement an allegedly invalid directive.
6   [1984] 1 WLR 892. In *Attorney-General v Observer Newspapers Ltd* [1986] NLJ Rep 799 he preferred the term 'balance of inconvenience'.
7   [1984] 1 All ER 225.
8   [1976] QB 122.
9   (1977) 121 Sol Jo 374.
10   [1979] FSR 337.
11   [1984] AC 130.

issue of writ and the motion for an interlocutory injunction the period immediately preceding the motion. The duration of that period since the state of affairs last changed must be more than minimal, having regard to the total length of the relationship between the parties in respect of which the injunction was granted; otherwise the state of affairs before the last change would be the relevant status quo.'[12]

These differences of judicial opinion serve to confirm the view that the preference expressed for maintaining the status quo lacks sound justification.

Finally, it has been argued by Gray that, irrespective of exceptions to *American Cyanamid*:

'A judge should be able to reach the same conclusion by applying the *Cyanamid* principles as he would have reached by the previous approach. So the difference between the pre-*Cyanamid* situation … and the post-*Cyanamid* situation … is superficial, a difference of appearance rather than substance, of approach rather than result.'[13]

But while it is true that the *American Cyanamid* principles do allow some flexibility, so that for example a judge eager to bring in his or her view of the merits of the case can do so by regarding the balance of convenience as equal, the principles *if applied* must affect results because, without a prima facie case hurdle to overcome, they must make it easier for a claimant to obtain an interim injunction. *Hubbard v Pitt*[14] is a good example, where the majority applying *American Cyanamid*, granted the interim injunction, whereas Lord Denning, applying the old law would have refused it. That many such examples are not forthcoming is best explained by the fact that important exceptions to *American Cyanamid* have been developed, and by the suspicion that, while purporting to apply Lord Diplock's principles, the judges have in fact been distorting them. But the submission is that, if applied, *American Cyanamid* does produce a change of result as well as approach. As Hammond writes:

'The classical model has been replaced by a balancing model. A cynic might contend that was merely window-dressing – that judges continued to do the same old things in the same old way – yet the reformulation of the remedy did in some cases affect the case-law results.'[15]

---

12 [1984] AC 130 at 140. Cf *Graham v Delderfield* [1992] FSR 313 where it was held to be the position at the date of the service, rather than at the date of the issue of the writ, that fixed the status quo.
13 'Interim Injunctions since *Cyanamid*' (1980) 40 CLJ 307 at 338–339.
14 [1976] QB 142.
15 'Interim Injunctions: Time for a New Model?' (1980) 30 UTLJ 249, 259.

(3) Criticisms of *American Cyanamid*

A feature of the post-*Cyanamid* case law has been the reluctance of many judges to follow the Lords' approach. A number of reasons may be suggested for its lack of popularity.

(i)   The mini-trial interim application was useful for parties, being a quick and relatively cheap means of achieving rough and ready justice. In Wallington's graphic phrase, 'The House of Lords has effectively closed down the economy-class option: we shall all have to travel in the Rolls – or not at all.'[16]

(ii) In many cases, the time factor and circumstances are such that the decision on the interim application ends the dispute, rendering a trial regarding a final injunction superfluous. In such cases, one cannot fairly decide the interim application on the basis of what is more convenient pending trial, and the merits of the claim must be regarded as decisive.

(iii) The basis of Lord Diplock's reasoning – that there is insufficient evidence and argument at the interim application to come to a sound conclusion on fact and law – appears not to be borne out by the reality for, as noted by one well-known barrister, in almost all cases that have proceeded to trial the decision has gone the same way as at the interim stage.[17]

(iv) *American Cyanamid* is detrimental to civil liberties. This follows from the fact that in assessing the balance of convenience, the courts have traditionally regarded temporary interference with economic interests as more serious than temporary interference with non-tangible interests, such as the right to continue a strike or demonstration, or to speak freely. Where the primary emphasis was on the claimant's establishing a prima facie case this mattered less. But Lord Diplock's removal of that emphasis makes it too easy for a claimant to infringe the defendant's civil liberties. Wallington has been particularly critical of this aspect of *American Cyanamid*; '... failure to bring into account the intangibles is only tolerable where at least an arbitrary assessment of the legal merits has been made, so that the conduct prohibited is at least *probably* unlawful. If there is no determination of the legal issues, it is intolerable that such a vital factor as the defendant's liberties be left out of account in assessing the balance of convenience.'[18]

---

16   (1976) 35 CLJ 82, 87.
17   Prescott (1975) 91 LQR 168, 169.
18   'Injunctions and the "Right to Demonstrate" ' (1976) 35 CLJ 82, 92.

(v)   Under *American Cyanamid*, the fact that the claimant appears to have a very strong case as opposed to a merely arguable one has no bearing except as a last resort. This seems unsatisfactory, for a very strong case is a factor that should outweigh whatever the balance of convenience would dictate.

(4) Exceptions to *American Cyanamid*

In view of the above criticisms, it is not surprising that the courts have recognised a number of exceptions to *American Cyanamid*, where the old law, or something similar to it, is applied.[19]

(a) **Where no action for a final injunction will reach trial**

This, the most important exception, is where the timing and circumstances are such that if the interim decision goes one way or, in some situations, either way it will resolve the dispute relating to injunctive relief without a trial.[20]

It would seem that this is what Lord Denning had in mind when in one of the first cases after *American Cyanamid*, *Fellowes v Fisher*,[1] in a judgment not agreed with by the majority, he said that *American Cyanamid* did not apply and the old law did, where '… it is urgent and imperative to come to a decision';[2] and he thought that this would be so in cases of industrial disputes, breach of confidence, covenants in restraint of trade, passing-off, and in many commercial cases. Lord Denning applied the same approach in several subsequent cases.[3]

However, more recent cases have established that Lord Denning's approach of listing the sorts of case that would automatically fall within

---

19 See Martin 'Interlocutory Injunctions: *American Cyanamid* Comes of Age' (1993–4) 4 King's CLJ 52. For an additional exception, not discussed below, see *Re J (a minor)* [1993] Fam 15. See also *Deutsche Rückversicherung AG v Walbrook Insurance Co Ltd* [1995] 1 WLR 1017 on the courts' reluctance to grant an interim injunction restraining a bank, on the grounds of alleged fraud, from paying on a letter of credit. Interestingly in Australia there were initial doubts as to whether *Cyanamid* should be followed, given its contradiction of the old law embodied in *Beecham Group Ltd v Bristol Laboratories Pty Ltd* (1968) 118 CLR 618. But more recently *Cyanamid* has been followed in, eg *Australian Coarse Grain Pty Ltd v Barley Marketing Board of Queensland* (1982) 57 ALJR 425; *Tableland Peanuts v Peanut Marketing Board* (1984) 58 ALJR 283; *Murphy v Lush* (1986) 60 ALJR 523. See *Meagher, Gummow and Lehane's Equity: Doctrines and Remedies* (4th edn, 2002) paras 21–350–21–375.
20 But it is not sufficient simply that the parties are likely to settle out of court following the interim application, for this is always likely: Newell 'Trade Unions and Non-Striking Members' (1981) 97 LQR 214, 217.
1   [1976] QB 122.
2   [1976] QB 122 at 133.
3   *Hubbard v Pitt* [1976] QB 142; *Dunford and Elliot Ltd v Johnson & Firth Brown Ltd* [1977] 1 Lloyd's Rep 505, and as agreed with by the other CA judges in *Office Overload Ltd v Gunn* [1977] FSR 39, and *Newsweek Inc v BBC* [1979] RPC 441.

this exception was too wide-ranging. In *Lawrence David Ltd v Ashton*[4] and *County Sound plc v Ocean Sound Ltd*[5] the Court of Appeal clarified, without doubting the exception itself, that *American Cyanamid* principles apply in the normal way to covenants in restraint of trade and passing off cases respectively. Lord Denning's judgment in *Fellowes v Fisher* was expressly disapproved as was the approach of the Court of Appeal in *Office Overload Ltd v Gunn*[6] (covenant in restraint of trade) and *Newsweek Inc v BBC*[7] (passing off).

Authoritative support for at least a modification of *American Cyanamid* where no action for a final injunction will reach trial came from Lord Diplock himself; for in *NWL Ltd v Woods*,[8] faced with a legislative reaction embodied in what is now the Trade Union and Labour Relations (Consolidation) Act 1992, s 221(2),[9] Lord Diplock was forced to concede that *American Cyanamid* could not be straightforwardly applied in industrial dispute cases. He said that this was so because, 'the grant or refusal of an interlocutory injunction generally disposes finally of the action: in practice actions of this type seldom if ever come to actual trial.'[10]

Further support for this exception was given by a strong Court of Appeal, even without Lord Denning, in *Cayne v Global Natural Resources*,[11] where the claimant shareholder sought an interim injunction to restrain the directors of Global from allegedly acting in breach of fiduciary duty by merging Global with another company. The claimant argued that the proposed merger was simply a means whereby the directors could resist the attempt by the claimant and other shareholders to remove them. In refusing the interim injunction, the Court of Appeal declined to apply *American Cyanamid* and referred to *NWL v Woods*, because in these circumstances the grant of the interim injunction would effectively decide the issue in the claimant's favour; for if granted the directors would be unlikely to resist removal by the claimant and, as the claimant and his supporters would then be directors, the proposed merger would be dropped.[12] As *American Cyanamid* was not being applied, the claimant

---

4   [1991] 1 All ER 385. Cf *Lansing Linde Ltd v Kerr* [1991] 1 WLR 251.
5   [1991] FSR 367.
6   [1977] FSR 39.
7   [1979] RPC 441.
8   [1979] 1 WLR 1294.
9   Below, pp 557–560.
10   [1979] 1 WLR 1294 at 1305. See also *Porter v National Union of Journalists* [1980] IRLR 404 at 406; Newell (1981) 97 LQR 214.
11   [1984] 1 All ER 225. See also *Fulwell v Bragg* (1983) 127 Sol Jo 171.
12   [1984] 1 All ER 225 at 232 per Eveleigh LJ, who thought also that a refusal of the injunction would decide the issue because the merger would then go ahead, the directors would successfully defeat the claimant and his supporters, and in practice this could not be reversed by a final injunction.

needed to show an 'overwhelming'[13] case, that is a prima facie case, and this he had failed to do. Kerr LJ in characteristically clear terms stressed that *American Cyanamid* should be restricted to cases where:

'... a trial is in fact likely to take place, in the sense that the plaintiffs' case shows that they are genuinely concerned to pursue their claim to trial, and that they are seeking the injunction as a means of a holding operation pending the trial.'[14]

Cayne should be followed and *American Cyanamid* ignored wherever the interim decision, one way or either way, will finally resolve the dispute relating to injunctive relief. This is supported by *Thomas v National Union of Mineworkers*:[15] Scott J, recognising that an action for a final injunction preventing the allegedly unlawful picketing of the claimants, who were working miners, would be unlikely ever to come to trial, followed *Cayne* and, in granting an interim injunction, in effect required the claimants to show a prima facie case that they would be entitled to a final injunction to restrain the picketing.[16] It is also supported by Kerr LJ in *Cambridge Nutrition Ltd v BBC*.[17] But the majority of the Court of Appeal in that case attempted to reconcile *Cayne* and *Cyanamid*[18] by elevating within the balance of convenience the importance of the claimant's prospects of success where a trial is unlikely. The Lords Justices were unanimous in discharging an interim injunction restraining the BBC from screening a programme (allegedly in breach of contract) about the claimant's low calorie diet.

(b) Trade dispute defence[19]

In reaction to *American Cyanamid*, the legislature added a new subsection (2) to the Trade Union and Labour Relations Act 1974, s 17, which is now contained in the Trade Union and Labour Relations (Consolidation) Act 1992, s 221(2). By this:

'Where (a) an application for an interlocutory injunction is made to a court pending the trial of an action; and (b) the party against whom the injunction is sought claims that he acted in contemplation or furtherance of a trade dispute, the court shall, in exercising its discretion, whether or not to grant the injunction, have regard to the

---

13 [1984] 1 All ER 225 at 233, 236.
14 [1984] 1 All ER 225 at 234.
15 [1986] Ch 20.
16 [1986] Ch 20 at 68.
17 [1990] 3 All ER 523.
18 See analogously the attempts to assimilate the Trade Union and Labour Relations (Consolidation) Act 1992, s 221(2) and *Cyanamid* in *Mercury Communications Ltd v Scott-Garner* [1984] Ch 37 and *Dimbleby & Sons Ltd v National Union of Journalists* [1984] 1 WLR 427: below, pp 559–560.
19 Davies and Freedland *Labour Law* (2nd edn, 1984) pp 765–777.

likelihood of that party's succeeding at the trial of the action in establishing any matter which would afford a defence to the action under s 219 (protection from certain tort liabilities) or s 220 (peaceful picketing).'[20]

Although this subsection is based on the first exception already examined – that is, it recognises that *American Cyanamid* would make it too easy for an employer effectively to end lawful industrial action for ever, since once stopped industrial action is very difficult to reorganise – it has given rise to its own interesting jurisprudence on whether and how the subsection fits in with *American Cyanamid;* and this issue remains relevant despite the subsequent development of exceptions to the defence (eg where there has been no ballot) and the narrowing of what is meant by a trade dispute.[1]

In *Star Sea Transport Corpn of Monrovia v Slater*[2] Lord Denning thought that the effect of what is now the Trade Union and Labour Relations (Consolidation) Act 1992, s 221(2) was 'to restore the previous law'[3] in cases involving the defence of acts done in contemplation or furtherance of a trade dispute. This should have meant that the interim injunction would be refused because, taking this defence into account, the claimant could not establish a prima facie case. But Lord Denning considered that, as there was an arguable question of law, the balance of convenience should determine the issue in favour of granting the injunction – an approach which resembled *American Cyanamid,* rather than the previous law. The two other judges without clarifying the relationship between s 221(2) and *American Cyanamid* simply thought that there was insufficient likelihood of the defence succeeding to outweigh the balance of convenience, which was in favour of granting the injunction.

Lord Scarman in *NWL v Woods*[4] considered that what is now the Trade Union and Labour Relations (Consolidation) Act 1992, s 221(2) could not fit within the *American Cyanamid* framework. But then, rather than simply reverting to the old law, he regarded the s 221(2) question as a third stage in the inquiry after the serious question to be tried and balance of convenience issues. This seems unnecessarily cumbersome, particularly since if the trade dispute defence is likely to succeed at trial, no interim injunction will be granted, irrespective of the answers to the first two stages. Nevertheless, Lord Scarman's approach is to be preferred

---

20 Where in contemplation or furtherance of a trade dispute, the Trade Union and Labour Relations (Consolidation) Act 1992, s 219 affords a defence to economic torts, and the Trade Union and Labour Relations (Consolidation) Act 1992, s 220 to peaceful primary picketing.
1   The meaning of 'trade dispute' is now contained in the Trade Union and Labour Relations (Consolidation) Act 1992, s 244; see *Mercury Communications Ld v Scott-Garner* [1984] Ch 37.
2   [1978] IRLR 507.
3   [1978] IRLR 507 at 510.
4   [1979] 1 WLR 1294.

to that adopted by Lords Diplock and Fraser. They considered that s 221(2) could be fitted within the *American Cyanamid* framework with the amendment that in these cases the claimant's likelihood of gaining an injunction at trial should be an important rather than a last resort factor within the balance of convenience. While, as we have seen, Lord Diplock's explanation of this modification was eminently sensible – the practical realities of industrial disputes mean that the grant or refusal of the interim injunction generally disposes finally of the claim – confining s 221(2) to a place within the balance of convenience potentially undermines the purpose of that provision: if there is a likelihood of the defence succeeding at trial, no interim injunction should be granted irrespective of other factors.

For a time, however, it looked as if even Lord Diplock was departing from his *American Cyanamid* framework in relation to what is now the Trade Union and Labour Relations (Consolidation) Act 1992, s 221(2). In *Hadmor Productions Ltd v Hamilton*,[5] in giving the sole judgment, he refused an interim injunction because of the very high likelihood of the trade dispute defence succeeding at trial and, although *American Cyanamid* and *NWL v Woods* were mentioned, his approach, with no reference to other factors in the balance of convenience, looked more like that of the old law. Furthermore in *Duport Steels Ltd v Sirs*,[6] the House of Lords, including Lord Diplock, did not even mention *American Cyanamid*.

But any hopes that *American Cyanamid* might be forgotten in the context of what is now the Trade Union and Labour Relations (Consolidation) Act 1992, s 221(2), particularly with the intervening decision in *Cayne v Global Natural Resources plc*,[7] proved shortlived for in *Mercury Communications Ltd v Scott-Garner*[8] and *Dimbleby & Sons Ltd v National Union of Journalists*[9] the Court of Appeal (under Sir John Donaldson) and the House of Lords respectively, continued to grapple with the assimilation of *American Cyanamid* and s 221(2). The approach adopted in these cases, differing from *NWL v Woods*, was that s 221(2) applies at an initial stage, so that presumably, if the trade dispute defence is likely to succeed, no injunction should be granted. Otherwise *American Cyanamid* applies in the normal way. 'As respects all other issues raised by way of defence to the action the criterion to be applied in order to make recourse to the balance of convenience necessary is the ordinary criterion laid down in

5   [1982] ICR 114.
6   [1980] ICR 161.
7   [1984] 1 All ER 225.
8   [1984] Ch 37.
9   [1984] 1 WLR 427.

American Cyanamid – is there a serious question to be tried?'[10] Curiously Lord Diplock thought that the practical realities that in *NWL v Woods* he had regarded as justifying modification of *American Cyanamid* no longer applied in an action against a trade union because now that a trade union could be sued an employer might well be interested in pursuing a claim for damages to trial. This is most misleading, for the important practical reality remains that to grant an interim injunction in an industrial dispute has the drastic effect of ending industrial action without the trial. Therefore, the justification for departure from *American Cyanamid* conceded in *NWL v Woods* remains as valid as ever. Furthermore, Lord Diplock was left without any coherent explanation as to why s 221(2) should have departed from *American Cyanamid*. But having said that, it is an ironic twist that the new approach adopted in these cases is far more acceptable than that adopted by Lord Diplock in *NWL v Woods*, and it seems to come very close to the old law. Indeed it merely serves to strengthen the view, indirectly supported by *Cayne v Global Natural Resources*, that it would have been preferable from the outset to have ignored *American Cyanamid* and to have regarded s 221(2) as restoring the old law in relation to cases involving the trade dispute defence.

(c) The need to protect free speech

Pre-*Cyanamid*, the principles governing interim injunctions in defamation (and injurious falsehood) cases were exceptional. The tradition that juries should hear such cases was one supposed reason for this. But the primary justification was the desire to protect free speech. As such, interim injunctions were to be refused wherever the defendant raised a defence, whether of justification, fair comment or privilege unless the defence would obviously fail at trial.[11] It has now been established in a series of decisions[12] that these old principles survive *American Cyanamid*, for as

---

10   [1984] 1 WLR 427 at 432 (per Lord Diplock).
11   *William Coulson & Sons v James Coulson & Co* (1887) 3 TLR 846; *Bonnard v Perryman* [1891] 2 Ch 269; *Fraser v Evans* [1969] 1 QB 349.
12   *Bestobell Paints Ltd v Biggs* [1975] FSR 421; *Trevor and Sons v Soloman* (1978) 248 Estates Gazette 779; *Harakas v Baltic Mercantile and Shipping Exchange Ltd* [1982] 2 All ER 701; *Herbage v Pressdram Ltd* [1984] 1 WLR 1160; *Al-Fayed v The Observer Ltd* (1986) Times, 14 July; *Khashoggi v IPC Magazines Ltd* [1986] 3 All ER 577; *Kaye v Robertson* [1991] FSR 62; *Holley v Smyth* [1998] QB 726. See also *Gulf Oil (GB) Ltd v Page* [1987] Ch 327 and esp *Femis-Bank (Anguilla) Ltd v Lazar* [1991] Ch 391 (similarly to defamation cases, the protection of free speech is an important factor in deciding whether to grant an interim injunction to restrain an alleged conspiracy to injure so that such an injunction should only be granted where the claimant has established a strong prima facie case). And the question of at least modifying *Cyanamid* to protect freedom of speech has also risen in respect of other causes of action such as, eg breach of contract: *Cambridge Nutrition Ltd v BBC* [1990] 3 All ER 523; *Secretary of State for the Home Department v Central Broadcasting Ltd* [1993] EMLR 253.

Griffiths LJ said in *Herbage v Pressdram Ltd*,[13] *American Cyanamid* would represent 'a very considerable incursion into ... [principles] based on freedom of speech'.[14] Indeed Martin has argued that interim injunctions for defamation are such an infringement of free speech that they should never be granted. 'If we are committed to the widest possible freedom of discourse on matters of public concern, the jurisdiction to make interlocutory injunctions, this undesirable judicial censorship, cannot on principle be accepted.'[15] Although put forward in respect of Canadian law, the argument is equally applicable here. But it seems to go too far, for the case against the defendant may be clear-cut and indisputable even at the interim stage. Nevertheless the argument does serve to highlight the importance of not weakening the test for interim injunctions in defamation cases, and thereby supports the courts' rejection of *American Cyanamid* in this context.

As regards freedom of expression protected under the Human Rights Act 1998, the position on interim injunctions has been specifically dealt with in s 12(3) of that Act. According to this, a court shall not grant an interim injunction restraining publication before trial, where this might affect the exercise of the Convention right to freedom of expression, 'unless the court is satisfied that the applicant is likely to establish that publication shall not be allowed.' This appears to be in line with the common law approach to defamation that has been set out above and constitutes a legislative departure from *American Cyanamid*. In *Cream Holdings Ltd v Banerjee*[16] the Court of Appeal, in upholding the grant of an interim injunction to restrain a breach of confidence, laid down that 'likely' in s 12(3) means that there must be a 'real prospect of success, convincingly established.' This was said to be a lower threshold for a claimant to cross, in order to be granted an interim injunction, than having to show that it was 'more probable than not' that an injunction would be granted at trial; but it was a higher threshold than the *American Cyanamid* test of there being a serious issue to be tried.

(d) Little factual or legal dispute

Some judges, like Walton J in *Athletes Foot Marketing Associates Inc v Cobra Sports Ltd*[17] and Bridge LJ in *Office Overload Ltd v Gunn*,[18] have recognised a

---

13 [1984] 1 WLR 1160.
14 [1984] 1 WLR 1160 at 1163.
15 'Interlocutory Injunctions in Libel Actions' (1982) 20 UWOLR 129, 140.
16 [2003] EWCA Civ 103, [2003] Ch 650, at paras 12, 83–86.
17 [1980] RPC 343.
18 [1977] FSR 39. Bridge LJ's approach was approved by the Court of Appeal in *Lawrence David Ltd v Ashton* [1991] 1 All ER 385 at 393, 396.

further wide-ranging exception, namely that *American Cyanamid* does not apply where there is little dispute on the facts and the law is not difficult.[19] This should be supported, for Lord Diplock's reasoning – that there should be no mini-trials on inadequate evidence and argument – is inapplicable to such a case. In similar vein, Sir John Pennycuick in *Fellowes v Fisher*[20] thought that it was particularly in cases 'depending in whole or in great part upon the construction of a written instrument'[1] that the prospect of success was within the competence of the judge hearing the interim application; and in *Official Custodian for Charities v Mackey*,[2] Scott J thought *American Cyanamid* inapplicable where there was no arguable defence to the claim. Particularly radical was the Court of Appeal's view in *Bradford City Metropolitan Council v Brown*[3] that *Cyanamid* was essentially concerned only with factual as opposed to legal disputes.

In *Series 5 Software v Clarke*[4] Laddie J built upon the idea, that the strength of the parties' cases on the facts or the law can usually be easily determined at the interim stage, to put forward a radical reinterpretation of *American Cyanamid*. According to this, the courts can always take into account any view that they can easily reach as to the relative strength of the parties' cases. The *Cyanamid* prohibition on examining the strength of the parties' cases therefore only applies where there are complex issues of disputed fact or law. In line with this, Laddie J controversially argued that *American Cyanamid* had not intended to change the traditional basis upon which courts had proceeded in relation to interim injunctions. He said,

'Lord Diplock did not intend ... to exclude consideration of the strength of the cases in most applications for interlocutory relief. It appears to me that what is intended is that the court should not attempt to resolve difficult issues of fact or law on an application for interlocutory relief. If, on the other hand, the court is able to come to a view as to the strength of the parties' cases on the credible evidence, then it can do so. In fact, as any lawyer who has experience of interlocutory proceedings will know, it is frequently the case that it is easy to determine who is most likely to win the trial on the basis of the affidavit evidence and any exhibited contemporaneous documents. If it is apparent from the material that one party's case is much stronger than the other's then that is a matter the court should not ignore. To suggest otherwise would be to exclude from consideration an important factor ...'[5]

---

19   The validity of this exception was left open in *Alfred Dunhill v Sunoptic* [1979] FSR 337.
20   [1976] QB 122.
1   [1976] QB 122 at 141.
2   [1985] Ch 168. See also *Attorney-General v Barker* [1990] 3 All ER 257 at 262 (per Nourse LJ).
3   (1986) 19 HLR 16. This derives some support from the reasoning of Lords Jauncey and Bridge in *R v Secretary of State for Transport, ex p Factortame (No 2)* [1991] 1 AC 603.
4   [1996] 1 All ER 853.
5   [1996] 1 All ER 853 at 865.

Despite its merits, Laddie J's reinterpretation has not overtly found favour in subsequent decisions. Rather, as Laddie J himself commented in relation to the approach of the courts prior to his decision, the courts have continued to exercise their discretion in this area 'by paying lip-service to the guidance given in *American Cyanamid* while in practice applying different criteria.'[6]

(5) An alternative approach

The present law on interim injunctions can most helpfully be summed up by saying that, while the approach in *American Cyanamid* is, on the face of it, that generally followed, there are extensive exceptions where the old law, or something very similar, is applied.

While this is a workable compromise, it is submitted that the criticisms made of *American Cyanamid* are valid and that the old law was preferable. But having said that – and this is the positive aspect of *American Cyanamid* – the old law could produce injustice to a claimant who failed to satisfy the initial prima facie test. To overcome this, the ideal solution would be to revert to the old law, with its emphasis on the strength of the claimant's case, but with the qualification that, if the action for an injunction is likely to go to trial, a claimant who can merely show an arguable case, should still be granted an interim injunction if the balance of convenience is overwhelmingly in the claimant's favour.[7]

(6) Special types of interim injunction

(a) Interim mandatory injunction

It has been consistently stressed that the courts are particularly reluctant to grant an interim mandatory injunction, a reluctance which reflects the fact that, while a final mandatory injunction is more drastic than a prohibitory one, an interim mandatory injunction is doubly drastic, being granted where the court cannot be sure of the merits of the dispute. In *Gale v Abbott*,[8] for example, it was said that an application for an interim mandatory injunction was '... one of the rarest cases that occurs, for the court will not compel a man to do so serious a thing as to undo what he has done, except at the hearing.'[9] Cohen LJ in *Canadian*

---

6   [1996] 1 All ER 853 at 857.
7   For other approaches, see Sharpe *Injunctions and Specific Performance* (3rd edn, 2000) paras 2.370–2.380; Leubsdorf 'The Standard for Preliminary Injunctions' (1978) 91 Harv LR 525.
8   (1862) 6 LT 852.
9   (1862) 6 LT 852 at 854.

Pacific Rly v Gaud[10] thought that an interim mandatory injunction was a 'very exceptional form of relief',[11] and this reluctance has again been stressed in more recent cases.[12]

This is not to say that such an injunction is never granted.[13] In particular, and seemingly reflecting a punitive approach,[14] an interim mandatory injunction has been ordered to undo an alleged tort because the defendant has tried to 'steal a march' on the claimant by, for example, speeding up building work allegedly interfering with the claimant's light so as to have the building completed before a pending court hearing.[15]

Furthermore, there is perhaps not the same reluctance to grant an interim mandatory injunction enforcing a positive contractual obligation. In this context, the interim mandatory injunction performs the role which, at trial, is performed by specific performance rather than by a final mandatory injunction. It is therefore apt to view the interim mandatory injunction as temporary specific performance. It has fairly recently been confirmed by the Court of Appeal in *Astro Exito Navegacion SA v Southland Enterprise Co Ltd, The Messiniaki Tolmi*,[16] that there is indeed jurisdiction to grant an interim mandatory injunction amounting to temporary specific performance: and in that case, which concerned the sale of a ship, such an injunction was granted ordering the defendants to comply with their contractual obligations by instructing their bank to release the purchase price before their letters of credit expired. To support its view on jurisdiction, the Court of Appeal referred to *Smith v Peters*,[17] where an interim mandatory injunction had been granted ordering the vendor of a house, in accordance with the contract of sale, to allow a named third party to make a valuation of the fixtures and fittings. Not cited, but just as relevant, is the well-known case of *Sky*

---

10 [1949] 2 KB 239.
11 [1949] 2 KB 239 at 249.
12 *Shepherd Homes Ltd v Sandham* (1971] Ch 340; *Hounslow London Borough Council v Twickenham Garden Developments Ltd* [1971] Ch 233; *Shotton v Hammond* (1976) 120 Sol Jo 780; *John Trenberth Ltd v National Westminster Bank Ltd* (1980) 39 P & CR 104; *Taylor and Foulstone v NUM* (1984] IRLR 445; *Locabail International Finance Ltd v Agroexport* [1986] 1 WLR 657; *Leisure Data v Bell* [1988] FSR 367, CA; *Jakeman v South West Thames RHA* [1990] IRLR 62; *Moran v University of Salford (No 2)* [1994] ELR 187, CA.
13 See, eg the injunctions ordering withdrawals of strike notices, which gave rise to contempt proceedings in *Express Newspapers plc v Mitchell* [1982] IRLR 465; *Austin Rover Group Ltd v Amalgamated Union of Engineering Workers* [1985] IRLR 162.
14 Sharpe *Injunctions and Specific Performance* (3rd edn) para 2.650.
15 *Daniel v Ferguson* [1891] 2 Ch 27; *Von Joel v Hornsey* [1895] 2 Ch 774. See also *Esso Petroleum Co Ltd v Kingswood Motors Ltd* [1974] QB 142.
16 [1982] QB 1248.
17 (1875) LR 20 Eq 511.

Petroleum Ltd v VIP Petroleum Ltd[18] where an interim injunction was granted, restraining the defendants from withholding supplies of petrol to the claimants' filling stations. Although the form of the injunction was prohibitory, it was mandatory in substance, as Goulding J's judgment recognises, and amounted to temporary specific performance of the defendants' contract to supply all the petrol required by the claimants.

Prior to *American Cyanamid v Ethicon* the judicial reluctance to award interim mandatory injunctions was often reflected by insisting, as a first requirement, that the claimant should show a strong or very strong prima facie case.[19] Lord Diplock in *American Cyanamid* can be taken to have disapproved of such a requirement because, although he did not expressly refer to mandatory injunctions, his reasoning criticising mini-trials at the interim stage appears to have been directed to all interim injunctions. However, as the balance of convenience will almost always be against granting a mandatory injunction – since to order the defendant to take positive action, particularly where restorative, is usually more of a hardship to him than the claimant's interim hardship – application of the *American Cyanamid* approach would be unlikely to lead to such injunctions being more readily granted.

However, it would appear that the courts continue to apply the pre-*Cyanamid* approach to interim mandatory injunctions on the ground that they are exceptional injunctions not covered by *American Cyanamid*.[20] That this should be so was expressly stated by the Court of Appeal in *Locabail International Finance Ltd v Agroexport*,[1] which was followed by Auld J in *Jakeman v South West Thames Regional Health Authority*.[2]

18 [1974] 1 WLR 576. Other examples are *Luganda v Service Hotels Ltd* [1969] 2 Ch 209; *Texaco Ltd v Mulberry Filling Station Ltd* [1972] 1 WLR 814; *Shotton v Hammond* (1976) 120 Sol Jo 780; *Peninsular Maritime Ltd v Padseal Ltd* (1981) 259 Estates Gazette 860; *Taylor v NUM* [1984] IRLR 445; *Parker v Camden London Borough Council* [1985] 2 All ER 141; *Land Rover Group Ltd v UPF (UK) Ltd* [2002] EWHC (QB) 3183, [2003] 2 BCLC 222.

19 *Hounslow London Borough Council v Twickenham Garden Developments Ltd* [1971] Ch 233; *Esso Petroleum Co Ltd v Kingswood Motors Ltd* [1974] QB 142. It should be remembered that when considering the availability of a final order in deciding whether to grant an interim mandatory injunction enforcing positive contractual obligations – ie in deciding whether there is a strong prima facie case (or, on *American Cyanamid*, a serious question to be tried) – the relevant principles are those of specific performance.

20 Indeed since granting the injunction will almost invariably finally resolve the claim without a trial, the exception discussed above, pp 555–557, is applicable.

1 [1986] 1 All ER 901. See also *De Falco v Crawley Borough Council* [1980] QB 460 at 481 (per Bridge LJ); *Leisure Data v Bell* [1988] FSR 367; *R v Kensington and Chelsea Royal London Borough Council, ex p Hammell* [1989] QB 518. Contra are *Meade v London Borough of Haringey* [1979] 1 WLR 637 at 657–658 (per Sir Stanley Rees); *Peninsular Maritime Ltd v Padseal Ltd* (1981) 259 Estates Gazette 860 at 868 (per Stephenson LJ).

2 [1990] IRLR 62.

A slightly different approach was taken by Hoffmann J in *Films Rover International Ltd v Cannon Film Sales Ltd.*[3] He considered that the basic question was not so much whether the injunction sought was prohibitory or mandatory but whether the injustice to the defendant if the application were granted and the claimant subsequently failed at the trial would outweigh the injustice to the claimant if the application were refused and he subsequently succeeded at the trial. And while he appeared to view *American Cyanamid* as inapplicable to mandatory injunctions he regarded the Court of Appeal's insistence in *Locabail* on a strong case for an interim mandatory injunction as merely laying down a guideline rather than a rule, which reflected the fact that mandatory injunctions, if granted at an interim stage, *generally* create greater risks of injustice to the defendant in the manner described than prohibitory injunctions. Applying that approach, Hoffmann J granted an interim mandatory injunction, enforcing a contractual obligation, even though the claimant could not establish a strong prima facie case.

Subsequently in *Nottingham Building Society v Eurodynamics Systems*[4] Chadwick J has clarified Hoffmann J's approach in a four point formulation that has been approved by the Court of Appeal in *Zockoll Group Ltd v Mercury Communications Ltd*[5] 'as being all the citation that should in future be necessary'. Chadwick J's four-point formulation was as follows:

> 'First, the overriding consideration, as for all interim injunctions, is which course is likely to involve the least risk of injustice if it turns out to be "wrong". Secondly, in considering whether to grant a mandatory injunction, the court must keep in mind that an order which requires a party to take some positive step at an interlocutory stage, may well carry a greater risk of injustice if it turns out to have been wrongly made than an order which merely prohibits action, thereby preserving the status quo. Thirdly, it is legitimate, where a mandatory injunction is sought, to consider whether the court does feel a high degree of assurance that the plaintiff will be able to establish his right at a trial. That is because the greater the degree of assurance the plaintiff will ultimately establish his right, the less will be the risk of injustice if the injunction is granted. But, finally, even where the court is unable to feel any high degree of assurance that the plaintiff will establish his right, there may still be circumstances in which it is appropriate to grant a mandatory injunction at an interlocutory stage. Those circumstances will exist where the risk of injustice if this injunction is refused sufficiently outweigh the risk of injustice if it is granted.'

---

3   [1986] 3 All ER 772. This is supported by *Meagher, Gummow & Lehane's Equity: Doctrines and Remedies* (4th edn, 2002) para 21–395.
4   [1993] FSR 468 at 474.
5   [1998] FSR 354 at 366.

In the *Nottingham Building Society* case itself, the interim remedy sought, and granted, ordered the delivery up of computer software in a case where Chadwick J was satisfied, with a high degree of assurance, that the claimant would succeed at trial.[6] In the *Zockoll* case an interim mandatory injunction requiring performance of a contractual obligation was refused.

(b) 'Without notice' injunction[7]

An interim injunction can be granted without notice of the application having been given to the defendant so that it has had no opportunity to be heard. Normally a 'without notice' injunction lasts until a named day (ie it is an interim injunction) when an application on notice can be made. Nowadays the most common 'without notice' injunctions are freezing injunctions and search orders,[8] which are governed by their own special principles.

But to justify an ordinary 'without notice' injunction the claimant, in addition to satisfying the usual requirements for an interim injunction, will need to establish that there are good reasons (most obviously, that the matter is one of urgency) for not giving notice.[9] Delay, whereby an opportunity to apply on notice has been unjustifiably lost, will bar a 'without notice' injunction. In *Bates v Lord Hailsham*,[10] for example, the claimant applied, without notice, for an injunction at 2 pm to prevent a committee, due to meet at 4.30 pm, from making an order concerning the abolition of solicitors' scale fees. The injunction was refused because the claimant had known of the meeting for some weeks and had had ample opportunity to make an application on notice. A further requirement of a 'without notice' application is that the claimant should act in good faith by disclosing all relevant facts to the court, including those prejudicial to its case, and failure to do so will lead to the injunction being discharged.[11]

An important additional restriction is imposed by statute on the power to grant 'without notice' injunctions in industrial disputes. By the Trade Union and Labour Relations (Consolidation) Act 1992, s 221(1), no injunction shall be granted against a defendant who is absent and is likely to raise the defence that he was acting in contemplation or furtherance of

---

6   Although not mentioned, it would appear that the order fell within the Torts (Interference with Goods) Act 1977, s 4: see below, pp 581–582.
7   Formerly called an 'ex parte' injunction.
8   Below, pp 568–569.
9   CPR 25.3, 25 PD.4.
10 [1972] 1 WLR 1373.
11 *R v Kensington Income Tax General Comrs* [1917] 1 KB 486; *Beese v Woodhouse* [1970] 1 WLR 586. Presumably there will usually also be a costs penalty.

a trade dispute unless all reasonable steps have been taken to give that person notice and an opportunity to be heard. In practice claimants appear to give, and courts accept as sufficient, about 24 hours' notice.

(c) Freezing injunction

A freezing injunction is what was previously known as a *Mareva* injunction.[12] This is an interim[13] prohibitory injunction, which is almost always granted without notice and usually restrains a person from removing assets from the jurisdiction or otherwise disposing of assets within the jurisdiction. In rare circumstances it may also extend to restraining the defendant from dealing with its assets outside the jurisdiction (so-called 'world-wide freezing injunctions'). Regarded by Lord Denning as 'the greatest piece of judicial law reform in my time',[14] the freezing injunction has the purpose of preventing a defendant frustrating the satisfaction of a monetary judgment that the claimant may get against it. Typically it leads to the freezing of a person's bank accounts. The injunction is governed by its own special principles, developed in the case law, and *American Cyanamid v Ethicon* does not apply. As it is designed to ensure that monetary remedies can be effective, rather than itself being a remedy for torts or breach of contract,[15] the freezing injunction lies outside the scope of this book, and no further consideration will be given to it.[16]

(d) Search order

A search order is what was previously known as an *Anton Piller* order.[17] The power of the High Court to grant such an order has been placed on a firm statutory footing by section 7 of the Civil Procedure Act 1997. It was described by Donaldson LJ as 'one of the law's two nuclear weapons',[18] the other being the freezing injunction. A search order is an interim mandatory injunction, which is almost invariably granted without notice and usually orders the defendant to allow the claimant to

---

12 Named after *Mareva Cia Naviera SA v International Bulkcarriers SA* [1975] 2 Lloyd's Rep 509. The new terminology is that laid down in CPR 25.1(1)(f).
13 This can include an injunction granted after final judgment, see above, p 513, n 18.
14 *The Due Process of Law* (1980) p 134.
15 It may also be granted in other contexts, eg family law.
16 Ie it assists enforcement. Hence it is best viewed alongside that large body of law dealing with the enforcement of monetary judgments. For detailed consideration of freezing injunctions, see Gee *Commercial Injunctions* (5th edn, 2004); *Clerk and Lindsell on Torts* (18th edn, 2000) paras 30–38–30–49. Neither a freezing injunction nor a search order can generally be ordered by a county court: County Court Remedies Regulations 1991, SI 1991/1222.
17 Named after *Anton Piller KG v Manufacturing Processes Ltd* [1976] Ch 55. The new terminology is that laid down in CPR 25.1(1)(h).
18 *Bank Mellat v Nikpour* [1982] Com LR 158 at 159.

enter its premises for the purposes of searching for, inspecting and seizing property infringing the claimant's rights or documents relevant to the claim against the defendant. It is given where speed and secrecy are vital to prevent the destruction or disposal of such property or documents. While developed to deal with cases involving intellectual property, a search order has been granted in other contexts such as matrimonial[19] and ordinary commercial cases.[20] Special principles have been formulated to govern search orders and *Cyanamid* does not apply.

Like the freezing injunction, the search order is best regarded as outside this book's scope. Primarily it is a means of ensuring that essential evidence is not destroyed. In this role it most obviously belongs alongside orders of specific disclosure and inspection,[1] and is a means by which the claimant is enabled to prove its case.[2] A subsidiary function is to preserve goods[3] that are likely to be the subject matter of an action brought by the claimant and are endangered. In this, the search order is like a preservation order made under CPR 25.1(c)(i),[4] and is most sensibly viewed as seeking to ensure that subsequent remedies gained in relation to those goods can be effective.[5]

6. THE CLAIMANT'S CONDUCT AS A BAR TO AN INJUNCTION

It has been considered convenient to discuss this as a separate head, since the six doctrines encompassed, apply whether the injunction is final or interim, prohibitory or mandatory, *quia timet* or not *quia timet*.

---

19 *Emanuel v Emanuel* [1982] 1 WLR 669.
20 *Yousif v Salama* [1980] 1 WLR 1540.
1   [1980] 1 WLR 1540 at 1543 (per Donaldson LJ); *Rank Film Distributors Ltd v Video Information Centre* [1982] AC 380.
2   Above, pp 3–4.
3   Hence an undertaking has to be given that articles obtained will be retained by the claimant's solicitors in safe custody – *Universal City Studios Inc v Mukhtar & Sons Ltd* [1976] 1 WLR 568.
4   Or an interim injunction to preserve property ordered under the courts' general jurisdiction to grant injunctions. See *Redler Grain Silos v BICC Ltd* [1982] 1 Lloyd's Rep 435; *Polly Peck International plc v Nadir (No 2)* [1992] 4 All ER 769; Sharpe *Injunctions and Specific Performance* (3rd edn) paras 2.700–2.710.
5   It therefore assists enforcement – above, p 568, n 16. Contrast interim delivery up *to the claimant*, below, ch 22. For general consideration of search orders, see Gee *Commercial Injunctions* (5th edn, 2004); *Clerk and Lindsell on Torts* (18th edn, 2000) paras 30–27–30–37.

(1) Serious breach of contract

A good example here is *Telegraph Despatch and Intelligence Co v McLean*,[6] where a prohibitory injunction to restrain a defendant from transmitting news in breach of covenant was refused, because the claimants were themselves in serious[7] breach of their contract with the defendant by selling the news-agency business. However, it may be doubted whether a defendant now needs to rely on this equitable defence since it can simply terminate for breach and may thereby also escape liability for damages.[8]

(2) He who comes to equity must come with clean hands

This is a wide-ranging doctrine,[9] whereby the court may refuse an injunction, where it considers that the claimant's past conduct, as revealed by the facts of the dispute, has been so improper that he does not deserve to be helped by the court's granting of an injunction. Clearly such conduct can take many forms. In *Hubbard v Vosper*[10] Megaw LJ considered that scientologists should be denied an interim injunction restraining publication of defamatory articles because of their own deplorable activities and beliefs; and in *Tollemache & Cobbold Breweries Ltd v Reynolds*,[11] no mandatory injunction ordering the removal of eaves trespassing into the claimant's air-space was granted because, inter alia, the claimant had acted pettily throughout.

On the other hand, in *Duchess of Argyll v Duke of Argyll*,[12] the claimant's own adultery and her own articles revealing some secrets of her former marriage did not prevent her from gaining an interim injunction on the basis of breach of confidence, to restrain her ex-husband publishing in a Sunday newspaper an account of her private life during their marriage. In an important statement, Ungoed-Thomas J said, 'A person coming to Equity for relief ... must come with clean hands: but the cleanliness required is to be judged in relation to the relief that is sought.'[13] This emphasises that the 'clean hands' doctrine is a relative one, by which an

---

6   (1873) 8 Ch App 658. See also *Goddard v Midland Rly Co* (1891) 8 TLR 126; *Litvinoff v Kent* (1918) 34 TLR 298.
7   The breach was not serious enough to bar the injunction in *Western v MacDermott* (1866) 2 Ch App 72; *Chitty v Bray* (1883) 48 LT 860; *Meredith v Wilson* (1893) 69 LT 336; *Hooper v Bromet* (1903) 90 LT 234.
8   Eg *General Billposting v Atkinson* [1909] AC 118.
9   For general discussion see Chafee 'Coming into Equity with Clean Hands' (1948–9) 47 Mich LR 877, 1065.
10   [1972] 2 QB 84.
11   (1983) 268 Estates Gazette 52.
12   [1967] Ch 302. See also *Grobbelaar v News Group Newspapers Ltd* [2002] UKHL 40, [2002] 1 WLR 3024.
13   [1967] Ch 302 at 332.

injunction will still be granted to someone whose conduct has been improper, if the defendant's conduct was that much worse.

(3) He who seeks equity must do equity

This maxim is similar to that requiring 'clean hands', but looks to the claimant's future rather than past conduct so that, by it, a claimant will not be granted an injunction against the defendant, unless he is prepared to do what is fair and right in relation to the defendant. With regard to breach of contract, for example, a claimant will be refused an injunction, unless he is ready and willing to perform his own obligations to the defendant. The classic authority is *Measures Bros Ltd v Measures*,[14] where it was held that employers, who had wrongfully repudiated an employee's contract,[15] could not enforce that employee's restrictive trading covenant because, inter alia, they were unwilling and unable to perform their side of the contract in the future.

(4) Acquiescence

In relation to equitable remedies for wrongs,[16] the defence of acquiescence requires that the claimant, actively or passively, has represented to the defendant that he has no objection to the defendant doing what amounts to a wrong against him and that the defendant has acted to its detriment in that belief.[17] Before the claimant can be said to acquiesce, he must be aware of the facts relevant to his remedy.[18]

In the leading case of *Shaw v Applegate*[19] the defendant had partly used his property for an amusement arcade in breach of a restrictive covenant with the claimant. The claimant had made no complaints about this for six years, although he knew about it, and in consequence the defendant had gone on to buy and install more amusement machinery. The Court

---

14   [1910] 2 Ch 248. *Shell UK Ltd v Lostock Garage Ltd* [1976] 1 WLR 1187 at 1199 (per Lord Denning); *Agricultural Supplies Ltd v Rushmere* [1967] 3 KIR 55.

15   Presumably, the employee could have terminated for breach, rather than relying on the equitable defence.

16   There should be no difference in approach whether the wrong be legal or equitable – *Habib Bank Ltd v Habib Bank AG Zurich* [1981] 1 WLR 1265. Acquiescence, often alternatively referred to as equitable estoppel, may also bar the claimant's strict rights, and indeed create new rights, in situations where there is no question of wrongdoing by the defendant: eg *Willmott v Barber* (1880) 15 Ch D 96; *Crabb v Arun District Council* [1976] Ch 179; *Taylor Fashions Ltd v Liverpool Victoria Trustees Co Ltd* [1981] 1 All ER 897.

17   *Bulmer Ltd and Showerings Ltd v Bollinger SA* [1977] 2 CMLR 625 at 682 (per Goff LJ). See also *Electrolux Ltd v Electrix Ltd* (1953) 71 RPC 23 at 34 (per Lord Evershed MR); *Habib Bank Ltd v Habib Bank AG Zurich* [1981] 1 WLR 1265 at 1284–1285 (per Oliver LJ); *Jones v Stones* [1999] 1 WLR 1739, CA (no acquiescence established).

18   *Re Howlett* [1949] Ch 767, 775.

19   [1977] 1 WLR 970.

of Appeal held that acquiescence barred the claim for a prohibitory and mandatory injunction. But damages in lieu were awarded, thereby showing that acquiescence can be a slightly wider defence for an injunction than for damages.[20]

In other cases, however, both an injunction and equitable damages have been barred. For example, in *Sayers v Collyer,*[1] where the defendant had broken a restrictive covenant not to use premises as a shop, but the claimant had turned a blind eye to this for three years, no damages, let alone an injunction, were awarded. Similarly in *Habib Bank Ltd* v *Habib Bank AG Zurich*[2] the claimant bank sought an injunction to restrain the defendants from passing off their business as the claimant's. It was held that the tort had not been made out, since there had been no misrepresentation: but even if it had been, the injunction (and presumably, although not mentioned, equitable damages) would be barred by acquiescence, constituted by the claimant's predecessors having worked closely with the defendants and having helped them to set up their bank. As Oliver LJ said, 'One's initial reaction looking at the history of the matter is that there could hardly be a plainer case of acquiescence than this.'[3]

It should be realised that acquiescence may operate not merely to bar equitable remedies, but also to extinguish the defendant's liability, so that no common law remedies are available either. In a case such as *Shaw v Applegate,* it was indicated that a higher degree of acquiescence amounting to dishonesty or unconscionability[4] would be required to extinguish liability and hence common law remedies. But such a distinction lacks any sensible rationale.[5] The preferable approach is that a lesser degree of acquiescence may bar an injunction than will bar damages, whether they are equitable or common law.

Finally in *Johnson v Wyatt,*[6] it was said that the defence of acquiescence is more likely to apply as a bar to an interim than a final injunction. In particular, this follows because a shorter period of acquiescence will suffice.

20   *Sayers v Collyer* (1884) 28 Ch D 103 at 110 (Fry J).
1   (1884) 28 Ch D 103. See similarly *Gafford v Graham* [1999] 3 EGLR 75, CA.
2   [1981] 1 WLR 1265.
3   [1981] 1 WLR 1265 at 1283.
4   [1977] 1 WLR 970 at 978 (per Buckley LJ); *Bulmer v Bollinger* [1977] 2 CMLR 625 at 681 (per Goff LJ).
5   Arguably, *Habib* supports this criticism, although there it was the distinction between legal and equitable *rights*, that was regarded as 'archaic and arcane'. See, similarly, *Gafford v Graham* [1999] 3 EGLR 75, CA.
6   (1863) 2 De GJ & Sm 18.

(5) Laches

(a) Final injunction

By the Limitation Act 1980, s 36(1), the usual six-year limitation period for torts or breach of contract does not apply directly to injunctions and it is unclear whether it applies 'by analogy' under the proviso to s 36(1).[7]

But what is clear is that the defendant may establish that the claimant is barred from an injunction under the doctrine of laches.[8] This doctrine applies where the delay by the claimant in seeking a remedy is such that it would be unjust to grant that remedy. While laches has often not been separated from acquiescence, as a distinct doctrine it lays down when delay by the claimant in seeking an equitable remedy will bar that remedy, other than where acquiescence can be made out. The essential difference is that it is not necessary for laches, as distinct from acquiescence, that there has been a representation by the claimant: pure delay, not constituting a representation, counts under the doctrine of laches but not acquiescence. But as with acquiescence, the claimant must have sufficient knowledge of the facts relevant to his remedy before laches can deprive him of a remedy.[9]

In the past it has sometimes been suggested that laches is not a sufficient bar to an injunction, and that the additional requirements of acquiescence are necessary.[10] This, however, has been departed from in more recent cases such as *Cluett Peabody & Co Inc v McIntyre Hogg Marsh & Co Ltd*[11] and *HP Bulmer Ltd v J Bollinger SA*,[12] where 'inordinate delay'[13] has been regarded as a bar in itself. In *Cluett Peabody* Upjohn J considered that a delay of 29 years from when the claimants first knew that the defendants were using their trade mark barred an injunction restraining the continued infringement of that trade mark. On the other hand, in the *Bollinger* case Goff LJ indicated that 16–17 years' delay in bringing an action in respect of a continuing passing off was not 'inordinate'.[14] One would expect that additional factors, such as consequential prejudice to

---

7   Under the Law Commission's proposals for reform, the standard limitation periods for breach of contract and torts (and equitable wrongs) would apply to claims for injunctions, albeit that the doctrine of laches (and acquiescence) would also apply within those periods: see *Limitation of Actions*, Law Commission Report No 270 (2001) paras 4.268–4.278 and Draft Bill, cl 34(2).
8   Limitation Act 1980, s 36(2).
9   *Lindsay Petroleum Company v Hurd* (1874) LR 5 PC 221.
10 *Fullwood v Fullwood* (1878) 9 Ch D 176.
11 [1958] RPC 335.
12 [1977] 2 CMLR 625.
13 [1977] 2 CMLR 625 at 681.
14 Also *Savile v Kilner* (1872) 26 LT 277 (20 years' delay no bar to injunction for continuing nuisance).

the defendant, will lead to a lesser delay being a sufficient bar (especially where the injunction sought is mandatory).[15]

(b) Interim injunction

What the court is here assessing is whether the claimant has delayed too long in seeking an *interim* injunction and hence much shorter periods of delay will bar this than would bar a final injunction. So in *Church of Scientology of California v Miller*[16] a delay of less than two months was held by the Court of Appeal to bar an interim injunction restraining an alleged breach of confidence; in *Legg v ILEA*[17] Megarry J came close to declining interlocutory injunctions because the claimants had been guilty of 12 weeks' delay; and in *Morecambe and Heysham Borough v Mecca Ltd*,[18] in refusing an interim injunction to prevent the defendants holding a beauty competition, Wilberforce J appears to have been influenced by the finding that the claimants knew of the relevant facts by about mid-December, but did not give notice of motion until April. Again, at the interim stage in *Bracewell v Appleby*,[19] Pennycuick V-C had refused an injunction preventing the defendants trespassing over the claimant's road to build a house, because of a few months' delay by the claimant. A four-month delay was also regarded as relevant by Megarry J in refusing an interim mandatory injunction in *Shepherd Homes Ltd v Sandham*.[20]

Even if the delay does not itself bar the interim injunction, one would expect it to be regarded as strong evidence that the interim harm to the claimant is not that serious, which is an important factor, particularly under *American Cyanamid*.

Where exactly delay (or acquiescence) fits within the *Cyanamid* principles is unclear. One might think that it would be applied separately, and would not be swallowed up in the balance of convenience. But this is not borne out in the cases.[1]

---

15 In *Ketley v Gooden* (1997) 73 P & CR 305 a delay of some 18 months, coupled with the fact that the damage to the claimant was relatively minor, led the Court of Appeal to refuse a mandatory restorative injunction.
16 (1987) Times, 23 October.
17 [1972] 1 WLR 1245.
18 [1962] RPC 145.
19 Referred to at trial by Graham J [1975] Ch 408 at 415. Unfortunately Graham J seemed to regard this as also relevant to the final injunction: contra is *Wrotham Park Estate Co v Parkside Homes Ltd* [1974] 1 WLR 798.
20 [1971] Ch 340.
1   Eg *Roussel-Uclaf v GD Searle & Co Ltd* [1977] FSR 125.

(6) Valid termination of the contract by the claimant

Where the claimant seeks an injunction to enforce negative or positive contractual obligations, that injunction is presumably barred where the claimant has chosen validly to terminate the contract. Although rarely discussed in relation to injunctions,[2] the law on this in relation to specific performance would seem to apply by analogy – once the contractual obligation has gone there is nothing to enforce.[3]

7. APPOINTMENT OF A RECEIVER

Although not an injunction, this seems the most appropriate place to consider the remedy of the appointment of a receiver (and manager) which goes beyond, but is analogous to, a mandatory enforcing injunction. That is, like a mandatory enforcing injunction the purpose behind appointing a receiver (and manager) as a remedy for a breach of contract or tort is to ensure that positive obligations are performed. This is achieved by the receiver himself performing the obligation or organising its performance.

In broad terms a receiver and manager is a person appointed to take in property (such as rents and profits), to recover property, and to carry on or superintend the business for which that property has been employed. There has long been an equitable jurisdiction to appoint a receiver and this power is now embodied in the Supreme Court Act 1981, s 37(1): 'The High Court may by order (whether interlocutory or final) ... appoint a receiver in all cases in which it appears to the court to be just and convenient to do so.' In the past such a power was hardly ever used to remedy a tort or breach of contract.[4] But some change may have been heralded by *Hart v Emelkirk Ltd*[5] and *Daiches v Bluelake Investments Ltd*.[6] In these two cases, receivers were appointed in interlocutory actions to collect rents and to organise the repair of flats, which defendant landlords had allowed to fall into a serious state of disrepair in breach of their repairing covenants. In the former, Goulding J said:

2   But this bar was implicitly accepted in *Thomas Marshall (Exports) Ltd v Guinle* [1979] Ch 227 at 239–243 (per Megarry V-C).
3   Above, pp 502–503. But this may well not bar a mandatory restorative injunction, which arguably does not depend on the continuing rather than past existence of the obligation.
4   Rare exceptions were *Riches v Owen* (1868) 3 Ch App 820; *Leney & Sons Ltd v Callingham and Thompson* [1908] 1 KB 79.
5   [1983] 1 WLR 1289.
6   (1985) 275 Estates Gazette 462.

'I know of no precedent for such relief, but I also know of no authority that forbids it under the provisions of ... the Supreme Court Act 1981, s 37 ... It clearly appears to me to be just to appoint a receiver in this case because it is done to support the enforcement by the court of covenants affecting property. It is also convenient because ... the properties are in a condition that demands urgent action.'[7]

That there is an unfettered jurisdiction to appoint a receiver (and manager) was confirmed in *Parker v Camden London Borough Council*[8] which also concerned a breach of repairing covenants. But the Court of Appeal there refused to exercise its discretion to make an appointment because it thought that, as the flats were mainly sheltered homes provided by the local authority for the elderly and infirm, an appointment would contravene Parliament's intention, under what is now the Housing Act 1985, s 21, that only a local authority should have responsibility for the management of such homes.

The appointment of a receiver (and manager) is clearly a convenient remedy to 'enforce' many continuing positive obligations, and it is therefore surprising that greater use has not been made of this remedy for breach of contract. Perhaps any judicial reluctance is explicable as resting on similar ideas to those underpinning the controversial constant supervision objection to specific performance.

---

7   [1983] 1 WLR 1289 at 1291.
8   [1986] Ch 162. See also *Evans v Clayhope Properties Ltd* [1988] 1 WLR 358 at 361 (although the actual decision was that the defendant could not be ordered at an interlocutory stage to meet the receiver and manager's expenses or remuneration).

Chapter 22

Delivery up

1. DELIVERY UP OF GOODS

(1) Introduction

This is the appropriate remedy for the claimant to recover its goods where the defendant is tortiously 'interfering' with them under the Torts (Interference with Goods) Act 1977. By the remedy the defendant is ordered to deliver the goods to, or to allow them to be taken by, the claimant. Delivery up therefore belongs alongside the mandatory restorative injunction as a remedy concerned to compel the undoing of a wrong.

Prior to 1854 the common law courts could not make such an order; the most they could do was to order the defendant to return the goods or pay their value at his option. This contrasted with the position in equity, where the Court of Chancery had power to grant delivery up of the claimant's goods, which it exercised where there was no adequate remedy at common law. By the Common Law Procedure Act 1854, s 78, the common law courts too were given the power to order delivery up, in any action for the detention of any chattel, without giving the defendant the option of paying its value and this is now embodied in the Torts (Interference with Goods) Act 1977. By the Torts (Interference with Goods) Act 1977, s 3, the following remedies are available in proceedings for wrongful interference against a person in possession or in control of the goods:

> '(a) an order for delivery of the goods and for payment of any consequential damages; or (b) an order for delivery of the goods, but giving the defendant the option of paying damages by reference to the value of the goods, together in either alternative with payment of any consequential damages; or (c) damages.'[1]

---

1   For the assessment of damages, see above, pp 248–251.

As the Act has abolished detinue, the actual torts for which delivery up can be ordered are conversion, as statutorily extended by the Torts (Interference with Goods) Act 1977, s 2(2), and trespass to goods.

(2) When will the courts order delivery up?

There is no reason to think that the Torts (Interference with Goods) Act 1977 has affected the principles governing when delivery up will be ordered. The primary principle, deriving from the remedy's roots in equity, is that delivery up will not be ordered if damages are adequate. At least if one puts the defendant's inability to pay (ie insolvency) to one side,[2] the same approach to adequacy has traditionally been adopted as for specific performance of a contract for the sale of goods and specific performance and delivery up are regarded as directly analogous remedies. For example in *Cohen v Roche*[3] McCardie J said, 'In my view, the power of the Court in an action of detinue rests upon a footing which fully accords with s 52 of the Sale of Goods Act 1893 ... The law is thus, I am glad to find, consistent in its several parts.' This also explains why cases dealing with delivery up for detinue are often used as authorities on specific performance.

In line with the approach to specific performance,[4] it can therefore be said that delivery up will not be ordered for most goods on the ground that damages will enable substitutes to be bought in the market. An extreme example is *Cohen v Roche* where delivery up was refused to a buyer of some Hepplewhite chairs (to whom property in the chairs had passed) because in McCardie J's view, citing Swinfen Eady MR's words in *William Whiteley Ltd v Hilt,*[5] '... the goods in question were ordinary articles of commerce and of no special value or interest.'[6] Again, therefore, the uniqueness of the goods is the most crucial concept in judging adequacy.

There are several excellent examples of the Court of Chancery ordering the delivery up of physically unique goods – that is, of goods possessing significant physical characteristics that very few, if any, other goods have. In *Pusey v Pusey*[7] it was the Pusey horn that was ordered to be delivered up; in *Somerset (Duke) v Cookson*[8] it was an antique altarpiece; in

---

2   See below, pp 579–580
3   [1927] 1 KB 169 at 180–181.
4   Above, ch 20.
5   [1918] 2 KB 808 at 819.
6   [1927] 1 KB 169 at 181.
7   (1684) 1 Vern 273.
8   (1735) 3 P Wms 390.

Fells v Read[9] some ceremonial ornaments; in *Lowther v Lowther*[10] a painting by Titian; and in *Earl of Macclesfield v Davies*[11] an order was made allowing the inspection of an iron-chest on the assumption that if it contained certain heirlooms they must be delivered up.

Goods may also be ordered to be delivered up, if they are commercially unique – that is where, although the goods are not physically unique, buying substitutes would be so difficult or would cause such delay that the claimant's business would be seriously interrupted. So in *North v Great Northern Rly Co*[12] the commercial uniqueness of 54 coal waggons underlay the acceptance that they could be ordered to be delivered up. Sir John Stuart V-C said:

'There can be no doubt that ... the coal waggons were of special value to him in order to carry on his business. The sudden sale of these waggons, without which the trade could not be conducted, must necessarily have inflicted serious injury by the interruption of his trade ... It cannot be pretended that the plaintiff could have got on a sudden 54 other coal waggons fit for his business as readily and promptly as he could have purchased 54 tons of coal or 54 bushels of wheat.'[13]

Similarly, the even more drastic remedy of interim delivery up under the Torts (Interference with Goods) Act 1977, s 4, was recently ordered in respect of 500 tons of steel lying in railway depots in *Howard Perry & Co v British Rly Board*[14] because, in view of the steel strike then taking place, the claimants could not hope to acquire any other steel in the short term, and hence non-delivery up of their steel could cause substantial disruption to their business. Sir Robert Megarry V-C said:

'... at present steel is obtainable on the market only with great difficulty, if at all. If the equivalent of what is detained is unobtainable, how can it be said that damages are an adequate remedy? They plainly are not ... All that the plaintiffs are losing, said counsel for the defendants, is the sale of some steel, and damages will adequately compensate them for that. I do not think that this is by any means the whole picture. Damages would be a poor consolation if the failure of supplies forces a trader to lay off staff and disappoint his customers ... and ultimately forces him towards insolvency.'[15]

Although there are no direct authorities clarifying this point, it appears to be the case that the analogy between delivery up and specific performance breaks down where the defendant is unable to pay (ie is

9   (1796) 3 Ves 70.
10   (1806) 13 Ves 95.
11   (1814) 3 Ves & B 16.
12   (1860) 2 Giff 64. See also the Canadian case *Farwell v Walbridge* (1851) 2 Gr 332 (delivery up of
     sawlogs).
13   (1860) 2 Giff 64 at pp 68–69.
14   [1980] 1 WLR 1375.
15   [1980] 1 WLR 1375 at 1383.

insolvent). As we have seen, specific performance will not be ordered so as to overcome the defendant's insolvency (at least where other creditors would be prejudiced).[16] If an unsecured creditor could simply obtain specific performance where the defendant is insolvent, the distinction between secured and unsecured creditors would be eroded. In contrast, if property in goods is retained by a seller (where the purchaser has become insolvent)[17] or has passed to the purchaser (where the seller has become insolvent),[18] the 'owner' of the goods is able to avoid the insolvency. This is the most significant consequence of deciding whether property in goods has passed or not. The owner is assumed to be entitled 'to take his goods out' of the trustee in bankruptcy's or liquidator's possession so that they are removed from the assets that are available for distribution among the insolvent's creditors. This 'taking out of his goods' appears to mean[19] that, in a claim for wrongful interference where the tortfeasor is insolvent, the claimant is entitled to delivery up of his goods rather than being left to a (personal) remedy of damages for their value. In other words, in contrast to specific performance, it appears that delivery up will be ordered of non-unique goods because of the defendant's insolvency.

An interesting theoretical question is whether, even with the exception just explained, the analogy traditionally drawn with specific performance as regards adequacy is a sensible one. As is shown by the ease with which the adequacy hurdle is overcome in relation to prohibitory injunctions for the breach of a negative contractual promise, adequacy is an elastic concept and one might have thought that the wide view of adequacy adopted in relation to specific performance, which confines that remedy to a secondary role, would be inappropriate where the claim is for wrongful interference.[20] Certainly it seems surprising that if the defendant steals and keeps the claimant's (non-unique) goods the claimant has no prima facie civil right to recover them but must first overcome a substantial adequacy of damages hurdle. Nor, contrary to the fears of McCardie J in *Cohen v Roche*, would the law be inconsistent if delivery up were to be easier to obtain than specific performance, for the

---

16   Above, pp 467–468.

17   This was the issue in, eg *Wait and James v Midland Bank* (1926) 31 Com Cas 523 and *Cheetham v Thornham Spinning Co* [1964] 2 Lloyd's Rep 17.

18   This was the issue in, eg *Re Wait* [1927] 1 Ch 606 and *Carlos Federspiel & Co SA v Charles Twigg & Co Ltd* [1957] 1 Lloyd's Rep 240.

19   An alternative explanation, which has the merit of avoiding any 'inconsistency' between delivery up and specific performance but depends on an assumption as to how a trustee in bankruptcy or liquidator will act, is that, while the owner is merely entitled to damages, a trustee in bankruptcy or liquidator will in practice prefer to hand over the goods to the 'owner' rather than being held personally liable for wrongful interference with them.

20   Arguably the Consumer Credit Act 1974, s 100(5) supports delivery up being easier to obtain; on termination of a regulated hire-purchase or conditional sale agreement, delivery up of goods wrongly detained by the debtor must be ordered unless 'it would not be just to do so'.

basis of each is fundamentally different. The former rests on interference with an existing proprietary right whereas the latter is simply given for breach of promise.[1]

Even where damages are inadequate, delivery up may still be refused.[2] For example, given its equitable roots, the courts may deny the remedy, while granting damages, because of the claimant's conduct, such as his acquiescence or 'unclean hands'. Whether the normal six-year limitation period for tort actions laid down in the Limitation Act 1980, s 2 applies to delivery up is not entirely clear. But, in so far as delivery up is treated as 'equitable relief', s 36(1) lays down that, as with specific performance and injunctions, the normal time bar does not apply directly although it might be applied 'by analogy'. But if there is no statutory limitation period, laches presumably does apply. Like specific performance and injunctions, delivery up may also be ordered on terms, for example that the claimant compensates the defendant for improvements made to the goods.[3]

(3) Interim delivery up

So far (with the exception of the discussion on the *Howard Perry* case) it has been assumed that delivery up is sought at trial. But delivery up may also be granted pre-trial.

(a) Torts (Interference with Goods) Act 1977, s 4

By this, and by CPR 25.1(1)(e), the court is empowered to order the delivery up of goods which are or may become the subject matter of subsequent proceedings for tortious interference. The delivery is to be either to the claimant or to a person appointed by the court for the purpose. Where there are good reasons (for example, in cases of urgency) delivery up may be ordered on an application made without notice as with interim injunctions.

Delivery up to a person appointed by the court, like a preservation order under CPR 25.1(c)(i), is best viewed as outside the scope of this book, since it seeks to ensure that subsequent remedies in relation to those goods can be effective and therefore belongs alongside the law on

---

1   Admittedly the maxim that 'equity treats as done that which ought to be done' blurs this line between obligation and ownership. A claimant who will be granted specific performance of the transfer of land (or goods) is treated, in equity, as being the owner from the time the contract was made.

2   Delivery up cannot be ordered against the Crown – the Crown Proceedings Act 1947, s 21(1)(b).

3   As expressly laid down in the Torts (Interference with Goods) Act 1977, s 3(7).

the enforcement of remedies.[4] But interim delivery up to the claimant is a straightforward remedy for tortious interference. It is the equivalent of delivery up granted at trial under the Torts (Interference with Goods) Act 1977, s 3, and from the claimant's point of view has the advantage of being available quickly without waiting for trial. There has been little discussion of the principles governing such delivery up but one would expect them to be analogous to those governing interim mandatory injunctions: for example, the claimant should have to show a strong or very strong prima facie case and that the balance of convenience favours the remedy.[5] In *Howard Perry & Co v British Railways Board,*[6] which is the leading case on this remedy, Megarry V-C ordered interim delivery up of commercially unique steel kept in the defendant's yards, and stressed that there was no need to show a risk of the goods being disposed of, lost or destroyed. He also explained that the order for delivery up could and in this case would require the defendant to permit the claimants to collect the goods.

(b) Replevin

Replevin is an interlocutory procedure of ancient origin by which a defendant can be ordered to deliver up goods taken from the claimant. Theoretically replevin is available for any trespassory taking of the claimant's goods, but in practice it has been used only where the defendant has taken the goods by wrongful distress. The modern procedure is laid down in the County Courts Act 1984, Sch 1.[7] The claimant whose goods have been seized applies to the Registrar, who will order the goods to be 'replevied to that party' provided he gives security to cover, for example, the probable costs of the action and the alleged rent or damage in respect of which the distress has been made, and with a condition of the security being that he will prosecute the action without delay in a county court or the High Court.

Now that the Torts (Interference with Goods) Act 1977, s 4 provides for interim delivery up, it may be that delivery up in an action for

---

4   See analogously search orders, above, p 569.
5   Above, pp 563–567. There is support for this in *Adventure Film Productions Ltd v Tully* [1993] EMLR 376; and *Nottingham Building Society v Eurodynamics Systems* [1993] FSR 468, above, pp 566–567 (although the remedy in this case was treated simply as an interim mandatory injunction without there being any mention of interim delivery up under the Torts (Interference with Goods) Act 1977, s 4).
6   [1980] 1 WLR 1375. See also *Secretary of State for Defence v Guardian Newspapers Ltd* [1985] AC 339.
7   As amended by the Courts and Legal Services Act 1990.

replevin will wither away. Certainly the Law Reform Committee, upon whose report the Act was based, hoped that s 4 would 'pave the way for the abolition of replevin.'[8]

(4) The action for the recovery of land[9] – a contrast to delivery up of goods

This common law action enables a claimant to recover possession of its land by ordering the defendant to give up his possession. But interestingly it is not a remedy for the tort of trespass to land as such. So, unlike a claim for that tort, the action for the recovery of land (formerly known as the action for ejectment) is necessarily available to an owner who is out of possession. Moreover, it is available to a claimant who was out of possession at the time of the unauthorised entry without any need to rely on the fiction of trespass by relation. Further differences from tortious trespass are that by the Limitation Act 1980, s 15(1) the limitation period is twelve years rather than six, and that the action rests to a greater extent than does trespass on the claimant establishing good title so that, for example, *ius tertii*[10] appears to be a good defence.

All this serves to emphasise the important theoretical point that in contrast (and in some commentators' views,[11] in enlightened contrast) to delivery up of goods, this remedy has retained its identity as a remedy within the law of property without becoming dependent on wrongdoing by the defendant. It also follows that recovery of land falls outside the true scope of this book.

2.   DELIVERY UP FOR DESTRUCTION OR DESTRUCTION ON OATH

Where there has been a tortious infringement of intellectual property rights (whether by infringement of copyright,[12] patent,[13] trademark[14] or design)[15] the courts have an inherent jurisdiction to order the defendant to deliver up to the claimant or the court for destruction, or himself to destroy, articles made in infringement of the claimant's rights or even in

---

8   18th Report, Cmnd 4774, para 97.
9   Lawson *Remedies of English Law* (2nd edn, 1980) p 203.
10   'The right to possession is in a third party.'
11   See Weir *A Casebook on Tort* (9th edn, 2000) p 483.
12   *Mergenthaler Linotype Co v Intertype Co Ltd* (1926) 43 RPC 381.
13   *Paton Calvert & Co Ltd v Rosedale Associated Manufacturers Ltd* [1966] RPC 61.
14   *Slazenger & Sons v Feltham & Co* (1889) 6 RPC 531.
15   *Rosedale Associated Manufacturers Ltd v Airfix Products Ltd* [1956] RPC 360.

some cases[16] the means of making those articles. At first sight the function of these alternative equitable final remedies appears most closely allied to that of the mandatory restorative injunction since they generally compel the undoing of what has wrongfully been done. But as the claimant's principal concern is not with the mere continued existence of infringing material (that in itself causing him no harm) but is rather with the harmful *use* of that material, the primary function of the remedies is best viewed as being to prevent acts infringing the claimant's rights. As such the remedies go one step beyond, and protect the claimant even more effectively than, a prohibitory injunction. The classic judicial statement on the remedies' function is Russell J's in *Mergenthaler Linotype Co v Intertype Co Ltd.* [17] He said:

> '[The plaintiff] is protected as to further manufacture of infringing articles by the injunction which he obtains, but there remains this, that so long as there is still what I might call infringing stock in the possession of the infringer, he may be subject to too serious and grave a temptation and may therefore be tempted to commit a breach of the injunction which he would otherwise not commit. Accordingly, in order to assist the plaintiff and as a relief ancillary to the injunction he has obtained, the Court may in its discretion make an order for destruction or delivery up of infringing articles.'[18]

This passage also supports the view that there is no power to order destruction where a prohibitory injunction has not been granted. But of course just because such an injunction has been granted does not mean that the courts will exercise their power to order destruction. On the contrary there is always greater reluctance to grant positive than negative orders and the courts are also likely to be influenced by the hardship to the defendant and the waste of resources involved. Certainly if the claimant's rights can be effectively protected by ordering something less than full destruction, this will be preferred. For example, in *Slazenger & Sons v Feltham & Co*[19] the defendant was ordered merely to erase the claimant's trade mark from tennis racquets, rather than being ordered to destroy all racquets bearing the trade mark; and in *Rosedale Associated Manufacturers Ltd v Airfix Products Ltd,*[20] where buckets infringing the claimant's design and moulds and dies used for making those buckets were ordered to be destroyed, it was explained by Lloyd-Jacob J that, in

---

16 *Rosedale Associated Manufacturers Ltd v Airfix Products Ltd* (1956] RPC 360; *Wham-O Manufacturing Co v Lincoln Industries Ltd* [1982] RPC 281 at 318.
17 (1926) 43 RPC 381.
18 (1926) 43 RPC 381 at 382.
19 (1889) 6 RPC 531.
20 [1956] RPC 360.

respect of the moulds and dies, destruction meant '... a modification such as to render them inoperable to make an article of infringing shape.'[1]

When the courts will order delivery up for destruction as opposed to destruction on oath is unclear: but there is support for the view that the choice is essentially a matter for the defendant,[2] unless he has shown himself to be untrustworthy.[3]

It is important to emphasise that these remedies are granted even though the claimant does not own the articles ordered to be destroyed.[4] This is the key to avoiding confusion with the different remedy of delivery up of goods examined above. It follows that, while a claimant granted delivery up of goods belonging to him is entitled to do what he likes with that property, a claimant to whom delivery up for destruction is ordered ought to destroy that property. Unfortunately the distinction between these remedies is clouded by the tendency of judges, practitioners and academics alike,[5] to omit the words 'for destruction' after delivery up to a non-owner. Understanding of the true purpose of the destruction remedies would be further enhanced if delivery up for destruction was always ordered to be made to the court, rather than to the claimant.

Although these remedies are clearly ideally suited for the tortious infringement of intellectual property rights, there are other torts to which one would have thought they might be equally appropriate. The most obvious example is libel, for a claimant who has obtained an injunction would be even better protected by destruction (or erasing) of libellous material. The explanation for the present confinement of the remedies is presumably that the intellectual property torts had their roots in equity and these are equitable remedies. But this is clearly not a justification and it is suggested that, although they are drastic remedies, delivery up for destruction or destruction on oath could be usefully extended to other torts.

In relation to infringement of copyright and design right,[6] the Copyright, Designs and Patents Act 1988, ss 99 and 230 give the courts a specific statutory power (irrespective of the grant of an injunction) to

---

1   [1956] RPC 360 at 368.
2   *Paton Calvert & Co Ltd v Rosedale Associated Manufacturers Ltd* [1966] RPC 61.
3   *Industrial Furnaces Ltd v Reaves* [1970] RPC 605.
4   *Vivasseur v Krupp* (1878) 9 Ch D 351 at 360; *Chappell & Co Ltd v Columbia Gramophone Co* [1914] 2 Ch 745 at 756.
5   A notable exception is Forrai 'Confidential Information – A General Survey' (1971) 6 Syd LR 382, 391.
6   Analogous provisions apply to infringement of a person's performer's or recording rights by illicit recording: Copyright, Designs and Patents Act 1988, ss 195 and 204.

order delivery up of infringing copies or articles, or anything designed or adapted for making infringing copies or articles.[7] Moreover, while the courts may require the material delivered up to be destroyed they can also simply order it to be forfeited to the copyright or design right owner.[8] That represents a difference from the remedies available under the inherent equitable jurisdiction: delivery up and forfeiture to the copyright or design owner (of material that is owned by the defendant) may be regarded as occupying a mid-position between delivery up of (one's) goods and delivery up for destruction.[9]

---

7   The courts' inherent jurisdiction is unaffected: see the Copyright, Designs and Patents Act 1988, ss 99(4) and 230(7). By s 233(2) damages only can be awarded for innocent secondary infringement of a design right.

8   Copyright, Designs and Patents Act 1988, s 114 (copyright); s 231 (design right). In effect the same remedy was previously available for infringement of copyright under the Copyright Act 1956, s 18 (now repealed): the copyright owner was treated as the owner of infringing copies and plates used to make infringing copies and could therefore seek delivery up of (his) goods for the tort of conversion.

9   The primary function of delivery up and forfeiture is probably to compel the undoing of a wrong: cf above, p 584.

Part four

Declaring rights

Chapter 23

Nominal and contemptuous damages and declarations

1. NOMINAL DAMAGES[1]

Many torts are actionable only on proof of damage. But torts actionable per se, as well as breach of contract, are actionable without proof of damage. One consequence is that even though the court is satisfied that the claimant has not suffered any damage, it is still entitled to damages for the defendant's breach of contract or tort actionable per se. Such damages are termed nominal and they comprise a trivial sum of money, usually about £2–£10.[2] Nominal damages are therefore in no sense compensatory and must be distinguished from a small sum of compensatory damages. Their function is merely to declare that the defendant has committed a wrong against the claimant and hence that the claimant's rights have been infringed. Given that the remedy of a declaration is specifically designed to serve this purpose nominal damages are superfluous and could happily be abolished. This is particularly so since what was previously an important practical consequence of an award of nominal damages has been removed by Devlin J's decision in *Anglo-Cyprian Trade Agencies v Paphos Wine Industries Ltd*[3] that a claimant awarded nominal damages should not necessarily be regarded as a successful claimant for the purposes of costs.

2. CONTEMPTUOUS DAMAGES

Rarely awarded other than by a jury in a defamation case, these are damages of a very small amount – usually of the lowest coin of the realm (at present 1p) – whose function is to indicate that, while the defendant has committed the alleged wrong (including a tort actionable only on proof of damage) the claimant deserves no more than a technical

---

1   Of the law on compensatory damages examined in Part One, the form of damages (ch 8) and limitation periods (ch 15) are also relevant to nominal (and contemptuous) damages.
2   An example of nominal damages being awarded is *C and P Haulage v Middleton* [1983] 1 WLR 1461 (£10); above, pp 67–68.
3   [1951] 1 All ER 873.

acknowledgment of the infringement of his rights, because of his own conduct in the matter.[4] In other words the derisory award amounts to a declaration of the claimant's rights combined with an admonition of the claimant. As it is difficult to see how the grant of a declaration can achieve this 'double-edged sword' effect, contemptuous damages justify their continued, albeit very limited, existence.

3.   DECLARATIONS

While all remedies impliedly declare what the parties' rights are, a declaration[5] is a remedy, generally regarded as statutory[6] albeit with equitable roots, by which a court simply pronounces on the rights or even the remedies of the parties. Available in relation to any sort of legal right, a declaration can quickly and easily, and without invoking any coercion, aid the resolution of a dispute or prevent one from arising. As Lawson wrote:

> 'If persons dispute among themselves as to their legal position, but are perfectly willing to respect and act upon it once they know what it is, there is no need to order them in any way. A mere declaration stating authoritatively their legal relations will suffice.'[7]

Prior to 1883, the Court of Chancery alone had the power to grant a declaration, and then this was exercised only where consequential relief was or could have been claimed. But by the Judicature Acts 1873–1875 and the accompanying Rules of the Supreme Court 1883, Ord 25, r 5, all divisions of the High Court were given power to make declarations 'whether or not consequential relief is or could be claimed'. It was this 'innovation of a very important kind'[8] that paved the way for the modern widespread use of declarations. The present procedural rule is CPR 40.20 which states, 'The court may make binding declarations whether or not any other remedy is claimed.'

---

4   Ogus *The Law of Damages* (1973) p 26; Waddams *The Law of Damages* (3rd edn, 1997) para 10.40. For examples see *Kelly v Sherlock* (1866) LR 1 QB 686; *Dering v Uris* [1964] 2 QB 669. A possible recent example was the £1 awarded to the claimant in *Grobbelaar v News Group Newspapers Ltd* [2002] UKHL 40, [2002] 1 WLR 3024 albeit that their Lordships (with the exception of Lord Millett who described them as 'derisory damages') called them nominal damages. A claimant awarded merely contemptuous damages is even less likely to recover his costs than one awarded nominal damages – *Martin v Benson* [1927] 1 KB 771.
5   See generally Zamir and Woolf *The Declaratory Judgment* (3rd edn, 2002); Young *Declaratory Orders* (1975); Lawson *Remedies of English Law* (2nd edn) ch 16.
6   *Chapman v Michaelson* [1908] 2 Ch 612; *Tito v Waddell (No 2)* [1977] Ch 106 at 259.
7   Lawson *Remedies of English Law* (2nd edn) p 231.
8   *Ellis v Duke of Bedford* [1899] 1 Ch 494 at 515 (per Lindley MR).

Early this century it was said that the discretion to grant a declaration should be exercised 'with extreme caution',[9] but in Lord Radcliffe's words giving the Privy Council's judgment in *Ibeneweka v Egbuna:*[10]

'... it is doubtful if there is more of principle involved than the undoubted truth that the power of granting a declaration should be exercised with a proper sense of responsibility and full realisation that judicial pronouncements ought not to be issued unless there are circumstances that call for their making. Beyond that there is no legal restriction on the award of a declaration.'

Denning LJ earlier spoke in similar vein in *Pyx Granite Co Ltd v Ministry of Housing and Local Government:*[11] '... if a substantial question exists which one person has a real interest to raise and the other to oppose, then the court has a discretion to resolve it by a declaration, which it will exercise if there is good reason for so doing.' So in modern times a declaration is readily granted.

It has also now been accepted that, while an unusual remedy, negative declarations (that the claimant is under no liability) can also be granted where they would serve a useful purpose. In Lord Woolf MR's words in *Messier-Dowty Ltd v Sabena SA (No 2),*[12]

'The deployment of negative declarations should be scrutinised and their use rejected where it would serve no useful purpose. However, where a negative declaration would help to ensure that the aims of justice are achieved the courts should not be reluctant to grant such declarations. They can and do assist in achieving justice ... [T]he development of the use of declaratory relief in relation to commercial disputes should not be contained by artificial limits wrongly related to jurisdiction. It should instead be kept within proper bounds by the exercise of the courts' discretion.'

All this does not, of course, mean that a declaration will never be refused. The claimant must have a real interest in the matter and must not be merely an interfering busybody. Nor will it be granted where no dispute or infringement of legal rights has yet taken place and the chances of that occurring are regarded as too hypothetical.[13] Moreover

---

9   *Faber v Gosworth Urban District Council* (1903) 88 LT 549 at 550.
10   [1964] 1 WLR 219 at 225. See also *Guaranty Trust Co of New York v Hannay & Co* [1915] 2 KB 536, 572 (per Bankes LJ); *Hanson v Radcliffe UDC* [1922] 2 Ch 490 at 507 (per Lord Sterndale MR); *Booker v Bell* [1989] 1 Lloyd's Rep 516; *Financial Services Authority v Rourke* (2001) Times, 12 November.
11   [1958] 1 QB 554 at 571.
12   [2000] 1 WLR 2040 at 2050. See also *Greenwich Healthcare National Health Service Trust v London and Quadrant Housing Trust* [1998] 3 All ER 437 (claimant granted negative declaration that defendant would not be entitled to an injunction or damages if claimant went ahead with a development).
13   *Mellstrom v Garner* [1970] 1 WLR 603.

the dispute must normally be as between the parties.[14] In Lord Diplock's words in *Gouriet v Union of Post Office Workers,*[15] '… the jurisdiction is not to declare the law generally or to give advisory opinions; it is confined to declaring legal rights, subsisting or future, of the parties represented in the litigation before it and not those of anyone else.' And in *Meadows Indemnity Co Ltd v Insurance Corpn of Ireland Ltd*[16] a declaration sought by a reinsurer as to the invalidity of a claim made under the head insurance was refused by the Court of Appeal on the ground that there was no contested issue between the reinsurer and the head-assured. Given its equitable roots, it would also appear, although there is little authority on this, that equitable defences relating to the claimant's conduct, such as laches, acquiescence and 'unclean hands', further bar a declaration.[17]

As a remedy for a tort or breach of contract a declaration is generally concerned to pronounce authoritatively that the defendant's conduct did or does amount to a tort or breach of contract. So in *Harrison v Duke of Rutland*[18] the defendant, on a counterclaim, was granted a declaration that the claimant was trespassing when he rode his bicycle along the defendant's road as a means of interfering with the defendant's grouse-shooting; and in *Louis Drayfus et Cie v Parnaso Cia Naviera SA,*[19] the claimants were at first instance granted, but on appeal refused, a declaration that the defendant shipowners were in breach of a charterparty. A claimant may also seek a declaration of the defendant's duties to him, so as to counter a threatened tort or breach of contract. In *Rajbenbach v Mamon,*[20] for example, the claimant tenant was granted a declaration of the defendant landlord's contractual obligations to him following the defendant's anticipatory repudiation of a contract under which the defendant was to pay the claimant £300 for vacating premises by a certain date. It is especially where the claimant is seeking to enforce obligations in a continuing contractual relationship that the declaration shows its advantages, for as Borchard has written:

---

14 An exception is where a health authority or relative or next friend seeks a declaration in respect of a patient: see, eg *Re S* [1995] 3 All ER 290, CA.
15 [1978] AC 435 at 501. See also Lord Wilberforce at 483.
16 [1989] 2 Lloyd's Rep 298.
17 It is unclear whether the reference to 'other equitable relief' in the Limitation Act 1980, s 36(1), includes a declaration. If not, the normal limitation periods for torts and breach of contract apply to a claim for a declaration (as they do if the 'by analogy' proviso to s 36(1) applies): but it appears that, as with injunctions and because of its equitable roots, laches and acquiescence apply, in any event, to a declaration.
18 [1893] 1 QB 142.
19 [1959] 1 QB 498; revsd [1960] 2 QB 49. See also *Burdett-Coutts v Hertfordshire County Council* [1984] IRLR 91.
20 [1955] 1 QB 283.

'The declaration rather than the more drastic and definitive coercive decree enables the parties to re-establish their questioned relations without irreparable injury. The declaration thus has a social advantage which should not be underestimated as an element in the administration of justice.'[1]

Two final points are noteworthy. First, in some cases the courts have found it useful to be able to grant a declaration, while refusing or suspending the more drastic remedy of an injunction.[2] Secondly, the courts now have power to award an interim declaration.[3]

---

1   *Declaratory Judgments* (2nd edn, 1941) p 554.
2   *Llandudno Urban District Council v Woods* [1899] 2 Ch 705; *Stollmeyer v Trinidad Lake Petroleum Co* [1918] AC 485; *Race Relations Board v Applin* [1973] QB 815.
3   CPR 25.1 (1)(b). For discussion of the appropriateness of granting interim declarations in order to assist banks in relation to the criminal law on money laundering see, eg *Bank of Scotland v A Ltd* [2001] EWCA Civ 52, [2001] 1 WLR 751; *Amalgamated Metal Trading Ltd v City of London Police Financial Investigation Unit* [2003] EWHC 703 (Comm), [2003] 1 WLR 2711. For the previous law, to the effect that the courts did not have power to grant interim declarations, see *Underhill v Ministry of Food* [1950] 1 All ER 591; *International General Electric Co of New York Ltd v Customs and Excise Comrs* [1962] Ch 784; *R v IRC, ex p Rossminster Ltd* [1980] AC 952; *Riverside Mental Health NHS Trust v Fox* [1994] 1 FLR 614; *Newport AFC Ltd v FA of Wales* [1995] 2 All ER 87.

Part five

Remedies for equitable wrongs

Chapter 24

Remedies for equitable wrongs

1. INTRODUCTION

Torts and breach of contract are termed common law wrongs because they were historically developed in the common law courts. Equitable wrongs are civil wrongs that historically were developed in the Court of Chancery. Despite the fusion of the common law courts and the Court of Chancery by the Supreme Court of Judicature Acts 1873–1875, much of the substantive law has not been fused. One example is the continued distinction between common law and equitable wrongs. In a rational fused system, nothing should turn on whether a civil wrong is common law or equitable. But that is not the present law.

Three introductory points on equitable wrongs and remedies for equitable wrongs should be made.[1] First, at the present time, equitable civil wrongs comprise breach of fiduciary duty, breach of confidence,[2] dishonestly procuring or assisting a breach of fiduciary duty,[3] and those forms of estoppel that constitute causes of action, in particular proprietary estoppel. Of these equitable wrongs, the most wide-ranging is breach of fiduciary duty which extends well beyond trustees. In Australia, New Zealand, and Canada, claims for breach of fiduciary duty have for many years been commonplace. In England it is only relatively recently that the potential of breach of fiduciary duty has been fully realised: it has therefore been something of a new departure for claims for 'professional negligence' against, for example, solicitors to be pleaded not only in contract and tort but also for breach of fiduciary duty.

Secondly, while it would have been possible to examine remedies for equitable wrongs alongside torts and breach of contract throughout this book, it was thought that it would aid clear exposition, and make the

---

1   See also above, pp 12–13.
2   See below, p 607, n 17.
3   *Royal Brunei Airlines v Tan* [1995] 2 AC 378, PC; *Fyffes Group Ltd v Templeman* [2000] 2 Lloyd's Rep 643; *Grupo Torras SA v Al-Sabah (No 5)* [2001] Lloyd's Rep Bank 36, CA; *Twinsectra v Yardley* [2002] UKHL 12, [2002] 2 AC 164; Mitchell 'Assistance' in *Breach of Trust* (eds Birks and Pretto, 2002) pp 139–212; Elliott and Mitchell 'Remedies for Dishonest Assistance' (2004) 67 MLR 16.

book easier to use, to devote this final chapter to remedies for equitable wrongs. The aim is to enable the parallels – and contrasts – with remedies for the common law wrongs to be easily understood.

Thirdly, while it is still essentially true that only equitable remedies are available for equitable wrongs, it is also true that the same, or similar, functions are performed by the equitable remedies for equitable wrongs as by the (common law and equitable) remedies for torts and breach of contract that have been considered in chapters 1–23 of this book. An important purpose of this chapter is to enable the reader to see clearly the coherence of remedial function across the divide between common law and equitable wrongs. In understanding this, the reader may find helpful the following table of primary functions and remedies for equitable wrongs which can be compared with, and seen to be largely consistent with, the equivalent table for torts and breach of contract in chapter 1.[4]

Remedies for Equitable Wrongs	
Primary Function	*Remedies*
Compensation	Equitable compensation. (Equitable) compensatory damages.
Restitution	(Equitable) restitutionary damages. Account of profits. Award of money had and received. Constructive trust.
Punishment?	Punitive damages?
Compelling performance (of positive obligations)	Mandatory enforcing injunction. Appointment of a receiver.
Preventing a wrong	Prohibitory injunction. Delivery up for destruction or destruction on oath.
Compelling the undoing of a wrong	Mandatory restorative injunction. Delivery up of material containing confidential information.
Declaring rights	Declaration.

---

4   See above, p 10. We do not consider in this chapter some specialised judicial remedies for breach of fiduciary duty: eg the removal by a court of a trustee (see Hanbury and Martin *Modern Equity* (16th edn, 2001) pp 522–524).

This chapter is structured according to the primary functions of the remedies for equitable wrongs. Its main sections therefore correspond with the four parts into which chapters 1–23 were divided, namely compensation, restitution and punishment, compelling performance or preventing (or compelling the undoing of) an equitable wrong, and declaring rights. A final section deals with two miscellaneous issues on remedies for equitable wrongs, namely interest and limitation periods.

2. COMPENSATION FOR EQUITABLE WRONGS

Common law compensatory damages are, at present, available only for common law wrongs, that is, torts and breach of contract. They are not available for equitable wrongs. So one cannot be awarded common law compensatory damages for breach of fiduciary duty or (although there is on-going debate about this)[5] breach of confidence. This historical anachronism (although opponents of the fusion of common law and equity would, no doubt, disagree with that description) leaves no great lacuna in the law because there is an analogous equitable remedy performing the same function of compensation. This is the remedy of 'equitable compensation' (sometimes labelled 'accounting for loss') which, until relatively recently, had been little discussed or analysed.[6] We shall also see that equitable damages, awarded in substitution for, or in addition to, an injunction under the Supreme Court Act 1981, s 50 (the successor to Lord Cairns's Act) may sometimes be awarded to compensate the claimant for equitable wrongs just as they may be for common law wrongs.

5 Below, pp 606–609.
6 The catalyst for greater use being made of 'equitable compensation' may have been the path-breaking article by Davidson 'The Equitable Remedy of Compensation' (1982) 13 Melb Univ LR 349. For other examinations of equitable compensation see, eg Tilbury *Civil Remedies* (1990) paras 3247–3254; Gummow 'Compensation for Breach of Fiduciary Duty' in *Equity, Fiduciaries and Trusts* (ed Youdan, 1989) pp 57–92; McCamus 'Equitable Compensation and Restitutionary Remedies: Recent Developments' in *Law of Remedies: Principles and Proofs* (Special Lectures of the Law Society of Upper Canada, 1995) 295, 298–332; Rickett 'Compensating for Loss in Equity – Choosing the Right Horse for Each Course' in *Restitution and Equity* (eds Birks and Rose, 2000) pp 173–191; Getzler 'Equitable Compensation and the Regulation of Fiduciary Relationships', ibid, pp 235–237; Conaglen 'Equitable Compensation for Breach of Fiduciary Dealing Rules' (2003) 119 LQR 246.

(1) Equitable compensation

That equitable compensation is a remedy available for breach of fiduciary duty has now been clearly established.[7] As we shall see below, the best view is that equitable compensation has absorbed, or been assimilated with, the remedy for breach of fiduciary duty of 'accounting for loss'. There are also proprietary estoppel cases where the monetary remedy awarded is best viewed as 'equitable compensation'.[8] The reasoning of the Privy Council in *Royal Brunei Airlines v Tan*,[9] and cases subsequent to it,[10] also indicate that the primary monetary remedy for the equitable wrong of dishonestly procuring or assisting a breach of fiduciary duty is equitable compensation, albeit that the traditional language of 'accounting as a constructive trustee' has often tended to obscure this.[11]

Peculiarly, there has been no English case in which equitable compensation has been awarded for breach of confidence.[12] Instead, the courts have tended to think of equitable damages awarded in substitution for, or in addition to, an injunction under the Supreme Court Act 1981, s 50.[13] As the standard remedy for breach of fiduciary duty is equitable compensation, it is odd that the same is not also true of breach of confidence.

The basic aim of 'equitable compensation', as its name suggests, is to compensate a loss. In other words, it is concerned to put the claimant into as good a position as if no wrong had occurred. It therefore has exactly the same function as compensatory damages. This is why the House of Lords in *Target Holdings Ltd v Redfern*[14] (the facts of which are

---

7   *Fry v Fry* (1859) 27 Beav 144; *Nocton v Lord Ashburton* [1914] AC 932; *McKenzie v McDonald* [1927] VLR 134 (equitable compensation on terms); *Re Dawson* [1966] 2 NSWLR 211; *Wallersteiner v Moir (No 2)* [1975] QB 373; *Bartlett v Barclays Bank Trust Co (No 2)* [1980] Ch 515; *Re Bell's Indenture* [1980] 1 WLR 1217; *Target Holdings Ltd v Redfern* [1996] AC 421, HL; *Bristol & West Building Society v Mothew* [1998] Ch 1, CA; *Swindle v Harrison* [1997] 4 All ER 705, CA.

8   Eg *Dodsworth v Dodsworth* (1973) 228 Estates Gazette 1115; *Baker & Baker v Baker* (1993) 25 HLR 408, CA; *Wayling v Jones* (1995) 69 P & CR 170, CA; *Gillett v Holt* [2001] Ch 210; *Jennings v Rice* [2002] EWCA Civ 159, [2003] 1 P & CR 8.

9   [1995] 2 AC 378.

10   See above, n 3.

11   For criticism of this phrase in this context, see Hanbury and Martin *Modern Equity* (16th edn, 2001) at 206; *Dubai Aluminium Co Ltd v Salaam* [2002] UKHL 48, [2003] 2 AC 366, at para 142 (per Lord Millett).

12   In Canada, 'equitable compensation' has been awarded by the Supreme Court for breach of confidence: see *Cadbury Schweppes v FBI Foods Ltd* (1999) 167 DLR (4th) 577.

13   See, eg *Attorney-General v Guardian Newspapers (No 2)* [1990] 1 AC 109 (per Lord Goff). In some cases, the courts have awarded damages for breach of confidence without discussing whether they were equitable or common law damages: see below, pp 607–609.

14   [1996] AC 421. See also *Gwembe Valley Development Co Ltd v Koshy* [2003] EWCA Civ 1048, [2004] 1 BCLC 131 at paras 142–160 (no loss caused by breach of fiduciary duty by director and therefore no equitable compensation could be awarded).

examined below)[15] was correct to say that there could be no equitable compensation where the loss would have been suffered even if there had been no breach of duty; that is, where the breach of fiduciary duty had caused the claimant no loss. Of course, and just as at common law, what is a loss and hence what is required in order to compensate will vary according to the duty broken and fiduciary duties may be positive as well as negative. If the duty broken was a failure to invest on behalf of a trust fund the aim of the compensation will be to put the beneficiaries into as good a position as if there had been that investment. If the duty broken was in stealing money from the trust fund, the aim of the compensation will be to put the beneficiaries into as good a position as if that money had not been stolen (ie to restore the money).

In principle, in order to put the claimant into as good a position as if the equitable wrong had not occurred, the equitable compensation should cover non-pecuniary as well as pecuniary loss (albeit that, as a matter of policy, there may be particular restrictions on this). Although there has as yet been no English case awarding equitable compensation for non-pecuniary loss, there is support in Canada for this.[16]

An important question is whether the same limitations that apply to compensatory damages also apply to equitable compensation. In other words do limitations such as remoteness, intervening cause, and contributory negligence apply to equitable compensation? The practical importance of this is that where a claimant has a choice of causes of action, so that the claimant may choose to sue for breach of contract, tort, or an equitable wrong, it may be advantageous to found the claim on the equitable wrong if the limitations that would apply to compensatory damages do not apply (or apply in a less restrictive way) to equitable compensation.

Examination of the cases in the common law world on this central question reveals that there is a fundamental conflict of opinion. On the one hand, there are those judges who consider that the limitations on common law compensatory damages, such as remoteness, intervening cause and contributory negligence, do not apply to equitable compensation. This was the opinion of Lord Browne-Wilkinson, giving the leading speech, in *Target Holdings v Redfern*. In emphasising that a trustee would be liable for breach of trust even if the immediate cause of the loss was a third party, his Lordship said, 'thus the common law rules of remoteness of damages and causation do not apply.'[17] This was also

---

15 Below, pp 604–605.
16 *M(H) v M(K)* (1992) 96 DLR (4th) 289, Supreme Court of Canada (equitable compensation for breach of fiduciary duty).
17 [1996] AC 421, 434.

the approach of the minority, led by McLachlin J, in the influential Canadian case of *Canson Enterprises v Broughton*.[18] Here a claim for equitable compensation was brought against a solicitor for breach of fiduciary duty in relation to the claimant's purchase of land. While all the judges in the Supreme Court of Canada concurred in the result, namely that the solicitor was liable for the claimant's loss but only until the intervention of third parties which in effect broke the chain of causation, the minority and the majority disagreed in their reasoning. McLachlin J for the minority said:

> '[This case] raises the question of whether the plaintiff can hold the solicitor liable for loss suffered by the plaintiff due to the negligence of architects and engineers in subsequent construction on the land. I agree with La Forest J that the solicitor's liability does not extend this far ... I base this result, however, in equity. I cannot concur in the suggestion in my colleague's reasons that ... damages for breach of fiduciary duty should be measured by analogy to tort and contract ... The basis of the fiduciary obligation and the rationale for equitable compensation are distinct from the tort of negligence and contract. In negligence and contract the parties are taken to be independent and equal actors, concerned primarily with their own self-interest. Consequently the law seeks a balance between enforcing obligations by awarding compensation and preserving optimum freedom for those involved in the relationship in question, communal or otherwise. The essence of a fiduciary relationship, by contrast, is that one party pledges itself to act in the best interest of the other. The fiduciary relationship has trust, not self-interest, at its core, and when breach occurs, the balance favours the person wronged.'[19]

So the argument of the minority was that common law limitations were not directly applicable to equitable compensation and that no analogy should be drawn with contract and tort. In other words, common law and equity are here different and should remain so.

This is also the view in Australia. In *Pilmer v Duke Group Ltd*[20] the High Court, in obiter dicta, said that contributory negligence was inapplicable to equitable compensation for breach of fiduciary duty. In a joint judgment, McHugh, Gummow, Hayne and Callinan JJ, said, '[I]n Australia, the measure of compensation in respect of losses sustained by reason of breach of fiduciary duty by a trustee or other fiduciary is

---

18 (1991) 85 DLR (4th) 129.
19 (1991) 85 DLR (4th) 129, 154.
20 (2001) 75 ALJR 1067. On the main point in the case, the majority of the High Court (Kirby J dissenting) held that a company, that is induced by a negligent report on a 'target' company to issue shares in order to acquire that target company, suffers no loss. For criticism, see Nolan and Prentice 'The Issue of Shares – Compensating the Company for Loss' (2002) 118 LQR 180. See also Oditah 'Takeovers, Share Exchanges and the Meaning of Loss' (1996) 112 LQR 424.

determined by equitable principles and these do not necessarily reflect the rules for assessment of damages in tort or contract.'[1] Again in *Youyang Pty Ltd v Minter Ellison Morris Fletcher*[2] the High Court of Australia (Gleeson CJ, McHugh, Gummow, Kirby and Hayne JJ) cited with approval the second part of the passage from McLachlin J's judgment in the *Canson* case set out above.

Taking the opposing view – that common law restrictions on compensatory damages should apply also to equitable compensation – are, for example, the majority in the *Canson Enterprises* case, led by La Forest J; the New Zealand Court of Appeal in *Day v Mead*[3] and *Bank of New Zealand v New Zealand Guardian Trust Ltd*;[4] and, as regards equitable compensation for breach of fiduciary duty comprising a failure to use care and skill, Millett LJ in *Bristol & West Building Society v Mothew*.[5]

In *Day v Mead*, where contributory negligence was applied to equitable compensation for breach of fiduciary duty by a solicitor, Cooke P said:[6]

'As Lord Diplock put it (in *United Scientific Holdings Ltd v Burnley Borough Council*)[7] law and equity have mingled now; the [Judicature] Acts did not bring to a sudden halt the whole process of development of the common law of England that had been so notable a feature of the preceding decades; the legislation placed no ban upon further development of substantive rules by judicial decision ... Whether or not there are reported cases in which compensation for breach of fiduciary obligation has been assessed on the footing that the plaintiff should accept some share of the responsibility, there appears to be no solid reason for denying jurisdiction to follow that obviously just course, especially now that law and equity have mingled or are interacting. It is an opportunity for equity to show that it has not petrified and to live up to the spirit of its maxims.'

And Millett LJ in Bristol & West Building Society v Mothew said:[8]

'Although the remedy which equity makes available for breach of the equitable duty of skill and care is equitable compensation rather than damages, this is merely the product of history and in this context it is in my opinion a distinction without a difference. Equitable compensation for breach of the duty of skill and care resembles common law damages in that it is awarded by way of compensation to a plaintiff for his loss. There is no reason in principle why the common law rules of causation, remoteness of damage and measure of damages should not be applied by analogy in such a case.'

1 (2001) 75 ALJR 1067 at para 85.
2 (2003) 196 ALR 482 at 492.
3 [1987] 2 NZLR 443.
4 [1999] 1 NZLR 664.
5 [1998] Ch 1.
6 [1987] 2 NZLR 443 at 451.
7 [1978] AC 904 at 924–925.
8 [1998] Ch 1 at 17.

This 'opposing' view is to be preferred.[9] Given the discretion open at common law in applying limitations, and the different approach to limitations that has been taken in respect of, for example, the tort of deceit,[10] there is no good reason for equitable compensation going its own separate way from compensatory damages. On the contrary, compensatory damages and equitable compensation should be regarded as identical in function – compensation – and identical in relation to the application of limitations.

It is also important to clarify that the remedy of equitable compensation has absorbed, or been assimilated with, the remedy of accounting (for loss).[11] The argument has been put that the latter remedy may operate differently as a remedy against a trustee than equitable compensation because it is concerned to restore a trust fund rather than to compensate. The account remedy, so it is argued, is therefore analogous to an action in debt (or specific performance) in contrast to equitable compensation which is analogous to an action for compensatory damages. Put another way, the account remedy, unlike equitable compensation, responds to a trustee's primary obligation rather than being a remedy for breach of a trustee's primary obligation. That there is this type of difference has been argued by, for example, Peter Birks,[12] Lord Millett[13] and, in detail, by Steven Elliott in his Oxford D Phil thesis.[14]

But that argument is inconsistent with the central reasoning of the House of Lords in *Target Holdings Ltd v Redfern*.[15] In that case the defendants were solicitors who were acting for mortgagees (the claimants) in relation to the purchase of property by C Ltd. In breach of trust the defendants paid over the loaned money (£1,525,000) from the claimants

---

9   Burrows 'We Do This At Common Law But That In Equity' (2002) 22 OJLS 1, esp 9–12; 'Fusing Common Law and Equity: Remedies, Restitution and Reform' Hochelaga Lecture 2001, esp 6–14.

10 Above, ch 6. For a case denying the applicability of contributory negligence to dishonestly-committed wrongs, whether common law or equitable, see *Corporacion Nacional del Cobre de Chile v Sogemin Metals Ltd* [1997] 1 WLR 1396: above, p 133, n 1.

11 Contrast the clearly different remedy of accounting for profits which is concerned to effect restitution and not compensation.

12 'Equity in the Modern Law: an Exercise in Taxonomy' (1996) 26 Univ of Western Aus LR 1, 46–47.

13 'Equity's Place in the Law of Commerce' (1998) 114 LQR 214, 225–227; see also Millett LJ's judgment in *Bristol & West Building Society v Mothew* [1998] Ch 1 at 18. Cf Parker and Mellows *The Modern Law of Trusts* (ed Oakley) (7th edn, 1998) 679–683. See also *Bairstow v Queen's Moat Houses plc* [2001] EWCA Civ 712, [2001] 2 BCLC 531.

14 *Compensation Claims Against Trustees* (2002). For the outline of his central argument, see Elliott 'Remoteness Criteria in Equity' (2002) 65 MLR 588, 590; Elliott and Mitchell 'Remedies for Dishonest Assistance' (2004) 67 MLR 16, 23–36.

15 [1996] AC 421. *Target Holdings* was distinguished by the High Court of Australia in *Youyang Pty Ltd v Minter Ellison Morris Fletcher* (2003) 196 ALR 482, noted by Elliott and Edelman '*Target Holdings* Considered in Australia' (2003) 119 LQR 545.

to the vendors prior to the completion of the sale and charge. That was a breach of trust albeit that a few days afterwards the completion of the sale and charge did take place. Subsequently C Ltd became insolvent and the claimants repossessed the property selling it for £500,000. The defendants argued that their breach of trust was technical only because the claimants had subsequently obtained the charge to which they were entitled. The breach of trust had not caused the claimants the loss they had suffered which was rather caused by the property having been overvalued so that the claimants' security was inadequate. The House of Lords agreed and held that there could be no equitable compensation and, although this was implied rather than expressly stated, *no account remedy* where, as on these facts, the loss would have been suffered even if there had been no breach of duty.[16]

However, applying the argument of Birks, Millett and Elliott, the House of Lords should have taken a different approach to the supposedly separate account remedy than to equitable compensation (even if ultimately the same result might have been reached on the facts) precisely because, like an action in debt or specific performance, the account remedy does not require loss to have been caused by the breach of fiduciary duty: the fact that the beneficiaries would have suffered the loss in question irrespective of the breach of fiduciary duty should have been irrelevant.

While historically that argument has much to commend it, it is hard to see why in terms of policy one would wish to retain a distinctive remedy of that type. A trustee does not contract to pay a particular sum to the beneficiaries and, if the beneficiaries would have suffered the loss even if the trustee had performed its fiduciary duties, it is hard to see why, as a matter of policy, they should have redress against the trustee for that loss. Put another way, to regard the trustees as being liable to a distinct account remedy appears to impose on them an unwarranted absolute duty to pay back into the trust fund the value of the moneys that, in breach of trust, have been paid out from it and not recovered. *Target Holdings v Redfern*, which is most naturally interpreted as having impliedly laid down that loss must have been factually caused in respect of the remedy of accounting (for loss), should be applauded in terms of policy

---

16 It seems far-fetched to argue (but see Parker and Mellows *The Modern Law of Trusts* (ed Oakley) (7th edn, 1998) 683) that the account remedy was erroneously forgotten about by counsel and their Lordships and that therefore the decision has no relevance to that remedy. Having said that, it would clearly have been preferable for their Lordships to have expressly mentioned the account remedy and to have anticipated expressly the type of argument made by Birks, Millett, and Elliott.

for (impliedly) rejecting older cases that may have supported the view that the accounting remedy can operate differently from the remedy of equitable compensation.

(2) Equitable (compensatory) damages

Equitable damages are damages awarded in addition to, or in substitution for, an injunction or specific performance under the Supreme Court Act 1981, s 50. We have seen in chapter 16 that they can be awarded, and can offer some advantages over common law damages, for a tort or breach of contract.

In respect of equitable wrongs, there appears to be no case illustrating the award of equitable damages other than for breach of confidence. But in principle there is no reason why, instead of equitable compensation, such damages should not be awarded for breach of fiduciary duty or dishonestly procuring or assisting a breach of fiduciary duty. Such damages would seem especially appropriate where the breach of fiduciary duty has not yet accrued and one is seeking damages for an anticipated breach. In that situation, it is unclear whether 'equitable compensation' as opposed to equitable damages could be awarded although, given that equitable compensation is an equitable remedy, it may be thought that there is not the same difficulty as where common law damages are sought.

Lest the point be lost, one should interject at this stage that all these technical distinctions between common law damages, equitable compensation and equitable damages bring no credit to the legal system. They are the irrational historical residue of an unfused system that should be swept away.

As regards breach of confidence, damages, arguably best viewed as equitable damages, have been awarded in several cases. These will now be examined under two sub-headings. First, the jurisdiction to award damages for breach of confidence; and, secondly, the assessment of compensatory damages for breach of confidence.

(a) The jurisdiction to award damages for breach of confidence

There is an on-going debate as to the jurisdiction to award damages for breach of confidence. This directly links to general questions about the fusion of common law and equity and as to whether breach of confidence should be recognised as a tort rather than as an equitable wrong. In particular, if common law damages, rather than equitable damages (or equitable compensation) are being awarded for breach of confidence, this may be interpreted as showing either that breach of confidence is now a common law tort or that, contrary to the traditional 'anti-fusion' view, common law damages can be awarded for an equitable wrong.

Whatever the attractions in principle, it is submitted that it cannot yet be said that breach of confidence (as a cause of action independent from breach of contract) is a tort. In so far as the judges have referred to, or discussed, this question, they have overwhelmingly viewed breach of confidence as an equitable wrong not a tort.[17] Assuming then that breach of confidence is an equitable wrong, the 'jurisdictional' question is whether the damages awarded have always been equitable damages or whether, on the contrary, the best analysis is that common law damages have sometimes been awarded.

In some cases the damages are most naturally viewed as equitable. In *Saltman Engineering Co Ltd v Campbell Engineering Ltd*,[18] having established that the defendants were in breach of an equitable obligation of confidence in using drawings to make special tools, the Court of Appeal refused an injunction to restrain use or sale of the tools, but ordered an inquiry as to damages, Lord Greene MR saying that damages could be awarded under Lord Cairns's Act '... to cover both past and future acts in lieu of an injunction.'[19] Again in *Seager v Copydex Ltd*[20] the Court of Appeal ordered damages to be awarded by the master for breach of confidence in manufacturing a carpetgrip invented by the claimant. Although no explanation was offered as to the jurisdiction to award damages, the most natural interpretation, given the claimant's application for an injunction, was that they were granted in lieu of that injunction under Lord Cairns's Act.

Similarly there are several cases in which the courts have accepted that damages in addition to an injunction can be awarded for breach of

---

17 See, eg *Attorney-General v Guardian Newspapers (No 2)* [1990] 1 AC 109 at 286 (per Lord Goff): '[T]he remedy of damages ... in cases of breach of confidence is now available, despite the equitable nature of the wrong ...'; *Wainwright v Home Office* [2003] UKHL 53, [2003] 3 WLR 1137 at para 18. See also Gurry *Breach of Confidence* (1984) pp 431–432. Cf Lord Nicholls (dissenting) in *Campbell v Mirror Group Newspapers Ltd* [2004] UKHL 22, [2004] 2 All ER 995 at paras 14–15 who seemed to envisage there as being a tort of misuse of private information that has grown from the equitable cause of action of breach of confidence; and in *Aquaculture Corpn v New Zealand Mussel Co Ltd* [1990] 3 NZLR 299, 301 Cooke P said 'Whether the obligation of confidence in a case of the present kind should be classified as purely an equitable one is debatable, but we do not think that the question matters for any purpose material to this appeal.' North has argued that breach of confidence is a tort: see North 'Breach of Confidence: Is There a New Tort?' (1972) 12 JSPTL 149. See also Law Commission Report No 110 (1981) *Breach of Confidence*.

18 [1948] 65 RPC 203.

19 [1948] 65 RPC 203 at 219.

20 [1967] 1 WLR 923.

confidence. In *Peter Pan Manufacturing Corpn v Corsets Silhouette Ltd*[1] for example, Pennycuick J said that, in addition to an injunction, the claimant had the option to claim damages or to take an account of profits (in fact the claimant chose the latter); and in *Ackroyds (London) Ltd v Islington Plastics Ltd*[2] Havers J, in addition to granting an injunction, ordered an inquiry into damages for breach of confidence. Although there was no explanation of the basis for the damages in these cases, it is natural to assume that they were additional to an injunction under Lord Cairns's Act.

However, in *Nichrotherm Electrical Co Ltd v Percy*[3] no application for an injunction had been made by the claimants and yet at first instance Harman J ordered an inquiry as to damages for breach of confidence. Unless one can make something of the fact that the claimants were also given leave to apply for an injunction it would seem that the damages cannot be regarded as equitable and that the decision is out of line with the other authorities. As Jones writes, 'Harman J's suggestion is mildly revolutionary in that, by implying that a damages claim can succeed independently of any prayer for equitable relief, it presupposes a fusion of law and equity.[4] Significantly the Court of Appeal[5] left open the question of whether there was jurisdiction to award damages in such a situation for breach of an equitable duty of confidence and instead upheld Harman J's decision on the ground that there had been a breach of a contractual duty of confidence where the jurisdiction to award damages was indisputable.

But the above interpretation of the cases is not the only one that can be offered. In particular it has been argued that, other than in respect of future acts, the damages in the above cases were ordinary common law, rather than equitable, damages.[6] Apart from the first instance decision in *Nichrotherm* the strongest point in support of this approach is that 'at first blush' one would expect damages in lieu of an injunction to cover only future and not past acts and, if so, the damages awarded for past acts, where no injunction was being granted, must have been given at common law. But Lord Greene MR in the *Saltman* case considered that damages in lieu of an injunction can cover past acts and ultimately this

1   [1963] RPC 45. See similarly the Australian case *Ansell Rubber Co Pty Ltd v Allied Rubber Industries Pty Ltd* [1972] RPC 811.
2   [1962] RPC 97. See also the Australian cases *Interfirm Comparison (Australia) Pty Ltd v Law Society of New South Wales* [1977] RPC 137; *Talbot v General Television Corpn Pty Ltd* [1981] RPC 1.
3   [1956] RPC 272.
4   'Restitution of Benefits Obtained in Breach Another's Confidence' (1970) 86 LQR 463 at 491.
5   [1957] RPC 207.
6   North 'Breach of Confidence: Is There a New Tort?' (1972) 12 JSPTL 149. North's view that the damages were common law underpins his main argument that breach of confidence is recognised as a tort.

seems a preferable view.[7] For it avoids the anomaly of the courts being able to grant equitable damages to cover past acts in addition to an injunction, but only damages to cover future acts where no injunction is granted.

Meagher Gummow and Lehane have strenuously argued that even the award of equitable damages in these cases was incorrect because 'wrongful act' in Lord Cairns's Act referred only to legal and not equitable wrongs.[8] In their view, the remedy in question in these cases should therefore have been recognised as being not damages but 'equitable compensation'. But if there was ever any force in this narrow view, the re-enactment of the Lord Cairns's Act power in the Supreme Court Act 1981, s 50, has surely removed it; for that omits any reference to the detailed circumstances in which there is jurisdiction to entertain an application for an injunction or specific performance so that the term 'wrongful act' is no longer included.

More recent cases have continued to 'skirt' the issue as to whether the damages are equitable or common law. So while in obiter dicta in *Attorney-General v Guardian Newspapers (No 2)*,[9] Lord Goff expressed the clear view that the damages were equitable, as being based on a generous interpretation of Lord Cairns's Act, the Court of Appeal in *Dawson & Mason Ltd v Potter*[10] awarded (compensatory) damages for breach of confidence without an injunction being granted or sought. A possible explanation for there being seen to be no problem with this was that, as in the *Nicrotherm* case, the breach of duty in question could have been viewed as purely contractual. In *Douglas v Hello! Ltd (No 3)*[11] Lindsay J referred to the remedy for breach of confidence as 'damages or equitable compensation'[12] and went on both to accept that aggravated damages[13] and to assume that 'exemplary damages (or equity's equivalent)'[14] were available for breach of confidence. And in *Campbell v MGN Ltd*[15] the House of Lords upheld an award of £2,500 damages for mental distress plus £1,000 aggravated damages without making any comment as to the jurisdictional basis of those damages.

---

7   This is supported by, eg *Elsley v J G Collins Insurance Agencies Ltd* (1978) 83 DLR (3d) 1.
8   Meagher, Heydon & Leeming *Meagher Gummow & Lehane's Equity – Doctrines and Remedies* (4th edn, 2002) para 23–105.
9   [1990] 1 AC 109, 286.
10   [1986] 1 WLR 1419.
11   [2003] EWHC 786, [2003] 3 All ER 996.
12   [2003] EWHC 786, [2003] 3 All ER 996 at para 203.
13   [2003] EWHC 786, [2003] 3 All ER 996 at para 275.
14   [2003] EWHC 786, [2003] 3 All ER 996 at para 273.
15   [2004] UKHL 22, [2004] 2 All ER 995.

(b) **The assessment of compensatory damages for breach of confidence**

Whether common law or equitable, damages for breach of confidence are principally compensatory (although, as we shall see, they may, possibly, also be restitutionary).[16] That is, their principal aim is to put the claimant into as good a position as if no breach of confidence had occurred.

Where the breach has been of a commercial (rather than a personal) confidence, one would therefore expect the damages to be assessed in a directly analogous way to damages compensating pecuniary loss for wrongful infringement of intellectual property rights.[17] Confidential information is very similar to, and may even be regarded as, intellectual property. This is borne out by the approach to damages of the Court of Appeal in *Dowson & Mason Ltd v Potter*.[18] The claimants were manufacturers of a part for lorries. They would not have licensed the use of confidential information (obtained by the first defendant and used by the second defendant) relating to that part (which comprised the names and addresses of the suppliers to the claimants of the various components for the part and the price paid for them). The claimants were awarded as damages their lost sales profits consequent on the breach of confidence. This was to assess damages on the same basis as for (other) cases of intellectual property infringement.

The Court of Appeal distinguished the controversial case of *Seager v Copydex Ltd (No 2)*.[19] This dealt with a breach of confidence claim in respect of a carpet grip. The Court of Appeal put forward an approach that differs somewhat from the general approach to assessing damages for intellectual property infringement. Drawing an analogy with damages for conversion, Lord Denning viewed the issue in terms of the 'value' of the confidential information. He went on to say that the value depended on the nature of the confidential information. If there was nothing special about it, ie it was the sort of information which could be obtained by employing any competent consultant, the value was the fee which a consultant would charge for it because, by taking the information, the defendant has merely saved itself the time and trouble of employing a consultant. But if the information was special, for example, if it involved some inventive step, its value would be far higher: '... not merely a consultant's fee, but the price which a willing buyer – desirous of obtaining it – would pay for it. It is the value as between a willing buyer

---

16 Below, pp 624–625.
17 See above, pp 261–263.
18 [1986] 2 All ER 418. See also *Talbot v General Television Corpn Pty Ltd* [1980] VR 224.
19 [1969] 2 All ER 718. This case also indicates that the standard of liability for damages for breach of confidence may be strict: cf above, p 261, n 2.

and a willing seller.'[20] It was suggested that this price might be calculated by a capitalisation of the royalties which the court thinks the defendant would have had to pay the claimant for the information.

But this approach is controversial for at least two reasons. First, Lord Denning's emphasis on the expense the defendant has saved makes it appear that he was more concerned to reverse the defendant's enrichment than to compensate the claimant's loss.[1] Secondly, assuming that he was concerned with compensation, there may be no reason to think that the claimant would have sold the special information rather than keeping it for the claimant's own use. In such a situation, the claimant's loss is likely to be better represented, as in (other) intellectual property cases – and as *Dowson & Mason Ltd v Potter*[2] has now established – by the lost profits from sales of goods or materials produced with the information.

Where the breach is of a personal, rather than a commercial, confidence, damages can compensate for non-pecuniary, as well as pecuniary, loss. This is shown by *Campbell v MGN Ltd*[3] in which the House of Lords upheld an award of £2,500 damages for mental distress plus £1,000 aggravated damages[4] made to Naomi Campbell, the celebrity model, for breach of confidence by a newspaper.

3. RESTITUTION AND PUNISHMENT FOR EQUITABLE WRONGS

(1) Restitution for equitable wrongs

As regards restitution for the four main types of equitable wrong (breach of fiduciary duty, breach of confidence, dishonestly procuring or assisting a breach of fiduciary duty, and proprietary estoppel), there is little to say in relation to the last two wrongs. This is because there appears to have been no English case in which restitution, rather than compensation, has been awarded for dishonest assistance or proprietary estoppel.

Should dishonest assistance ever trigger restitution?: ie should it be a restitution-yielding wrong? The closest analogy is with the economic torts for which restitution has not traditionally been available, although strong arguments can be put forward that it ought to be. For example, on Birks'

---

20   [1969] 2 All ER 718 at 720.
1   Below, p 624.
2   [1986] 1 WLR 1419, CA.
3   [2004] UKHL 22, [2004] 2 All ER 995. See also *Douglas v Hello! Ltd (No 3)* [2003] EWHC 786, [2003] 3 All ER 996, at para 275, where it was accepted that aggravated damages can be awarded for breach of confidence, albeit that, on the facts, no such damages were awarded.
4   See above, p 339.

view that it is the moral quality of the wrongdoing that is particularly important,[5] it would appear that, given their standard of liability, restitution should generally be available for the economic torts and for dishonestly procuring or assisting a breach of fiduciary duty.[6]

Similarly, the monetary remedies for the wrong of proprietary estoppel, have not been restitutionary but have been compensatory and concerned to protect the claimant's expectation[7] or, occasionally, reliance interests.[8] That is not surprising given that proprietary estoppel is closely akin to breach of contract in resting on a breach of promise or conduct equivalent to a promise; and restitution has not traditionally been available for breach of contract. Whether following *Attorney-General v Blake*[9] it will be and *should* be more widely available turns on the issues concerning restitution for breach of contract considered in chapter 17, above.

In contrast to dishonest assistance and proprietary estoppel, restitution (as we shall see in the next two sections) has been a common response to breach of fiduciary duty and breach of confidence through the remedy of accounting for profits. Indeed it has sometimes been assumed that restitution is so central to these wrongs that the claimant cannot alternatively claim compensation for them. That is incorrect. As we have seen,[10] compensation, through either the remedy of equitable compensation (sometimes referred to as accounting for loss) or equitable damages in substitution for, or in addition to, an injunction, is readily available as an alternative to restitution.[11]

---

5   Birks *An Introduction to the Law of Restitution* (rvsd edn, 1989) pp 326–327.

6   This is supported by *Warman International v Dwyer* (1995) 182 CLR 544 (account of profits ordered for 'dishonest assistance' of Dwyer's breach of fiduciary duty). It was also accepted as regards 'dishonest assistance' (by a briber) in obiter dicta of Toulson J in *Fyffes Group Ltd v Templeman* [2000] 2 Lloyd's Rep 643. It is further supported by the Law Commission. In *Aggravated, Exemplary and Restitutionary Damages* (1997) Report No 247, para 3.51 and Draft Bill, cl 12, it recommends that, irrespective of any other power to award restitutionary damages, they may be awarded to a claimant for an equitable wrong (or tort) where the defendant's conduct shows a deliberate and outrageous disregard of the claimant's rights. An equitable wrong is defined as a breach of fiduciary duty, breach of confidence, or procuring or assisting a breach of fiduciary duty: paras 5.44, 5.54–5.55, and Draft Bill, cl 15(4).

7   See, eg *Baker & Baker v Baker* (1993) 25 HLR 408; *Gillett v Holt* [2001] Ch 210. See also *Jennings v Rice* [2002] EWCA Civ 159, [2003] 1 P & CR 8 (expectations protected if 'proportionate'). See generally, on the question of the extent to which expectations are protected by proprietary estoppel, Moriarty 'Licences and Land Law: Legal Principles and Public Policies' (1984) 100 LQR 376; Cooke 'Estoppel and the Protection of Expectations' (1997) 17 Legal Studies 258; Gardner 'The Remedial Discretion in Proprietary Estoppel' (1999) 115 LQR 438.

8   *Dodsworth v Dodsworth* (1973) 228 Estates Gazette 1115 (in effect protecting the reliance interest).

9   [2001] 1 AC 268, HL.

10   See above, pp 599–611.

11   The claimant must elect between compensation and restitution for the wrong: see above, pp 15 and 388–390.

(a) **Restitution for breach of fiduciary duty**

(i) *Secret or unauthorised profit*

There have been many cases of fiduciaries, usually trustees or company directors, being required by the remedy of an account of profits to disgorge unauthorised profits made out of their position as fiduciaries.[12] The duty is a strict one: no unauthorised profit can be made. Although the courts do have a discretion to give the fiduciary an allowance out of the profits made to remunerate him for his skill and time, it is no defence for the fiduciary to establish that he was acting bona fide and in the best interests of the beneficiary. The leading cases are *Regal (Hastings) Ltd v Gulliver*[13] and *Boardman v Phipps*.[14]

In the former, the claimant company, Regal, owned a cinema and wanted to acquire two other cinemas. The directors found that Regal could not itself afford to buy the cinemas so they put up much of the money themselves by creating a subsidiary company in which they themselves took 2,000 £1 shares, the company's solicitor took 500 £1 shares, outside purchasers took 500 £1 shares and Regal took 2,000 £1 shares. The two cinemas were bought and subsequently the shares in the subsidiary company were sold at a considerable profit (£2 16s 1d profit per share). Regal, now under new directors, sought to recover the profits made by the former directors from the sale of the shares in the subsidiary company. The House of Lords held that the former directors were liable to account to Regal for the profits made. Although they had been acting bona fide, the fact remained that they had personally made unauthorised profits out of their fiduciary position as directors.

Viscount Sankey said:

> '... the respondents were in a fiduciary position and their liability to account does not depend upon proof of mala fides. The general rule of equity is that no one who has duties of a fiduciary nature to perform is allowed to enter into engagements in which he has or can have a personal interest conflicting with the interests of those whom he is bound to protect.'[15]

---

12 In addition to the two leading cases examined in the text, see *Keech v Sandford* (1726) Sel Cas Temp King 61; *Parker v McKenna* (1874) 10 Ch App 96; *Boston Deep Sea Fishing & Ice Co v Ansell* (1888) 39 Ch D 339; *Re North Australian Territory Co, Archer's Case* [1892] 1 Ch 322; *Cook v Deeks* [1916] 1 AC 554; *Williams v Barton* [1927] 2 Ch 9; *Industrial Development Consultants v Cooley* [1972] 1 WLR 443; *Canadian Aero Services v O'Malley* (1974) 40 DLR (3d) 371; *English v Dedham Vale Properties Ltd* [1978] 1 WLR 93; *Queensland Mines Ltd v Hudson* (1978) 52 ALJR 399; *Hospital Products Ltd v United States Surgical Corpn* (1985) 156 CLR 41; *Guinness plc v Saunders* [1990] 2 AC 663; *Warman International Ltd v Dwyer* (1995) 182 CLR 544; *Nottingham University v Fishel* [2000] ICR 1462; *CMS Dolphin Ltd v Simonet* [2001] 2 BCLC 704.
13 [1967] 2 AC 134n.
14 [1967] 2 AC 46.
15 [1942] 1 All ER 378 at 381.

In Lord Russell's words:

'The rule of equity which insists on those, who by use of a fiduciary position make a profit, being liable to account for that profit, in no way depends on fraud or absence of bona fides; or upon such questions or considerations as whether the profit would or should otherwise have gone to the plaintiff, or whether the profiteer was under a duty to obtain the source of the profit for the plaintiff or whether he took a risk or acted as he did for the benefit of the plaintiff, or whether the plaintiff had in fact been damaged or benefited by his actions. The liability arises from the mere fact of a profit having, in the stated circumstances, been made. The profiteer, however honest and well-intentioned, cannot escape the risk of being called upon to account.'[16]

And according to Lord Wright:

'... both in law and equity, it has been held that, if a person in a fiduciary relationship makes a secret profit out of the relationship, the court will not inquire whether the other person is damnified or has lost a profit which otherwise he would have got ... Nor can the court adequately investigate the matter in most cases. The facts are generally difficult to ascertain or are solely in the knowledge of the person who is being charged. They are ... hypothetical because the inquiry is as to what would have been the position ... or what he might have done if ... interest had not conflicted with duty.'[17]

In *Boardman v Phipps* the claimant was a beneficiary with a 5/18ths beneficial interest in the Phipps trust. The trust property, inter alia, comprised shares in a company. The defendants, who were another beneficiary and the solicitor to the trustees, sought to improve the value of the shares. Using information acquired while acting as agents for the trustees the defendants embarked on a skilful operation whereby they acquired for themselves the majority of shares in the company. The value of the shares in the company rose sharply so that the defendants' operations were profitable for themselves personally and for the trust holding. The claimant beneficiary nevertheless brought an action claiming a declaration that the defendants held 5/18ths of their shares on constructive trust for him and that they should account to him for 5/18ths of the profit they had personally made. The House of Lords by a three–two majority (Viscount Dilhorne and Lord Upjohn dissenting) granted the declaration sought and held the defendants liable to account as constructive trustees for the profit they had made. *Regal Hastings* was followed. Although the defendants had been acting bona fide, this did not alter the fact that they had made their gains out of their position as agents for the trustees and hence while acting as fiduciaries to the

---

16   [1942] 1 All ER 378 at 386.
17   [1942] 1 All ER 378 at 392.

beneficiaries and the beneficiaries had not authorised their scheme. However, it was stressed that the defendants should be entitled to a liberal allowance for their work and skill.[18]

The minority's reasoning was that to order a disgorging of profits was too harsh. The normal strict rule against unauthorised profits acquired by a fiduciary ought not to apply here where the fiduciaries had acted in good faith and the trustees, on behalf of the beneficiaries, had made it clear that they were not interested in any scheme to obtain majority shares in the company.

Two points should be made on those two leading cases. First, it is clear that the account of profits remedy awarded was restitutionary. It cannot realistically be reanalysed as compensatory. If the fiduciaries had not gone ahead with their schemes because unauthorised, the beneficiaries would not have otherwise made the gains that were required to be disgorged.

Secondly, in *Boardman v Phipps*, as is commonplace in this area of the law, constructive trust terminology was used. The personal liability to account was described as being a liability to account as a constructive trustee. The importance of imposing a constructive trust is that it makes the beneficiary the equitable owner of the unauthorised gains thereby affording priority if the fiduciary is insolvent. The terminology also appears to make clear, although this may follow in any event, that the trustee is under a personal liability to account for unauthorised gains made from the initial unauthorised gain. Whether a constructive trust should be imposed – and indeed whether it was being imposed in *Boardman v Phipps* – will be considered below in comparing bribe cases.

(ii) Bribes or secret commission

The law is most easily described by examining three leading cases, *Lister & Co v Stubbs*,[19] *Reading v Attorney-General*,[20] and *Attorney-General of Hong Kong v Reid*.[1] Taking the second case first, Reading was a Sergeant in the British Army serving in Egypt and, in return for bribes totalling £20,000, he sat on several occasions in his military uniform on lorries illegally

---

18 See also *Nottingham University v Fishel* [2000] ICR 1462. No such allowance was given, and *Boardman v Phipps* was distinguished, in *Guinness plc v Saunders* [1990] 2 AC 663.
19 (1890) 45 Ch D 1.
20 [1951] AC 507.
1 [1994] 1 AC 324. Other cases on bribes include *Metropolitan Bank v Heiron* (1880) 5 Ex D 319; *Boston Deep Sea Fishing & Ice Co v Ansell* (1888) 39 Ch D 339; *Mahesan S/O Thambiah v Malaysian Government Officers' Cooperative Housing Society Ltd* [1979] AC 374; *Islamic Republic of Iran Shipping Lines v Denby* [1987] 1 Lloyd's Rep 367; *Logicrose Ltd v Southend United Football Club Ltd* [1988] 1 WLR 1256; *Petrotrade Inc v Smith* [2000] 1 Lloyd's Rep 486; *Fyffes Group Ltd v Templeman* [2000] 2 Lloyd's Rep 643. It is also well established that the amount of the bribe or compensatory

transporting alcohol thereby avoiding their inspection by the police. Ultimately he was found out, court-martialled, sent to prison and £19,325 was seized by the Crown. He claimed recovery of that money. The House of Lords refused that claim. On the contrary, the Crown was held entitled to the money because in accepting bribes to sit in his military uniform Reading had been acting in breach of his fiduciary duty to the Crown as his employer. He was therefore liable to account for the bribe or to pay it over in an action for money had and received. The fact that the Crown had not lost anything was irrelevant: the measure of relief, as in all bribe cases, was therefore indisputably restitutionary.

One peculiarity of the bribe cases, as illustrated by *Reading*, is that, as an alternative to the equitable remedy of accounting for the bribe, the claimant has an action for money had and received. The latter is a common law remedy and, on the face of it, flouts the conventional dogma that common law remedies cannot be given for equitable wrongs.[2] One radical explanation would be that the common law remedy is responding to a breach of contract: ie the breach of an implied term in the employment or agency contract. Support for this could be found in the vagueness of the fiduciary label. But this would then contradict the traditional view, prior to *Attorney-General v Blake*,[3] that there could be no restitution for breach of contract. As there is no logical, as opposed to historical, reason why common law remedies should not be given for equitable wrongs, probably the better view is that the bribe cases represent a long-accepted, but little appreciated, exception to the 'no fusion' dogma.

The issue in *Lister v Stubbs* and *Attorney-General of Hong Kong v Reid* can be expressed by asking, is the fiduciary a constructive trustee of the bribe?: that is, is the bribe owned in equity by the beneficiary?

Lister v Stubbs gave a negative answer to these questions. The defendant was the foreman buyer for the claimants. He accepted a bribe of £5,541 from particular suppliers in return for showing them favouritism in orders. The defendant had invested some of that bribe in land and other securities. What the claimants sought in this action was not restitution of £5,541 (which they were clearly entitled to) but rather an order that the defendant should stop dealing with the investments and should hold them for the claimants. That order was refused.

---

damages (for the tort of deceit or, more realistically, inducing a breach of contract or for the equitable wrong of dishonest assistance) can be recovered from the briber; see, eg the *Mahesan*, *Logicrose* and *Fyffes* cases. Recovery of the bribe from the briber probably cannot be justified on restitutionary principle. Cf Birks *An Introduction to the Law of Restitution* (1989) pp 337–338.

2   Hanbury and Martin *Modern Equity* (16th edn, 2001) pp 24–26.
3   [2001] 1 AC 268.

In a very clear statement, exploring the implications of accepting the claimants' argument, Lindley LJ said:

'One consequence, of course, would be that, if Stubbs were to become bankrupt, this property acquired by him with the money ... would be withdrawn from the mass of his creditors and be handed over bodily to Lister. Can that be right? Another consequence would be that, if the appellants are right, Lister could compel Stubbs to account to them, not only for the money with interest, but for all the profits which he might have made by embarking in trade with it. Can that be right? It appears to me that those consequences show that there is some flaw in the argument ... the unsoundness consists in confounding ownership with obligation.'[4]

On the face of it, therefore, *Lister v Stubbs* meant that the bribe cases were treated differently from the unauthorised profit cases in that the fiduciary did not hold bribes on constructive trust.[5] Goff and Jones criticised this distinction and suggested that *Lister v Stubbs* was wrongly decided. They wrote:

'This decision emphatically marks off the secret commission cases ... an honest fiduciary, such as Mr Boardman, who is deemed to have abused his position of trust, is a constructive trustee of his profits, even though he acted in the best interests of the trust and his beneficiary gained over £20,000 from his intervention. In contrast the corrupt agent, or Sergeant Reading, is simply obliged to account for the value of his bribe.'[6]

That type of criticism has since been dispelled, and the remedial difference between the bribe and unauthorised profit cases removed, by the Privy Council in *Attorney-General for Hong Kong v Reid*[7] which refused to follow *Lister v Stubbs*. The defendant, a Crown Prosecutor and ultimately Director of Public Prosecutions in Hong Kong, had accepted bribes so as to obstruct the prosecution of certain criminals. He was convicted of criminal offences and imprisoned. The Hong Kong government successfully sought to establish that three properties in New Zealand, bought by the defendant using the bribe, were held on constructive trust for it so that its registration of caveats on the title of the three properties was valid. Lord Templeman contrasted the bribe cases with authorities

---

4 (1890) 45 Ch D 1 at 15.
5 It was followed on this point in, eg *Islamic Republic of Iran v Denby* [1987] 1 Lloyd's Rep 367; *Attorney-General's Reference (No 1 of 1985)* [1986] QB 491.
6 Goff and Jones *The Law of Restitution* (4th edn, 1993) at pp 668–669 (this passage does not appear in the latest 6th edn, 2002, having been overtaken by subsequent cases). See also, eg Needham 'Recovering the Profits of Bribery' (1979) 95 LQR 536, 540–545; Finn *Fiduciary Obligations* (1977) para 513.
7 [1994] 1 AC 324. For a consideration of the consequences for criminal law, see J C Smith '*Lister v Stubbs* and the Criminal Law' (1994) 110 LQR 180.

on other unauthorised gains made by fiduciaries, such as *Keech v Sandford*,[8] and referred with approval to an article by Sir Peter Millett criticising *Lister v Stubbs*.[9] Lord Templeman said:

> 'The decision in *Lister & Co v Stubbs* is not consistent with the principles that a fiduciary must not be allowed to benefit from his own breach of duty, that the fiduciary should account for the bribe as soon as he receives it and that equity regards as done that which ought to be done. From these principles it would appear to follow that the bribe and the property from time to time representing the bribe are held on a constructive trust for the person injured. A fiduciary remains personally liable for the amount of the bribe if, in the event, the value of the property then recovered by the injured person proved to be less than that amount.'[10]

Although *Attorney-General of Hong Kong v Reid* is technically of only persuasive authority, the very firm opinion of the Privy Council suggests that, in practice, *Lister v Stubbs* has been overruled. This has been confirmed by the recent case of *Daraydon Holdings Ltd v Solland International Ltd*[11] in which Lawrence Collins J applied *Reid*, and distinguished *Lister v Stubbs*, in holding that a bribe acquired in breach of fiduciary duty was held on constructive trust.

But not everyone disagrees with *Lister v Stubbs*. On the contrary, the powerful voices of Birks[12] and Goode[13] have long argued that the case was correct and that there is generally no justification for imposing proprietary, rather than personal, restitution to strip gains made by a wrongdoer. They principally argue that a proprietary restitutionary remedy is not justified other than where there has been a subtraction from the claimant's ownership. In Birks' terminology, the claimant must have a 'proprietary base.'[14] In contrast to where a trustee has misappropriated his beneficiary's equitable property, there is normally no

---

8   (1726) Sel Cas temp King 61.
9   'Bribes and Secret Commissions' [1993] RLR 7.
10   [1994] 1 AC 324, 336.
11   [2004] EWHC 622 (Ch).
12   Birks *An Introduction to the Law of Restitution* (revised edn, 1989) pp 387–389, 473–474; 'Personal Restitution in Equity' [1988] LMCLQ 128.
13   Goode 'Ownership and Obligation in Commercial Transactions' (1987) 103 LQR 433, 441–445; 'Property and Unjust Enrichment' in *Essays on the Law of Restitution* (ed Burrows, 1991) pp 215–246, esp 242; 'Proprietary Restitutionary Claims' in *Restitution, Past, Present and Future* (eds Cornish, Nolan, O'Sullivan and Virgo, 1998) pp 63–77. Finch and Worthington 'The *Pari Passu* Principle and Ranking Restitutionary Rights' in *Restitution and Insolvency* (ed Rose, 2000) pp 1–20 reach the similar conclusion, at pp 19–20, that 'unjust enrichment claimants merit proprietary status but disgorgement claimants do not.' See also Crilley 'A Case of Proprietary Overkill' [1994] RLR 57; Rotherham 'The Recovery of the Profits of Wrongdoing and Insolvency' [1997] CFILR 43. Note that Goode also argues that a form of proprietary remedy (he labels it a 'remedial constructive trust') which protects the interests of D's creditors is justified where D makes a 'deemed agency gain' (ie a gain which D was bound in equity to make, if he made it at all, for C).
14   Birks *An Introduction to the Law of Restitution* (revised edn, 1989) pp 386–389.

such proprietary base here because a beneficiary does not own the bribe or the unauthorised gain before the (alleged) constructive trust takes effect.

In the *Daraydon Holdings* case, Lawrence Collins J pointed out that the facts were distinguishable from *Lister v Stubbs* because the bribe, having been taken out of the contract price paid by the claimants, did come from the claimant's property. The facts therefore did fall within the 'proprietary base' justification. But on Collins J's primary reasoning, supporting *Reid*, this was not crucial. In his view, a constructive trust should be applied in all cases of gains made in breach of fiduciary duty. He said,

> 'There are powerful policy reasons for ensuring that a fiduciary does not retain gains acquired in violation of fiduciary duty, and I do not consider that it should make any difference whether the fiduciary is insolvent. There is no injustice to the creditors in their not sharing in an asset for which the fiduciary has not given value, and which the fiduciary should not have had.'[15]

With respect, however, it is hard to see why a victim claiming restitution for a wrong should have priority on the wrongdoer's insolvency given that a compensation-claimant does not have such priority.[16] Compensation should rank above restitution as a remedial response to a wrong; and while, unlike wrongfully acquiring gains, loss caused by a wrongdoer does not swell the wrongdoer's assets, one can say that, by the wrongdoer failing to pay compensation, his assets on insolvency are greater than they should have been so that, in that indirect sense, the creditors are sharing in assets which the wrongdoer should not have had.

One would have expected it to follow from Birks' support for *Lister v Stubbs* that he considered *Boardman v Phipps* to be wrong. But he argued that nothing turned in that case on the constructive trust terminology used: it was superfluous. *Boardman v Phipps* merely imposed a personal restitutionary remedy. Contrary to the common assumption the decision was, in his view, consistent with *Lister v Stubbs*.

It is hard to agree with Birks' startling re-interpretation. Admittedly the cases on the equitable wrong of dishonest assistance show that the courts do sometimes adopt constructive trust language that is indisputably unwarranted (clearly so in that area, as is well-recognised, because the defendant has commonly not received any property).[17] And it is true that no order was made in *Boardman v Phipps* that the defendants

---

15 [2004] EWHC 622 (Ch), para 86.
16 Burrows 'Proprietary Restitution: Unmasking Unjust Enrichment' (2001) 117 LQR 412, 427; *The Law of Restitution* (2nd edn, 2002) p 72.
17 Hanbury and Martin *Modern Equity* (16th edn, 2001) p 306.

should transfer the shares to the claimant. But a declaration that the defendants held the shares on constructive trust was made[18] and it must follow that the claimants would have been entitled to priority had the defendants been insolvent. Even if Birks were right on *Boardman v Phipps* itself, he would be fighting against both the consistent use of constructive trust terminology by the judiciary and the widespread assumption of commentators that this means that a beneficiary is entitled to a proprietary restitutionary remedy for unauthorised profits.

The quantum of restitution for equitable wrongs is a distinct policy question. Even though factual causation is satisfied, in that the gain would not have been made but for the wrong, it may be too harsh to the defendant to strip it of all factually caused profits however far removed from the wrong. Constructive trust terminology prima facie indicates that the fiduciary is liable for any profit made from the initial gain. In contrast, it is clear from Lindley LJ's reasoning in *Lister v Stubbs* that he considered fiduciaries liable to account only for the bribe and not for gains made from investing that bribe. In fact the distinction is not quite as sharp as may at first sight appear because of the judicial discretion – exercised in *Boardman v Phipps* – to afford a fiduciary an allowance for his time and skill in making the profit.

It is submitted that this discretion to make an allowance affords the courts the necessary flexibility in deciding on the appropriate quantum of restitution. The application of an allowance, and its amount, may turn on a variety of factors such as the degree of skill and effort expended by the wrongdoer and whether the wrongdoer was acting honestly or not. Indeed one can argue that an account of profits reduced by the discretionary allowance is analogous to the discretion the courts have, in the context of restitutionary damages for torts and breach of contract, in deciding what constitutes the reasonable sum that, hypothetically, the parties would have bargained for to allow the 'wrong'.[19] In other words, both appear to be mechanisms enabling the courts to strip what they consider to be the appropriate proportion of the wrongdoer's profits.

Whatever the correct answer to the *Lister v Stubbs* debate, one must not lose sight of the uncontroverted starting point, namely that restitution can be, and commonly has been, granted for breach of fiduciary duty (including on a strict liability basis). Is this justified?

Jackman argues that it is, because trusts and other fiduciary relationships are facilitative institutions that merit special protection.[20]

---

18   This is made clear by the report of Wilberforce J's judgment in *Phipps v Boardman* [1964] 2 All ER 187, 208.
19   Above, pp 374, 379–384, 407.
20   'Restitution for Wrongs' [1989] CLJ 302, 311–314.

The imposition of restitution for breach of a strict fiduciary duty is therefore no more surprising than restitution for strict liability in the proprietary torts. On his view, the judicial discretion to make an allowance for the fiduciary's skill and time will primarily be exercised where the fiduciary aims bona fide to make the beneficiaries (perhaps as well as himself) better off and is successful in so doing and reflects the consistent idea that the moral quality of the wrongdoing is a discretionary factor going to the quantum of restitution not to whether it is justified in the first place. Birks also considered that restitution for breach of fiduciary duty is justified. The bribe cases fit his primary 'cynical wrongdoing' justification for giving restitution for a wrong.[1] Moreover, Birks went beyond his primary test to argue that a policy of 'prophylaxis' also justifies restitution on a strict liability basis for unauthorised gains made in breach of fiduciary duty.[2]

(b) Restitution for breach of confidence

It is clear that, as an alternative to compensatory damages, a claimant is entitled to an account of profits for breach of confidence at least if that breach was intentional. It is possible that he is alternatively entitled to restitutionary damages. Those restitutionary damages are equitable (awarded in substitution for, or in addition to, an injunction under Supreme Court Act 1981, s 50) or, possibly, common law damages.[3]

That an account of profits can be awarded is shown by, for example, *Peter Pan Manufacturing Corpn v Corsets Silhouette Ltd*[4] where the defendants had manufactured and sold brassieres knowingly using confidential information obtained from the claimants. And in *Attorney-General v Guardian Newspapers Ltd (No 2)*,[5] the *Sunday Times* was held liable to account for profits made in publishing, in breach of confidence to the Crown, the first extract of Peter Wright's book, *Spycatcher*, that publication having taken place before the information had reached the public domain. Lord Keith said of an account of profits:

'The remedy is, in my opinion ... to be attributed to the principle that no one should be permitted to gain from his own wrongdoing. Its availability may also, in general,

---

1   Birks *An Introduction to the Law of Restitution* (rvsd ed, 1989) pp 326–327. This is also supported by the Law Commission: see above, p 612, n 6.
2   Birks *An Introduction to the Law of Restitution* (rvsd ed, 1989) pp 332–333, 338–343.
3   The discussion above, pp 606–609 of the jurisdiction to award damages for breach of confidence, in the context of compensatory damages, is equally relevant to restitutionary damages.
4   [1964] 1 WLR 96. See also *Ansell Rubber Co Ltd v Allied Rubber Industries Pty Ltd* [1972] RPC 811; *AB Consolidated v Europe Strength Food Co Pty Ltd* [1978] 2 NZLR 515.
5   [1990] 1 AC 109.

serve a useful purpose in lessening the temptation for recipients of confidential information to misuse it for financial gain.'[6]

And in Lord Brightman's words, 'the only remedy available to the Crown is the inadequate remedy of an account of profits, on the basis that the *Sunday Times* unjustly enriched itself and should therefore be stripped of the riches wrongfully acquired.'[7]

Although there is no case law on this, it would seem clear that, as with breach of fiduciary duty, in awarding an account of profits for breach of confidence the courts have a discretion to afford the defendant a liberal allowance for work and skill.

In none of the English cases has it been held that the gains made in breach of confidence are held on constructive trust.[8] But in the difficult Canadian case of *LAC Minerals Ltd v International Corona Resources Ltd*[9] a constructive trust was imposed for breach of confidence. In negotiations for a joint venture between them, the defendants acquired from the claimant information about the mineral potential of some land. The defendants subsequently outbid the claimant in buying that land and set up a successful gold-mine on it. The majority of the Supreme Court of Canada held that the claimant was entitled to a constructive trust of the land as a remedy for the defendants' breach of confidence, subject to an allowance to the defendants, secured by a lien, for expenses in developing the mine that the claimant itself would have necessarily had to incur.

La Forest J, giving the main majority judgment, rejected the argument that a proprietary restitutionary remedy is only justified where the claimant has a pre-existing right of property. He said:

'... it is not the case that a constructive trust should be reserved for situations where a right of property is recognised. That would limit the constructive trust to its institutional function and deny it the status of a remedy, its more important role. Thus it is

---

6   [1990] 1 AC 109 at 262.
7   [1990] 1 AC 109 at 266. Lord Goff's general comments on restitution for wrongs at 286 are also of interest.
8   But in obiter dicta in *Attorney-General v Guardian Newspapers (No 2)* [1990] 1 AC 109 at 288 Lord Goff tentatively suggested that the copyright in *Spycatcher* might be held on constructive trust for the Crown. See also *Service Corpn International plc v Channel Four Television Corpn* [1999] EMLR 83 at 90–91; *United Pan-Europe Communications NV v Deutsche Bank AG* [2000] 2 BCLC 461, CA.
9   (1989) 61 DLR (4th) 14. In *Cadbury Schweppes Inc v FBI Foods Ltd* (1999) 167 DLR (4th) 577, the Supreme Court of Canada has subsequently stressed that, in Canada, the imposition of a constructive trust is discretionary and dependent on the particular facts of a case. It was there held that compensation for breach of confidence, and not a proprietary remedy, was appropriate (the claimants not having sought an account of profits). See Abdullah and Hang 'To Make The Remedy Fit the Wrong' (1999) 115 LQR 376.

not in all cases that a pre-existing right of property will exist when a constructive trust is ordered ... it is not necessary, therefore, to determine whether confidential informa- tion is property ...'[10]

The objection to this approach is that, to the extent that it imposes proprietary restitution for a wrong, it unjustifiably sacrifices the interests of a defendant's creditors.[11] And for what positive reasons? La Forest J suggests the following: 'Having specific regard to the uniqueness of the Williams property, to the fact that but for LAC's breaches of duty, Corona would have acquired it, and recognising the virtual impossibility of accurately valuing the property, I am of the view that it is appropriate to award Corona a constructive trust over the land.'[12]

It is hard to accept that difficulty of assessment is a valid reason for preferring a proprietary, as opposed to a personal, restitutionary remedy for a wrong. And even if a justification for a constructive trust could lie in there having been an unjust enrichment by interceptive subtraction,[13] that should surely have meant that the constructive trust existed from the date when LAC acquired the property.

Wilson J appeared to think that the constructive trust was being imposed as a compensatory remedy:

' ... the only sure way in which Corona can be fully compensated for the breach in this case is by the imposition of a constructive trust on LAC in favour of Corona with respect to the property. Full compensation may or may not have been achieved through an award of common law damages depending upon the accuracy of valuation techniques. It can most surely be achieved in this case through the award of an *in rem* remedy.'[14]

A merit of that approach is that the remedies of specific performance and delivery up suggest that, at least where the subject-matter is unique, difficulty in assessing compensation for a wrong can constitute a valid ground for preferring a proprietary remedy. But on the facts to impose the constructive trust as a means of ensuring full compensation rested on the unrealistic assumption that, had there been no breach of confidence,

---

10   (1989) 61 DLR (4th) 14 at 50.
11   Goode 'Property and Unjust Enrichment' in *Essays on the Law of Restitution* (ed Burrows, (1991) pp 215, 239–240; Gummow 'Unjust Enrichment, Restitution and Proprietary Remedies' in *Essays on Restitution* (ed Finn, 1990) pp 47, 78; Birks 'The Remedies for Abuse of Confidential Information' [1990] LMCLQ 460, 463.
12   (1989) 61 DLR (4th) 14 at 52.
13   For the concept of 'interceptive subtraction', see Birks *An Introduction to the Law of Restitution* (rvsd edn, 1989) pp 133–139.
14   (1989) 61 DLR (4th) 14 at 17.

not only would the claimant have developed the mine itself rather than jointly with the defendants but also would have developed it as profitably as the defendants had done.

The minority (Soprinka and McIntyre JJ) preferred to award compensatory damages. The remedy of an accounting of profits had not been in issue and they thought a constructive trust inappropriate because, on their view of the facts, the extent of the connection between the confidential information and the acquisition of the property was uncertain.

If we now turn from an account of profits to restitutionary damages, the possibility of such damages being awarded for breach of confidence primarily derives from the Court of Appeal's judgment in *Seager v Copydex Ltd (No 2)*,[15] which we have already examined in detail in respect of compensatory damages. The defendants had inadvertently (ie subconsciously) used confidential information in manufacturing a new style carpet-grip. Lord Denning said that if there was nothing special about the confidential information, damages for breach of confidence should be based on the fee the defendant saved by not employing a consultant to acquire that information; whereas if the information was special, damages should be assessed according to what a willing buyer would have paid for it.

The former is restitutionary. The latter can be analysed as either compensatory or restitutionary: it represents either what the claimant has lost by not selling to the defendant or a third party, or what the defendant has gained by saving itself the expense of paying for the information.

The Court of Appeal appeared to think that an account of profits was not an appropriate remedy.[16] Although the reason for this was not given, the obvious explanation is that, in contrast to the *Peter Pan* and *Spycatcher* cases, the wrongdoing was not intentional in *Seager v Copydex*.

As we have seen,[17] although there was no discussion in *Seager v Copydex* as to the jurisdiction to award damages, the most natural interpretation is that they were equitable damages being given in substitution for an injunction.

There is further support for the award of restitutionary damages for breach of confidence in Sir Donald Nicholls V-C's judgment in *Universal Thermosensors Ltd v Hibben*.[18] In assessing the defendants' damages on the claimant's cross-undertaking supporting an interim injunction restraining

15   [1969] 1 WLR 809.
16   *Seager v Copydex Ltd* [1967] 1 WLR 923 at 932.
17   See above, p 607.
18   [1992] 1 WLR 840.

the defendants' breach of confidence, the Vice-Chancellor deducted the damages the claimant was entitled to 'for the benefits they derived from the wrongful use of its confidential information, in particular (but not exclusively) by saving themselves the time, trouble, and expense of compiling their own list of contacts without reference to the plaintiff's records.'[19] He referred to *Seager v Copydex* and to the 'user principle' by which 'the plaintiff ought to be paid by the defendants for the use they made of the plaintiff's confidential information even if the plaintiff suffered no loss of profits in consequence'.[20] Although he thereby used clear restitutionary reasoning, the strength of this is weakened by the fact that the Vice-Chancellor also described the damages as compensatory; and, despite the wrongdoing being intentional, he thought that the claimant was not entitled to an injunction (nor, by inference, to an account of profits) because that would put the claimant in a better position than if there had been no breach of confidence.

Is restitution (whether through an account of profits or restitutionary damages) for breach of confidence justified? Jackman's 'facilitative institution' analysis neatly reconciles the main cases.[1] A relationship of confidentiality (whether confidential information is property or not) is a facilitative institution which merits special protection by the courts. On this view, *Peter Pan*, the *Spycatcher* case, and *Seager* are all justifiably restitutionary with the difference between the remedy of an account of profits and restitutionary damages being one of quantum turning on the secondary factor of the moral quality of the wrongdoing. Birks analysed *Seager* as awarding compensation only which would leave the other leading cases as explicable on his primary test of cynical wrongdoing.[2]

(2) Punishment for equitable wrongs

It is a controversial question whether punishment, most obviously through punitive damages, can be awarded for an equitable wrong. Those who argue against the fusion of common law and equity argue that punitive damages, being a common law remedy, simply cannot be awarded for an equitable wrong. And there is no indication that equitable damages or 'equitable compensation' have ever included a punitive element.

---

19   [1992] 1 WLR 840 at 858–859.
20   [1992] 1 WLR 840 at 856.
1   See above, pp 620–621.
2   Birks *An Introduction to the Law of Restitution* (rvsd edn, 1989) pp 326–327. Cf Birks, at pp 345–346 which relies on his subsequently abandoned 'anti-enrichment wrong' test. See also Law Commission Report No 247, para 3.51 and Draft Bill, cl 12; above, p 612, n 6.

But leaving aside history, it is hard to see why as a matter of principle or policy punitive damages should be confined to torts. In *Kuddus v Chief Constable of Leicestershire Constabulary*[3] a cause of action limitation on punitive damages was rejected. And although the language of their Lordships was confined to torts, the majority's reasoning would suggest that there is no reason why punitive damages cannot be awarded for equitable wrongs.

The Law Commission recommended that punitive damages should be available for equitable wrongs. It argued that there was no reason of principle or practicality to exclude equitable wrongs from a rational expansion of punitive damages and said that it was 'unsatisfactory to perpetuate the historical divide between common law and equity, unless there is very good reason to do so.'[4] It argued that it would be wrong as a matter of policy to allow punitive damages for the tort of deceit and yet to deny them for dishonest breach of fiduciary duty or dishonest breach of confidence. Indeed one might argue that punitive damages are historically even more suitable for equitable wrongs than common law wrongs given that, as we have seen, restitution for equitable wrongs – stripping away gains – is a commonplace remedy, whereas it is still somewhat unusual for torts (and even rarer for breach of contract).

This now derives support from Lindsay J's judgment in *Douglas v Hello! Ltd (No 3)*.[5] While refusing punitive damages for breach of confidence on the facts – because the defendants' wrongful conduct had not been sufficiently outrageous – he said, after considering *Kuddus*, 'I am content to assume, without deciding, that exemplary damages (or equity's equivalent) are available in respect of breach of confidence.'[6]

Furthermore, although the contrary position has been taken in Australia,[7] there is support from New Zealand and Canada for punitive damages being available for equitable wrongs. In the well-known decision of the New Zealand Court of Appeal in *Acquaculture Corpn v New Zealand Green Mussel Co Ltd*,[8] a majority held that, in addition to compensation, punitive damages could be awarded for breach of confidence albeit that, on the facts, they were not merited. Cooke P, giving the majority's decision, said:

---

3   [2001] UKHL 29, [2002] 2 AC 122. See above, ch 18.
4   *Aggravated, Exemplary and Restitutionary Damages* Report No 247 (1997) para 5.55.
5   [2003] EWHC 786, [2003] 3 All ER 996.
6   [2003] EWHC 786, [2003] 3 All ER 996 at para 273.
7   *Harris v Digital Pulse Pty Ltd* (2003) 197 ALR 626 (NSWCA). For criticism see Edelman 'A "Fusion Fallacy" Fallacy' (2003) 119 LQR 375. See also *Bailey v Namol Pty Ltd* (1994) 12 ALR 228 at 238 (Federal CA tentatively doubting, without deciding, the point, whether punitive damages can be awarded for equitable wrongs). The position is also left open by McDermott 'Exemplary Damages in Equity' (1995) 69 ALJ 773–774.
8   [1990] 3 NZLR 299.

'Whether the obligation of confidence in a case of the present kind should be classified as purely an equitable one is debatable, but we do not think that the question matters for any purpose material to this appeal. For all purposes now material, equity and common law are mingled or merged. The practicality of the matter is that in the circumstances of the dealings between the parties the law imposes a duty of confidence. For its breach a full range of remedies should be available as appropriate, no matter whether they originated in common law, equity or statute ... [A]pplying the foregoing approach as to the available range of remedies, we see no reason in principle why exemplary damages should not be awarded for actionable breach of confidence in a case where a compensatory award would not adequately reflect the gravity of the defendant's conduct.'[9]

Following on from this in *Cook v Evatt (No 2)*,[10] Fisher J in the New Zealand High Court added exemplary damages of NZ$5,000 to an account of profits of over NZ$20,000 for breach of fiduciary duty. Citing *Acquaculture*, he said, 'Exemplary damages may be awarded whether the cause of action is founded in law or in equity.' [11]

In Canada in *Norberg v Wynrib*,[12] punitive damages were awarded for the tort of trespass to the person or, in the opinion of McLachlin J, for breach of fiduciary duty, where the claimant sued her defendant doctor for sexual assaults on her that she permitted in return for being prescribed drugs to which she was addicted.

It is submitted that, as in New Zealand and, it would seem, Canada, English law should allow the award of punitive damages for equitable wrongs as well as torts. Punitive damages can serve a useful function and it is irrational to rule them out on purely historical grounds.

4. COMPELLING PERFORMANCE OR PREVENTING (OR COMPELLING THE UNDOING OF) AN EQUITABLE WRONG

(1) Injunctions

In this section, we are concerned to clarify that injunctions, granted or refused according to similar principles as have been discussed in relation to torts and breach of contract,[13] are also available in respect of

---

9   [1990] 3 NZLR 299 at 301–302. In contrast, Somers J dissented on this aspect of the reasoning saying, at 302, 'equity and penalty are strangers.'
10 [1992] 1 NZLR 676.
11 [1992] 1 NZLR 676 at 705.
12 (1992) 92 DLR (4th) 440. See also, eg *Mcdonald Estate v Martin* [1995] CCL 1142 (Man CA); *Gerula v Flores* [1995] CCL 8583 (Ont CA).
13 See above, ch 21.

equitable wrongs. One technical difference is that, as common law compensatory damages are not available for equitable wrongs, there is no 'adequacy of damages' hurdle that a claimant seeking an injunction for an equitable wrong needs to overcome. However, at least in relation to prohibitory injunctions, this is unlikely to be a significant difference in practice because that hurdle is easily overcome in respect of prohibitory injunctions for torts and breach of contract. Moreover, while there may be no 'adequacy of damages' hurdle for injunctions for equitable wrongs, the courts, in the exercise of their general discretion to refuse an injunction, might do so on the basis that equitable compensation or equitable (compensatory) damages is a more appropriate remedy.

It is well established that a beneficiary may be granted an interim[14] or final prohibitory injunction to prevent the continuation or repetition of a breach of fiduciary duty or to prevent a threatened breach of fiduciary duty. So, for example, prohibitory injunctions have been granted to prevent a trustee in breach of trust, from completing a detrimental contract for the sale of trust property;[15] or to restrain a proposed distribution of trust property contrary to the terms of the trust;[16] or to restrain a sale of trust property where the vendor was not complying with statutory requirements for the sale.[17] Mandatory enforcing injunctions have also been ordered against trustees ordering them to carry out their positive fiduciary duties.[18] Analogously, but going one step further, the court has jurisdiction to appoint a receiver to ensure that the duties owed by a fiduciary are performed.[19]

In respect of proprietary estoppel, orders to convey land – corresponding to specific performance of a contract to convey land –

---

14 Albeit that the injunction was refused, one of the most important decisions on the correct approach to interim injunctions, where a trial is unlikely to take place, concerned an alleged breach of fiduciary duty by company directors: see *Cayne v Global Natural Resources* [1984] 1 All ER 225, above, pp 556–557.

15 *Dance v Goldingham* (1873) 8 Ch App 902.

16 *Fox v Fox* (1870) LR 11 Eq 142.

17 *Wheelwright v Walker* (1883) 23 Ch D 752; *Waller v Waller* [1967] 1 All ER 305 (interim injunction).

18 *Foley v Burnell* (1783) 1 Bro CC 274; *Fletcher v Fletcher* (1844) 4 Hare 67. The constructive trust ordered by the Supreme Court of Canada in the very difficult case of *Korkontzilas v Soulos* (1997) 146 DLR (4th) 214 may be best viewed as being concerned to enforce the defendant's positive fiduciary duty rather than as being restitutionary: see Burrows *The Law of Restitution* (2nd edn, 2002) pp 501–502.

19 Supreme Court Act 1981, s 37(1): see above, p 575. For a receiver appointed in respect of a fiduciary duty, see *Middleton v Dodswell* (1806) 13 Ves 266.

have been made;[20] and, in other cases, the courts 'treating as done that which ought to be done' have declared that, in equity, the expected right over another's land already exists.[1]

Interim or final prohibitory injunctions have also been commonly granted to prevent a breach of confidence.[2] As regards interim injunctions, an important question is whether the approach in *American Cyanamid v Ethicon*[3] applies given that, as we have seen,[4] that approach is not applied to the tort of defamation and similar free speech issues may be in play in restraining a breach of confidence. The case law on that question is unsettled.

On the one hand, in *Schering Chemicals Ltd v Falkman Ltd*,[5] concerning a television film, and *Francome v Mirror Group Newspapers Ltd*,[6] dealing with a newspaper article, interim injunctions were granted to restrain breach of confidence apparently on the application of *American Cyanamid*. Similarly in *Attorney-General v Observer Newspapers Ltd*,[7] where an interim injunction was granted to restrain two newspapers publishing confidential information disclosed by a former member of the British secret service in his book *Spycatcher*, the Court of Appeal thought that in this context a proper approach was to grant the injunction unless the court was satisfied that there was a serious defence of public interest which was *very likely* to succeed at trial. Again in *Attorney-General v Guardian Newspapers Ltd*,[8] in a further round of the *Spycatcher* litigation, interim injunctions were upheld by the House of Lords apparently on the application of *American Cyanamid* principles.

---

20 *Dillwyn v Llewellyn* (1862) 4 De G F & J 517; *Pascoe v Turner* [1979] 1 WLR 431.
1 *Inwards v Baker* [1965] 2 QB 29; *Crabb v Arun District Council* [1976] Ch 179; *Re Basham* [1986] 1 WLR 1498; *Gillett v Holt* [2001] Ch 210.
2 *Peter Pan Manufacturing Corpn v Corsets Silhouette Ltd* [1964] 1 WLR 96; *Duchess of Argyll v Duke of Argyll* [1967] Ch 302 (interim injunction: see above, p 570); *Francombe v Mirror Group Newspapers Ltd* [1984] 1 WLR 892 (interim *quia timet* injunction); *X v Y* [1988] 2 All ER 648. See Sharpe *Injunctions and Specific Performance* (3rd edn, 2000) paras 5.130–5.180. See also *Instil Group Inc v Zahoor* [2003] EWHC 165 (Ch), [2003] 2 All ER 252 (injunction to restrain a breach of confidence, in respect of legally privileged documents, refused on the facts). For the impact of interim injunctions, preventing a breach of confidence, on third parties, see *Attorney-General v Times Newspapers Ltd* [1992] 1 AC 191; *Attorney-General v Punch Ltd* [2002] UKHL 50, [2003] 1 AC 1046; *Jockey Club Ltd v Buffham* [2002] EWHC 1866 (QB), [2003] QB 462. The Law Commission in *Breach of Confidence* Report No 110 (1981) paras 6.110–6.112 recommended that the courts should be empowered (or, on the better view, should use their existing powers) to make conditional injunctions, whereby the claimant should pay fair compensation for wasted expenses incurred by the defendant before it knew, or ought to have known, that the information was confidential: cf the 'compensated injunction,' discussed above, p 525.
3 [1975] AC 396.
4 See above, pp 560–561.
5 [1982] QB 1.
6 [1984] 1 WLR 892.
7 [1986] NLJ Rep 799.
8 [1987] 1 WLR 1248.

In contrast, in *Woodward v Hutchins*[9] the Court of Appeal drew some analogy to libel cases in allowing a newspaper to publish articles about the private lives of the claimant pop singers, written by their former publicity agent, and this was also Lord Denning's approach dissenting in *Schering*. This latter view is further supported by *Lion Laboratories Ltd v Evans*.[10] The question here was whether an interim injunction should be granted to restrain publication in a newspaper of admittedly confidential information regarding the accuracy of the claimant's intoxication instrument being used by the police to test the breath of drivers. The Court of Appeal refused the injunction because the defendants had satisfied the court that at trial they would have a strong defence of public interest. *American Cyanamid* was not applied, and the approach adopted was somewhat analogous to that for defamation, although the court was anxious to stress that the public interest needed to be far more clearly made out than did the defence of justification for libel. 'To be allowed to publish confidential information the defendants must do more than raise the plea of public interest; they must show "a legitimate ground for supposing it is in the public interest for it to be disclosed".'[11] This seems sensible. For while breach of confidence should probably be easier to restrain by interim injunction than defamation – since once made public, confidentiality is destroyed for ever, whereas a lost reputation can be won back – where free speech is in issue, the courts should again be slow to grant an interim injunction, amounting as it does to prior censorship. Certainly *American Cyanamid* should not be applied.

This latter approach derives further support from the Human Rights Act 1998, s 12(3). According to this, a court shall not grant an interim injunction restraining publication before trial (where this 'might affect the exercise of the Convention right to freedom of expression') 'unless the court is satisfied that the applicant is likely to establish that publication shall not be allowed.' This constitutes a legislative departure from *American Cyanamid*. In *Cream Holdings Ltd v Banerjee*,[12] an interim injunction restraining a breach of confidence was upheld and the Court of Appeal laid down that 'likely' in s 12(3) means that there must be a 'real prospect of success, convincingly established.' This was said to be a higher threshold than the *American Cyanamid* test of there being a serious

9   [1977] 1 WLR 760. Prior *to American Cyanamid*, see *Fraser v Evans* [1969] 1 QB 349; *Hubbard v Vosper* [1972] 2 QB 84.
10   [1985] QB 526.
11   [1985] QB 526 at 528 (per Stephenson LJ citing Lord Denning in *Woodward v Hutchins* [1977] WLR 760 at 764).
12   [2003] EWCA Civ 103, [2003] Ch 650. See also above, p 561.

issue to be tried but a lower threshold than having to show that it was 'more probable than not' that an injunction would be granted at trial.

What the above examination of the case law has shown is that, as one would expect, prohibitory and mandatory injunctions (whether final or interim) are available for equitable wrongs on similar principles to those applying to injunctions for the common law wrongs.

(2) Accounting for loss?

As we have seen above in discussing equitable compensation,[13] it has been argued by some that the equitable remedy of accounting (for loss) available against a trustee is different from equitable compensation. According to that argument, accounting for loss is analogous to the award of an agreed sum or specific performance. It is a monetary remedy compelling performance of a trustee's positive obligations. But although this argument was not specifically addressed by the House of Lords in *Target Holdings Ltd v Redfern*,[14] that decision has impliedly rejected the view that the accounting (for loss) remedy can operate differently from equitable compensation. In other words, it appears that, whatever the historical position, there is no longer an equitable monetary remedy (as distinct from a mandatory injunction) compelling performance of a trustee's positive obligations.

(3) Delivery up in relation to breach of confidence

(a) Delivery up of material containing confidential information

A claimant can be granted delivery up of material containing confidential information belonging to him.[15] This is a remedy for the equitable wrong of breach of confidence[16] and is analogous to delivery up of goods for tortious interference with goods[17] although, a fortiori, no common law damages can be awarded and hence no usual adequacy hurdle needs to be overcome. Delivery up of material containing confidential information is a remedy concerned to compel the undoing of a wrong.

---

13 See above, pp 604–606.
14 [1996] AC 421. See above, pp 604–606.
15 *Alperton Rubber Co v Manning* (1917) 86 LJ Ch 377; *Industrial Furnaces Ltd v Reaves* [1970] RPC 605.
16 See, eg *Industrial Furnaces Ltd v Reaves* [1970] RPC 605; Gurry *Breach of Confidence* (1984) p 411; Law Commission Report No 110 *Breach of Confidence* paras 4.102–4.104.
17 See above, ch 22.

(b) Delivery up for destruction or destruction on oath

As with tortious infringement of intellectual property rights,[18] so with breach of confidence, the courts have an inherent jurisdiction to order, and have ordered, a defendant to deliver up to the claimant or the court for destruction, or himself to destroy, articles made in breach of the duty of confidence owed to the claimant.[19] This remedy is best viewed as being to prevent a breach of confidence and as going one step beyond a prohibitory injunction.[20]

It is important to realise that this remedy is granted even though the claimant does not own the articles ordered to be destroyed.[1] This is the key to avoiding confusion with the different remedy of delivery up of material containing confidential information. It follows that, while a claimant granted delivery up of confidential information belonging to him is entitled to do what he likes with that property, a claimant to whom delivery up for destruction is ordered ought to destroy that property.

5. DECLARING RIGHTS

Equity has no concept of nominal (or contemptuous) damages so that these cannot be awarded for an equitable wrong. This creates no difficulty or lacuna because the function of nominal damages is simply to declare rights and this can be done more straightforwardly and openly by a declaration. Declarations are available on the same principles in respect of equitable rights as they are for common law rights. All that has been said about declarations in chapter 23 therefore applies analogously here. As a remedy for an equitable wrong, a declaration will generally be concerned to pronounce authoritatively that the defendant's conduct did or does amount to an equitable wrong.[2]

---

18 See above, pp 583–585.
19 *Prince Albert v Strange* (1849) 2 De G & Sm 704; *Peter Pan Manufacturing Corpn v Corsets Silhouette Ltd* [1963] 3 All ER 402; *Ansell Rubber Co Pty Ltd v Allied Rubber Industries Pty Ltd* [1972] RPC 811; *Franklin v Giddins* [1978] Qd R 72.
20 See above, p 584.
1 *Ansell Rubber Co Pty v Allied Rubber Industries Pty Ltd* [1972] RPC 811.
2 Note also that, in respect of proprietary estoppel, declarations of the claimant's equitable proprietary rights (that were promised by the defendant) have been made: see above, p 629, n 1.

6. MISCELLANEOUS ISSUES ON REMEDIES FOR EQUITABLE WRONGS

In this section, we consider two issues not so far dealt with in this chapter: (pre-judgment) interest and limitation periods in respect of remedies for equitable wrongs.

(1) Interest

There is an inherent equitable jurisdiction empowering the courts to award pre-judgment interest on equitable remedies. In so far as the equitable remedy is 'for the recovery of a debt or damages' a statutory power to award simple interest is also conferred by the Supreme Court Act 1981, s 35A. In *BP Exploration Co (Libya) Ltd v Hunt (No 2)*[3] Lord Brandon interpreted those words widely as covering any monetary remedy, whether common law or equitable. He said:

> 'In my opinion, the words "any debt or damages", in the context in which they occur, are very wide so that they cover any sum of money which is recoverable by one party from another, either at common law or in equity or under a statute of the kind here concerned.'[4]

In some cases in which equitable remedies have been granted, compound rather than merely simple, interest has been awarded. But it appears that this power is confined to cases of fraud or breach of fiduciary duty;[5] and there are suggestions that it is further restricted to where the monetary remedy is restitutionary (ie an account of profits) rather than compensatory.[6]

An opportunity to develop the law was presented to the House of Lords in *Westdeutsche Landesbank Girozentrale v Islington London Borough Council,*[7] albeit that this case was concerned not with remedies for wrongs but restitution for the cause of action of unjust enrichment. The claim was a common law restitutionary claim for money paid under a void interest rate swap transaction. Unfortunately, by a bare majority (Lords Goff and Woolf dissenting), their Lordships decided that compound

---

3   [1983] 2 AC 352.
4   [1983] 2 AC 352 at 373. The statute he was there referring to was the Law Reform (Frustrated Contracts) Act 1943.
5   *Wallersteiner v Moir (No 2)* [1975] QB 373; *President of India v La Pintada Compania* [1985] AC 104; *Westdeutsche Landesbank Girozentrale v Islington London Borough Council* [1996] AC 669; *Kuwait Oil Tanker Co SAK v Al Bader* [2000] 2 All ER (Comm) 271 at 339–344.
6   *Westdeutsche Landesbank Girozentrale v Islington London Borough Council* [1996] AC 669 at 701. For a strong argument to the contrary, see Elliott 'Rethinking Interest on Withheld and Misapplied Trust Money' (2001) Conv 313, esp 335–336 citing, eg *Gilroy v Stephens* (1882) 30 WR 745.
7   [1996] AC 669.

interest could not be added to the restitutionary remedy. To develop the equitable jurisdiction to award compound interest beyond its two recognised categories (fraud or breach of fiduciary duty) was felt to be unacceptable as outflanking the Legislature's decision to allow simple interest only under the Supreme Court Act 1981, s 35A (and before that under the Law Reform (Miscellaneous Provisions) Act 1934, s 3(1)). Lord Lloyd also argued that to allow the award of compound interest might cause uncertainty and consequent litigation, for example as to the rate to be awarded. In contrast, Lords Goff and Woolf dissenting saw the award of compound interest, in the instant case, as essential in order to achieve full and proper restitution; and there was thought to be no countervailing good reason for refusing to extend the equitable jurisdiction.

Given that the House of Lords has, therefore, not seen fit to extend the equitable jurisdiction to award compound interest, it is not surprising that the Law Commission has recommended a reform of the Supreme Court Act 1981, s 35A. The recommended reform would give the courts a general power to award compound, rather than simple, interest on debts and damages.[8]

(2) Limitation periods[9]

As regards breach of trust, the crucial provision of the Limitation Act 1980 governing limitation of actions is the tortuous s 21. The basic regime of that section is that there is a six-year limitation period, running from the date when the right of action accrued,[10] for a breach of trust (s 21(3)) but that actions for fraudulent breach of trust or to recover trust property or its proceeds are excluded and have no statutory limitation period (s 21(1)).

The position in relation to breach of fiduciary duty (other than by an express trustee) has recently been the subject of judicial controversy. In *Nelson v Rye*[11] Laddie J held that, while laches applies, no statutory limitation period applied to a claim by a musician for an account of profits for his manager's breach of fiduciary duty. His reasoning was that a breach of fiduciary duty per se has no statutory limitation period; and

---

8   *Pre-Judgment Interest on Debts and Damages*, Law Commission Report No 287 (2004). See above, p 349.

9   The Law Commission has recommended that the same limitation regime should apply to remedies for equitable wrongs as for torts and breach of contract but that the discretion to refuse an equitable remedy under the doctrine of laches (or acquiescence) should still apply: see Law Commission Report No 270 *Limitation of Actions* (2001) paras 4.101, 4.268–4.278, 4.293.

10   This is the date of the breach of trust: *Thorne v Heard and Marsh* [1894] 1 Ch 599.

11   [1996] 1 WLR 1378.

a breach of fiduciary duty that gives rise to a constructive trust, which he thought was the position on the facts of the case, falls within the Limitation Act 1980, s 21(1)(b) which says that there shall be no limitation period. However, in *Paragon Finance plc v DB Thakerar & Co*,[12] which was concerned with the remedy of equitable compensation, the Court of Appeal regarded that reasoning as incorrect. It was helpfully explained that a constructive trust imposed or recognised as a response to a wrong does not bring a claim within s 21. That is, on the facts of *Nelson v Rye* there was no breach of trust within the meaning of s 21. But nor was it correct that breach of fiduciary duty per se has no statutory limitation period because historically the six-year period laid down for breach of contract has been applied by analogy to a non-contractual breach of fiduciary duty under the power now contained in the Limitation Act 1980, s 36(1).

This has been confirmed in subsequent cases which have applied a six-year limitation period to claims for equitable compensation[13] or an account of profits[14] for breach of fiduciary duty.

Where there is no statutory limitation period applicable to the equitable wrong – as is the case in respect of, for example, breach of confidence – the equitable doctrine of laches applies to equitable remedies for the equitable wrong.[15]

Finally it should be noted that, as with injunctions (and, it seems, declarations) for torts and breach of contract,[16] so with injunctions (and, it seems, declarations) for equitable wrongs, the doctrine of laches applies.[17]

7.   CONCLUSION

The fact that both legal and equitable remedies are available for the common law wrongs (torts and breach of contract)[18] is one good reason

---

12   [1999] 1 All ER 400.
13   *Cia De Seguros Imperio v Heath (REBX) Ltd* [2001] 1 WLR 112, CA
14   *Gwembe Valley Development Co Ltd v Koshy* [2003] EWCA Civ 1048, [2004] 1 BCLC 131: but, by analogy, to the 'fraud' exception in the Limitation Act 1980, s 21(1), it was held that on the facts there was no statutory limitation period.
15   Limitation Act 1980, s 36(2). As regards 'equitable damages', it appears that, because they are given in addition to or in lieu of an injunction or specific performance, they will be barred if the injunction or specific performance would be barred by laches: see above, p 361. It has been held, in the context of a monetary remedy for breach of trust that, where there is a statutory limitation period, laches does not apply: *Re Paulings's Settlement* [1962] 1 WLR 86 at 115 (per Wilberforce J) approved [1964] Ch 303 at 353, CA.
16   See above, pp 573–574, 592, n 17.
17   For an example of laches barring an interim injunction for an alleged breach of confidence, see *Church of Scientology of California v Miller* (1987) Times, 23 October: above, p 574. In respect of injunctions (and declarations) for equitable wrongs, it appears that laches applies even if there is a limitation period under the Limitation Act 1980.
18   See above, pp 11–12.

for treating law/equity as a purely historical and not a rational division. This chapter indicates another. For while it is essentially true, as the non-fusionists stress, that only equitable remedies are available for equitable wrongs (although this is coming under increased pressure in relation to breach of confidence), it is also true – as this chapter has shown – that the same, or similar, functions are performed by the remedies awarded for equitable wrongs as by the remedies for torts and breach of contract. In other words, the functions that have been identified in this book as being performed by the remedies for torts and breach of contract – compensation, restitution and punishment, compelling performance, preventing (or compelling the undoing of) a wrong, and declaring rights – are also the functions (subject to there being some doubt about punishment) that lie behind the remedies for equitable wrongs. As was explained in chapter 1,[19] there is therefore a coherence in remedial function for civil wrongs that transcends the common law/equity divide. So, for example, to treat breach of fiduciary duty as a tort, giving rise to purely tortious remedies, or proprietary estoppel as a breach of contract, giving rise to solely contractual remedies, would produce no real change in the range of functions performed by the available remedies. All this illustrates that, in the context of remedies for civil wrongs, those who argue against the fusion of law and equity merely seek to perpetuate an historical and not a rational division.

---

19 See above, p 13.

Index

[all references are to page number]